The

INDOMITABLE
Gertrude
Green

To order additional copies of *The Indomitable Gertrude Green,*
by Max W. Hammonds, call 1-800-765-6955.

Visit us at **www.reviewandherald.com** for information on
other Review and Herald® products.

The

INDOMITABLE

Gertrude Green

Max W. Hammonds

REVIEW AND HERALD® PUBLISHING ASSOCIATION
Since 1861 | www.reviewandherald.com

The Review and Herald® Publishing Association publishes biblically based materials for spiritual, physical, and mental growth and Christian discipleship.

The author assumes full responsibility for the accuracy of all facts and quotations as cited in this book.

Scripture quotations marked NASB are from the *New American Standard Bible,* copyright © 1960, 1962, 1963, 1968, 1971, 1972, 1973, 1975, 1977, 1994 by The Lockman Foundation. Used by permission.

This book was
Edited by Penny Estes Wheeler
Cover designed by Trent Truman
Interior designed by Tina M. Ivany
Cover photo of trees and mountain: © iStockphoto.com/KingWu
Typeset: Bembo 11/14

PRINTED IN U.S.A.

14 13 12 11 10   5 4 3 2 1

Library of Congress Cataloging-in-Publication Data

Hammonds, Max W., 1943-
  The indomitable Gertrude Green / Max W. Hammonds.
      p. cm.
1. Green, Gertrude, 1907-2002. 2. Seventh-Day Adventists—Biography. 3. Nurses—Biography. 4. Missionaries—China—Biography. 5. Nurses—China—Biography. I. Title.
  BV3427.G695H36 2009
  266'.673251092—dc22
  [B]

                    2009039418

ISBN 978-0-8280-2499-0

CONTENTS

Some of the people you'll meet in this book . . .

Ashley—a poverty-stricken Chinese child whom Gertrude befriended.

Ruth Atwell—the matron of the language school in Nanking, China, in 1937. Another of Gertrude's spiritual mentors.

Dr. Geneva Beatty (Jones)—supportive friend of Gertrude and resident physician from America who came to be the main obstetrical doctor at the Shanghai Sanitarium.

Allen and Mildred Boynton—superintendent and nurse at the Range Road Clinic in Shanghai. Old friends of Gertrude from Porter Memorial Hospital in Denver, Colorado.

Elder William Branson—president of the China Division and soon to be president of the General Conference of Seventh-day Adventists

Pastor Chang—Chinese pastor of the Yencheng Mission Church. Another spiritual mentor for Gertrude.

Mr. Chen—a Christian Chinese national and teacher in Gertrude's language school. His child's death led to the opening of Gertrude's unofficial clinic and to a deeper understanding of the Chinese people.

Elder Jerald E. Christensen—experienced pastor in China and newly-appointed director of the Yencheng Mission.

Leatha Coulston—widow of Elder Coulston and director of the Shanghai Sanitarium Nursing School whom Gertrude replaced.

Dr. Charles and Grace Dale—pathologist and nurse who became Gertrude's close friends and clinic helpers at the Nanking Language School and later confidants at the Shanghai Sanitarium.

Lillian Nothstein Edwards—Gertrude's friend and fellow emergency room nurse under the special tutelage of Dr. Haysmer.

Mr. Otis G. Erich—trained as a nurse, but functioned as the secretary-treasurer of the Honan Union Mission.

Mr. Fan—the trustworthy pharmacist at the Yencheng Sanitarium and Hospital.

Matilda June Follette—an obstetrical nurse. Known as "Follie" to her friends.

Elder Samuel Frost—a China Division official.

Lena Christina Schwader Green—Gertrude's mother and closest confidant. A first generation daughter of German immigrant parents.

Ruth Green—Gertrude's younger sister.

Elder and Mrs. Hartwell—the chaplain and his wife of the Shanghai Sanitarium and Hospital. An older couple who took solicitous interest in the young Gertrude.

Lillian Havens—a friend of Gertrude's from Union Springs Academy (New York) and a fellow nursing student at New England Sanitarium Nursing School.

Dr. Clyde Haysmer—surgeon at the New England Sanitarium and Hospital. One of Gertrude's early spiritual mentors.

Dr. William Holden—medical director and father figure to the Portland Sanitarium and Hospital.

Dr. Hwang Dzi-gin—a Chinese national physician, cultural and spiritual mentor to Gertrude. Father of Dr. Paul Hwang. Dr. Hwang Dzi-gin was martyred at Chiao Tuo Tseng.

Dr. Paul and Thelma Hwang—the son of the martyred Dr. Hwang Dzi-gin, and his wife. Medical director and treasurer of the Yencheng Sanitarium and Hospital during Gertrude's second posting there. Both became close personal friends of Gertrude.

Rachel Landrum—office secretary for the China Division in Shanghai.

Major General Li Deh Shem—Chinese general. A Roman Catholic Christian.

Dr. Herbert Liu—medical director of the Range Road Hospital during the siege of Shanghai by the Communist Chinese Army.

Gert and Marvin Loewen—friends of Gertrude from the language school.

Miss Ma—a Chinese nurse who accompanied Gertrude and the others on the long bicycle trip into Yencheng.

Dr. Raymond and Zora McMullen—American physician and his wife who arrived in Yencheng only months before the Chinese Communist Army forced everyone out of Yencheng.

Ed and Eileen Meisler—chief cook and the superintendent of nurses at the Shanghai Sanitarium and Hospital in 1936.

Dr. Harry and Marie Miller—the China Doctor. Gertrude's enigmatic employer and sometimes nemesis, and his second wife.

Two young Mennonite women—Mennonite missionaries who befriended Gertrude.

Dr. Winston Nethery—medical director of the Yencheng Sanitarium and Hospital during Gertrude's first posting there.

Olga and John Oss—expatriate workers of German descent who stayed in Shanghai during the Japanese occupation and were in Shanghai during the assault and occupation of Shanghai by the Communist Chinese Army.

Prof. Paul Quimby—Gertrude's Bible teacher at Union Springs Academy in New York. Later the superintendent of the China Training Institute at Chiao Tuo Tseng, China.

Dr. Wells Allen Ruble—superintendent of the New England Sanitarium and Hospital and admiring employer. The father figure Gertrude did not have in her own father.

Herbert Smith, Jr.—the adolescent son of Thelma Smith.

Thelma Smith—widow of Elder Herbert Smith who was martyred in the interior of China. Bible worker and treasurer for the Yencheng Sanitarium and Hospital and a close personal friend of Gertrude.

Elizabeth Stemp—Gertrude's dance teacher.

Anne Stratton—assistant nursing school director of Portland Sanitarium and Hospital. Gertrude's co-conspirator and confidant.

Mr. Cecil Tang—nursing supervisor of questionable character at Yencheng Sanitarium and Hospital.

Dr. Tsao—Chinese physician at Yencheng Sanitarium and Hospital.

Mr. Wang Shueh Wen—energetic, innovative, and entrepreneurial nursing supervisor at the Yencheng Sanitarium and Hospital.

Elder Merritt Warren—president of the Central China Union Mission and leader of the refugee group escaping from the interior of China. Spiritual mentor to Gertrude.

Nellie Wilkinson—wife of the district pastoral leader. Friendly, artistic, and easily frightened.

PREFACE

Writing a book is a journey. The beginning gives but a faint hint of the destination and the joy that is in the trip.

This book began when I, with my family, was on missionary assignment as a physician and novice administrator at the Bangkok Adventist Hospital in Bangkok, Thailand. Across the compound's open courtyard from our house lived the much older director of the midwifery program, Gertrude Green. During compound holiday celebrations we became acquainted with who she was. During conversations with other longtime residents we got to know about her— her single-mindedness, her compassion for national workers, her fame among the citizenry of Bangkok, and her explosive temper.

My wife, Cari Jo, experienced this last trait firsthand during a public confrontation in the courtyard over some misdeed of our 9-year old son, Christopher. My wife heard Gertrude screaming at the top of her voice and ran down to see what crisis had occurred. She discovered that Gertrude was upset because some of her outside orchids had been put in danger of toppling over by Christopher climbing nearby. Cari Jo apologized and retreated to our apartment with Chris, then returned to Gertrude's apartment to confront her with her inappropriate public behavior as a missionary. To Cari Jo's surprise, Gertrude was a gracious hostess and humbly horrified at how her performance had come across. Cari Jo and Gertrude became close friends for the duration of our service in Bangkok.

In 1986, close friends from our home town, Walla Walla, Washington, Steve and Barbie Dickerson and their daughter, Christy, came to Bangkok where Steve served as the construction manager for the new wing of the hospital. Barbie found herself a hospital patient, birthing their son, Matthew, under the close supervision of the obstetrical department, including Miss Gertrude Green. Later, Steve told me that Gertrude had an interesting life story that should be shared with a wider population than just the compound residents and her retinue of friends. He and I discussed the fact that someone should write the story down before it was lost. In December, 1988, we moved from Bangkok to Hendersonville, North Carolina.

Gertrude retired in 1993, joining her friends in an independent living facility, the Fletcher Park Inn, in Hendersonville, North Carolina. It happened to be just across the street from where I practiced anesthesiology at the Park Ridge Hospital, a Seventh-day Adventist healthcare institution. During gatherings of former missionaries (otherwise known as game nights) we renewed our acquaintance with Gertrude and visited her several times in her small apartment.

In 1997, after having personally heard parts of Gertrude's story, and having heard more of it from other friends, I approached her with the idea of writing it down.

"Why would you want to do that?" she asked. "I haven't done anything so special."

"Actually, you have," I answered. "You have lived a most remarkable life—one that can inspire others. Let me hear your story and let's see if I can tell it in an interesting way." And thus began a four-year adventure of trying to fit in visits to Gertrude's apartment while she lived her busy life—luncheons, hair appointments, shopping trips—and I carried on a full-time career as an anesthesiologist.

I began by sitting Gertrude down and asking her to tell her story from beginning to end. Being a novice writer, I initially tried to take notes as she talked but soon found that this would not work. I couldn't concentrate on what she was saying, her nuances of body motion and hand movements, and write at the same time. After the first hour and a half session, I took along a tape recorder and kept peripheral notes about *how* she said things, not what she said.

Gertrude tired easily after an hour or so. Therefore, our sessions were not very long, and because they were interspersed through a number of months it took some time for her to complete it. I was surprised to discover that her story was not about her 42 years in Thailand. In her mind, her story was about her early life growing up in Rochester, New York, about her education at Union Springs Academy and the New England Sanitarium and Hospital, and about the years she spent in China. For her, those seemed to be the defining years and I did not press her to tell more. I let her tell the story in the way she remembered it, saying, "Tell it to me the way you always tell it when someone asks you to tell your story."

The result was five or six hours on audio tape—Gertrude telling the story of her life with my prompting whenever she seemed to struggle with a particular memory or needed a reminder of where she was in the story.

Then we began again. After transcribing the tapes verbatim, I asked her to go back over her story, incident by incident, filling in the details such as where in the room the window was located, the color of the bed covers, what so-and-so looked like, and so on.

"Why do you want to know that?" she'd asked, incredulously.

"Because I want others to be able see what happened just as clearly as you saw it," I explained. "Only you know these details. I want the story to be as much alive for the people who read it as it is for you."

At that time I told her that there were three reasons why I thought her story needed to be written:

First, she had led a life that few others had ever imagined and people would find it interesting. Second, she had set an example that would inspire some to want to serve as missionaries. And finally, her story was so compelling that I believed people would pay good money to read it, money that could be put into scholarships for nurses and nursing schools.

Gertrude told me that she would like to see any money earned go to her nursing school. Her original nursing school, New England Sanitarium and Hospital, had closed but she had received her B.S. in Nursing from Columbia Union College (now Washington Adventist University). She thought that would be a fine place to set up such a scholarship. With that agreement between us, she began filling in the details of her life story while I continued to run the tape recorder and take notes.

The second time through we got as far as her early childhood and nursing school memories—and then she died on March 12, 2002.

I suppose that, had she lived, this story in its present form would never have been written. On her death I was forced to dig deeper and search more widely for information that I would never have found otherwise.

On several occasions Gertrude had told me that she had no photographs or papers from her time in China. She said all had been lost during the numerous times she had had to evacuate on a minute's notice. So I did not search her closets or her numerous desk drawers for information.

But now, with my primary source gone, I went to her address book and wrote to everyone listed there. Then I called and made appointments to see every person who'd responded—most were in California—individuals who had shared her China experience with her (not many at this late date) or those who might have insights into what China was like during the time she lived there.

Meanwhile I was working a *locum tenens* (temporary position) as an anesthesiologist in Springfield, Massachusetts. From there I made trips to the Atlantic Union College library, located near Boston, to the New England Sanitarium near Stoneham, and to Rochester, New York.

At the library, Karen Silverthorn, the archives librarian, showed me the locked archives room where I discovered the entire set of bound volumes of the *China Division Reporter*, the church newsletter of daily and monthly happenings in China—including ship sailing times and dates, descriptions of hospital buildings, and pictures of people. She also directed me to the home of Oreen Smart, the former office secretary and nurse of one of Gertrude's mentors, Dr. Haysmer. Ms. Smart gave me valuable insights into the New England San, its personnel, its grounds, its nursing school—and she provided pictures. As I walked the now deserted grounds of the New England San, I found the visuals Gertrude would have seen—the houses, the nursing school building, and her dearly loved Spot Pond.

In Rochester, I met Gertrude's brother Fred Green and his wife Dottie. Interviewing them I learned more about Gertrude's mother and also the names of significant people in Gertrude's early life. Then as I was about to leave, Dottie said, "Oh, by the way, I went back to Gertrude's apartment and saved all the things that I thought shouldn't be thrown away. Would you like to see them?"

Remembering that I had asked Gertrude about pictures and papers, I politely said that it would be fun to see Gertrude's things. We went to the basement where Dottie showed me the trunks that Gertrude had sent home from China and some of the coats and a Chinese wedding dress that Gertrude had sent to her mother for safe keeping. As we were about to go upstairs, Dottie said, "Oh, yes. Would you like to see Gertrude's diary?"

"What diary?" I exclaimed.

She placed in my hand the blue diary Gertrude had been given at the New England San going away party. In my hand I held five years of Gertrude's life, day by day accounts, persons and places named, dates and events detailed. I had Gertrude back!

"Oh, and I have the letters that Gertrude wrote to her mother from China," she offered. "Her mother kept them all, you know. Would they be of any interest?"

"Would they!"

Now I had Gertrude's thoughts and aspirations that she would tell only to her mother—as well as her life. And then the story really began to unfold.

I traveled to California where I met and interviewed Dr. Geneva Beatty Bedelius, Gertrude's roommate and confidante in Shanghai. From her I got a completely new perspective on Gertrude's personality, a view which helped me to step away from seeing the unfolding story only through Gertrude's eyes. She was able to fill in the information about Gertrude during her stay with Geneva in Long Beach. After visiting her and realizing the value of her perspective, suddenly everyone else's stories became revealing and essential.

I visited and interviewed Dr. Paul and Mrs. Thelma Hwang, both of whom lived through the horrendous days of Gertrude's second time of service at Yencheng. They described details of the life and work at the Yencheng San, the buildings and the layout of the compound, the characters of the people that only those who lived there could have known. Dr. Hwang also gave me his violin, rescued by Elder Warren during the arduous walk out of the interior of China. He asked me to give it to Elder Warren's daughter when I saw her, as his token of devotion.

I also visited Mrs. Ollie Mae Robbins, Mrs. Minnie Woods, and Mrs. Florence Howlett (all now deceased) all of whom lived and worked in Shanghai and/or in China before and after World War II. They gave invaluable insights into life in China: the buildings, the roads, the railroad cars, the various compounds and institutions.

Also in northern California I visited Helen Lee, the daughter of Elder Merritt Warren, and delivered Dr. Hwang's violin. She understood the Oriental significance of such a gift. She was able to identify, in pictures, people that heretofore had no names. She was able to read the Chinese in the pictures, to tell me about the cars and trucks that were used, and to describe medical treatments in use then.

Finally, I visited Mrs. Elizabeth Hamlin, the daughter of Dr. Nethery. She had pictures of Yencheng. She had letters Gertrude had written to her father during that particular time. I also received, for the second time, a personal opinion about Gertrude from someone who knew her—her father, Dr. Nethery. This, along with the opinion of Dr. Beatty, increased my understanding of Gertrude's character as no amount of my own imagination could have.

Another piece of Gertrude's life was filled in when I visited the library at the Walla Walla University School of Nursing campus in Portland, Oregon. The librarian, Bruce McClay, found files containing stories, pictures, maps, newsletters, yearbooks, and even the report of the accrediting organization that had come to evaluate the nursing program. That piece of Gertrude's life was filled in.

Then came a trip to Washington, D.C., and the offices of the General Conference of Seventh-day Adventists for a perusal of the archives where Bert Haloviak and his assistant Eucaria Galicia made pictures and maps available.

Finally, my wife and I joined a group tour of China. Although the other members of our group were there to see the sights, I was there to see where Gertrude had lived and worked. Many questions needed to be answered: Where were the mountains she mentioned between Yencheng and Wuhan where the bandits were hiding? What does Wuhan look like? What does Shanghai look like? What about the countryside, the farm compounds, the haystacks?

Flying to Wuhan by myself, I met a tour guide who showed me the city, then put me on a Chinese train for Beijing, a train that followed the same rails that Gertrude had traveled. I saw the bread loaf haystacks, the countryside farm compounds, and the mountains. I saw the *hutongs*—the rabbit warren housing areas of Beijing that replicated the housing areas of Nanking that Gertrude would have known. I walked the Bund of Shanghai and rode a boat on the Yangtze River. I got a feeling for the country Gertrude had grown to love—China.

Besides the people and the travel, there were the books. Besides large reference books on the history and geography of China, I reviewed and considered the information of *In Spite of Danger* by Mary Ogle, the life of Thelma Smith; *Light the Paper Lantern* by Ruth Wheeler—the missionary experiences of Merritt and Wilma Warren in China; *Invisible Escort* by Rose Christensen—the missionary experiences of Jerold and Rose Christensen;

Yankee on the Yangtze by Paul Quimby with Norma Youngberg—outlining the experiences of Paul Quimby in China, and *China Doctor* by Raymond S. Moore—the life of Dr. Harry Miller. All of these described persons who knew and interacted with Gertrude. Some of them told the same stories that she told and helped to corroborate—or deny—the accuracy of her story.

Despite the loss of Gertrude, I had her story in more detail and with more accuracy than if I had stuck to her memories only. In fact, I had a more detailed description of Gertrude's character than she could have given, and from the perspective of those who worked with her, respected her, and loved her.

Despite all the research and the compiling of notes, pictures, and interviews, the resulting story was of necessity a historic novel. It could not be otherwise. To make the story come alive, as I had told Gertrude, there needed to be conversations, scenes, incidents flowing into incidents and a story line that placed Gertrude's story in real time.

To the best of my ability—from all that I had learned about Gertrude—I tried to recreate the story as true to her character as I could envision. Though I created dialogue and imagined the setting and the unfolding of the scene, I insured that each major incident described in the book actually happened or, from the evidence, easily could be construed to have happened. With the exception of six or eight letters that I imagined Gertrude to have written to tell part of the story, every letter is a real letter, or a compilation of several letters all written at about the same time, and is quoted *verbatim,* except for some spelling corrections. Except for the minor fill-in characters (the coolies, the villagers, the market venders), there are no pretend people, no composite characters. I had gathered enough material to know who was present or likely to be present when each and every event took place. Except for a very few Chinese names that were not available, every student, every doctor, every person who plays even a minor role is called by their given name, including Chinese students who were frequently given Christian names when their families became Christians.

As I developed the story, I kept one guiding principle uppermost in my mind. This is Gertrude's story, told as she would tell it, from her perspective, giving her opinions of events, administrations, cultures, people and their motives, right or wrong. In some instances, Gertrude did not hold a very high opinion of some people, some groups or some institutions, an opinion not always shared by others. In time she discovered that some of those opinions were wrong and the narrative reflects this growth on her part. In some instances she never changed her opinion, but right or wrong, they are her opinions as she felt them and understood them at the time.

To that end I allowed the reader to "sit on Gertrude's shoulder" and hear her thoughts as well as listen to her interact with her environs. I intended that the book would not be about the Adventist church, nor about China, or even about being a missionary. While all of these were contributing forces, the book is intended to be a chronology of Gertrude Green's life, an unfolding of the events of history, her interactions with other people, and her own thoughts and decisions that molded her and made her the woman she became, developing from a preteen dancing star to a missionary nurse who helped lead 51 men, women, and children out of the interior of China in the dead of winter—on foot.

If I have succeeded, it is because the material with which I worked was so compelling. If I have failed, it is because I was unable to convey the intense drama and character struggle that took place in the life of Gertrude Green. I was never in doubt that the story was worth telling. My only doubt was whether the author was up to the telling of it.

In addition to all the above people who shared their expertise, their stories and their resources, I must acknowledge the help of four other people.

The first is Stephen Chavez, managing editor of the *Adventist Review*, who, at the General Conference session in Toronto, took me under his busy wing and hustled me over to the Review and Herald Publishing Association booth, personally introducing me as someone who'd had a poem published in the *Adventist Review*. He broke the ice and let me know that someone might think I had a good idea.

The second is Jeannette Johnson, acquisitions editor at Review and Herald Publishing, to whom I was introduced. She took my calls, read my unfinished manuscript in its early stages, encouraged me with e-mails, and generally let me know that she was eager to see the rest of the book—and when could I get it to her? It was encouragement that this novice writer needed to hear.

The third person is Steve Dickerson, a former manager of writers and copy editors and a prepublication technician at Coffey Communications in Walla Walla, Washington. Steve is a published author in his own right and one of my best friends. He received faithfully each chapter as I wrote it and skillfully critiqued it with spelling and grammar corrections, as well as questions, such as, "What did you mean by . . . ? I didn't follow you." "Did you realize that you used the word 'd——s' twice within two lines of each other?" "This paragraph may be confusing to the reader; how might you make it more clear? Would this phrase be more helpful?" Without Steve's guardianship this manuscript would have bled red ink at the publisher's office.

The fourth person I must acknowledge is my wife, Carolyn Jo, more affectionately known by her friends as Cari Jo, or just Cari. All writers who are successfully married know that an understanding spouse is absolutely essential to the long hours spent laboring over the keyboard, trying to achieve just the right turn of phrase. Cari has suffered through the reading of chapters, my messy office with stacks of papers everywhere (she doesn't have to clean in there or live in there, but she says she has to look at it!), and my disappearances in the afternoon, in the evening, and on weekends in order to write.

And finally, this book is a product of the encouragement and the inspiration of the Holy Spirit who had to deal with a melancholic writer who was unsure of his calling and uncertain of his ability. This book has belonged to the Lord from its inception, and it is to His glory that it is written.

—Max Hammonds, MD, retired
Kenneth City, Florida
January 4, 2009

PROLOGUE

Let no one be mistaken. Gertrude Green was a dancer.

Not that anyone would suspect it. At 91 years of age she was no longer light on her feet. Stooped with osteoporosis, she walked slowly and carefully as a result of her recent knee surgery. Her right ankle drooped from a loss of the elevating tendon and caused her right foot to drag slightly, giving her a hesitating gait. Her wavy gray hair lay closely coifed atop a bowed head and a wrinkled face.

Only her eyes gave her away. Laughter and life radiated from her gray-green eyes as they quickly took in all that happened around her. While her mouth might be openly laughing in a moment of fond remembrance and pensively closed just as quickly in another, her eyes, now wrinkled with too much sun and too much responsibility, consumed her surroundings. Her eyes absorbed, and through her eyes she responded—showing gray when she was pensive or sad, turning emerald green when she was excited or angry. Her eyes were a barometer of her emotions and a harbinger of her reactions to the world.

Gertrude had the mental agility required to coordinate her thoughts and movements with those around her. She could quickly learn and retain a complex series of required actions, especially physical ones. At 91, her mind was still a sponge in search of the water of knowing: knowing what was about to happen, knowing what was required of her and how it could be done. And while her body was no longer capable of physically standing on tiptoe, in her mind, even now, Gertrude Green could dance.

The clicking of the metal joints of her walker was the only sound as Gertrude carefully negotiated her way toward the third floor conference room where the Bible study was being held. She moved slowly down the carpeted halls of the Fletcher Park Inn, past the apartments of the others who had also moved to Fletcher, North Carolina, in their retirement.

The nameplate on each door marked the current location of a complex life, now mostly lived out. Attached under each nameplate or arranged beside each door was a small packet of dried flowers or a crayon drawing of a great-grandchild or a picture of the occupant. To some it might seem as if the doors and hallways were filled with clutter. But to those who lived here, this was their last attempt to say, "I lived a full life, and I am still alive."

As she shuffled past, Gertrude noted and mentally checked off each door and the individual it represented. She related to these lives as she had always done. They were people, creations of God, and therefore to be respected, cared for, worked with. She was not naturally emotional and did not get intimately involved with anyone. But people were important to her. They were her friends, her work, her reference points in life—so that no matter how important or unimportant any individual might be in the world, to Gertrude they were all precious and worthy of her attention.

Because of her recent surgery and the slowness of her progress, Gertrude arrived late and the discussion had already begun. She took a seat near the back of the room, easing into the upholstered chair with some difficulty, her knee not wanting to bend to the 90 degrees required. But Gertrude willed it to respond. Her sharp eyes swept the room, noting quickly who had come and who was missing. Only after doing this preliminary "bed check" did she focus on the speaker and the discussion in progress.

Dr. Schwarz, a retired history professor from Andrews University, stood before the group, all five-and-a-half feet of him. His healthy crop of salt-and-pepper hair and equally full and colorful moustache suggested a man of considerably younger age than his 70 odd years. At Andrews he was known as a knowledgeable and engaging teacher, easily approachable and at once a friend and confidante. These qualities worked equally well in relating to the gray heads and sharp minds in the group before him so that the teaching dialogue was more like a conversation between old friends. With many in the group being former pastors or missionaries, the discussion was lively and everyone spoke confidently and without embarrassment.

Everyone there had heard discussions of the book of Revelation before. He was not going to surprise many of them with any new or radical ideas about the seven churches or the four horsemen or the two-horned beast. So he engaged them instead with a personal application of the various ideas presented in the book.

"Of the seven churches of Revelation, only Smyrna and Philadelphia have the distinction of receiving no rebuke from the Lord," he said.

Many knowing heads nodded in obvious agreement.

"And both of these churches have something else in common. Does anyone know what that was?" he asked with the smile of a teacher who has found a nugget the students had not anticipated.

The distinctive rustle of very thin pages peculiar to Bibles filled the room. Several small discussion groups whispered their tentative findings to each other as everyone sought out the hidden manna he had so cleverly dropped. Then several hands shot up.

"Yes?" he said as he pointed to a plump lady in a pillbox hat. He had noticed her at previous meetings, remembering the hat which she always wore to religious services and the small earrings, both indicative of the fact that she was not a Seventh-day Adventist. He was glad for her willingness to respond and wanted to affirm her.

"Margaret here helped me," she admitted, embarrassed but obviously pleased, indicating her friend and seatmate. Smiles blossomed around the room and knowing nods as she stood.

"It says in Revelation—uh—chapter two and—uh—verse 10 that there is a tribulation coming for Smyrna," she said.

Gertrude noted that the woman spoke haltingly, attempting to describe the chapter and verse in what might be considered complete, liturgical phrases. It sounded odd to one who was used to giving Bible references in a quick, foreshortened manner. Gertrude smiled sympathetically at the woman's discomfort, remembering her own difficulty reading scripture in public.

"And in Revelation—uh—chapter three and verse 10 it says that the church of Philadelphia can expect an hour of testing." Here she stopped speaking and read with her Bible held closely to her round, spectacled face, "'which is about to come upon the whole world, to test those that dwell upon the earth.'" She was obviously pleased with herself and squeezed the arm of her friend in thanks for the help as she sat back down.

"Very good," Dr. Schwarz said with genuine warmth in his voice. His engaging smile spread spontaneously under his huge multicolored moustache. "There is coming a tribulation on the earth, a time of trouble. And . . . yes?" He acknowledged another hand which had quickly been raised.

A very tall, erect, and thin man rose to his full height from his chair. Obviously he was used to speaking only while standing. Dr. Schwarz guessed he was a former pastor.

"Daniel 12:1 mentions this same time of trouble," he announced authoritatively.

Again thin pages rustled as scholars sought the text. The former pastor waited, as he had always done, until everyone in his congregation had found the passage.

"'Now at that time,' he read, 'Michael, the great prince who stands guard over the sons of your people, will arise. And there will be a time of distress such as never occurred since there was a nation until that time; and at that time your people, everyone who is found written in the book, will be rescued'" (NASB). He stood quietly for a solemn moment and then sat without further comment.

"Thank you for that excellent addition," Dr. Schwarz said in his firm, warm teacher's voice. "A time of distress, a time of trouble," he repeated for emphasis. "And your people will be rescued out of it." He looked about the room, watching for facial reactions of the former missionaries, pastors, and church workers who had seen their fair share of trouble.

"After all your lives of difficult decisions and unusual living situations"— as he knew many in the room had personally experienced—"can you imagine a time of trouble such as has never occurred? What will that be like? For you, personally, do you think?"

He knew what answers he would get as he'd posed this question to his classes at Andrews University. Of course, the responses from this older group were little different from the ones given by the young undergraduates in his classes there. Many could not imagine much worse times. Some were expecting family breakups and church disruptions, even closings. Some voiced a desire not to have to go through such a time while others reminded these fearful ones of the promise to be rescued.

In the back of the room Gertrude heard these exchanges and followed them with care, noting who made what remarks. She was not one to speak up in public meetings, especially now that her voice was no longer strong and had developed an old woman's crackle. But Dr. Schwarz's question had touched her deeply, suddenly and sharply, as when an ax strikes wood and splinters it with a mighty *crack,* or when a hypodermic needle suddenly pierces the skin. She was carried back to a time of trouble she had known, a time of trouble that had indelibly imprinted her with a lifelong response to life, like a birthmark on a baby or a brand on the flank of a steer.

As if on cue, she felt anew her anguish at the senseless death of Mr. Chen's child, the thrill of opening Dr. Miller's new hospital in Wuhan, and the grinding exhaustion of an obstetrical nursing career derailed by the Great Depression. Her nostrils filled with the nauseating odor of her own fear as she heard again the penetrating crescendo whistle of falling bombs and the quietly insistent request of Elder Warren for her to play the organ for the Communist generals. Her numbingly cold feet on the long bicycle trip to Yencheng became her numbingly cold feet in the railroad coal car surrounded by murderous soldiers. In rapid succession her nursing experiences in Stoneham, Massachusetts, and Shanghai, China, ran together—a cacophony of eager questions from hopeful young nursing students, pitiful cries of suffering soldiers, the labored breathing of fevered patients under the stony gaze of their high-placed relatives, and the quiet sobbing of a fellow missionary who had lost her infant at birth far from her family in a foreign land.

While she could not recall with clarity all the aspects of her experiences, she remembered without question what she had learned about trouble and about fear and about expectations. And she began to rise from her seat.

Those nearby saw her struggle with her walker as she stood. Some even reached out a hand as if to help, though they could not reach her. What they could not know and could not see were her thoughts—thoughts which traveled back to the beginning where she was being prepared for her time of trouble.

Dr. Schwarz recognized her and waited for her to rise. When she finally gained her feet, he spoke.

"Yes, Gertrude?" he said quietly.

Chapter 1

THE YOUNGEST DANCER

Gertrude!" Mrs. Lena Green called from the kitchen. "Get ready for supper."

There was no answer.

"Gerrr-truuude! Where is that child?" Mrs. Green said with irritation. She looked toward the dining room door, her hand holding the fork she'd just used to stir the cabbage, poised in midair. With her sister visiting from New York, she wanted everything to be just so.

Although she knew that 4-year-old Gertrude had just been in the dining room, out of motherly habit she quickly took in the whole of the backyard through the window over the kitchen sink. No Gertrude in the sand box, or in the double swing under the big elm.

As Lena Green strode purposefully into the dining room, her sister, Anna, setting the last of the plates on the table, looked up with a down-set mouth and a shake of her head.

"She's headed down the front steps in her blue coat and pushing her doll buggy."

"Gertrude!" Lena cried, running toward the front of the house.

Bursting through the front door, she dashed across the porch and down the steps, the edges of her apron flapping about her thighs like the tip ends of wing feathers.

"Gertrude!" she called after the retreating blue figure now going up Bryan Street. "Where are you going?"

Gertrude stopped, turned, and calmly considered the person who looked like she was trying to fly but without leaving the ground.

"I'm going to see Miss Blue." she said, her small, sharp voice carrying on the cool evening air.

"But it's supper time," her mother cried. "You can't go now."

"No, Mother," Gertrude said matter-of-factly, "I must go now and see Miss Blue."

She turned back to her small buggy and pushed it to the large white house that stood vacant at the end of the block. Head held high and her short legs striding as she'd seen adult women do, she proceeded up the walk. Then she climbed to the top step, turned, and elegantly seated herself on the edge of the wooden porch. Looking out over the neighborhood, she held in her hand a pretend cup of tea which she occasionally brought to her mouth while seemingly chatting with one or two pretend individuals seated with her.

Hands on her hips, Lena Green watched again as the scene that Gertrude had acted out so many times before unfolded—Gertrude going to visit the mysterious "Miss Blue," becoming the famous "Miss Blue." Lena gave a twist of her head and closed her eyes as if seeking for understanding, a small smile of approval playing about the corners of her mouth. Gertrude was going to be someone famous. She knew it for sure.

The smile became a frown as Lena turned her head and caught sight of the grocer across the street. He stood rocking on his heels, his fingers interlaced and his hands rounded like a trough across his ample stomach as if to catch the amusement running down from his wide grin and onto his shirt and grocer's apron. When he saw that he had been observed, he quickly brought his hand up to cover his mouth, spilling his mirth, and retreated hastily into his store.

"She is a willful child, Lena Schwader Green." Anna's voice spoke from the darkness of the porch behind her.

Startled to find another observer, Lena turned quickly to face her second accuser. She drew in her breath as if about to speak but held her tongue. She had more important things to discuss with Anna than Gertrude's behavior. She needed her sisterly advice, not her ire.

Glancing back up the street to the distant porch and the small blue figure sipping imaginary tea, Lena said, "She will be famous some day," and walked back to her own house.

"Mrs. Green, I think she has a natural gift." Elizabeth Stemp bobbed her head for emphasis, her round face bright with excitement, her curls bobbing in counterpoint from the back of her head where her hair was pulled tight all around and caught in a double comb.

Betsy, as she was known by her dancing students, stood in front of the coffee table and couch. Backlit by the front window, she appeared to be surrounded in a halo of flame, adding more fervency to what she had come to tell Mrs. Green.

Like a floating feather, Lena slowly collapsed on the couch, partly from weakness and partly from excitement about what Betsy had just said.

"Do you think she can do this?" she asked in a whisper of astonishment and disbelief.

"Believe me, Mrs. Green, she can do it, all right," Betsy told her, now striding about the room. "She has poise and excellent carriage. And she is a quick study. She is ready for a professional dance career on the stage."

"But she is only 7 years old. Do they really want someone that young?" Lena asked, shaking her head. Walter, her oldest, was studying the piano and Ruth at 5, was already showing an interest in the violin. Gertrude was learning to play the piano—but her first love was dancing.

"She wants to be a second Anna Pavlova," Lena said, speaking aloud her private thoughts.

Betsy beamed, bursting with the honor that would come to her as the teacher of this prodigy. "The director of the theater watched her perform today. He was really smitten. Says he'll write a part in his next production especially for her."

Then realizing what Lena had asked, she stopped pacing and turned to face Lena Green, the pride of the moment succumbing to practicality.

"Gertrude has been studying with me for more than three years now. They don't care how old she is. They want her," Betsy said with conviction. "She is very good."

"Yes, I know," Lena mused. "I've watched her practicing in her room." Then looking at Betsy with sparkling green eyes and her widest smile she said, "Well, I suppose you should tell Gertrude."

"Mate, stain, play, cane," droned three children's voices simultaneously from below.

Walter, now 16, Gertrude, age 9, and little Ruth, only 7, were reciting together for the elocution teacher down in the front room. Frederick, at age 2,
was too young to participate. He was in his room taking his nap.

From where she was sitting in her bedroom at the sewing machine, Lena
could hear their strong voices running through the vowels. There would be
no trace of the German accent in *her* children. She straightened for just a
moment to rest her back while she listened.

"Cat, fan, back, ram."

Lena bent over the sewing machine again. She was making another costume
for Gertrude's next performance. It was something Greek, certainly something
a little less jazzy than the last production. Lena, a good conservative Lutheran,
had been a little embarrassed to be seen coming out of the theater after that one.

Although she had not missed one of Gertrude's performances, George, her
husband had not seen any. *He's almost never here,* Lena thought, *always traveling
on a buying trip.* But even she was unable to convince herself that this was the
real reason.

"He's a good provider," she said out loud, and she believed it.

It was his excellent job at the shoe factory that made possible the music
and elocution lessons and the material to make Gertrude's costumes. "I'll
not complain over a little alcohol," Lena said firmly to herself. To confirm
her conclusion and bolster her belief, she listened again.

"Star, farm, lark, army."

Lena smiled in satisfaction.

"Did you get all your bags?" shouted Betsy Stemp, laughing and dragging
her wood slat steamer trunk to the edge of the curb.

"I have only these two," Gertrude laughed in return, swinging a suitcase
from each arm. "I travel light." During the summer she had grown almost
as tall as her dancing teacher and more lithe.

"Especially when you let me bring all the costumes," Betsy carped. Then
searching the crowded Bronx street she added, "Where's a taxi when you
want one?"

Gertrude set her bags on the curb next to the small metal-bound trunk
and stepped into the street, searching the tangle of rushing vehicles for a flash
of yellow.

"You want to get back on the curb, dearie?" Betsy chided with mock firmness. "Your mother will not be happy if I write and tell her that her 11-year-old daughter was run down in the streets of New York like a street urchin."

"That's why I'm here this summer taking dancing classes from Professor Kosloff," Gertrude shot back. "To be light on my feet."

"At five dollars a lesson, let's hope he can teach you some good sense at the same time. Have you no fear at all?" Betsy asked with increasing concern.

Halfway into the street Gertrude turned and looked at her with puzzlement, trying to recall something she was afraid of. At the sound of a horn and the screech of brakes she leaped lightly back onto the curb. Betsy covered her eyes and shook her head in disbelief.

"Yes. Yes, I do," Gertrude responded. "But not much." She unconsciously smoothed her blue silk jacket, straightened her posture, and standing on tiptoe, began again to search the traffic—this time from the curb.

"Was your uncle very mad when you told him that we were going to live across town?" Betsy asked, looking back over her shoulder at the small music shop and the equally small apartment above it, crowded between similarly flat-faced and ugly brown shop houses.

"Actually, I think he was relieved that we wanted to go. With five kids plus the two of us, all in three rooms, I think we were a bit much for him." Gertrude spoke over her shoulder, not taking her eyes from the stream of cars and buses in the noisy street. "Besides, he thought we were taking more than our share of the bed bugs."

"Oooohh!" Betsy moaned. The memory of last night's battle with the little red bugs made her suddenly scratch at her left shoulder. "How do you get rid of these awful creatures?"

"I don't know," Gertrude shouted, waving frantically as a yellow cab with a black and white checked band about its middle turned the corner at the end of the block. "But I'll bet I find out," she called back as she leaped in front of a startled bus driver and through the stream of traffic, flagging down the unsuspecting taxi driver in the opposite lane.

"Lift it just a bit more," Lena Green huffed.

Gertrude struggled with the heavy dining room table and watched her mother pull the edge of the rug from under it. She let the table down with a thump.

Every Saturday afternoon for the last six months they had gone through this same exercise, rearranging the dining room to make space for Gertrude's dance class of 7, 8, and 9-year-olds. And Gertrude wondered at her mother's untiring patience at this disruption in her well-kept house.

"Why do you do it?" Gertrude asked, leaning on the table and catching her breath.

"Why do I do what?" her mother asked as she took her place at the opposite end of the room on the far corner of the rug. They had performed this ritual so frequently that they took their places and performed it with no conscious thought, conversing as if they were sitting quietly in the kitchen.

"Why do you allow me to take apart your beautiful dining room every week—and help me to do it?" Gertrude asked as she moved to her corner of the rug.

They began to roll the dark red and ochre Persian rug toward the table that now sat against the wall. When the rug was rolled and pushed against the table, Lena Green placed both her hands against the small of her back and stretched herself into a full upright position. Gertrude watched and winced in sympathy and wondered again to herself, *Why?*

"For the same reason I sent you to New York two summers ago. And for the same reason I sew all of your costumes. And for the same reason I have taught you to be hard working, frugal, and organized," her mother said, standing up to her full height but with a twinkle in her eye. "You will be someone famous someday and I want to be the proud mother of such a person."

Gertrude chuckled at her mother's assurance of future pride as she turned and hurried upstairs to change for class. But with each step she climbed, Gertrude determined again and again in her heart to live up to those expectations.

"And because I love you, Gertrude," her mother added quietly as she watched her maturing young daughter gracefully ascend the stairs.

Chapter 2

THE UNSETTLING CHANGE

It was a cool evening, September 29, 1921. Autumn in New England had arrived early and the leaves were already in the full flame of their coloring in Rochester, New York. Gertrude hardly saw them, if she noticed them at all. Having just turned 14 on the 25th of September, she was consumed with being what she had decided to be in grade school and what she had now become: an exceptional dancer.

It was already dark as Gertrude made her way home from her teacher's house where she spent every spare minute when she was not teaching her own dance classes or in school. She skipped lightly through the rustling leaves from the street corner in front of her old grade school to the vacant lot on the opposite corner under the dim yellow of the street light.

As she crossed the street Gertrude could see the firemen at the station on the corner. They were old friends of the family and were familiar with the four children whose backyard touched their station. She waved to the man standing in front of the firehouse and he waved back, recognizing the tall, skinny oldest daughter of the Green family.

Gertrude seemed tall because she was thin, but actually she was not quite as tall as her mother's five-foot-three. But everyone said she was an exact replica of her mother. Her oval face was bounded above by medium length brown hair worn like a frame around her head, parted in the middle and combed down in a childish way to ringlets at the sides. Her strongly outlined jaw was softened somewhat by a wide mouth and straight teeth.

But her most striking feature was her gray-green eyes which were mature beyond her years, as if they could see into the future while being acutely focused on the reality of her immediate surroundings. Her brows softly curved over each eye, giving her face a deceptively quiet look, not revealing the drive or the intellect that lay just beneath.

Though she used glasses for reading she never wore them while dancing. She needed her eyes as part of her overall persona. She didn't want them hidden behind glasses. Besides dancers—or the characters they portrayed— did not wear glasses.

When she saw no lights on in the house, Gertrude wondered if she'd arrived home before her mother. She broke into a run and hurried up the familiar steps past the rocking chairs and the glider on the large porch. She had lived in this house all her life and was as familiar with it as she was with her dancing shoes. This house and those shoes, they were her life.

At the front door only darkness greeted her. Never one to be afraid, she accepted its invitation eagerly and hurried through the living room, throwing her coat on the chair.

She was alone in the house. Passing through the dining room, her hands skipping along the backs of the chairs, she thought of her father, George, who was either on a buying trip or at one of the local bars. He was a quiet alcoholic who would occasionally rant about and throw the dining room chairs down the stairs into the basement, but he was a good provider and a hard worker at the baby shoe factory. Though hard on the dining room chairs, he was seldom present in her life.

Her older brother, Walter, now 21, had his own room upstairs. He worked downtown as a clerk in a tobacco shop. But just now he was probably following in his father's footsteps at the bars.

Her father never struck any of the family members. But his drunken fits and her brother's wasted life turned Gertrude against the thought of any marriage where she might be trapped like her mother. She had her dancing, and that would be enough.

As she made her way through the familiar dark to the kitchen, she considered where the rest of her family might be. Mother probably had 6-year-old Frederick and 12-year-old Ruth with her. It was good to have some quiet time before all the commotion started with their return.

Mother. Gertrude gazed out the kitchen window as she'd seen her mother do so often to watch the children at play in the large backyard where the sandbox and playhouse were. Mother was usually there to greet her when she arrived home from a performance or a practice. Mother was so proud of what she was doing with her life. She came to every performance and had supported her two summers ago when she had studied in New York under Kosloff.

But Mother wasn't here tonight. For most of this summer's evenings she hadn't been here. She'd been attending some kind of church meetings. Now these meetings had been moved to a local theater. Her family were Lutherans, had always been Lutherans, so Gertrude didn't know why her mother was so taken with these meetings.

And this new church was strange. They met on Saturday mornings. Her mother had tried to get Gertrude to attend some of the meetings, but Gertrude was busy every evening and every weekend. She was preparing for a new show and trying to keep up with teaching her students. This fall she'd started high school which just added more to her already busy life. She simply had no time to go to any meetings.

Gertrude turned on the kitchen light, straightened the vase of flowers on the table, and began washing up a few leftover dishes. Like all the other children, Gertrude had her jobs in the house. She was the washer of dishes, the duster of furniture, and the dance teacher. She was neat like her mother and had learned the value of order in her life. Her busy life demanded self-discipline and her mother had been a kind and gentle teacher.

"Thank you, Mother," she whispered to herself as she went to her room to await her mother's return.

Around 9:00 o'clock Gertrude heard a rustling at the front door. Mother was arriving with the younger ones. Gertrude got to the living room just as her mother was taking off her coat.

"Hello, everyone," Gertrude said.

"Hi, Gertrude," said Frederick. Mother always insisted on no nicknames, not even among family members.

Gertrude smiled, anticipating a response from her sister's usually cheerful disposition. But Ruth looked at her with large, worried eyes and walked up the stairs without speaking.

"How was your day, dear?" said her mother, kissing her lightly on the cheek. "Frederick, you run upstairs and get to bed."

"Yes, Mother," he replied as he skipped up the stairs behind Ruth.

"I was able to get home early since there's no performance for another six weeks," Gertrude said. She had, in fact, just finished a production and would not be in rehearsal for a while.

"I'm glad. You work too hard, you know." Her mother wearily flopped into the armchair.

Gertrude stood in the middle of the floor observing her mother's face. Casual observers would have called them sisters. Both had long oval faces, full mouths, and wideset, gray eyes which could turn green with a flair of emotion. Both would be considered pretty, except for the lines around the eyes and mouth of her mother which gave away the extra years of worry and care. They made her look drawn and tired.

We are *like sisters*, Gertrude thought. *We share so much of this life, and Father, and this house. We even share my dancing.* It was because she recognized the close kinship of this shared experience that her mother's next comment shocked her.

"I want you to go with me tomorrow to the Seventh-day Adventist church," Mother said.

"But Mother, you know I have to teach tomorrow. Besides I just started school again and I really have no interest in what they're doing at that church." Gertrude was not being disrespectful. She would never do such a thing to her mother. But she really did not want to go.

"I know, dear," her mother said carefully. "But they are going to have something very special tomorrow morning. I don't know what it is, but they call it Thirteenth Sabbath."

Gertrude saw the almost pleading look in her mother's eyes. What did her mother want her to see?

She knew her mother diligently studied her Bible in the evenings up in her room. But Gertrude did not understand this sudden fixation on religion. All their lives Mother had taken the children to the Lutheran church every Sunday. Gertrude had been confirmed after dutifully memorizing and reciting her catechism. But this summer her mother had changed. She was more excited, more consumed by this new church. What was it? Should she go see for herself?

Gertrude turned and walked slowly across the length of the living room as these thoughts went through her mind. Then she returned and sat in the chair near her mother. Just a small stand holding a picture of Grandmother Green stood between them. Finally Mother spoke.

"Gertrude, I have not pushed you all this summer. I knew that you were busy and that you were not interested in this new church. But, please, Gertrude, for me. Please come tomorrow and see for yourself."

Maybe it was the hint of her grandmother's German accent coming out in her mother. Maybe it was Gertrude's own curiosity in this thing that so interested her.

"And you don't know what it is they are going to do," she heard herself saying.

Lena Green leaned over and touched her daughter on the arm. "No I don't, dear, I'm sorry. But please. For me. Please come."

"Well, my dancing classes aren't 'til the afternoon. So I guess I can come in the morning," Gertrude said confidently, now that she'd thought of a plan to continue her life around this new obstacle.

Her mother's face glowed in the lamplight. "Thank you, dear," was all she said. But the sereneness of her face and her lighthearted step up the stairs to her room said much more.

Gertrude undressed in the darkness of the room she shared with Ruth. Her thoughts were on the face of her mother and how she had looked before their conversation and afterward. She jumped when Ruth spoke out of the darkness.

"What are you going to do, Gertrude?"

"Oh, you startled me. I thought you were asleep."

"No, I'm not asleep. I'm worried about . . . Mother." Ruth's voice broke just a little as she spoke the last word.

"Why are you worried about Mother?" Gertrude asked, quickly coming to the side of her sister's bed. "Are you all right? What's the matter?"

"Well, I don't know." Ruth suddenly poured forth her story. "I just know that Mother's become sadder and sadder all this summer. She gets real quiet when we walk home from the meetings. And I hear her praying for you and Father and Walter at the meetings all the time. I know she has been especially praying for you."

"Has she said anything to you, anything about why she's worried?" Gertrude questioned.

"No. You know she doesn't talk to me like she talks to you. But I just know she's worried about you."

Ruth was quiet as she considered her next words. Then she sat up on the side of the bed and looked earnestly at her sister. Gertrude could feel her eyes staring at her in the dark.

"Gertrude. What are you going to do?"

"What am I going to do about what?" Gertrude asked, becoming even more confused by the intensity of emotions whirling around her.

"What are you going to do about tomorrow? I mean, are you going with us?"

"Is that what this is all about? The meeting tomorrow? Yes, I'm going," Gertrude said, still trying to understand her sister's concern.

"On the way home tonight, Mother said she hoped you'd come. She wanted you to come so much!" Ruth was so relieved that it sounded as if she were about to cry again.

"Well, I am going with you all tomorrow," Gertrude said with relief. "Now you lie down and sleep and stop worrying over me." She hugged her sister and fluffed her pillow as Ruth snuggled down into her bed.

Gertrude walked quietly to her own bed and crawled into it. The covers were so cozy, so like home. She wondered what tomorrow would bring and how this kind of emotion had developed around her—here in her own home—without her seeming to notice.

But now she was going to the meeting tomorrow and everyone seemed relieved. She had a plan and everything was going to be all right. She rolled up in a ball snugly on her side and quickly slept.

Chapter 3

THE NEWEST CONVERT

Gertrude, Ruth, Frederick, and Mother emerged through the front doors of the old theater building where the church meetings were being held. Elder O. D. Cardey, a short, energetic young man in a black suit, stood at the door, shaking hands and making earnest eye contact with church members and visitors alike. Gertrude knew him from the summer months when he had come to the house to study with Mother. But she had never heard him speak in public until today and had not been introduced to him.

"Well, good morning, Mrs. Green," he said warmly. "And whom do we have here?" he asked, extending his hand to Gertrude who was tall enough and looked old enough to be Mother's younger sister.

"This is my oldest daughter, Gertrude," Mother said proudly.

"Well, Gertrude, is it?" he said, responding to her firm handshake with a gentle grip of his own. "I think you have not been here before, have you?" He kept looking into her eyes and waiting for a spark of interest.

Surprisingly, Gertrude met his gaze with a steady eye of her own.

"No, sir. I have not," was all she said. But she kept looking at him as if there were more to be said or a question to be answered.

Pastor Cardey was an astute judge of character. *Here is an earnest seeker of knowledge*, he mused to himself. *What will it take to awaken her?*

"Well, I hope we see more of you, young lady," he told Gertrude.

Then they were out on the sidewalk and walking toward home. Mother was walking beside Gertrude and Ruth, Frederick skipping ahead of them, Mother glanced toward her older daughter and ventured a question.

"What did you think, Gertrude?"

"They have a lot of missionaries, don't they, Mother?" were the first words that popped out of Gertrude's mouth. The new experiences of the morning were so many that Gertrude hardly knew where to begin. But that was what she said.

"Yes, they have many missionaries," Mother said quietly.

"And this idea of Sabbath. That's very new, isn't it? I mean, we never learned about that in Lutheran catechism." Gertrude was running through all the ideas she had heard that morning and popping them out in no particular order. "And the service was so very much like our own, but there were no robes or candles."

Ruth looked over her shoulder, trying to see Gertrude's face, while continuing to walk. She stumbled over cracks in the sidewalk twice, nearly falling the second time.

"Watch where you're going, Ruth, dear," Mother cautioned. "You don't want to fall and ruin your Sabbath dress."

Mother is using all these new words, Gertrude thought. What had started out to be just another Saturday had suddenly turned into a "Sabbath" day. Now the sky was a different color and everything had changed.

Suddenly Gertrude said, "Mother, I want to come to the—u'mmm—Sabbath meetings with you again next week, if I may?"

Mother tried not to smile too broadly, but the green in her eyes sparkled like emeralds as she said, "Of course, dear. I would love for you to come with me. But what will you do about your dancing classes on Saturday morning?"

"I think I will have to change them," Gertrude said. *I will have to change a lot of things,* Gertrude thought, but she said no more. She just walked home with her mother and her sister and her brother on her first Sabbath day.

"You what?" cried Betsy Stemp.

"I am giving up my dancing," said Gertrude calmly.

"But you can't! How can you do this to me?" Betsy cried, tossing her head wildly and flinging her arms about in a violent dance of anger and fear. "How can you do this to yourself? What are you thinking?" Her teacher struggled to find the words to express her horror at what Gertrude had said so matter-of-factly.

"My life is changing and I am making some new choices," Gertrude said.

Her 30-year-old teacher was showing a side of herself that Gertrude had never seen before. Gertrude had never seen her so visibly upset. In fact, this kind of anger was totally new to Gertrude. It made her nervous and uncertain as to what to do. Not even her father in his drunkenness got this angry, at least not at her. She began to back away from this maelstrom of emotion, easing toward the front door and escape.

Just two weeks after her first Sabbath, Gertrude had come to Betsy's house to tell her of her new life. Initially, she had not intended to make these changes. But in characteristic style, once Gertrude knew what she wanted to do, she set about doing it without any further questions or doubts. What she did not understand was that other people do not necessarily accept these changes so quickly or calmly.

"I don't understand what has happened," Betsy said, trying to be more calm. She had stopped pacing and stood facing Gertrude, her countenance forcibly restrained into a benign, quizzical frown.

In the ensuing silence, Gertrude realized that her teacher had meant her statement to be a question and was waiting for an answer.

"This last summer my mother started going to some church meetings," she began quietly. "Two weeks ago she invited me to go with her. And in those two weeks I have come to the conclusion that I am not going to have a career in dancing. In fact, I am not going to dance at all."

"Not at all?" her teacher asked incredulously. "Is there some law against dancing in this new religion of yours?" she added sarcastically, moving a step closer to Gertrude.

"Actually, I don't know what the Seventh-day Adventists say about dancing. But I do know that it is no longer for me. I'm going to do something else with my life . . . make it count for something," Gertrude added almost to herself. She paused as she realized she had found an answer to a question she'd asked herself only subconsciously.

"But all that time we spent together. That summer in New York. Doesn't any of that mean anything to you?" Betsy was losing control again. She turned away and strode two or three steps back to try to remove herself from this irritation. But when she turned, Gertrude was still there and the reality of what she had been saying struck Betsy Stemp hard, like a strong wind, a wind that tore her sails down and left her lying helplessly adrift.

"What am I going to do?" she finally managed, hoisting her arms in surrender.

"I'm sorry," Gertrude offered. "I didn't know this would upset you so much." She genuinely had not realized how her decision would affect her teacher. Gertrude slowly began to understand that her dancing had meant more to her teacher that it had meant even to her. She wasn't sure why, but it surely was true.

"I'm sorry," she said again, not knowing what else to say, and again began to back toward the door.

"What about your students?" Betsy suddenly queried. "What have you done about them?"

"Oh, I've found others who are willing to take them on," Gertrude said truthfully.

"But you didn't send them to me, did you?" Betsy said, her voice rising again.

"No, I thought you were busy enough," Gertrude offered, recognizing a swamp where she didn't want to founder. She really had thought her teacher would not be the right teacher for them, but she did not say so.

Now she had her hand on the doorknob. She turned it as she said quickly, "I'm sorry." And she left.

Spring was a long time in coming, as was usual for Rochester, New York. Mountain ridges of snow dominated the middle of the streets and the curbs, thrust up and sculpted like the Catskills by the latest glacial efforts of the snowplows. In the late afternoon of this March day with no natural sense of compass direction, Gertrude just sat and rode through these mountains to wherever the city bus would take her.

The bus ride across town to and from the new school was a long one. Gertrude had to catch the bus going up Lyle Avenue and State Street to Main Street. Then she had to wait for the bus which would take her out to Browning Memorial Seventh-day Adventist Church. The school was in two rooms in the church basement. And now in the dim light of the late afternoon, she was riding the buses home in the opposite direction.

Gertrude had finished her seventh grade in the neighborhood school across the street corner from her house. She had attended the eighth grade in the local junior high school and had started her ninth grade there. But as the winds of change blew into her life, Gertrude, curious and uncharacteristically submissive, went where they took her.

When Gertrude began attending the Browning Memorial Seventh-day Adventist Church, she found they held a church school in the basement. She met and immediately liked the two teachers, Mr. Benny Preston who taught the upper grades and his wife, Ethel, who taught the lower grades. Her mother, of course, was supportive and said they would find the money to put Gertrude in church school. Thus Gertrude found herself on a one-hour crosstown bus ride every morning and evening.

Both in school and in church Gertrude began to hear and quickly devour the truths of the Bible. She did not understand everything she heard and she did not find some of the concepts easy to incorporate into her life. But for the most part, Pastor Cardey's observation was correct. Here was a bright mind, waiting to be taught.

Gertrude soon discovered that her foundations for a scholar's life had been poorly laid. She found herself struggling with the simplest math problems and the easiest English sentences. During her lower grades she had devoted all her time to her dancing and nothing to her school work. Now it was becoming increasingly clear to her that she would have to work harder than she had at her dancing just to pass the ninth grade. And struggle she did.

As she gazed out on the city cradled in the soft, cold arms of winter, Gertrude recalled a confrontation with her English teacher, Miss Schneighberger, last year in the eighth grade. She had asked Gertrude to stay after class to talk with her. Gertrude could not imagine what for.

"I am sorry, Gertrude, but I cannot pass you in English. You really don't know anything," she'd said with quiet candor to the school's star dancer.

Gertrude was as stunned as if she had been slapped across the face. As she gazed into the concerned eyes of her teacher, she sensed the gnawing of an emotion she had never faced before—the fear of failure. Action was necessary, but what?

"What can I do?" she finally blurted out.

"You need to study what I give you."

It didn't quite make sense to Gertrude. Hadn't she been doing that? And yet, here was failure becoming ever more real, as real as the desk and the teacher sitting before her.

Mother will be heartbroken, was her first thought. *But I must try something.*

Summoning all her resolve, she pleaded most earnestly, "Will you give me a chance to try?"

And for the next several weeks, she did try. Gertrude raised her hand in class for every question. She handed in all of her assignments. And she tried to give her studious best to all her work.

Later, Gertrude again presented herself after class and asked, "Miss Schneighberger, do you think I have improved any?"

Miss Schneighberger gazed at her hopeful pupil. Sighing quietly, she said aloud, "Well, to tell you the truth, Gertrude, your brains are all in your feet."

Gertrude did pass. But now in this new school more than ever she felt the weight of poor scholastics covering her up, smothering her, just as the snow outside the bus window smothered the city.

Gertrude stepped down from the bus with her arms loaded with books. Fortunately she had to walk only a half block along Dewey Street to reach her house. She passed the fire station and waved to her friends there.

At the corner, she looked across the vacant lot to her right. There was the front yard of her home just down Bryan Street—the mulberry tree with light green hints of foliage at the tips of its branches, the large front porch with the rockers and the old glider, the big blue spruce at the corner of the house. At least this part of her life had not changed.

"How was your day, dear?" her mother called as she came through the front door. "I'm in the kitchen."

Gertrude made a detour through the dining room, dropping her books on the table. Mother was always in the kitchen. It was her workroom, her sewing room, her throne room. *Mother is queen here,* Gertrude thought as she came through the door.

"Good evening, your majesty," Gertrude said in mock submissiveness, curtsying gently, almost to the floor. She had not lost her gracefulness even though she had stopped dancing.

"Good evening, yourself, you silly girl," said Mother as she turned from the sink to peck her on the cheek. She turned back to her work. "So how did the scholar do today?"

"Oh, Mother, I am struggling so." Gertrude sighed. But then she quickly recovered her usual optimism. "But I am improving in English. Mr. Preston said so again today."

"Good for you." Mother carried the colander of green beans to the stove and placed them in the pressure cooker for supper. She struck a match and lit the gas burner under them. Then she turned and sat in a chair opposite where Gertrude perched on the edge of her own chair at the kitchen table.

"I've been thinking about your schooling," Mother said with her usual directness.

"I have, too. All day long," Gertrude echoed.

"No. I mean what you're going to do after this year."

Gertrude crossed her arms on the table and looked at her mother more intently, especially at her eyes. *You can always tell when Mother is serious by her eyes,* thought Gertrude. *They get larger and the gray disappears. Only the green remains.*

Mother was composing herself, settling in for one of their girl-to-girl talks. There was a moment of silence as she straightened her dress and touched her hair. The rich spicy smell of the kitchen hung in the air.

Gertrude waited respectfully. *Mother is always thinking about our future. I wonder what she's planning now.*

"Have you thought about what you'll do next year, Gertrude?" Mother finally asked.

"Well, no, I haven't really," Gertrude said. "I don't actually know what I can do." She thought she knew where Mother was going with this one. "I know I can continue at Browning Memorial. They teach 10 grades there now, but Helen and I would be the only ones in that grade. And I don't think that's a good choice for me. But where can I go? Do I have to go back to the public high school? I don't think I have any other choice, do I, Mother?" The words tumbled out like so many heavy rocks, much in the same order and with the same haste as Gertrude was thinking them. Then she stopped. *Mother obviously has an idea. What is it?*

"What about the new academy . . . Union Springs Academy? Have you thought about going there?"

"Oh, Mother, I couldn't possibly. I mean, we can't afford it, can we?"

Gertrude's face was the picture of disbelief but her voice was hopeful. "Can we?"

"If you are going to be somebody, Gertrude, you have to have an education. And that includes a religious education as well. I don't know what you're going to do with your life. But I think going back to the high school would be a step in the wrong direction, don't you?" Mother asked earnestly.

"Yes, Mother, I do. But can we afford it? Father's job is not as good as it used to be."

"How do you know these things?" her mother questioned.

"Well, I notice things," said Gertrude looking around at the kitchen. "I notice that you're not buying as much as you used to. And you're making more of our clothes than you used to."

"Well, it's true," said Mother with a sigh of resignation. "But don't you worry about the money, *liebchen*. I have a few ideas that I'm looking into."

"But what do you think?" Mother asked with a smile. Her eyes lit up as she reached across the table to touch her eldest daughter. "Would you like to go to Union Springs Academy?"

"Oh, yes, Mother. I would like to very much," Gertrude answered, touching her mother's hand in return.

"Good," Mother said, rising from the table. "Then we'll plan on it."

Gertrude watched Mother turn to the stove and adjust the flame. Then she stepped to the sink as if to say that their serious conversation was at an end. Gertrude bit her lip in a moment of contemplation and then she spoke.

"Mother, why was the Lutheran minister here last Sunday evening?" she finally asked.

Mother, rinsing the colander, stopped with her hands in midair and held them there for a long moment. Gertrude, watching the shocked reaction, realized that she'd asked a far more serious question than she knew.

Her mother turned slowly, placed both of her hands on the edge of the sink behind her, and leaned back on it for support. Gertrude saw her mother's eyes go to gray, almost to tears.

She saw sorrow cross her mother's face that she had not seen since Grandmother Schwader had died.

"Why do you ask, Gertrude? What did you hear?" Mother asked softly.

"Well, we didn't hear anything, really," Gertrude said quietly. "Ruth and

I were trying to keep Frederick entertained downstairs so we couldn't hear anything." She paused, looking at her mother for an answer. "But the minister was up there in your bedroom—with you and Father—for a very long time. We finally took Frederick over to see the fire trucks and when we got back, he was gone."

"And I hope he never comes back," Mother said, her face suddenly becoming German hard and her eyes more piercing. "Gertrude, he wanted me to divorce your father."

"Oh, Mother," Gertrude gasped, raising her hand to her mouth as if to stifle the thought, "Why, whatever for?"

"Because I left the Lutheran Church," she said as she crossed her arms in defiance. "Because I became a Seventh-day Adventist."

Gertrude felt her face go hot and then cold. *What will become of us,* she thought. *What will happen to my brothers and my sister? And to my chances to go to academy? And to Father. Poor Father.*

Mother saw the color drain from Gertrude's face. She came quickly and knelt close beside her chair, putting one hand in Gertrude's lap and stroking her hair with the other.

"I think he was trying to threaten me," she explained in a quiet but strained voice. "Or he was trying to make your father angry, get him to react. But he didn't, of course. As you know, your father doesn't care much about any religion, Lutheran or Adventist. And I was too shocked to be as angry as I am now."

"But you aren't going to do it, are you?" Gertrude asked, searching her mother's face.

"No, dear Gertrude," Mother said, squeezing Gertrude's hand, "I'm not going to divorce your father. It would be foolish and very unchristian, not to mention cruel to your father."

Mother looked into her face, "You do know I love him, don't you?" she said most earnestly.

"Yes, Mother, we all do," Gertrude sighed. She could read in her face the pain her mother endured because of her father's drinking and what it was doing to his health and to his job.

"But the Lutheran minister is gone and I shall put it all out of my mind," Mother said as she rose and returned to her work at the sink. "I think you shouldn't worry about it either." Then she turned and looked at Gertrude earnestly, as a confidante. "And I don't think you should discuss this with Ruth or Frederick, OK?"

"Yes, Mother, I know," she said as she nodded her head. And she did know—that it would only worry the others; that these things were best kept quiet between friends.

Absently, Gertrude got up and began to set the table for supper. She carried the plates into the dining room, stacking them next to her books. As she was placing her books on the floor beside the hutch, Mother called out to her.

"Gertrude, what are we going to do with those costumes in that trunk in your room? We need to move the trunk to make room for Ruth's things."

"I don't know, Mother." she said without thinking, getting out the every-day silverware. "Maybe just store them in the attic, I guess."

Chapter 4

THE STRUGGLING SCHOLAR

Just south of Lake Ontario in New York State, between Rochester and Syracuse, lies a necklace of dangling baubles called the Finger Lakes. Counting from east to west, Lake Cayuga is the fourth of these. At the southern end of this lake is the town of Ithaca and Cornell University. At its northern end is Waterloo, some distance to the west, and Auburn to the east. And one-fifth of the way south from the northern end on the east side of the lake is the small Quaker town of Union Springs.

At least it was a Quaker town when, in 1857, they purchased the Presbyterian three-story brick school building and its surrounding 33 acres up in an oak grove area known as The Hill. The Quakers established a modern, nationally renowned educational center known after 1876, as Oakwood Seminary. It was in continual operation until a fire destroyed the upper floors of the main building in 1918.

In 1921 the newly reorganized New York Conference of Seventh-day Adventists was seeking to consolidate its two previously separate academies and move to a new property to establish a work-study "family school" boarding academy. For the small sum of $5,000, they purchased the previous Quaker Academy and Union Springs Academy was born.

In response to an aggressive recruiting campaign by the principal, Professor Claude Shull, the Bible teacher, Dr. Paul Quimby, and the math teacher, Gerald Miles, 94 students came to Union Springs Academy in the fall of 1923. One of them was an unbaptized, non-church member and former dancer named Gertrude Green.

In the early afternoon sun of a late August day, Gertrude alighted from the New York Central coach car that brought her from Rochester. She was alone. Other passengers, preoccupied, went about their business of arriving and leaving. The usual bustle of activities surrounding a train station flowed around her, but no one was waiting for her or stepped forward to greet her.

Gertrude had been teaching dancing classes, riding buses, and carrying her mother's confidential conversations all alone for some years now. So being by herself was neither fearful nor confusing.

After checking about her once more to make sure she had not missed a welcoming party, Gertrude stepped briskly along the train side platform, suitcase in hand, to where the train hands were unloading the trunks from the baggage car. She arranged for her trunk to be kept at the station until she could find out what arrangements could be made to take it up to the school. Then she walked to the reception window and spoke to the man in the green visor who sat in the shadows inside the station.

"Please, sir," she said in a firm, even voice, "could you direct me to Union Springs Academy?"

The man looked up from his work and returned the even gaze of this short, thin girl with the bobbed brown hair. "You're one of those Advent students, aren't you?" he said with some knowledge.

This was his second year to watch these well-mannered students arrive in the fall in their nearly look-alike uniforms, especially the girls in their sailor suits, carrying their suitcases and adolescent lostness in plain sight. But he noted that this one was different. She returned his gaze with the confident eyes of a seasoned traveler. Yet she was asking the way to the school, so she must be new here, even though she was not new to being on her own.

"Yes, sir," Gertrude answered politely. "This is my first year here and I don't know the way to the school. So if you could kindly direct me, I would be most obliged."

"You just go out that away," the station man said, now half rising and pointing out through his window, "to Seminary Street. It's not a very long walk up the hill and you'll see it right off."

Gertrude thanked him kindly. She turned and walked the short distance to the steps at the end of the station platform, over which hung the usual sign, marking the town as "Union Springs." Gertrude marched down the steps and into her new life as an academy student.

The walk up the hill of Seminary Street was a pleasant stroll. The tall elm trees and telephone poles reached out to arch over the gravel road and provide shade from the warm afternoon sun. To Gertrude's surprise, houses and a church with a tall steeple lined the street all the way to the top of the hill. She had expected the school to be out in the countryside as there was said to be a farm and some acreage attached to the property.

When she reached the top of the hill, she saw a large three-story red brick building set back from the street. It occupied the very top of the hill like a fortress, yet seemed to be trying to conceal itself among the surrounding tall trees. In fact, it almost seemed to be two buildings, one facing west toward the lake and the other, crowned with a cupola, facing in the opposite direction. A narrower section of the same height stretched between the two buildings, joining them like a doubletree between two horses.

A veranda fronted the end of the building that faced the lake. It looked like it might serve as the front of the school. So Gertrude marched up Grove Street and then up the long flight of stairs that led to the veranda and the large door that seemed to be the entrance.

As she stepped into the darkened interior, Gertrude found herself in a small alcove, sparsely furnished, which contained a reception desk and several office doors. There was no one at all in this outer chamber. The first door to her left marked "Principal" was closed, but the door next to it stood open. As if she were working out a maze, Gertrude proceeded to the open door.

A woman in her late 20s, willowy despite her fully bloused sleeves, and modern with her hair cut in the new shorter style, looked up from behind her large desk.

"Hello," she said as she stood and extended her hand across her desk, "I'm Bernice Andrews, the preceptress. Welcome to Union Springs Academy."

"Hello," said Gertrude, stepping into the room and taking her hand briefly. "I'm Gertrude Green. From Rochester."

Gertrude admiringly noted that Miss Andrews wore what was commonly known as the "reform dress," a long-sleeved white blouse with high collar gathered at the throat and a three-quarter length full, dark skirt over simple laced shoes with low heels. Her appearance was modestly becoming, if a bit old-fashioned.

"I've come to Union Springs Academy for my tenth grade," Gertrude added. Feeling awkward in the presence of higher authority, she retreated a few steps toward the door.

Responding instinctively to her discomfort, Miss Andrews deliberately abandoned her safe haven behind the desk. As she spoke, she moved casually around her desk and leaned against its front. Gertrude sensed her friendly intentions and began to relax.

"It seems I am the only one here at the moment," Miss Andrews said. "But I think the others will be returning from dinner soon." She paused, noting that Gertrude carried only her suitcase and no lunch basket.

"Have you had anything to eat today?"

"Yes, ma'am. I had breakfast." Gertrude tried not to look hungry. It was now past 1:00 o'clock. Gertrude did not want to take charity, but she didn't have the money to spend. In fact, she was very much in trouble in that department.

"I do have a problem that I need help with," she said tentatively.

Gertrude set her suitcase down and opened it to take out her small purse. Retrieving what was left of her money, she held it out with both hands in front of her, like a worship offering, for inspection. She spoke rapidly, her large eyes imploring dispensation.

"I worked very hard this last summer and earned enough money to get ready for school. And Mother helped me to make most of my clothes. I had $15 dollars when I left home in Rochester. But I had to buy my train ticket and then I didn't have enough to buy my lunch." She stopped to draw a breath and hurried on. "And I really need a job so that I can stay in school."

She stopped speaking and stood there. All that morning Gertrude had been processing her financial situation. She longed for an academy education, a dream she had shared with her mother. During the entire trip from Rochester she had worried that she might have made the trip for nothing. What if she didn't have the enough money, could not earn enough money, and would have to go home?

"H'mmm, I can appreciate your dilemma," Miss Andrews said as she sympathetically traced the anxious lines of the small face before her, "but I think that will not be a problem." She held up both hands, refusing to examine the money offered. "We'll talk about this with Professor Shull, the principal, later. We have an excellent work program here and I'm sure something can and will be arranged."

She raised herself from her perch on the front of her desk and extended her hand. "But first, how about we go downstairs to the dining hall and find some free lunch, shall we?"

Gertrude's shoulders relaxed and her eyes smiled for the first time since leaving Rochester. She hid her money away in her small purse, carefully closed her suitcase, and followed Miss Andrews out the office door. As she leaned slightly left to counterbalance her suitcase, she remembered her trunk at the train station.

"Miss Andrews," she said, suddenly coming to a stop in the outer office, "my trunk in still at the train station. How can I get it up to the school?"

Miss Andrews paused at the door.

"One of the boys earns his money by carrying up the trunks. But we can arrange that later." *My, how this child does worry,* she thought.

Again Miss Andrews beckoned and Gertrude followed her through the large, open doorway to the veranda.

Chapter 5

THE NEW ROOMMATE

During the next three years, Gertrude became quite familiar with the dining hall and the kitchen. Just as she had enjoyed doing at home, her assigned work duties included washing the evening dishes in two large tubs, one for washing and one for rinsing and drying. One of the boys worked with her, washing the large pots used in food preparation. Always one for a bit of fun, Gertrude sometimes joined the boy in splashing water on one another, making the work more like play and making the time go faster.

Gertrude enjoyed the friendship of many of the boys. At the Saturday night marching exercises and at the girls' reception she was accompanied frequently by one of her male friends, but she never gave serious thought to any of them. The indelible memory of the pain in her mother's eyes over a life with an alcoholic husband caused her to applaud the Victorian separation of the sexes at the academy.

Gertrude shared a room with Catherine Cushman, the niece of the Bible teacher, Professor Paul Quimby. Their room was on the third floor in Sunset Hall, the end of the seminary building facing west, separated by solid plaster walls and locked doors from Cooledge Hall, the boys' end of the building. Facing north, their window allowed them to look out over the electrical generator building next door and into the attached rolling farm acreage which provided employment for many of the boys. The arduous climb up the three flights of stairs from her work in the kitchen to her third floor room was no problem for the legs of a former dancer like Gertrude.

Returning to her room one evening, Gertrude found several of her friends gathered there. They were talking excitedly with Catherine about the upcoming Home Talent Show being organized by Miss Blakney, the music teacher. As Gertrude entered the room, two of the girls were practicing the duet they'd be singing. Another group of three were discussing the piano solo one of them would do. And a third group was discussing a reading.

For just a moment Gertrude stood watching these would-be entertainers, remembering her own previous performances to much more sophisticated audiences in Rochester. Her mind tried to span the gap between where she had been then and where she was now. But the gap was too wide. She had already crossed it and could not go back. The best she could do was to realize just what a different world Union Springs really was.

When Catherine saw Gertrude watching from the doorway she ran to her and pulled her into the whirlwind of girl talk that filled the room.

"Gertrude," she asked loudly, "what are you going to do for the Home Talent Show?"

Gertrude was the immediate focus of everyone's attention.

"Oh, I don't think I'll do anything," she demurred. Her mind raced over ground these girls had never dreamed of even as she tried to retreat from the center of the room.

"Don't you know how to do something? Don't you have some hidden talent?" one of the girls asked, a hint of sarcasm in her voice.

"Yes, I play the piano," Gertrude said, turning to face the speaker, quickly adding, "but I don't think it's good enough to perform in front of others."

"Well, you must know how to do *something*."

Gertrude looked around the room at her new friends. She saw in Catherine's face that she wanted to help, wanting to say something, or wanting Gertrude to do something.

Deliberately Gertrude walked to her bed, reached under it, and withdrew her suitcase. As all eyes watched she took out one of her favorite dance costumes and smoothed it out on the bed. Then she carefully placed her ballet shoes beside it. She could not have said why she had kept them with her, perhaps a last remembrance of the dancer she had been, perhaps an attachment to her mother who'd lovingly encouraged and supported her by making her costumes.

Soon she stood before them in her favorite Greek sheer, her headband in place, and her glasses on the bed with her school clothes. As she took her position, head held high, arms delicately rounded above her, everyone fell back to the edges of the room, leaving the center empty. She rose up on her left foot rigidly pointed to the center of the earth. Her right foot floated at her left knee then gently extended straight out in front of her.

The music began in her head and Gertrude began to dance. She floated in twirls. She glided above the floor, seeming not to touch it. Her arms and her legs became extensions of her mind as she relived once again the beauty of what she once had wanted to be. The room was utterly silent.

She landed from a small leap and took two steps on her pointed toes. Then looking around she stopped and slowly lowered herself to stand flat-footed as normal humans do. The dream and the music faded and she returned to the present. Suddenly feeling self-conscious and out of place in her costume, she stepped to the bed where her school clothes lay.

"Gertrude, I didn't know," Catherine said, just above a whisper.

Gertrude turned to face them.

"I am . . . I was a dancer, a very good dancer."

She felt her courage returning and with it a conviction that she had discovered something about herself which she had not understood previously.

"But when I came to understand that Jesus loves me, I knew I could not be a dancer"— here her voice choked for just a moment—"and love Him in return. I don't know how I knew that, but I did. So I gave it all up. And I have not danced for the last two years—until now."

She reached up and took off her headband and put on her glasses, breathing easier, returning to herself.

"I wanted you to know what I was before. And that now, I want to live for Jesus. So I will never dance again."

As she began to take off her costume and put on her school clothes, the girls quietly left the room. When she'd finished dressing, only Catherine was there, busying herself on her side of the room. Gertrude sat on the edge of her bed, staring at her hands in her lap.

Then Catherine sat on her bed and looked across at her.

"What *will* you do with your life, Gertrude?"

"I don't know," she answered honestly.

"Uncle Paul—uh—Professor Quimby said that you really talked a lot about Mr. Rainey's Alaska presentation at Sabbath dinner last week. That you were really keen on going there someday."

"I do like the cold." Gertrude smiled, remembering the thrill of the cold wind when the students went ice skating on Lake Cayuga or tobogganing on Seminary Street.

"Maybe you could be a missionary to Alaska," Catherine said.

"Maybe. But I don't know what I would do there . . . as a missionary." Gertrude finally looked at her friend and smiled. "I'm not even baptized yet, so I don't think they will take me. Not yet anyway."

Every spring, V. O. Punches led the Colporteur Band at the academy, training 20 to 30 students for selling Christian literature the following summer. Between her sophomore and junior years Gertrude participated heartily in selling *Life and Health* magazine door-to-door, because doing so, she received a 10 percent discount on her school bill. This would help her mother, who continued to search for ways to stretch Father's ever-shrinking paycheck.

In the middle of the summer of 1924, Gertrude made the decision to be baptized. O. D. Cardey, who had seen her as a bright mind, had the privilege of lowering her into the watery grave and bringing her forth into newness of life. Was her decision made that first Thirteenth Sabbath? Or when she had faced her dancing teacher? When she and her mother had planned for her to attend the academy? Or was it in that third floor dorm room at Union Springs Academy—the day she stopped dancing for good? Through all of these experiences and more, Gertrude decided. Now she would live her life for Jesus. But just how she would do that was yet to be discovered.

Gertrude's senior year in 1925-26 found many changes at the academy. Gerald Miles, the math teacher, replaced Professor Shull as principal. Professor Quimby, the Bible teacher and pastor, and his wife, the English teacher, were also gone. And their niece, Catherine, had not returned.

In her place was a new roommate, Gertrude's sister, Ruth. After finishing 10 grades in the Rochester public school system, with the encouragement of her mother she'd joined Gertrude at Union Springs Academy. Gertrude reveled in her role as big sister, introducing Ruth to all her favorite activities including "shopping" on Town Day.

In the latter part of April, as Spring kissed the elm trees with green lips along Seminary Street, Miss Severs, the new music teacher, accompanied eight girls on an afternoon visit to the small town of Union Springs. This was a special outing because these girls had maintained an excellent grade average in their respective classes and an excellent grade in their deportment. Since Gertrude was doing so well in her classes, she was able to go. Ruth, of course, had no difficulty with her grades. Gertrude thought Ruth was a genius.

"Do you know why I love to come to town? Do you?" Gertrude asked as she peered into the next large-windowed store.

"No, I cannot imagine," Ruth said, obviously bored with being dragged from store window to store window.

"Because I love to go shopping," Gertrude said, not hearing her sister's tired voice.

"But Gertrude, you never spend any money," Ruth said with sudden, sharp exasperation.

Gertrude bent at the waist to peer in the window at some item on the floor, then turned and shaded her eyes with her hand to see the shadow of her sister's face.

"Of course I don't spend any money," she said sharply. "How could I, with Mother selling men's ties on the street to keep us in academy? But if I had the money, I know what I'd buy. And I'd know where to get it at the best price," she added to clinch her argument.

"You should be a lawyer," Ruth said, folding her arms in reluctant resignation.

"What I should do," Gertrude said, straightening herself, "is sweeten your disposition." Then she smiled, "And I know just the place. Come with me, young lady."

She grabbed her sister's hand and started running with her down the street and around the corner.

"Hold up!" shouted the laughing Ruth, clutching her purse and trying to keep up. "I can't run like you can."

The two girls arrived at the Drug Store and Soda Shop laughing and gasping for breath. The tinkling of the small bell above the door announced their arrival to the three other girls who were already sitting on the stools in front of the soda counter.

"Gertrude, Ruth, come join us," they shouted.

"Two ice cream chocolate fudge sundaes, please," Gertrude called out.

Gertrude and Ruth piled onto the two stools next to their friends. They looked like five little matching mushrooms, all coifed with rounded, ear-length haircuts and dressed in matching brown middies, bobbing toward one another as if a light forest breeze where blowing along the soda shop counter. And this is where Miss Severs found them when it was time to go back to the academy for supper.

Later that evening, after completing her work assignment in the kitchen, Gertrude was the first to arrive at their large corner room on the second floor. She went immediately to their shared study desk under the west window that faced the lake. The brilliant sunset, which she usually loved to watch from this vantage point, was ignored tonight. Facing the last month of her senior year, Gertrude was going to wring every last drop of education from her remaining time, as if still trying to make up for all the information she missed in grade school.

"I'm home," Ruth cried as she came through the door clutching three envelopes. She propped herself up on her single bed just inside the door, her back against the wall, and scanned the addresses.

"There's a letter from Mother," she said. Both she and Gertrude knew that Mother wrote every week.

"And there's one here from the New England Sanitarium and Hospital," she reported. She held it up to the light as if trying to see what was in it.

Gertrude leaped out of her chair, nearly knocking it over. Ruth handed over the letter with a quizzical look.

"Why are you getting a letter from them?" she asked.

"I applied for their nursing program," Gertrude said, standing in the middle of the floor and gingerly holding the letter at arm's length, hesitating to open it.

"I didn't know you were interested in nursing," Ruth said.

Saying nothing, Gertrude slowly drew the letter to eye level and opened the envelope. Her eyes carefully read each word, hardly daring to believe what it said. Then she clutched it to her chest and sank to her knees on the floor just in front of her sister.

"They have accepted me."

Her eyes shone with a thousand lights as she beamed at her sister.

"Well, of course, they accepted you, silly," Ruth responded. "Why shouldn't they?"

"I didn't think my grades would be good enough," Gertrude said, looking again at the letter to make sure she had read it correctly. "You're the brainy one, you know," she added, smiling now at Ruth. "I've always said you have your brains and mine, too."

"You do just fine," Ruth encouraged. "The letter proves it."

Ruth flopped around like a large seal until she was lying on her stomach across her bed with her legs propped against the wall. She beamed at her big sister sitting in front of her.

"What were you so worried about?"

"Oh, you know," Gertrude said, suddenly busying herself with retrieving the scraps of the envelope she'd dropped on the floor. "The algebra class that I failed my first year here and had to take it over by correspondence from Fireside. You know, I just thought that maybe . . ." Her voice trailed off as a curtain of worry covered her face.

"Well, it didn't seem to bother them," Ruth said, gesturing at the letter. "So stop worrying. You're in, kid."

With that, Ruth jumped off the bed and hugged her sister for a long time as they both sat in the middle of the floor in their dorm room.

Then Gertrude, ever practical, held her sister at arms' length and said, "And what are you going to do with your life? You'll have to go through this next year, you know."

"Who, me?" Ruth asked nonchalantly. She disentangled herself from Gertrude's grasp and stood, distractedly turning to smooth the cover on her bed. "I'm going to play the violin and do concerts all over the world."

"Then why are you taking the pre-medical course here at the academy?" Gertrude asked, taking on the mothering role.

"Because it's the only one that interests me," Ruth said, trying to escape her sister's sharp mind. "Besides I want to go to Atlantic Union College, I think. And that's the only course the academy has that gets you ready for college." She turned and sat on her bed, wrinkling her brow with seriousness. "I don't know, Gertrude. There aren't many things that a girl can do. I just have to get ready."

"Well, we can sew," Gertrude said. She looked around at the curtains they'd put up and at the clothes they had helped their mother make for them.

"Oh, it helps all right, but I don't think that's going to feed us," Ruth retorted. "We need something a little more practical, I think—like nursing." She looked approvingly at Gertrude as if she were now the big sister. "Is that what you're going to do in Alaska?"

"Alaska?" Gertrude asked with genuine surprise and shock.

"The girls told me that the Senior Class will in the yearbook says something about you're going to be a missionary in Alaska," Ruth explained.

"Oh, that."

Gertrude stood up and straightened her skirt, brushing off the idea.

"In my first year here, Mr. Rainey made a presentation about Alaska, and I said I thought it would be an adventure to go there because I liked the cold." She retreated to the chair at the desk. "Everyone else thought I wanted to be a missionary. That's all."

Before Gertrude could turn around and begin her studies again, Ruth remembered the letter from their mother.

"Before you start again, let's read Mother's letter."

As Gertrude settled herself more comfortably on the chair, Ruth opened the letter and began to read.

Chapter 6

THE STUDENT NURSE

"Gertrude!" Lillian called, hurrying down the hall with her arms full, "Gertrude, wait for me."

Gertrude, who was almost to the stairwell with her own valuable treasures collected in the maze of offices, turned to see who was calling her. Lillian Havens, small of frame and brunette like Gertrude, was half running, trying not to lose her pile of books, papers, and uniforms held loosely in both arms in front of her like a dinner tray. Gertrude waited for her at the top of the staircase. Lillian and she had been classmates at Union Springs Academy and now they were both registering for the nursing course in Melrose near Stoneham, Massachusetts.

"I just never thought there'd be so much to do to get ready for nursing," said Lillian, gasping for breath as they walked together down to the first floor of the New England Sanitarium and Hospital. "I've spent all morning going from office to office. I think I have signed my name to every piece of paper there is."

Lillian backed into the outside door and held it open as Gertrude sidled through with her precious bundle of books and clothes.

"And the money!" Lillian said as they began the walk to the student nursing dorm, "Can you imagine—$40!"

"Yes," Gertrude managed, lost in her own thoughts about the $40.

Lillian noticed her friend's quiet response. She squinted against the sun and tried to look sideways into Gertrude's face. But Gertrude's eyes were half closed and downcast, focused on the bundle in her arms.

"Gertrude?" Lillian asked, "Is there a problem with the $40?"

"No, no problem."

Gertrude squared her shoulders, took a deep breath and gazed back at her friend, her eyes now brightening.

"No problem," she repeated. "I don't have it, is all."

"You don't," Lillian gasped. "But they let you register, didn't they? I mean, you have all your things, your books and all." She nodded at the load similar to hers in Gertrude's arms. "What happened?"

"Well, I had $40 when I started out for the train in Rochester," Gertrude said with a snort of disgust at herself. "But I had to buy my train ticket, of course. And I had to have something to eat. It's a long train ride to Boston. I guess I forgot about those things when I started out." She shook her head at her lack of planning, the curls at the ends of her brown hair bobbing and weaving like Christmas tree ornaments.

"But not to worry," she added, smiling, "I did this when I first went to academy and I can do it again here."

"Do what?" Lillian asked.

They'd reached the front door of Langwood Hall, the student nurses' dormitory. Both shifted their load so they could manage to open and hold the large front door as they entered the three-story structure. The downstairs parlor was full of new students, now scowling to figure out their room assignments, now laughing to greet old friends—some both at the same time. Around the edges a few second and third-year students were watching the new "probies" arrive for the first time. The place hummed like a commuter station at rush hour.

Gertrude and Lillian worked their way through the clusters of soon-to-be classmates to the back stairs that led to the upper floors.

"Do what?" Lillian repeated when they were in the back hallway and away from the noise.

"I'll have to work out the other $25," Gertrude said as she rounded the stair post and began the climb up. "I'll have to work waiting tables in the dining room for a while but it'll be all right."

"Wow," was all Lillian could manage as she tried to keep up with Gertrude's rapid ascent.

"I stop here," Lillian said as they reached the second floor landing. "Where are you going?"

Gertrude had already begun the climb up the next set of stairs. She stopped and turned on the third step and said, "I'm in the small room at the top of the landing and around to the left. Why don't you come up when you've changed and we'll go to supper."

"OK," Lillian said as she thought about one more flight of stairs to climb. Then she turned and struggled hurriedly down the hall.

Gertrude continued on up the stairs to the landing, made the left turn, and came to the door to her room. She just managed to edge open the door with her hand and to deposit her supplies on her bed. Then she walked to the window and opened it, taking a deep breath of the breeze which gently blew the curtains aside to freshen the room.

Gertrude gazed out for just a moment at the new world that was to be her home for the next three years. Although the hospital blocked her view to the left, she could see the lawns and many of the buildings on the huge campus of the sanitarium. Several houses—lived in by some of the doctors, she understood—were connected by walkways and all cascaded down the hill past the semicircular drive at the front of the property. Trees and bushes cuddled up to and embraced the homes. It occurred to Gertrude that she should enjoy the view now because she probably wouldn't see much of it in the future, considering her work schedule for the next several months.

She turned and gathered her books and papers, carrying them to the small desk across the room. As she began to lay out the blue probie uniforms on her bed before hanging them in her closet, Gertrude heard a knock at the door.

"Come in," she called.

Lillian rushed into the room, swishing about in a circle to close the door, at the same time flaring with her left hand the skirt of the new plain blue dress she now wore.

"Isn't it just awful?" she cried as she turned another full circle. "And they're all exactly alike!"

"Oh, I don't know," Gertrude replied. "They aren't all that different from the uniforms we wore at the academy." She took off the blouse and jumper she'd worn from Rochester and hung it in the small closet at the other end of the room.

"Well, they weren't all alike," Lillian said, flopping on the bed.

"Almost," said Gertrude as she put on her own blue uniform that she'd wear for the next six months. "I guess we are now officially on probation—since we have on our 'probie' uniform." She turned about to see how it looked and realized it was about as plain as Lillian had said.

Gertrude laughed. "Let's go show it to the world!" she said, opening the door and waiting for Lillian to join her.

For the next six months Gertrude and Lillian, and the rest of the girls in the class of 1926, lived in their probie uniforms whenever they were on duty—which was almost every waking moment.

They rose at 5:00 a.m., dressed, and hurried to the sanitarium kitchen. There they got the carts loaded with trays for the patients' breakfasts. For the next hour and a half they delivered the breakfasts to the patients on their assigned floors. After a brief time to eat their own breakfast they hurried to their first class of the day, hydrotherapy. After an hour-long lecture, they gave treatments to patients who came to the hydrotherapy room from both the hospital and the outlying cottages on campus. In addition, in certain situations, some of the hospital patients had to be treated in their rooms.

Usually the treatments were finished just in time for them to go back to the kitchen to pick up lunch trays which they delivered during the next hour. With barely enough time for their own lunch they rushed to their afternoon classes—anatomy, physiology, and nursing techniques. In the late afternoon some of the hydrotherapy treatments had to be repeated, or sometimes they had a short break. At supper time they repeated the trek from kitchen to patients' bedsides with the supper trays.

If they were lucky, they had the rest of the evening off for study, but sometimes they had evening treatment assignments as well. There were so many patients that almost every probie was involved in the treatments until 9:00 p.m.

Finally, on a rotating basis, sleeping duty was assigned. No, not to give the student nurses time to sleep! Usually sleeping duty involved sleeping in the room of a patient who might require something during the night. But sometimes the patient was especially sick or needed around-the-clock care. Then the nights were long and the time for sleep was short. The student nurse would have just enough time to run back to the dorm and climb the two or three flights of stairs to change into a fresh uniform before the breakfast trays had to go out again.

Five-fifteen one Friday morning in early December found Gertrude climbing the stairs to the second-floor landing as Lillian was coming down.

"Gertrude!" Lillian gasped, stopping to stare at the apparition before her. "You look just dreadful. What happened?"

Gertrude, climbing much slower than her usual pace, looked up into the startled face of her friend, and slowly grinned.

"I'm a sight, aren't I?" she managed, trying to smooth her hair. "It's the last night of a long week."

"What have you been doing?" Lillian rushed down the stairs, taking hold of Gertrude's hand as if to steady her. "What kind of patient did you have?"

"Oh, she wasn't very sick actually," Gertrude said, patting Lillian's hand, "but I've had to stay awake almost every night this week and count the number of times she turned over in her sleep. I just don't know how I'm going to stay awake today in class," she added weakly, leaning against the large banister.

"Whatever did they want to know that for?" Lillian asked, slowly shaking her head.

"I don't know," Gertrude said. "I just know that I'm going to get some sleep tonight. That's all."

Gertrude continued her climb up the stairs as Lillian, assuaged in her concern and remembering her own duties, dropped her friend's hand and rushed down to her own early morning assignment.

"Yes, get some sleep tonight," she shot back over her shoulder. "You don't want to miss the party tomorrow evening."

Saturday evening after sundown was party time in the parlor for those lucky enough not to have weekend duty. And Gertrude, refreshed after a good night's sleep, was in the center of it all. Carrying a tray of cups steaming with hot cider, she returned to her group of friends just as Lillian crossed the parlor to join them.

"And who is this sweet young lady?" quipped one of the girls, "I don't believe I recognize you without your blue dress."

"Oh, you silly," Lillian said, snatching one of the cups from Gertrude's tray.

Gertrude set the tray on the large maple coffee table as the other girls began helping themselves to the steaming spiced cider. Lillian slid in beside one of the girls on the loveseat, wiggling to make room for herself. Gertrude stood at the end of the coffee table, the unofficial hostess and mother hen over her brood of five chicks.

"Who are all the guys from AUC, Gertrude?" one of the girls asked coyly.

"Well, let's see," Gertrude began, trying to remember each of the names of the more than a dozen boys she'd already met tonight who had come up from Atlantic Union College.

"Who's that big guy you were escorting around, Gertrude?" another one asked.

Then the whole group laughed, thinking Gertrude would be embarrassed. In truth, they were all reticent to meet the college guys, preferring to stay in their safe covey in the corner. They were amazed at Gertrude's apparent brazenness in introducing herself and actually shaking hands with strangers, especially male strangers who were all their own age.

Undisturbed and generally unaware of the thoughts of her friends, Gertrude turned to see the guy they were referring to.

"Oh, that's Harold Schultz," she said. Turning back to the group she added, "He's been here before. He wanted to meet one of the girls in our class. So I introduced him." She sipped her cider as several just shook their heads in amazement. Gertrude did not seem to know any strangers.

"I think those guys are here just to find a wife," someone offered.

"Of course they are," Lillian said. "Most of these guys are going to be pastors and they know they have to have a wife before they can get a call to a conference to take a church."

"Don't they have girls at AUC?"

"Yes," Gertrude said, "but nurses make the best pastors' wives, especially if they go overseas as missionaries."

For a moment everyone was quiet as they contemplated the fate of those nurses who might be enticed into such a relationship.

"We haven't lost any of our classmates, have we?" one girl asked.

"Not yet," Lillian replied. "The girls from the class ahead of us tell me that usually one or two probies drop out. But so far, we haven't lost anybody."

"Well, it's sure not because the work isn't hard enough," someone quickly said.

Everyone laughed, remembering the long hours they all endured.

"But we've all survived thus far," Gertrude said. Then moving quickly, she grabbed the hands of Lillian and the girl next to her and pulled them to their feet. "Come on, girls, let's go meet the fellas. We need to know them before the marching starts over in the gym. Unless you want to march with each other."

With the group of five in tow like a flock of reluctant partridges, Gertrude headed for the young men on the other side of the parlor.

The solemn capping ceremony, held in January at the end of their first six months, was all that Gertrude had hoped it would be. Each nursing student walked forward to receive her white cap and candle. While one of the older nurses portrayed Florence Nightingale holding her lamp, each student then passed by the Lady with the Lamp and lit her candle, repeating the time-honored ritual of passage from probie to nurse, accepting the responsibilities of the profession.

While Gertrude waited and watched for her turn, she thought about the patients who had passed under her care in the last six months and whether she had done well as their nurse. She had done well in her studies so far, she knew that. They had covered so much information, yet she needed to know more. She couldn't seem to get enough of learning now. What did she need to know next?

Then she heard a voice call her name. As the others had done, Gertrude stood and walked slowly forward. With a smile, the preceptress handed her a cap and candle and Gertrude moved toward Florence Nightingale. She bent to light her candle. Gertrude Green, the former dancer, was becoming some-body—maybe not somebody famous—but certainly somebody. Then she took her place with her classmates as they were transformed from probation-ary students—probies—to full-fledged first-year nursing students.

The February sky hung heavily gray and close to the earth and Gertrude and Lillian wrapped their worn winter coats closer about them. The fog, pal-pably wet, poured like a waterfall over the hospital and roiled about in the space between the hospital and the chapel, boiling up over the two young women, reducing the sun to an orange smudge directly overhead.

"I'll be glad when I can earn enough money working in the dining room to buy one of those nursing capes," Gertrude said. With one hand she held her coat collar closed around her throat, clutching her Bible close to her face with the other. Her white nursing smock hung conspicuously below the dark green border of her coat.

"I'm sorry you're going to miss Sabbath dinner at the Haysmers," Lillian said as they hurried to get under the protective overhang of the hospital.

"It's OK." Gertrude turned her head only slightly in the wind and smiled around the edge of her Bible. "I was glad they asked me to help. I think it's a good idea to give the nurses some time off on Sabbath. They shouldn't have to work the whole day and miss the Sabbath blessing."

"But don't they usually ask the second and third-year students to do these special shifts?" Lillian returned.

"Well, it looks like I got an early promotion," Gertrude laughed. "Besides it's for only four hours. How hard can that be?"

"See you later then," Lillian shouted as she hurried down the walk behind the hospital and disappeared into the thick, gray mist.

Gertrude hastened through the back door of the hospital and rushed up the back stairs, taking the steps two at a time. When she reached the South Ward on the third floor, she was warm and had slowed to a walk. She shrugged out of her coat and hung it in the back of the ward office, straightened her hair, and went looking for the graduate nurse she was to relieve. She found her at the far end of the ward, passing out the lunch trays to her patients.

"Hello, how can I help?" Gertrude greeted, moving up quietly beside Flo Wainwright who was facing the end of the patient's bed.

"Oh, bless your heart," Flo said, her blond head touching cheeks with Gertrude as her hand gave Gertrude's shoulder a squeeze. "I'm so glad to get a bit of time off. It's Gertrude, isn't it?"

Gertrude nodded and smiled, pleased that she'd agreed to share the Sabbath burden with this fellow nurse.

A fellow nurse, Gertrude said to herself. *I'm really going to work as a nurse.* Her scalp tingled and her face flushed with the thrill of this new realization.

"Well, let's finish handing out these trays and I'll tell you about the folk here on my end of the ward."

For the next 20 minutes, the two girls worked and whispered together like old comrades while Gertrude got acquainted with the patients and the routine on the ward. Being a first-year student, she had experienced very little of the regular nursing work, and she certainly had never had responsibility for a whole section of the ward.

Finally they arrive at the bed of the last patient, wreathed in the smell of room deodorizer.

"And this lady is totally bedridden. I already fed her earlier," Flo said with a wave of her hand at the tray in the corner of the cubicle. "But you have to turn her every two hours to keep her from getting bedsores." Flo shook her short, blond ringlets. "We've worked very hard to keep her skin soft without any breakdowns, I can tell you that."

She turned to go.

"Well, that's everyone."

"That's fine," Gertrude said, still gazing at the last patient. "I'll be OK."

After about 10 steps Flo turned and called out. "Oh, and by the way. She has to be catheterized at 2:00 o'clock." Then she hurriedly left.

Gertrude appraised the frail, shriveled wraith before her, curled up on her side like an insignificant comma. The poor thing was totally unaware of her surroundings. She made not a glimmer of a response when Gertrude addressed her by name and tried to roll her over on her back to get the pressure off of her right hip.

But the patient could not lie on her back. Her legs were permanently contracted into the sitting position and hovered above her body, an unstable weight on a pendulum waiting to fall to one side or the other when Gertrude let go of her. Her legs could not be straightened. In fact, they could hardly be separated.

In nursing techniques class, Gertrude had learned about catheterization; at least, she had heard the lecture and seen the pictures in her textbook. But she had never catheterized anyone under the guidance of an instructor, let alone by herself. And this was not the ideal patient to start on, one who could not cooperate and who could not even get into the proper position. Gertrude made the patient as comfortable as she could, now turned on her left side, and left the room to attend to her other duties.

What am I going to do? Gertrude asked herself as she cared for her other patients, watching the hands of the clock move inevitably toward 2:00 o'clock.

Not wanting to appear inept but wanting to get some help, Gertrude looked for the other nurses on ward duty. She found two of them working on charts at the central desk. As Gertrude approached the desk, she began to speak to the two of them collectively.

"I have a totally bedfast patient down there at the end."

She turned and pointed to the end of the ward. One of the nurses looked up and seemed to glance in the direction Gertrude indicated. Gertrude thought she saw a glimmer of understanding flit across her eyes.

"I'm going to need some help at 2:00 o'clock to catheterize her."

The understanding eyes nodded in recognition of the problem and quickly returned to the work they were doing.

Are you really going to help? Gertrude thought as she walked back to her end of the ward. *I think she understands how difficult that is going to be even for someone who's done it before.*

She turned to watch the two nurses rapidly writing in their charts. As one of them abruptly rose from her chair and hurried to the far end of the room, Gertrude gradually began to understand that they each had their own difficult patients and their own busy schedules. Maybe they could help, and maybe they couldn't. As she went about her other work Gertrude continued to worry.

Gertrude looked up again at the clock above the door of the ward. Five minutes to two. With a sigh of resignation she walked to the supply room and gathered the catheter, basin, prep solutions, and sterile gloves. When she passed the main desk, she reminded the understanding eyes working there that she'd need some help. In response, she received a perfunctory wave of the hand and an unreassuring nod of the head. But the eyes did not rise from their seat or follow Gertrude down the hall.

As she walked along the corridor of curtained cubicles in the ward, Gertrude's thoughts went from *What will I do* to *How will I do this?* to *Let's see, . . . if I did it . . . this way maybe . . .*

Bringing a small table alongside the bed, she laid out her equipment, remembering the lecture she'd attended and beginning to recall the steps of the technique. Then thinking practically and logically, Gertrude worked out in her mind an approach to her problem and proceeded to carry it out. The technique worked wonderfully. And soon Gertrude had the procedure finished, the equipment tidily cleaned up, and the patient comfortably turned and now resting on her right side.

When she walked past the front desk to put everything away, the understanding eyes looked up in surprised recognition and asked if she still needed any help.

"No," Gertrude said, "it's all done and everything turned out all right." But to herself she said, *I'm just glad it's over and I hope I never have to do that again.*

Chapter 7

THE GREAT DEPRESSION

The next years passed rapidly. Gertrude literally worked her way through her last two years of nursing and after graduation accepted a yearlong position working in the physical therapy department.

Then came a momentous decision. Ever in pursuit of more education she moved to Boston and enrolled in a six-month obstetrical and gynecological nursing course at Boston Lying-In near the Harvard Medical School. Graduating from nursing school in the spring of 1929, and moving to Boston a year later, Gertrude, like many others, became entangled in the early years of the Great Depression at a time when she had few friends, no close family with financial means, and almost no income.

Throughout these later nursing school years and into her Boston experience, Gertrude frequently wrote to her sister—an attempt to share her life with someone close to her, a life which had descended from one of fulfilling work among supportive comrades in an environment of plenty to one of privation, want, and loneliness.

New England Sanitarium
Langwood Hall
Sabbath Afternoon
October, 1928

Dear Ruth,

It is a quiet Sabbath afternoon and I do not have to work. So I am taking this opportunity to write to you. I have just arrived back at my room from dinner at the home of Dr. and Mrs. Haysmer. He is a surgeon on the staff and lives in one of the nice houses on the circular drive near the front of the sanitarium. All of the staff physicians invite the nursing students to their homes on occasion, especially the second and third-year students that they know.

Their home is lovely but not so large as our house in Rochester. Mrs. Haysmer is a very plain woman, but quite pleasant. She is obviously in charge of her home and everything that happens there, including her husband. It is sure funny to watch Dr. Haysmer as just another person in her household, instead of the surgeon in charge that we see in the hospital.

You would be interested to observe, I think, the contrast between their very strict habits of living and eating and their very pleasant demeanor towards the guests and students in their home. Being a new Adventist myself, I am trying to learn seriously how Dr. Haysmer's habits of living reflect on his attitude toward others. I am not always so generous or so patient as he seems to be. I have a lot to learn about how a Christian behaves.

My new room this year is in a different building altogether from where I was for the last two years. Maybe you can remember that I was on the third floor of the nursing dorm during my first and second years here. Well, now I'm in the new stone building, the new addition. But we still have only one bathroom for the entire floor of people. And I am by myself again. But I think it's grand because I can study when I want and come and go as I want.

Mother tells me you started taking the premed course last year and are now thinking of going to Loma Linda for medical school. I am not surprised. I always said you had your brains and mine, too. You could put a book under your pillow at night and by morning you would know everything in it. Oh boy, am I proud of my little sister!

How are you managing to earn the money for your schooling there at Atlantic Union College and for medical school? I am working extra shifts whenever I can so that Mother does not have to pay for any of my schooling now. I know Father's job is just about gone and she can barely keep the house going as it is.

Did I tell you that we lost a student from our class last year? She married Harold Schull, a young ministerial student from there at AUC. You probably know him or his father. He is the pastor of the Boston Tabernacle Church. We sometimes go into Boston for church if they are having something special and I have met his mother who is very nice. But I am sorry that our fellow student will not be finishing her nurse's training. I understand they will be going to China as missionaries and I think that would have been useful training for her.

I will close for now as I am going on a walk with several students here. It is so rare that we have any time off. I want to make sure I get to walk outside in the beautiful weather. Please write when you can.

Your loving sister,
Gertrude

Langwood Hall
New England Sanitarium
April 28, 1929

Dear Ruth,

I am just grabbing a quick break to write to you between studying for exams and night duty at the hospital. Graduation is approaching faster than I can get ready for it. And soon I will be finished here and graduated.

Actually I won't be totally finished here as I have been offered a job in physical therapy. I think I will be doing some teaching of the first-year students as well as some of the therapies myself. And I'm hoping to spend more time in the maternity ward as I really love that part of nursing very much. Our first year here was hydrotherapy and the basics of nursing. Then last year we were deep into the various areas of nursing: hospital wards, outpatient, operating room, and so on. But this year we are seeing all the special areas like obstetrics and anesthesia. I have been doing both and enjoying it lots—especially the obstetrics.

Mother says you are finishing at AUC this year and will be going to medical school next year. I didn't know that would happen quite so soon. I had hoped to be able to see more of you when I finished my schooling here. You know my prayers will be with you out there in California.

Mother and her two sisters are coming here for my graduation. I think she is making more of this than is necessary. But it seems that her girls, at least, are making something of themselves. I'm sure she is very happy for both of us.

I am managing to do some sewing for Mother in my spare time. I think she needs all the money I can send her since she did so much for us when we were at home.

Must run as duty calls.

Love as always,
Gertrude

Harvard Medical School
Boston Lying-In Hospital
October 5, 1930

Dearest Ruth,

I have a short breather between patients so I am going to answer the letter you sent as I have been promising myself I would do for some time now.

As you can see by the return address I am at Boston Lying-In and, boy, am I ever busy! I'm in here at 7:00 every morning for classes and techniques and I'm working until all hours learning how to deliver babies. And I know you are probably doing the same out there in California in medical school. But I find it such a wonder to assist in bringing a life into the world. And such a lot of work! I am also participating in a research project on the use of some new medicines for obstetrics. So I am staying very busy.

Actually I'm staying with Uncle Henry—you know, the one who has the music store out in Roxbury. So I have to get up very early to catch the bus to the hospital. I think I am a terrible nuisance to them, getting up so early and getting breakfast and all. I am thinking of moving to something closer to the hospital. I can work in the call schedule for obstetrical nurses when I finish my course here and continue my work on the research project and probably make ends meet OK. The times are hard here for some but so far it has not affected me or the delivery of babies.

You may ask why I am working so hard to get further education. I am carrying out some instructions I received from Mother at my graduation eighteen months ago. You will remember that Mother and her two sisters came to Stoneham for the graduation.

Well, while we were relaxing during one of our quiet times that weekend, Mother said she hoped I would not get married right away but would practice my profession for at least five years before getting married. I laughed and said, "Five years. Just think, I will be too old then to get married."

But Mother was quite serious. She said, "Well, you know, one of our relatives got married right away when she got through with her education and didn't practice any of the things she had learned. When she tried to find a job, she had a hard time because she had no experience. I'm just telling you for your own good. You don't have to do this. But it would be nice if you practiced for a few years. And then if you had to come back—if something happened—if you had to go back to work, you would have the experience."

Well, I could have told her that I wasn't thinking of marriage at all but I didn't because she is so hopeful for you and me. But as of right now, I can't think of a single boy who interests me in the least. But I am working hard to get the experience and loving it more and more.

Write when you can. I love receiving your letters.

As ever,
Gertrude

Boston, Mass.
March 15, 1933

My dearest sister, Ruth:

I do not think I will be sending this letter to you as I think it would be too discouraging. But I just must simply tell someone who cares about me what is happening to me here. And it will be enough if I can write to you, even if I don't send it.

I have been trying for so long to keep everything together, to keep going. But it is becoming impossible to do. But I really need to start at the beginning.

When I finished my course two years ago, I thought I would be able to earn money in the rotating call schedule for obstetrical nurses and do very well. And for a while it seemed to work out. I was living in the extra room of a young couple who had an apartment almost directly across the street from the hospital here. I could get to the hospital by just walking across the street. But these people moved away and I had to find another place not quite so convenient in a hotel, again in a spare room with another couple. It was fine and I had my own telephone and could be on call from there. But then the calls did not come quite so often.

Actually, there were just more of us in the call rotation. As the hard times became more severe, more nurses were willing to be in the call rotation. We all have to take our turn, waiting for the next patient to come in. When we are assigned to a patient, we stay with that patient until she is discharged. But we don't get another patient until our turn comes round again in the call schedule. We get five dollars for each twelve hour shift we do. But when we don't have a patient, we get nothing. Sometimes I have gone for a week with no patients at all.

Now I am down to no money at all. Most of what I had saved working at the New England San in the hydrotherapy department I spent on my classes here. And now I am barely able to keep up with my rent. I have found a small deli close to the hospital where I can eat for about thirty-five cents. But I can afford only one meal every other day.

No, I have not written to Mother or told this to anyone else. I know that everyone is having a very hard time now. And many do not have any jobs at all. So I feel very fortunate to have something at least. But I don't know how much longer I can hold on.

I do have one friend. He's an intern at Boston City Hospital and is in about as bad shape as I am. He at least has his lodging and meals taken care of at the hospital but he has no extra money to spend.

When we have time off at the same time, he comes to visit me here in my room. We have no money so we cannot go to concerts or even shopping, which you know I love to do. But it wouldn't matter if we could because I must stay right here all the time in case I get a call for another patient.

We actually have a good bit in common and find a lot to talk about. And when he is not here, I am able to get a lot of reading done. But I do wish I could go walking in the parks or just get away from these four walls . . .

The letter was never finished and never sent. On an unusually warm spring day in late April, 1933, Gertrude returned home to Rochester to live with her mother.

"Gertrude! Gertrude, dear, are you up yet?"

Gertrude, scrunched down under her sheet and bedspread, could hear her mother's bright and cheerful voice in the kitchen below. She wasn't sleeping, hadn't been sleeping for more than an hour now. How could you sleep when the sun came up so early on these long June days? But she still felt too tired to get out of the bed.

It wasn't that she couldn't get up. She'd been getting up before 5:00 o'clock for years now. It was the dark, oppressive blanket of the last two years in Boston that lay so heavy upon her. The memory of those years seemed to smother her in its folds so that the labor of breathing tired her, made her too weak to move.

Even as the voice from below stopped speaking, Gertrude heard the soft padding of feet ascending the staircase. In a moment the door to the room she used to share with Ruth slowly swung open and her mother's graying head and smiling gray-green eyes appeared around its leading edge.

"How are you doing today, dear?" Mother asked. She padded softly to the window, pulling back the curtains and opening the window, permitting a breath of lilac fragrance to mix with the stale air. "Let's let a little of God's precious fresh air in here, shall we?" She began to bustle about the room, picking up items on the dresser and setting them down again, pretending to straighten them, trying to appear busy, waiting for Gertrude to speak.

The activity motivated Gertrude to come out of the cave of her bed. Like an awakening bear, she shuffled to one side and then to the other. Then she stretched one arm straight up and slowly rose to a sitting position, satisfied she had made some progress.

Her mother stopped bustling about and stood near the open window with one arm outstretched and slightly bent, watching. She held open the side curtains in one hand lightly as if assisting the emergence of a moth from its cocoon, yet not wanting to interfere, wanting the creature to emerge in its own time and at its own pace.

"I suppose I should be getting up," Gertrude finally managed. She pushed the sheet down to her waist, revealing the blue nightgown with the lace across the bodice, the nightgown Ruth had sent her for Christmas the year she had gone to Boston. "What time is it?" she asked, letting her hands fall into her lap in exhaustion.

"It's after 7:00 o'clock," her mother answered quietly, standing very still, her eyes sparkling a brilliant green with interest. For a long moment there was no sound but the ticking of the kitchen clock downstairs and the buzz of a bee in the lilacs near the window.

Her mother's standing there so quietly yet so intently made Gertrude nervous. She had to do something. With great effort she pushed the covers aside and slowly slid to a sitting position on the right side of the bed, the side away from the window. The motion made her feel stronger and she quickly stood up beside the bed.

Her mother drew a breath in and out sharply through her nose and dropped the curtain.

"I have some nice, warm cream of wheat ready when you come downstairs," she said. Dropping her gaze she started across the red and blue oval rag rug that lay between her two daughters' beds, gaining momentum as she reached the door. She left it standing open, an invitation.

"I'll set the bowl on the table," she said and left.

Gertrude examined her face in the bathroom mirror. The eyes were a dull gray and pinched. The mouth was grimly set in a straight pencil line from cheek to cheek, the lips pressed tightly together as if to protect themselves from a drought.

"This will not do, Gertrude," she said severely. "This simply will not do."

She reached up with both hands, grasped a cheek wrinkle between the thumbs and forefingers, and forced the cheeks up in a farcical smile. The comical effect was immediately followed by a spontaneous, openmouthed grin that jerked the now smarting cheeks from her grasp. Her chest heaved with two quick chuckles and the dark cloud of the past two years developed a crack right down its middle.

For the last two months, Gertrude had stayed at home and said nothing to her mother about what had happened. And her mother had not asked. They had talked about the Depression, the closing of the shoe factory, and the loss of Father's job. They had discussed the Browning Memorial Church and its activities, and the new church school teachers. But they'd never discussed the heavy darkness of depression that hovered so palpably over Gertrude that she sometimes thought it must be literally visible to her mother. And now with a silly grin, the oppressive heaviness began to crack. The darkness seemed to be drawn to each side like heavy, folded stage curtains and the stage lights were coming up.

Gertrude's laughing mouth settled into a pleasant smile. The arches of both eyebrows that for months had almost met each other over a hill of wrinkles just above her nose now flattened out, curving outward and down, and the wrinkles disappeared altogether. Her eyes began to catch some of the stage light, bringing out the green-ness of life in them. And Gertrude recognized the 26-year-old, pleasantly smiling young woman in the mirror as herself.

The telephone on the kitchen wall began ringing. Gertrude heard her mother pick up the earpiece on the fourth ring.

"Yes, Marie."

"Yes, we'll take the call."

"Gertrude, the operator says there's a long distance call coming in from Melrose, Massachusetts. Isn't that near Stoneham? You'd better come down and take it," she called out with her hand over the mouthpiece.

Melrose? Who would be calling from Melrose? Gertrude thought, as she quickly threw on her house robe and clumped down the stairs in her bare feet.

"Yes? Hello?" she said breathlessly into the mouthpiece of the dull black box on the wall, the black ear piece pressed tightly against the side of her head.

"Yes, hello," came the voice at the other end of the line, "Is this Gertrude Green?"

"Yes, yes it is," she responded.

"This is the New England Sanitarium and Hospital. We heard that you were home and we were wondering—that is, if you have no other plans— would you consider taking a position with us here again?"

Crackles of static on the line garbled certain syllables, but Gertrude heard plainly enough not to have to ask the voice to repeat the message. She grabbed at the mouthpiece on the box, covering it with her hand, and whispered emphatically, "They want me to come back to the San!"

Mother said, "Well, I think you'd better talk to them—instead of to me."

But she was more interested in the new life in Gertrude than in the prospect of a new job for her in Massachusetts.

Gertrude took her hand off the mouthpiece and tried to smooth her hair. She cleared her throat and struggled to get control of her voice.

"Hello? Hello?" the voice on the line repeated.

"Yes, hello," Gertrude said with as much composure as she could muster. "Yes, I'm here. And yes, I would be interested."

"We were hoping you'd say that," the voice continued. "We have just lost our department director and would like to offer you the position of director of hydrotherapy. This would be more responsibility than you had when you were here before. But we remember that you were a very good teacher. This position, as you know, is mostly about teaching the first-year students and leading the hydrotherapy treatments for women. You would be working with a man who is leading the hydrotherapy for men."

During the long explanation, Gertrude began to realize the enormity of the responsibility she was being offered and the heavy blackness began to gather and settle over her once again. But she straightened her shoulders with sudden seriousness of purpose and spoke quickly and firmly into the mouthpiece.

"Yes, I understand the responsibilities that accompany the job. I worked in that department for a year. I enjoyed the work immensely and I am certain I could do the job quite well." She took a deep breath. "When do you want me to report to work?"

Chapter 8

THE CLINIC MANAGER

One last thought." Gertrude spoke loudly to get the students' attention again at the end of the class, "Keep them warm. I know it's called the 'cool down' period but a Swedish massage is to warm them up and relax them. You must let them cool down gradually. If you let them get cold in the 'cool down' period, you will have undone what you just spent an hour doing. Their muscles will tighten up and all your work will have been wasted. Don't let them get cold!"

With that admonition ringing in their ears, Gertrude sent most of the first-year nursing students scurrying out to the hydrotherapy booths to begin seeing their first morning outpatients. "Olive, Vera, and Hazel," she called out. "If you would, please help me with the rounds of the cottages."

"Who are these guests in the cottages?" Vera asked, as they made their way to the rear of the sanitarium and out into the crisp New England autumn air.

Gertrude paused a moment to take in the riot of color in the maples and birches marching across the grounds between the homes and the guest cottages. She loved New England's autumn.

"Some of the patients at the San are here on a longer term basis . . ." Gertrude spoke over her shoulder as she swiftly climbed the few short steps to the higher walkway that led to the cottages. The nursing students scrambled to keep up.

Gertrude was now approaching the first of the cottages on the upper level.

"This patient has been here since the first week of September. He has dropsy as well as diabetes and you will soon see why the one condition compounds the other." She continued to teach even as they approached the door.

"As a result, he is unable to come down to the hydrotherapy sessions in the main building and we must come up to him, at least for now." She turned her attention to the cottage and rapped lightly on the door. "I've been working on reducing the swelling in his legs to where he can come down to the main building," she said as she peered through the small glass windows in the door.

A plump, round face radiating Dutch good humor peered back at Gertrude from within. And a short, round woman of 60, in full apron over plain gingham with a tightly rolled braid at the back of her head opened the door.

"How does she keep this up?" Hazel whispered to Olive as they brought up the rear of the entourage into the cottage. "She was up early this morning doing anesthesia in the operating theater."

"Come along, girls, and don't dawdle." Gertrude's voice was soft so as not to be heard by the matron of the house. But it had just enough sharpness to make the girls quickly enter and shut the door.

It was a typical day for Gertrude. She had been called at 3:00 a.m. to assist with anesthesia in the operating suite. At 6:00 a.m. she was released to get her breakfast in time to meet with her first hydrotherapy class at 7:00 o'clock. Following the instructional time, the nursing students had to be supervised as they treated both outpatients and the cottage patients until noon. In the afternoon the inpatients who required more frequent physical therapy received their second treatments of the day. At 4:00 o'clock. Gertrude would have a class of second-year nursing students for one hour of gynecology instruction. Because of her special training at Boston Lying-In, she was the obvious choice to carry this responsibility. Then, if she were on call, she would supervise the students in their third hydrotherapy and massage session in the evening, getting patients ready for sleep. If she were lucky, she'd have the evening off after supper to prepare her classes for the next day.

For the next six months, Gertrude's schedule followed much the same routine—the days filled instructing others; the evenings—when they were hers—filled with self-instruction. Her eyes were bright green and snapped when she spoke. The smile playing about the corners of her mouth could harden to a full, even line as she sharply critiqued languid or lazy students. She was relentless in her pursuit of knowledge and no less intense with those under her. "More education and hard work" was her singular advice to those who sought it. Among the nursing students and the hospital staff she was developing a reputation as one with high praise for those who pursued excellence and low tolerance for those who didn't try.

In midwinter, after the rush of the Christmas holiday, a fellow instructor found Gertrude in the rear of the hydrotherapy lab at the massage table with a student and a patient during the afternoon hydrotherapy session for inpatients.

"You have just had a summons to come to the office of Dr. Ruble," she whispered in Gertrude's ear.

"Dr. Ruble?" Gertrude spoke louder than she had intended and several heads turned to look her direction. "What does he want?" she said more quietly.

"I don't know," was the reply, "but the matron of nurses delivered the message herself," she murmured. "I'll take over here," she said, moving into place as Gertrude backed out of the cubicle, "She said he wants to see you now."

Gertrude glanced quickly in the full-length mirror that hung at the end of the physical therapy exercise room and absentmindedly touched the edges of her tightly waved short, brown hair. Wisps of it had again escaped, from under her graduate nurse's cap. Her attention to this detail demonstrated the seriousness of her summons as she almost never paid any attention to her sharp oval face with the straight set generous mouth and the serious gray-green eyes.

It wasn't that she was uninterested in being attractive. She spent the usual feminine time each evening in setting her naturally curly hair and each morning in applying a light touch of face powder to soften the highlights of her sharp features. It was just that she was intensely focused on her responsibilities as director of physical therapy and head of the female hydrotherapy section. Mr. Furmin, the head of the male hydrotherapy section, was the only man of significance in her life now, and he was married.

Gertrude paused by the large bay windows on the second floor, looking out over the calm blue waters of the lake that lay just beyond the road in front of the sanitarium. The San was set on a hill with a semicircular drive that ran up the hill and down again, encompassing a spacious, park-like lawn that was now covered in snow. For a moment Gertrude envisioned the buds and blossoms of spring in this most beautiful of settings. While she didn't mind the cold or the heat, Gertrude harbored a special love for the glory of spring and the blaze of autumn.

Seeing no one at the reception desk, but knowing she was expected, Gertrude knocked on the door marked Medical Director.

"Come in, please," called a strong but gentle male voice.

Dr. Wells Allen Ruble stood behind his desk. Gertrude could see that he was much older than the other physicians on staff, probably in his mid-60s. His eyes, made smaller by his thick-lensed glasses, peered over a wide nose and close-trimmed moustache. His open square face showed ample lines and creases engendered by years of responsibility. Behind his desk he seemed somewhat diminished from the height Gertrude remembered from previous meetings. His thin, slightly stooped frame, thinning gray hair, and wire-framed glasses over large ears reinforced the appearance of frailty, as of a great weight on his shoulders, bearing him down.

But as he stepped quickly from behind his desk, he seemed to come to life, taking on increased stature and youth, his eyes twinkling and his mouth parting in a warm smile. Gertrude immediately felt the power of the fatherly person which staff physicians, as well as other hospital employees, attributed to him. Dr. Ruble was the highly respected medical director of the New England Sanitarium and Hospital.

"Come in, Miss Green," he said, motioning toward a grooved and corded green wingback chair in front of his desk.

Gertrude seated herself at attention on the edge of her chair, both feet in white nursing shoes planted firmly on the floor. Dr. Ruble reclined in a similar chair opposite her, trying to strike a more relaxed pose. She watched his observation of her alert, attentive posture and tried to prepare herself for the intensity of business it portended. At last he spoke.

"I see that, in fact, you *are* the no-nonsense person I was led to believe you were."

Gertrude did not know where this was leading and did not know how to respond, so she said nothing at all. She continued to gaze at him confidently and intently, awaiting his further word.

After a few moments of silence, Dr. Ruble moved forward in his chair in an attempt to meet the intense gaze of this young and attentive nurse. She was obviously not frightened by this sudden call to his office nor was she intimidated by his position or his reputation. In fact, she was closely observing his actions and minutely dissecting his character. Suddenly he felt he was the one being interviewed and not her. He dropped his gaze to the carpet.

"I think I have begun this rather badly, Miss Green."

Dr. Ruble stood uncomfortably and looked away to the far corner of his office. Walking to the edge of his desk, he placed a hand on it as if to steady himself.

"Please permit me to begin again."

He looked down at his shoes to collect his thoughts, then raised his eyes to find her gaze still fixed intently on him. He returned the gaze with equal strength and spoke again.

"I do want you to know that we appreciate very much the work you have done here," he said, hoping to put her and himself more at ease, but without much success. Dr. Ruble was used to controlling conversations by his genteel demeanor or by his "elder statesman" role, neither of which seemed to faze Gertrude.

"Actually, this shouldn't be all that hard," he said aloud to himself, touching his glasses at the temple, raising his eyebrows and chuckling momentarily at his own discomfiture.

Then slipping into a clipped British accent which betrayed his nine years in England he said, "Let's come right to the point, shall we? Yes, well. We are looking for an individual with just your strength of character and attention to duty to manage the outpatient offices for us.

"I'm sure you noticed that no one is sitting at the desk out there in the lobby. We, that is, the six of us physicians who work out of this cluster of offices here, are in need of a good manager, organizer, and scheduler. Do you think you could manage that for us, Miss Green?"

Returning his steady gaze, she said, "I'm sure I could try, Dr. Ruble. But what about my other duties in hydrotherapy—and my students?"

She was bursting with questions but succeeded in maintaining an outward calm. Her only sign of nervousness was to move both her hands that had been folded in her lap to the arms of the chair and grasp quite firmly the gnarled, wooden ends of the green velvet armrests. *What about my students? My evening classes? And my half day off to go shopping?* she mentally fretted. In her mind Gertrude saw the building blocks of her once orderly life being tumbled about and reordered by a hand beyond her control.

Dr. Ruble, long in the business of reading people, caught this motion and relaxed inwardly, happy to find that his new office manager had other emotions besides serious intensity.

"I am sure you will find this new position quite time consuming," he said confidently, feeling a bit more in control of the conversation. "I have taken the liberty of asking the director of the nursing school and the hospital matron of nurses to help you to find a replacement in the hydrotherapy and physical therapy department."

Now Gertrude wrinkled her brow and lowered the corners of her mouth into a firm straight line at the thought of someone, even the medical director, interfering in her life without having asked her. She was about to express her objections to this when another, more worrisome thought intruded. This one was so overwhelmingly powerful that she spoke it aloud without thinking.

"When is all this supposed to take place?" she asked with more worry now than anger.

Watching and understanding the gamut of these rapidly changing emotions, Dr. Ruble tactfully replied, "I was hoping, personally, that you might start next Monday—if that is quite convenient. I know it would be a great help to me."

For the first time Gertrude dropped her gaze from his eyes, searching for an answer first in her lap and then over his shoulder and through the corner window that looked out over the snow-covered front lawn of the hospital. She sank with a deep sigh, allowing her head to recline among the ridges of upholstery on the back of the chair as if overtaken by a great tiredness from too much thinking.

Dr. Ruble quietly stepped behind his desk and sat down, taking off and toying with his glasses, allowing Gertrude time to adjust to this sudden rearranging of her life.

"I know that you enjoy learning new things, Miss Green. So I am hoping that this next part of your new position will lessen somewhat the shock of all these changes being asked of you."

Gertrude shifted her eyes back to Dr. Ruble. Her eyes were softer, more gray now, not so intense as they were questioning, blinking once or twice as if adjusting to a new brightness of the light from the window.

"The emergency room is really an extension of our offices here, so we are—that is, I am—asking you to be the director of the emergency room as well. This means you will be required to take X-rays, read, and describe what you see. And that means you will need to learn this skill, from Dr. Haysmer, our surgeon."

"You will be taking this training with Mrs. Lillian Nothstein Edwards, one of our other graduate nurses, a classmate of yours as I remember. She will be our X-ray technician in the daytime and you will be the director of these medical offices. In the evening, you and she will alternate covering the emergency room and taking the X-rays as necessary." Dr. Ruble now felt free to state the full extent of what he wanted Gertrude to do, confident that he had won her over and that this encounter was about to be concluded.

Gertrude's face and eyes brightened at the thought of learning something new. She also realized that she would be very busy, far too busy to continue in the hydrotherapy department. Her eyes shifted to look again at Dr. Ruble, this time with sparkle, turning green at the thought of a new adventure about to begin, and she smiled.

Dr. Ruble placed his glasses on his face and spoke more quietly now. "While you will be keeping the schedules and appointments for all of the physicians here and looking after all the offices, I especially want you to be my office nurse, assisting me in my examination of patients and looking after my office. I have needed this for some time now. And I think I have . . ." He stopped speaking for a moment to consider what he was about to say, thought better of it and left the thought unfinished. "Well, we shall see, shall we not?"

He stood and Gertrude understood that the interview was over. She popped out of the chair like a released spring and stood confidently in front of the expansive oak desk. Again she returned his gaze evenly as she spoke, "Yes, Dr. Ruble, I believe we shall see."

She turned and walked quickly to the office door, passed through it, and quietly shut it behind her.

Chapter 9

THE PERPETUAL STUDENT

At 7:00 o'clock the next Monday morning Gertrude was sitting comfortably in a chair in the small office used as a conference room and classroom just off the main X-ray department lounge. Dr. Haysmer had lost no time initiating their classes in reading X-rays, beginning this week, he had announced, with chest films.

Through the open door Gertrude observed a sudden whirlwind of activity with short bobbed brown hair on a frame somewhat more amply endowed than Gertrude. With a flurry of coats and scarves flying, a rush of small feet under a white uniform blew into the small office.

"Good morning, Lillian," Gertrude sang out with a smile to her former classmate.

"Oh, Gertrude," Lillian gasped, out of breath, "I was so afraid I would be late to my very first class with Dr. Haysmer. Just let me sit down and catch my breath."

With a loud exhalation of air that squeaked like an old Model-T at the instant it is shut off, Lillian collapsed into another roundbacked chair beside Gertrude. She stole a glance at Gertrude out of the corner of her eye and both girls fell into fits of laughter. This was Lillian's signature entrance into every classroom she had ever attended since she had started as a nursing freshman at the New England San.

"Lillian Nothstein Edwards," Gertrude managed in the midst of her laughter, "you haven't changed a twitch in the nine years I've known you."

"Well, I am married now, you know. That's different," Lillian shot back in mock defensiveness, shaking her short, brown curls. "We do live on the other side of Stoneham and I have to ride the bus all the way over here," she added, leaning over to pick up an itinerant glove that had escaped her coat pocket.

"Well, you needn't have rushed so this morning. Dr. Haysmer is still in surgery finishing an emergency appendectomy so we have a few minutes to collect ourselves."

Gertrude settled herself in her chair and again stared at the chest films hanging on the X-ray viewing boxes suspended from the wall. Lillian followed her gaze but only momentarily, preferring to face people rather than X-rays.

"I've taken lots of these," she confided, "and I'm pretty good at it, but I've never bothered to try to read them."

Gertrude reached out and patted Lillian on the arm reassuringly, without taking her eyes off the viewing boxes.

"Oh, don't worry about a thing, dear. I've looked at lots of these. You help me learn how to take them and I'll help you learn how to read them."

As Gertrude glanced at Lillian's youthful face for a response, she recognized the worry lines as ones her mother used to wear. Lillian had a husband now and a home to concern her as much as reading X-rays. Gertrude felt fortunate to be without those burdens in addition to all she was doing at the hospital. But Lillian had them both. More intently, Gertrude turned in her chair to face Lillian, who was now beginning to concentrate on the X-rays.

"What about the call schedule? Does Cleburn understand that you will be here all night every other night and every other weekend?" As she spoke, Gertrude watched for the reaction she knew would come.

"Oh, yes," Lillian said, sitting up straighter and trying to look more resolved than she felt. "We've talked about it. He knows that it is what has to be for now. And that it won't be like this forever." She sighed bravely. "It'll be OK."

She softly folded her hands in her lap and looked at them, becoming uncharacteristically quiet. Gertrude tried hard to grasp how difficult a decision this had been for them both.

"Good morning, ladies" barked a firm, tenor voice from the doorway, filling the room and startling them both, causing them each to catch a hand to their mouths to stifle simultaneous gasps of alarm.

The small, wiry figure of Dr. Haysmer strode into the room. From his short, closely trimmed hair and angular face to his lean, athletic body and fitted business suit, he was every inch the man of precision and control, the exacting surgeon. But his twinkling eyes and the mirth at the corners of his mouth revealed what Gertrude had observed in working with him in the operating room, a genuine concern for his patients and a droll sense of humor in dealing with students. He was to be respected, but not to be feared.

"Are we ready then?" he asked on reaching the front of the room and glancing at them both. "These," he said, pointing to the first radiograph, "are the shadows of the magnificent organs of the chest."

The next several weeks flew by as Gertrude began the arduous task of understanding the working patterns and offices of six busy physicians. She learned their schedules and their various preferences. She memorized their names, each wife's name, and their children's names. She found their instruments and wrote up the cards for their procedures. She scheduled their patients and their surgeries. Gradually she became the organizer of their lives.

The physicians in turn soon learned that Gertrude could be trusted to keep them on schedule, closely organized, and well supplied. From an office where they had to do everything for themselves, they progressed to an environment where their every need was met before they even asked.

As the medical director, Dr. Ruble saw many important personages interspersed with his many private patients and his clinics. As Dr. Ruble's private nurse, Gertrude organized both his office schedule and his corporate schedule. Soon every morning he found a neatly handwritten list of his appointments and clinics on the right hand corner of his desk, listing the individual, the appointment time, the expected in office time, and any quiet respites for reading, writing, or contemplation. He knew he had chosen wisely when he had asked Gertrude to take charge of their outpatient clinic desk.

During one unusually quiet late morning, Gertrude scurried down to the X-ray department to see if Lillian could go to lunch. She slipped through the back door of the department marked Staff Only and saw the red light shining above the door to the film development room. She knocked on the door quietly so as not to startle whoever was within.

"Lillian," she called out, "are you in there?"

"Yes, I'm here," came a muffled voice amid a splashing of water and rattling of trays.

"Can you get free for a bite of lunch?"

"As soon as I finish this batch of films." came back the distant voice. "I don't have another scheduled procedure until 1:00 o'clock."

"I'll run down and get us a table." Gertrude scooted out the back door and down the dark stairs for a quick dash across the campus to the nurses' cafeteria.

When Lillian arrived 25 minutes later with tray in hand, Gertrude was sitting at a far table with her food in front of her, patiently waiting.

"It was the only one available when I came in," she apologized.

"Suits me," Lillian replied, flouncing into her chair with hungry resolve. After a quick prayer over their meal, she continued, "I never get to see much of you anymore. Now that our classes with Dr. Haysmer are over, I wonder if you're still alive."

"You know I'm still alive, silly," Gertrude managed around her first mouthful. "Who do you think is taking all those pictures on the nights you aren't here?"

"I know," Lillian sighed. "I just miss seeing you after all those mornings together."

"Well, you'll be seeing more of me soon," Gertrude warned over her peas and onions. "I'm going to be down your way again for awhile to learn about fluoroscopy from Dr. Haysmer."

"You never stop learning, do you?" said Lillian in genuine amazement.

"Nope. 'Hard work and more education'—that's my motto," Gertrude confirmed, attacking her food rapidly as she talked.

"And shopping," Lillian chided, pointing with her fork. "Don't forget shopping."

"And shopping," Gertrude agreed, and then added with a grin, "and the symphony."

"When are you going again?" Lillian was now getting into her own food with gusto, knowing that her time for lunch was short.

"Tomorrow night while you're on call," Gertrude said with a grin. "If I can get off in time, Mr. Sanderson can take me to catch the train in Melrose. I can ride right downtown to the symphony and the stores. Or I can get the bus from here to Stoneham and take the bus into Boston. It's only a short walk from the bus station to where I want to go."

For a short while Gertrude was dreaming of the symphony concerts that she loved and both were quietly busy with their food.

Then she peered up at Lillian over her glass of milk and asked, "How are you handling all the night work?" She'd stopped eating, watching Lillian's face for signs of worry or distress.

Lillian snorted through her nose and threw Gertrude a quick, nonchalant glance. "Don't worry about me. I'm fine. Yes, there are some long nights." She continued eating without showing any concern. "But I'm able to sleep most nights—at least some—just like you do."

Lillian stopped eating as well and fixed Gertrude with her own penetrating blue eyes. "I'm fine, really." She flashed a quick smile and Gertrude relaxed.

"Bet you can't guess who came into the office yesterday," Gertrude said, picking up her fork again.

"Nope. Can't guess," was all the reply Lillian could give in the middle of her sandwich.

"Dr. John Harvey Kellogg." Gertrude played out the name like fishing line.

"Wow," Lillian said in true appreciation.

"Yep. I think he taught Dr. Ruble in medical school or knew him when he was going to med school. I'm not sure which." Gertrude paused a moment to think, then continued eating. "Dr. Ruble says Dr. Kellogg makes a trip east every year to see him and other students he had in the past years."

"He's quite an old man now, isn't he?" Lillian asked.

"Yes, but surprisingly spry. And very good-natured."

More silent eating as plates were cleaned up and drinks finished.

"Lillian, how are you doing with the casting work?" Gertrude asked as she stood up to take her tray to the window.

"With what?"

"You know, putting on casts in the Emergency Ward."

"Gertrude, I don't put on casts. I let the doctors do that."

"But you never know when you might have to put on a cast," Gertrude countered. "Dr. Haysmer and some of the other physicians are showing me how to do it. It's sort of like putting on the top crust of an apple pie, you know."

"Gertrude, you are a case," Lillian cried out as she turned the corner and was gone out the door and across the campus to the X-ray department.

Later that evening during a lull in the emergency traffic, Gertrude wrote to her sister, Ruth. Because of her constraints of time and money, instead of traveling, Gertrude wrote letters continuously to everyone who was dear to her: her mother, her sister, her younger brother, and her many friends from academy and nursing school. Letters were her major means of expressing love to those far away and her major hedge against loneliness.

New England Sanitarium
Stoneham, Mass.
November 11, 1934

My dearest sister, Ruth;

Today is Armistice Day. I wonder how many are remembering what it means and if it has any meaning in the face of all that is happening in Europe these days. They are hard days for us all. The financial situation for Mother is no better than before. But I think it's a miracle that she has not lost the house. Somehow she is managing to keep everything together and look after Father, Walter, and Frederick. I am hoping the boys are still helping her with the expenses since Father no longer has his job and no longer is able to work—because of his condition.

It is also hard to write about your present situation because I don't know what you want to say about it or what I should say about it. I know from Mother that you graduated from medical school this last spring. But the polio kept you from graduating last year with your class. Mother says you are thinking about going into Psychiatry since your arms do not work well enough or steady enough to do Ophthalmology as you originally wished. I hardly know how to express to you my grief for you over this. I am very near to tears even as I write as I know you probably will be also when you read this.

But my greater grief is hearing that you are thinking of dropping out of church because of the great tragedy that has befallen you. God has preserved you to accomplish some good yet in this life. Yet I am trying to understand the great grief and anger you must feel at having your medical career largely altered and your violin totally taken from you.

Mother tells me not to say this—but I do not know what else to say—I am praying for you. I know others have said that and that it has made you only angrier when nothing seemed to happen. How I wish Dr. Magan could still be visiting you. But now that you are moving on in Psychiatry, you probably will not be seeing him much. Since our academy days much has changed for us both.

If you remember, there was an intern at the Boston City Hospital who used to see me some while I was at Boston Lying-In. He came to visit me here the other day but I found that the old feelings are gone and I am much too occupied with my work to think about or desire his company or the company of any male. I think I will not see him again.

On a lighter note, I am planning a shopping trip to Boston tomorrow evening and will probably go to the symphony later. I enjoy it even more when I realize the years I spent there and was unable to go because of finances. I am so happy to have a secure job here at the New England San. And I take great satisfaction in the work I am doing for Dr. Ruble and all the other physicians. And I smile as I realize that you are one of those physicians now. You always were the smart one.

There are patients coming in so I will close—
with much love,
Gertrude

PS—I will be starting classes at Simmons College in Boston. They are able to give me the Liberal Arts classes I need in English, math, and so on, that I cannot get here or at Atlantic Union because I need to take them at night. So will be traveling to Boston two or three nights a week, when I am not on call. I know the bus schedules so this should not be too hard. Love.

Chapter 10

THE PROFICIENT TEACHER

Even though it was December, there was no snow on the ground as Gertrude sat absorbing the view from her third-story window in the Glenhurst Building behind the main hospital structure. It was long before sunrise. Only the street lights sparkled through the bare branches of the trees huddling among the buildings on the grounds of the hospital complex. No nursing students went out or into the nursing dorm. Very few lights glowed in the doctors' homes lining the semicircular drive in front of the hospital. The Doctors Bond were obviously awake, at least she probably was. Perhaps she was just getting home after delivering a baby. Gertrude's gaze stopped at Dr. Haysmer's house where early rising was a religious act. It, too, was dark. But it was only 4:30 a.m.

Gertrude had just gotten back to her compact room after seeing an obstetrical patient in the emergency ward for belly pain. It made for a very early start for her day.

More than Lake Cayuga stretching beyond the academy campus at Union Springs, more than the big oak, the lilacs, and her playhouse in her own familiar back yard in Rochester, New York, this was without doubt her most cherished vista—the New England Sanitarium campus as it faced Spot Pond, quiet and in the moonlight. For six of the last nine years this had been her home and she loved it. And it wasn't just the lake and the park-like setting. It was the people and the memories and the security she felt here. This was now her home. She mused on how long she would work here, perhaps her whole career. Perhaps 30 years.

Reminded of the time and her tiredness by an irrepressible yawn, she turned away from the window back into the deep shadows of her darkened room, lay down on her bed, and slept until 6:30.

Just after Dr. Ruble's third patient of the morning, the director of the nursing school appeared at his door and was admitted without Gertrude's knowledge. Five minutes later Dr. Ruble leaned his head out of his door and said, "Gertrude, could you step in here for a moment?"

When Gertrude entered the office, she saw Amanda Sloane, the rotund nursing school director, stuffed into the green wingback chair in conversation with Dr. Ruble. Miss Sloane smiled, causing Dr. Ruble to look up and see Gertrude standing at the door with a quizzical look which plainly said, *What's she doing in here? She's not on your schedule.*

"Gertrude, come in please," he said kindly. "We've been having a conversation, actually an extended conversation over several days. But, to the point, Miss Sloane here seems to feel that you could help her."

Miss Sloane stood with surprising quickness accompanied by her warmest smile, and addressed Gertrude.

"Miss Green, I have senior students who will be going out into the nursing world within the next four months who have no experience in office nursing. Your outpatient clinic is the talk of the campus. And I have been trying to convince Dr. Ruble that there is still time in this school year to rotate some of our senior students through your clinic. I know you haven't had any students here previously, and that their presence would be an added burden on your already busy schedule, but—can you help us?"

"Gertrude," Dr. Ruble added quickly, "I have reiterated to Miss Sloane how busy your schedule already is with the clinic, the emergency room, and the afternoon gynecology classes. But she insists that I at least ask you. What do you think?"

Although he was speaking as if to protect her from intrusions, Gertrude could read the pleading in his eyes to help. Her right hand passed lightly in front of her eyes, adjusting some wayward strands of hair as she internally adjusted her morning timetable, guarding her face from revealing too much while she considered the situation. Gertrude knew she could be too sharp in answering such questions if she spoke impulsively.

Her right hand slowly drifted down to join her left hand and be held at her waist. At the same time a small sigh escaped as scenes of students and more classes flashed through her mind's eye. Then dismissing her emotional reactions, Gertrude began to process the situation and her options.

She taught because new nurses needed to be taught, but the outpatient clinic had taken her away from fulltime teaching. She loved the challenges of the outpatient clinic. But she loved teaching and she missed the interaction she used to enjoy with the students in the hydrotherapy classes. Could these two loves be combined? These would be senior students with clinical experience, she silently reasoned. They wouldn't require such intense watching, only a little direction. A fleeting smile crossed her face as her eyes brightened, first for Dr. Ruble and then for Miss Sloane.

With a nod to make it seem more positive, she responded cautiously, "Of course, I can help. What can I do for you?"

"As you know, we have no extra teaching staff. In fact, we're a little short right now." Now it was Miss Sloane's turn to plead with her eyes and her voice. "Could you teach them?"

"How long do I have to prepare?" Gertrude asked quietly, having now decided.

"One month. I was hoping to start the first six students in January and the second six in mid-March."

"I think that should be sufficient time to prepare the appropriate class material," Gertrude said impassively, thinking to herself, *Now we can get on with the schedule for today.*

She smiled at both of them to signify that the problem was solved and life could now continue. When neither of them moved or responded, Gertrude turned to Dr. Ruble.

"Shall I prepare your next patient, Dr. Ruble?"

"Uh, yes. Of course, Miss Green. Thank you."

Gertrude smiled again, turned, and left the office, leaving the door ajar to signal that Miss Sloane should do likewise so that the day could continue uninterrupted.

The iron rail bed, the chest of drawers with the oval mirror, the standing wardrobe—all stood heavily in the darkness, each taking on bulk from the surrounding shadows until the room felt close and crowded. Spraying a dim sunburst of fuzziness on the wall, the single-bulb lamp on Gertrude's desk cast downward a small, perfect, yellow circle of light. Her hands folded in a position of supplication before her face, Gertrude perched on her desk chair on the edge of the brightness, staring down at the white paper before her, considering the activities of the day.

She was aware of books and articles concerning office nursing, but she wanted to avoid the didactic material in favor of a more practical class. She wanted the girls, the students, to experience the real world of nursing; not just hospital nursing, but the world of physicians and patients and lab tests and examinations the way it really happened. If she could capture for them what it was really like, they could leave the nursing school seeking jobs with actual experience to their credit and some confidence in their pocket.

No. No books, she thought. *This will be a hands-on class with real tasks and real responsibilities to organize their work and their time.*

Since the class of 1935 was small, she immediately intuited the rotation of her six student nurses and her six clinic physicians. The matchup was obvious. Every two weeks she would rotate each student to a different physician so that each would be exposed to at least three different practice styles and three different kinds of procedures. She didn't want the students to learn the procedures so much as to learn how to prepare for running an office—how to read a doctor's need before it was asked, how to keep the appointments, the patients, and the doctors organized, how to clean and resupply without being unavailable. To her organizing mind all this had seemed obvious almost from the beginning.

But what to teach in the classes, she mused, tapping her pencil on the desk. *Where to start? What to teach first? What second?*

She drew six columns on her paper and wrote each of the doctors' names at the head of a column. Under each name she began to list every daily activity for that doctor and the nursing activities that accompanied it. As the columns grew longer, certain nursing duties started repeating themselves in the various columns and a pattern began to emerge. Gertrude began making horizontal lines, dividing the work into specific nursing tasks, and a plan for teaching took shape.

Several large blocks of information assembled themselves and Gertrude wrote them down as a unit. "Preparation for the Day" included making a schedule for the doctor and the nurse, noting anticipated procedures and instruments needed, gathering supplies for the exam room, and tidying the doctor's office to be presentable to the public. "Assisting With an Examination" included dressing and undressing the patient, privacy issues for the patient and the family, knowing what instruments were needed for each procedure, anticipating the physician's movements during the examination, and resupplying the room after each examination.

As the teaching plan emerged, Gertrude outlined how each unit would be taught, with what examples, and in what order. Soon a mere six weeks seemed a woefully short time to fit it all in. But beginning the first week of January, the nursing school would have its class in Office Nursing.

"Miss Green, can you step down here for a minute?"

Madaleine sounded desperate this time. She had her head out the Instrument Room door and was fairly shouting. Gertrude came almost on a run.

"Madaleine, don't shout so," Gertrude admonished, coming through the door. "The patients in the waiting area can hear every word we say if we speak too loudly. And we must always appear calm and in control."

"I know, Miss Green. I'm sorry." Her words tumbled over each other like spilled marbles. "And I'm sorry to be so much trouble today. But I can't seem to find anything I need." These last words were said with a catch in her voice. She was almost in tears with exasperation and anger.

Madaleine was one of Gertrude's best students so Gertrude had put her with Dr. (Mrs.) Bond, the gynecologist, because of the greater number of procedures and instruments. But today had not gone well. Madaleine had been furiously searching through the tall wall cupboards. Several drawers were also pulled out. But she obviously had not found what she needed.

"Madaleine, what are you looking for?" Gertrude spoke more sharply than she intended.

Madaleine whirled about, the tears just beginning in the corners of her eyes.

"I need a large speculum for Dr. Bond. We've already used the two we have in the exam room. And I couldn't get into the sterilization room because I couldn't see in there for all the steam. I had hoped I wouldn't need another one. But now I do . . . and . . ."

With a quick motion of her hand to the corner of her eye, Madaleine smeared the tears down the side of her cheek.

"Oh, Miss Green. I feel like such a failure today," she said in a much smaller voice.

Gertrude moved quickly to the far end of the room, stooping and opening a lower cupboard door.

"I have a stash of instruments for just such days as these," she said as she reached to the back of the lower shelf and retrieved a small, sterile, wrapped bundle. Standing up she handed it to the student nurse. "You are doing very well, Madaleine," she encouraged. "It's just been a tough day. Buck up, dear, and give them your best professional smile. Now out you go."

Dutifully Madaleine smiled through the tears, cleared her throat, and made for the door.

I must do something about that sterilizer room, Gertrude told herself as she started down the hall to check on Rose who was working with Dr. Joy.

Dr. Genevieve Joy Ubbink was the new pediatrician who'd just come to the sanitarium and hospital in August. She used her own last name of Joy while working in the clinic, though she was married to Mr. Richard Ubbink who was employed in the finance and billing office. Dr. Joy was from Rochester and, therefore, had made an instant connection with Gertrude. Gertrude was going to take her "shopping" soon, which meant talking about home and all that they had in common.

Because Dr. Joy was new, all of her procedures and instruments were unfamiliar to the others. Gertrude had given Rose, her other excellent student, a chance to work with her, organizing the pediatric exam room and finding out what Dr. Joy needed and how she wanted things done. So far, Rose was having a much better day than Madaleine.

Gertrude waited in the hall until she saw Rose going quickly from Dr. Joy's office to the exam area. Gertrude quickly fell into step with her as the two of them walked down the corridor together.

"How are things going, Rose?" she asked quickly.

"Very well, Miss Green," Rose answered calmly. "I have the cabinet spaces organized and the frequently used instruments all in their places."

She is obviously pleased with herself, as well she should be, Gertrude thought.

Then aloud she said, "I want you to explain to the other students what you did and how you worked it all out—when we meet for class tomorrow at 1:00 o'clock. OK? This is an experience they can all learn from."

"Yes, Miss Green," Rose said as she opened the exam room door and slipped in.

And it will be a good chance for you to think through all that you have done and organize it for others to consider, Gertrude mused. *There's no time like the present to begin preparing future teachers.*

Gertrude made her rounds through the clinic, checking on Geraldine, who was assisting Dr. Haysmer, and Alice, who was looking after Dr. Ruble for the afternoon. In the morning Gertrude had the clinic to herself. This was when she got her scheduling work done and Dr. Ruble had most of his private patients and administrative appointments. But the afternoon was full of the students.

The lecture class was at 1:00 o'clock before the afternoon clinic began an hour later. The clinics ran until 5:00 o'clock with each of the girls being assigned to look after one of the physicians and Gertrude looking after them all. Gertrude's gynecology class had been moved back to 5:00 o'clock, immediately following the clinic.

Gertrude's problem student was Mary whom she had placed with Dr. (Mr.) Bond, the internist. It was one of the easiest assignments in the clinic but Mary was having trouble functioning in the office setting. She'd not had any trouble on the wards. In fact, she was the star of the class according to her other instructors. But when left to herself to organize her work, to figure out what needed to be done, Mary lacked self-confidence and seemed at a loss.

Yesterday Mary had folded and put away the linens newly arrived from the laundry. Gertrude had a special way of stacking the sheets in the linen supply room so that each sheet came off the pile without dragging the next one to the floor. She had learned this from her mother and taught it to her students. But Mary had not learned it from her mother or, apparently, from Gertrude. Today when the girls went to get their linens to set up for the afternoon clinics, the sheets came piling out onto the floor two and three at a time.

I'll have to spend some extra time with her, I guess, Gertrude thought as she hurried down the hall toward Dr. Bond's office.

With her mind on Mary and not on her immediate surroundings, Gertrude was almost run down by Geraldine who stumbled blindly out of the sterilizer room, enveloped in a white cloud. Deftly stepping aside at the last moment, Gertrude quickly gained her own footing. Her left hand shot out, catching Geraldine by the collar of her white pinafore and spinning her around before she could run into the opposite wall.

"Geraldine, what happened? What's going on?"

Geraldine had spun to a stop and collapsed in a sitting position on the floor in the middle of the corridor. With her nursing cap on the floor beside her, she sat, looking about her in bewilderment, more dazed than injured.

"Geraldine," Gertrude said, kneeling down beside her, "are you all right?"

"Yes'm. I think so," she mumbled, slowly getting her bearings and looking up at Gertrude. "I needed to run instruments for Dr. Haysmer and I couldn't wait for the steam to clear from the last run. I tried to get the instruments out of the sterilizer but the steam was all around me and I couldn't see."

She got to her feet slowly while one of the other students retrieved her cap. Gertrude rose with her, holding her arm and steadying her.

"I couldn't find the door," she continued, now reliving the last few moments and speaking more rapidly as she did. "I got confused and the steam seemed to be getting hotter. When I finally found the doorknob I just got out as quick as I could." Turning suddenly to Gertrude she became apologetic. "I'm sorry, Miss Green. I'm sorry for the mess and confusion."

Gertrude's mouth had settled into the firm straight line the students had learned to fear. Her eyes were beacons of green but they were not focused on Geraldine.

"Never you mind, Geraldine," she said in a voice as hard as steel. "This was not your fault. But I am about to find out whose fault it is."

Turning from the group of gaping girls, Gertrude marched down the corridor speaking out loud to no one in particular.

"I have been trying to get someone to deal with that sterilizer room for long enough. I have sent messages and got no responses. I have talked with people and got no action. I have had enough."

She marched past Dr. Ruble who had just come out of his office to see what all the commotion was about. Gertrude paid no attention to him, neither looking at him nor speaking to him. When he saw the drawn eyebrows and the firm step, heard the sharpness of her voice as she spoke aloud—although to no one he could see—he quickly withdrew into his doorway as if trying to avoid being burnt by a passing forest fire. When she had passed, he stepped out again into the corridor and shook his head knowingly, pitying whoever was about to be the recipient of all that heat.

As she walked, Gertrude cooled and considered and planned. She had a knack for speaking without thinking and she was trying to correct this trait which had not been especially effectual. This particular situation had not been remedied by requests or talks, she fumed, but it certainly would not respond to tirades either.

Gertrude was dealing with the business manager of the hospital, the one who held the purse strings, approved all the purchases, and ordered all the maintenance. Despite her repeated requests for his personal assistance, so far this particular item was not high, apparently, on his to-do list. This would call for cleverness. As she walked, Gertrude formulated a plan.

The business manager's office was five doors down from Dr. Ruble's office. When Gertrude reached the door, she turned in and quickly strode past the receptionist, ignoring her stare of surprise. She opened the door to the man's office and walked in.

"Mr. Place," she announced calmly, managing a small smile while hiding the fury that burned within. "Would you come here? I have something I want you to see right now."

E. L. Place had just finished a particularly arduous task and was looking for a short break. He did not perceive the veiled iron in Gertrude's voice or her posture.

"Of course, Miss Green," he said, "What is it?"

Without answering, Gertrude turned and marched out of the office. Mr. Place, close behind her, raised his arms and shrugged his shoulders in apparent ignorance to his receptionist as he stepped from the office into the corridor. When he turned into the hall, he went the wrong direction out of habit and had to turn and hurry after Gertrude who was halfway to the clinic area.

When he caught up with her, Gertrude was standing in front of the sterilizer room door which was now closed. She watched him approach as a cat watches a bird. The students knew better than to stand and gawk. They were hidden discretely in the linen room, listening.

Just as he arrived in front of the door, Gertrude reached for the door as if about to enter and he prepared to follow her. She smiled with her lips but her eyes held him with a steady gaze. She backed up, still holding the door-knob, as if to let him enter first.

"Here," she said, "I want you to see this."

In one swift motion she opened the door, shoved Mr. Place inside, and closed the door behind him. She had performed this feat so quickly that only a wisp of steam hung in the corridor as if she were a magician and had made Mr. Place disappear in a puff of smoke. A small gasp and a giggle from the linen room revealed that more than ears were at work in there.

In a moment Mr. Place realized that the door was not locked and opened it from the inside, emerging in a larger cloud of steam than that in which he had disappeared. For a long moment he met the steady gaze of Gertrude's fierce green eyes. Finally he lowered his eyes, swinging his head around and looking back into the sterilizer room which was slowly exhausting itself into the corridor.

"Yes, I see there is a problem," he said quietly.

He turned and walked slowly down the corridor, back to his office. The next day a technician from maintenance came and installed an exhaust fan in the sterilizer room.

Chapter 11

THE MISSIONARY CALL

On a bright, beautiful Sabbath afternoon Gertrude pushed open the front door of Glenhurst Dorm and stepped onto the porch. Quickly crossing the lawn, she stopped under the thick boughs of the tall horse chestnut tree that grew in the front right of the building, momentarily shielding her eyes from the late July sun. Immediately after church she'd gone to her room to change into more casual clothes for Sabbath dinner at the Larson's. Her eyes had grown accustomed to the room's comfortable dimness and she paused now while they adjusted to the bright sunlight.

She reached up with her right hand and rubbed the back of her neck, holding her hand firmly in place for just a moment, trying to imagine why she felt so uncomfortable. She rounded up her shoulders and let them fall in place, but the feeling would not subside. She finally decided that she felt awkward because she was not in uniform and tense because she was not on call.

It's odd to have one whole day to myself, she considered. *No wonder I feel strange.*

As she strolled past the old carriage house where the hospital cars were now kept and down the walkway that led to the stairs that marched up to the front of the hospital, she remembered the reason for the dinner and picked up her pace. It was a welcome dinner for Dr. Roland White and a much belated welcome to the sanitarium for Dr. Joy. It would not do to arrive after the guests of honor.

Dr. Larson's house was the third of the three doctors' houses along the right side of the semicircular drive that ran in front of the main hospital building. Gertrude bounded up the stairs, rapped twice on the door, and let herself in. She had been here for numerous Sabbath dinners and knew Mrs.

Larson expected her to let herself in. She'd managed to arrive before Dr. Joy but not before the Bonds as they lived just next door.

"Hello, Gertrude," came a full-bodied baritone from the living room.

"Hello, Dr. Haysmer. Happy Sabbath," Gertrude responded as she headed directly for the small kitchen at the back of the house.

"How can I help?" she offered.

"Oh, Gertrude," Mrs. Larson said, turning her head ever so slightly to make sure she knew who it was who'd come to help. "Bless your heart, dear. Yes, if you wouldn't mind, could you mash the potatoes? The masher is in the middle drawer. Mind the knives on the left, dear."

Gertrude marveled at how Mrs. Larson, small and plump and always dressed so properly, could be raising a young daughter, be so well organized, and have such a neat house for Sabbath. *She must have had a mother who trained her well,* thought Gertrude, as she pushed the steel masher down carefully on the firm, white potatoes that had already been peeled.

With the arrival of Dr. Joy and her husband, dinner was served. Dr. Haysmer and his wife sat at one end while Dr. and Mrs. Larson sat at the other end of the large dining room table. It had been moved into the center of the living room to accommodate everyone. Dr. and Mrs. Ruble sat in the middle on the side next to the fireplace with Dr. Albert Bond, the internist, and Dr. Katherine Erickson-Bond, the gynecologist to his left. To his right near the corner sat Dr. Joy and Mr. Richard Ubbink, her consort, as he liked to refer to himself. Dr. Roland White with the other physicians from the clinic and Gertrude sat on the opposite side. It made for an impressive table.

These are my physicians, Gertrude thought. She smiled as she looked about at those she cared for each day. She settled into her chair and noted that her previous discomfort was dissipating. These were her people and she was back in her element. Although she was the only nurse present among the physicians, she was perfectly at ease. She knew that her contribution to the clinic made all of their efforts more effective and that they were deeply appreciative.

When the entree and side dishes had made their second round and were safely set aside, Dr. Ruble stood and cleared his throat in three little staccatos in his napkin. Everyone quieted their conversation.

"As frequently happens in our institutions," he began, "we have lost some people this last year and are gaining some people again this year."

Everyone smiled and nodded at the guests of honor. Dr. Haysmer sat back in his chair and folded his arms, turning and leaning slightly toward his wife, who was almost a head taller than he, as if for support, and prepared himself for the speech.

"We were very sad to lose Dr. Cramp. He was an especially valuable part of our team here. But his absence has been filled by Dr. Roland White, our new eye, ear, nose, and throat doctor."

The smattering of applause began to the right of Gertrude and traveled down the table like a wave, catching Dr. Haysmer unaware. He almost lost his balance while trying to unfold his arms and join in somewhat belatedly. Although no one else noticed, Mrs. Haysmer caught Gertrude's eye and they smiled as if they shared a private joke, stifling chuckles but saying nothing.

"Dr. Albert Bond and Dr. Katherine Bond will be going on a short vacation soon. I dare say Dr. Larson will be put to it to cover all the patients while Dr. Albert is gone."

Everyone looked and nodded at Dr. Larson.

"And perhaps Miss Green can see some of Dr. Katherine's postpartum patients while she is away."

It was Gertrude's turn to smile as everyone nodded in her direction.

Must make a note of that, Gertrude added to her mental checklist. *That was a suggestion, not an idle comment.*

"And it is our great pleasure to welcome Dr. Genevieve Joy to the San." Again the applause. "As she has been here for almost half a year, it seems silly to be introducing her to you. But I do want her to know that she is a welcome addition and has already become a valuable part of the staff here." Dr. Joy smiled while her husband slipped his arm around her shoulders. Gertrude sensed a tight bond there and was glad for them.

Dr. Ruble seemed to hesitate, not knowing what more to say. Gertrude saw him look up and far away and waited, knowing by his face that reminiscence was coming. She was not wrong.

"Of all the hospitals where I have worked and all the medical staffs it has been my privilege to serve," he said finally, "this has been the most pleasurable." He looked about him at the upturned faces. "And you all have been major contributors." Then he caught Gertrude's eye and added, "All of you."

Gertrude nodded demurely, smiling closed mouthed as was proper. The satisfaction of the moment closed her green eyes to slits of light.

As Dr. Ruble began to sit, he rose again suddenly.

"Oh, by the way. Dr. Harry Miller, the vagabond doctor from China, will be visiting us this next week . . . I think. I never quite know when he'll pop in." This last he added almost as an aside to his wife who also knew from medical school days how unpredictable Dr. Miller could be.

"He is one of my oldest and dearest friends. But watch him." He pointed a warning finger at them all around the circle in what Gertrude thought was a curious mixture of mirth and seriousness. "Don't let him catch you up in his net. When he comes home like this, it's usually because he's looking for more people to go overseas. And I don't want to lose any more of you than we already have." He smiled at the Drs. Bond. "God speed to you during your time away." And he sat down.

The next Tuesday morning just before Dr. Ruble's first appointment, Gertrude sensed a presence and looked up into a pair of large blue-gray eyes set in an equally large, square, handsome face, topped by a shock of slightly curly, somewhat unruly, silver-tipped dark brown hair. The boyish smile and the touch of snow at the temples were incongruous and confused any attempt at an estimate of age.

"Dr. Miller." Gertrude held his gaze. "Good morning," she said as if she had been expecting him all along.

She casually checked the schedule under her left elbow, mentally rearranging the appointments. She knew Dr. Ruble would want to see him as soon as he arrived. She looked up again

"I think Dr. Ruble can see you now. Shall I announce you?"

"That's not necessary. He knows I'm coming," Dr. Miller said as he turned and headed for the door. Gertrude's gaze following him.

He moves like a large mountain, she thought, analyzing what she'd seen. *His eyes are warm but his mind is somewhere else, thinking about something else.*

Gertrude returned to her work and gave him no further thought.

The week continued unseasonably warm even for July in Stoneham, Massachusetts. By the end of it, Dr. Miller had kept the trail into Dr. Ruble's office equally warm, appearing at least three times in as many days. Dr. Ruble said little to Gertrude about his visits, but she could tell he was becoming more troubled as the week drew to an end.

This only added to Gertrude's difficulties as this was the time, midway through the quarter, when her senior students must begin to function in the doctors' offices on their own. Now Gertrude purposefully left them to their own devices while staying vigilant to step in and intervene when a problem arose, seeing such situations an opportunity to teach or to guide or to encourage. This was much more difficult than having students trail around behind her and certainly much more strenuous even than looking after the clinics by herself.

The outpatient clinics, the emergency ward, the gynecology classes, helping out with anesthesia and the operating room in her spare moments, and working on her classes at Simmons College were quite enough to keep her busy. Now she had the added burden of Dr. Miller's visit and his obvious upsetting of Dr. Ruble and his schedule.

From the previous Sabbath dinner's discussion with Mrs. Ruble and others, Gertrude had learned that Dr. Ruble was much older than Dr. Miller. They had known each other at Battle Creek College where "junior" Wells Allen Ruble had been ahead of "freshman" Harry Miller by two years. But while then Professor Ruble was teaching at Claremont Union College in South Africa, Harry Miller, the student, was catching up. By the time Wells Allen Ruble had decided to attend medical school at the American Medical Missionary College in Battle Creek in 1902, Harry Miller was just finishing at the same institution, now ahead of his friend, in medical education at least, by several years.

Perhaps the long life experience of the older Wells Ruble clicked with the intensity of the young Harry Miller, causing them to become close friends. Or perhaps it was a particular medical subject they both found interesting. Whatever the circumstances, Gertrude knew they enjoyed being together. But now their friendship had wreaked havoc with Dr. Ruble's appointment schedule.

As the week wound to its conclusion, Gertrude observed Dr. Ruble in long periods of preoccupied thought when he should have been seeing patients. At other times, such as when she was arranging his exam room after he'd seen a patient, she would catch him staring at her with a sad, sympathetic, almost fatherly expression. While he had always been kind and considerate in their professional relationship, this was quite uncharacteristic. Gertrude hoped that with

Dr. Miller's departure, the worries that came with him, whatever they were, would also depart and things would settle back into their routine.

Nursing shoe heels clicking on wooden floors announced Gertrude's arrival in the halls of the outpatient clinic a few minutes before 7:00 a.m. She was early this morning as she wanted to arrive before Dr. Ruble. She and Dr. Ruble met early every Monday to discuss the coming week's events: patients he'd be seeing, the progress of the students, or any other current topic of clinic interest. As she turned the corner to the last hall she was thinking that today would surely include a discussion of Dr. Miller, maybe even what had been troubling Dr. Ruble all last week.

Gertrude slowed her pace almost to a stop as she saw that Dr. Ruble's office door was ajar, the narrow shaft of light from his desk lamp competing for space on the floor with the already bright morning light from the east windows.

His desk lamp is on, she thought, examining each bit of evidence as she gathered it, rapidly finding the logical conclusion at the end. *He turned it on when he arrived, while it was still dark. He's been here since before sunrise.*

Without even stopping by her desk, Gertrude walked directly to his office door and gently pushed it open. He was deep in thought, a much older man working behind a very large desk. Gertrude saw captured before her—as if in a framed picture on a wall—a depiction of the weight of responsibility he carried for the San. He was as she'd seen him at that first interview, revealing sagging shoulders and thinning gray hair over larger-than-life ears, appearing smaller than his true height, dwarfed by the enormity of his task.

Dr. Ruble looked up and saw her standing in the doorway. Always the gentleman, he quickly stood.

"Gertrude. Come in. Good morning." As he motioned her to a chair, his face smiled brightly but his voice spoke with a sigh.

Gertrude studied the now familiar face as she walked in and took her seat in the green wingbacked chair in front of the desk. *Whatever had him upset last week,* she decided after a moment of study, *he has resolved.* His face was the picture of composure though his eyes still radiated fatherly concern. But the lines of worry around his eyes were gone. Gertrude set back in her chair to wait for him to speak.

Dr. Ruble settled into his chair and looked across the vast expanse between them, holding her gaze for just a moment.

"Dr. Miller wants you to go to China," he said.

"Oh, no!" Gertrude blurted, sitting up straight as if the chair back had suddenly become hot. "I mean . . . why? Why me?"

Dr. Ruble allowed a small, fleeting smile of appreciation to cross his face. *How like Gertrude,* he thought, *to never consider that she might be the one Miller was after.* To Gertrude he said, "Dr. Miller has established several hospitals in China—in Shanghai, in Nanking, and in some place further up the river. He is in desperate need of nursing help, especially nurses who can run a nursing school and run his clinics at the same time."

Again Dr. Ruble smiled at her, knowing she would not believe this to be true of herself. As if to prove him correct, Gertrude sat bolt upright in the chair, her mouth slightly opened, her eyes wide in disbelief.

"When Dr. Miller came to see me last week," he continued, "he asked me to give him the best nurse we've got in this institution. Naturally I said, 'All I can tell you is—my own nurse—she is the best. But I don't want to lose her.'" He paused. "But Harry Miller is a good talker."

At that, Dr. Ruble chuckled to himself, remembering some long-forgotten memories from college which illustrated what he'd just said about Harry Miller. Then he became quite serious. He stood and walked from behind his desk to the south-facing windows that were still partly in shadow, pulling back the drapes and looking out as if hoping to find the right words. Gertrude's eyes followed him, turning herself entirely around while holding tightly to the arms of the chair as if at any moment it might abandon her, leaving her suspended in the air.

Dr. Ruble turned to her. "Dr. Miller wanted to talk with you, to ask you. But I told him I would talk with you myself."

He dropped his hand from the drapes and began to walk slowly back to his desk.

"You know I've been thinking about this all last week . . . how to ask you."

"Yes. I knew you were thinking—worrying about something," Gertrude said, finding her tongue and her emotions simultaneously.

Dr. Ruble stood beside his desk and placed his right hand on its corner, drawing his attention to what was displayed there. Although he was not one to gather mementos, he gazed across the various pieces of his past arranged on the desk: the gift letter opener, the paperweight from Scotland, the small statue from South Africa. These were the memories of his life now lived. What would Gertrude receive in the future? He looked her full in the face and spoke with prescient conviction.

"I don't want you to go, Gertrude. We have never had anyone do here what you have done. But . . . your life may be out there and not here." He cleared his throat and continued. "I will not stand in the way of the Lord. If He has sent Miller here to take you away, then you should go."

"But I'm not going," Gertrude said with a nervous laugh. "I know nothing about China. I have not given *any* thought to being *anywhere* but right here at New England San. And I am certainly not going to go off to China with a doctor just because he shows up one day and asks me to!" These last words were spontaneously explosive and Gertrude immediately regretted having spoken so rashly.

"I do not mean to sound disrespectful," she attempted an apology, "but I find it very disturbing for others to presume that I would—"

Interrupting her, Dr. Ruble raised his right hand from the desk with his index finger extended. He brought it quickly to his lips while staring directly at her. Without speaking, he asked for her silence and received it.

"Miss Green," he said softly, "I would suggest you pray about this before you make any hasty decisions."

His steady gaze met hers. She opened her mouth as if to speak but he still held his finger to his lips and she thought better of it. Unconsciously she began to erect an emotional barrier of resistance to all who would attempt to reorder her life—especially to men.

Dr. Ruble's eyes bored in while his face softened. As she gazed at his face, Gertrude saw penetrating wisdom and genuine warmth of concern. This which broke through her resolve, restoring her rationality. Gertrude long knew that he had years of experience in the Lord's work. Now that experience was telling her something.

"Pray about it," he repeated.

"Do you think I should consider this?" she asked, her voice rising, her face reflecting her mental state of confusion.

"Yes, I think you should," he said, raising his left hand so that his index fingers met while the rest of his fingers folded together. He pressed them both to his lips pensively in a moment of silence, then lowered them to his chest as if in prayer.

"I think you should discuss it with others that you trust. I think you should consider the possibility that the Lord may be calling you to missionary work in China. And I think you should pray about it."

Gertrude looked down into her hands now lying helplessly on her lap but found no answers. When she had come to the hospital this morning, her life had been neatly arranged before her, far into the future. Suddenly everything was turned upside down. Here was a call—was it a call?—from the Lord. She wasn't sure and didn't know how to find out.

Gertrude looked up at Dr. Ruble and saw a warm fatherly smile on the face of a friend.

He knows what this is like, she thought. *He's had this experience before. And he knows.*

As if in answer to her unspoken thoughts, he said, "This time comes to all of us. Pray about it, Gertrude."

Then Dr. Ruble shrugged his shoulders and stretched himself with a sigh as if he'd been able to finally set down a very heavy burden.

"This is probably enough talking for this morning, eh what?" he said, lapsing back into his English mannerisms. "Let's let everything else rest for a bit and gather ourselves for the day's work."

As he turned to walk behind his desk, Gertrude did just that. Resolutely she gathered herself from the various places where her thoughts had taken her and walked from the room, making no further comments or sound. It was as if she'd only been passing through and had not wanted to be a distraction. When Dr. Ruble remembered a patient who'd called over the weekend and turned to mention him, Gertrude was gone.

New England Sanitarium
July 25, 1936

Dear Mother,

I am sorry to be writing you in such an abrupt manner but I need your help. Actually, I need your advice. I received the most unsettling news of my life from Dr. Ruble this last Monday. Dr. Harry Miller, the missionary doctor from China, has been visiting here. He is a close friend of Dr. Ruble and has been here for the last week. Dr. Ruble tells me that Dr. Miller wants me to go to China as a missionary nurse.

I am sorry if this is a shock to you. I can tell you that it was to me, too.

I hardly knew what to say. I told him I had no intention of going to China. I hardly knew where it was and I don't speak Chinese and I don't have any plans other than to stay right here.

Dr. Ruble was very firm. He said I should pray about this. He said the Lord may be calling me to the mission field and I should ask those I trust for advice. Well, there isn't anyone I trust more than you, Mother. So here is my situation.

Dr. Harry Miller, the China doctor, wants me to go to China and help him in his clinics and hospitals and to run the nursing schools, wherever they are. I tell you I have no experience running a nursing school. I have taught a little here at the New England San but I haven't ever run a school.

I think you can tell by how I am running on so, that I am very confused. I don't know what to do. I don't want to refuse the Lord if He is calling me. But I don't know how to find out. Do you know how to find out?

Please write me and tell me what you think. Oh, how I wish you were here so that we could discuss this. But do write and "talk" to me.

Your loving daughter,
Gertrude

Chapter 12

THE PRAYERFUL LIFE

For the next week Gertrude worked in silence. If her students had thought she was aloof and emotionally removed from them before, they now found her almost absentminded. Her teaching and thinking were still as sharp as ever. But her critical attention to little details was less and her sharp correctional remarks were almost nonexistent. They had no way of knowing that Gertrude's internal workings had radically altered. She was praying—almost constantly.

Gertrude had prayed before, but not this intensely. She prayed morning and evening. She prayed through her meals. Even in the quiet moments of the clinic schedule she found herself contemplating God's direction in her life. She took Dr. Ruble's advice and she prayed.

"Dr. Haysmer, may I speak with you—when you have a moment?"

Gertrude was peering around the slightly opened door of Dr. Haysmer's office. His last morning patient had just left and he was sitting thoughtfully at his desk, his mind momentarily blank and at peace. Gertrude started to withdraw and close the door, but he called out to her.

"Miss Green! Come in now."

She opened the door and again peered in.

"Come in now, if that is convenient for you," he said more quietly, smiling and symbolically clearing his desk, rearranging a few papers as he prepared his mind for what was about to come. He knew that when Gertrude wanted to talk, she required his undivided attention.

"Dr. Haysmer," she began, still holding the door open, "I need some advice. Spiritual advice."

"Come on in, Gertrude," he encouraged, "Sit down." He reached in his desk drawer and brought out his Bible, placing it on the desk in front of him.

She sat across from him, her face lined with worry, her hands fidgeting. He folded his hands on the desk, waiting for her to speak.

"Dr. Haysmer, I don't know what to do," she began at last, still staring at her hands. "Dr. Ruble tells me that Dr. Miller wants me to go to China as a missionary. And I don't know what to say."

"Say 'yes,' of course," he responded quickly. "It's a wonderful opportunity to serve the Lord."

"But I don't want to go," she replied emphatically, looking up quickly to see if she'd been too abrupt. "That's the problem. I don't want to . . . I don't know what I want."

She now had his full attention. He was aware of a spiritual battle which Gertrude did not see.

"Dr. Ruble told me I should not be too quick to respond, that I should pray about it."

"He's right. It is a wonderful thing to be called by the Lord to be a missionary."

"But how do I know I was called?" she said in genuine confusion. "I only see Dr. Miller flying in here on the spur of the moment and trying to spirit me off to China. Where is the Lord in all of this?"

He thought for a moment then asked, "And did you pray?"

"I am praying constantly," she told him, leaning forward in her chair. "But I don't think I know how to pray. And I surely don't know the answer."

Opening his Bible, he said, "Let's look at one of the great prayers of the Bible and see how the answer came and under what conditions." Deftly flipping the pages, he found the passage. "In 2 Chronicles, chapter 6, we find Solomon giving one of the most wonderful prayers of the Bible at the dedication of the new temple. But I want to concentrate on the answer, which came to him in a dream.

"It's in chapter 7, verse 14, and God is speaking. It says, 'If my people, which are called by my name, shall humble themselves, and pray, and seek my face, and turn from their wicked ways; then I will hear from heaven, and will forgive their sin, and will heal their land.'"

He looked up to see if Gertrude was following what he was saying. She was so focused intently on his Bible and on his face that her eyes met his with a longing for understanding. He was gratified and continued.

"There are four significant words in that passage, four conditions of answered prayer. Did you see them?"

Gertrude's face was a question mark but she still sat forward listening and gathering in.

"The first word is 'my' as in my people and my name. It means we see ourselves as belonging to Him." He paused a moment, letting the words sink in, hoping to erase the questions in her eyes. "The second word is 'humble.' It means that we are prepared to set aside our will and submit to His will."

He was numbering the words with his fingers, extending his left-hand fingers one at a time while his right index finger counted them slowly for emphasis and for understanding.

"The third word is 'seek.' It means we are actively asking. The Lord can work for us only as we give Him permission. And the fourth word is 'turn.'

"Is there anything in your life that would prevent the Lord from answering your prayers?" he asked abruptly.

"I don't think so." And she really could not think of anything that would stand in the way.

"Good," he assured her. "Then let's look at the other three. Do you belong to Him?"

"I was baptized," she offered, not really knowing what he was asking.

"That's good for starters," he smiled. "But do you consider yourself His child? If not, that's one topic for your prayers. Offering yourself as His child, putting yourself in His hands, so to speak—which leads to the second word. Have you surrendered to His will—humbled yourself?"

In answer to her quizzical look, he continued, "Have you told God that whatever He decides for you, you will do? Even going to China?"

"Oh!" she gasped. This was a new thought and a revelation.

"I see you have found another topic for prayer." He smiled again. "And that takes us to word number three—seek. Actively asking Him to lead, wherever that might be." He could see a softening of her wrinkled brow, the beginning of understanding in her face, and he pushed on. "It says 'seek my face.' It means to trust Him, Gertrude." He paused in a moment of introspection. "It is a hard thing for people like you and me, Gertrude, to learn to trust Him when we are so used to being in charge."

Gertrude was so startled at this revelation of vulnerability on his part that she almost jumped in her seat. But as she considered his statement, the glow of a shared experience and understanding lit her green eyes.

Then her eyebrows knitted together, her eyes beginning to gray, as the next question presented itself.

"And my prayers? I mean, what do I say?"

"Talk to Him as a friend, as if you trust Him," Dr. Haysmer said quietly.

"Then what do I do?" Gertrude asked, while in her mind she assembled the steps he had outlined as if she were learning a new nursing procedure.

"Ahh. That's the hard part." He removed his glasses and looked away, thinking back to another time. Then turning back at her, he pressed forward one more time. "Now you must wait."

"Wait? Wait for what?" she said impatiently. Thinking he had made a mistake, she almost said, *What procedure has a 'wait' in it?*

"Why, wait for the answer, of course." he chided, smiling at her impatience. "Have you read David's prayers in the Psalms?"

"David is too emotional," she shot back, shooing away this pesky idea with her hand.

"Perhaps you and David have more in common than you know."

He pursed his lips at the thought. He replaced his glasses, leaned forward, and turned a few more pages in his Bible.

"'Wait on the Lord: be of good courage, and he shall strengthen thine heart,'" he read slowly. "'Wait, I say, on the Lord'" (Psalm 27:14 KJV).

Gertrude frowned with intense consideration. She needed an answer. How long would she have to wait? How long would Dr. Miller wait?

"And how will I know the answer?"

"You will know," was all he said. "Abraham knew. Moses knew. Elijah knew. And you will know." He said this last in a whisper and closed his Bible.

Two weeks of prayers later Gertrude had her answer. Her mother's letter arrived telling her that she certainly should not go to China. It would not do her career any good to be overseas while others were here in the States getting further education and picking up the choice positions in nursing. With Dr.

Ruble, Gertrude had an excellent position with a physician of distinction. And she should make good on that relationship as she moved up to a higher position in the nursing department at the New England Sanitarium and Hospital or at one of the other sanitariums newly opened by the denomination.

After getting out of clinic and finishing her gynecology class, Gertrude had gone to the mail room where she found the letter. She hurried to the second floor outpatient clinic of the Main Building, hoping to catch Dr. Ruble in his office, knowing he would be finishing his paperwork before he went on his evening rounds.

As she approached the office door and reached to open it, she thought she heard voices. She was familiar with the second voice but did not recognize it. She knocked. The voices stopped.

"Dr. Ruble?" she called out, her voice lifted in a question.

"Yes, Gertrude, come in," came the cheerful, familiar voice of Wells Allen Ruble, MD.

As she opened the door, he continued, "We've just been talking about you."

Dr. Ruble stood behind his desk, his right arm extended in greeting, his left sweeping toward the other person in the room. Gertrude paused in the doorway and followed his gesture. Sitting in the green wingback chair was Dr. Harry Miller.

"Miss Green," he said as he rose to his full imposing height. He was a large man, both tall and broad. But his genuinely warm smile and open face kept those he met from being intimidated.

Gertrude was rarely intimidated by anyone, but she was shocked to find the very person she had been thinking about now in her presence. For the moment she was speechless.

"Gertrude, come in," Dr. Ruble said again, encouraging her and breaking the silence that had settled over the office.

As a gazelle guardedly watches a lion, Gertrude kept her eyes on Harry Miller as she took the other seat in front of Dr. Ruble's desk. As she sat, Dr. Miller folded himself into his own chair. *What's he doing here?* she wondered, perching on the edge of her chair, ready for flight.

In answer to her unspoken question Dr. Ruble said, "Dr. Miller has just returned from his recruiting tour into the South. He decided to stop by and see what answer might be coming about his request for a nurse. And we have been discussing your somewhat— u'mm—troubled consideration of his request."

"I didn't know I was the topic of everyone's conversation," she said, looking at him sharply. The thought that there might be more than one lion in the room crossed her mind.

"Gertrude," Dr. Ruble said, lowering himself carefully into his chair, "you have become such an essential part of our work here. Anything that troubles you, troubles the rest of us. That's why I have been explaining to Dr. Miller that we do not want you to go to China."

Embarrassed by her outburst, Gertrude blushed behind lowered eyes. As she did so, she saw that Dr. Miller was taking in this conversation with some amusement. But the amusement in his eyes was not directed toward her. She blushed even more at the discomfort she had caused Dr. Ruble, but she found Dr. Miller more interesting because of it. She began to relax.

"Dr. Ruble is correct," Dr. Miller said, deciding he should speak on his own behalf. "He has been telling me about all the various things you do here at the San." He smiled at Dr. Ruble, "But I'm afraid he has only been making my case for me. Because you are such an excellent nurse in so many areas— clinic, X-ray, emergency, anesthesia, operating room, hydrotherapy—these are the very reasons I need you—or someone very like you—in China."

Warming to his topic, he uncoiled himself and sat forward.

"We have just opened our twelfth hospital in China, in Canton. And we are running out of capable people to run them all. We have several excellent national doctors as well as our own missionaries. But we are hard pressed right now to meet the needs everywhere." He spread his hands expansively.

"Now that I am no longer the president of the China Division, I can spend more time with the expanding medical work. But I need help, Miss Green." He held her intently in his gaze. "Won't you please come help us?"

Gertrude was moved by his plea, even moved to respond, when she remembered why she had come and the letter in her hand.

"But I can't," she blurted out, waving the letter in the air like a flag. "My mother says I should not go to China."

"Your mother?" Dr. Ruble broke in, obviously confounded.

"When you and I discussed this," Gertrude quickly explained, "you said I should talk with people I trust. So I wrote my mother." She lowered the letter to her lap and looked at it longingly. "She is the closest friend I have and I value her opinion greatly.

"She feels I would be endangering my career as a nurse by going overseas. And I think I agree with her," Gertrude said with finality. "So I think I shall not go."

"Is that the answer to your prayers?" Dr. Ruble asked gently.

"It's the only answer I've received so far," Gertrude said firmly.

"May I see the letter?" Dr. Miller asked, holding out his hand.

"Why, of course," Gertrude said, handing him the letter and envelope.

He studied them intently, both the letter and the envelope, turning them over as if he were memorizing them. He handed them back to her, but said nothing.

Again silence hung like a curtain in the room, each person insulated from the others by his own thoughts.

Don't they see that I can't go against my mother's wishes? Gertrude said to herself, clutching her paper talisman in both hands. *What would Mother do if I went overseas? Ruth is in California and the boys—well, the boys—are they much comfort to Mother? I just can't go.* As these thoughts swirled in her head, she stood suddenly and spoke.

"I'm sorry to have disturbed your conversation." she announced as she took control of the direction of her life, addressing them each in turn. "I only came to tell you, Dr. Ruble, about receiving this letter." She held it up. "Dr. Miller, I will pray for the success of the work in China." He nodded to her with grave eyes and a serious countenance, but made no reply.

Gertrude marched out of the room. She moved quickly down the hall and descended the back stairs, glad to have this decision made so quickly for her. *Now that that's done,* she said to herself as she headed for the cafeteria, *the next task is to get some supper.*

Chapter 13

THE FATEFUL DECISION

Two weeks later a second letter from her mother arrived.

> 88 Bryan Street
> Rochester, New York
> August 14, 1936

My dear girl,

You must be wondering why I would write you again so soon. So I will get right to the point. I had the most enlightening conversation with a very interesting man, Elder Frederick Griggs, the newly elected president of the China Division.

He told me that Dr. Harry Miller had telegraphed him to come see me. He apparently sent along the directions to our house, because when I answered the knock at the door, there he was beside the old green glider with his hat in his hand.

He is a very distinguished looking man, mustached, with his eyeglasses perched on his nose and attached to the lapel of his coat by a handsome, silk ribbon. When I told the women at church, they said he was a famous teacher here in the States and in China. But all this does not tell you why I am writing to you.

I invited him in and we sat in the living room. We talked about China and the mission work there and about Dr. Miller asking you to go to China. I told him that I did not think it a good idea for you to go because your career as a nurse was just getting started.

He listened politely. Then he began to tell me of the wonderful work the church is doing in China—the training school for ministers and workers, the churches in many large cities, the national workers who have taken up the work for their own people and the hospitals.

He said that under Dr. Miller's guidance they now have twelve hospitals and are constructing another in a place called Wuhan or Wuchang, something of the sort.

Then he said something very special. He said it was time for people to set aside their plans for a career, which brings glory only to themselves, and, instead, begin to use their talents for the finishing of the work. He then took out his Bible and read the passage from Philippians, chapter 2 about Christ, who set aside His own plans in order to come to this earth and carry out the work His Father had for Him to do.

I was very touched, Gertrude, as you can see. And I could see that the Lord might be calling you to be a part of this work.

I had always hoped that you would be here, near me. But maybe that is not what the Lord has in mind. I certainly don't know what He has in mind. But I wanted to write and tell you that if you decide that you want to go to China, or that you are being called to go to China, I would be willing to give you up to do it. And I would pray for you every day while you were there.

Before he left, Elder Griggs had a very nice prayer for your father and all of us here in the house. It was one of the nicest prayers I have ever heard. And I don't remember anyone praying so earnestly for our family as he did. Then he asked me to write you and tell you how I felt about this call.

I know that this decision has to be yours. I cannot make it for you. But I know that the Lord is doing marvelous things in China. And I wish that I could go and help, I was so moved by what Elder Griggs told me. But maybe the best I can do is send you—for me.

I pray for you daily, as I do for all my children, but especially for you and Ruth, since you are both far away from me now.

Please write me and let me know what you decide to do.

Your loving mother,
Lena Schwader Green

Gertrude sat at her window on a beautiful Sunday morning and gazed out. The view was a familiar one, the back side of the hospital with the new surgical-obstetrical wing attached to the main building, the old horse barn—now used for automobiles—and just barely visible beyond, Langwood Hall, the nursing dorm where she had spent her earliest days as a student. Her eyes followed down the new concrete walk from her apartment in Glenhurst through the small gap between the hospital and the other buildings to the spacious lawn and the expanse of Spot Pond and beyond.

How many times had she gazed over this same scene and pictured herself working here, living here for a very long time? This was home.

This was where she had learned her nursing skills, her anesthesia skills, her hydrotherapy skills. She taught here and worked here—and belonged here. Dr. Ruble and Dr. Haysmer and Dr. Joy. Her clinic and her girls in the out-patient clinic office classes. Was she supposed to leave it all?

"Why leave all this?" she said out loud, overcome with the enormity of the changes she now faced.

She was praying again. As she did now every morning, she was praying almost audibly for guidance and understanding and answers . . . and patience.

"Dr. Miller says that all the skills and all that I have learned to do are exactly what he needs in China," she murmured to herself and to God. "Is that why I have learned all of these things?" Her hands were folded in her lap but her head was not bowed. Her eyes were open and she was looking out longingly at her home.

"Don't they need these skills here, as well?"

The four words of Dr. Haysmer's Bible study crept into her mind—"my" and "humble" and "seek" and "turn." For more than a month now she had been thinking about her relationship to the Lord. Dr. Haysmer had said to become "His child and learn to trust Him."

She was His child, had been His child in the morning worships and the evening vespers at school. In her morning and evening devotionals she had been His child. He had guided her through all the years of her dancing, and the struggles with school, and the difficult three years at Boston Lying-In when she had almost starved both physically and emotionally. In the good times and in the hard times—He had guided her through them all.

Now she wanted to trust Him.

But could she give up her home and "family" here? Could she surrender her will to Him? "Miss Blue," the alter ego of her childhood, would have had a hard time surrendering her will to anyone. But she was Miss Green—the teaching terror, as she had overheard her students describe her when they thought she couldn't hear—the cold fish. The aloof Miss Green.

"Father"—this word was hard to say and it stuck in her throat—"Father, help me to surrender. I know I am willful and hard-driving, which is a good thing . . . sometimes. But just now I want to surrender . . . to Your will. Show me the way. Please."

Now the tears were beginning to run down her high cheek bones, dripping onto her starched lapels. She quickly brushed them away with both hands but could not stop them from flowing.

"I am seeking Your way and not my own. Help me learn to trust You."

A childhood picture of Jesus from her Lutheran catechism appeared in her mind. Jesus with the kind face and warm eyes was holding children and talking with them. She could learn to trust such a friend if she knew He was like that, a being with the kind eyes of Dr. Ruble and the strong, steady voice of Dr. Haysmer. She felt very much like a child just now, in need of a lap to sit on.

"It's the waiting that's hard," she said again out loud, getting control of her emotions.

Then don't wait, came the suggestion. *You know what to do. You have always known what to do. Just do it.*

The thought was so overpowering, she gasped as if she'd been struck in the chest. It was not the waiting and it was not the doing that was hard. It was the change she dreaded.

"Then strengthen me for the change—and all the changes that may come my way," she prayed as fervently as she knew how. It was not a prayer of emotion, but of action.

Gertrude was not crying now. She was preparing for action, which she knew how to do. Plan and execute. She could do that. It was the unknown that frightened her.

"Then I will place the unknown in Your hands," she said firmly.

It was Monday morning again. As Gertrude approached Dr. Ruble's office door, she stopped to touch the letters that said "Medical Director." When the voice beckoned from inside, she knew he could see her silhouette through the opaque glass door. She pushed open the door and entered as she'd done so many times before.

"Good morning, Miss Green." Dr. Ruble was standing behind his desk, beckoning her to a chair.

Gertrude stood in front of his desk and placed the long, white envelope in front of him. She did not want to sit, did not want to prolong this morning's encounter. Their eyes met and his asked, *Are you going to sit?* and her's answered, *No.* Then he sat and opened the envelope, taking out the neatly typed sheet of paper.

"Oh, I see," he said, reading the first few lines and now comprehending her mood. "So you have decided to go to China."

"The Lord sort of decided for me," she answered, still not totally comfortable with the thought.

He watched her struggling with the idea and averted his eyes.

"Your resignation. All typed out, I see."

"Yes. I wanted it to look official. I came over and did it on the office Underwood. My typing classes from Simmons College," she explained.

"Of course," he responded, thinking of all the classes she had taught and taken simultaneously, and shook his head in disbelief. "You've prayed about this, then?" he asked, looking at her most earnestly for any sign of wavering.

"Harder than I have ever prayed in my life." Gertrude shuddered as she reviewed the last 24 hours. "I have placed my life in His hands. I will let Him take care of the unknowns." She spoke with increasing resolution until she began to believe it herself. Then she half smiled. "I will miss being here."

"And we will miss you," he responded, placing the letter on his desk in an effort to find something to do.

A gulf opened between them which Gertrude palpably felt. But she did not reach across it. She let it fill with silence, somehow knowing it would be like that in the future—the leaving and the gulf and the silence.

"They will want to have a going away party for you in the gymnasium," he said, breaking the silence. "Everyone likes to say farewell and bring presents."

"Good," she said, "I like parties. But I won't know what to say."

"Oh, I'll make the speeches," he smiled with a small, audible snort. "It goes with the job." He gestured about the room as if taking in all the hospital and the grounds, the apartments and the employees, the leave-takings and the welcomings.

And Gertrude suddenly saw the enormity of his responsibility and understood why his desk always looked so big to her and he always looked so small behind it. Only as he stepped away from his desk did he take on the proportions of a normal man.

"Can we talk about the coming week?" he asked, laying aside the moment. "I have some special patients coming in tomorrow."

"Of course," she replied, remembering it was the time of their regular Monday morning meeting. She perched on the edge of the green wing-backed chair and gave him her complete attention.

Chapter 14

THE CALIFORNIA TRIP

Gertrude swung open the screen door and stepped out onto the porch of her mother's house. Although her father still lived there, it seemed that this was now her mother's house because she was the one earning the living. Since what they were calling the Great Depression had destroyed his baby shoe business, her father had not been employed except in bending his elbow at the local bars. Walter still worked at the tobacco shop and helped with expenses, but it wasn't his house, nor Frederick's.

The house was the same but the people in it were getting older—Father and the boys, but especially Mother. Her hair was almost totally gray. She still wore it in the short, wavy bob that had shocked Gertrude in the 1920s. Her face was more wrinkled, more lined, more careworn.

But she still stood as straight as ever, the picture of German sturdiness. Her smile was the same—warm and homey, like freshly baked bread.

Gertrude gathered the mail from the box and retreated inside. She searched through the envelopes in her hand and found what she'd been waiting for since she'd arrived in the middle of September. It was an official envelope from the General Conference of Seventh-day Adventists in Washington, D.C. Dropping the rest of the mail on the dining table, she headed for the kitchen and Mother, opening the envelope as she went.

"It finally arrived," she announced as she scooted out a chair and sat at the kitchen table to read it.

Her mother turned from the sink, wiping her hands on her apron, and sat next to her. She watched while Gertrude read in silence. There were several sheets of paper, probably with instructions of what to take and when to go, but she waited quietly until her daughter finished.

When Gertrude looked up, she chided, "Well, don't keep it all to yourself. What do they say? A mother needs to know these things."

Gertrude smiled and handed over the introductory letter.

"It just says what I already knew," Gertrude said. "They're placing a regular call for me to go to China."

"But when," her mother laughed, "and where and how?" She leaned toward Gertrude affectionately. "How long do I have you here until I lose you again to this Dr. Miller?"

Gertrude hurriedly thumbed through the remaining papers. "It says here the boat to China doesn't leave San Francisco until November—h'mm—November 13." She looked at her mother with widening eyes. "That's only four weeks from now," she gasped.

"They didn't give you any extra time, did they?" her mother scolded in the direction of the anonymous "they."

"But I can't take much with me," Gertrude quickly noted, her finger on the lines of a page. "They say I shouldn't take but one suitcase and one or two trunks, if necessary."

"If necessary," her mother scoffed. "You're going to be gone for five years on one suitcase?"

In order to keep her mother from exploding with curiosity, Gertrude handed over the papers with a grin. "Here. Read this before you pop," she laughed. "They say that the seasons change radically and I can't possibly take everything I need. They suggest I buy what I need when I get there—furniture, clothing, mostly everything of a personal nature, I think."

"And your family pictures and the precious things they gave you at the going away party at the San," her mother added.

"I will take only what I can really use," Gertrude said, thinking of some of the impractical things she'd received from well-meaning friends. "I'll need my books and my notes and my instruments. Those for sure . . . and . . ." She looked into her mother's eyes and saw the real message being conveyed.

"Mother. I won't forget you." Gertrude reached out to her mother across the table. "I'll write as often as I can."

"I know you won't forget, *liebchen*," her mother said, her eyes moistening. "But my Gertrude, she has become somebody." Tears added a sparkle to her eyes.

"Just another missionary, Mother," Gertrude said with a sigh, "who must now decide what to pack." Her hand withdrew from her mother's arm even as her mind returned to the pragmatic problem of which clothes to take and which to leave behind.

"Yes, we'll have to start packing right away," Mother agreed, her gaze leaving the now blurred pages, her head falling forward to meet her hand as she lightly rubbed her forehead to hide her eyes and her emotions. She dropped the papers onto the table, scattering them, and rose quickly from her chair, returning to her sink and the snap beans soaking there. The introductory letter slid off the edge of the table and quietly settled to the floor.

Slowly Gertrude lowered the remaining papers in her hand, a small smile playing around the corners of her mouth.

"Mother, what did you just say?"

Her mother quizzically looked around over her shoulder, not understanding the intent or the tone in Gertrude's voice.

"I said that we have to start packing. What?" she asked. The smile and the green glitter of joy in Gertrude's eyes stopped her hands in midair, the water dripping from them, ticking off the seconds of silence that hung in the quiet kitchen.

"You said 'we.' You said 'we' need to start packing."

"Yes and I . . . Oh, Gertrude, I couldn't!" Her wet hand flew to her mouth, green bean stems clinging to her forearm.

"Yes, you could," Gertrude encouraged. "You could visit Ruth and we could travel together. And have a little more time," she added softly.

"We could see some of those places Ruth is always talking about in her letters," Mother said, warming to the idea. She turned from the sink, the beans a past memory. "And we could go shopping for some of the things you still need for China." Now she was leaning over the table, her face reflecting the excitement that had been only Gertrude's a moment before.

"Mother, I have only one trunk," Gertrude laughed, bending to retrieve the dropped letter from the floor. "But, yes, shopping would be fun."

"And maybe, maybe we could talk with Ruth about the church?"

Gertrude felt the search of her mother's eyes on her back. She looked up from her crouched position to see reflected in her mother's eyes the same questions about Ruth that had puzzled her. Her mother's face was asking for wisdom and Gertrude didn't have any.

"I don't know, Mother," she said as she straightened. "I think we should be careful with that subject. She's been through an awful lot."

"But we have lots of people out there that we know. And Ruth will know where they all are," Gertrude said, recapturing the magic of the moment. She watched the worry lines around her mother's eyes soften in a quick smile as the visiting possibilities took charge of her thinking.

"We do have family out there, you know, and we could visit the Corts and . . . How long do we have?" her mother asked. The realities of time and family suddenly intruded. "And who will take care of your father? Oh, Gertrude, how can I?"

"Walter and Fred can look after Father," Gertrude said almost sharply as she began to pick up the papers from the table. "But as for us," she smiled and reached out to pat her mother's hand, "*we* need to get packing."

The train ride was a long one, filled with hours of talking, sewing, visiting with other passengers, and occasional stops in cities of interest. Southern California was a wonderland of places to see, people to visit, shopping trips, and 75-degree weather in November. Gertrude packed her long winter coat with the fur collar in her trunk.

Ruth expertly maneuvered her car from Route 60 onto U.S. 101, heading north and west out of Los Angeles toward Camarillo and the state mental hospital located there. Having settled her mother for a morning of reminiscence with the Corts, Gertrude sat in the passenger seat, marveling at her sister's ability to drive. In all of her traveling to and from Stoneham and Boston Gertrude had never driven a car. Trains and buses and Walter had taken care of her transportation needs. But Ruth seemed to accomplish this marvelous feat as if by second nature.

"Where did you learn to drive?" Gertrude asked, turning herself about in the seat to see her sister better.

"L.A. is a big place. It's spread out all over," Ruth replied, signaling her turn. "Out here in the valleys there are no trolleys. You have to drive or not go anywhere." She threw an appreciative smile at Gertrude. "Besides it's not so hard to learn. You should try it."

Gertrude watched her sister's face, looking for any drooping of the muscles, any telltale signs of weakness from the polio. But if anything, Ruth's long, angular features were sharper than Gertrude had remembered. Her mouth was set in a straight, firm line and her eyes darted about rapidly, quick and sure, and serious.

"You're looking for signs of the disease, aren't you?" Ruth offered with a small smile. "It didn't affect my face. Only these." She held out one gloved hand and Gertrude saw the faint tremor. "No one would even notice it, except under a microscope."

Gertrude remembered the dreams of the academy junior student who planned to be a violinist and an eye surgeon.

"I'm so sorry, Ruth," Gertrude said, reaching out to touch her sister's gloved hand.

Ruth withdrew it quickly, avoiding the touch, and continued driving.

"I wish I could have been here," Gertrude offered, trying to close the space which had suddenly opened between them.

"Oh, it's all right, Gertrude," Ruth said. She smiled at her sister as she checked the traffic coming into the highway from the right. "We've all had a lot to deal with in the last few years."

"Didn't anyone come, I mean, didn't anyone help you?" Gertrude was remembering now the lonesome letters from Ruth during her bout with polio in medical school, the loss of her dreams, and the bitterness.

"Dr. Magan. He came. But that was all."

"*The* Dr. Magan? The president of the university?" Gertrude knew of him through Dr. Ruble's correspondence.

"Yes. He was very kind. But even he had nothing to offer—except prayers." Ruth's eyes began to moisten. "Even he couldn't explain why God would let such a thing happen." Now her voice hardened and Gertrude saw her grip the steering wheel ever tighter. "If that's all Christians have to offer . . ." She began the sentence like a mantra she had said often, but left it unfinished.

"Mother is worried about you," Gertrude said, studying the face of the sister she loved. "She wanted to talk with you about church but I wasn't sure that was a good idea."

Ruth turned her face fully in Gertrude's direction and smiled through her moist eyes.

"Thanks. I'm not sure," she offered honestly. "And I know Mother can be unrelenting sometimes." She turned again and gave her full attention to the road.

"So now my little sister is a psychiatrist. That's not so very different from the way I remembered her," Gertrude mused out loud, wanting to relieve the tension.

"And my older sister is a missionary," Ruth laughed. "I seem to recall something about that in your past somewhere."

And for the next several miles Gertrude sat quietly in her seat and reviewed in her mind the enormity of the changes that the word "missionary" had brought into her life. Dr. Miller. China. Traveling by train across the United States. Crossing the Pacific Ocean. What lay before her? What would be asked of her next?

After a few miles Ruth said quietly, "Change is OK, sis. You'll be able to handle it." She looked directly at Gertrude, "You're strong, Gertrude. You have always been able to handle it."

Gertrude's face flushed while her mind frantically looked for a retort.

"Do you read minds as well, Doctor?"

"It goes with the territory."

Chapter 15

THE LAST GOODBYE

During their time in Los Angeles, Mother had been staying with the Henry Corts and Gertrude had gotten her own small apartment on Pennsylvania Avenue, preferring to be alone as she had in the past. But tonight Mother had walked home with Gertrude to help with the last-minute packing.

"What are you going to do with all these pairs of hose?" Mother called from her kneeling position in front of a steamer trunk, hose lying all about her.

"They'll fit in the corners," Gertrude said as she entered from the small bedroom, her arms carrying the steamer rug, a going away gift from Dr. Ruble that she'd been using at the foot of her bed. "Besides if it's as cold as they say, I'll need them all." She laid the rug carefully in the trunk on top of her winter coat.

"They're all gifts from various people," she added, picking them up in her fists and stuffing them down in the corners. Then she was gone again into the bedroom.

Industrious as she was, Mother was astounded at the flurry of activity wrought by her oldest daughter. She got up slowly and sat in the chair next to the three-tiered piecrust table. Leaning against the fringed lamp on the top tier was an envelope with several important-looking documents peeking out.

"Are these papers important?" she called, picking them up to examine them.

"Yes," Gertrude said, coming in almost out of breath with the last of her uniforms and her nursing cloak draped over both arms. "Those are the visas for Japan and China that Len Bohner and I got two weeks ago. Thanks," she said, taking them from her mother and placing them with her shoulder bag.

"I can't forget them or they won't let me in."

"You remember Len and Peg Bohner and their son, Buddy, don't you?" Gertrude was now in the kitchen rummaging through the cupboards. "He was that tall boy in academy who became the financial manager at New England San."

"Of course you do," Gertrude added with a shake of her head as she came back into the room. She remembered that her mother had just met them at church two nights ago.

"You have a lot on your mind, *liebchen*," Mother said, using her German diminutive of affection. "Maybe I should go and let you finish this yourself."

Gertrude was standing in front of the trunk, arms folded, staring down at it like a magical mirror as if to discern what she might have forgotten. She looked up at her mother and saw the gray eyes of tiredness and the worry lines . . . and something else. But what?

"Are you worried about Ruth?" Gertrude guessed, only half attentive. "I had a talk with her in the car when we went to visit her hospital in Camarillo the other day." Gertrude didn't offer to repeat what it was they'd said. Her mind was still occupied with the train tickets that must be bought tomorrow and the sailing date four days hence.

"Yes," Lena Green said, rubbing her eyes, "but I'm thinking about you right now."

Gertrude unfolded her arms as she came around the trunk to kneel down at her mother's feet. As she did, the tumult of planning and packing gave way to the thought that this would be the last time she would see her mother for five years. *Don't get so busy that you overlook her*, she told herself crossly.

"I'll miss you, Mother," she said, looking up into the eyes that were so much like her own.

"I will miss you, too," her mother responded, stroking Gertrude's hair as if she were a little child.

"And I'll write every week," Gertrude promised, "so that you'll know everything is all right. You know I'm good about writing."

"Good. Please do."

"The day before Thanksgiving seems like a popular day to be going somewhere on a train," Henry Cort shouted over his shoulder as he turned his forest green Packard into the parking lot of the Southern Pacific Railway station. He had to wait for several other cars to clear the way before he could park.

"The *Asamu Maru* sails the day after Thanksgiving and I have to be on it," Gertrude replied from the back seat. "I would have been gone two weeks ago if there hadn't been a dock strike. Now everything is being done in a hurry—Thanksgiving or not."

Almost before Henry could stop the car in a space across from the station's main entrance, Gertrude popped out of the rear door. Excitedly searching for her new traveling companions, but not wanting to impolitely abandon her mother's friends who'd brought her to the station, Gertrude stood on tiptoe at the rear of the car, one hand shading her eyes and the other one holding the large black hat perched on the back of her head. As Henry retrieved her suitcase and trunk from the rear of the car, she continued to dance from foot to foot, craning her neck, her new black dress lifting almost to her knees.

"Gertrude, you look like a crow hopping about," her mother laughed as Evelyn Cort helped her step down from the running board at the other rear door.

"I'm trying to see over the crowds for any sign of Len and Peg Bohner," Gertrude told them, still straining.

"Oh, there they are!" she shouted, waving excitedly with both arms. Gertrude turned, grabbing Mr. Cort by the arm. "Henry, do be a dear and bring along the trunk." Then grabbing the suitcase from his hand, she dashed across the parking lot, one hand holding the suitcase and one hand still holding her hat.

"You'd think she was back in academy," Mother said to Evelyn with a look of apology.

"It's just the excitement of the trip, Lena," Evelyn soothed, as she guided Mother by the elbow across the parking lot toward the station. "We're OK. Come along, Henry."

As Mother and the Corts approached the group gathered in the shade of the eaves, Gertrude saw a surprised look of recognition flash between her mother and the tall man with the pince nez.

"Professor Griggs," Mother said, offering her hand. "What a surprise."

"Mrs. Green, how good to see you again," he responded, taking her hand with a nod of his head and an abbreviated bow.

Gertrude and her friends had stopped talking to watch this display of old world courtly ritual. As Professor Griggs quickly introduced his wife and his son to Lena Green, Gertrude caught her mother's eye with a quizzical smile. Mother raised her eyebrows quickly with a coy smile of her own and turned to shake the hand of Mrs. Griggs. *Mother, you never fail to amaze me*, Gertrude thought.

Then the conversations began again, all at once and all together.

"Here, Henry, let me help you with that trunk," offered Len Bohner to Mr. Cort who was struggling with Gertrude's trunk toward the luggage room check-in.

"Thanks," Henry panted, "It's the last one of three. Gertrude had me bring the others and three suitcases down already. We can just add this one to the rest. I know the procedure."

Len Bohner stood openmouthed and stared in Gertrude's direction wondering why one woman could possibly need three trunks and three suitcases.

"Fred and I are here visiting our son, Donald, at Loma Linda," Mrs. Griggs was telling Mother as they began walking into the station. "But we never miss an opportunity to see off our missionaries, especially when they're going to our division."

"Come on, Buddy," Gertrude shouted as she and Peg Bohner grabbed Peg's small son by a hand on each side and ran through the doors of the station, leading the group to the back of the building and the loading platform.

Gertrude and the Bohners had already been on the train once, securing seats for themselves in the day coach. Now they returned to their small universe of new and old friends milling about on the platform with all the other passengers, making small talk and waiting for the inevitable.

"All aboard!" came the call. "All aboard!"

As if this were the starting gun for a marathon of affection, pecks on the cheek, hugs, and handshakes erupted across the platform. What had been an amorphously moving mass of people coalesced into knots of community, small solar systems that were drawn across the loading platform by the gravitational pull of the railway cars.

Gertrude was everywhere, hugging Mrs. Griggs, touching Dr. Donald Griggs on the arm, thanking Evelyn Cort for looking after Mother.

"Mr. Cort, thank you for getting my trunks on board," she remembered courteously with a peck on the cheek that left him flustered and red-faced while his wife laughed at his embarrassment.

The last-minute addition to the group of Martha Jane Ruble Carruthers, daughter of Dr. Ruble, touched off another round of squeals of delight and hugs all around as Gertrude introduced her to the others.

"Gertrude, Peg, we'd better get on board," Len Bohner called out as he mounted the three steps leading up to the day coach carrying his wiggly son, Buddy, in his free arm. As if to emphasize his warning, the steam engine far down the line shrieked a blast of imminent departure.

Being the stranger from out of town and not a member of the families gathered there, Mother had gradually slipped to the back of the group. Sensing her absence, Gertrude quickly scanned the group until she saw her standing there, small and quiet, in the shadows of the station's huge overhanging eaves. Gertrude ran to her and hugged her tightly.

Mother returned her hug firmly and held her for a long time. Then she held her at arm's length and the two sets of gray-green eyes, that were so much alike, embraced.

"Good-bye, Mother," Gertrude said quietly.

"Good-bye." Mother could not find the strength to say the words but only mouthed them.

Over her shoulder Gertrude heard the thunder of car couplings rolling down the long train. Holding her broad, black hat in place, she turned and sprinted the few feet to the short stairway. Clutching the railings beside the door, she jumped into the coach as the train began to move.

She strode up the aisle to her seat where Buddy was waving through the window back to the people they'd left on the platform. She could have looked out the windows and watched them as she walked up the aisle and took her seat, but she did not. Nor did she gaze out the open window longingly or wave her handkerchief as others were doing. Nor did she cry.

Gertrude's mother had taught them as children to be economical in their efforts and to give attention to the task at hand, while spending little time on emotional display. Therefore, once the decision was made to go and that hurdle was passed, Gertrude wasted no time or energy on tears or regrets.

As she settled into her seat, Gertrude spoke to Buddy who was up on his knees in his seat with his head resting on his folded arms on top of the open window. He turned and smiled but couldn't hear her. Peg and Len had their heads together, holding hands and talking in the seat just in front of them. As she felt the train gather speed Gertrude turned once in her seat and looked back.

Mother and the Corts stood at the back of the platform where she'd left them, fading into the shadows of the roof over the station, becoming smaller and smaller in her mind. Gertrude turned in her seat and faced resolutely toward San Francisco.

Chapter 16

ARRIVING IN CHINA

Crossing the East China Sea in the winter from Nagasaki, Japan, to the mouth of the Yangtze River guarantees rough seas and harsh weather. Gertrude, however, was an excellent sailor. She relished the brisk air, had no seasickness, and took daily walks on the rolling decks of the Japanese ship Shanghai Maru.

At noon on Sunday, December 20, 1936, Gertrude stood at the railing in the bow of the ship. Bundled into her dark winter coat with the heavy fur collar, her head wrapped in a scarf, she was prepared to record and remember for all time her first glimpses of China and Shanghai.

Oh boy, this is a cold wind, she thought, ducking inside the salon for the third time since 10:00 a.m. *I wonder if China is always like this in the winter.* Since entering the Yangtze River, the steamer had been struggling through a cold, steady northwest wind straight into its bow.

Gently turning, the large passenger liner skirted the two large islands on her port side at the mouth of the Yangtze, entering the quieter waters of the Wangpoo River. As the ship swung into the deep channel near the northern bank of the river, the large land mass to starboard shielded those on deck from the steady blow. Gertrude stepped out of the salon to the open deck.

Her ears were immediately assaulted by the deep-throated bellowing of the large oceangoing cargo ships in the main river channel joined by the hooting horns of the smaller steamships and tugs. Boats were everywhere.

Gertrude marveled at the intricate dance of the river traffic. The smaller boats did a rapid foxtrot around the promenade of the giant ocean liners and freighters. In the midst of these the sampans, some with sails and some with oars only, danced their careless jigs and flings, always weaving and bobbing out of harm's way with impeccable timing. Gertrude wanted to applaud their choreographer, whoever she was.

Like floating loaves of bread sitting side by side eight to 12 deep from the shore, houseboats lined the riverbanks on both sides. At least Gertrude thought they must be houseboats because of the laundry. Even in the cold wind of December, shirts and pants, both large and small, flapped from poles protruding from the long, squat, sausage-shaped homes on the water.

Gertrude's darting eyes quickly sorted through the aerial markers of life for probable sightings of children. There! On the butt end of a—"junk," was it?—squatting on a thin platform suspended high over the water were two small boys who must surely be as cold as the air she now breathed. While she was bundled up in her winter warmest, they wore no coats, hats, or mittens, only the drab gray pants and shirts such as those hanging empty and lifeless above them on their mother's drying poles.

And then she saw them, drab to almost invisibility, yet teeming, undulating like bees in a hive, the masses that covered the hundreds, no, *thousands* of houseboats—sampans, someone had told her—that lined the river. They were swarming with life: mothers cooking, fathers fishing, and more children running, sitting, clambering. Bordering the margins of this living organism and occasionally joining themselves to it were venders, fishermen, dock workers, roustabouts, those going and those returning from the market, entering and exiting this hive of activity on the watery edge of Shanghai.

Here was the consuming passion of her life—people. And here were more of them in obvious need of basic sanitation than she had ever seen assembled in one place, even in Boston. Her eyes, straining to see them all at the same time, grew tired. She closed them tightly, then opened them and allowed her gaze to drift upward.

Her eyes grew wide and her mouth opened in an unexpressed gasp as she became aware of the bustling streets and the gray stone masses towering over the sampans—the Bund of the Shanghai waterfront.

From the rococo clock tower on her left to the neoclassical columned building before her to the solid marble edifice on her right, every architectural style from every culture in Europe was present. Not even in New York did this many large buildings of varied styles stand so close to each other in so confined a space.

"I thought China would be . . . well, I don't know what I . . . more backward," she stammered out loud, letting her mind express itself to no one in particular.

"All passengers please assemble in the lounge on the main deck for passport inspection."

The loudspeakers repeated the message twice in Japanese and then in English.

Focused so sharply on her initial reactions to China, Gertrude turned abruptly, momentarily thinking the loudspeaker was addressing her personally. Then laughing at her foolishness, she hurried to join the other passengers on the main deck.

Papers, official people, lines, and the cacophony of three languages being spoken simultaneously greeted her as she slipped through the side door into the main deck lounge. She pushed her way through the crowds as she saw others doing until she was in the proper line and rubber-stamped through— an official visitor to China. She followed the lead of those going to purchase Chinese money, all the while watching the swarms of shoving, fighting, grabbing coolies on the dock just below her who seemed to assault the passengers as they disembarked with their luggage.

"Miss Green! Oh, Miss Green!"

Someone was calling her name.

"Miss Green! Gertrude Green!"

It was a man, a Caucasian man with wavy graying-brown hair, who stood head and shoulders above the Chinese around him.

"Dr. Miller," Gertrude whispered in shocked recognition. "Dr. Miller!" she shouted as her right hand shot up and waved vigorously from side to side.

Dr. Harry Miller strode up the gangplank, parting and passing through the grappling coolies and the suddenly attentive officials. In a moment he stood beside her at the head of the gangplank.

"Well, Miss Green, I thought we had lost you," he said as his eyes searched the deck immediately around her. "We didn't know until the last moment that you had been switched to the *Shanghai Maru*.

"Well, I'm certainly glad you found out," Gertrude shot back nervously. "I was not looking forward to facing those coolies down there."

"How many pieces of luggage do you have, Miss Green?" he asked with some puzzlement and a bit of irritation, ignoring her concerns.

"Why, uh . . . , nine." she answered, following his gaze around her in confusion, her mind racing to catch up. Then realizing she was completely empty handed, she quickly added, "I'll get some help to retrieve what I have in my stateroom."

With a deckhand heavily laden, Gertrude returned 10 minutes later with two suitcases, a small cabin trunk, and several parcels.

"Let's give these to Mr. Shull down there," Dr. Miller said, pointing toward a tall, thin man standing behind a large, black Dodge truck with plank sides on the wharf below. The man gave a half smile, as if he understood a secret that Gertrude did not yet grasp, lifted his hand and wiggled his fingers up at them. Dr. Miller grabbed the small trunk and a suitcase and charged down the planks. "Then let's get your trunks out of the hold. If we wait til they bring them out, it'll be midnight," he shouted over his shoulder.

Gertrude rushed down the gangway and up again trying to stay with this man who knew what he was doing and was intent on getting it done quickly. As she arrived at the gaping maw of the ship's hold, she saw Dr. Miller disappear over the edge into the blackness beyond.

"Miss Green, do you know where your trunks are? What do they look like?" came his voice from the interior.

Catching the spirit of this race against—what, she did not know—Gertrude motioned the deckhand into the hold and quickly slipped over the edge herself, landing lightly on a palette of crates two feet below.

As her eyes adjusted to the darkness, she saw two dozen Chinese workers, a Japanese sailor, and one tall American doctor trying to force their way through the maze of luggage thrown together in the hold. Avoiding the difficulty of walking on the already crowded floor, Gertrude jumped over to a box and away from the light coming into the hold from above. Squatting down she peered about for a better vantage point then sprang to the top of a trunk, ignoring the stares of the now bemused Chinese men around her ankles.

"I think I see them over there," she called out, pointing to a stack of steamer trunks and packing crates against the far wall.

Speaking rapid Chinese, Dr. Miller soon had all the workmen in the hold moving every obstruction to the elusive luggage. In fire brigade fashion the trunks were passed up over the other cargo. And soon the deckhand and Dr. Miller lifted first one, then the other trunk up over the edge of the hold and onto the deck. In a short time, Gertrude and her nine pieces of luggage stood on the wharf beside the Dodge truck with the Chinese characters on its side and "Shanghai Sanitarium" written above them, waiting for the customs inspector.

"So that was your introduction to our home away from home," Chaplain Hartwell chuckled as he lowered himself into a large armchair. The Hartwells had been invited along with all the new, incoming missionaries for Christmas dinner at the home of Ed and Eileen Meisler on the hospital compound just outside of Shanghai.

"And to our tenacious Dr. Miller," Eileen Meisler added as she handed Gertrude a cup of steaming cocoa. "He knows how to shake a leg."

"And get everyone else to shake one, as well," Gertrude laughed. "I think between the two of us, we shocked the poor coolies out of a year's growth." As everyone laughed, she turned sideways on the couch. "Shouldn't I be helping with the dishes?" she called over her shoulder.

"No, dear," Eileen said as she retreated into the kitchen, "Ed and I can clear these away quite nicely. You just sit and let that hot drink soothe away your cold."

Gertrude held her cocoa close to her face and let the hot steam slowly penetrate up through her nose into her head. The rich scent of warm chocolate reminded her of other Christmases: toboggan outings at the academy and parties at the New England Sanitarium. The warm memories together with the hot chocolate almost made her cold symptoms disappear.

Just like the families I've know before, thought Gertrude. The Meislers had cordially invited her to spend Christmas dinner with them. But when she'd arrived, the hospital chaplain and his wife were also there along with Ada and Leighton Holley, newlyweds just arrived last summer. *Everyone seems to have someone to look after.* Gertrude smiled to herself.

"We feel so at home here," she heard Ada say, as she cuddled up on the couch close to her husband of eight months. And Gertrude smiled as she realized that others also sensed they were being adopted into the close family on the Shanghai compound on Rubicon Road.

"But you haven't told us about the rest of your trip," Leighton said, extracting himself from his wife's comforting clasp and sitting forward. "We heard about the dock strike and the Japanese ship. But what else happened?"

Happily animated when telling stories, Gertrude took up her adventuresome travelogue where she'd left off during dinner. Unable to sit still for more than a few sentences, Gertrude deposited her cup on the short table before her and bounded to the center of the floor where she began to mimic the actions of the characters she was describing. She soon had the group in stitches over the antics of the Japanese stewards, the unusual tastes of the international foods, and the friendly but tense relationship between Elder Jacobs, who was making an around the world trip and the Presbyterian priests and Catholic monks who were on their way to China.

As they listened, each missionary relived their own boat trip "across the pond" and were soon adding interesting or amusing bits of their own stories. Some were about personal sacrifices made and some were of humorous social catastrophes barely avoided. And all added to the total picture of being a missionary.

Gertrude took her seat and retrieved her warm cocoa as the humorous stories waned but the serious talk continued unabated. She listened and filed away information until she began to understand what each of them had left behind and why they were so far from home on this Christmas day.

"And now Gertrude, what about Shanghai?" Mrs. Hartwell asked, standing, as always, close beside her husband. "Let's return to you, my dear. What have you seen in your short time here?"

"Yes, what do we need to show you?" Ada chimed in, always ready for a lark.

"What haven't I seen is more like it," Gertrude shot back gasping in mock exhaustion. "Dr. Miller has nearly run my legs off. First it was to a staff meeting at the Sanitarium and then to the milk factory and then to the clinic and then various compounds all over town. But why so many compounds?" she asked abruptly, gazing about.

"The Ningkuo Road Compound was enough for the early work," Elder Hartwell responded as the eldest of the group. "But with the Division offices, the college, Far Eastern Academy, the press, and all the housing, we just got full up there. The East China Union offices were moved to Yuyuen Road, and the clinic, of course, was downtown. The Sanitarium was begun out here on Rubicon Road," he concluded with a shrug of his shoulders and a quick smile of resignation, "and the rest just sort of happened."

"Well, there sure is a lot of it." Gertrude said emphatically. "And everyone seems to speak Chinese. I watched Mrs. Coulston teaching her nursing class—in Chinese!"

"Have to," Ed Meisler said. "Most of the Chinese who work for me in the kitchen at the San don't speak English. I have to speak Chinese or not get the work done." Eileen and the Hartwells nodded their heads in agreement.

"The publishing work is the same," Leighton said. "I can't speak the language and I struggle every day."

"So you're coming to Nanking with me?" Gertrude asked hopefully.

"Yes, as soon as we can get away."

"That's the whole purpose of being here," Elder Hartwell added thoughtfully, "to communicate the gospel of Jesus Christ."

"Yes, I suppose so," Gertrude said, wondering what it was she would have to share after she learned to speak Chinese. It was tough enough to share the gospel in English.

"And the Chocolate Shoppe," Gertrude shouted, suddenly remembering, causing Ada who sat next to her, to jump closer to her husband.

"What about it?" Mrs. Hartwell laughed as did everyone else at poor Ada's expense.

"I thought it was a chocolate shop!" Gertrude joined the laughter now at her own expense. "But it wasn't. We went there for dinner and it was delightful."

"Yes, many of us go there often because it can be very inexpensive," Eileen said.

"And such a pleasant break," added Ed, the sanitarium cook.

"And . . . so inexpensive," Mrs. Hartwell repeated, smiling at her own small joke, ever the practical leader of their home.

"So you've seen some of the downtown?" Eileen now took an interest.

"Oh, but I've seen more than that," Gertrude interrupted, now excited. "I went shopping and got several things to mail home. I found the post office and mailed them out yesterday."

"Yesterday?" Eileen asked, adjusting her glasses as if to check the reality of Gertrude's bravery.

"Yes. I decided to find my way to town by myself and managed it all very nicely before getting my hair done for Christmas." Gertrude touched the back of her head lightly with her hand, a satisfied smile on her lips.

"Well, well, my dear," Elder Hartwell said thoughtfully, stroking his chin with his hand. "You're here less than a week and already running around Shanghai by yourself. And in a rickshaw, too, I'll wager. I think you will do, Miss Green," he added approvingly with a wink. "I think you will do very well."

Chapter 17

LEARNING THE LANGUAGE

Shanghai, China
Tuesday, Dec. 29, 1936

Dear Family at home and at the New England San,
Please excuse me while I include all of you in this letter. I have so much to write about that I fear I will play out before I can write it over and over enough to write to each of you individually.

First of all, please note that the dire prophecies of my impending seasickness were without foundation. And all such persons are to be proclaimed false prophets. Ha. Ha.

The ocean voyage over here was magnificent as I have told several of you already. Even my romantic life. As some may have already heard from the Bohners, they enjoyed great fun at my expense when a dashing young English gentleman insisted that I dance with him on the ship during one of the concerts. I had a most difficult time trying to explain to him why I could not. As you may know, the Bohners changed ships in Japan and are on their way to the Philippines. I miss them.

In Japan I visited numerous shrines where incense sticks are burned and numerous prayers are said to the idols kept within. This, if for no other reason, was a keen reminder as to why so many of us are coming over here to spread the gospel. The students in our school here in Japan are making kimonos to sell in order to earn their way through school, much as many of us did in the States. Mother, I am arranging to send some of them your way that you might sell them and make a profit for yourself. I will be helping you and the school in Japan at the same time. I think you will like the excellent workmanship.

I have been having a wonderful time since I got here. There have been Christmas parties at the nursing dorm and parties at the home of the Meislers. They have taken me in and adopted me along with the Holleys, a newly married couple who will be in my language school which starts next Tuesday. But for now I am enjoying just settling into the luxurious life of a lady—no work to do—and I am loving every minute of it. I wouldn't be anywhere else for all the tea in—well, you know where.

I must tell you about the medical facilities where I will work when I return from language school. The Range Road Clinic is actually the old Red Cross Hospital and sits right on the street in the heart of the Chinese district. It is a six-story building with the clinics on the first floor, the operating room—which is booming—on the second floor, the patient beds on the next two floors, and apartments for workers on the top two floors. It is kept very clean and has activity everywhere, including lots of children.

The Shanghai Sanitarium is built way out of town at 150 Rubicon Road and is such a wondrous place I can hardly begin to describe it. The entryway has carpeted floors and a chandelier and plush seats—gifts, I am told, of Mrs. Chiang Kai-shek and her sister-in-law, Mrs. Shaw. The building is set on a wonderful layout of grounds, the rooms are all large and airy. But most stunning of all is the food.

The food is served to the patients in the dining room. It is not a cafeteria but food is served at the tables. There are always fresh vegetables and fresh salads. There are linen napkins, not paper ones, and even the initials of the San are embroidered on the corner.

I am continuing my old habit of shopping on my half day off as I did at New England San., only now it is Shanghai and not Boston that I visit. I went to the business district by myself on the day before Christmas and should have several things arriving for many of you in the next few weeks. I had to get personal shopping done now because I leave for Nanking, the capital of China, on Tuesday next where the language school is now located.

I will be at the language school for one year, I think. I may stay in Nanking only until June as the school closes. Then everyone moves to a cooler place for the summer, either Peking or some place in the mountains. I imagine I will be very busy then and not have so much time to write. So I wish you the greatest of success there at Melrose, a place I shall always call home.

Your sister and daughter,

Gertrude

On Tuesday, Jan. 3, 1937, Gertrude and her traveling companion, Dr. Mary Wilkerson, left the Shanghai Railroad Station at 8:00 a.m. on the Capital Limited. They arrived in the afternoon in Nanking in time for dinner at the China Language Institute at 6 Shanghai Lane.

The language school was the dream child of Elder W. A. Scharffenberg. He wanted to establish the best Chinese language school in China, attracting embassy people, business people, and missionaries of other denominations as well as serve the needs of the Seventh-day Adventist denomination. The school, originally established in Shanghai, moved to the new capital, Nanking, in the summer of 1936, to be near the center of the activities surrounding the government of General Chiang Kai-shek that had so recently established itself in China.

In reality, the language school resided in a large stucco, multigabled, two-story Western style house with many porches, wings, and dormers. Being located in the International Section, it was surrounded by other houses of similar style outside and similar intentions inside, being the places of residence for other overseas businesses trying to establish a foreign foothold in a culture more than 5,000 years old.

The downstairs held the kitchen, the common dining room, and the class-rooms. The upstairs was divided into apartment rooms that could accommodate up to 15 or more students and their families. The teachers lived in the surrounding neighborhoods but, being Chinese, were not permitted to live on the same grounds as the school. Despite its small beginnings, the school was well established. And despite its church affiliation, it had already earned a good reputation in the international and business community.

"Gertrude, what a stunning dress," June Knight gasped. She stood in the middle of the upstairs hall watching as Gertrude closed the door to her room behind her. "Did you make that yourself?"

"I bought the material at the market," Gertrude smiled, self-consciously smoothing the green brocade long gown. "And I cut it out. But I had the seamstress sew it together." She turned halfway round so that Mrs. Knight could appreciate the excellent workmanship in the back.

"They do such wonderful work here," June said, touching the gown at the waist and around the zipper. "I wish we'd had this kind of help available in the States."

"And at these prices," Gertrude noted. "We'd best hurry," she added. "We don't want to keep the boys waiting." Tearing their attention away from the dress, they both turned and hurried toward the stairs leading to the parlor.

"Miss Atwell, if you will please take your seat at the head of the table," Frank Knight called out as he stood at attention in the doorway of the dining room. A dish towel lay neatly over one arm and his apron bib covered his white shirt and tie. As Ruth Atwell, the school matron, approached him, he bowed stiffly at the waist and indicated her seat with a courtly wave of his arm. Ruth, done up in her best Sabbath dress, stifled the broad smile that normally rested on her round, cheerful face. However, her twinkling eyes betrayed her good humor even as she tried to maintain a serious demeanor while gracefully taking her seat. The mood of the evening was echoed as several chuckles followed her into the dining room from the others waiting in the parlor to join her for her birthday party.

"Miss Green, if you will." Now it was Clarence Krohn's turn to summon a party goer. He was likewise adorned in a large bibbed white apron tied securely over his shirt and tie. He offered his arm and escorted Gertrude to her usual place next to Miss Ruth. Both men had cooperated in preparing this evening's meal and both were now enjoying the role of maitre d' with relish. And they had insisted that everyone else dress their very best for this special "night on the town" dinner.

By turns the two honorary chef/waiters seated their wives and Clarence's little girl Eva Mae, who, like all children, was fast becoming friends with Gertrude. Then the Holleys were seated at the far end with the singles scattered among the other chairs. Although each one found themselves in the same place they occupied at every meal at the old dining table, Frank and Clarence made it seem an evening of royal presentation as each was escorted to their place of honor.

The "two chefs," as they were now dubbed by their housemates, continued to strut and sway like bobbing penguins about the table, serving each course accompanied by "ahhs" of approval or giggles of shocked surprise. But every course was edible and some were delicious. The two chefs had done even better than they had boasted and everyone was impressed.

"Daddy, come sit by me," Eva Mae called out in her small 8-year-old voice.

"Yes, Clarence, come eat," his wife added with gentle humor. "Everyone has been served far more than they ever hoped to receive from the likes of you two."

"Hear! Hear!" came a chorus of affable voices. Clarence and Frank took their seats to lusty applause. Then for the next few minutes the dining room was awash in the sound of clinking of silverware against china.

"Has anyone been on a good bicycle trip lately?" Leighton asked with unmasked sarcasm. Several snickers and a few chokes of laughter slipped out around mouthfuls of food. Gertrude's face reddened, knowing she was again the butt of this ongoing joke. But before she could speak, Dr. Mary Wilkerson came to her rescue.

"Now, Leighton Holley, you're riding that old horse to death," she lectured, her short, golden brown curls bouncing with each shake of her head. But a broad grin broke the lines of her pudgy face despite her best efforts to conceal it. Around the table the snickers that followed her own poorly concealed mirth were infectious and soon everyone was laughing at the memory of Gertrude's return in the rickshaw, holding her broken bicycle in her lap.

"I'll have you know I'm doing quite well riding my bicycle." Gertrude bit off the words with icy preciseness. "I haven't been arrested for reckless driving in more than two weeks. I've managed not to kill anyone in more than a month." Her green eyes were snapping now. "I should think that would qualify for clemency, Mr. Holley."

The table was silent. Everyone looked at their plates and kept eating—except Eva Mae. She sat there with big round eyes looking at Miss Green and wondering how her new friend could change like that in an instant.

Gertrude returned her gaze, receiving in full the rebuke of disbelief from the startled face of this little girl. Gertrude closed her eyes and wrinkled up her mouth in frustration.

"What's wrong? What did I say?"

Her eyes rolled heavenward as she shook her head at everyone's touchiness. Her hands settled to each side of her place setting as a small sigh escaped.

When she felt the soft pat and caress of the back of her hand, Gertrude looked up into the smile of Ruth Atwell. Gertrude saw no anger and felt no rebuke. But what was Miss Atwell trying to say? She did not speak, just shook her head slowly and smiled, as Gertrude's mother used to do.

"I'm enjoying my bicycle immensely, now that it's repaired." Gertrude offered, wanting to restore the congeniality of the evening. "It certainly beats having to put up with that smart aleck rickshaw puller," she added.

"Yes, I had him the other day," June Knight put in, thinking this would be a safe topic. "He loves calling us 'foreign devils' even when he's asking us to hire him. He thinks we don't understand what he says."

"It's the Chinese way," Miss Atwell cautioned with an edge in her voice. "They use sharp humor and biting sarcasm to cover their own discomfort, even to each other. And they don't think you understand. But it is one of the advantages of really learning a language," she added, softening, patting Gertrude's hand, "the ability to know when someone doesn't really mean what they say."

"Well, I for one am glad to be learning their language," Gertrude said. "I was able to catch more than half the sermon last Sabbath. But, I can tell you, that first sermon in Chinese . . . what a total loss."

"Where do you suppose Mr. Scharffenburg was able to find such excellent teachers?" Ada asked between bites.

"Mr. Hahn teaches such a good Sabbath school lesson."

"And Mr. Chen who got us all started on our first words." And each student in the house began to praise their favorite teacher.

"Ah, Mr. Chen," Leighton spoke with modulation, eager to return to being the pastor he was. "He has an interesting history." And all quieted as he began his tale. "He's the only Christian in his home. Even as the father in the family, he has very little power over those in his household because he believes in the foreigner's religion." He folded his hands over his plate pensively. "He pays a high price to be a Christian."

"Well, the price I'm paying is to be in this language school only three months," Dr. Wilkerson piped up, "and having to learn three times faster than the rest of you."

While the others commiserated with Dr. Mary about her short time with them, Gertrude's mind wandered back over her own schedule for the last five weeks. Up at 7:00 o'clock every morning and to breakfast by 7:30. Ten new words to learn every day at 8:30. Private tutor for an hour starting at 9:30. Recess at 10:10. Conversation practice in groups of five from 10:30 to 11:15. Writing until noon. Lunch break til 2:00 o'clock. Reading from 2:00 to 2:30. And review of the day's activities until 3:45. And not one word was to be spoken in English. All had to be in Chinese. No wonder she could now understand most everything being said in church. No wonder she was so tired at the end of the day that she needed a warm bath before supper to enable her to relax. Her mind just swam with Chinese . . .

"Gertrude. Gertrude!"

Gertrude shook her head, blinked her eyes, and focused on the present. Nearly everyone had left the table.

"Gertrude, dessert will be served when we get out the Monopoly game. Dinner is over. Come." It was Dr. Mary beckoning to her from the parlor room door. Only Eva Mae sat with her mother at the end of the table slowly finishing her vegetables.

"Sorry," Gertrude said, rising quickly. "Just thinking about . . . oh, never mind what I was thinking." She laughed quietly over her daydreaming as she walked around the table.

"Monopoly!" she said, halting. "Oh, no. Frank Knight wins every night. Now, quick," she said, grabbing Mary's arm and rushing for the stairs, "let's go devise a strategy to beat him for once."

Chapter 18

DISCOVERING THE CHILDREN

For the next six weeks the snow fell, the Chinese lessons continued, and the Monopoly games were won by someone other than Gertrude. Following language school, on nice days her afternoons were filled with bike riding and shopping. Writing letters and playing the piano in the parlor occupied snowy afternoons.

On most weekends, Gertrude played the piano for church and assisted Miss Atwell in handing out tracts in the market, where everyone was curious to see what the "foreign devils" were giving away in English. On some weekends she caught the noon train to Shanghai for more intense shopping on Sunday before dashing home on the late train Sunday evening or the "tardy" train Monday morning.

One special Sunday diversion was a frosty outing to the Ming Tombs with the Holleys and the Olsens who'd come over from Shanghai. And one Friday Gertrude hopped a noon train for a warm weekend "homecoming" visit with Professor and Mrs. Quimby, her academy Bible and English teachers, who now taught at the China Training Institute in nearby Chiao Tou Tseng.

Frequently her market purchases were set aside to be shipped home or to be given away to the children she met on the street. Dressed in ragged, dirty clothes, many without proper winter coats or warm winter shoes, the children flocked around the foreigners because they could not contain their curiosity. And Gertrude was drawn to them, often giving balloons or peanut brittle to them.

One child in particular arrested her attention. Early every morning Gertrude looked over the edge of her balcony and saw a young boy, bigger than his playmates, carrying a large flat basket. He stooped down and scratched into the ground at the side of their compound, sifting through the ash heap. He had a round face and a wide smile, but was too shy for spontaneous conversation as he went about his sooty task. Plying him with peanut brittle and her new Chinese language skills, Gertrude eventually discovered that he was looking for charcoal clinkers which he put in his basket and took home to his mother for fuel. Her heart went out to him and he became her favorite. Although he would not tell her his Chinese name, her term of endearment for him was Ashey.

★★★

The only hint of the war in far away Northern China was the presence of seven U.S. gunboats lying just off shore in the river. Gertrude and several of her friends were invited to dinner one Wednesday evening by Dr. Ekvall, a Seventh-day Adventist physician, stationed aboard the *USS Pansy*. They were told that the gunboats were there for the evacuation of U.S. citizens, if that became necessary, but that it was highly unlikely. Gertrude was relieved to know that the war would be staying in the north.

> 6 Shanghai Lane
> Nanking, China
> Sunday, April 4, 1937

Dearest Mother,

I am trying to write to you once every week but sometimes I get so busy that I fall behind. Please forgive. I do so love getting letters here. There are several weeks that go by before anything comes and I wonder if people have forgotten me. Then with the arrival of the next mail boat I get several letters and am awash in good wishes and fond memories of home.

Dr. Mary Wilkerson has returned to Shanghai where she is to be interning for the next year. But her place at the Monopoly table has been taken by Dr. Charles and Mrs. Grace Dale. They arrived at the end of March and are scheduled to be here for the next six months. I for one am glad to see them arrive. Dr. Dale plays a mean game of Monopoly and Mr. Knight is no longer the only winner.

Do you remember Mr. Chen, my first teacher? He taught me my first words and how to write them. His youngest child, a two-year-old, is somewhat weak and frequently ailing. I have been to his house to see the child and have spoken with Dr. Dale. He seems to think the child will be all right. I hope so. Mr. Chen is the only Christian in his family and wants so much to raise up his children in the Lord. But he has a hard go of it with no support from his parents or from his wife or her family. In China, family is everything.

You asked about babies to send home to you. Believe me, if I could I would. There are so many children roaming the streets, many with little more than the clothes on their backs. I hear stories from Mr. Hahn about infants who are murdered by their parents at birth because they cannot take care of them. It is not considered a crime here but a way of preserving the lives of those already in the home from one more mouth to feed. My heart goes out to them and I think I am falling love with these little ones of the streets.

I am having another dress made from material I got on an especially good bargain in the linens market. The Chinese have cloth here even superior to what comes from England.

I have also purchased a new radio. The old one has been repaired twice and has finally given up the ghost. The radio is sometimes the only way we can get news of the outside world. Much of what passes for news here in China is rumor pumped up by fear and anxiety. We are always glad to hear the BBC.

The next shipment of kimonos should be arriving there from Japan. You have asked for kimonos with dragons on them. The Japanese don't put dragons on their kimonos but the Chinese do. When I am in Shanghai next, I shall find a source of Chinese kimonos and have some with dragons sent on.

I am glad to hear that Ruth has gotten a raise. Maybe she can get control of some of those medical bills. I hope so. I was encouraged to hear that Father now has work. I pray he will be able to hold on to this situation.

I must close for now as we are preparing to go on a boat ride and picnic with Elder Cormack who is visiting from the General Conference in Washington, D.C. He was the one, you remember, who contacted me and made the arrangements for my coming to the Far East.

Please write soon.
Heaps and heaps of love from your loving daughter,
Gertrude

Gertrude jumped when she heard the crash of the garbage pails followed by laughter and crying. She dropped her writing pen and rushed outside to the edge of her balcony. There in the snow sat Ashey in the middle of the scattered garbage and the pails. The other children were running wildly around him, pushing him and hitting him, laughing and pointing.

"Stop that!" Gertrude shouted in English. "Stop that this instant!"

The children all stopped and looked up at the White foreigner speaking from heaven. Then, laughing, they pointed at Gertrude as they began hitting Ashey again, looking at Gertrude for a reaction. Gertrude found her Chinese tongue.

"I will call down the ancestors to strike you," she shouted in her best Mandarin.

The children stopped hitting the boy and looked up to consider this new, more serious assault from above. Some of the less brave began to back away.

"I am coming down right now to take care of you," she called to Ashey as she made a dash for the door and the stairway. Many of the children, thinking this last comment was directed at them personally, began screaming and running in all directions. As he was passing, one big boy smacked Ashey on the head one last time, knocking off his round cap. A smaller child, in her mad dash for safety, stumbled over the cap as it rolled away. Her brother grabbed the cap, thinking it was hers, and pulled her after him behind the wall to the next compound.

"Gertrude, what's happening?" It was Grace Dale who almost got run down on the stairway.

"It's Ashey!" Gertrude shouted in her face in Chinese as she passed. "They're attacking him!" Grace, the new student in the school, spun around in confusion at the unfamiliar Chinese language as the fury of Gertrude hit the front door.

"Ashey! Are you all right? Are you all right?"

Gertrude, dressed only in her afternoon lounging dress and pumps, towered over the huddled Chinese boy. Her hot breath spewed clouds of steam into the cold, clear air. A dragon, he was sure, if there ever was one. He'd stopped crying when the children shot away, running for their lives. Now he huddled close to the ground, his hands over his bare head, looking up at this puffing giant. Saved, only to be devoured!

Gertrude knelt in the snow, extending a hand to lift up his trembling chin.

"Are you hurt?" she asked quietly in Chinese.

He shook his head.

Gertrude's practiced eye quickly scanned him for cuts or bruises. The attack had been more noise than substance. She sighed in relief, then gasped as she saw the scabs and sores on the bare head. *What is this? Cradle cap? Ringworm?* She reached out now with both hands and began to search through the scabs and sparse wisps of hair. *What a mess!* And all hiding under that cap!

"Ashey." She scrunched down even lower and lifted up his head so that their eyes were level. "Ashey. Come into the house with me. I will wash your head and make it better," she said slowly.

The boy tried to pull away, but Gertrude held him firmly with one hand and touched his cheek where the tear stains were still evident.

"Come with me, Ashey. I won't hurt you." She smiled into his eyes, her green eyes sparkling.

Slowly he stood and allowed himself to be led into the parlor where Gertrude set him on the tall, straight backed chair nearest the door. Grace Dale was standing at the door as they passed, and followed them in.

"Don't let him leave," Gertrude barked to Grace as she hurried out again. "I'm going for some soap and water. I have to clean him up before I can tell what he needs." She headed for the bathroom and the towels.

When Gertrude returned, Grace was kneeling in front of the boy, wiping away the tear stains as Gertrude had done. Ashey sat with his head bowed, afraid to look up at the fine and strange world of the foreigner. Grace slipped aside as Gertrude approached with a basin of steaming water, towels, and a small medical case.

Carefully Gertrude applied a soaking wet towel to Ashey's head, patting and caressing the scabs to yield to the warm water. As the dried scum came loose, Gertrude saw round, red lesions with clear centers and no hair, covering almost all of the child's head. She applied soap now to the towel and gently rubbed away the bits and pieces of scab that still clung to the diseased scalp.

"He will never have any hair," she said to Grace in English. "It's ringworm."

"How do you treat it?" Grace asked, her eyes wide with curiosity.

"Tar paste. Every day for weeks," Gertrude said, thinking out loud as she continued the cleansing. "I will have to apply it every day until the lesions begin to heal." But how to cover the tar? What would he keep on his head? "Ashey, where is your cap?" she asked gently in Chinese.

Again the boy visibly flinched and looked down when he heard himself addressed in Chinese by the name Gertrude had given him. Again Gertrude lifted his head to make eye contact and smiled disarmingly. "Where is your cap?" she repeated.

"I don't know," he replied so quietly as to almost not be heard. Gertrude strained to catch his Mandarin. "I lost it, or they took it."

"Miss Atwell," Gertrude shouted, making Ashey flinch once more. She turned. "Grace, can you find Miss—."

"Yes, Gertrude." The round face and wavy gray hair of Miss Atwell appeared around the parlor door followed by her short, stout body.

Gertrude stood now, dirty towel in hand, in deference to her school matron.

"Miss Atwell," Gertrude tried to modulate her voice, avoiding the sound of command. "Would you happen to have a round Chinese cap that Ashey could wear? I need to treat his head with coal tar paste and he seems to have lost his." She waved the towel in the boy's direction.

"Yes. Yes, I think we do," Ruth said and turned to fetch it.

After applying the coal tar paste to his scalp, Gertrude showed Ashey the new cap, not so unlike his own, only much cleaner and with no frayed edges. She gently placed it on his head and instructed him not to remove it. She would take it off tomorrow, wash his head again, and reapply the medicine. As she spoke he began to relax and looked at her voluntarily for the first time. Gertrude's eyes lit up as she smiled in return and led him to the door.

"You love him, don't you?" Grace stated as she watched the boy cross the street and disappear around the edge of the compound wall.

"Of course," Gertrude replied without turning, trying to hide the catch in her voice. "He's a child in great need." Then she turned and faced Grace. "And there are so many of them."

"Gertrude, it's only noon. Where are you going?" Mrs. Krohn called over the railing to the disappearing figure descending the stairs.

"I know." Gertrude looked up from the landing and waved. "Mr. Chen's 2-year-old is sick again. Dysentery this time." She turned and started down. "I'll be back for dinner."

When Ada Holley walked into the 2:00 o'clock reading class, she nearly dropped her books and tablet. Gertrude bent over her tablet at one of the student desks, practicing her Chinese characters.

"Gertrude, what are you doing here? Mrs. Krohn told us at lunch that you wouldn't be home until this evening."

Gertrude looked up with a big smile. "The boy is doing better than I expected. I actually got him to drink something for me." She laid down her pencil and pushed back from the table. "The mother is the biggest challenge actually," she said thoughtfully.

"How is that?" Ada asked, sitting down beside her.

"She is so resistive to any ideas from a Westerner. I think it has something to do with Mr. Chen being a Christian." She shook her head. "I had to talk and talk just to get her to agree to give him water."

"I know," Ada said. "They think if they can't eat, they shouldn't drink."

"And he looks so dehydrated, Ada," Gertrude said, leaning toward her as if for affirmation. "If she would just give him the water or the broth." Gertrude sat back in resignation. "I'll go check on him after school. We'll see." She leaned over her tablet and picked up her pencil.

"How's the little boy?" Leighton asked as he leaned over his bowl of rice soup, his hand poised for another spoonful.

Gertrude's eyebrows and shoulders rose in uncertainty. "I don't know, really," she managed. Her eyes were pinched and tired. "I wish he looked as good now as he did at noon." She gazed into her own bowl as if for wisdom. "I'll go see him in the morning."

Mr. Chen, drained of color from lack of sleep, was present for the new words class at 8:00 o'clock Wednesday morning, but Gertrude was not. Nor did she come to the afternoon classes. She appeared once in the early afternoon to collect her fomentation pads and was gone before anyone could ask her how it was going.

In fact, Gertrude spent the day at the Chen household, doing fomentations and a hot foot bath in the late afternoon. While she was able to get the child to drink for her, he didn't seem to improve. He needed intravenous hydration but the mother would not let Gertrude take him to the hospital.

On Thursday Gertrude went to Ganlow Hospital by herself to talk with the American doctor. Gertrude told him that she suspected pneumonia and he suggested herbs he thought the mother would allow the child to take that would slow the diarrhea. They talked about the limitations of treating the little boy while he remained at home. Both agreed that the key was hydration and the problem was the mother. In the afternoon Gertrude returned to the child's bedside to force oral fluids because she was sure his mother wasn't doing it when Gertrude was not there. The fomentations were helping keep the chest congestion clear but the child was gradually failing.

The next morning Miss Atwell was standing just inside the dining room when Gertrude came through the front door.

"I think you'll just make your first class," she said quietly. "We missed you at breakfast."

Startled, Gertrude turned to see her stepping out of the shadows into the entryway. Gertrude's face relaxed with a large sigh when she saw the kindly eyes, but a smile was long in coming. "He's seems to be rallying," she managed to say before slipping down the hall to the classroom.

But at noon he was no better, nor at 4:00 o'clock when classes let out. With Mr. Chen now home and at his bedside, Gertrude again gave the 2-year-old fomentations and a hot foot bath for the pneumonia, and he seemed a bit better. She went to a corner noodle shop for a bite as she had been offered nothing by Mrs. Chen, and returned at 7:00 o'clock. Then as she watched with Mr. Chen, the boy gradually grew weaker and weaker. He died a little before 10:00 p.m.

Mr. Chen sat by the small bed in the robe he always wore to class, old and faded, worn at the knees. He always appeared to be too old to have young children, Gertrude thought. How does one guess the age of the Chinese? But tonight his face seemed to be anciently lined as with the sadness of all the Chinese who over the centuries had ever lost small children to disease.

"Thank you, Miss Green," he said in polite Chinese.

"It is nothing," she replied, hoping she had conveyed the right sentiment.

A moment of silence hung quietly on the air.

Then in English, "He was my youngest. I had hoped I could raise him in the Lord."

Not knowing what was the proper thing to do, Gertrude slipped out of the small room while Mr. Chen sat by the bed with his head bowed, not crying. She let herself out of the house and walked the few blocks toward home, looking at the stars in the cold night sky and wondering what it was all about.

She had lost patients before, even this young. But never under such difficult circumstances—in such a divided home, and in the Chinese culture where she did not know what was the proper thing to say to console the family or how to carry out the nursing role for the bereaved. *I have much more than language to learn here,* she decided as she turned onto Shanghai Lane.

Chapter 19

OPENING A CLINIC

During the next several weeks, every day after school, Gertrude treated Ashey's head with the tar paste then carefully placed his cap on his head and sent him home. When his head was clear of scabs, Gertrude positioned him in a chair she'd set on the lawn and gently shaved away all of his remaining hair, then painted his head with iodine. As a reward for his faithfulness she also gave him a large piece of Miss Atwell's special home baked bread with strawberry jam, some of the first to come from the Chiao Tou Tseng farm. As Ashey was finishing his bread and Gertrude was placing his cap on his head for the walk home, Mr. Chen came out of the house and stood watching on the steps.

"You come back in three days and we'll see how your head looks," Gertrude instructed in excellent Mandarin. "And we will also see if there's more bread and jam." This last word she said in English because she did not know the word in Chinese. She patted Ashey on the shoulder and sent him on his way.

The boy scooted across the street with quick shuffling steps, singing "Jesus Loves Me" at the top of his lungs.

"Now I wonder who taught him to sing that song in Chinese?" Mr. Chen remarked—in Chinese.

"I did, honorable teacher," Gertrude answered without turning around.

"You have a way with the children, Miss Green."

"I tell them stories from the Bible. But they mostly like to sing." Gertrude's gaze followed Ashey until he disappeared. *It's all I know how to do,* she thought to herself.

"They are easy to love, honorable teacher." Gertrude turned and bowed in his direction.

He came down the steps holding out his folded hands in front of him. It was as if he were about to offer her something, she thought. Then he stopped.

"I would be honored if you would come to my house again, Miss Green." She detected a bit of strain in his voice. "My youngest child—now—also has sores on his head as that young man did. Would you come and treat his head with your medicine?" The faint trace of a smile flickered through his eyes.

"The honor would be mine, honorable teacher," she replied, bowing again. This was a test of her ability to function in China. She knew it. And Mr. Chen knew it. "Would it be convenient to come now?"

"Now is an excellent time," he replied. He stood for a moment, fixing her with his gaze.

What have I done wrong? she wondered as she held his gaze with her own. *Why is he staring at me?* she thought as her eyes narrowed with irritation.

"You are an excellent student, Miss Green," he said finally. "You will do well here in China as a missionary. Very well. But you should not look at your teacher with a steady gaze. It is not respectful."

"I understand, honorable teacher," she said, dropping her gaze to the ground. "I will collect my medical supplies and come to your house quickly." Again she bowed.

Mr. Chen smiled to himself and continued out of the compound to his house.

When Gertrude arrived at the Chen house, it was as Mr. Chen had said. The youngest boy did indeed have the same sores as Ashey had, and Gertrude set about applying the same remedy. The wife again took no interest in her ministrations but neither was she resistive. It was as if the incident of the previous child had never happened. Gertrude gave the boy instructions and told him she would return the next day at his father's request to repeat the treatment.

The next afternoon, medical bag in hand, Gertrude made her way down the narrow crooked street toward Mr. Chen's house. Doorways and green-tiled gables stuck out in all directions from the small houses that seemed to be propped against one another at every odd angle. Small courtyards of potted plants and scrawny dogs appeared momentarily through low dark archways.

Clotheslines and drying poles reached out over the dark passageways to touch the clotheslines and drying poles of their neighbors. Everywhere was the sense of closeness and community.

Because of the intensity of her previous errands, Gertrude had never quite noticed how tightly packed, how densely populated this neighborhood was. Everything, the walls, the overhanging rooflines, and, she supposed, the families who lived within them, were so closed in, so on top of one another, not at all like the space she was used to. Yet, if she lived here, it might seem as just one big extended family. That would be an awful lot of people who would know your business she pondered. For sure, the people in this part of the world, at least, lived very close to the earth and to each other.

Where are the children? There had always been children and people in the streets when she'd come before. She had had to dodge around them in her haste, even late at night. Now there were none.

As she turned a sharp corner in the narrow lane, she could hear the noise of a small crowd just ahead. She would just have to work her way around it, saying something polite in Chinese as she did so. Not stop to stare at whatever was the attraction. Just move on.

Then the children began to come toward her and surround her. They were coming from the low archway leading to Mr. Chen's small courtyard, laughing and pointing as Chinese children always did when they were curious. *What's happening?*

As she ducked her head through the archway, she saw Mr. Chen's youngest child seated on a stool in the middle of his mother's herb garden, cap in hand, waiting for her treatment. All around the edge of the enclosure, keeping a safe distance but wanting to see this strange sight, were children and their mothers—waiting for her to begin.

"A thousand pardons, Miss Green." It was Mr. Chen emerging from his house, bowing and bowing as he approached her. He was genuinely embarrassed. He was now the petitioner.

Another test, Gertrude thought, her mind racing. *They are all watching, including his wife who is quietly standing in the shadows. What is the right thing to do? They must know he teaches school and that he is my teacher. He will lose face if I act superior. But will they have any respect for my medicine if I act inferior?*

She smiled and bowed. *Mr. Chen, help me,* she said to herself. But she knew he could not. The pressure on him was too much.

"Miss Green," he said in English, "it is my wife. She told all the neighbors ..." He paused and extended his arms wide, his face a painting of shame and humiliation.

"Honorable teacher," Gertrude addressed him in Chinese. The crowd became hushed. "I have come as you requested," she said, adopting the same wide armed stance as he had done and bowing. "It is an honor to treat your beautiful child. Come, honorable teacher," she said as she moved toward the young boy on the stool. "I will present what I am doing for your approval."

Mr. Chen smiled, his eyes connecting with Gertrude's for only a split second. Then he inserted his hands into the long sleeves of his robe and walked, head held upright, to where Gertrude now examined the boy's head.

"Bring me some water and towels," Gertrude commanded, green eyes looking straight at the wife.

Mrs. Chen never flinched but a small motion of her hand sent a young girl—*a daughter, perhaps?*—scurrying into the house. She returned so quickly with the basin and towels that Gertrude knew they must have been waiting just inside the door.

"Thank you most kindly," Gertrude said politely, nodding to the mother as she took the articles offered by the daughter. Then she began the ritual of the soaking and the cleansing, explaining each step to Mr. Chen as if asking for his approval. He, in turn, stood near, arms folded into his gown, nodding as he would have for a student recitation.

As she worked, Gertrude heard the low buzz of conversation beginning again. By twos and threes the children and their mothers edged closer to the action. Gertrude talked above the rising din, explaining supposedly to her teacher what she was doing.

As she had hoped, their curiosity knew no bounds. Soon the treatment area was a mass of curious hands touching and wondering tongues questioning. And Gertrude tried to answer all the honest enquiries while still addressing Mr. Chen. A classroom in a courtyard, she decided. Really no different than taking freshman probies out to the cottages to see the hydrotherapy patients.

When the last of the tar paste was applied and the cap set gently on the boy's head, Gertrude turned and addressed Mr. Chen once more.

"Is there any other service I might render to you, honorable teacher?"

"Yes, Miss Green. I think there is. Many of these children also have problems," he said as one who is now overseer of the welfare of his neighbors as well as master of his home. "I think the mothers would like it very much if you would look at their children as well."

"I would be very honored to do so," she responded. *Oh boy, Gertrude, what have you gotten yourself into?* she thought as she took in a deep breath. *There must be 25 kids here and I'll bet they don't all have ringworm.*

"If you will all line up, I will examine you one at a time"

Gertrude looked over her shoulder to see Mrs. Chen coming to fetch her son. Gertrude tried desperately to smile with her eyes. There was just a pause and the sad questioning face of Mrs. Chen, and she was gone. There were some Chinese puzzles for which Gertrude knew she had no answers. Quickly, surgically, Gertrude cut off the emotional loss of not connecting with Mrs. Chen and switched her clinical mind to the curious, raucous children milling about her.

Mr. Chen was now the grandfather of them all, gently prodding the children into line until the queue wound around the garden and back in under the willows overhanging the compound wall.

Gertrude turned. "It looks like it's time for clinic," she said under her breath as she picked up the stool the young boy had vacated and approached the head of the line.

On Wednesday of the following week 10 to 15 additional children were waiting to see "the doctor" at Mr. Chen's house. On Thursday, when Ashey returned for his final examination, he was accompanied by three friends who politely removed their caps and bowed their heads for examination. Gertrude knew she needed help.

"I need help, and that's a fact," Gertrude said as she sat down on the piano bench facing Charles and Grace Dale who'd followed her into the parlor which also served as the entryway to the house. Charles sat on the stuffed and corded maroon loveseat with the carved arms which backed against the stairway, his spectacles framing his boyish face under a short shock of wispy blond hair. Dark haired Grace sat close beside him, her right hand resting on his knee. Her usually smiling round face was drawn down in a frown of perplexity. They both sat forward, extending themselves in sincere concern for their housemate.

"Whatever is the matter?" Grace asked, looking at Charles and then at Gertrude, worry lines creasing her brow.

"I need a doctor," Gertrude said, nodding her head for emphasis, looking at the floor and not at them.

"Are you sick, Gertrude?" Charles asked, now sharing his wife's anxiety.

"Oh, no," Gertrude looked up, eyes wide in innocence. "I'm fine. But my patients are not."

"Your patients?" Charles asked, drawing himself up and shaking his head, trying to follow the conversation. "What patients?"

"I found a young street urchin with ringworm on his head and treated him."

"Yes. Ashey. We know," Grace said.

"Not so hard to do," Gertrude waved her hand at the small effort. "But now he has friends who have come with him who have similar problems. And they want to be cared for." Now she transfixed the Dales with her eyes. "I visited Mr. Chen's young son who also had ringworm. And now there is a whole neighborhood of children and their mothers who are seeking treatment. It started out as a lesson in Chinese and now it's become a clinic. They are so pathetic, Charles. They need help."

"Well, I agree they probably need help but I don't see . . ." Charles began.

"They have typhoid and dysentery, skin infections and abscessed teeth, tuberculosis and things I don't recognize. Charles, I'm only a nurse and I'm in over my head. I need a doctor," Gertrude pleaded.

"How would you care for these children?" Grace asked, wondering what Gertrude was considering. "Where would you get the medicines?"

"Well, I don't think the medicines are a problem." Gertrude had already considered this particular angle. "I've talked with the doctor at Ganlow Hospital. He is willing to help with some of the vaccines from the government supplies. And what we don't get there, I'll talk to Dr. Ekvall about."

"Who is Dr. Ekvall?" Charles asked.

"Dr. Ekvall is an Adventist physician on the gunboat USS Pansy. I met him over dinner one night." Gertrude now leveled her gaze at Charles. "Charles, I need help. I can't do this alone."

Charles sat back on the loveseat in stunned silence. He looked from his wife to Gertrude with questioning eyes. "I thought I was here to learn Chinese," he said with a short laugh. But neither his wife nor Gertrude seemed to catch the humor of the moment. He cleared his throat, trying to comprehend the sides of the box that were quickly closing in on him.

"Gertrude, I'm a pathologist, not a family doctor," he said desperately. "I wouldn't be much good at treating these people."

"You wouldn't need to treat them," Gertrude coaxed. "I can treat them— once I know what they have. I need your skills in recognizing their illnesses."

"I'll help," Grace said, smiling at her husband and patting him on the leg. "We can all help, can't we, Charles?"

"Well, yes, certainly. I suppose we can all help." Charles raised his arms in resignation. "What do you want me to do, Gertrude?"

"Are you busy at 4:00 o'clock this afternoon, Doctor?" she asked with a smile.

Chapter 20

BECOMING A MISSIONARY

6 Shanghai Lane
Nanking, China
Wednesday, May 12, 1937

My dearest Ruth,

Radio is a wonderful invention. I am listening to the coronation of King George the IV while writing to you. Imagine being able to hear what is happening halfway round the world. I don't think this coronation will mean much to the folks in Rochester, but it is big news out here where what the BBC broadcasts is what people talk about.

It has suddenly gotten very warm here. The roses are in bloom and I am able to share them with everyone, especially the little "ash kids," the ones I told you about who go through our ash heap every day.

Which reminds me, have I told you about our clinic here? Dr. Charles Dale, a pathologist in the language school, and his wife are helping me run a clinic for the children in the neighborhood. It's not like a clinic in the States. This clinic meets out of doors in Mr. Chen's courtyard. And the ailments are a mixture of all the overseas diseases you ever heard of. We have had help from several sources in finding the medicines and the means to help these people.

I just love these Chinese people. They have hearts of gold and appreciate what one does so much.

Actually most of the people we have been seeing for the last six weeks are just about well which will be just about right. The language school will be moving, along with everyone else who can get away, to the mountains of Kuling for the summer. They say if you think you are sweating now, just wait until you have been in Nanking in the summer. So we are not waiting. The first week of June I will pack what I need for the summer and leave the rest of my things here for when I return in September. I am ordering a camphor chest from Shanghai to store things so they will not mold.

It is two weeks until final exams for the second quarter of language school. I am studying furiously. You would love my printing of Chinese characters. Remember how artistic I am? Ha. Ha. I will do third quarter in Kuling this summer and fourth quarter when I return in the fall. Then I will be ready to return to Shanghai and begin my work here in China as a missionary.

Yesterday I went to town and got the mosquito netting that I am told we will need. From now on I will be sleeping "under cover." Malaria is still a prevalent disease here and a killer, too, especially of little children.

I will be visiting Chiao Tou Tseng again next weekend. That's our farm and training school where all the strawberries come from. We have them at almost every meal now. Mrs. Blanchard wants me to visit and I think I shall one more time before I go to the mountains.

The world seems to be looking up for us Greens. Fred has a new Plymouth, I hear. And papa is working steadily. Walter has given his girl the go by but one can never tell what these men will do next. They sure surprise one greatly. And you seem to be doing well with your increase in salary.

I am fine here. Do not worry about the rumors of the war over here. It is very far away and likely to stay that way. I think we are in more danger from malaria than from the Japanese.

Now that it is warm, the Chinese fans are coming out. They are very pretty. I will get one and send it to you.

Your loving sister,
Gertrude

Twenty-six miles to the east of Nanking lay a fertile plain of gently rolling hills bordering on the Yangtze River, guarded on the northwest and southeast by mountains usually shrouded in mist. In the midst of this verdant rural paradise the Shanghai-Nanking locomotives passed through the little railroad town of Chiao Tou Tseng. A short walk or rickshaw ride along the tracks to the east and north of this village was the 130-acre site of the China Training Institute.

Begun in Shanghai by Dr. D. E. Rebok as the China Mission College, China Training Institute or Chiao Tuo Tseng, as it was more commonly known, was moved to its rural setting in 1925. Far from the demands of the city and the political strife of the nation, here it would be possible to more clearly teach a new philosophy of education: the combination of manual labor and academics, the close cooperation of teachers and students, and the democratic ideals of Christian service. These ideas were quite foreign to China where a strict demarcation, socially and culturally, separated those who worked with their hands and those who worked with their minds, those who taught and those who learned, those who led and those who followed.

It was the dream of Dr. Rebok and the teachers and staff who followed him, that from these grounds there would emerge new Chinese leaders who would one day assume the responsibilities for the work of the Seventh-day Adventist Church in China.

The rickshaw puller turned in at the main gates and trotted up the tree-lined narrow road that wound through the strawberry fields and lush green gardens. Gertrude leaned forward to better observe the students and their teachers working side by side in the long vegetable rows that ran together in the distance to the river's edge.

The peace and tranquility of this place, she thought as she watched the red brick buildings in the distance growing ever larger. *What a contrast to the crowded, hectic life of Shanghai and Nanking*

But it is the people who live in those congested cities who buy the strawberries that make this school possible. She wrinkled her brow, frowning, trying to understand. *Some of life's puzzles are not so easily solved,* she observed.

The rickshaw puller looked back questioningly but Gertrude directed him past the two boys' dormitories and the tree lined semicircular drive of the main school building. She was headed for the president's office where Professor Quimby would be finishing his work just before the Sabbath began.

The one story school office building sat immediately adjacent to the main building, surrounded by shrubs and flowering trees now in full blossom. Gertrude climbed down and paid the man the fare that had been haggled over at the railroad station. At the door she turned and took one last look at the unspoiled pastoral landscape cradled in the arms of the surrounding mountains before opening the door and stepping into the dark interior.

Professor—that's how Gertrude would always remember him—Paul Quimby stood framed in his open office door, the light shining through his thinning hair. His wide mouth was opened in a generous smile, his arms extended in greeting.

"Gertrude, Gertrude, come in, do come in," he welcomed in his profuse style. He shook the hand that she extended to him. "Welcome again to Chiao Tuo Tseng, strawberry capital of the world," he added, knowing how much Gertrude loved the delicious red fruit grown here in abundance.

Gertrude entered the small office crowded with the accouterments of responsibility. She marveled again at how he was able to tastefully arrange a large executive desk, a meeting table, two chairs, and book shelves into such a small space. A full quarter of the 2,000 volumes in his library lined the walls to the window at the far end.

Gertrude stopped short, having barely entered the room. The shadow at the edge of the window moved and turned, becoming a Chinese man of medium short height, totally bald and wearing round, dark-rimmed glasses. His long gown was close woven, lined and edged, yet all of one color, elegant and simple.

Gertrude gazed at the inscrutable face. The effect was like coming under the sudden, sharp scrutiny of an owl. She felt like prey. She could only return the steady gaze with questioning eyes of her own, her body frozen in place.

Professor Quimby awkwardly wriggled between Gertrude and the door frame, trying to enter the room.

"Gertrude," he said, standing erect and grasping for his professional composure, "may I introduce Dr. Hwang Dzi-gin, one of our teachers here at the China Training Institute."

Gertrude said nothing and did not move. Her initial fear was now replaced with anger at herself for feeling intimidated. She had met doctors before, but not a Chinese doctor. Then the anger dissipated into curiosity as she stepped forward for a better look.

Dr. Hwang stood motionless as stone. Then slowly as a tall pine might bend in the wind he doubled at the waist, leaned forward, then gracefully returned to the upright position.

"Miss Gertrude Green," he said in perfect English.

Gertrude halted, recognizing her error in not bowing first or in lowering her eyes in respect to the teacher. Yet she was confused as to what to do next, her Chinese training and her American curiosity sending simultaneous, confusing signals which left her unsure of a proper response.

"Dr. Hwang," she finally managed, offering no hand and not remembering to bow.

"Perhaps if we all sat down," Paul Quimby offered, "we would be more comfortable."

"I was startled," Gertrude said sharply, turning on him hastily, then recognized the offer of help for what it was and smiled. Turning to Dr. Hwang she said in her best Chinese, "I am most sorry, honorable doctor. I am honored to make your acquaintance."

"It is nothing," he answered in English. "Let us sit as Paul has suggested."

"I was frightened at first," Gertrude said with utter candor, speaking to Dr. Hwang as she would have to Mr. Chen. She stood beside one of the two straight backed stuffed chairs, waiting for Dr. Hwang to sit before seating herself directly opposite him.

"It is understandable," he said, nodding his head, still unsmiling. "It is not commonly known that a serious Chinese face hides a smile and a smiling Chinese face is dangerous."

"Or confused," Gertrude added.

"Which can also be dangerous," Dr. Hwang noted, a twinkle showing itself in his eyes. "I see you are studying the Chinese in more than language, Miss Green."

She leaned forward as if to come closer to this man of wisdom. "I have come to know some wonderful people in your beautiful land, Dr. Hwang."

Unconsciously sensing that she was in safe waters, Gertrude launched into a description of her encounters with the Chinese of Nanking, especially describing the clinic in Mr. Chen's courtyard, the puzzling attitude of Mrs. Chen, and how it all began with the death of his son. Dr. Hwang listened and commented, answering unasked questions and asking probing questions of his own.

During the unfettered exchange, Paul Quimby, mostly unnoticed, pulled out a straight chair from the conference table and sat quietly. His gaze shifted from one to the other of the two before him as one would observe a tennis match, marveling with keen interest at the almost instant rapport. The conversation, he noted with growing appreciation, was in English and Chinese as each of the players volleyed, switching easily from one language to the other whenever a word or phrase was unfamiliar or when they wanted to make themselves better understood.

"But he is a Christian, Dr. Hwang," Gertrude said with eyes now moist in sadness. "They placed his son's small coffin outside the city walls and left him there. He couldn't even give him a Christian burial."

"Because he is a Christian, he has little power in his home," Dr. Hwang spoke quietly but firmly. "He must reserve his confrontation for a greater battle. For now, he must not risk losing this one. For in so doing, he would lose face and all chance for influence later."

"I would have protested," Gertrude said with shameless indignation.

"And you would not now have your clinic, Miss Green." Dr. Hwang brought home the lesson with a snap of his owlish eyes.

"I think saving face has its disadvantages," she tried to counter.

"But he who has no face to save is thought impudent and ill-bred." Dr. Hwang raised his arm and hand to make his point. "His advice is not heeded and his opinion is lightly thought of since he takes no risk when giving it."

Gertrude considered this last thought carefully, looking away and breathing deeply as if to inhale the wisdom of it.

"But if he has face to save, he may not be able to give an opinion when it is needed," she said quietly. She looked up at Dr. Hwang with a smile. "It is a puzzle, honorable teacher."

"Just so," he nodded.

"This has been a more interesting encounter than I had ever anticipated," Paul Quimby said, breaking the silence and startling Gertrude with the sudden realization of his presence. "I have known you to be loquacious, Gertrude. But I've never known you to take up so quickly with strangers— and in two languages!"

"I like the Chinese," she said, turning to him, her cheeks reddening at the thought of undue familiarity. "I think I am more comfortable with the Chinese than I am with Westerners," she added impulsively, her voice tinged with defiance.

"And do you think you would make a good Chinese?" Dr. Hwang asked guardedly.

"I can think of worse things to be," Gertrude returned, forgetting whom she was addressing.

"Can you think of something better to be?" Dr. Hwang's question snapped in the air and hung there. His voice begged an answer from her; Gertrude could feel it. But she could not think of what to say.

"Being a Christian," he said most earnestly. "You are a missionary and a Christian, Miss Green." Now he leaned toward her and spoke passionately. "My beloved country has rejected the Lord. My people have rejected God's mercy and now I feel that God has rejected them. I sense a terrible foreign power which has rejected God will control this nation. Dreadful times are ahead for my people and my country.

"Miss Green, you have already begun your work as a missionary with compassion and genuine concern. But we need the missionaries to be Christians, Miss Green, to set us the example that all who will may follow and escape what is about to happen to us."

"Just so, honorable teacher," she said softly. "Just so."

Chapter 21

WRITING FROM KULING

The last of May and the first two weeks of June ushered in the long pre-dicted humid mosquito season. Lying under their netting each night in damp sheets, the language school students eagerly anticipated their escape, along with many other missionaries, to the cool mountains of Kuling.

The journey from Nanking to the river town of Kiukiang by steamer re-quired two days in clear sunshine and balmy river breezes. The bus ride from Kiukiang deposited the nine missionaries from the language school at the bottom of the mountain in the chill of the predawn. The three-and-one-half hour, eight-mile trip up the mountain carried in wicker sedan chairs through clouds and cold rain, introduced the chilled and soggy missionaries to their new mountain home.

Throughout the summer Gertrude kept her mother apprised of the situation in Kuling, her progress in language school, the sunny but humid weather, and the war in the north that crept slowly but persistently southward.

China Language Institute
Kuling, China
Sunday, June 27, 1937

Dearest Mother,

Here comes another weekly epistle. I try to write to you every week al-though sometimes I don't make the deadline. So much has changed.

We are settling in nicely into our little town in the sky, 2,000 feet up ac-tually. Kuling is a small village at the top of the mountain but with stores, post office, and everything grand. There are no level places on the mountain top so the houses are built all over, including ours which is high above the road. I nearly die climbing up here but it is so nice when you get to the top.

The house is made of stone with a large living room and big fireplace and one end is used as a dining room. There is a bedroom and private bath downstairs and a nice kitchen and three bedrooms upstairs, with a bath. There is a perfect view from the house when the clouds are not surrounding us—pine groves, walks, waterfalls, three swimming pools—far better than California ever thought of being. Since I got here I have been running all over this mountain and enjoying every minute of it, oh boy! But I am out of breath most of the time.

I left most of my things in Nanking at the mission compound and moved up here only the bedding and clothing that I would need for the summer. Everything has to be carried up the mountain by coolie. In one place a thousand stairs go almost straight up!

Since I will be staying only two and one half months, send your mail to me at 150 Rubicon Road at the Shanghai San and they will forward it on. I expect to be back in Nanking in the fall for the last quarter of language school. Although I may not. I am anxious to get to work.

Not everyone is here in Kuling who was in Nanking. Miss Atwell did not make the trip, staying behind to look after the house. Dr. and Mrs. Dale have gone to Shanghai. Dr. Miller is going to Hankow to open the Hankow Sanitarium and Clinic. They need three doctors at Shanghai San so the Dales have returned there early.

Holleys and Krohns are here and the Knights have also come after going to Hankow to set up their house there. (He is still winning all the Monopoly games now that Charles Dale is gone to Shanghai.) Millers will be coming here later in the summer and Loewens are coming from Shanghai. Mrs. Loewen, Mrs. Holley, and Mrs. Knight are all expecting within the next two months. It will be like a nursery here then. The ladies who are expecting have a hard time climbing up to the houses but are thankful they are away from the heat in the cities down on the river. I have to take it easy when we all go to town shopping. I can't just go swooping along like I usually do.

I will be moving to a different house as soon as Professor Morse and his wife come. She is Dr. Miller's sister. We will all move into #85 and the others will be moving into this place.

The third quarter of language school starts next week. I have been studying with Mr. Hahn but he shows up only when he wants to. Rainy days and days in the clouds I am studying by myself. When the clouds come down it is all dreary and closed up, can't even see the trees in the yard.

We don't see as much of the Chinese life up here as we did in Nanking. There are only foreigners and the rich Chinese who are here for the summer—and the people of the village.

Should I send more kimonos? Have you sold the ones that have arrived already? I don't want to load you down. I cannot send the silk that you asked for as the duty would be far too high. But I am sending a box of fans, hand embroidered guest towels and Chinese scissors that can cut anything and stay sharp. Everything is so cheap here. I have not heard from Ruth in a while, hope everything is OK with her.

Well, I will get on with writing more letters to others.

Loads and loads of love, your daughter with xxxxoooo
Gertrude

China Language Institute
Kuling, China
Sabbath, July 31, 1937

Dear Mother,

It is so beautiful up here and the air is wonderful when it's not raining—which it is doing now. This week we have had thunderstorms every day but fortunately the sun always comes out in the afternoon. When it's this rainy all our shoes get moldy; I can watch them mold overnight. The black suitcase is moldy and my dresses are moldy. Even one's hair smells moldy and has to be washed to keep it from smelling bad. When the sun comes out this afternoon I will take everything outside for a good airing out.

Our servant has been sick this week so Mrs. Morse and I are doing our own laundry and ironing, the first I have done since being in China. Otherwise we have been studying all day or walking and swimming every day when it isn't raining. A week ago last Wednesday we walked seven miles to Paradise Pools, downhill going and uphill coming home all the way. There was a beautiful waterfall and the pools were like crystal.

My Chinese is doing fine. Did I tell you I got 95 percent on my second quarter exams? I didn't think I could ever learn but it is sinking in slowly. I can understand almost all of the sermons on Sabbath now and the Sabbath School Lesson discussion. I even bought a New Testament in Chinese and English. But I do miss Adventist Youth Missionary Volunteer meetings on Friday nights. I think I have been going to the youth meetings every Friday night since Academy, including in Shanghai and now I miss it. But here we usually spend Friday evening at someone's house, usually at the Krohns' or here at our house.

Coming home from our hike to Paradise Pools we passed a Buddhist temple. We all went filing in and saw no one but we could hear mumbling. Then in the shadows of the dingy room we could see priests all squatted down while the head priest was reading prayers. There was a big, old idol in the center of the room way up high. The whole atmosphere gave me the creeps. Then they started chanting. Boy, was I glad to get out of that place.

Mrs. Knight added a little boy to the growing nursery here today. Mrs. Holley had her baby two weeks ago and Mrs. Loewen is soon to follow. Of course they can't go shopping with us now which we do on days when it rains and keeps us from hiking.

I bought two beautiful vases with the thousand-flower design. Kiukiang is the city where dishes and vases are made so I got it for half price. I feel so sorry for the Chinese; they sell so cheap and hardly make a living.

There is always someone coming to the door to sell something: fruit vendors, blanket vendors, cobbler, tailor, carpenter, tinsmith, barber, laundry, dry cleaning, yard workers, or cooks. We have no electricity or running water. We use kerosene lamps and have the water brought to us so we are interested in some of the things they have to sell.

Have you heard anything about the war in the north between the Chinese and the Japanese? You may see it in the papers. We don't get much news being way up here. It is hard to believe there is such a thing as war. I don't know much about it but I can tell you I should like to get a sock at those lousy Japanese, always making trouble for poor China. But the Chinese have taken about all they can stand and are coming up with a good fight.

If the war gets too bad and starts coming down this way, we may all have to get out of China. But we know we can depend on our U.S. Consulate which is responsible for every American citizen. The U.S. has lots of gun boats that can take people somewhere else. And there are thousands of marines to protect us. They tell us that if things get too bad an extra force can come up from Manila. But I don't think anything like that is going to happen.

This last week the Japanese took over Peking and Tientsien entirely but we are all in the safest place in the world up here in the mountains. They wouldn't come way up here in this little place just to fight because there is nothing to be gained by it. Time will tell, but I think it will stop pretty soon because the Japanese have what they want now.

I am glad the check from the General Conference is arriving now so you can pay my insurance. I received your letter and the one from Mrs. Schlegel with the green guest towel and the lovely handkerchief. I am sorry but the stamp from the airmail letter you sent I have already given away. Give my love to Fred and Elaine. Hope papa has work again real soon. Don't worry about me, I am fine.

Loads of love, your loving daughter
Gertrude

China Language Institute
Kuling, China
Tuesday, August 24, 1937

Dearest Mother,

I am going to write this letter but land knows if it will ever get to you and if it gets to you, can't imagine how long it will take.

It is raining now day and night without stopping—how dreary. We have had three typhoons in the last two weeks. I can't imagine where all the water comes from. The large Chinese umbrellas are nice for walking to and from language school but the raincoats don't help much when there is a cloud-burst. It even rains in the house and seeps in every possible crevice.

I sure wish I could be there for Ruth's visit home. She tells me that the Cort girls are both married and living with their mother. I would rather be doing what I am doing than be tied to some poor guy who can't even support you. What a life. Where do you suppose they are all sleeping in that house?

I am sure glad I am not staying in Shanghai right now. The fighting broke out there a week ago Sunday. If it continues, there will be absolutely nothing left of the place when they are through. One of the largest hotels, the Cathay, in the International Settlement was struck by a bomb.

The American Consulate has called for all Americans to move out of the Chinese district and into the International Settlement where it's supposed to be safe. That means that the Sanitarium and the Clinic, which are both in Chinese territory, now have not a soul in them.

The trains have been cut off between Shanghai and Nanking so there is no more shopping for a while. The airplane service for mail has been stopped and no boats can get up and down the river. So I don't know when this letter will reach you.

The last few days Japanese planes have been flying over Kuling. There are no bombs here but they have been bombing Kiukiang. They destroyed a cotton mill there, killing several people. It makes us anxious every time we hear the bell telling us that the Japanese planes are coming. Pretty soon we can hear the motors. When the signal goes off, every light must go out immediately so they cannot see Kuling.

All of our workers have been evacuated from Shanghai except for Professor Griggs, Elder Longway, Dr. Dale, and Mr. Morris, the treasurer. Most of the rest have been removed to Hong Kong or Manila. We even received orders from Professor Griggs to evacuate Kuling right away but then another telegram arrived telling us to wait until Mr. Scharffenberg arrives to direct us. So we are still sitting here waiting for him to arrive tonight. I have nearly all my things packed and can leave any time. But I don't think anyone knows what will happen.

At the meeting last night at the American School the authorities discussed with us about whether we should evacuate. The American Embassy people told us we would all be safe where we are and should not go to interior stations. It would be easier to evacuate us from where we are if it came to that. They may still evacuate all the Americans in China to the U.S. but for now they tell us that Kuling is safe.

All my things are in Nanking except for my summer things here. I imagine I can say goodbye to everything there and count myself lucky if I get any of it back. Pastor and Mrs. Hartwell—from Shanghai San—have been in these situations before when they had to evacuate and were allowed to take only one suitcase. They were in the interior of China during the civil war in 1927 and said they lost everything several times. So they did not want to be stationed in the interior any more but wanted to be in Shanghai. Now they are having to go through it again. They are anxious to return to Shanghai to see what is left of the compound and the Shanghai San.

I am sorry for rambling on so about the war but that is what we talk about now all the time. I am safe here. Don't worry about me. The Lord looks after and takes care of His children. We have our American gunboats that will be waiting for us.

I will curtail letter writing to others for now because of the expense of airmail. And I am not sure if even the airmail is going to get through. The Japanese shoot at every plane they see. I am holding my money with me. We cannot get it out of the banks so easily as they are closed down for one or two days at a time. So I am holding $100 to go on if need be.

I will try to write to you every week depending on where I am. But I am not sure if the letters will get out. Don't worry. We are fine in Kuling.

Your loving daughter,
Gertrude

Chapter 22

HIDING FROM THE WAR

The cold mountain air was clear of everything except stars. This high up they shone brilliantly against a black and cloudless sky. The rain and thunderheads of the early afternoon had all blown away, and now even the wind was gone. What a perfectly beautiful night, Gertrude thought. One would never know that there was a war on somewhere.

Down below, the mountainside was pitch black in the stillness. When the warning bell had rung, all the lights had gone out as if snuffers had been lowered over each house. It was as if Kuling had vanished from the earth.

Which is what they want the Japs to think, Gertrude mused. *What a life. I am here continuing my language studies just as if nothing has changed. And in Nanking and Shanghai people are dying by the hundreds in terrible fighting.*

Gertrude stepped out off the porch to look at the northeastern sky.

Don't see any planes, she thought, *probably another false alarm.*

She turned and headed up the steps and was quickly engulfed by the shadows of the darkened house.

The birthday party tonight for Ada Holley had been early and small. Both the Knights and the Holleys had newborns who needed to be in bed. And the brownies had been as hard as bricks. Gertrude had mixed them right but the cook had left them in the oven too long. Gertrude headed toward the kitchen to see what could be done for a better day tomorrow.

This was a new house but, like all the others, it harbored the dampness of humidity and the odor of mildew. Gertrude moved carefully as she made her way in the dark through the large living room to the back. She and the Loewens, Marvin and Gertrude, had moved in with the Knights in #130 to consolidate housekeeping now that some of the others had gone. Although it was dark, the layout of the house was similar to the others. Gertrude glided through the dining area like a wraith, bumping into nothing, making almost no sound.

"Oh, my goodness!" Mrs. Loewen cried when Gertrude silently opened the door into her backside. She jumped forward and sideways, banging her protruding abdomen against the kitchen chairs at the table. She managed to hold onto the sugar canister but almost fell in the process.

"Oh, my dear, I am sorry," Gertrude rushed to her side and grabbed for where she thought a chair should be, pulling it out and slipping it under her before she fell. "I didn't know you were in here."

"Well, I guess we were both as quiet as mice." Gert Loewen laughed as the shock quickly abated. "I don't suppose the Japanese heard us, do you?"

"Not likely." The two laughed together in the darkened kitchen. "They have bigger fish to fry than us. What are you doing in here, Gert?"

"Probably the same thing you were going to do, I bet," Mrs. Loewen said, now serious. "Trying to do something to make up for the brownies. Although for the life of me I can't imagine what I could do in the dark."

"And we can't light the stove, at least not until the all clear bell rings." Gertrude shook her head at the foolish motherliness of them both.

Gert Loewen, large with child, said nothing. Gertrude could hear her breathing heavily.

"Gertrude, I'm frightened."

Bending slightly in the dim half light from the window, Gertrude searched the shadows with her outstretched hand until she found Mrs. Loewen's up-turned face. Moving more confidently, she slipped both arms around her shoulders and drew her close.

"I'm not exactly in the best physical shape to be running," Gert said with a small chuckle.

Gertrude released her and groped for a chair in the dark, trying to move it noiselessly on the linoleum.

"And it's not for me so much. I'm worried for Marvelyn and the new baby," she stumbled on. "If we'd known what was about to happen, I mean . . . well, we might not . . ." The unfinished thought was transparently clear in Gertrude's mind. In times like these what were a mother's thoughts—of family and fear and sudden uncertainty? As Gertrude sank down in her seat, she pictured Marvelyn, Gert's little 3-year-old, probably sleeping in the big downstairs bedroom with her father. So much had changed for them all. So many unknowns.

What had she been reading just this morning?

"'God is our refuge and strength, a very present help in trouble,'" she quoted. "I was just reading that this morning, consoling myself with the thought. 'Therefore will not we fear, though the earth be removed, and though the mountains be carried into the midst of the sea.'"

Gertrude folded her hands on the table before her in a small, silent prayer of thanksgiving. Even as she quoted the words for Mrs. Loewen, she felt a calm wash over herself, more comforting than many assurances of American gunboats.

Funny how the words of an ancient psalm from a desert country of long ago could bring such peace in a pitch dark kitchen in the middle of the modern war-torn Orient.

There is something mysterious about those words . . .

"Gertrude?" There was a breathiness to Gert's voice.

"Yes?"

"I think it's time."

"Time for what?"

"Time for the baby," Gert said as the all too familiar pressure in her abdomen slowly subsided.

Gertrude sat at the far end of the large living room near the comfort of the fireplace. The air outside was suddenly crispy cold. *No spring or fall in China*, she thought, *just summer and winter. And now winter has come.*

Leighton Holley seated himself quietly in the large armchair opposite the fireplace. He wanted to comfort her but did not want to intrude so he waited until Gertrude looked up before speaking.

"Where's Ada?" she asked quietly. "In the kitchen?"

"Yes. I left her with Mrs. Krohn to make the Sabbath dinner." He was cautious, not rushing.

"Good," Gertrude said. "The Knights should be here momentarily from church." She tried to marshal her thoughts, insisting on some proper order, then added, "I baked a cake and made the pudding." It was all that came to her, she was so tired.

"I should think you have done all you could, Gertrude," Leighton offered.

Gertrude looked up into his face. He seemed so young—like Fred, her brother.

"You look so very tired, Gertrude. When have you had a full night's sleep?"

"Not since Sunday," she said, her eyes now widening, revealing a far distant light of green.

"What have you been doing?" Leighton watched a door open in her mind and encouraged her to come forth.

Like a dammed-up waterfall, Gertrude spilled out, releasing the pressure that had kept her going for the last five days. Resurrected from her exhaustion, she sat forward, speaking with her hands and her mind and her heart, her eyes moist but not overflowing. And with the retelling, she relived the long, hard labor and the birth and the struggle . . . and the death and the funeral of the child.

With all the pastoral skill he knew, Leighton kept his gaze fixed on Gertrude's animated form. He listened intently, his fingers folding and un-folding in each other. But in a separate recess of his mind he considered that his own newborn daughter was alive and well—and facing the dangers of the war that now surrounded them.

When Gertrude finished, she leaned back into the warmth of the large chair, suddenly comfortable like a bed, her eyes closed.

"Where's Marvin?" Leighton asked, knowing the answer, giving her more opportunity to talk.

"In the bedroom with her." she answered, never opening her eyes. "Has been since we brought her home."

"And how has Gert held up?" He genuinely did not know the answer to this one.

"Remarkably well," she answered, opening her eyes and sitting erect, speaking for herself and for Mrs. Loewen, drawing strength from the know-ing. "Getting stronger." And Gertrude, herself feeling stronger, was able to stand, refreshed.

Leighton was staring into the fire and did not notice her movements. While Gertrude was ascending, he was descending into his own thoughts about his family and the war.

"Thinking about the telegram—from Elder Frost?" Gertrude inserted herself into his world.

"H'mm?" he mumbled, looking up as if surprised she was standing there, one hand on the fireplace mantle. "Yes—yes. The evacuation and where we will go . . . and how."

"You will all travel together." It was her turn to reassure.

"As far as Hankow," he said. "After that I'm not sure where the Knights and the Krohns are assigned." His brow furrowed as his thoughts turned to the person who was now comforting him.

"And what will you do, Gertrude?"

"I'll have to stay here and look after Gert," she said, repeating the decision she had already made. "Marvin is going into Kiukiang on Tuesday for supplies. So I'll stay here and look after Gert and Marvelyn. She isn't ready to travel yet."

"And besides," she added with a small smile, "it's still safe up here on the mountain."

Chapter 23

RUNNING FROM THE ENEMY

On Tuesday evening Marvin Loewen returned from Kiukiang with Gertrude's shoulder cosy and the supplies—and news.

Canton was being bombed heavily every day. Notice had been given to all foreigners in Nanking to get away, that it was about to be bombed. The Hankow-Canton railroad would also be bombed after Tuesday next. After that, all transportation in and out of Kuling would be gone. There would be no more supplies coming. They would all have to leave, ready or not.

Friday evening Gert was able to sit up to the table as they celebrated Gertrude's birthday with a small party.

Tomorrow I will be 30 years old, she thought as she watched the reunited family enjoying the end of the ice cream and her birthday cake which she'd made from the tail ends of the sugar and flour. *Seems like too old. Maybe I'll have to start counting backward now.* She smiled at the thought.

On Sunday and Monday the packing and the cleaning proceeded in earnest. On Tuesday morning Marvin Loewen walked beside his wife as she was carried down the mountain in a sedan chair. Gertrude was in the chair just behind with Marvelyn in her lap. At the bottom of the mountain Elder Effenberg met them with his car for the drive to the mission compound.

Having deposited Marvelyn in the front passenger seat, Gertrude relaxed quietly in the backseat against the window, watching the passing countryside. As they approached the city the wreckage of buildings and homes along with the scattered remains of wagons, broken furniture, and shredded clothing spoke of the devastation of war imposed on Kiukiang.

"Are you being evacuated, too?" asked Gert who was tucked safely between Marvin and Gertrude in the back seat.

"We think we're going to be here for a while," Pastor Effenberg responded, steering carefully around a horse cart, avoiding a family of five on foot who seemed to have everything they owned piled on their backs. "We're kind of a way station on the run to Hankow," he chuckled. "We have to keep a supply of goods here for those who are passing through. Wednesday after the Schroters come in, I'll be making a run with him on the riverboat to Nanking to see what we can find to bring back here."

"Nanking?" Gertrude was suddenly alert and thinking. "All my things are in Nanking. Do you suppose I could go with you?"

"Don't see why not, if you're up to a little excitement."

On Thursday afternoon, despite the warnings of further bombing, Gertrude was standing on the deck just under the wheelhouse of the steamer *Wangpoo* headed for Nanking on a rescue mission of her own.

Knit one. Purl one. Knit One. Purl two. Knit one. Drop One. Gertrude slowly and carefully followed the knitting pattern for her sweater, the needles in her hand moving cautiously. She was trying to knit and carry on a conversation with Gert and already had had to pull out two rows where the pattern was totally out of line. She didn't really mind so much because she had been deeply moved by the devastation of the war and wanted to talk about it with someone.

"There was no gasoline there so we had to travel by horse-drawn cart," Gertrude said, watching her needles carefully. "We had to go slowly because of the bomb craters in the middle of the major streets.

"There were big guns all along the wall facing the river. And antiaircraft guns placed all around the major city buildings and the railroad station."

"Did you have any air raids while you were there?" Gert asked anxiously.

Click, click, click, click. The needles moved now faster and now slower, providing the comfort of the familiar in the face of the unknown.

"That was the interesting part," Gertrude said, looking up, her hands temporarily motionless. "There wasn't one warning bell rung the whole time we were there. On Friday we went to the compound, got what Mr. Schroter needed and retrieved all my trunks and boxes. We came back to the steamer Sabbath afternoon and started home without one incident."

Sitting here in this comfortable chair in the Loewens' living room in Kiukiang, knitting, it was hard to remember just how she'd felt. *The war is so real when you're in it and so distant when you're not,* she thought. Right now it was all so matter of fact.

"It wasn't until we were on the river," she said, her eyes counting the stitches, her hands moving again, "that we saw the Japanese planes flying in over Anching. There were explosions on the ground and puffs of smoke all around the airplanes. Thank goodness they were interested in Anching and not in us. We were kind of exposed out there in the middle of the river."

Hearing a sharp intake of air and a quick sigh, Gertrude looked up. Gert had her hand to her mouth, staring hard at her, eyes wide.

"Weren't you frightened?" she asked breathlessly.

For a moment Gertrude was back on the boat hearing the firing of the guns and watching the airplanes diving at the city.

"Gert, I'm very glad I got my things out of there. But I feel much safer back here where we're under cover," she said. "Even with the rubble all around us, the war doesn't seem so real until you can hear the sounds. Then it is terrifying. I'd be glad not to be on that boat again."

She shook her head with a grimace and began moving the knitting needles in their slow cadence. Marvin Loewen, a Saint Bernard of a man, all jowls and a large chest, appeared in the doorway.

"Letter for you, Gertrude," he said in his deep bass voice, crossing the room and holding out the envelope.

Gertrude could tell by the scrawled address that it had been hastily written. But it was on the stationery of the Honan Mission, West China Union. *Unusual*, she thought, *they usually send telegrams.*

"Elder Warren," she said, scanning and editing the letter as she shared it out loud. These days everyone was interested in every scrap of information no matter to whom it was originally sent.

"He wants me—no, he is instructing me—to come to Hankow to work in the new clinic and sanitarium there. Since there are no boats or trains going to Shanghai, he says the committee has decided to assign me temporarily to the Hankow Sanitarium and Clinic."

"But how will you get there?" Gert asked, their latest conversation playing again in her mind.

"I doubt that little item crossed their minds," Gertrude snapped. Here were some more people—men—trying to control her life. "Do they understand that there's a war out here?"

"Oh, I think they know about the war," Marvin smiled, his strong, square jaw creased with mirth, his massive shoulders heaving in a heavy, silent chuckle.

"Probably," Gertrude laughed at herself.

Marvin turned at the sound of the front door of the house being opened.

"Gertrude! Gertrude Green."

"I'd know that voice anywhere," Gertrude said with a shake of her head. She laid aside her partially completed sweater and stood facing the door.

"Dr. Miller, welcome," she said as the tall doctor with the curly mop of graying hair strode through the archway.

"They told me I'd find you here. Are you ready to go?" he asked expectantly, hands on hips.

"Go? Go where?"

"Hankow, of course. I stopped by to pick you up on my way from the meetings in Shanghai. Didn't you get the message?"

"You just came from Shanghai? How?"

Gertrude's mind raced for a moment to catch up, to figure out what was happening. Then she stopped. Her eyes flashed green and narrowed with irritation. This man had the unpleasant habit of appearing out of thin air and immediately demanding that she dash off with him to wherever. Her hands went to her hips as she faced him squarely.

"I just this minute received a letter from Elder Warren, *asking* me to come to Hankow. I have had no time to pack or prepare for a sudden departure." Her steady gaze held his eyes captive.

"H'mmm," he said, looking away. "The call was sent out two weeks ago. The telegraph lines are probably down." He hardly paused for a breath. "Well! How soon can you be ready?" His face was now covered with boyish good humor. But Gertrude wasn't buying it.

"Dr. Miller," she fired back, "do you know there's a war on out there?"

His smiled faded but the eyes remained soft and distant.

"My fight is not with the Japanese, Miss Green."

"Do they know that?"

"My fight is with illness and disease," he said, ignoring her comment. "I have a hospital in Hankow that needs your excellent nursing skills, Miss Green. If you do not come now, I will lose you because there will be no way for you to get to Hankow or to Shanghai. And you will be evacuated with the rest of them to Hong Kong."

He paused and closed his eyes for a moment as if contemplating the loss. With two fingers he rubbed the bridge of his nose up and down, then slowly opened his eyes and with a slight twist of his head silently awaited her answer.

In a boat on the river again. *O, Lord, do I have to?* she prayed. Gertrude's shoulders visibly sagged.

And what about Gert? Who will look after her? Gertrude cast a wishful eye at Mrs. Loewen, seeking a refuge, an escape. But Gert misread it and thought it was compassion.

"I'll be fine, dear," Gert said with a nod of her head and a tilt of her chin to show bravery. "You go on."

"What about language school?" Gertrude asked wistfully of no one in particular.

"The language school has been split up," Dr. Miller said. "Two of the teachers are now in Hankow and the rest have gone south."

"I have the last boat to Hankow waiting at the dock. Miss Green," he implored with his voice and his eyes. "Will you come help us?"

"Of course I'll come," she said. A small shudder passed through her as she closed her eyes and contemplated the boat and the river.

"Thank you," he said quietly.

Gertrude stood in the middle of the room and watched her life turn over. Marvin walked down the short hallway to the back of the house to retrieve her unopened trunks. His wife stepped up beside Gertrude and touched her lightly on the shoulder.

"Come, dear, it's my turn to help you pack."

Dr. Miller had disappeared altogether.

Twenty minutes later Gertrude came down the hall with the last of her suitcases to find Dr. Miller waiting just inside the front door beside the rest of her luggage.

"I assumed your baggage had not diminished since arriving in China," he said with twinkling eyes. "So I planned accordingly."

"What do you mean—planned?"

Dr. Miller opened the front door to reveal six rickshaws waiting in the street.

"Your planning was impeccable as usual," Gertrude sighed in resignation, "but can you foresee everything?"

She paused to search his face for wisdom and security. "Like what the Japanese will do to us on this little steamboat of yours?"

Shaking her head slowly, she headed for the closest rickshaw with her old black suitcase in hand.

"No one can foresee everything, Miss Green," he said quietly to her retreating form.

When every trunk and box had been safely loaded into the six rickshaws, Gertrude gathered the coolies about her in a huddle and instructed them carefully to watch each other and to stay together. She knew it would be easy to get separated in the throngs of refugees now living in the streets of Kiukiang.

She also knew that the coolies would not try to run away or steal her things. The Chinese were uninterested in Western clothes or articles, preferring their own heavy, practical fabrics to the light and easily torn garments of the Caucasians. But they were insatiably curious and could easily be distracted by some unusual sight or commotion. And the streets were full of such these days.

"I will have the full price and an extra two coppers for each of you when we reach the docks," she said in the local dialect, jingling her bag of small coins in the air for all to see. "Now see that you stay together."

While she climbed aboard, sitting between her black suitcase and the brown plaid one, the coolies scrambled for their rickshaws and got in line as she had instructed them. As her own coolie turned out of the compound and into the street, Gertrude grasped the frame of the rickshaw and half standing, turned to look over her right shoulder to inspect the following entourage. Each was in his place as she had directed. It had started well.

The streets flowed as with a muddy tide of humanity, eddying about protrusions, flowing around corners. Carts being drawn by men and by horses jostled with men and women carrying great superstructures of boxes or bags stacked high above their heads. Small wheelbarrows and other homemade conveyances added noise and weight to the seething flotsam and jetsam which parted and streamed by in the wake of Gertrude's convoy.

Along the edges floated the communal lives of the refugees, people living in every small crack and cranny, every burned-out building, discarded box, or open doorway. Gertrude could almost reach out and touch the hollow faces of fear with eyes that held no hope as they floated by. And her heart was torn by their suffering.

I will be of no use to anyone if I don't get to Hankow, she admonished herself as she looked over her shoulder once more to check on her line of rickshaws.

And then she saw them, coming out of the sun, a dozen small, dark objects in the sky growing rapidly larger, bearing down on the city. The coolie pulling her rickshaw heard the noise of their engines at the same time and turned his head also to look in their direction. With the combined noise of the approaching aircraft engines and the sudden ringing of the church bells, the irrepressible river of humanity around Gertrude paused for a moment and stopped flowing and looked up. Then it erupted in chaos.

Towers of boxes crashed to the street as coolies dropped their loads and ran. Eight human pullers abandoned their wagon which slowly careened across the road and into a market stall scattering onions and green and yellow peppers in colorful profusion. A screaming mother snatched her two small boys from the path of a wildly charging horse-drawn cart which was now bearing down on Gertrude in her rickshaw.

"RUN!" she screamed at the coolie pulling her rickshaw, leaping up and beating the sides of rickshaw with her open palms. "Run for the docks!"

But she need not have shouted. The coolie had seen the path of the strafing guns and was moving before the words were out of her mouth. With a lurch he scampered to the edge of the road, crushing the peppers in the street and stumbling over the onions. Regaining his feet he dashed for the nearest corner and turned left out of the line of fire and toward the dock.

Gertrude fell backward into the seat and almost over the right edge of the rickshaw as it tipped and skidded around the corner. As she slid to her knees on the floor, she could just peer over the rickshaw's edge and see two more of her caravan turning the corner and following her at a dead run. Then she instinctively ducked down as one and then another bomb exploded in the rail yards just beyond the market street behind them.

"O, Jesus, Jesus, save us. Please save us," she sobbed from the rickshaw floor as it swerved and careened down the street. When the world around her belched out an unending series of explosions so close as to be palpable, she rolled herself into a tiny ball and thrust her fingers in her ears, tears streaming down her face in terror.

"Miss Green, get out!" Two strong arms were lifting her up.

She looked up into piercing blue-gray eyes that penetrated her terror.

"Get out now," he said firmly. "They will be coming back." He stood her on her feet. "We must go now."

The coolies, four of them, streamed past her, carrying her luggage onto the steamboat. She could see the captain standing at the railing, pointing, shouting—first at the coolies, then at the sky. *There are only four coolies,* she realized. *Where are the other two?*

As she started to turn toward the street, Dr. Miller grabbed her by the arm and forcibly led her to the gangway. He took the small bag of coins that hung from her hand and threw it in the direction of the nervous coolies on the dock.

"This way, Miss Green," he whispered in her ear. "This is the way. Walk ye in it."

She looked up at him, eyes wide in confusion and consternation.

"But my luggage . . . ," she began, pointing back to where the second wave of bombers was beginning to make its run.

"Can be replaced in Wuhan," he finished her sentence sensibly. "But *you* cannot be. Come."

As the fury of antiaircraft fire again poured into the sky over Kiukiang, the steamboat belched smoke and fire from its tall stack. The paddlewheel beat the water to froth as the boat pulled away from the dock and the bombs and the war, heading up river for Hankow.

Chapter 24

WORKING WITH AN ENIGMA

In 1937 the Yangtze River divided China into two diverse halves. To the north the land was drier, the climate was harsher, the people were politically more aggressive, and the staple food was wheat. To the south the land was wetter, the climate was milder, the people were politically more subdued, and the staple food was rice.

Likewise the railroad line that connected Peking (Beijing) and Hong Kong divided China into two diverse units. To the east of this line the land was river and canal flood plains of intensive farming. The cities were large and metropolitan, international commerce exported China's exotic merchandise to foreign countries through bustling port cities, the people were ethnically Chinese, and the civil authority was a national government, either Chinese or Japanese. To the west of this line the land was mountainous, the cities were small and colloquial, international commerce imported goods from all the bordering countries and hinterlands on China's vast western frontier, the people were a polyglot of obscure cultures and ethnic groups, and the civil authority was the most powerful local landlord, warlord, or bandit chief.

At the exact crossing point of these two geosocial boundaries lay the ethnically diverse and politically shifting city of Wuhan—in actuality two cities, each reflecting the cultural background of its particular side of the river. On the south bank of the Yangtze River stood Wuchang, one of the historically venerated political and religious centers of China, replete with ancient government office buildings, spacious private gardens, and unique religious shrines.

On the north bank was Hankow, the bustling commercial center. This was home to some of the earliest established foreign enclaves into which poured the rich diversity of merchandise arriving by rail, water, and caravan from all over western, northern, and southern China and from which spewed forth the river steamers on the Yangtze River laden for world markets.

In the fall of 1937 Wuhan received a new influx of imports—war refugees from the north and the east. Joining the incessant waves of farmers, merchants, and villagers was the Nationalist Chinese Government of Generalissimo Chiang Kai-shek, moving from Nanking with all its government officials to take up residence in the old buildings in Wuchang. In addition, from Mongolia to Shanghai all foreign nationals—business and government officials and missionaries—were ordered by their respective organizations to evacuate to Wuhan or Hong Kong.

To care for this rapidly growing population, Dr. Harry Miller was struggling to complete his thirteenth Chinese sanitarium and hospital outside of Wuchang and a medical clinic in the heart of the Hankow business district. To equip, staff, and run these institutions, he had several excellent missionary nurses. But he remembered the efficient administrative, teaching, and organizational skills he had seen in operation at the New England San in the summer of 1936. Because of the war, Gertrude could not return to the Shanghai San and he had gotten permission to "borrow" her for the Wuhan San to help get it up and running.

"Gertrude, where are you?" Blanche Sevrens said aloud to herself as she ducked under the edges of the large overlapping umbrellas and hurried through the narrow aisles between the stalls. "One minute we're looking at shoes and the next minute you're gone."

Blanche turned left into the cloth and clothing section, ignoring the vendors vying for her attention as she swept past them. Her eyes scanned the stalls ahead for the tall Caucasian who would stand head and shoulders above the Chinese merchants.

According to Gertrude the mud and rain last Sabbath at the new sanitarium's church services had "made a perfect mess" of her favorite brown pumps. This morning Blanche had brought Gertrude downtown to the Exchange Market to look for new shoes. But since their arrival at the large open market, it was Blanche who kept getting lost, or more accurately—left behind.

"Blanche!"

Blanche spun around to see an arm and hand signaling like a semaphore flag above a mountain of bolts of muslin. The arm sank from sight as Blanch navigated around a beachhead of brown, fibrous mattress stuffing and spied Gertrude and her diminutive Chinese counterpart haggling with great gusto over her latest bargain.

"This material is just perfect for the sheets and the curtains we need at the San," Gertrude whispered behind her hand as the young Chinese woman turned to get permission for yet another lowering of the price.

"Well, you certainly didn't need me here," Blanche laughed. She watched appreciatively as Gertrude expertly finalized the deal and arranged for delivery.

"Oh, but I do," Gertrude said, slipping her arm through the crook of Blanche's elbow. "You know where all the bargains are, dearie."

Blanche quickened her pace to match Gertrude's long strides. Like a panther seeking prey, Gertrude constantly turned her head from side to side as her eyes hunted through the rich profusion of colors and textures for the bargains she knew were hiding there.

"Dr. Wang brought me downtown last week and showed me all around," Gertrude said. "He took me to the People's Palace and the Exchange Market and the Bund. But I knew you'd know where the real bargains were."

"But where"—*gasp*—"did you learn to shop like this?" Blanche managed between quick breaths.

Gertrude stopped and turned, taking Blanche's two hands in her own. She held her new friend at arm's length and smiled wistfully, her lips tightly closed. Her eyes were moist and twinkled with emotion.

"I learned to shop for bargains with my sister when we were in academy," she said, looking over Blanche's shoulder to a memory far away. "But," she added, raising a finger of instruction and smiling broadly, "I learned to haggle in Boston. Some of the best hagglers I know are good Irish Catholics."

Abruptly she turned and strode away. "Now where was it you said they have desks?"

Blanche caught up with her and gently steered her across the street to the furniture shops.

"Come in, Miss Green."

Gertrude recoiled from the door as if it were alive and had just spoken to her.

How did he know I was out here? she thought as she pushed through the now inanimate door and stepped into the world of Dr. Harry Miller.

Stacks of books and papers lounged about the room on the floor and available table space. Against the wall opposite the large desk, the bookcase housed a menagerie of papers and reports that leaned over the edges of the shelves as if searching for a way of escape. Only the desk with its ink blotter and pen set seemed tame and under control.

How unlike Dr. Ruble, Gertrude mused as she gazed about on the organized chaos. *No old world tradition here—or sentimentality. Just a busy man in a hurry. A man who knew I was outside his door.* This last thought wrinkled her brow as she caught sight of Dr. Harry Miller in the far corner bent over a writing desk, scribbling furiously.

"I saw your feet under the door," he said without looking up.

How does everyone know what I'm thinking? Gertrude pondered.

Dr. Miller raised his head and smiled disarmingly, his piercing blue-gray eyes a mixture of mirth and mystery.

"Besides who else would be here in an empty clinic building at 7:00 o'clock in the morning?" he asked as he bent to finish the last sentence. He picked up the finished pages and carried them across the room, placing them neatly stacked on the far left corner of the empty desk top. With a turn of his large head, he held Gertrude in his full gaze.

"I was hoping to catch you before your day started," she responded, grabbing at her turn in the conversation, remembering the urgency of her visit, the reason for her early morning appearance. "I was hoping to discuss some things I've been observing . . ."

"My days start very early," he interrupted without really hearing her. "We have not started an operating schedule so I was able to begin my writing at 5:00 o'clock this morning. Normally I would be operating now," he said absently, looking at the wall behind her as if reading his daily schedule there. Then seeing her again, he said, "But let's discuss your position here. Then you can share your ideas."

"OK," she laughed, folding her arms as she readjusted herself mentally, "What is my position here?"

"May we sit, Miss Green?" he said, still standing behind the desk. He motioned to the corner of an already crowded chair that faced the desk.

"Of course."

Gertrude perched on the edge of the chair, trying not to disturb the papers which occupied the greater portion of the seat. Dr. Harry Miller quickly followed her lead, sitting in his own chair behind the large oak desk. He folded his hands in front of his face, his elbows resting on the desk, his eyes just visible over his knuckles.

I only see but part of you, do I, Doctor? Gertrude caught at the thought as it sprinted past her consciousness.

"As you know, you are officially assigned to Shanghai Sanitarium," he began. "They want you as their director of nurses and they are not willing to release you."

"Is the Shanghai San open now?" she asked in surprise, remembering the news of the invasion.

"No," he said. Lines and shadows of pain passed over his face at the reminder. "Most of our workers have been evacuated from there to Hong Kong or Manila. The school, the hospital, the press . . ." As he talked, his hands began to move, folding and unfolding, reaching into the air for emphasis, revealing an intensity of emotion that his steady gaze did not betray.

You have big hands for a surgeon—large fingers, Gertrude noted. She filed away a mental reminder for glove sizes to order.

"They can't use you right now, but I can." His hands paused in midair, arresting Gertrude's attention. "I am trying to get the clinic and the sanitarium started here and I need your help, Miss Green."

"And the war is interfering with that," she offered in amusement.

"Just a bit." His eyes softened in the mirth.

"But you already have excellent staff here," she returned, sharpening to the point of the moment.

"Mrs. Wilkinson is an excellent director of nurses," he nodded, his hands moving again. "And Miss Ragsdale and the others all have their assignments and are quite competent. But I need someone to help me."

"I don't understand," Gertrude said with genuine confusion.

"I am trying to start the clinic here in Hankow and the sanitarium and hospital in Wuchang at the same time. Usually I have one or the other up and running as a base of operation. But the rapidity of events has forced me to begin both at the same time."

He paused to see if Gertrude was following. Her head bobbed vigorously as if answering his unasked question about her comprehension and he continued.

"I know you have been out inspecting the San with Mr. Wood and you have been shopping with Mrs. Sevrens for supplies for the clinic. You can already see what needs to be done. That's what I need. Eyes and ears, hands and feet to see the obvious needs and to push with perseverance to get them done." His blue-gray eyes blazed with the rising intensity of his own personal efforts. "Can you do this? Can you help me?"

What do you want me to be? Gertrude puzzled in her mind. *You are the China Doctor. I am only a nurse.*

"Do you need a personal office nurse—an assistant—what?" Gertrude was trying to phrase his request in terms that she understood as a nurse, trying to visualize his need in a particular job she could grasp, categorize, and do.

"Whatever you want to call it. It doesn't matter." His hand waved it away in uncharacteristic irritation. "Can you help me?"

Gertrude heard his whispered question as a plea, delivered with the intensity of a mission call from the heart of this doctor who loved China and had already sacrificed a great deal of himself for it. She wanted desperately to respond.

"Of course, I can help you," she answered. Her hands reached out to him, clutched at thin air, and shook with mounting frustration. "But in what capacity? I can't just go barging in on Mr. Boynton and tell him I want money for things without some modicum of authority."

His eyes softened and his mouth twitched slightly into his famous boyish grin. "All right. Let's say you are my personal office nurse—at least temporarily—for the sake of the Shanghai Sanitarium and Hospital. I think they will go along with that."

"Then we should have a regularly scheduled meeting where we can discuss …," she began, relieved at the appearance of a bud of an organizing thought.

"I have no regularly scheduled meetings, Miss Green. I'm too busy. And I travel a great deal."

"But when will we talk? How will I know …?"

"We will talk," he said dismissively. Then quickly he asked. "Where are you staying?"

She blinked at the abrupt change of direction in the conversation but answered objectively, "I am staying temporarily with the Warrens and eating with your son, Clarence, and his wife. It allows me to continue my language studies at the Navy YMCA with Mr. Hsu in the evenings."

"H'mm."

Gertrude could see that he wasn't listening—at least not to her.

"The Sanitarium and Hospital needs your attention the most. Maybe you could move out there." He was musing more to himself than to Gertrude, his eyes shifting to the back wall again as if to see beyond them into tomorrow.

"But the clinic is about to open."

"We'll let Mrs. Wilkinson worry about the clinic." He returned to the present and focused on Gertrude once more. "Help her, of course, to get the clinic opened. You can function as her assistant. But the Sanitarium needs your attention—the operating theaters, the clinic rooms, and the wards. We aren't nearly ready for the influx of patients that's coming."

When Gertrude had withdrawn from the inner sanctum of Dr. Miller, she contemplated the multiple threads that together made no pattern at all, the myriad questions that had no answers.

What kind of office do I work out of? How do I get the money to make purchases for the clinic or the San? Where do I begin? And whose assistant am I? she asked herself, knowing all the while that these were questions Dr. Miller would not answer. *Dr. Miller's job is to dream and plan. My job is to make this particular part of the dream come true.*

She paused in the hallway.

"Where do I begin?" she said again—aloud. "With Mrs. Wilkinson, of course."

She turned abruptly and retraced her steps, striding resolutely toward the nursing office.

Chapter 25

ORGANIZING A HOSPITAL

2 Rue Clemenceu
Hankow, Hupeh, China
Sunday, October 16, 1937

Dearest Mother,
Let me begin by telling you that I am perfectly safe and sound here in Hankow in central China. A lot of wonderful folks met me at the dock and ushered me to our mission compound in the French Concession. I caught a cold on the boat up here and have had it ever since because of the nasty, rainy weather. But I will not complain since it keeps the Japs away. In fact, there have been no air raids in a week and a half. The Japanese planes don't come here as it is too far and they don't have the room to carry bombs as well as enough gasoline to get back home.

Dr. Miller is opening the new sanitarium across the river in a place called Wuchang and about five miles out from there. Such a gorgeous place you have never seen.

The buildings, thirteen in all, are not all quite done but will be in another month or so. The sanitarium is a gorgeous structure of gray granite, four stories high. The floors inside are all of terrazzo. And the girls' and boys' dorms and the doctors' and workers' houses are all of red brick. They are all situated to look out over a lake about the same size as Spot Pond at Melrose, but here the lake is nearer the front of the sanitarium building and the view is simply breathtaking.

I have been living here on the compound with the Warrens. But as soon as the clinic is open and up and running, I will move to the San and live with Dr. and Mrs. Miller in their house where I will have my own room and bath that looks out over the entire lake. The people in Nanking will send my studio couch and my bicycle if they can be shipped out. And we found a dresser for $14 and a Governor Winthrop desk for $18 in the Exchange Market, but will still need some chairs. So the new place should be quite comfortable in no time at all.

Your letter recently arrived was dated July 26. Got here October 12; not bad. You said that K.O. Brown's shirts were not very good. Please send his measurements again and I can have them redone here. This place reminds me much of Boston and is even better than Shanghai in many ways. I am afraid you won't get any more kimonos from Japan. I will not buy their stuff, especially when you see what they are doing to China, so many innocent people killed and beautiful cities ruined. But here in Hankow I have forgotten all about such a thing as war and am busy getting ready for this beautiful new San.

My big question is how long will I be here? I cannot go to Shanghai San because of the fighting there. And they won't release me to work here permanently. So I am in limbo and staying busy while I wait.

It is getting colder here and I am beginning to feel it. Must close for tonight. Heaps and heaps of love and kisses.

Your daughter,
Gertrude

"But we shared Sabbath school and church yesterday with the Chinese," Gertrude insisted. She pointed about with her chin in the delicate fashion she had learned from the Chinese, indicating all the White faces gathered in the special back room of the restaurant.

"It just seems funny that we're not sharing our Chinese banquet tonight with the Chinese."

"Well, dear," Wilma Warren said in her quiet voice, "sometimes it's just nice to be able to share with a few English speakers for a change. We do live most of our lives in their language and in their culture." Her chopsticks hung poised in midair as if holding another thought between them. She seemed about to speak again but her chopsticks opened and the thought fell away. The chopsticks descended to her plate.

Elder Warren and Dr. Miller exchanged glances over their rice bowls but allowed Mrs. Warren's gentle reply to suffice for them all.

"So how have you been spending your time since you helped me move out to the San?" Marie Miller asked. "I hardly ever get to see you now that I'm out there."

Gertrude immediately shifted her focus of intensity and began a description of her busy schedule. She told of cleaning with Mrs. Phang on the opening day of the new clinic on the Hankow compound, of shopping with Mrs. Sevrens for office supplies, of planning classes and duties with Mrs. Wilkinson. She ended her exhaustive recitation describing her evening studies with Mr. Hsu in the language school at the YMCA.

"I am trying so hard to get my fourth quarter of language study done," she finished emphatically. "I want so much to help these dear people of China."

"Me, too," Dr. Miller said, his eyes twinkling as they engaged Gertrude for a full 15 seconds of silence.

"Of course you do," Gertrude said, suddenly flustered, red coloring rising up to her ears. "Of course you all do."

She looked around at them all. The Warrens, whose triangular faces and expressive eyes looked enough alike to be brother and sister, had spent all of their married lives in some part of western or central China. Dr. Miller had spent his entire professional career building up the hospital work. And Marie Miller had given up her own career in the States to come join him when the first Mrs. Miller had died in Central China.

"How silly of me to carry on so," she said, now gazing at her hands fidgeting in her lap. "Of course you all do."

"Don't feel foolish, Gertrude," Elder Warren laughed, inciting the others into their own self-conscious chuckles. "It's good to hear the enthusiasm of the new crop of young people."

"Makes us feel that we have new workers who love these precious people and this work as much as we do." Mrs. Warren spoke warmly, her head bobbing up and down for emphasis, her wavy hair dancing in time with her words.

"Well, I do feel like the young one here," Gertrude joked, setting aside her embarrassment and turning her wit on her table mates. "I am eating with my 'older' landlords, both present and future."

Dr. Miller laughed at his own expense, but the Warrens exchanged puzzled glances.

"Gertrude's going to be moving out to the San and living in our extra room," he told the Warrens. "So she can be nearer her work there."

"At the boss's insistence," Gertrude mumbled, avoiding his gaze by attacking her plate again.

"You use chopsticks very well," Wilma Warren observed. "How did you learn so quickly, Gertrude? It took me forever."

"I had excellent teachers," Gertrude said, looking up. "I've tried to adjust to all the new experiences here," she added, thinking of her multiple houses, her shopping sprees, and her time at language school in Nanking and Kiukiang.

"Except for one," Dr. Miller observed quietly into his rice bowl.

Gertrude's eyes were on her plate, her head down. She met no one's quizzical glance and said nothing.

"What is it, dear?" Marie Miller asked as she reached across the table toward Gertrude.

"The air raids," Dr. Miller murmured in the silence.

"Sometimes those Japanese make me so mad," Mrs. Warren snapped so uncharacteristically that her husband looked at her in amazement. "Destroying this beautiful country!" she finished.

"I'm like that, too," Gertrude said quietly, "but only when I'm writing to Mother. But when the air raids start—like last night. They dropped 36 bombs before they went away!"

"You counted them?" Wilma asked.

"And 12 last Sunday evening." Gertrude said as her voice dropped to a whisper. "Then I'm not so very angry . . . as I'm frightened."

"We all have burdens, don't we?" Marie said, her long face and large eyes more solemn than usual. "You worry about the war and I worry about the children."

"The children?" Gertrude asked, gazing up out of her own anxieties.

"I'll be returning to the States next month," Marie said. "The children . . . ," was all she could manage to add before her voice choked. Even Dr. Miller was pensive as he squeezed his wife's hand.

"We each one have our own particular hardship," Merritt Warren considered, drumming his fingers on the table in thought. "For each of us it's something different. But it's something that makes us worry, makes us afraid. And it is a genuine problem, well worth being concerned about.

"For Marie, it's the children; for Gertrude, it's the air raids. For me, it's the workers, our Chinese workers. And for you, Harry, well, I don't know what it is."

Dr. Harry Miller's smile was tight-lipped but he said nothing.

"In each case, it is something over which we have no control," Elder Warren continued. "And that's when we must exercise faith. Place that worry, that fear, whatever it is, in the Lord's hands. And leave it there."

"My faith," Gertrude thought out loud. "My mustard seed faith. How I pray that the Lord will increase it."

"He will," Elder Warren reassured her, "in His own good time."

"Speaking of time," Dr. Miller interjected looking at his watch, "Gertrude, we have an appointment at 4:30 in the morning with a pair of tonsils."

"I'll be there, Doctor," she said with a smile. "If you think you're up to it."

"Oh, I'm up to it," he assured her with a twinkle. "It's good to have an operating theater again—and someone to run it."

Chapter 26

LOOKING OUT FOR DR. MILLER

For the next three weeks Gertrude did more than run the operating the-ater. During the first week, in addition to several tonsillectomies, she managed to clean and bring some semblance of order to Dr. Miller's office and to establish herself as his assistant in the clinic and at the hospital. When he was occupied elsewhere, Gertrude crossed and recrossed the Yangtze in small water taxis, sometimes twice a day, shopping on both sides of the river for supplies for the Hankow clinic and glassware for the OR at the San in Wuchang. By the time Friday evening came, she had been able to do a little personal washing, go to language school for two hours, attend the com-pound sundown worship, and go to bed early at the Warrens.

Bang! Bang! Bang! Someone was beating furiously on Gertrude's door.
"Gertrude! Wake up!"
"What. . . . ?"
Gertrude sat up in her bed, groping for consciousness.
"What's wrong? What time is it?" she called in a fog, trying to orient herself.
"I'm sorry," Mrs. Wilkinson said, rushing into Gertrude's bedroom in her housedress, her hair tied up in a scarf. "It's 10:30 at night, Gertrude," she gasped. "But I need your help now." She snatched up a plain cotton dress that had been flung over the back of a chair and held it out to Gertrude. "Come help me. Please. They've just brought 64 wounded soldiers in to the clinic."

Hurrying through the front door of the clinic building, Gertrude was still adjusting her uniform—which she'd insisted on wearing—and pinning her nursing cap in place. Immediately in front of her she saw Dr. Miller kneeling between two of the 14 cots that had been placed in rows across the length of the reception hall.

These must be the least critical, she reasoned. *They're not being kept near surgery or the lab.* She quickly strode toward Dr. Miller who was examining a patient with arm and leg burns.

"Miss Green, is that you?" he asked without looking up.

"Yes, Doctor."

"Do we have a pneumothorax kit? I have a patient on second floor that has a sucking chest wound and needs drains and stabilization."

Gertrude thought for a moment. "We don't have one made up but I'll get one for you."

"Meet me on Second Floor in about 10 minutes," Dr. Miller said, turning his attention back to his patient and the student nurse who was taking his orders.

Gertrude hurried to the OR trying to remember where she'd hidden the hard-to-obtain rubber tubing to protect it from being pilfered.

For the next four hours Gertrude, Mrs. Wilkinson, Dr. Miller, and the student nurses cleansed, dressed, splinted, and stabilized the soldiers who were scattered throughout the four floors of the clinic. Fortunately none of them required emergency surgery. Then after checking on the students and staff who would stay with the new patients, Gertrude returned to her bed and her interrupted sleep.

At 7:00 a.m. Gertrude was back at the clinic. While others on the compound were on their way to church, she supervised the staff and students as they changed dressings and cleansed wounds. She followed Dr. Miller on his rounds and made sure his orders were taken clearly and were understood, especially by the student nurses. In the sterile supply area she organized a group of students to make up more dressing trays. And it soon became obvious that there would not be enough dressings or dressing trays after tomorrow morning's treatments.

"Gertrude, what a pleasant surprise," Marie Miller said, opening the door to her red brick home on the Wuchang compound across the river from the clinic. "Do come in out of the rain. The folks just left from Sabbath dinner but you're welcome to the leftovers."

"No, ma'am, I can't stay," Gertrude said. She was wrapped in her furred brown coat and stood under a large, dripping umbrella. "I'm on my way to the San to prepare dressing trays for the wounded we got in clinic last night."

Marie nodded with the understanding that all doctors' wives have of emergencies.

"I'm wondering if I could come by later for a bite to eat," Gertrude said, shivering slightly in the coolness of the rain. "And I'm wondering if I could stay tonight in my new room. I know it's not quite ready yet, but by the time I finish it'll be too late to cross back over the river at a decent hour." She hated having to make this modest request, feeling that she was intruding, imposing herself where she was not yet officially moved in.

"Gertrude, of course you can stay here," Marie reassured her. "You just come over when you get done. I'll have something hot and comfy ready for you when you get here."

On the first river taxi that crossed the Yangtze Sunday morning Gertrude had her dressing trays boxed, stacked and covered, protected from the weather, and on their way to the clinic.

During the next two weeks, in the daylight hours Gertrude assisted Dr. Miller in the clinic and did anesthesia for his surgeries while her evenings were spent making preparations to open the San. She sewed together long strips of excellent quality Chinese linen to make sheets for the wards and the OR. She used a heavier cloth to make curtains to hang between ward beds. It would have been nice to make window curtains, too, but that was out of the question with so much other work to be done.

In her spare afternoons she shopped for supplies or struggled to keep up in language school. Fortunately Mr. Hsu was an old friend and understood her dilemma, giving her individual help when she missed particularly important classes.

At night Gertrude slept in her new room in the Miller house. Her window had a magnificent view overlooking the lake. But she hardly ever saw it in the daylight to appreciate the fine view or to spend a few pleasant moments reminiscing about Spot Pond at the New England San.

"Dr. Miller, we cannot do surgery here at the San." Gertrude's tone was insistent and her voice steady.

"Unfortunately, Miss Green, the patient is here and not at the clinic. He cannot be transported across the river without the loss of more blood." Dr. Miller was equally insistent and towered over her by at least 16 inches.

Not to be intimidated, Gertrude rose up on the balls of her feet, almost dancing on her toes, her green eyes snapping at every word. "There are no lights, Doctor. It is dark. There is no heat, Doctor. It is winter. There is no running water on the wards, Doctor. The hospital is not ready to open." Gertrude's last words rang with a resounding echo off the floors like the gauntlet of challenge they were intended to be.

Dr. Miller shifted mentally, parrying the frontal attack, looking for the flank and the weakness. "I know you have been working here every night . . ." he began.

"Yes, I was here late last night so that you now have a working autoclave, Doctor." Gertrude continued the assault, not seeing the flanking move.

"I know that we're not entirely ready for patients, Miss Green. But if we do not operate, this patient will die." Dr. Miller held her in his steady gaze, exerting all his strength to keep his hands purposefully at his sides, not moving about in any way to be seen as threatening. He let the one logical statement that all nurses must respond to sink in. "The patient will die."

Gertrude lowered herself to a flatfooted stance. She cast her eyes about for a way of escape and found none. Looking back into Dr. Miller's face she saw intensity and purpose but not anger. Slowly she pursed her lips in thought as she took a deep breath and exhaled audibly through her nose. She gave up. Dr. Miller had won.

"I'll find the generators and see what we can do about the lights in the OR, Doctor," she said as she turned to go. "But I don't think we have any plasma over here,"

"This won't take long," he said to her retreating form.

Even as Gertrude's mind worked out a plan to complete the operation, every fiber of her being trembled at having lost a confrontation with Dr. Miller. He could be so stubborn!

Then a thought, totally unbidden, slowed her resolute stride to a slow walk. *The Chinese have a saying that you only fight with those you love.* She pondered this for a moment, placed it next to the idea of Mrs. Miller's leaving for the States next week, and of herself living in the Miller household during that time.

The Chinese will see the situation and will draw their own conclusions, she mused. *I'll have to move back to the clinic,* she decided easily enough. *Besides I'm spending most of my time at the clinic and I'm doing too much running back and forth. I'll have to get my trunks moved back over there.* And with that little problem cleared away, she quickened her pace and turned up the side hall.

> 2 Rue Clemenceu
> Hankow, China
> November 16, 1937

Dearest Mother,

This is only a short note tonight to send along with the Christmas presents. Clarence Miller and his mother are returning to the States tomorrow and I wanted to send these things with them as it is much safer and faster than trusting to the mails these days. I am sending a blouse directly on to Ruth which Clarence will mail for me. You might see it if she is coming home for Christmas this year. There is material here for you to make a lovely tablecloth. The Chinese-made linen is so wonderful, much better even than what we used to get imported from England.

The work at the San and at the clinic is picking up. We have more soldiers coming in every day from the battlefields. Two more were operated on at the San. And many are on the wards at the clinic. The Japanese are advancing up the river, pushing the refugees and the soldiers ahead of them into Wuhan. So we don't lack for something to do.

I am still working on my language school. It is hard going as I have to squeeze it in around the work at the clinic. But because of all the patients and the surgery, I have moved back to the clinic and it is easier to get to school now.

I will write more soon when I have time. Heaps of love and kisses.

Your loving daughter,

Gertrude

Tuesday evening, a week after Marie Miller had left China, Gertrude worked until late on the operating room cupboards at the San. Staying overnight with Mrs. Sevrens, she gave anesthesia for early morning surgery with Dr. Miller before catching the early river taxi to be at the clinic by 9:00 a.m.

As Dr. Miller entered the outer clinic area, Gertrude, hearing the noise of the opening door, looked out through the registration window and gasped. Dr. Miller had on a three-piece suit as usual. But the coat was blue pinstripe, the vest was dark brown wool, and the pants were navy serge. Before he could pass any pleasantries with anyone, Gertrude came tearing through the waiting area.

"Dr. Miller," she said, grabbing his arm and forcibly moving him, "come with me. This way, please." She steered him around behind the reception windows and into his private office by the back hallway.

"What happened?" she implored, when she had gotten him through the door.

"Whatever do you mean?" he asked innocently, looking around.

"Your clothes," she said pointing. "They don't match."

He looked down at his coat, then held it open, examining his other apparel. He looked up at Gertrude with a sheepish grin on his face.

"I guess I was in a hurry," he said, trying to be disarmingly cute.

"Well, I guess you were," she said. Then coming closer for a more critical look, she walked around him. "And your socks; they don't match either. Did you dress in the dark?"

He turned to the left in a half circle, trying to follow her examination tour. Then turning his head to the right, he met her eyes full on coming around the other side.

"Dr. Miller, you haven't shaved."

He put his hand to his face, feeling the stubble. Slowly his boyish grin was replaced by genuine embarrassment. He looked up under his arched eyebrows for an explanation, but finding none, said nothing.

"Dr. Miller, you can't appear in public like that," she lectured him. "Your clientele are the elite of China. From the Generalissimo on down, they are well aware of proper Western dress. And I think they would be highly insulted if you were to see them while you are dressed so slovenly."

"But I was preoccupied with my schedule. I am very busy today." He tried to be curt.

"It doesn't matter," she cut him off. "Your position demands that you dress the part. Your patients will think you have no respect for them and that is highly insulting in China. You know that."

"Yes, I know that," he sighed, nodding his head. He raised his hands in a shrug of resignation. "Since Marie has been gone, I've had no one to help me get dressed in the morning."

"What?"

"She lays things out for me so that I don't have to search for them." He smiled through misty blue-gray eyes. "She lets me think about other things. It's the chink in my armor, Miss Green. I don't know these things."

Suddenly she smiled, then laughed, "Well, I won't tell them if you don't."

"No, Miss Green. I won't tell them," he laughed gratefully in return.

"When is your first appointment?" she asked more seriously.

"Ten o'clock, I think."

"Well, I'll get someone to delay them a bit. You go upstairs and find a prep razor and do something about that stubble."

He rubbed his chin again with a bit of humor.

"I'll run out to the San," she mused, mentally calculating how much time she had. "I'll lay out a few things in the guest bedroom for you. Then I'll find the mates to those things you have on. And we'll keep a set of things here at the clinic for you, just in case."

"Thank you, Miss Green," he said in a soft voice.

"You just stay out of sight until I get back," she shot back. "If Mrs. Chiang Kai-shek sees you like that, I won't be able to face her at the next reception party. I'm just saving my own skin."

Gertrude shook her head, her shoulders shaking in silent laughter, as she headed for the door.

Chapter 27

LEAVING IN THE FACE OF FEAR

2 Rue Clemenceu
Hankow, China
Tuesday, Dec. 7, 1937

My dear Ruth,

Oh, you wouldn't believe how famous your sister is. All the famous people I get to meet. But I doubt they will remember since they come in at the most horrendous hours. Generalissimo Chiang Kai-shek's secretary came into the clinic at 9:00 p.m. a week ago Monday. The staff were all so frightened they called me to get him supper and get him settled for the night. I didn't get to bed until midnight.

Things are progressing here. The sanitarium opened for its first official civilian inpatient on the day before Thanksgiving. And now that the San is opened, nursing classes have begun and I am teaching again—hydrotherapy and gynecology and clinic work.

Just like schools back home, we had our week of prayer beginning on December 3 and ending this next Sabbath. We are all praying for an end to the war. And I am always praying for you, dear sis.

And we have plenty of cases for the nurses in the hospital and the clinic. The war is getting closer. There are more refugees pouring into Hankow every day and many wounded soldiers come to the clinic for surgery and care. The air raids are increasing also, probably once or twice a week, so that we hardly pay any attention to them.

We had a lot of surgery this last week as Dr. Miller was getting ready to go to Manila and was getting everything caught up. Dr. Wang does a good job and I try to encourage him. But the patients always seem to know when Dr. Miller returns. And the census goes up.

While Dr. Miller is gone I have been working extra hard on my language studies. I am trying to get my fourth quarter finished and the exam done before he returns because, when he returns, I won't have the time.

I also have a little time for recreation now that he is gone. I can attend some of the excellent concert and lecture series that they have at the Navy YMCA. So don't worry about me. I am having a wonderful time here being busy and enjoying the good life. It is getting colder so I have gotten a new coat with fur collar. It gets cold here in the winter. I hope you can get home this year for Christmas. It would mean so much to Mother.

Your loving sister,

Gertrude

Gertrude could barely sit still. She had come to the Wuchang train station to see the Loewens on their way, but her mind was racing through the busy schedule of the day ahead.

"Oh, Gert, I've just got to get back to the clinic," Gertrude moaned. "I'll miss supper and the Friday night Week of Prayer session." She turned again and strained to look out the station windows for any sign of the train going to Hong Kong. "I need to be there for the nursing students, if nothing else," she said, turning around on the wooden seat to face Gert Loewen. "I'm sorry. There are so many of our people going through right now I can't see everyone. But you and Marvin are special. I wanted to see you off."

"Don't worry, Gertrude," Mrs. Loewen said, patting her hand. "We'll be fine."

Gertrude looked over her shoulder and spotted him first. Then Gert turned around on their end of the crowded bench and saw her bear of a husband coming from the stationmaster's office. He was picking his way through the boxes and bundles of hundreds of Chinese and foreign refugees that spilled from the wooden benches and covered the floor with noodle bowls, sleeping infants, and forlorn elderly. As he approached, he held out his arms in a silent "I don't know" and shook his head.

"Gertrude's got to go," Gert told him as Marvin approached.

Marvin shrugged. "The stationmaster doesn't know when the train will arrive."

"Well, waiting won't make it come any faster," Gertrude laughed as she stood up.

"Gertrude, will you be all right?" Mrs. Loewen asked, still clinging to her hand. "I'm just remembering what you said about the air raids in Kiukiang."

"I'll be fine," Gertrude said with a laugh, patting Gert's hand as Marvin put his large arm about her shoulders. "I'm busy enough not to notice so much. I just finished the fourth quarter language exam yesterday, the nursing school has started, I'm teaching every day, and Dr. Miller is coming home tomorrow." She patted Gert's hand again and squeezed it. "I'm too busy to be afraid." Then she pulled away, tugging her coat around her.

"We'll not forget you, Gertrude," Marvin said as his wife began to dab at her eyes.

"You have a safe train ride to Hong Kong," Gertrude called out, almost stepping in the middle of a family eating supper.

"Oops, I better watch it. Godspeed." She waved, then turned her attention to the crowd.

"Lord, help me to believe what I just told them," Gertrude whispered as she picked her way toward the entrance to find a rickshaw back to the river-front.

After Dr. Miller returned, the clinic and the surgeries began again in earnest. Sunday was a full clinic day with surgery in the evening. Tonsillectomies were scheduled for the next three days. And the faculty of the nursing school met almost nightly to finalize the curriculum for the new academic year.

"Gertrude. Gertrude, did you hear?" Blanche Sevrens called as Gertrude whisked by the administration offices.

Blanche bounded out of her chair and raced to the door. Balancing on one foot, she grasped the thick wooden frame with one hand and poked her head around the door just as Gertrude slowed her pace to see who'd called to her.

"Did you hear?" Blanche lowered her voice to a conspiratorial whisper. "The American Consul has ordered all Americans out of Hankow."

"Why? What happened?" Gertrude asked, coming to a stop, half turning.

"Don't know for sure," Blanche whispered, moving into the hall now on both feet, her left hand still resting lightly on the doorjamb. She was looking for girlfriend conversation, for a friend to talk with about this latest piece of news, to discuss options. What did it all mean?

"There's going to be a special radio broadcast—from Manila—on Wednesday night. Something about a special train."

"H'mmm," Gertrude considered aloud. "Dr. Miller and I will be eating with the Warrens that evening. I guess we can listen to it there."

As her mind set aside the temporary interruption and reconnected to the task at hand, Gertrude turned and resumed her rapid pace toward the clinic. Stunned and abandoned, Blanche was left to conspire alone in the hallway.

"Most interesting," Merritt Warren said as he reached over to the sideboard to switch off the small Zenith radio. "I wonder how long they've been contemplating this action?"

"You mean the special evacuation train?" Wilma Warren asked as she stood up to clear away the dishes. Gertrude watched her, detached, and did not rise to help.

"H'mm, yes," Elder Warren answered, moving his water glass to where his wife could reach it. The fingers of his right hand marched in place on the table. One part of his mind was attentive to his wife while another part was already running through the list of expatriate workers. Who should be on the train and who should stay behind?

"They seemed pretty certain of their facts, didn't they?" Dr. Miller commented, addressing no one in particular. He stared absently at his empty white dinner plate, his large hands resting quietly on the table on each side of it.

"Well, those facts certainly weren't designed to help us digest our suppers," Mrs. Warren commented, coming through the door from the kitchen to gather up the bowl of greens and the bread plate.

"Oh, I think they were intended to be broadcast at just exactly this time." Elder Warren nodded to the small mantel clock also sitting on the sideboard, focusing on the moment at hand. "We were all supposed to receive it just at supper time. Make sure we were all listening." He continued nodding his head as if in confirmation of his own words.

"Nanking is gone," Gertrude said, still sitting in stunned immobility at the table, trying to digest the unbelievable news about the loss of the southern capital of China.

"One wonders what is happening at Chiao Tuo Tseng," Elder Warren said, his voice quiet and strained.

"And how soon the Japanese Army will be here," Gertrude added, coming to life, rising from her chair.

"Soon enough," Elder Warren said resignedly. "Soon enough."

Then grasping his responsibilities as the Mission president, he turned and addressed Dr. Miller. "Harry, we'll have to put into action our evacuation plan, the one we were discussing in Administrative Council."

Then turning to his wife as she came through the kitchen door on her return trip, he said, "And you and the children will need to be on that train."

"And I'll be on that train, too," Gertrude said, standing behind her chair, gripping the gnarled tops of the uprights with white knuckles.

"Gertrude, you can't." Dr. Miller cried out, his voice hard and edgy.

"That's a decision she'll have to make for herself, Harry," Elder Warren said with deliberateness. "Everyone will have to."

Dr. Miller ignored the comment from his right. He pushed his chair back from the table, twisting his entire body around in the chair to face his personal office nurse. His hands rose imploringly.

"Miss Green, I need you," he said, his voice strained and struggling for control. "I need you here. The hospital. The nursing school."

"And the war, Doctor," she said, her green eyes burning brightly. "In Kiukiang on the dock you were intent on getting me out of harm's way. Now you seem to be intent on keeping me in it. Or is it that you are more concerned about your precious hospitals than you are about the people who work in them?"

"Gertrude!"

Silverware clattering to the floor, Wilma clapped her right hand to her mouth as if trying to hold back the words Gertrude had just said, as if by covering her own mouth she could catch what Gertrude had released. Her left hand fluttered around her heart, feeling the hurt and the pain and the fear that was so palpable in the room.

"No," Dr. Miller said, looking at Mrs. Warren, raising his own hands to stave off further criticism. He turned to catch Elder Warren's reaction and lowered his eyes at what he saw.

"No, it's OK," he said quietly, turning in his chair to face the table, folding his hands in his lap. "It's OK. She might be right."

"I'm frightened, Dr. Miller," Gertrude said with tight-lipped control. "Every time those air raid sirens go off, I want to jump under my bed or under a table. I want to stick my fingers in my ears, and just—scream."

As Mrs. Warren instinctively moved toward her, Gertrude held her at bay with a stiff right arm. Her voice became husky, cracking in the strain to be audible.

"I am not afraid of very many things," she said. "But I am scared to death of bombs and airplanes—and war. I don't want to die!" She bit her lower lip, the green eyes misting over. "I don't know what you have to do. But I want to leave while I can." The brave right arm so stiff in resistance just moments before shook slightly and fearfully drew back to her body.

This time when Wilma reached out toward Gertrude, she was not rebuffed. With a sweeping motion of her arms she gathered Gertrude like a rumpled blanket. Although she was shorter and smaller of frame, she held Gertrude as one might hold a child, head drooping on the shoulder, left hand rubbing the nape of the neck comfortingly.

With her eyes closed Gertrude did not cry. Exhaustion from holding in the fear and anxiety for so many months now consumed her. In quiet resignation, she stood there, holding on, being mothered.

"I can't give up, Miss Green," Dr. Miller said into his lap. "China is my life."

The massive head with its sad and lonely blue-gray eyes turned to her.

"I buried my first wife in Yencheng in 1907, after being in China for only two years. During the last 30 years of my life I have given my heart to China. The 13 hospitals built all over China, they are my children. The Chinese people are my family. I can't abandon my family."

"I'm sorry, Dr. Miller," Gertrude said from the comfort of Mrs. Warren's motherly shoulder. "I love these people just as I know you do."

Holding on to Mrs. Warren and the chair standing before her, she raised her head and then her whole body to an erect posture.

"But I can't help them," she said quietly, "I can't function as a nurse. Not in the middle of a war."

On December 25, 1937, the *Christmas Express*, flags of every country represented painted on the roofs of the passenger cars, pulled into Hong Kong filled with the expatriates of many countries evacuating the central part of China, including Gertrude Green. Allowed only two suitcases and her spacious brown shoulder bag, for the third time she was forced to leave an area of China with less luggage than she'd brought in.

General Conference of Seventh-day Adventists
Tacoma Park, Washington, D.C.
January 2, 1938

Mr. and Mrs. George Green
88 Bryan St.
Rochester, N.Y.

Mrs. Mary Barnett
394 Birr St.
Rochester, N.Y.

Dr. Ruth L. Green
c/o College of Medical Evangelists
Los Angeles, Calif.

Dear Friends:

We are endeavoring to keep in touch with the State Department concerning matters relating to the movement of our missionaries from place to place in China, and a recent word from the Department tells of a cable to hand from the Consul General at Hankow, stating that included in a group of American citizens who traveled from Hankow and Changsa on a special train, December 23, 1937, for Canton and Hong Kong was Miss Gertrude Mary Green.

The mails from some parts of China are somewhat irregular of late, and it may be that this word as to the present location of Miss Green will be of interest to you.

With best wishes,

Yours sincerely,
A. W. Cormack

3 Robinson Road
Hong Kong, China
January 25, 1938

Dearest Mother,

Well I was sure happy to hear from you when I received your airmail letter last night. I just jumped all over for joy to hear that you got your Xmas box and no duty and that you liked everything. And that everyone else liked the things I got them. I get the biggest thrill when I send something and people really appreciate it.

Since being in Hong Kong I have been busy fixing up a place for myself to live. There are so many people coming to Hong Kong there is hardly any place to live. As you can imagine, I wasn't able to bring many of my things from Hankow so I have had to sort of start over in housekeeping here.

The house where I live is so crowded that I had to fix up a cute little corner in a hallway on the second floor landing just above the staircase. I bought a secondhand wardrobe with a drawer in the bottom which serves as part of my wall and a place to hang my clothes. Then I have a screen for the other wall behind which I have a lot of empty wooden boxes piled one on the other and fixed with Canton crepe as a bureau. I have a mirror over it, a wooden table and a chair and my radio goes nicely there. My cot is outdoors on the roof porch which makes it very nice since the weather is so lovely just now, like California only better.

There is only one bathroom for four families plus me up here on the second floor and the refrigerator for my milk is downstairs but I get up early before the others and manage quite nicely.

I am staying very busy in this beautiful city. Language school started the first of this month—my second year, first quarter—and now I have time to study. I am eating with the Loewens and sightseeing with the Knights who are also here. I attended Winter Council meetings all last week. I get to go to Young People's MV every Friday night and Sabbath School and church in the afternoons on Sabbaths. So I am quite busy and happy here. I just wish you could come and see this place sometime.

And Mrs. Sevrens and I go shopping in this duty-free port almost every day. You would not believe the markets they have here. They have one street we call cloth street where every single store is a cloth store. Then they have an egg street, a silk street, a flower street, and a snake street. One rarely sees a cat on the streets here because the Cantonese people eat cats and snakes and rats. Up north the Chinese don't do that but down here they do.

There is one street where Chinese women fix and comb other Chinese ladies' hair. And on another street there are all these men who sit behind tables and write letters for people. You see there are so many people who cannot read or write in China so they pay someone to write for them. Then the person who gets the letter has to pay someone to read it for them.

I am buying things for the Wuhan Sanitarium and sending them back with Dr. Pang when he returns there. I got a letter from Dr. Miller telling me some of the things he needs. He also told about the Nationalist Chinese government that is moving further west to Chungking because the Japanese are getting so close. I am sure glad not to be in Hankow now as they have bombs dropping almost every day.

Last Friday some of our workers left on a French boat for Shanghai. The Winter Council decided that things are settled enough there to try to open some of our institutions again. I also heard that I will be going there soon. I will try to get this letter to you quickly by getting it on the China Clipper that is leaving here for the U.S. I would like to get K. O. Brown's measurements so that I can get his shirts remade here before I leave Hong Kong.

For tonight I will say bye-bye. Remember me to everyone there. Heaps of love to my darling mother. As ever, your daughter,

Gertrude

Chapter 28

RETURNING TO SHANGHAI

In its easterly course the Wangpoo River turns sharply north for about five miles before turning east in its search for the Yangtze River, the East China Sea, and the Pacific Ocean. On the western shore of this short five-mile section lay the harbor and the heart of Shanghai, the Bund, the waterfront. In an area five miles wide and extending approximately 10 miles inland, the international community had established here—as they had in other coastal cities of China—their "spheres of influence," little replications of their respective countries, complete with familiar architecture, infrastructures, businesses, and governments that were not embassies, but extensions of the sovereignty of their countries.

Collectively the entire area was known as the International Settlement. Within it the British and American areas lay to the north, staying south of the Soochow Creek except to cross it near its mouth and extend along the waterfront several miles eastward. The White Russian section lay immediately south of this area and a bit west of the Public Recreation Ground, a large open park and horse racing track immediately west of the downtown business district. The French Concession occupied the southern edge along the Siccawei Creek, extending from the waterfront, circling north around the ancient walled Chinese City, and reaching to the extreme western edge of the settlement at Avenue Haig.

Within the International Settlement, the various foreign powers shared their own independent telephone, electricity, and trolley systems, established their own banks and their own unique mass transit systems (red double-decker buses in the British areas and green one-level buses in the Frenc-

Concession), and cooperated in the running of an efficient central city government. Within the International Settlement all businesses were owned by foreign companies and all housing was occupied by Caucasians. Every day, from the Chinese communities which surrounded it for many miles on every side, the International Settlement imported the street sweepers, the dock workers, the maids and housekeepers, the lower echelon of office workers and middle management who interfaced with the Chinese manufacturers and tradesmen. But the International Settlement was a complete and self-contained social and political world unto itself—and safe from the war which surrounded it.

As the tender glided up to the floating dock in the dim light of dusk, Gertrude could just make out the round face set in a full wreath of thick, dark hair that was Grace Dale. She was standing quietly among the two dozen Caucasians crowded behind the restraining rope, meeting returnees to Shanghai. Like the others, Grace held up a sign with the words, "Welcome" in big letters. Below it was Gertrude's name.

"I didn't expect anyone to be here this late in the evening," Gertrude told her, happy about the surprise. They walked up the sawn boards spanning the space from the floating dock to the rickety wooden pier which reached out to them through an undulating sea of houseboats into the dark river. "Isn't there a curfew or something?"

"Curfew isn't until 9:00 o'clock," Grace answered. "Besides it's not strictly enforced here in the International Settlement like it is over there." She nodded toward the mouth of the Soochow Creek about 200 yards to the north.

In the gathering darkness Gertrude could make out dark, amorphous structures on the other side of the creek with almost no lights showing anywhere, no sign of life or movement.

The progress of the disembarking passengers stopped as the front ranks collided with the waiting coolies and customs officials on the permanent docks on shore. Gertrude and Grace were left to gaze into the living quarters of the Chinese family floating next to the pier.

"This isn't where we used to dock, is it?" Gertrude commented, now noticing the close proximity of the masses to the usually protected foreign passenger traffic.

"They moved the docking areas south of the creek during the bombing. Too much danger of a stray bomb." The line began to move again.

"You're traveling light," Grace observed. Gertrude carried a suitcase in each hand and a long strapped, light brown bag hung over her shoulder. "Can I help? Be careful of the edge there." Grace motioned toward the last of the overlapping wooden boards which was set at an odd angle.

"Sure." Gertrude handed over the left-hand suitcase, then clutched the shoulder bag with her free hand to balance herself. "Don't want to go tumbling off of here. I'm sure-footed but I'm not much in the mood for a swim," she laughed, "at least not in that river."

"We were permitted only two suitcases when we left Hankow on the train. My trunks and the camphor chest are still there." Gertrude turned and looked back at the floating dock, past the tender moored there, to the *SS Shoenhurst* anchored in the river beyond the sampans, now all clustered south of the creek mouth near the shore. "The rest of the stuff . . . this is a lot different than the first time I arrived in Shanghai." She turned to Grace with a big grin. "But I guess that doesn't matter much right now, does it?" She laughed as she began climbing up the concrete steps which led to the street level.

Because it was a strange bed, Gertrude awoke first. A dim early light crept in from the adjoining bedroom which had the only window in the apartment. Slowly and quietly she propped herself up with her pillow, reclining thoughtfully against the wall as she gazed about the unfamiliar room at the three other sleeping forms. They were easy to see in this small cubicle that was formerly a living room, made smaller by the three cots and single bed tucked into it.

That's Mrs. Leatha Coulston down there, Gertrude thought as she peered over the foot of her cot to the only bed with a real headboard. Gertrude remembered her from the time she visited the nursing school in Shanghai and saw her teaching in Chinese. At the time it had seemed such a wonderfully impossible feat. Now Gertrude had done the same in Wuhan.

Gertrude turned her gaze toward the metal hospital bed on her right near the open bedroom door. "Miss Matilda Follette. Been in China for many years," Gertrude murmured from memory. As if on cue, the sleeping form turned over with the accompanying protest of creaking springs but did not awaken. *She doesn't like her first name, does she?* Gertrude smiled at the unconscious response of the sleeping older woman. Miss Follette preferred her middle name—June. *But one of her friends last night called her—h'mmm—Follie,* Gertrude remembered. *I'll need to be a friend before I can use that name, I think.*

The other iron-framed hospital bed by the front door to the apartment held a smaller form. *Dr. Geneva Beatty came to Shanghai as part of her vacation and became the OB-GYN department. That must be some story,* Gertrude mused.

"Good morning, bright eyes," came a voice from the kitchen door to Gertrude's far right.

Gertrude turned with a smile to see the tall, thin form of Eileen Meisler framed in the doorway, a baby bottle in her hand. She waved to the new mother.

"Good morning."

"Someone's hungry." Eileen held up the bottle and waved it as she glided ethereally in the dim light toward the bedroom door, the steam from the warmed bottle trailing behind.

Gertrude could hear small rustling sounds but no crying. Ed was in there with the new baby. *Five adults and a baby in two rooms with a small kitchen and a bath.* Gertrude thought about the crowded conditions in Hong Kong. *At least I'm not sleeping out on the porch.*

H'mmm. One bathroom. Now that sounds familiar. With that thought Gertrude was up and moving, and the first in line of several who rotated through the single washing facility and the small kitchen during the next hour.

Ed Miesler, as the chief cook at the sanitarium, was the first out the door. "Come have lunch on me at the San." He smiled at Gertrude as he spoke. Then turning slightly he threw a "Good-bye, honey" over his shoulder and was gone.

Dr. Beatty and June Follette, huddled together like two conspiring sisters, were deep in conversation about patients as they left. They usually worked together in the obstetric suite and needed an early start on rounds. Eileen Meisler, the head of the nursing school, was fussing with the baby on her way out and thinking about her schedules and her staffing. She just waved and closed the door.

"What would you like to do today?" Leatha Coulston called from the bathroom. As Superintendent of Nurses she'd waited until last to take her turn for she didn't need to be at the hospital quite so early.

"Oh, I'll just unpack," Gertrude said, a quizzical look on her face as she gazed about the room that had no closets and no chests of drawers. "Then I thought I'd look around town. Maybe go shopping." *A sure cure for the moving-in blues,* she thought.

"Mind if I go with you?" Leatha asked, sticking her gray, curly head out of the bathroom door. "I don't actually need to go to the hospital today. We aren't very busy these days, you know."

Gertrude straightened and her eyes brightened. "I'd love that."

"It looks about like I remembered," Gertrude said, looking south across Joffre Avenue into the French Concession. Trolleys ran both directions with overhead electric lines crisscrossing and cluttering the space above the street. Horse-drawn carts and some pulled by men crowded the center of the road. Wheelbarrows, sedan chairs, and rickshaws all competed for passengers. The peddlers and beggars and bundle carriers scurried about, staying out of the way of these mechanical conveyances and the occasional steampowered or gasoline powered lorry. Horns and shouts and grunts and growls of men and animals filled the air. "The smell is the same," she said, wrinkling her nose, "but it's more congested. More people than I remember." She turned to Leatha for an explanation.

"It's the refugees," Leatha observed, squinting into the bright sunlight. "If we were to walk back up to the racetrack," she pointed over her shoulder, "you'd see that they've taken over the entire place—plus every empty lot and space in the entire Settlement."

"Where'd they come from?"

"These are people who escaped during the Japanese takeover of the Chinese sections. And the workers who were trapped here. Their families escaped, sneaked in or swam the creek to join them—away from the bombs and the guns. They're not supposed to be here, but . . ."

Gertrude shuddered slightly, thinking of her own escape from Wuhan.

"Let's walk up to Yates Avenue and see the shops up there," Leatha suggested, motioning for Gertrude to follow. "I think you'll find Wing On's and all the rest still where you left them."

"And the Chocolate Shop?"

"Still there. It's all within walking distance from the hospital."

The two women picked their way around a string of sidewalk vendors and noodle stalls, fending off the calls to buy with a smile and a shake of the head.

"Where's the hospital—now, I mean?" Gertrude asked when they walked side by side again.

"Just about two blocks that way on the Rue Moliere." Leatha pointed south. "It's only 50 beds. But it's enough for now. We're all confined to a pretty small space."

"Like the apartment," Gertrude laughed. "Is everyone living like that?"

"Some, including the nursing students, are out at the East China Mission on Yu Yuen. Some are in apartments like ours in the White Russian section here. But most haven't returned yet from the evacuation," Leatha explained, keeping such a steady pace that Gertrude had to concentrate to keep up.

"What about Ningkuo Road and the clinic and the San?" Gertrude was thinking of other places where people might be staying.

"Much of Ningkuo Road was destroyed. Some of the houses, the college, and the publishing house are completely gone. It was too close to the Chinese areas." Leatha turned and looked at Gertrude with—*hard eyes or haunted, which?* Gertrude tried to decide but could not. "We can't go out there except by special permission from the Japanese. No one is out there except those who were left there to look after it."

Gertrude thought of the little narrow paths and the cute iron gates, the houses and buildings all in neat rows, and tried to imagine it destroyed.

"But the war never came here?"

"No, not right here." Leatha's eyes said more than her words.

Gertrude looked around at the little island in the middle of the big war and wondered.

"But we can go out to the San—out on Rubicon Road," Leatha explained with a lighter voice, "if you don't mind my driving. We can't use the hospital driver since the Japanese still have that area closed to Chinese traffic. It's beautiful out there and we can pick the flowers and bring them back to the hospital. Would you like to do that this afternoon?"

"Yes, that would be . . . interesting," Gertrude said, still wondering what life was like beyond this safe island.

Chapter 29

LIVING ON AN ISLAND

On Tuesday Gertrude began her work as head of the OR, replacing Lydia Siebold who had gone on furlough to the States when the attack on Shanghai began in September. Like many others, she had not yet returned.

The only case scheduled for the week was a Caesarean section with Dr. Beatty. Yet despite the light work load, Gertrude caught her usual return-to-country cold. By Thursday she was running a fever and coughing so hard that Dr. Butka, the chief physician, ordered her off the wards and Mrs. Coulston took her home and put her to bed. For the next two days, the occupants of the apartment took turns nursing Gertrude back to health.

On Sabbath Gertrude was well enough to attend Sabbath school and church at Yu Yuen Road and walk the few blocks with June Follette to the hospital for lunch. In the overcrowded dining area they shared a small table with Mrs. Olga Oss, a woman of German ancestry who looked like a grown up "Heidi" with golden hair, merry eyes, and a broad smile between round, pink cheeks. After lunch Olga invited Gertrude and June to join her on a Sabbath walk to the Range Road Clinic. June was reluctant but Gertrude chided her with, "Come on, June, it's not that far."

"We'll catch a British omnibus over on Edward the VII Avenue and take it across town to Peking Road," Olga explained confidently. "Then it'll be just two blocks walk to cross the Soochow on Chekiang Road. It will be a nice walk up to Range Road from there."

The bus ride was slow as the route skirted the east side of the race track. June and Olga had seen it all before and were deep in a serious conversation.

But Gertrude sat near the window pondering the throngs of refugees packed into every available empty space. Makeshift tents, lean-to's, and small board and metal shacks had been erected wherever space and the local authorities allowed. The resulting congestion on the roads brought the usually crowded street traffic almost to a standstill. Some of the side streets were completely clogged and closed to all but pedestrians.

So many destitute people in the middle of such prosperity. *What do they eat or drink? Who is helping them? How can they live like this? Does anyone care about them?* The conundrum of stark survival and callous complacency left Gertrude stunned into silence.

As the three women walked up the street from Peking Road, Gertrude remarked on the amazing decrease of traffic and people.

"There's nowhere for them to go," Olga said. "All the traffic stops at the creek."

"But I thought the International Settlement crossed the creek here." Gertrude's gaze was fixed on the barricade on the bridge where two Japanese soldiers stood watching them.

"It did—all the way to Range Road," June said from behind her friends. Her usually serious face was now even more somber. As the older of the three, she had some trouble keeping up. Now she'd gradually slowed her pace until she trailed the others by five or more yards.

"The Japanese decided to stop the Chinese traffic into The Bund by controlling the bridges on the creeks," Olga said quietly. "We haven't had any problem crossing but we can't take our Chinese students over there into Chapei."

"You do have your pass, don't you?" Olga turned suddenly with consternation.

"Yes, of course," Gertrude said with a laugh, holding up her pass. "In this town you almost can't cross the street without it." She chuckled and winked at Olga who smiled and reached out a hand encouragingly to wave June forward. June remained in the rear but managed a weak smile and a wave of her pass as well.

"Good for you. OK, let's go talk to these boys."

The two men appeared to be barely into their twenties. But as the three women approached the barrier, both guards moved forward, their guns with fixed bayonets carried across their chests like pike poles. Olga Oss smiled and bowed, her hands folded in front of her. Gertrude followed her lead but never took her eyes off of the two warriors standing on the far side of the barrier.

As Olga moved toward the pedestrian bypass around the barrier, the younger of the two guards stepped sideways and blocked her path. Olga stopped and held up her pass but the young man frowned and vigorously shook his head.

"I am an American and I want to pass," Mrs. Oss said with a steady but friendly voice.

"No!" he shouted. "No pass."

"But why not?" Mrs. Oss was obviously surprised by this show of obstinacy.

"No have man. No pass!" The guard was obviously enjoying his exercise of authority.

Gertrude watched a smirk of contempt spread across the face of the older guard. While bombs might be deadly, Gertrude thought, smart-alecky young boys were certainly nothing to be afraid of. And what was that remark about not having a man along?

When Olga moved forward to gently challenge his youthful exuberance, the young guard raised a stiff right arm and pushed an open palm very near to her face.

"No pass!"

"This is just about enough," Gertrude said aloud to herself. "These boys are no older than the ones in the nursing class." Gertrude's voice grew louder as she slowly moved forward.

"Now see here!" Gertrude spoke with the staccato fire of a drill sergeant. "That's no way to treat an American citizen." With her finger pointed like a gun she advanced on the startled young guard who began to back away.

Olga tugged at her arm as she passed but Gertrude shook her off. Only when she reached the barrier did Gertrude notice that the older guard was advancing with his bayonet pointed at her. She stopped talking and glared at him but did not turn her accusing finger toward him. His eyes were locked on hers. And neither gave way.

"I think we should find another way," Olga said quietly.

Slowly Gertrude lowered her arm. "Well, you can just keep your old bridge," she snapped. She turned and stalked away, grabbing June's trembling hand and dragging her along.

As Olga retreated behind Gertrude, she looked back to see the older guard now berating the younger one. But Gertrude, shaking with anger, marched straight off the bridge with never a backward glance.

The next day Olga accompanied the girls to church at the Marine Camp just north of the race track on Bubbling Well Road. She called it "making friends for if and when we ever need them." After the service Gertrude was surrounded by a sea of orange-trimmed dark blue uniforms as she regaled the young Marines with an animated retelling of the confrontation at the bridge. They all applauded when she fired off, "I don't see how we can just stand around and do nothing while they are destroying this beautiful country."

Although the young Marines knew almost no one at the hospital, the "Battle at the Bridge" story spread like spilled milk at breakfast, quickly and quietly among the hospital workers, especially among the student nurses. The Japanese, at least a small contingent of them, had learned what many before them had come to appreciate—the frank and fiery Miss Gertrude Green was an ardent ally to those under her watchful care and a fearsome opponent to those who crossed her.

On March 25 the new class of probies of the Shanghai Hospital received their caps. As Gertrude watched each candle receive a flame from the lamp of "Miss Nightingale," she remembered her own probie year at New England Sanitarium and Hospital, her time as a student there, and the years of nursing that followed. That's what she had come to China to share. But here in Shanghai she felt disconnected and misplaced.

Standing in the reception line serving the refreshments, Gertrude wanted to be of service, not just to run the operating room or an outpatient clinic. She wanted to teach these Chinese and Russian and English students the skills and compassion of her profession. As the young women and men of the new class received a small saucer of delicacies from her hand, she spoke to them in the appropriate language, congratulating them and joking with them about surviving the probie experience. But no student received what Gertrude most wanted to give—herself.

For now Gertrude had only the few surgeries in need of anesthesia, the operating room to organize, and the study of the Chinese language. The nursing classes were small and the school would not take any new first-year students until May. Leatha Coulston was still the superintendent of nurses and would not leave on her furlough for another month. Gertrude must be content to spend her time shopping with the girls, eating Chinese food at Sun Ya's or American food at the Chocolate Shop, and playing games in the evening with the Dales and others who lived on the East China Union compound.

51 Rue Moliere
Shanghai, China
Saturday, April 17, 1938

Dearest Mother,

Well here I am, tomorrow is Easter and spring is here. I just came off duty at 9:00 tonight and found out there is a boat going out tomorrow, so wanted to get a letter off to you.

I received your letter this week and was sorry you had such a miserable cold. I had a swell one a while ago, but it has gone now and I am feeling very well. The weather is very warm and we are all into summer clothes already. I don't like awful hot weather to come so quickly.

I am working every day but we are not so very busy. Also I am studying Chinese one hour every day, second year and second quarter. I am learning anatomy and medical terms so that I can teach better in Chinese.

Our house is less crowded now. Ed and Eileen Meisler and baby have moved over to the Range Road Clinic apartments and Mrs. Coulston has packed and is staying at Yu Yuen Road prior to going home on furlough. So there are just the three of us girls here. We all three sleep in the bedroom and have the living room to fool around in. Our kitchenette is also less crowded and we are quite nicely fixed up.

With Meislers and others from the hospital now living at the Range Road Clinic, the traffic is flowing nicely across the Soochow Creek. Before this the Japanese were not allowing the Americans or their Chinese servants to cross the creek. But now that we have someone living over there, the bridges are open and the passes for the servants are working again.

The attitude of the Japanese and their uppity ways are more than I can stomach sometimes. Their soldiers are rude to everyone on the street. And they are frequently drunk and disorderly and certainly have nothing to be proud of, the way they have destroyed this beautiful country. But everyone says to be patient and put up with it so that we can get the clinic open and running again.

We certainly will not have the Shanghai Sanitarium on Rubicon Road open any time soon. The soldiers in the fighting out there just made a wreck of everything. The buildings are all still standing but they just went through the San destroying everything. They took furniture out in the yard and left it in the rain. They tore up the carpets and broke down the grand chandelier in the front lobby. They ran their bayonets through the large cans of food and ruined them. And now Rubicon Road is the area that the Japanese have decided to close to all traffic. So I don't know how we will ever open it again.

The division compound on Ningkuo Road is gradually being repaired and restored. The homes should be usable soon but the publishing house was totally destroyed and will have to be replaced. Miraculously the Chinese church was untouched and I will be going out there soon for Sabbath when things are open for travel. I enjoy listening to the sermons and the lessons in Chinese and it is good practice for me.

Tomorrow I am going to Easter services at the Marine Church just north of here. And that reminds me to tell you about what we are planning for the Sunday before Mother's Day.

There is a yearly custom here for each American family in Shanghai to entertain some American Marines for dinner. I am invited to help Elder and Mrs. Hartwell with their entertaining at their house on the Mission Compound.

The idea is that these boys are over here to protect all of us and we want to give them an opportunity to have a real dinner in a real home for one day. The boys are really pleased to do this and we will have a lot of fun doing it.

After the dinner we are planning some music, games, and readings. I will be accompanying Mrs. Hartwell who plays the marimba. And then each of us will do one of the readings. I am looking forward to it a lot.

I also received a letter from Walter saying that he got his tie and likes it very well. If his friends want one like it I will have to get it from Hong Kong, the only place where I know I can get them. And K. O. Brown's shirts went out just the other day and then I got a letter from him asking about them. Tell Aunt Mary that the ginger comes from Canton, China, and I cannot get it in Shanghai. I will see about ordering more when I check into the ties.

Elder Griggs brought my trunks and my camphor chest when he came from Hankow. So I will keep them at Yu Yuen Road until I have a larger place to stay. He says to please remember him to my mother. He still speaks of you and says how lucky I am to have you for a mother, as if I didn't know that already!

The other things I have left behind in so many places are just gone, I guess. The furniture and all, the desk and the chest of drawers, they were just all too big to move so quickly. And now that the Japanese are moving into these areas like Nanking and Hankow—they are just gone. I am learning to close my eyes and turn away from this world's goods and it can't be helped.

I am safe here and enjoying myself immensely. I will close with heaps and heaps of love to you from your loving daughter,

Gertrude

Chapter 30

WORKING OVERTIME

Gertrude held open the door as Leatha Coulston stepped into Sun Ya's Chinese Restaurant. The place was smaller than its reputation suggested. But it was especially popular with the Americans of Shanghai because the congenial owner spoke some English and seemed to remember everyone by their first name, a custom he thought was very American.

"The hospital is getting busier these days," Gertrude said when the server had gone to fill their order. "Dr. Butka is happy that there's more surgery to do."

"No surgeon is happy unless he's working," Leatha observed with a smile. "It's too bad that he's leaving just as things are beginning to pick up." She settled back in her chair. "But then a lot of us were just getting our feet under us."

"You'll be missed," Gertrude said quietly.

"I'm sure you will fill in nicely, Gertrude." Leatha smiled even more broadly and leaned forward, her eyes twinkling. "From what I hear, you have the fire for crossing bridges of all kinds."

"It takes more than fire." Gertrude colored and lowered her eyes with embarrassment. She knew everyone had heard about the bridge incident. "Sometimes fire is exactly *not* what is needed. Or ice either for that matter." Gertrude looked up at her companion with admiration and respect, as if trying to draw something of her character to herself. "Actually I'm praying for more of your steady-as-she-goes approach."

"When I first arrived in Shanghai," Gertrude tried to explain, "I saw you teaching the nursing students in Chinese. I thought it was so amazing. I wanted to be able to do it, too." Gertrude's hands came up out of her lap to the tabletop to assist in the thoughts she found hard to put into words. "You were my model. And I kept you in my mind all the while I was in language school in Nanking—until all the war started. And everything changed."

"You are too kind, my dear," Leatha demurred. But then more seriously, "But the war is not over yet. And we have a new surgeon, Dr. Harold Maurer, coming. And a new class of nursing students, both English speakers and Chinese nationals."

"Yes, Mrs. Meisler says we'll need to split them and teach all of our classes twice. Once in English and once in Chinese."

"And the summer season with all of its infectious diseases is just around the corner." Leatha ticked off on her fingers the various challenges she saw coming. "And graduation. As the Superintendent of Nurses you still have a lot of wars to fight."

"Well, I for one am looking forward to graduation," Gertrude laughed, "because we can use the help on the wards. They won't be students any more and can pitch in like the rest of us."

"Which means a new work schedule," Leatha said more to herself as if it were still her responsibility.

"Yep, I've been thinking about that," Gertrude agreed. "But right now I'm hungry. Where's the food?" she asked, looking around for the waiter.

Although Dr. Maurer was unknown to the average resident of Shanghai, within two weeks of his arrival every one of the hospital's 50 beds was full and more patients were admitted every day. The hot season began in mid-May, and the crowded conditions among the refugees brought the infectious diseases Leatha had predicted, including typhoid, tuberculosis, and meningitis. All this added to the hospital's overcrowding and the long working hours of the limited nursing staff.

As the new Superintendent of Nurses, Gertrude was grateful that the graduation exercises made five more nurses available for her revised work schedule. But her own hours were now long and arduous. In addition to her superintendent's duties and working day, evening, and night shifts on the wards, she continued to run the OR, give anesthetics, and assist with X-rays.

When the new class of nursing students began May 24, Gertrude was asked to teach as she'd hoped she would be. Although it only added to her already crowded schedule, the shortage of instructors made it necessary and Gertrude was delighted to do it. In her heart, giving personal care to her grateful Chinese patients was equaled only by the personal satisfaction she derived from teaching the eager young minds of her nursing students. But the added burden stretched her endurance, emotionally and physically, to the breaking point.

> 51 Rue Moliere
> Shanghai, China
> June 15, 1938

Dearest Mother,

I am on night duty now for two weeks so am getting a lot of writing done. I take care of the operating room and am on duty on the ward as well so I never seem to get done until late in the afternoon or evening even when I am working days.

Our surgery work has increased markedly. And with the large number of infectious disease cases like typhoid and tuberculosis, we are just kept hopping all the time. We all had to get our typhoid and cholera shots recently and I have started sleeping under a mosquito net, although I think the risks of getting malaria are pretty small.

It has been quite hot until the last few days. It has been raining for the last five days straight and the water is up to people's knees in some places. In order to cross the street one must take a rickshaw. And it is still raining outside. At least it cools off the hot weather if nothing else.

There are so many refugee camps all over Shanghai in old buildings or mat sheds set up on empty lots. In each camp thousands are all crowded together in such filthy conditions as you can't imagine with beggars and dirty little children everywhere. And all they get is two bowls of rice per day with no vegetables or anything else. I don't know how they are able to survive all huddled together like that.

Along with the Red Cross and several doctors in town, we have secured a former school building and have made a Refugee Maternity Center. All the refugees who are expecting babies will move to the camp on the grounds next to the school building. Then they can all be cared for in the hospital which will hold about 100 patients. Dr. Beatty and Miss June Follett from our sanitarium are taking charge of it. In fact, they opened a week ago Monday with three patients and more on the waiting list

Our own hospital holds only 50 patients and is now much too small and not at all suitable for all the people we are treating. Recently we found a much better location right on the main street of Shanghai, Bubbling Well Road, and we will be moving the hospital in the next three or four weeks. The American Marines had been living in this place and just moved to another location. It isn't so marvelous but is 300 percent better than where we are now.

Last month we graduated five nursing students from our nursing school program. With the help of June and Geneva we had a party for them afterward at our house. I took some pictures and will send you some so you can see our lovely Chinese nurses. They are very nice girls and I just love them so much.

I went out this evening with a crowd of people to Sun Ya's, a Chinese restaurant where we get excellent food. I especially like the fried noodles with mushrooms and sauce. Rice, of course, is always the main dish for the people in the south of China. But in the north they eat only noodles or other wheat flour products.

Afterward we went to the Chocolate Shoppe, an American run place, and had ice cream. They also have the most delicious sandwiches I have ever tasted including a three-decker that is dipped in batter and deep fried. Oh, boy, is it ever delicious!

If someone wants to get a tablecloth like yours, it would be more reasonable to get it now. The exchange on Chinese money for gold is very good; yesterday it was $6.50 to $1.00 US. It dropped today to $5.50 but that is still very excellent. Tell her to let me know.

The war continues here with the Japanese making steady progress toward Hankow. They are dropping bombs there every day and I am glad not to be there. Dr. Miller is still there and is still very busy.

There is a boat going out tomorrow so Dr. Beatty and I will make our usual little trip to the boat with our letters. That way we are perfectly sure they will get on their way and not be opened by the Japanese censors.

But I will be careful on the way. The last time we went walking down there, I got a whole gob of spit on my forehead. Someone had spit out of a third-story window and it was my bad luck to be just under that window.

You never can tell what is coming down on you. China is a great place and I like it. Something new every minute.

Well, I will close for tonight, hoping you are well and enjoying the summer. Heaps of love to my dear mother from her darling daughter,

Gertrude xxxxoooo

"I think it must be the Fourth of July," June Follette said loudly, standing in front of the closed bathroom door.

"No, it isn't," came the voice from the other side. "It's only the third."

"Well, it's been so long since you went in there, I guess it just seems like the calendar changed over." June danced from foot to foot in her bathrobe, clutching her towel, impatiently waiting her turn in the tub.

Gertrude lay sprawled on the living room sofa, the damp ringlets plastered to her forehead by the humidity and heat, only vaguely aware of the conversation. She had gotten home first and had had her turn in the tub, lying in the cold water trying to cool off. When Geneva and June came home from the Maternity Center, she had surrendered her place to them. Now, after being up most of the night, she was too hot and too exhausted to listen to or participate in the banter that was a natural part of three working girls all living in the same small apartment.

"This is what we get for complaining about the incessant rain." The wet, wrapped, diminutive figure of Geneva Beatty appeared in the now open bathroom doorway.

"Yeah, it's now too hot to breathe." June's taller blond figure rushed past Geneva and closed the door. "You didn't change the water, did you?" she called out amid splashes and settlings.

"No, dearie," Geneva said, drying her short brunette curls, "There's no water to waste. And besides, we can't afford it."

"Gertrude, are you OK?" Geneva paused her vigorous hair toweling, concern spreading over her face. She retrieved her owlish spectacles from her dressing gown pocket and peered more closely at the prostrate form spread-eagled on the sofa.

Gertrude peered up at her languidly through one raised eyelid, then closed it. Arching both eyebrows in a weak effort at exercise, she slowly retrieved her arms until her hands cupped her face. Brushing them over her cheeks and chin with a waterless washing motion, she released a grand exhalation and sat up.

"What happened last night?" Geneva queried, her towel now working again.

"Two appendectomies—in a row."

"And p.m. shift the night before, and double shift covering for a sick nurse the night before that, plus all the administrative work and the OR. Gertrude, when are you going to run out of steam?"

"I don't know."

Geneva shook her head, fluffing her hair. "How many patients yesterday?"

"The hospital is full and beyond capacity. They are jamming up the wards and lying in the waiting room." Gertrude stretched out again, slipping into semi-consciousness. "We have to move the hospital before we start parking them on the lawn."

"The maternity center is full to the brim. But Follie and I aren't trying to cover both day and night," Geneva said as she turned and headed for the bedroom.

From out in the hallway came a shout and a crash followed by running feet and a pursuit.

Gertrude sat bolt upright, eyes wide, mind and heart racing.

"Good grief and little fishes," she cried as her feet hit the floor. "Can't we have some peace and quiet around here?" Grabbing the doorknob, she flung open the door. "What do you think this is, a dormitory?" she screamed into the hallway. The simultaneous slam of the door almost drowned the last syllable. "Why does everyone have to live right on top of me?"

"What was *that*?" June called from the bathroom. She'd leapt from the tub, grabbed a towel for cover, and now peeked around the door frame.

As Gertrude whirled around, her snapping eyes met June's questioning face wreathed in dripping hair and Geneva's worried face now poised above a lace collar. The rattle of the doorknob wrenched her back to her supposed tormenters in the hallway. Gertrude grabbed the door and jerked it open, advancing on whomever was standing there. It was Grace Dale. She stood in the hall with her cupped hand extended, empty of the doorknob that had suddenly been snatched away.

"Hi. What's all the noise?" Grace smiled and sidled past Gertrude's stony, smoldering statue into the small living space which housed them all.

"Ask her," June snorted, retreating into the bathroom.

"Too hot," Gertrude mumbled as she shuffled to the sofa, her shoulders now sagging and her eyes half closed.

"Then let's go out," Grace offered, "Get out in the breeze and out of this stuffy hole."

"Great idea," Geneva said with a hopeful lilt, slipping on her loafers.

"Not 'til I've finished my soak." June's voice echoed from the tub.

"You've been in there long enough," Gertrude snapped.

"Have not!" came the retort.

"I just got out, Gertrude," Geneva said, her head cocked in wonderment and concern.

"I know," Gertrude sighed, crumpling again. "I'm just too hot."

"And too exhausted to make good sense." Grace advanced her biggest smile. "Come on, Gertrude, it will do you good to get out."

Gertrude smiled weakly and gave a knowing little nod of her head.

"Where to?" June called out.

The other three girls looked at each other. "Shopping!" they said in unison and began laughing at the universal panacea for all women.

"And then to Sun Ya's for supper," June said as she came dripping to the door.

Gertrude's face contorted into a frown. "Aw, we always go there. Let's go to the Chocolate Shoppe."

"Come on, Gertrude. You know you like it there," Geneva chided.

"I do not!" Gertrude shouted. "I hate that fresh guy there who always calls us by our first names." Her lip shot out as her eyes clouded over. "I don't want to go there. I never get to do what I want to do!" She leaped off the sofa and ran crying into the bedroom.

"What happened?" Grace asked, eyes wide as she sank onto the vacated sofa.

"Just being her cantankerous self." June's peeved face disappeared into the bathroom.

Geneva shook her head. "Too many late night surgeries, too little sleep, too much work."

For several minutes Geneva Beatty and Grace Dale sat looking alternatively at each other and at the floor, searching for the answers to these common problems that plagued them all and finding none. The crying from the bedroom stopped and only the occasional gurgle of water echoed from the bath. The weight of heavy humidity quietly smothered them all.

Then Gertrude appeared in the bedroom doorway, dressed in her cotton blouse and plaid skirt. Her eyes were dry and her hair was tucked under a broad brimmed hat.

"To keep the sun off," she said, adjusting it slightly. "Ready to go," she added with big smile.

"Where to?" Grace ventured, confused by the sudden appearance of this congenial apparition.

"Oh, it doesn't matter," Gertrude smiled again. "I'll be all right once I get my shopping legs under me." She walked smartly to the front door and opened it for them.

"OK," Grace said lightly as she rose up. "Let's go."

"Follie, are you coming?" Geneva called, hesitating.

"No, I'll stay here where it's cool . . . and calm," came the quiet reply.

"Sorry, June," Gertrude sang out as she gently closed the apartment door.

At the end of the next week, June Follette moved out of the cramped apartment and into her new living quarters at the East China Union compound on Yu Yuen Road. She explained to Dr. Beatty that, because of the increased number of patients it would be more convenient for her to live closer to the maternity center.

Chapter 31

RUNNING AT BREAKNECK SPEED

The refugees living at the race track across the road had never seen such a flurry of activity on Bubbling Well Road. Just two weeks ago the U.S. Marines moved out their office desks, their barracks furniture, and armored vehicles. Today the Seventh-day Adventists were moving in hospital beds, their medical files, operating room equipment—and more than 50 patients.

Gertrude and her staff had spent the whole month of July preparing for this day—July 26. Sundry supplies, old patient records, clinic charts, and office furniture, were moved in a full week before. All the operating room equipment was brought in on July 25, and no surgery was scheduled for the 26th. Even the outpatient clinic was closed. Gertrude devoted the entire day to moving the patients, their beds and furniture, and the nursing stations. She scheduled every nurse available in a double coverage to discharge the patients as they exited 51 Rue Moliere and to readmit them as they entered 526 Bubbling Well Road.

Gertrude used every available hospital conveyance and borrowed more. Some of the patients who could walk were sent by rickshaw. Some post-op or seriously ill patients were moved in their beds. Every patient was accompanied by a student nurse, and every patient must be accounted for. In addition, Gertrude also kept track of the moving of the X-ray department, the lab and pharmacy, and the outpatient clinic. These departments could afford to be closed only one day.

In mid morning, after receiving the first transferred patients, the nurses reported to Gertrude that the water was not working anywhere in the new facility. While the maintenance people began to track down the reason, Gertrude arranged for water to be brought over from the old facility with each patient. By midnight the outside temperature still hovered in the 80s. But all the patients had been safely transferred and the new facility was ready to open for business on Wednesday, July 27, at the new address.

For the next three days the normal hospital routine suffered as nurses struggled with items not stored in their usual places, other hospital departments not fully functional, and the lack of water which defied attempts to flow through pipes and into faucets. The convenience of having twice the space to work in was a relief. But the news of the bigger facility had gotten out and the outpatient department was twice as busy, with admissions soon following suit. During the daytime Gertrude worked helping the departments and wards get settled. She spent much of those first nights doing anesthetics as an emergency surgery occurred on each of the first two nights. By Friday evening things were beginning to settle and Gertrude was ready for a quiet dinner and some social time.

"Gertrude and Geneva! How good of you to come all this way." Eileen Meisler met them at the top of the stairs on the sixth floor of what had been the Range Road Clinic. "Supper will be ready shortly," she said as she led them into the first room on the left from the hallway. "I'm expecting Ed to be back from the hospital any minute now."

Gertrude noted the cracked ceiling and the spots of plaster missing from the walls.

"The bombs fell pretty close around here, didn't they?" she said.

"Just behind that school across the street."

Gertrude looked closely as Eileen pointed past them to the room across the hall and out its cracked window to an abandoned schoolyard and a partially destroyed building.

"All the rooms on that side of the building are too badly damaged to live in."

"That was a bit of a hike up those stairs," Geneva said, falling into a straight-backed library chair tucked under what served as the dining table. "So how are you making out here?"

"Well, we've taken over all the rooms on this side of the hall," Eileen said, hurrying across the floor to look in the pot on the small oil burning stove.

"They were all dorm rooms for nursing students way back when. But now we have a home here, just somewhat scattered out. Want to come see?"

Eileen led the girls back into the hall, stopping at each old dorm room and pointing out how they'd been made into a living room, a bedroom, the baby's nursery, and at the end of the hall, an office.

"Are you here all by yourselves?" Gertrude asked, looking out again at the devastated buildings all around.

"Oh, mercy, no," Eileen laughed. "There are several servants and hospital helpers living downstairs in some of the old clinic rooms. And a lot of the nurses are living down there as well. It's much closer to Bubbling Well Road and easier to get to. All the buses run right past the crossing at the bridge over the Soochow."

Gertrude screwed up her face in thought, calculating travel time and inconvenience from her present house and from here. She nodded in agreement as the numbers fell into place.

"So what's happening at the apartment?" Eileen asked as they ambled back down the hall toward the delicious scents of supper.

"I hardly ever see the place," Geneva said, pushing her large, round glasses back up on her nose. "Follie and I spend most nights sleeping at the Maternity Center. The number of babies being born and the refugees who have them is just too staggering to comprehend."

"And you?" Eileen peered closely at Gertrude's drawn and tired face.

"Oh, I'm as guilty as the next," Gertrude chuckled, blushing under the fervent gaze. She found a seat near the door and collapsed into it. "The Chinese nurses, bless their hearts, all try. But most of them are new graduates. And the few of us from the States are carrying most of the load. I've been working so late I never see the place either." She thought again of how much closer Range Road was to the hospital. "By the time I'm done at night, it's just too far to go home."

"Why not move over here?" Eileen offered. "I'm sure the hospital would be glad to have another foreigner in this place. Helps to keep the bridge guards friendly and access open for the Chinese workers."

"H'mm." Gertrude grimly remembered her first encounter with guards at the bridge.

"I can move over to Yu Yuen Road because it's closer to the maternity center," Geneva said. "Actually, I can move my *things* over," she added with a shrug of resignation, "but I'm sure I'll be spending all my time at the center and will probably never see whatever place they put me in." They all nodded, knowing that the work load would continue unabated until the people who'd left during the bombing returned or were replaced by others returning from furlough.

"What a bunch of Sad Sacks," Ed Meisler proclaimed, standing in the doorway, his suit coat over his arm.

At his voice, Gertrude jumped. "Oh—you!" she gasped, reaching up and swatting him on the arm. "You horrible man," she said with a laugh, "scaring poor, defenseless women in the middle of a war zone."

"Yes, so defenseless," Ed said as his tall frame strode over to the stove and peered into the pot simmering there. "Seems I remember a certain young lady on a bridge . . ."

"Never you mind now, dear," his wife said as she followed closely behind him, snatching the lid from his hand and shooing him away from the stove. "Go talk to the girls while I finish up this business in here. And don't wake the baby."

On Sunday morning Gertrude, now an expert mover, rounded up the faithful Dodge truck and two Chinese helpers and moved to the Range Road Clinic building. The crossing over the Soochow was uneventful. The guards at the gates barely glanced at Gertrude's pass as they swung open the striped poles and the old wood-sided truck rumbled across.

Perhaps this won't be so hard after all, Gertrude thought as they drove the remaining five blocks through the crooked, rubble-strewn streets of the now Japanese occupied sector. But for the next four weeks, Gertrude learned just how hard it could be.

For those who worked days at the hospital, the crossing of the Soochow Creek Bridge was a daily ritual, morning and evening. Each person slowly approached the pedestrian gate and the guard, so as not to surprise him. Then they bowed very low to show subservience to the guard. With her pass extended, Gertrude had to wait while the guard examined it and anything else she might being carrying, if he was so inclined. If he wanted to be particularly insolent, the guard would go inside the guard shack to "check the list," leaving the supplicant standing shamefacedly, earning the ire of others in line who were being held up by someone who had to be "checked on." For Gertrude, who frequently returned late at night, passing the guard was only the beginning of a five-block gauntlet of drunken sailors and soldiers who haunted her path to the Range Road clinic building.

"Gertrude, what did you do?" Geneva Beatty's eyes were as round as her glasses and almost as big.

"I ran, of course," Gertrude managed around a mouthful.

"Ran from what?" Grace wanted to know, setting her tray on the small cafeteria table as she joined them. It was now 1:30, and only a few late-lunch customers dawdled at the tables near the windows in the hospital cafeteria.

"Oh, Grace, Gertrude has had the most horrendous and frightening adventure you can imagine," Geneva gasped as if she'd been running herself.

"Mercy, child," Grace laughed. "I've never seen you so excited. You're usually Miss Calm and Collected."

"Well, I've dealt with some pretty unusual people at the maternity center," Geneva said, trying to calm herself, "but I've never been chased by drunken sailors."

"What!" Grace's dark eyes grew big as she turned abruptly to Gertrude who was calmly eating her greens and cornbread.

"The same thing happens about every other night," Gertrude said with a shrug, looking up at them both. "Well, not exactly that way," she added when their mouths both dropped open. Then she took another bite, ignoring the fact that they were both holding their breath in expectation.

"Come on, Gertrude, tell it!" Grace cried.

"OK, OK," Gertrude said as she swallowed and dabbed at her mouth with her small, rough, brown paper napkin. "I had already gone through the checkpoint there at the bridge. The guard had gone back into the shack and I had gotten down to where that first road comes in on the right, you know, just past where the General Hospital was?" The girls nodded, mesmerized already.

"I'd just gotten into the shadows of that bombed out building on the right when I heard them urinating on the side of the building back in there." She was gesturing directions now with her fork. "There were three drunken sailors in there. I could here them talking and laughing and I could hear three distinct voices. They didn't see me at first when they came staggering out of the alley, and I shrank back into the shadows, hoping they wouldn't notice me. But I think it just took a bit of time for them, through their clouded brains, to recognize me as Caucasian.

"You know how usually in the daytime they'll shout at you or call you names or something. Well, at night they're bolder and will come right up and get in your face. I didn't want to deal with them in a dark part of the street so, when they came toward me, buttoning up their pants as they came, I put my head down and began walking fast up toward Range Road. When they started shouting at me, I ignored them and kept on walking." She paused. "Then I heard them hurrying after me, shouting, 'Lady, lady.' That's when I started to run."

"Oh, dear!" Grace said, her right hand rubbing her forehead and coming to rest on the side of her face.

"See what I mean!" Geneva said emphatically, leaning forward, not touching her food.

"But how could you outrun them?" Grace asked breathlessly.

"I was the fastest runner in my school. And I'm still good on my feet," Gertrude said firmly. After the slightest pause then she added, more cautiously, "but last night the Lord put wings on my feet. I fairly flew up to Boone Road and was crossing it on a tear when I heard another voice with authority shout out something in Japanese. I didn't know if he was shouting at me or at them and I didn't stay around to find out. It wasn't until I got to Range Road and turned right that I even looked back to see that no one was following."

Grace sat back in her chair, shaking her head in disbelief.

"See what I mean?" Geneva repeated, now finding something of interest on her plate.

"Gertrude, how long can you keep this up?" Grace demanded.

"Running every night?" Gertrude asked, her eyes crinkling and the corners of her mouth turning up.

"Now, I'm serious," Grace said, suppressing her own laughter. "I mean working all day and all night, too. And now you're adding road races as a nightcap. Really, Gertrude."

"I know." Gertrude lay down her fork, the laughter fading from her eyes, her face gradually sagging into tiredness. "I need to find another apartment, somewhere closer to the hospital. One of these nights I'm going to lose the race," she said, her face cracking with a grin.

"You need more than a new apartment, Miss Green," Grace declared, mustering up her seriousness. "You need a vacation."

"A vacation?" Geneva asked, her fork pausing in mid bite. "You've got to be kidding."

"I'm not kidding." Then gesturing toward Dr. Beatty, Geneva added, "And it might do you some good, too, young lady."

"Me?" And Geneva stopped eating again.

"Truth is, we're all working too hard," Grace said, her voice reflecting her own weariness.

Gertrude stopped eating and looked at her two companions. The lines around the eyes, especially of the young obstetrician, spoke volumes about the amount of sleep she wasn't getting. Even Grace's eyes reflected back to Gertrude the same bone tiredness that comes of too much responsibility and too few people to share it. As a sense of her own weariness grew in her mind, Gertrude realized that Grace was right. But what to do about it?

"You got some ideas?" Gertrude asked.

"Over the next month we have several people coming back from furlough," Grace said with measured cadence. "Each of us has people we could trust to carry our responsibilities . . . for a while."

"How long a while?"

"Ten days."

"You've been thinking about this for some time, haven't you?"

"I know the boat and the sailing time and the destination," Grace said.

"Where?" Geneva asked, always ready for an adventure.

"Japan."

Gertrude visibly stiffened.

"It's really inexpensive," Grace quickly offered. "And there's no war . . . there."

"And I know a friend in Nikko who can take us to the temples there," Geneva said, excitedly buying in.

"And we can go shopping in Kobe," Grace added. "And stay at the San in Tokyo."

"And see the Olsens and the Thurstons," Gertrude said as she caught their enthusiasm. "And I could buy some more kimonos to send home to Mother and exchange enough money at the bank to actually pay for the trip."

"You can?" Grace asked in surprise.

"You bet."

And just that quickly three heads bent together, bobbing and nodding over the cafeteria table, as three minds planned a short respite from the refugees, and the border guards, and the hectic pace that had become their China.

Chapter 32

FOCUSING ON THE WORK

"Gertrude, are you still here?"

Grace Dale and Geneva Beatty strolled arm in arm to the deck chair where Gertrude lounged, eyes closed. At their question, she opened one eye and peered up at them.

"Of course," Gertrude grinned. "I'm just around the corner from our third-class cabins. And I can hear the concert ever so much better from here."

"I meant—still sitting," Geneva said saucily. She pulled a deck chair up close to Gertrude and plopped down with a puff of exhaustion.

Gertrude waved her hand dismissively. "Mercy, child! I've been up since 5:30 and made the rounds of the deck a dozen times."

"Sounds like Japan was just the ticket for our favorite head nurse, u'mm, Doctor?" Grace pulled up her own chair to face the other two.

"I'll say," Geneva laughed. "And I don't know if I like her better tired or rested."

"Well, I hope you can stand me, Miss Dale," Gertrude said in mock disdain, "since we're going to be neighbors as soon as we get back to Shanghai."

"I didn't know you were moving over to Connaught Road, too," Geneva said. She leaned forward and shaded her eyes to look at Grace.

"Yes, my Charles is arranging for our things and some of Gertrude's heavier furniture to be moved while we're on this trip."

The three friends sat together in silence, gently caressed by the warm sun, the brisk wind, and the salt spray, each lost in her own silent thoughts.

"Do you feel more connected or more disconnected?" Grace asked after a few minutes.

"To what . . . or from what?" Gertrude tried to follow this new train of thought.

"You know, from everything, from God—maybe, or from the purpose of your life." Looking into blank stares Grace struggled to make her friends understand. "Whenever I'm in the middle of the ocean I feel a sort of disconnect from the rest of life, like it's not really there, like I'll just float on the ocean for ever and ever."

"Amen," Gertrude added, closing her eyes.

"I'm serious," Grace protested.

"Me, too," Gertrude replied. "It was just what I needed, to be disconnected for a while."

"From everything?"

"I don't know. Maybe."

"I guess I'm lost on this one," Geneva sighed. "I'm still looking for my purpose in life."

"Well, one of the purposes in life is to eat," Gertrude said, suddenly sitting forward. "And that reminds me that we have an appointment for dinner tonight in the cabin of the fifth mate, Mr. McDonald."

"So that explains the early morning strolls on the deck," Geneva said knowingly.

"But, Gertrude, what do you know about him?" Grace admonished.

"Don't worry about Gertrude," Geneva joked, "always lots of boyfriends, but never a beau."

"Just disconnected." Gertrude smiled reassuringly. "For a little while, just disconnected."

"Students. If I could have your attention . . ." Gertrude spoke in both Chinese and English, translating for herself and instantly getting the attention of the new freshman nursing class. The tiny classroom in the second floor back hall was barely able to contain the desks of the seven students and the Superintendent of Nurses who for the next hour would be their teacher.

"It is my pleasure to welcome you to your first anatomy class at the Shanghai Sanitarium and Hospital Nursing School."

Gertrude was pleased that they all seemed attentive and at ease with her Chinese pronunciation. "Thank you, Mr. Hsu," she murmured quietly to herself.

"I pray that you are comfortably moved into your rooms out on Yu Yuen Road. I know that some of you will be a bit crowded when the other new students arrive from Hankow."

Gertrude thought of the Japanese air raids and invasion forces that were even now attacking Wuhan and shuddered inwardly. *Dr. Miller, what of your fight against disease now?* she thought fearfully.

"I know that Thelma and Peter are living with their families and not with the rest of you." The round smiling Chinese face of Thelma Chang and the strong Russian countenance of Peter Ivanov looked up innocently at her from the second row of desks. "But they will have their own special problems of transportation in getting here each morning in time for worship—which is at 6:00 a.m.—sharp. Don't be late."

She watched the shock march across their faces as the reality of her pronouncement settled into their consciousness. *One of the first lessons of the new probies,* she thought, *is the appreciation of how early nursing duties begin.*

"There will be two classes for anatomy, one in English and one in Chinese." She watched the faces of Thelma and Peter visibly relax. "And I will be teaching both of them."

And last year at this time I was amazed that Mrs. Coulston was teaching in Chinese. Gertrude smiled at herself, pleased that she had gotten at least one of the purposes in her life correct.

The building at the China Division Headquarters where the English church services were held was damaged beyond repair. But the Chinese Church building was far enough removed from the Ningkuo Road compound that it had suffered no obvious structural damage. Consequently, as soon as travel was allowed into the area, both the English speakers and the Chinese conducted services there, holding separate Sabbath schools but sharing a combined Divine Service at the 11:00 o'clock hour.

As Gertrude headed up the few steps leading to the heavy oak doors of the entry vestibule she spotted Grace and Charles Dale talking with Thelma Chang and a young Chinese man who looked vaguely familiar. As she approached the group, she puzzled over his narrow facial features and large expressive eyes. The short stature and thick black hair cut in the European style were commonplace for young Chinese men. *Do I know you?* she thought.

"Gertrude," Dr. Charles Dale called out, "Come and meet these young people." He came down and escorted her up the steps by the elbow.

"I know Thelma already," Gertrude said, offering her hand. "Happy Sabbath, Thelma."

"Miss Green," Thelma responded.

"And this young man looks vaguely familiar." Gertrude spoke as she turned, retrieving her hand and offering it to him.

"This young man is famous, Miss Green," Charles said warmly. "A translator for the Division—so you might have seen him in the cafeteria, maybe—a singer on our new radio program, and a medical student at St. John's Medical School where I teach half time."

Gertrude noted the pride in Dr. Dale's eyes and the corresponding reverence in the youthful but solemn Chinese face that looked from him to her.

"Paul Hwang." The young man introduced himself in a crisp, firm voice as he took her hand.

Gertrude's eyes perceptibly widened as her mouth opened without speaking.

"The son of Dr. Hwang?" she finally managed.

"The same. My father." A shadow of emotion lent a slight tremor to the otherwise proud statement. "Did you know him?"

"I met him—once—at Chiao Tuo Tseng." Gertrude recalled the owlish face and the fatherly demeanor that had so captivated her. "I am so sorry about his death."

"He was murdered," Thelma said sharply.

Paul turned slightly and placed a restraining hand on her arm, but said nothing.

Interesting, Gertrude thought. *Here is a budding Oriental relationship that has evolved to the point where the Chinese girl can insert herself into the conversation of the Chinese boy without retribution. Or is it that she is from Australia and is unaware of what is proper? Or is it just that she is very forward?* Gertrude smiled at her own Oriental bent of mind which allowed her to make these cultural observations while maintaining an innocent expression.

"Paul is singing for special music today." It was Grace who broke the spell.

"I play the piano for the choir and for special music sometimes," Gertrude said. "If you should need me to accompany you in the future, Brother Hwang, I would be most happy to be of service."

"I shall remember," Paul said, releasing her hand with a slight bow but no visible trace of a smile.

A serious Chinese face holds a smile and a smiling Chinese face is dangerous, Gertrude recalled from the father of this serious young man, carefully concealing her own joy with this new friend.

> 526 Bubbling Well Road
> Shanghai, China
> November 27, 1938

Dearest Mother:

I sure wondered what happened at home because it had been over six weeks and no letters came from anyone. Then this last week a letter came up from Hong Kong by Clipper and I was certainly glad to hear from you. I can write to you every two weeks as that is the only time the Canadian ships leave for America. No American "Dollar Line" ships come here anymore so we are dependent on the Canadians for our mail and all passengers, coming and going.

We sure are busy at the hospital all right. The place is full and of course that always means a lot of work for me. I am studying medical Chinese and teaching in Chinese and English. And as the Superintendent of Nurses, I schedule and run the operating room, give anesthesia occasionally, and still take my shifts working in the wards. Miss Ragsdale has come from the central part of China, from Yencheng Hospital where the fighting is, and Mrs. Paul has returned from furlough with her husband, who is a physician. They will both work and that will help me out so much. It will cut my burdens in half and I won't mind one bit since I have been doing the work of about three people.

This month is a busy one for me. I have been getting ready for Christmas, wrapping and boxing up all the Christmas presents to send home. I had them ready two weeks ago but the boy who was to mail them somehow had trouble and did not get there before the post office closed. I sure could have crowned him. Now I will have to mail them tomorrow on the boat and hope they get there on time.

I am also getting ready to move into my new apartment at Hamilton House which is only two blocks from The Bund. It is a beautiful place with hot water and steam heat—no more coal buckets for me! My studio couch, carved desk and bookcase will look really swell with the baby grand piano in the big room. And I will be able to practice one hour every day. With an all-electric kitchen and a large closet with built in drawers I will be all settled in by the first of next week. There is twenty-four-hour elevator service and from my sixth-floor balcony I can see all the boats going up and down the river. A pretty ritzy place, I'd say! And the week after I decided to move in, they lowered the monthly rent by $10. That didn't make me mad!

I will be living there all alone as Charles and Grace Dale have moved out to Rubicon Road. So I am glad for lots of friends although I have to travel some to see them. My new friend, Paul Hwang lives out on the Yu Yuen compound to be nearer the medical school where he is a medical student. And June Follette lives out there, too, to be nearer the maternity center. Dr. Geneva Beatty lives there but she will be leaving the middle of this next month.

Everyone had a sort of surprise birthday party for me this last September at June's apartment. I decided I am getting old at 31 years of age. Turns out it was about the last bash that the four of us will have before we all separate.

Now for some bad news. Mrs. Griggs had a severe heart attack and Dr. Griggs had to resign his position here as China Division President and take her home. We were all sad to see them go under such circumstances. And I know it will make you sad also, as I know you remember him from his visit to the house.

I am sorry you did not like the summer kimonos they sent to you from the school in Japan. All of us here have them and just love wearing them. It is exactly what the Japanese wear in the summer time. The colors are so vivid that, on the streets when you see the Japanese, it is just one mass of color. I suppose to appreciate them more you really ought to see the Japanese people with them on for yourself.

Don't worry about sending the money for them until you have a chance to sell them. And if you can't sell the summer ones, don't bother to send the money. But if you do sell them, send me $2.00 for each one that you sell as that is what it cost me. If you can sell them for more, keep the money for yourself. But I can't send any more of them unless I get enough money to cover their cost because I don't make very much and living is very high here in Shanghai. You can send the money by money order.

Must close as it is getting time for supper and I don't miss any meals. Remember me to everyone there.

Heaps of love from your loving daughter,

Gertrude xxxxxooooo

Chapter 33

STRUGGLING WITH LOSS

"Gertrude, hurry up! The Bransons are about to disembark," Geneva called from the gangway above her.

Gertrude waved in acknowledgment while trying to concentrate on mailing her packages.

"And this one is going to Rochester, New York," she said as she slid the large box through the iron-grilled window to the uniformed young woman at the counter. She anxiously glanced up and over her shoulder while waiting for her change. *Won't do to be the one holding everyone up, especially since it's the new president of the Division.* Gertrude's thoughts expanded to all the people who were coming every month to Shanghai, now that the war was in full swing in the central part of China. *Well, the extra help is certainly appreciated,* she mused as she turned quickly from the postal window, clutching her money.

Gertrude jolted to a stop, her arms pinned in front of her. Two escaped pennies cascaded to the floor and rolled to a stop against the bulkhead. Where there had been an open corridor, Gertrude now stared at a wall of blue worsted wool and gold buttons.

"My dear Miss Green, what a pleasant surprise."

"Mr. McDonald," Gertrude responded as she looked up into a smiling, ruddy face topped with thick blond hair. "We do seem to be bumping into each other," she laughed as she quickly released herself from his arms and bent to retrieve the straying coins.

"I'm sorry, Miss Green." McDonald stepped back, bowing slightly, trying to recover. "U'mm . . . I was wondering . . ."

"I'm sorry, Mac," Gertrude interrupted, "but I have people waiting for me." She stepped forward to brush past him in the corridor.

He placed his large hand on her left arm, arresting her progress.

"Please, Miss Green, . . . Gertrude."

She looked into the earnest pale blue eyes under his shaggy brows and paused.

"The *Empress of Canada* will be in port for two weeks this time and I don't know how to contact you." He paused for breath. "I was wondering if I might call on you, perhaps take you out to tea . . . some place you might know."

Gertrude's eyes sparkled as a small smile teased the corners of her mouth. She bit her lip to control it. Carefully she placed her small right hand on the back of his hand that still rested on her arm.

"Of course, Mr. McDonald," she said quietly. "I would be very pleased. You may call for me at the Shanghai Sanitarium and Hospital on Bubbling Wells Road. I never miss a meal."

"I don't know how you do it, Gertrude," Mrs. Hartwell said as she brought the china tea service into the living room. "Your piano accompaniment follows along ever so nicely behind my marimba. And my husband says I'm not the easiest person to follow." She laughed at her own little joke.

Gertrude laughed with her. "I get to practice all the time because I have a baby grand piano at my apartment at Hamilton House."

"When do you practice—after midnight?" Mrs. Hartwell laughed again. "You always seem to be at the hospital."

"Well, I don't bang when I play and, so far, no one has complained." Gertrude took a sip from her cup. "What is this?" she asked. "It's delicious."

"It's a blend I found in the market—of barley and some other local herbs." Mrs. Hartwell held her own cup to her lips. "The Chinese do make other things to drink besides tea."

Gertrude slowly set her cup in its saucer and considered for a moment. "I don't have anyone staying with me anymore, so I can practice the Christmas program whenever I want to." She thought again of how much she cherished her solitude and quietness. "In fact, I can do pretty much whatever I want to."

"Don't you have anyone to share morning worship with?" Mrs. Hartwell mused, not really hearing. "Chaplain and I enjoy the Morning Watch reading together every day."

"Oh, no. I always have my own worship by myself," Gertrude said. She unconsciously pursed her lips trying to remember the last time she'd read her morning devotional.

Gertrude looked up to see Mrs. Hartwell pondering, her head cocked to one side in puzzlement.

"The Dales used to share an apartment with you, didn't they?" she probed.

Gertrude set down her cup and dabbed her mouth. "Yes, and Dr. Beatty and June Follette and the Meislers—they all used to be my roommates. But now that we have more space we've gone our separate ways."

"Aren't you lonely?" Mrs. Hartwell continued her search.

"No, not really." Gertrude smiled. "Besides I have lots of new friends such as Ethel Porter and Dorothy Wheeler. In fact, several of them are helping me to plan a going away tea for Geneva Beatty before she leaves in two weeks." Gertrude chose one of the small cookies from the silver tray.

"A *tea*?" Mrs. Hartwell latched on.

"That's what Mr. McDonald calls it. It's a dinner, you know."

"And who is Mr. McDonald?" Mrs. Hartwell didn't try to hide her piqued curiosity.

"The fifth mate on the *Empress of Canada*, the boat we sailed on three months ago," Gertrude said offhandedly, taking a bite of cookie. "He's Canadian, but his father is from Scotland and his mother is from France."

Mrs. Hartwell carefully set down her cup on the Chinese nest of tables next to her chair. "Is he an Adventist boy?" she asked hopefully.

"U'mm . . . I don't think so. He's probably Presbyterian." Gertrude didn't know what church he might attend and really didn't know why that was important.

"Do you think that's wise?" Mrs. Hartwell sat well forward in her seat, trying to come closer to her young charge.

Gertrude stopped eating and reconsidered the past two minutes of conversation. "You're worried about me, aren't you?" Her eyes narrowed slightly.

"Shouldn't I be?"

"I don't think so. It's only a dinner invitation." Gertrude forced a smile, but to herself, she thought, *And besides, you're not my mother.*

"Well, whatever you think, dear," Mrs. Hartwell said, sitting back in her chair and forcing her own smile. "I just worry about our girls, you know." She paused. "Just let your conscience be your guide. That's what I always say."

The various nationalities living within the International Settlement strove mightily to create an atmosphere of normalcy amidst the obvious and over-whelming evidences of war all around them. Large, multinational corporations that profited from both sides of the conflict and embassies that represented their countries' financial as well as political agendas cooperated monetarily in promoting a calm reassurance in the minds of those whose physical presence in Shanghai guaranteed the continuing influence of the organizations they represented. Embassies hosted big-name entertainers on tour. Corporations sponsored museums and libraries. Wealthy individuals and cultural connoisseurs sponsored and promoted participation in local symphonies and mass choirs. There was no current celebrity of ballet, opera, theater, or literature who was a stranger to the expatriates of Shanghai.

"I just love the symphony," Mrs. Maurer bubbled, straightening her skirt as she followed Gertrude from the ladies room. "We used to go all the time in the States and I was afraid we wouldn't have that opportunity here. I'm so glad you asked us to attend."

"Yes, I used to go to the Boston Symphony when I was in Melrose," Gertrude answered, not looking at her companion, hurriedly excusing herself through the crush of ladies in the small hallway.

"Are you all right?" Mrs. Maurer asked when they emerged into the lobby.

"I'm fine . . . now," Gertrude whispered, leaning close to her companion. "I just don't like close spaces."

"I wondered," Mrs. Maurer answered. "You seemed to be preoccupied all evening."

"Just been thinking about the hospital board actions," Gertrude said, frowning and shaking her head, trying to drive away the memories of the last week.

The square frame and bald head of Dr. Maurer approached from the open door of the salon. "Well, ladies, are we all set to return?" he asked, rubbing his hands together as if to warm them.

"I was just telling Gertrude how grateful we are for her invitation tonight," Mrs. Maurer prattled. "And she was saying how upset she was at the hospital board actions."

"That's not what I said." Gertrude looked sharply at her tattler.

"I'm sorry, my dear, what were you saying?" Mrs. Maurer was smooth as honey.

"I was just saying that . . . well, I wasn't expecting to be voted out as the Superintendent of Nurses and be replaced by Mrs. Paul, that's all." Gertrude tried to control her sharpness but failed utterly.

"I think some thought you would be pleased," Dr. Maurer interjected. "We knew how busy you all have been without any help for so long. Just wanted to spread the work around." He wrinkled his brow as if truly concerned. "Mrs. Meisler was also replaced by Ethel Porter as Director of the Nursing School. Do you think she is upset as well?"

"I don't know how she felt," Gertrude shot back, "but I know how I felt." Gertrude turned away, flustered and blushing at such a display of emotion in front of people she hardly knew.

"Oh dear, Harold," Mrs. Maurer said earnestly, "Do you think they were too hasty?"

"Actually, we wanted to free up Gertrude here to take charge of opening up the Range Road Clinic in February," he confided. "That's not officially announced yet, mind you," he added as Gertrude turned to him with a puzzled look. "But I was just discussing it with Elder Branson and Dr. Paul this last Friday."

"Doesn't anyone talk to the nurses anymore?" Gertrude fumed as her mind shifted gears and shot into overdrive. "Do you know how much planning that will take?"

"All in good time, Miss Green," he responded with an edge in his voice. "It is still at least six weeks away. And we will consult with you when the time is right."

Mrs. Maurer stepped between the combatants. "Isn't it time to return to the concert, Harold?"

Dr. Maurer glanced about at the dwindling crowd in the lobby. "Yes, my dear, I think it is." He touched his wife lightly on the elbow while sweeping his free arm toward the open salon doors. "Ladies, Beethoven's Third awaits us."

Gertrude turned quickly and strode toward the darkened concert hall, leaving the Maurers to bring up the rear.

"Doctor, you are being totally unreasonable."

"No, Miss Green, you cannot. And that is final."

Ed Miesler could hear the conversation even from the end of the hall in the administrative wing. He approached the open heavy wooden door and reached to close it, fearful of what the Chinese workers might think of this Western style confrontation.

"Ed," Dr. Maurer called out. "Ed, please come in." Dr. Maurer appeared at the door, opening it wider.

"I'm sorry, sir," Ed Meisler said as he entered the office. "I couldn't help overhearing. I thought I would just close the door." He stopped short when he saw Gertrude standing in front of the desk, her arms crossed, her green eyes snapping in defiance.

"Come in," Dr. Maurer said brusquely. "Have a seat."

"But no one else is seated," Ed observed, looking from one to the other. He turned back to the door. "Perhaps if I just left."

"No," Dr. Maurer commanded, then more softly, "please stay." He sat heavily in his large swivel chair behind his desk. "Miss Green and I are having a disagreement. Perhaps you can help."

"I don't know. I can try."

Gertrude eyed him warily, not knowing if he were friend or foe and suspicious of the answer.

"Miss Green is taking another trip to Japan and wishes to take some money with her," Dr. Maurer said. "Two hundred dollars, U.S."

Ed Meisler gasped. "Whatever for. It costs only six dollars for the fare."

Gertrude's fiery eyes settled on Ed in dark confirmation of her previous misgivings about whose side he would be on.

"Besides, it's illegal to carry that much money out of China in Chinese currency or in U.S. dollars," Ed added, recognizing the seriousness of the conversation. "You could get you and us in a lot of hot water, Gertrude."

"Do you know what the exchange rate for U.S. dollars is here in China?" Gertrude shot at him.

"Yes. It's $6.50 Chinese to $1.00 U.S."

"And do you know what the exchange rate is in Japan for Chinese dollars?"

"Yes. It's about three to one . . ." Ed paused, realizing what she was doing. "You're taking money from here and exchanging it twice and making more money."

"Almost doubling it, actually," she said smartly. "And do you know what we get paid here, Mr. Meisler?" She began to advance toward him. "And do you know how expensive it is to live here, Mr. Meisler?"

"Gertrude, it's illegal."

"Not for tourists."

"You're not a tourist."

"I am when I'm in Japan."

"It's not about the money," Dr. Maurer said quietly.

Gertrude turned, eyes burning hot. "Then I'd like to know what it is about." She placed both hands squarely on the desk and leaned forward as if she were about to spring up and perch on it like a hawk. *Where do these men get off telling me what to do?* she wanted to shout. *Why can't people just let me be?*

"It's about *Who* you work for, Miss Green," Dr. Maurer continued with hands folded on top of each other. "It's about *Who* I work for; *Who* we represent. And I am not referring to the hospital or to the church. I work for the Lord."

Gertrude blinked, first at Dr. Maurer and then at Ed Meisler.

"Men," she muttered sardonically. She retreated from her perch and slunk out of the office, leaving the door ajar.

On January 15, 1939, Gertrude and Miss June Follette began 11 days of cruising on the *Empress of Canada*, touring and sightseeing in Japan, buying kimonos to send home, and exchanging enough money in various banks to pay for the trip.

Chapter 34

LOSING THE PURPOSE

In the middle of March the Shanghai Hospital School of Nursing held a capping ceremony for the new probies, making them full-fledged student nurses. Gertrude's contribution to this joyous occasion was to celebrate with a party for her students and her friends.

The party was held at the Yu Yuen flat of June Follette and Ethel Porter because it was closer to where everyone lived than Gertrude's spacious apartment at Hamilton House. Grace Dale and Dorothy Wheeler helped plan the party. Ed Meisler organized the menu and procured the necessary food items through his connections with the cafeteria. Just the same, everyone knew that this was Gertrude's party.

Dressed in the latest just-below-the-knee-length acquisition from Wing On's, she circulated among the various groups of guests, picking up conversations, adding touches of humor, hearing news tidbits.

"Did you see Elsie Liu in the full body cast we did this last week?" was the hilarious lead line into the topic of discussion among the Chinese nursing students who had just been capped.

"They thought I had TB, but I thought I was getting a hernia from carrying all that water up to the second floor." Gertrude listened as Thelma Chang explained to a mixed group of Asians and Americans in the far corner of the kitchen why she had dropped out of the nursing class. Gertrude noted that Paul Hwang was standing next to Thelma, obviously still smitten with her.

Gertrude brought a tray of cookies to the young graduate nurses talking with Ethel Porter, the new director of the nursing school. "You see him in surgery all the time, Miss Green. What do we need to know about Dr. Truman, the new surgeon?" one of the nurses asked. Her reply—"That he is a surgeon, girls. That should tell you everything you need to know"—got a chorus of laughs and knowing nods.

"I see Dr. and Mrs. Paul came," June Follette whispered as she sidled up to Gertrude who stood at the stove pouring more cups of hot cocoa. "Did you invite them?"

"Sure," Gertrude said with a big grin. "I met with her and got everything all straightened out."

"I bet you did," June said, glancing toward the Pauls who were deep in a discussion with the Hartwells on the living room sofa.

"I did," Gertrude said seriously. "We're going to the Chocolate Shoppe next Tuesday evening for dinner. Want to come along and see?" Gertrude scooped up her tray of hot cocoa and headed for the group clustered around the piano.

"I wouldn't miss it for the world," June called after her, chuckling to herself and shaking her head in disbelief.

"Gertrude, what's this I hear about your moving again?" Grace Dale asked as Gertrude set her lacquered tray on the top of the upright piano. "I thought you liked your apartment."

"Correction: I *love* my apartment," Gertrude said emphatically to Grace and Eileen Meisler, who was sitting at the keyboard. "And I have no intention of moving." She lowered her voice. "It's Dr. Maurer again," she said, looking around for unintended listeners. "He thinks my apartment is too expensive. But he has another think coming. My apartment is heaven and I've waited too long to find just the sort of place I wanted."

Eileen continued to play one of the latest popular melodies while Gertrude reached for the tray, taking a cup for herself. Halfway through the chorus, Eileen paused in her playing and gazed up at Gertrude.

"Do you ever wonder if this is what it's all about?" she asked. "I mean, just parties and work and shopping and eating at Sun Ya's?"

"Nope, I never do," Gertrude said cheerily. She lifted her cup in a playful toast. "I love what I do and I love where I am. And that tells me everything I need to know." Carefully she took a cautious sip of the hot liquid.

In late April each year the China Division held a Spring Council in Shanghai—or elsewhere if the pressures of war demanded it. Here the presidents of unions and missions in the China field, and the directors of hospitals, schools, and publishing houses reported on the year's progress in the work of taking the gospel to the war-torn country of China.

Whenever she could throughout these two weeks, Gertrude attended the evening meetings to hear personally told stories of missionary peril and God's miraculous interventions. These stories were almost always followed by passionate sermons of exhortation for all church workers, wherever they were assigned, to bravely follow in the footsteps of these pioneering examples. Gertrude loved the excitement and thrill of the adventure stories. But the exhortations left her cold and unmoved. In fact, they didn't touch her at all.

"Dr. Quimby, Dr. Quimby!" Gertrude called to the retreating form.

Paul Quimby turned his spare frame about and immediately recognized his former student. He threaded his way through the hurrying throng now exiting from the meeting.

"Gertrude, what a pleasant surprise," he said as he took the gloved hand she extended to him. "It's been a long time since Union Springs Academy. How are you doing here in the middle of this war?"

"We're all managing quite well," she said, deftly deflecting the conversation from herself. "I thought you were in the interior—or were going there." She squinted, trying to remember that particular report from last night's meeting.

"We're talking about making a trip to see what the situation is at the old college site in Chiao Tuo Tseng. But we still must get travel passes from the Japanese."

Gertrude made a face. "They're in control of everything outside of the International Settlement," she snapped.

"Not quite everything," he assured her, patting the worn black Bible he held in the crook of his arm, then added, "Weren't the Loewens and the Holleys with you in Nanking?"

"Yes! Have you seen them?" Gertrude's demeanor changed abruptly as she thrilled at the thought of her old friends.

"They're here from Chungking. Just got in last night, I believe." He smiled at being able to bring such happy news. "I think they're staying with the Hartwells at the Yu Yuen Road compound."

Although it was located just to the west of the official confines of the International Settlement, Jessfield Park was a frequent getaway for foreigners living in Shanghai. It was outside the Settlement boundaries and under the control of the Japanese, so no Chinese refugees were encamped there. Adopting an attitude of Oriental monarchial benevolence, the Japanese allowed the foreigners the use of the park as a generous gesture, just as if they had planned it to be seen as such.

On Sabbath afternoon, Gertrude accompanied Chaplain and Mrs. Hartwell, Ada and Leighton Holley, and Marvin and Gert Loewen in strolling through one of the few open stretches of green grass in China that did not stink of gunpowder or human waste.

"It's so good to see all of you here again, safe and sound," Mrs. Hartwell said as she looked around at the couples following them across the grounds. Gertrude, walking closely beside Gert Loewen, gave her shoulder a squeeze as she gazed around fondly at her friends who had experienced so much with her.

Despite the 18-month-old who toddled beside her mother, the Holleys were holding hands like newlyweds. *No surprise there,* Gertrude noted to herself. But the Loewens walked closer than Gertrude remembered until she observed that Marvelyn wasn't walking in between them. She'd been left in Chungking in the care of trusted friends, the round about trip to Shanghai being thought too dangerous for a small child. Still Gertrude thought that Gert Loewen had a certain glow about her that was not at all natural for a mother who was missing her daughter.

Chaplain Hartwell stood under a large tree heavy with the young, green shoots of spring. "So much has happened since Gertrude and the Holleys joined us for Christmas," he said as he watched Gertrude and Mrs. Hartwell spread two blankets on the ground. "And someone else was there, wasn't there?"

"It wasn't us," Marvin Loewen offered, squeezing his wife's hand.

"It was Ed and Eileen Meisler," his wife reminded him.

"Oh sure," he said, seating himself next to his wife on the blanket. "Now I remember."

Gertrude noted with admiration—and some envy—the look of years of understanding pass between this husband and wife. *I've never shared a look like that with anyone,* she considered, wondering why.

Then she turned to the Holleys who were making a family nest for the baby across from her. "So where did you go when you left Peking?" Gertrude began.

"We were transferred to Hunan Province near Yencheng," Ada said, grabbing at the baby who was trying to stand up and walk away.

"But the war was so unpredictable, we've just been moved from one place to another," Leighton added, smilingly watching his wife struggle with 25 pounds of independence. "The hardest part," he said looking up at Gertrude, "was leaving behind those whom I had just trained, knowing they could not escape the war as easily as I could." Gertrude read the pain of loss in his eyes. *You've seen more than you're sharing, haven't you, Leighton?* And she wanted to know more.

"Were you ever in any real danger?" Gertrude leaned closer to them, sensing that they possessed something she knew was missing in her life here in Shanghai.

"No," Ada said confidently, "The Lord was always near."

"I just hope He was near those we left behind," Leighton murmured.

"Didn't Miss Ragsdale come from Yencheng?" Mrs. Hartwell asked, knowing the answer but looking for more news.

"She came out when we did," Leighton answered, "She was the Director of Nurses there but the war was coming too close, even for her."

"Will she try to go back?" Mrs. Hartwell persisted.

"No one will be going back there," Leighton said in a low voice.

"Actually she's going home on furlough," Gertrude said, thinking of the pert young lady who'd been such a cheerful addition to the nursing staff in those early, busy days.

"We were in Honan Province, near Wuhan," Marvin said, anticipating Gertrude's next question when he saw her take Gert's hand and squeeze it. "But we moved to Chungking when the offensive push came our way."

"And I took the Christmas evacuation train to Hong Kong," Gertrude added. "It all seems like such a long time ago." Then remembering, she said, "And Dr. Miller?"

"In Manila, I think," Leighton put in. "Overseeing some project there."

"His heart is forever in the work," Chaplain Hartwell observed.

And he doesn't see the war, Gertrude thought, wondering at such blindness in an obviously brilliant man. Suddenly she looked up, her green eyes carefully searching first the face of Gert and then Marvin. "So why are you here? Why didn't you stay in Chungking?"

"I probably wouldn't have come, except . . ." He looked at his wife for permission.

"I'm pregnant again," Gert said, demurely lowering her eyes.

"Oh, my dear," Mrs. Hartwell gasped, fanning herself.

It's the way women have been reacting to that news for thousands of years, Gertrude thought as she patted Gert's hand. *Shocked at the public announcement and relieved that it wasn't them.* Out loud she said, "Did you check with one of the doctors? What do they think?"

"Dr. Truman doesn't see a problem—this time," Gert said, trying to produce a small smile which quickly faded.

"We've prayed about it, Gertrude. It's in the Lord's hands," Marvin said simply, his strong arm gently draped over the shoulder of his wife.

In as few words as possible, Gertrude explained to the Hartwells what the Holleys already knew, the tragic end of Gert Loewen's last pregnancy. As she did so, she watched Marvin's eyes brim with tears and felt Gert's grip tighten even as she buried her face in her husband's shoulder. Such personal sadness Gertrude had not known, except in others.

"Makes our lives here seem pretty simple," Gertrude said aloud, unconsciously retreating from the painful memories in Kuling of the tragic loss of Gert's second child. "Just work and parties and shopping and eating at Sun Ya's." She adjusted her feet which were tucked under her, mentally searching for a place of comfort and finding none.

"Just leave the Japanese alone and they'll leave you alone." Gazing around the group she added, "No great crisis and no need for the Lord." In the silence that followed, Gertrude was stung by a moment of self-awareness. She turned abruptly and addressed Chaplain Hartwell directly. "Am I missing something here?" she asked.

He shrugged and nodded slowly. "Could be" was all he would say.

Chapter 35

CARING FOR AN OLD FRIEND

"Yes, Miss Li. I heard my rings on the paging system," Gertrude said sharply, balancing on the ball of one foot with the other leg bent at the knee to stretch her higher above the tall counter. She peered intently down at the second-year nursing student who was engrossed in her charting and had not seen her approach. "Did you need me for something?"

"Miss Green, ah-h-h-h, yes," the student nurse said, groping for the truant paper partly hidden under a medicine tray. "The people in obstetrics sent a message. One of their patients is asking for you. Mrs. Loe-wen, I believe it says." The Chinese student pronounced the English name as if it were Chinese with the accent on the second syllable and looked up for confirmation of her efforts. But Gertrude was gone.

"Gert, are you all right?" Gertrude burst through the door of the ward and quickly scanned the four beds for the dear friend who carried the same name as she did.

Gert's pinched face attempted a brave smile as she waved from bed number three. "I think I'll be OK," she said as Gertrude rushed to her bedside. "I was just running a little fever with my stomach cold," she said in hushed tone, "and Dr. Truman thought I ought to be in here. Just being cautious, I guess." With lowered eyes, she offered her damp forehead where Gertrude placed her open palm for a long moment.

"I see the students are sponging you with cold compresses," Gertrude said, pulling up the wooden chair next to the bed and plopping into it. "Mercy, girl, you gave me a scare."

"I'm sorry," Gert said, her eyes still lowered and her mouth tight, "I didn't want to be any bother."

"You're not a bother, silly," Gertrude said. Then noticing the downcast eyes, she hunched forward and found Gert's trembling hand. "What's the matter?" she asked, as she leaned further forward, trying to see up into the soulful face.

Gert raised her eyes, brimming with tears. "I'm afraid," she whispered.

"Oh, Gert." Instantly Gertrude was sitting on the side of the bed, holding her hand, brushing clinging wisps of wet hair out of her eyes. "It's going to be all right." She gazed earnestly into the sad eyes. "It's going to be all right," she repeated, wishing it to be so.

"I just don't want to lose this one, too." Gert spoke haltingly, her lower lip quivering. She clutched Gertrude's fingers tightly. "And I need help."

"I'm here, Gert."

"I can't go home," Gert said, fighting to control her tears. "I won't be able to get back here if I have trouble this time. Chungking is too far away and too primitive." Her struggle allowed her to say nothing more but her eyes pleaded for help.

"Of course you can't go home," Gertrude said, patting Gert's hand between hers. Then without hesitation, adding, "You're going home with me—as soon as Dr. Truman thinks you're able."

"Oh, Gertrude, I couldn't."

"Oh, yes, you could. You and Marvelyn." Gertrude stood and placed Gert's hand under the covers with a professional reassuring pat. "Now you get well while I talk with Marvin about getting everyone's things sent to my apartment." She grinned. "You'll be fine. You'll see."

Gertrude hurried back to the X-ray department which competed mightily with her time in the operating room. *Just a few more films to file and then I'll go find Marvin Loewen,* she thought as she grabbed up the large pale green envelopes stacked on the desk.

"Miss Green."

Gertrude stared up into a bespectacled, cherubic face, full-cheeked, with a boyish grin, and covered by a straw stack of hair.

"Elder Branson," she said, shocked to see the President of the China Mission in the hospital.

"I was wondering if you could stop by my office tomorrow." He continued to lean into the doorway, smiling. "We have an opening, actually a critical position, in Yencheng." He was nothing if not straightforward. "I'd like you to go there and fill it."

"Your office?" Gertrude said, trying to digest the message in smaller bites. "Yes. At 2:00 o'clock?"

"Yes, I can." Gertrude scrambled to understand what he had just said and think of her schedule at the same time. "OK . . . thank you . . . I think."

"Very good. I'll see you then," he said, and was gone.

> 526 Bubbling Well Road
> Shanghai, China
> July 8, 1939

Dearest Mother,

Another week has passed and this is Sabbath, but I haven't been out of the house yet today. I had a cold, but the last three days I have had diarrhea so I decided I didn't need to go to church or anywhere. Actually it has been raining hard all week. When it rains like that, the Chinese don't go to church. It even wiped out the big Fourth of July picnic planned out at the old San on Rubicon Road. So that day I just stayed at the hospital and worked. We had four heavy operations yesterday and one today, but I just couldn't make it in and asked someone else to go.

You have asked several times before about my bicycle. I presume some Jap is riding it around Nanking as I left it there when I escaped and I do not have it anymore. If I should move out to Rubicon Road it would be nice to have one again. But in the Shanghai traffic I would get killed for sure.

The streets here are very different than at home. Besides cars, streetcars, and buses we have double-decker buses, rickshaws, wagons with coolies pulling them, wheelbarrows, horses and carriages, and people walking in the streets instead of on the sidewalks—and loads of bicycles of all kinds. I walk in the streets all the time but I wouldn't ride a bicycle out there.

Mrs. Loewen is living with me for two months until her baby comes. I think you remember her. She is the one I knew in Kuling who had the baby who died. Her daughter Marvelyn is also with us. She had dysentery this last week. So many children die with this here in China and I did worry till she got over it. But she is up and around now and I surely feel a load off my shoulders.

I need to talk with you about the $10.00 postal money order you sent to me. You see, the post office has a set rate of exchange and it is always the lowest rate in town. If I had accepted the money I would have received only $60 in Chinese since the bank rate for the day was $10.50 for each American dollar. I would have lost $40. I am not so rich that I can keep the post office supplied with money so I told them to send it back to you.

There are other ways to send the money such as "American Express Money Order"— those small blue slips of paper just like you send in the U.S., a personal check or a bank draft. I can get full draft for any of these. But the Post Office is the worst way to do it. The others I can hold until the exchange rate is up, like today when the exchange is $14 for each American dollar. So I hope you won't mind that I sent it back to you.

In fact, just keep the money. I am sending a camphor chest home that I know you will enjoy. The man making it will ship it for me and you can pay for the shipping when it arrives. Use this money and the money you get from the shopping baskets and the Chinese scissors that I sent. If you keep the money, then you will have the money to pay for it.

I have a big surprise for you. I am having something made for your birthday and Christmas present for this year. It is a beautiful black winter fur coat. Of course it is expensive but so much more reasonable than you could ever get in America. My problem is getting it to you. I will ask Miss Ragsdale, who is going home on furlough, to take it to the White Memorial in Los Angeles and then write to Ruth to pick it up there and mail it or take it to you this fall. You mentioned that you wanted a new winter coat with a fur collar but a whole fur coat will be much warmer and look very nice. People will think you are Madame Astor with a new fur coat.

I will be moving again. Elder Branson asked me to go to Yencheng to be the Director of Nursing in our hospital there. It is our largest hospital in China with 150 beds, three separate buildings for men, women, and TB patients, besides a large academy of 400 students. Elder Branson asked me to go a few weeks ago and at first I was very undecided. But I guess I am getting tired of the constant noise and terrible traffic here in Shanghai. Yes, it sounds like a big job but I guess there is no other way.

They say it is the nicest mission compound we have in China. I am told they have a swimming pool and tennis courts and wonderful fruit, peaches and apricots,—and strawberries! It is located in the central part of China in Honan province. This part is still held by the Chinese which of course means it will be slow getting letters in and out. And I will have to take all my own food supplies as the railroad lines have been cut. And I won't be able to take most of my Chinese things with me, like my carved desk and my dyed rugs. I certainly don't want to drag them up there and have them get lost. So I will be sending those things home as well with Miss Ragsdale, who was the head nurse in Yencheng for the last five years. This is my opportunity to get them home so if another war breaks out over here I will not have to worry about losing them.

She tells me that I will have my own apartment with a living room, two bedrooms, dining room, kitchen, and bathroom. Sounds nice, huh? This will be even nicer than my apartment here. By the way, my rent was going up by $30 next month and I was going to have to give it up anyway and move out to the Rubicon Road compound as soon as it was opened. But now I am told by Elder Branson to just sit tight here. They are planning to move me to Yencheng in August or September.

Well, I will close for now. I hope you enjoy the things I am sending home and that they get there all in one piece. Remember me to everyone.

With heaps of love to my dear mother,

Gertrude xxxxoooo

Chapter 36

CHANGING HER PLANS

Marvin Loewen was a big man and hard to miss, striding down the short hall to the four-bed ward near the end of the obstetrical wing. As Gertrude came toward him from behind the nursing desk, he spied her and quickened his pace.

"I got here as quickly as I could," he puffed. His eyes asked a thousand questions that Gertrude did not want to answer.

"Dr. Truman thought it was just a cold—on Sabbath—but he put her in the hospital anyway." Gertrude struggled for professional detachment. Her eyes brimmed over as she spoke but she did not look away. "But yesterday she had more trouble and we had to do a C-section to try to save the baby. But the baby didn't make it." Gertrude watched the hope die in his eyes as his large shoulders sank under the weight of the news.

"Is she in there?" Marvin asked huskily, inclining his head toward the ward.

With wet eyes and a mouth held in a firm, thin line Gertrude nodded. He turned and swiftly entered.

Gertrude didn't go home for the next three days. She spent her daytime teaching and working in the operating room and X-ray and her nights at Gert's bedside on the obstetrical wing. Except for some gas pains Gert Loewen did quite well physically. But the emotional pain was almost unbearable—for everyone.

"Hi." Marvin's voice spoke out of the early morning darkened hallway. Gertrude looked up from the nursing desk and gave him a tired smile. She rose as he approached the circle of light which marked out the boundaries of the all-night nursing vigil.

"Good news," she said. "It looks like she'll be able to go home today. Dr. Truman was in early, before his surgery started." She smiled again, encouraging a similar response from him, although he looked away before speaking.

"We've been talking, Gertrude," he said, avoiding her gaze. He hesitated. "She can't come home with me, to Chungking, I mean."

Gertrude heard his voice falter and wondered at the terrible strain they were enduring together now. *One of the blessings of not being married,* she thought. She waited and did not speak.

" I think . . . actually, we think she will do better if she goes home to be with her family for a while." He looked up, his head twisting to one side, like a little boy seeking approval or asking permission.

Gertrude desperately wanted to reassure this big man who stood before her all alone in the dark. "What do you mean . . . go home, Marvin?"

"She just needs to be near those who love her," he explained. Then a look of fear passed over his face. "No, no. We're doing OK." He smiled as his hands rose defensively, simultaneously, to wave off any other ideas. "We'll be fine. It's just the war . . . and the tension and . . ." He wavered as he sought a more acceptable explanation.

"And you need someone to go with her." It wasn't a question but a statement of fact.

"Well, actually, I hadn't thought of a way yet."

"But I have. Look, Marvin, Monday, the thirty-first of July, is my last day of work." Gertrude came out from behind the desk to reach him. "And I'm ready to go on a small vacation. Elder Branson says they're not ready for me to go to Yencheng just yet, that I should take a few days off." She stood facing him, head tilted up, wanting earnestly to implant hope. "I can accompany her on a boat to Japan and spend time with her. I'll see her safely off to America and return to Shanghai in no time. And I won't even be missed. What do you think?" She planted her hands jauntily on her hips.

"I would be so grateful," his deep voice rumbled with controlled emotion. "I can't get away and she can't go alone . . ." he started to explain.

"It's OK. I understand," she said, touching him lightly on the arm. "You're just lucky I'm not a very expensive chaperone. Now you go on in there and see if she's awake and I'll get us all ready for discharge." Gertrude pushed him playfully toward the door, then turned back to the desk and the nursing tasks at hand.

Asama Maru
August 17, 1939

Dearest Mother:

Well, here I am on the boat and having a glorious time of it. Tomorrow we arrive in Yokohama. We had a good time shopping in Kobe today just looking around. I want to buy everything I see but of course I don't have the money for that.

The ship is very nice and so is the food. It is so much fun to travel and one meets so may interesting people.

You will remember the friend I told about, Gert Loewen, who was staying with me. Well, she had to have a C-section and the baby died. The poor thing nearly went to pieces because she lost her last baby when we were all up in Kuling at the language school. So I am accompanying her and her daughter, Marvelyn, to Yokohama where I will put her on the boat to America. She is doing much better now. The ocean breezes have been good for her and we have had some good conversations. I sometimes wish I could just stay on this boat until it reached America but, of course, I can't do that.

When I get to Yokohama I plan to go to Lake Yamanoka at the foot of Mt. Fuji. Everyone says it is very beautiful and wonderful for swimming, hiking, eating, and boating and a good place to rest for a change. I have my return ticket but I am not sure how long I want to stay there or whether I will go see some more places. Elder Branson said I might take to the middle of September as it is very indefinite as to when I can go to Yencheng.

The American Consulate has refused to let any women and children go to the interior of China because of a nasty anti-British campaign that has become anti-American and anti-foreigner. So all my further plans must wait at least until I get back from vacation.

If I don't go to Yencheng when I come back from my vacation, I am planning to take some singing lessons and piano lessons. There is a good teacher here, a Russian lady, where I tried out my voice. She said I had good material to work with, so I think I might start when I return.

In your last letter I received your $12.00 by Postal Money Order from the sale of the kimonos. You'll probably be sore at me, but I am sending it back when it arrives. As I said before, I don't want to be the one paying all the postal people their salaries. At the Postal rate I could get only 72 Shanghai dollars. The rate of exchange in the banks was 17 to 1 and two days later it was 25 to one. At that rate I could be getting 300 Shanghai dollars. So unless you want to send an American Express Money Order, don't send it; just keep it. I think you can get American Express in Sibley's—at least you used to.

Well, they are ringing the dinner bell here on the boat. And you know me, I never miss a meal. I will sign off for now and write later, maybe from the lake resort.

Heaps of love and hugs from your loving daughter,

Gertrude

"Gertrude! Have you seen Marvelyn?" Gert Loewen frantically rushed across the observation deck between the rows of great wooden lounge chairs.

"Yes, she's with me," Gertrude laughed. "Where could she be, silly? We're all on the boat together."

Gert's eyes cast about wildly, still searching, darting to the railing and the open ocean beyond. Her hand clutched at Gertrude's arm.

"I just thought . . ." She turned to face Gertrude, tears welling up. "I . . . I was afraid . . ."

Gertrude gathered her up in a gentle embrace.

"And I thought you were doing so well," Gertrude whispered into her ear. "I'm sorry I gave you such a fright."

Gert slowly extracted herself and dabbed at her eyes with a well-worn hanky which she had retrieved from her skirt pocket. "I was . . . I am . . . I'll be all right," she said through trembling lips that tried to smile. "I'm still a bit shaky." She sat on the end of the nearest lounge chair as if she were too tired to stand up any longer. Slowly her hands began to smooth the wrinkles from her skirt, arranging the pleats, trying to establish some kind of order.

Gertrude bent at the waist, her right hand lightly drawing Gert's shoulders forward, bringing their faces close together. "Are you OK?" she asked quietly, searching Gert's eyes for the truth that Gert might not know herself.

Gert squinted up into the sun, closing one eye as she returned her gaze and smiled. "Yeah, I'm OK," she said as she rubbed the now irritated eye with the back of her hand. "Where did you say Marvelyn is?"

"She's back there in the cabin with Mr. Richards," Gertrude said as she stood and looked back over her left shoulder to the forward part of the ship where the officers' quarters were located.

"Who?" Gert strained forward to peer around Gertrude as if she might possibly see him.

"Oh, you know, dear," Gertrude said with a dismissive wave of her hand, still gazing forward, "that nice young man we met this morning at breakfast, Dick Richards, the fifth mate on this boat." Gertrude turned to her companion, extending her hand in invitation. "Come," she said lightheartedly as she began moving away, "we've been invited to his cabin for a private dinner."

Aboard *Empress of Japan*
Aug 24, 1939

Dearest Mother,

Well, here I am traveling again. You will probably have received my letter written on the boat going to Japan. I told you I was going to the mountains for ten days, but when I landed in Yokohama I changed my mind and stayed only one day. I saw Gert and Marvelyn Loewen off on the *Asama Maru* to America. Then I returned to Shanghai where I caught this boat which is going to take me on a nice sea cruise, first to Hong Kong and then to Manila in the Philippines.

I have never been there. So I will take a one-and-a-half week trip around the Orient and see the world—or at least this part of it. I will arrive in Hong Kong tomorrow at 7:00 a.m. and I will spend the day looking around and having a good time. Then I will be on my way to Manila where I will visit Ruth Atwell, the lady who was our house matron at the language school in Nanking. This is much more fun than staying in the mountains all by myself.

You always meet such nice people on the boat and we always have good food. I am riding third-class, but on this boat that is good. I have a cabin all to myself. I go in swimming every day and I am having an elegant time.

I have a cute outfit I wear on the boat: a blouse and a pair of shorts, and a cute pair of red sandals and red socks. The buttons on my blouse and shorts are red, so it all matches.

When in Shanghai yesterday I received your last two letters which came by air mail. I was glad to receive them and hear that you are having such a good time visiting Union Springs on weekends. I cannot imagine why they are sending the boxes I mail to you to New York City. That is funny. Hope you get it all OK. I have quite a few things in those boxes that it wouldn't be nice to lose, like the thousand-flower vases I bought.

Things are looking very bad in Europe right now and here the Japanese are making everything very hard. They are trying to block off Hong Kong and Shanghai so I don't know if this boat will even make it back. I guess it is a good thing I am going to Manila because it is at least American territory.

I will mail this in Hong Kong and maybe send it air mail—will see how much it costs.

You sure have a daughter who likes to gad about and I sure do love it. I wish you were here to go with me, but perhaps someday. I still don't know when I can get to Yencheng.

Loads and loads of love to my darling mother.

Gertrude

Chapter 37

ADJUSTING THE FOCUS

W ell, Gertrude Green!" Ruth Atwell exclaimed as she opened the door to her small apartment. "What a wonderful surprise." Ruth's round face wreathed with smiles as she reached for Gertrude's hand, drawing her forward. "Come in, my dear. Come in." Amid giggles of greeting from both, Ruth held the door while Gertrude sidled in.

Entering the spartan but comfortable sitting room, Gertrude set her small overnight suitcase in the middle of the floor and surveyed her surroundings. She noted the large, bulky standard issue "missionary" furniture tastefully interspersed with Filipino wicker pieces. *So like her,* Gertrude thought, *practical, yet homey.* Straight ahead she spotted a small kitchen and off to her left was a door or a hallway that probably led to a bedroom or two.

"It reminds me of Nanking," Gertrude said, turning to Ruth as she shut the door. "You were always so good at making places feel comfortable."

"Thank you, my dear, but I didn't have quite so much to work with here," Ruth said. "The transition here to Manila was a sudden one for all of us. And I think that some have not yet fully recovered." She motioned Gertrude to a doily-laden overstuffed chair which, with its table and festive lamp, occupied one whole wall of the small room. "Sit and talk. Catch me up on your life in Shanghai." She quickly sat opposite Gertrude and leaned forward expectantly. "And tell me what in the world you're doing here."

Gertrude collected her thoughts as she considered the short, round woman across from her. Ruth could have been her older sister by at least a decade. *What's so special about this woman?* she mused. *I'm not sure . . . except she is very nice and very practical. A little bit like my mother and has my sister's name.* And that thought made Gertrude smile.

"Actually I was in Japan putting Gert Loewen on a boat to the United States. Do you remember the Loewens?"

"They came later in the summer to Kuling, didn't they?"

"Yes, she was one of the pregnant ones."

"Weren't they all?" Ruth laughed. She rose abruptly. "You want to come in the kitchen for a glass of pineapple juice? I'm in love with the stuff myself."

"Sure." Gertrude followed her into the tiny room where a table had managed to hide itself in the corner. She chose the chair against the wall.

"We were all in a hurry to leave that summer." Ruth's voice rumbled from within the cavity of the refrigerator, giving voice to her memories of the hectic evacuation of Kuling.

"But Gert Loewen was about to deliver, and I stayed with her."

As Gertrude's voice got noticeably quieter, Ruth's face appeared above the open refrigerator door.

"And she lost the baby," Gertrude continued.

"I didn't know."

With the pitcher of juice in one hand and two glasses balanced in the other, Ruth expertly nudged the fridge door closed with her knee. "We were scattered a lot in those days," she said, placing the pitcher on the small table. "Some of us to the Philippines and some to Hong Kong."

"And some to the States," Gertrude added as she steadied the large tumbler Ruth set before her. "They didn't come back for some time. And we were really busy for a spell in Shanghai." Ruth began filling the glass of her guest. "But when they all came flooding back, they didn't need me anymore."

Startled at the sudden change in Gertrude's voice, Ruth looked up from her pouring and spilled juice over the edge of the tumbler and onto Gertrude's hand.

"Oh, I'm so sorry," she said as she hastily set the pitcher on the table and grabbed for a towel lying on the sink. "I'm so clumsy."

"Not to worry," Gertrude laughed while wiping her hand. "I won't melt."

"So what do you do with all your free time?" Ruth tried to sound casual as she wiped up the last of the spill.

"Well, it's not free time, exactly," Gertrude struggled to explain. "I'm still working—or I was until July 31. It's just time . . . it's like . . . I don't know, like something's missing."

"We all become missionaries for different reasons," Ruth said as she laid the wet towel in the sink, then turned to Gertrude. "So why did you come to China?"

"It changed." Gertrude watched herself run her fingers around the rim of the tumbler. "At first I came because Dr. Miller asked me to. But then I got to language school and got interested in the children and in Mr. Chen. You remember?" She looked up.

"I do indeed. Very much," Ruth said earnestly, folding her arms in front of her.

"I seemed to have a purpose . . . the people." Gertrude looked at the tumbler again. "Then, when I went to Wuhan, Dr. Miller was struggling so to get the new sanitarium up and running." She shrugged with a short laugh. "But that got interrupted by the war."

"Yes, didn't we all?" Ruth added.

"And then I went to Shanghai." Gertrude sat back as if to think about that move from a safe distance. "There was so little help, you know, and so much to do. And yet—" Gertrude searched the room for the words.

"What?"

"There were all the fun things," Gertrude said with a smile. "The shopping and the restaurants." She sat forward, her hands reaching for expression. "Shanghai isn't like any other city in China. There are so many attractions." Her arms waved helplessly.

"And now you are here." Ruth tried to help. "Don't they need you there?"

Gertrude folded her hands over her tumbler. "Actually Elder Branson told me to take some time off because they're trying to get me to Yencheng."

"Isn't that Dr. Miller's first hospital?"

"His first clinic was in that area. But, yes, he started there. And now Yencheng is the largest Adventist hospital in China—with several separate hospital buildings and an academy and a nursing program."

"But you aren't going?"

"I can't go." Gertrude wrinkled her face in frustration. "The American Consul won't let us travel. That is, won't let women and children." Gertrude's eyes flashed green fire.

"Although for the life of me I don't know what the difference is between men and women."

"And now you're here?" Ruth spoke the words more like a question.

"Yes. I was supposed to go to a mountain retreat in Japan. But I met someone on the boat." Gertrude stopped abruptly and the fire in her eyes died.

"Met someone?"

"Yes. The fifth mate," Gertrude said lightly. "Dick Richards."

"And now you're following him around the South China Sea?"

"I'm not following him!" Gertrude drew back defensively, her voice shrill.

"Let's see," Ruth mused, "from Japan to Shanghai, to Hong Kong, to Manila." She nodded knowingly. "I'll bet he knows the difference."

"What difference?" Gertrude shot back.

"Between men and women."

Gertrude's face turned a bright crimson as she lowered her eyes.

"I wonder what they call it when an ambassador is absent without leave?" Ruth gazed at the two-burner gas stove, avoiding eye contact.

"What do you mean?" Gertrude looked up curiously.

"In the military when someone is missing without permission, they call it AWOL—absent without leave." She now held Gertrude in her steady gaze.

Gertrude sat up straighter. "But I have permission to be gone."

"But not from your ambassadorship," Ruth said with a shake of her head.

"What are you talking about?"

"In 2 Corinthians 5:20 Paul says, 'Now then we are ambassadors for Christ.'" Ruth placed both hands on the table, yet not coming too close. "Ambassadors represent their country. They move among the foreigners in the country where they reside. But they never forget where home is. They always remember that they are there to represent the homeland.

"And as missionaries we are here to represent Christ." Now Ruth leaned ever so slightly toward Gertrude. "To whom have you presented your ambassadorial credentials lately?"

"But I have worship with the students every morning," Gertrude hotly protested. "And I pray with the patients every night."

"Good."

"And I'm just taking a little vacation from work." Gertrude bristled up as her green eyes flashed again. "Surely ambassadors get a vacation, don't they?"

"Yes, they do." Ruth held her gaze steady, though maintaining a soft tone. "But even on vacation, they are still ambassadors. Now that you aren't at the hospital anymore, what are you doing? Where is your posting?"

Gertrude sank back in her chair as if she were a blow-up doll and the all the air had suddenly escaped. "I don't know." Her eyes softened as she searched Ruth's face for the answer. "How do I find out?"

"Most ambassadors send a wire and ask for instructions," Ruth suggested. "Christians call it prayer."

"But I have prayed." Gertrude's voice strained in her appeal. "And there's been no answer."

"So you wait for instructions."

A flicker of recognition budded in Gertrude's eyes. She slowly folded her hands on the table in front of her and studied them. "That's what Dr. Haysmer said," she mumbled to herself.

"Who?"

"Dr. Haysmer," Gertrude offered a bit louder as she half smiled. "He's a surgeon I knew at the New England San. I told him I wasn't good at waiting on the Lord."

"Whatever we are not good at . . . ," Ruth repeated knowingly, then smiled. "The Lord always makes sure we get lots of practice with whatever we're not good at."

"And you don't think Dick Richards is a part of that waiting?" Gertrude asked, looking up.

"Do you?" Ruth said with a slight twist of her head.

"Probably not." Gertrude withdrew her gaze as her cheeks reddened.

Ruth said nothing, just looked kindly toward her friend.

"I feel so foolish," Gertrude added, examining the thumbnail of her left hand, rubbing it slowly, testing its edge as if it were a knife.

"Why?" Ruth asked carefully.

"For playing around in Shanghai." Tears began to slide ever so slowly down

Gertrude's cheeks. "For being on that boat. For coming here." She raised her eyes in supplication.

"But you aren't here by accident," Ruth offered as she reached across the gulf that separated them, touching Gertrude lightly on the arm. "God makes sure we go where we need to go and receive what we need to receive. He's still in charge, you know."

Gertrude flashed an embarrassed smile as she brushed away the water from her cheek with her forefinger.

"When's the last time you ate?" Ruth asked.

"Is that a Chinese question?" Gertrude grinned as she thought of the common Chinese "hello" greeting: "Have you eaten?"

"It's a question for a dear friend who looks famished," Ruth responded, smiling in return.

"It's been awhile. Any suggestions?"

"Just like that?" Grace Dale asked as she maneuvered her bicycle across the cindered racetrack and onto the grassy infield.

"Just like that," Gertrude responded as she struggled through the deeper cinders near the edge of the racing course.

Gertrude followed Grace's example by clambering off her bicycle and easing it to the ground. Grace had already stretched herself full length on the grass, lying on her back and gazing up into a clear and warm September sky, her hands behind her head.

Gertrude stood and surveyed the vast refugee village that now engulfed what used to be the Race Track located directly across Bubbling Wells Road from the Shanghai Sanitarium and Hospital. It was a much safer place to ride bicycles than on the streets, and in the lazy midmorning was relatively free of curious children in rags who might follow the foreigners, pointing and laughing. She sat down beside Grace and picked up two blades of grass, holding them close and inspecting them.

"Just sent him a note?"

"Yep. And pajamas."

"Pajamas?" Grace rose up laughing. "Whatever for?"

"I didn't want him to think I was giving him the brush off," Gertrude said, her impish grin reflecting in her eyes before it formed on her face.

"But I was." Her face quickly sobered while she studied the grass more intently.

Gertrude looked sideways at the girl who was her substitute sister. She could share things with Grace, things she could not share with others. And Grace always knew what to say and when not to say it. Like now, as Grace returned her gaze with understanding and silence.

"What are you going to do now?" Grace asked.

"Well, I'm going to Yencheng," Gertrude said, tossing away the blades of grass, "as soon as they tell me I can. In the meantime . . . I don't know." She leaned back on her arms to let the cool autumn breeze play tag with the warm sun on her face. "I told Elder Branson I was ready to go but he says he can't risk sending me alone. Crossing the battle lines and boundaries between the Chinese and Japanese is still too risky."

"Are you working at all?" It was as if Grace knew the salve that would sooth the wounds of inactivity for Gertrude.

"Actually, I have been." Gertrude leaned forward, her hands now in her lap, contemplating that which gave her purpose. "They called me to do special nursing on Mrs. Miller."

"Botilda Miller, the Bible worker?"

"Yep, the old German lady, Mrs. Marie Miller's aunt. She had typhoid fever and has a bad heart. It was touch and go there for a while." Gertrude paused. "You know what she said?" she asked, gazing over at Grace. "When she got better, she began asking me all about my experiences here in China, what I had done and what I was going to do. She was real easy to talk to, like an old aunt, you know. And when I told her about trying to go to Yencheng, she just leaned over and patted my arm and said, 'All in good time, dearie. The Lord has His plan. Just wait on the Lord.'"

"Sounds familiar, doesn't it?" Grace raised her eyebrows and gave a short laugh.

"Waiting and praying occupies a lot of my time." Gertrude nodded and laughed as well.

"And your friends are praying right along with you," Grace added softly.

When the Range Road Clinic opened in October, Gertrude was asked to run the outpatient department. When the new nursing class began, immediately after graduation, Gertrude was asked to teach some of her old classes. And as Christmas slid into January, Gertrude was gradually reabsorbed into the routine of the Shanghai Sanitarium and Hospital. But the nights at Sun Ya's and the days in the classroom were not the same. She prayed and she waited for the Lord to tell her what to do—about Yencheng, about Shanghai, about life.

Chapter 38

PREPARING FOR THE TRIP

What was undoubtedly snow in the interior of China fell as rain in Shanghai. The trees were not yet in full bud in late February but the hint of what they were to become perched dripping on the tips of every twig and stem awaiting the warm signals of spring to burst forth.

In the freshly washed promises of the coming spring the China Division compound was healing itself after the long winter of occupation of the buildings and grounds by the Japanese. Over the past year many of the decorative low walls had been repaired and many of the houses had been cleaned and restored. The new publishing building, recently opened, was in full operation. The iron gates in front of the headquarters building hung vertically again on their newly mounted hinges while new bright red brick work and fresh mortar contrasted sharply with the old faded facade in the adjacent walls. Here and there small heaps of rubble remained as a reminder of the recent occupier and the ever-present war.

Alighting from the trolley, Gertrude hurried up Ningkuo Road toward the Division compound, under her umbrella and wrapped in her long fur coat. The air was cold and the rain intensified the heavy, prespring drabness. But her step was quick and her eyes were lit with a warmth from within. Gertrude was undaunted by the tailings of winter. She was going to Yencheng.

She walked briskly through the large iron gates (locked only at night) and made a sharp right turn into the housing section of the compound, then approached the house where Thelma Smith was staying. Slipping through the gap in the low wall where the small decorative iron gate used to hang, Gertrude avoided the bungalow's formal front entrance and headed directly for the back door. Then seeing a shadow in the windows of the house mimicking her progress, racing toward the rear of the house, Gertrude broke into a run. But before she could reach the back steps the door flew open to reveal the laughing face of Thelma Smith.

"Welcome," Thelma managed to gasp and laugh at the same time. "Dr. Nethery says he's not sure he can survive a trip with two foolish schoolgirls." Thelma was shorter than Gertrude by three or more inches, a bit stocky in the shoulders, but trim and dainty in her movements. Unlike the popular newer styles, her hair was cut long and curved down to cover her ears suggesting a conservative bent. But her laughing brown eyes and dark smiling face revealed a heart that naturally reached out to the world.

"Well, you can tell Dr. Nethery for me that these two schoolgirls will ride circles around him and his bicycle on the way to Yencheng," Gertrude said as she came up the steps and entered the small kitchen. She folded her umbrella and placed it just outside the door on the stoop.

"Maybe you should tell him yourself," said a large, square-shouldered man who almost entirely blocked out the sunlight coming through the door from the living room.

"Maybe I'll do that very thing," Gertrude countered as she shrugged her coat into Thelma's outstretched arms. She turned to warily eye the balding man whose head almost touched the doorway lintel. "It's been some time since I was accused of being a schoolgirl."

"Maybe it's been too long since you acted like one," Winston Nethery replied, his smile splitting the whole lower half of his face.

"Could be," Gertrude agreed, pushing her way past him into the living room.

"Hello, Herbert," she said, spying Thelma's 11-year-old son who sat dwarfed in a large overstuffed chair, solemnly observing the foolishness of his elders. His tousle of brown hair topped a face that was a smaller copy of his mother's.

"Have you got room for me in that big chair?" Gertrude asked.

"Sure," he said with a grin. He perched up on the arm of the chair, his legs drawn up like a leprechaun, and patted the seat below him.

"Don't put your feet on the chair, son," his mother chided as she entered the living room behind Dr. Nethery.

"Yes, ma'am." He stretched his legs out to dangle over the edge of the arm.

Gertrude plopped into the seat beside the boy and gave his knee a squeeze as she traded smiles with yet another child who saw her as an older version of himself: inquisitive, fun-loving, and prone to break the rules on occasion.

As the four new friends of three weeks duration settled into another planning session, Gertrude quickly scanned her mental dossier on each of her future traveling companions.

Dr. Winston E. Nethery—the football player-sized medical director of the Yencheng Hospital and previously of several other hospitals in China. In the early winter he had guided his pregnant wife, Marie, and their young son, Winston James, across the Chinese-Japanese battle lines to Shanghai to place her in the care of an experienced OB-GYN physician and to purchase much needed supplies for the hospital compound. Being too far from Chungking and having the railroad bridge destroyed by the Chinese to keep the Japanese from taking the town, Yencheng's isolation required a personal pedestrian caravan to and from Shanghai every time supplies ran low. Since the end of December Dr. Nethery had been shopping for supplies and waiting for permission to return. The red tape and forms, the continual trips to the American and Japanese embassies, and the interminable questions had caused him to refrain from securing many of his precious supplies, especially the ones likely to perish in the interim.

From the first time Gertrude had observed his calm, detached attitude and ready smile in President Branson's office, she had taken an instant liking to him. She thought then that he would be fun to work with. So far, she had not been disappointed.

Thelma Smith—a trained Bible worker and widow of one of the earlier missionaries. She was close to Gertrude's age. She had recently returned from furlough and was working as the temporary cashier at the China Division offices while waiting to go to Yencheng as the mission treasurer and Bible worker. Prevented from going to the interior of China on the same grounds as Gertrude, Thelma was praying for Dr. Nethery's efforts to get permission to return so that she could accompany him.

Gertrude had occasionally seen her around the Division compound and sometimes on Sabbath at church, but they had not become acquainted until

Elder Branson drew them together three weeks ago. Thelma had proved to be a thoughtful counselor and adept shopper for household as well as administrative needs, occasionally checking with and representing Marie Nethery who was not returning on this trip. Dr. Nethery would come out and retrieve his wife after the birth of their baby.

Herbert Smith, Jr.—Thelma's 11-year-old son. He was well mannered, adaptable, curious without being a nuisance, and companionable. In spite of the death of his father and the continually disrupted nature of his educational and home experience, Gertrude thought that he was one of the most pleasant children she'd ever encountered.

And, of course, there was Gertrude. Just when it seemed that her prayers were unheard and the waiting would go on forever, everything happened at once: the message came from Elder Branson, the meeting in his office with Thelma and Dr. Nethery, the shopping and the planning sessions—and the trip was on.

When the Lord waits, it seems like forever. And when He moves, it seems like a whirlwind. Biblical instances of both possibilities came to mind, and she inwardly smiled at her own slowness to comprehend the lessons of life. *Like learning Chinese,* she told herself, *learn it one step at a time.*

"Are all your bicycles in good working order?" Dr. Nethery asked.

Instead of walking or riding in sedan chairs the four intrepid travelers were riding bicycles during the pedestrian part of the trip. They thought riding the bikes would be easier, as well as good exercise. And the bicycles would be fun once they got to Yencheng.

"Yep," they answered in unison.

"Herbert and I have been riding all over the compound," Thelma said.

"And I've been riding at the racetrack with Grace Dale," Gertrude chimed in. "We even tried riding in the streets of Shanghai. I almost got run down by an omnibus."

Thelma gasped at the near accident and the possible consequences for their trip.

"There aren't any omnibuses where we're going," Dr. Nethery said with a knowing smile. "And the roads aren't paved like here on the compound," he added looking at Herbert.

"Oh, I think we'll all do splendidly well," Herbert said with a confident nod.

"U'mmm" was Dr. Nethery's dubious response.

"Well, I have two announcements," he said after a moment's pause. "The first is that we have another traveler joining us: Miss Ma, a Chinese national of indeterminate age."

"Aren't they all?" Gertrude said as she tried to remember Miss Ma's face, tried to separate it from all the other Chinese she knew. "She's a nurse, isn't she? It seems like I remember her from the San."

"Yes, and an excellent one," Dr. Nethery noted. "She worked in Yencheng before the war and wants to return. It's her home."

"Will that be a problem crossing the Japanese lines?" Thelma asked, ever the thoughtful planner.

"The Japanese don't think so," Dr. Nethery said with a scowl that suggested he wasn't so sure. "I wondered the same thing myself."

"And the second announcement?" Herbert asked with bursting curiosity.

"Oh, yes," Dr. Nethery said as if just remembering, "We leave in a week."

"Oh, you pill!" Gertrude shouted in mock disgust. "You knew this all along and didn't tell us." She picked up a small, red pillow by the chair as if to throw it at him while he feigned a duck of his head.

Even as she laughed at their antics, Thelma had already set to work thinking seriously about what was to be done next.

"Then we have to begin ordering the perishable items," she said in her most officious accountant's voice and got up to fetch a pencil and paper to make notes.

Now that the date of March 6 had been set for departure, the crating and shipping of all the supplies purchased previously began in earnest. In addition, the perishables—50 pounds of flour, 100 pounds of sugar, five pounds of baking powder, plus cans of almost every kind of fruit and vegetable—were purchased and added to the growing shipping manifest. As the railroads were still operating from Shanghai to Pengpu, all of these plus the travel cots, bedding, and the bicycles were shipped directly ahead to where Elder Larsen and Elder White, holding colporteur training seminars, could receive them. Dr. Nethery had assured the other four that excellent accommodations would be available in Nanking and Pengpu and they would not need their sleeping gear until the bicycle part of the trip began beyond the railhead at Pengpu.

"How long will it take us to get to Nanking?" Herbert asked again. His eyes were on the rain-washed train window.

"About five hours," his mother answered patiently—for the third time. She ruffled his hair as she gazed over his shoulder at all the missionary families huddled under umbrellas near the departing tracks of North Station. The Japanese had erected the temporary building where they all stood in the mud to replace the bombed out hulk of the original North Station. Yet it back-shadowed them all, reminding her of the unusual conditions in which she lived her life and raised this son, all she had left of her murdered missionary husband.

Gertrude turned toward the seats behind her to watch this exchange of familial love between Thelma Smith and Herbert. Then she noticed Winston Nethery in the seat behind them. A somber expression had replaced his usually broad grin and his right hand pressed against the window as if wanting to reach out through the window pane. His attention was on Marie Nethery, a long-haired, full-figured woman made more so by her pregnancy. She stood at the front of the crowd, holding the hand of a small, quiet boy, Winston James Nethery, Jr. otherwise known as Jim or Skippy. She bent awkwardly, at the same time pointing upward, trying to direct her son's attention to his father's face framed by the train window.

Miss Ma, her straight black hair cut squarely all around just under her ears, sat quietly in the seat beside Gertrude, her Chinese lunch pail in her lap, her long, warm Chinese coat buttoned up under her chin.

Looking about her and above her on the luggage racks Gertrude thought about the 190 crates, boxes, bicycles, and luggage accompanying them to Yencheng—around 30 pieces per traveler. While most had been sent ahead, they'd checked 36 pieces of luggage on this train and were carrying nine with them here in the car.

Wouldn't Dr. Miller be amused, she laughed to herself. *And he thought I had a lot of stuff when I first arrived in China.*

At the last minute Gertrude turned and waved to June who'd welcomed Gertrude into her apartment when her lease ran out at the end of March. *Follie is a good friend now, just when this part of my life is ending,* Gertrude reflected. *I knew it would take a long time to get to know her.* As she sat reminiscing over her many other Shanghai friends who were waving from under the station roof overhang, the train lurched and began moving forward. *Time to move on,* she announced to herself and faced forward as the train pulled away into the downpour.

The downpour had become a drab, gray drizzle by the time they arrived at the Nanking railway station five hours later. From her purse Gertrude retrieved the pictured ID pass issued by the Japanese and proceeded through the customs station. This was just one of many which had been set up at every conceivable itinerant spot in Japanese-occupied territory to catch contraband goods, illegal travelers, and guerrilla Chinese soldiers. Anxiously she observed as, first, Miss Ma, and then Thelma and Herbert were waved through without even a perfunctory search of their luggage.

"Where is Dr. Nethery?" Thelma asked as she trotted dutifully along behind Gertrude's purposeful strides toward the street.

"He went ahead to hail a taxi."

As she emerged from the station into the gentle misting rain Gertrude stopped abruptly in midstride. To avoid a collision, those following closely behind her popped out like popcorn kernels to her right and left. Now they stood staring at the ancient contraption to which Dr. Nethery beckoned them like a good porter with a broad grin, a short bow, and a sweep of his arm.

"What is that?" Gertrude asked, pointing at the dilapidated 1920's vintage Dodge touring car.

"Our taxi," he said, maintaining his Cheshire cat imitation.

"Looks like something playing hooky from the junk heap," she quipped.

"It'll get us there," he retorted, abandoning his servile stance and stuffing them all into the back two seats along with their luggage. He hopped in the front seat next to a young boy who sat next to the driver.

"And what is the young boy—?"

Before Herbert could complete his question, the touring car stopped in mid-traffic. To the accompaniment of horns and human curses, the young coolie leaped over Dr. Nethery, rushed to the front of the car and cranked it back to life with three quick turns of the crooked tool he carried. While Herbert attempted to stand to watch and his mother tried to pull him back in his seat, Gertrude sat chuckling and shaking her head incredulously.

After five miles of rattles, bumps, and two more cranked resurrections, the old car wheezed to the front of a well-appointed Japanese hotel.

"Stay here. I'll be right back," Dr. Nethery instructed, striding for the front door.

After thinking for a moment, *And this is the man who got us this taxi,* Gertrude hopped out and hustled after him into the hotel. She arrived just in time to hear the sucking sound of wind whistling between the teeth of the embarrassed Japanese proprietor and the exclamation, "Sorry, no rooms." Gertrude's green eyes cut a withering swath among those at the reception desk as the proprietor valiantly called every friend in the hotel business and Dr. Nethery, avoiding her gaze, encouraged him.

A voice behind her made her jump, biting off the invective she was about to unleash.

"Now I know how Joseph and Mary felt when there was no room for them in the inn," young Herbert offered with a grin.

Gertrude answered his infectious good nature with a sigh of resignation and a shake of her head. "Oh, well, there's nothing for it," she laughed as she and Herbert retreated from the hotel lobby to wait with Thelma in the old taxi.

At 10:00 p.m., after a four-hour tour of all the full hotels in Nanking, they were all soundly sleeping on straw ticks with dirty quilts for covers in two rooms of a run-down Chinese inn. It wasn't the fancy hotel Dr. Nethery had promised, but for now they were too tired to care. It was, in fact, to be the nicest hotel of the whole trip!

Chapter 39

SLEEPING UNDER CHINESE QUILTS

"Gertrude, get up," Mrs. Smith insisted, vigorously shaking the moribund form next to her. "The taxi is here for us."

"But he's not supposed to be here til 8:00 o'clock," Gertrude objected, keeping both eyes tightly shut.

"The Chinese can't tell the time except by the sun, and it's not up yet," Thelma lamely offered. "But if we don't get this taxi, there may not be another one and we'll miss our train."

"If they'd stop bombing the trains at night . . . ," Gertrude began but gave it up when the fetid smell of the quilt under her nose jerked her to full consciousness and forced her out of her straw tick. "When did they last wash these quilts?"

"Good morning, Miss Green," Miss Ma said, bowing from her corner of the room. "They only wash the bedding at the end of the season. If they wash it too often, it will fall apart."

"Well, they missed this one at the end of last season," Gertrude said with a laugh, bowing to Miss Ma.

"Any ideas for breakfast?" Dr. Nethery's rich bass voice penetrated the thin walls from the next room. "Herbert and I are starved."

Gertrude and Thelma exchanged knowing glances.

"Just like a man." Thelma was the first to say aloud what they were both thinking.

"How about we snatch out some of the lunch sandwiches?" Gertrude suggested with a quizzical look at Thelma. Thelma nodded.

"OK, I'll get the rest of the luggage out to the taxi," the voice from the other side of the wall responded. "You girls liberate those sandwiches."

The early arrival of the taxi proved to be heaven sent. The ride to the dock at the river, the ferry ride across the Yangtze, and the slow passage through customs placed the five intrepid travelers at the train station with only moments to spare. With the Japanese in charge of the rail system, departures were prompt and those not aboard were left standing at the station without apology.

"Quickly now," Dr. Nethery wheezed, winded after running from the front of the rail station, "you girls get on board and find us a compartment. Herbert and I will pass up the luggage to you through the window, Chinese style."

"When in Rome . . .," Thelma offered as she set down her small case and scrambled up the train steps.

"Down here, boys!" It was Gertrude waving out of an open window, three spaces down.

"How did she ever . . .," Herbert gasped out as he scampered after Dr. Nethery, dragging three suitcases.

"Just made it," Winston Nethery said, steadying his large frame against the wall of the narrow corridor in the swaying railcar. He patted Herbert on the back for a job well done and ushered him on ahead to where the women were holding the compartment and a place to sit down.

Startled at who he saw in the compartment, Dr. Nethery, abruptly straightened up and struck his head on the low door frame. With one hand on his injured pate, he awkwardly returned the bows of two middle-aged Japanese men in business suits who, standing in front of the seats they'd previously occupied, were repeatedly bowing while trying to steady themselves in the swaying train car.

"It's a very pleasant train, don't you think?" Gertrude said from the opposite bench seat. "And ever so much cleaner than the one we had yesterday."

Herbert squeezed in between his mother and Miss Ma on the bench next to Gertrude.

"Yes, ever so much cleaner," Dr. Nethery said, taking the remaining seat next to their Japanese traveling companions. "Leave it to Gertrude to find a compartment with men," he added under his breath, hoping his seatmates did not speak English.

Gertrude shrugged with a twinkle and a roll of her eyes and a coy little smile as she too settled back for the ride.

Dr. Nethery sat up with a start. "Are we there already?"

"I think this is Pengpu," Thelma guessed, arising slowly from her own nap and peering out the window, searching for some familiar landmark.

"Then we'd better get off this train or we'll be headed for South China," Dr. Nethery said as he jumped from his seat, jostling his Japanese seatmates awake. "Out the window, girls," he shouted as he ran for the steps with Herbert hot on his heels.

With genuine smiles and unhelpful bows the Japanese men assisted the girls in shoving the suitcases and boxes through the window into Dr. Nethery and Herbert's waiting arms. Gertrude worked hard at maintaining her Oriental calm demeanor while inwardly seething at having to work around the inept help of two overly polite, self-appointed Japanese goodwill ambassadors. As the train pulled out of the station, Gertrude stood next to the others on the station platform, straightening her dress while waving to her departing friends who were still leaning out of the compartment window. "Sometimes you can be too polite," she noted to no one in particular.

"Well, friends," Dr. Nethery happily announced, "we are now halfway to Yencheng."

"Yes, two days to go the first half," Gertrude observed, picking up her well-traveled black suitcase and boxes. "And 12 days for the other half. Another 260 miles yet to go!"

Pengpu was experiencing the same glut of Japanese immigrants and Chinese refugees that had filled Nanking. The hotels that Dr. Nethery had remembered as being conveniently empty were all full. Gertrude could see them spending the rest of the evening looking for a hovel to sleep in and ending up again with unwashed quilts over straw ticks.

"Let's go see if there's room for us at the little Seventh-day Adventist Church," Dr. Nethery said hopefully.

The church in Pengpu was struggling to retain its membership in the face of the chaos of war which hung heavily over this city situated so close to the main battle lines. Therefore, the church leadership had sent Elders Larsen,

White, Hsu, and Hwang to conduct a colporteur institute to train door-to-door Christian book sellers in preparation for holding more formal evangelistic meetings. When the little group of weary travelers arrived, they found the church building packed with church workers from around the province, all of them sleeping on the floor at night, according to Elder Dallas White who had stepped out to greet them.

"And the four of us are sleeping in the small room in the back," he added, "which we would gladly share with the men in your group."

"But that leaves the girls out on the street, doesn't it?" Gertrude finished his thought for him with a bite in her voice.

"Yes, I'm afraid that is not a good solution, is it?" He paused to consider, noting the look of exhaustion on the faces of the women and the dejected exasperation of Dr. Nethery. "Why don't Dr. Nethery and I go look for a place for all of you to stay," he suggested. "And the rest of you can wait in the church."

As the flickering lanterns of the Chinese market welcomed the dark of evening, Elder White and Dr. Nethery headed off into the crooked streets and tight clusters of buildings surrounding the church while Gertrude and Herbert led the rest of the group into the dark church interior to wait.

Two hours later Winston Nethery strode into the rear of the church announcing loudly, "I've found a place that is so bad, even the Chinese won't stay there. But they have beds."

"And quilts, too, I'll wager." Gertrude spoke from recent memory of the night before.

"All the stuff we packed for the trip," Herbert noted with less than his usual enthusiasm, "and all of our blankets—none of it is here yet."

"Come on, Gertrude," Thelma muttered in weary acquiescence. She dragged herself from where she sat and picked up her bags. "We've had it worse."

Gertrude sighed. "Yes, but I don't know when."

"Oh! Oh! Thelma! Oh, help me!"

"Gertrude, what is it?" Thelma sat bolt upright in her bed, groping for her flashlight. "A rat! A rat ran right across my bed!" Gertrude was dancing barefoot on the dirt floor beside her bed, vigorously shaking the soiled quilt that had covered her. "It ran right over me!"

Dr. Nethery and Herbert arose like ghosts in the eerie, dust-laden half-light and peered over the four-foot high bamboo poles that served as walls to separate the sleeping compartments that were supposed to represent rooms. Miss Ma sat upright in her bed, holding the quilt tightly around her body but saying nothing. Gertrude, in her nightgown, was examining her cot in the glare of Thelma's flashlight.

"Gertrude, what happened?" Dr. Nethery was still uncertain as to why all the commotion.

"There are rats in this filthy hole you brought us to," she spat out.

"Gertrude, I'm sorry."

"I will not stay here another night, I tell you. I will not do it," she cried, turning on him and shaking with undiluted anger and fear. And then she melted and began to sob. "I never should have come," she wept, sinking down on her cot, holding the stained quilt up to her face to hide her shame. "I just can't stand it. I just can't. I just can't."

"Gertrude, I'm sorry," Dr. Nethery repeated. "I'll find another place to-morrow, I promise."

"It will be all right," Thelma said to him, going to Gertrude and sitting next to her on the cot. "We'll be all right in a little while." She draped her short, strong arm over the shaking shoulders of her much taller new sister and drew her close. No one got much sleep the rest of the night.

The following day Dr. Nethery moved the group to another questionable location for a second attempt at a good night's sleep. In the morning, Elders Larson and White invited the five travelers to join them for an early breakfast.

"Well, Gertrude, were there any more rats last night?" Elder Larsen was clever and friendly, quick to lighten a serious incident with charitable humor. Gertrude had liked him from the moment she met him.

"Not unless they played little stringed instruments and sang in high pitched voices," she retorted with her own joke. Herbert nearly choked on his breakfast as Thelma laughed at Elder Larsen's puzzled expression.

"We got a better place all right," Thelma informed him. "But Dr. Nethery got us out of hell and into a Japanese brothel."

"A geisha house," Dr. Nethery quickly informed the group of nine who were sharing breakfast in an upstairs Chinese restaurant. Giggles and laughter at his expense rounded the table as the entertaining events of the night at the geisha house were retold several times in both English and Chinese.

"It was clean and there were no rats," Gertrude concluded with a twinkle in her eye for Dr. Nethery. "I've never slept better in my life, serenades and all," she added, bringing on another fit of giggles from Herbert. "It was lovely and the quilts were clean . . . which is more than I can say for this dirty table-cloth." She lightly fingered the white cotton rag which covered the table before them.

"Now, Gertrude," Elder White warned her good-naturedly, "don't be critical of the proprietor. He has given us his idea of service especially because there are ladies present. We got no such treatment as a tablecloth until you three ladies arrived." Thelma nodded demurely to the compliment and Miss Ma hung her head and blushed behind her napkin in the proper Chinese way.

"Well, the food is certainly excellent and no complaints there," Gertrude said, taking a second helping of the vegetable dish, "and we'll have to thank him for that blessing."

"Especially if we have to stay here for awhile," Dr. Nethery noted to the consternation of all, "as all of our freight has still not arrived." Mumbles and furtive glances rippled among the four other travelers over that bit of news.

"I've been thinking about that," Elder White said, laying down his chop-sticks. "What if you were to take what is here now and what comes on Sunday and go on to Yencheng?"

"Especially since our bicycles are here," chimed in Herbert, still stuffing his mouth and receiving a severe look from his mother.

"Especially since your bicycles are here," Elder White agreed with a smile. "And I'll bring what comes in the next few days with me on my itinerary out there next week."

With affirmative nods and glances around the table, Dr. Nethery readily agreed.

"But not until after the Sabbath," Elder Hsu said enthusiastically. "You cannot believe how the church here has grown in just the last few weeks."

Indeed the next day Gertrude was surprised and pleased to see the large congregation that filled the small church building and spilled out into the street. As she sat in the stiff wooden pews sharing in the English–Chinese sermon, she was grateful again for the Sabbath rest which over the years had become her time to gather her thoughts and her fears and share them with the God she had come to China to serve.

You've given me a new sister in Christ and a new nephew, she prayed silently. *And I think I understand my new assignment.* She paused to consider the mysterious stimulus of nursing students and hospital ward work and tingled with excitement at the thought of being the person in charge again. *The rollicking high adventure hasn't been too stressful,* she mused. *And for once I know where I'm going and why.*

Chapter 40

CYCLING INTO THE INTERIOR

Monday noon, March 11, 16 large rubber-wheeled carts, each pulled by a single coolie and carrying 350 to 400 pounds of freight rolled through the western gates of Pengpu. They were preceded by four missionaries on bicycles, two of them females, much to the delight of the crowds of Chinese who lined the streets, pointing and laughing. Miss Ma, the fifth missionary, who was actually returning to her hometown, followed the bicyclers in a rickshaw. And another rickshaw followed behind her for any who might find riding their bicycle a little too strenuous, although each one was sure they would not be the one needing it.

The caravan was allowed to pass the customs officer at the edge of town because Elder White had informed him that they were carrying medicines. The customs officer had a sister who was a nurse in the next town; thus the caravan received a roundabout family inclusive blessing. They quickly passed from the view and the thoughts of the curious in Pengpu, hoping to make 25 *li*—approximately eight miles—before nightfall.

But a major obstruction blocked their way, the Hwai River, one of many rivers they would have to cross on their way to Yencheng.

"They will soon learn that Dr. Nethery speaks Chinese and drives a hard bargain," Thelma said, holding her long coat shut against the stiff, cold wind. "I watched them talking excitedly when they saw him coming down the bluff. But now they're not so sure."

Gertrude, clad in heavy Chinese pants and her long black coat with the fur collar, stood beside Thelma, peering over the edge of the precipice at the cluster of boatmen on the riverbank below. A few of them were huddled around Dr. Nethery and the head coolie who was also the guide on the trip. Dr. Nethery was shaking his head vigorously and indicating with his fingers how much he would pay.

Gertrude's eye quickly calculated that the small, flat-bottomed boats could carry only one cart at a time. Crossing the swift flow and rowing back up the other side against the current would take at least half an hour per boat. She quickly did the math of five boats ferrying 16 carts plus the rickshaws and the bicycles.

"We're going to be stuck here for two hours unless things get moving," she said, turning away and walking back to pick up her bicycle.

"What's the holdup, now?" Thelma asked five minutes later when Dr. Nethery trudged up the road over the edge of the bluff. His white shirt and vest ruffling in the wind, he was shaking his head as he looked back at the group by the river, now joined by several of the coolies.

How can he stay warm when he never wears a coat? Gertrude pondered as she approached from the other direction. *The man never tires and never gets cold.*

Winston Nethery dusted off his hands as if trying to remove a bad stain. "The argument now is over who will be in charge of the crossing, the coolies or the boatmen," he said, glancing back again.

"Well, I'm for getting across now," Gertrude fumed as she wheeled her bicycle past them, over the edge of the bluff and down the road toward the river.

Two and a half hours later the caravan had crossed the river and was on its way toward the little town of Hwai Yuan.

As they approached the mud and brick arch that served as the city gate, they saw a Caucasian woman hurrying through the crude structure toward them. Ever ready to exchange information with someone who spoke unbroken English, the cyclists pushed on through the strong headwind with renewed energy. As they approached she stopped short, waiting for them to come to her.

"Oh, dear," she said as Dr. Nethery and Herbert reached her, "you aren't who I thought you were." When she realized how odd and inhospitable her greeting sounded, she quickly added, "I'm sorry. That was rude of me. I'm from the Presbyterian Mission here in Hwai Yuan."

Gertrude watched the woman extend her hand as she and Thelma rode up and stopped their bicycles close behind the men.

"I'm Dr. Winston Nethery from the Seventh-day Adventist Mission Hospital in Yencheng," Dr. Nethery said, shaking her proffered hand. "We're on our way there with supplies that we hope will last for a while . . . maybe 'til the war is over . . . but I don't think so," he added with a shrug and a sheepish grin at his lame joke.

"Probably not," she agreed. Turning to the women who had not heard her opening remarks, she repeated somewhat hopefully, "I'm from the Presbyterian Mission and I was out here because I thought your party was two missionaries that are coming to join us here." When everyone sat stupidly on their bicycles, staring at her in exhaustion, and did not respond, she said, "But since they're not here and you are, and since you look like you could use some supper and a good night's sleep, why don't you come with me and we'll put you up for the night?"

"Do you have real beds?" Herbert asked in a whisper.

They did.

Early the next morning, Thelma sat scrunched down in the ditch, ducking her turbaned head into the full fur collar of her long coat and out of the wind that whistled overhead. Herbert huddled close to his mother, his short-brimmed hat tugged tightly on his head, his hands retracted into the sleeves of his sweater. Gertrude in peaked cap and long fur-collared coat sat on her haunches peering over the edge of the ditch to the road they had recently traversed.

"I don't see them coming yet," she said, hunkering down with the others.

"Tell me again," Thelma asked, shaking off a chill, "why we are riding our bicycles in this biting cold headwind?"

"Because we thought it would be better exercise than riding in the rickshaw and more fun than walking," Gertrude said, tucking her very cold hands into her coat and trying to get her back comfortable against the back wall of the ditch.

"Then why are we sitting here in this ditch?" Thelma persisted in her query.

"Because we're resting and waiting for the carts to catch up," Gertrude said, peering over the edge once more. "And because the wind is cold up there." She pointed up over the edge with her gloved hand.

"And why am I rubbing my ankles and my bruised knee?" Thelma played out her mocking charade by rubbing her ankles that really were sore.

"Because you keep falling off your bicycle when it jumps out of the ruts in the road." Gertrude started to giggle at the memories of both of them lying on their sides in the road with their bicycles on top of them. And Thelma laughed with her.

"You guys should be on the radio, Mom," Herbert deadpanned. "You're so-o-o funny."

"Maybe we'll check into that when we get to Yencheng," Gertrude said, poking him in the ribs and making him jump. Spotting the lead cart coming around the distant bend, Gertrude clambered out of the ditch. "Better get going or we won't be able to get around those carts once they pass us," she instructed. Gallantly Herbert and Thelma followed her over the top.

At 1:30 the group ate a lunch of tinned mandarin oranges and tins of cold beans, standing next to their bicycles, with crowds of the curious laughing and pointing at what these strange foreigners ate. By 4:30 Dr. Nethery began riding ahead, looking for a secure place for them to stop for the evening, an enclosure large enough to place all the carts safely inside and with a small building for the missionaries to be out of the cold and away from the prying eyes of the ever-present onlookers. At 6:00 o'clock the first carts of the caravan began gathering inside a small farm compound on the outskirts of Hanchahu.

"I'll speak with the head coolie and get the other men settled for the night," Winston said, dismounting. He ducked his tall frame beneath the corrugated tin roof and leaned his bicycle against the front wall of a large mud hut.

"Let me dig out my Primus stove and fix us some supper," Gertrude added, disembarking in like manner and heading for the baggage on the lead cart.

Thelma and Herbert parked their bicycles next to the others. They followed Gertrude to the lead cart where they began taking down the cots and bedding. Herbert headed for the mud hut with his arms full of quilts.

"Speak to the man in charge here about keeping the villagers out of the compound," Gertrude urged Dr. Nethery who turned his head toward her and nodded vigorously even as he spoke in Chinese with the coolies clustered around him.

Gertrude turned from stirring the tomato soup simmering on her miniature camping stove as Dr. Nethery came through the small door of the hut. He closed it firmly in the faces of several small children who had attached themselves to him. Gertrude shook her head. "What's so interesting about us?" she asked in disgust.

"They've never seen a White person, some of them," Miss Ma offered from her corner. "And they have never seen food come from a can."

Gertrude returned to her soup stirring, trying to imagine how interesting a bunch of windburned, dirty, exhausted missionaries might be.

"I spoke to the farmer who owns this place," Winston said. He examined the haystack in the corner, looked for droppings from the previous occupants whose smell pervaded the small, dark interior, and counted the cots prepared for the evening. "I told him we wouldn't pay him if he didn't keep the people away from the hut tonight." Satisfied with his inspection, he pulled a small bench from the corner and eased himself down near a box positioned in the middle of the tiny room. The small oil lamp sitting there gave out a dim light and a small amount of inviting heat.

"Good luck," Thelma chuckled. "I couldn't find a moment of privacy out on the road—not a quiet bush or boulder anywhere—if you know what I mean. And I thought there was no one around out there at all—until I needed to be alone." All joined in her embarrassed laughter as they each had experienced the same inconvenience during the day.

"Those were the last of the Japanese, those guards we passed before lunch?" Herbert asked.

Dr. Nethery nodded. "We're now in Free China. We'll see how long it remains that way." With worried eyes he glanced at Thelma who silently passed on the thought to Gertrude who was pouring the tomato soup into their tin cups.

"What have you got there?" Dr. Nethery asked as Gertrude served each of them a dumpling-like mass that had been deep-fried some time in the past but was now a hard ball.

"Chinese cakes," Gertrude said. "Miss Ma says they are a delicacy here in this area because they're made from wheat."

"And onions," Miss Ma added. "They taste good when onions or some other vegetables are cut up in them. But it's been a bad year for crops and these do not have any onions." She proceeded to crumble her cake into her soup. The rest observed and followed her example.

"And all the fields we saw today are wheat?" Herbert asked. He'd saved a bit of his cake and was biting into a small, hard lump. It broke apart and turned to crumbs in his mouth.

"It's too cold to grow rice this far north," Miss Ma told them in her heavily accented English. "Everyone here grows wheat."

"It's very dry, like crackers," Herbert informed them. "No taste." He wrinkled his nose and stuck out his tongue as he added the remnants of his cake to his soup.

They ate in silence, appreciating the warmth of the soup after riding all day into the steady, cold wind. As each finished eating, they washed their utensils in hot water and rinsed them in a pot of water that Gertrude had simmering on her stove.

"Look at all those faces!" Gertrude said, pointing to the small window set in the front wall. Every pane was filled with faces behind faces, crowding forward to see what strange things the foreigners were doing. "What do they want?"

"Maybe they want to see why you needed to buy so much hot water from the farmer's wife," Thelma suggested. "They think it is such a waste to be using water to wash dishes."

"Well, it wasn't particularly clean, even when we got it," Gertrude said, thrashing about in the water as she washed her bowl in vigorous irritation. "She'd been boiling eggs in the water, so I covered up the taste by adding the soup."

"And don't you waste a bit of it," she said as Winston stared at his partially emptied bowl now held at arm's length. "The water cost us a pretty penny, I'll have you know. And I won't have you throwing it away."

Miss Ma and Thelma laughed heartily when Dr. Nethery snatched his bowl away from the outstretched hands of a still-hungry Herbert. He quickly tucked it under his chin and greedily began finishing the last few spoonfuls.

"I'm too hungry to throw it out," he said around the spoon in his mouth. "And I'm certainly not giving it to you, young man."

With laughter Herbert swung his snapping fingers in an arc of disappointment.

"Can you go see what can be done about those incessant faces at the window?" Gertrude asked, her voice rising. "I just can't stand having someone watching me constantly."

"Sure," Dr. Nethery said, handing his empty cup to Herbert who took it to the basin to wash it. "I'll go out there and see whom I can threaten." He rose to go to the door, then paused. "Herbert, you might want to set up your cot and mine here in front of the door—just in case someone decides that viewing us from the crack in the door is just not close enough."

Herbert waved the cup he was washing in a salute of assent as Dr. Nethery quickly stepped outside accompanied by the scrambling sound of retreating feet.

The next three days were a grueling, monotonous repetition of their daily existence. Breakfast was eaten standing as the five travelers huddled fully dressed around a small oil lamp. The first two hours of the day they were bitterly cold, but by midmorning it began to warm up. At noon they were the local source of entertainment, eating a lunch of cold canned beans and dried fruit before an audience. They spent the middle of the day hiding under heavy wraps and face coverings to protect themselves as much from sunburn and wind chapping as from the cold. By late afternoon they were searching for a large enclosure for the night's safety. Supper was soup or noodles accompanied by local produce or Chinese wheat cakes, with vegetables if they were lucky. Exhausted sleep came under the ever-present watchful eye of the curious villagers.

The wheel ruts in the hard-packed road could be a useful channel for the coolies pulling their carts. But they were a constant source of jarring bumps and painful spills for the bicycle riders. After an especially spectacular accident, the bicycle would be placed on one of the carts while the agonizing victim rode in the rickshaw for a few hours of recuperation. While Thelma and occasionally Herbert were the recipients of this care, the usual convalescent was Gertrude, rubbing her sore parts, stumbling about on her cold, blue feet, and loudly bemoaning her decision to ride a bicycle to Yencheng. Dr. Nethery was never a rickshaw rider.

Almost every day presented them with one or more rivers to cross. When possible, this was done on bridges—each one in various stages of disrepair because of the ravages of war activity. Sometimes they had to buy or rent boards from the local villagers to make the bridges passable. And the coolies would have to be convinced, usually with money, that the bridges were secure enough to carry them and their load. Occasionally the rivers were crossed in small rowboats, repeating the interminable processes of bargaining and cajoling and the power struggles of the first day's crossing.

During this protracted sojourn Gertrude observed up close, as few foreigners had, the intimate village life of rural China. She studied the farm compounds, the surrounding brown fields that awaited spring planting, the remnants of the bread-loaf style haystacks close to the animal pens, the families planting the early spring vegetables. In the villages she saw small girls with bound feet, a painful, terrible custom frowned on in Shanghai as foolish and old fashioned, and men with Manchu queues, a style and a loyalty that had been abandoned in the eastern provinces with the establishment of the Sun Yat Sen Republic.

Gertrude was observing the real China that had thrived for thousands of years on rural production and intense loyalty to tradition, honor, and a rigid hierarchy. And every day's travel brought her 90 *li* deeper into the midst of this China she would now call home.

Chapter 41

ENDURING THE SECOND WEEK

"What's the holdup now?" Having retraced half an hour's travel, Gertrude coasted up to Dr. Nethery who was standing astride his bicycle beside a cart with one end of its axle resting on the ground.

"Broken ball bearing. The carts are beginning to fall apart," he told her staring at the wounded cart. "The coolie has gone back to the last town to get another wheel. We used the last of our spares this morning."

Etched on his face Gertrude saw the weariness of leadership which he kept well concealed beneath lighthearted humor during their evening meals. She'd seen this same numbing fatigue in Dr. Ruble at New England San and in Dr. Miller in Wuhan. They had both needed her assistance as Dr. Nethery needed her now.

He glanced at her out of the corner of his eye, too tired to raise his head. "Would you go ahead and find us a place for the night?" he asked quietly. "I need to stay here to make sure our porters don't find another reason for dawdling." He cast a managerial gaze over the coolies lounging about on the ground and the 16 idle carts.

"Delighted to," she said eagerly, anxious to be helpful. "The Lord will find us an especially nice place tonight. It's Friday night, you know. The Sabbath is approaching." She nodded at the westering sun.

"So it is." His face brightened. "It will be a pleasant surprise for the coolies that we don't travel on the Sabbath. But I won't tell them until after we get in tonight." His little-boy grin had returned.

An hour and a half later in a small, round mud hut, Gertrude carried a steaming pot of noodles from her Primus stove to the two short boards set up as a table around which the group had gathered.

"Who did you say was our proprietor for these two fine rooms tonight?" Dr. Nethery asked, reaching for the noodle pot.

"He's a young boy, about Herbert's age I'd guess," Gertrude said, tousling Herbert's hair as she sat down next to him. "But not nearly so clever."

"He's clever enough to be renting these rooms and looking after his sick mother," Herbert observed, glancing at his own mother.

"H'mmm. I wonder what her problem is?" Dr. Nethery cradled his spoon on the edge of his tin cup. Gertrude watched professional concern and compassion transform his face and replace his hunger. He turned to Miss Ma. "Do you think we can see her?" he asked.

"The boy says she has a devil." Miss Ma's statement startled them all into silence.

"That's silly," Gertrude said spontaneously, the first to recover her tongue. "She probably has some medical problem that they don't understand."

"Silly or not, it's real for them," Thelma replied gently. "For the people in these rural areas, superstition and the fear of spirits is the explanation for all their troubles that are unexplainable. Their genuine medical situations are frequently compounded by the fear of the devils."

"So how can you tell which it is?" Gertrude grappled with this new twist on medical theory.

"It may be both. We can't be sure unless we see her," Dr. Nethery said. "Miss Ma, can you get the boy to let us examine her?"

"I will try, Doctor," she said, rising from the low stool where she sat.

Gertrude secretly admired Miss Ma, a Chinese national who openly lived her Christianity while retaining her common touch with the non-Christian people around her. Her gentle demeanor and quiet ways dispelled the fear and distrust that the people felt in their distress. As she quieted their anxieties, they were made ready for her prayers for them which invariably followed every treatment she administered. Gertrude knew how to pray for patients. But there was something more, something subtle, that made Miss Ma special. "There's a lesson here for you, Gertrude," she said quietly to herself. "Learn it."

On careful examination Dr. Nethery found a deep-seated abscess on the old mother's left thigh, not yet ready to open. Gertrude suggested warm charcoal compresses to draw it to a head. But Dr. Nethery thought that bringing it too rapidly to a head might cause even more pain. He suggested that they give the woman pain medicines and penicillin, sedate her for the evening and see what her own body defenses would do by morning if given some pain-free time.

The medical care of the old woman by the "foreign missionary devils" was the talk of the village, drawing a huge crowd. When the press of the inquisitive masses threatened to break down the door to the small mud and thatch house, Dr. Nethery arranged for several Chinese soldiers to stand guard. For the first time on the trip Gertrude and her friends slept through the night without shining white teeth showing at every window.

"What did she say?" Gertrude asked at the leisurely Sabbath lunch the next day.

"She still says she has a devil in her," Miss Ma replied quietly.

"But wasn't she better this morning?" Gertrude asked incredulously.

"Her leg was better," Dr. Nethery noted with a nod of his head, "but her belief in the spirits remains undaunted." He continued slurping his noodles from his chopsticks without pause.

'Well, what are we going to do?" Gertrude wanted to know.

"About what?" Dr. Nethery asked with a full mouth, leaning over his tin cup.

"About her belief in the spirits. We've treated only half the problem, Doctor."

"What would you have us do, Gertrude?" Dr. Nethery chuckled. "That kind of problem will not be cured by penicillin or any other medicines that I am aware of."

"Well, I know—but . . ." Gertrude floundered in the web she had begun to weave.

Thelma laid her chopsticks on the rim of her cup. "She may be better but she is not convinced. Her belief in the spirit world was taught her from the time she was a small child. And a lifetime of beliefs cannot be easily changed." Thelma reached out with both hands, seeking Gertrude's consideration of her thoughts. "Besides, it's the Holy Spirit's job. We've done our part to suggest an alternative to what she believes."

"But how will she know?" Gertrude pleaded, not wanting to let go. "Who will tell her?"

"I will tell her," Miss Ma said quietly, "this afternoon." She fixed Gertrude with intense black eyes. "A hurried project is soon destroyed, Miss Green. The elder brother of faith is patience; he brings strength and not weakness."

Self-consciously Gertrude lowered her green eyes to the wisdom of the Orient. *So that's the lesson,* she thought humbly. *At least, one of them.*

"Well, let's not keep patience waiting any longer, shall we?" Thelma said, nodding to Herbert who had slipped away quietly to his mother's secret horde of delicacies.

Herbert stepped forward from the shadows proudly displaying a large can of Del Monte peaches in his outstretched hands.

"It's time for a Sabbath treat," Thelma announced to her wide-eyed companions.

"Where's Gertrude?" Dr. Nethery stood waiting beside his bicycle with Herbert next to him as Thelma coasted to a stop in front of them.

"She's on the rickshaw again." Thelma pointed back up the road. "She fell twice and started crying." Thelma paused to catch her breath, wrapping her coat tighter against the bitter cold wind. "Said she couldn't go another inch on that bicycle, her feet were so cold."

Dr. Nethery could see the rickshaws coming around the bend with Miss Ma in the lead and Gertrude in the next one behind her. Together he and Herbert pushed off toward the village just ahead of them, staying ahead of the carts. Thelma, still astraddle of her bicycle, desperately hopped along several steps with one foot on the ground and one foot on the pedal, trying to get started before the carts arrived and pushed her to the rough side of the road and certain disaster.

At the customs house in the village, an older, wiser Chinese officer studied Dr. Nethery warily as he explained that they were missionaries on their way to Yencheng with medicines for the hospital.

"You look like Russian," the Chinese guard said, thrusting his uplifted chin, pointing it at Dr. Nethery accusingly.

"I am an American who has been on the road for more than a week."

Dr. Nethery stroked his heavy growth of beard, realizing it was the cause of his accusation.

"Uhhh. Look like Russian," the guard said again. Averting his eyes, he waved him on through the short pole gate without charging any duty.

As the carts passed, the old guard closely scrutinized each one, trying to meet the eyes of each coolie. When a porter could not meet his gaze, he would stop the cart and search through the boxes and bundles secured there. On the sixth cart he found what he had been looking for, packages of cigarettes wrapped in straw matting, stowed carefully between the missionary boxes. With one finger the guard poked through the matting and discovered his quarry.

At once the caravan stopped as the coolies descended on the guard house, simultaneously threatening the coolie who had been caught and pleading with the guard for leniency. But the old guard stood his ground, his muscular arms folded over his chest, glowering at the protestors in triumph.

Gertrude came stomping back from her rickshaw to where Winston Nethery stood by the road, watching the proceedings with a wry smile.

"They got caught, didn't they?" she demanded.

"Yep," he said with a chuckle and a shake of his head. "I don't know how they're going to work this out. But I'll bet they aren't going to leave all those cigarettes here." He now turned his smile on Gertrude's ire, making her even angrier.

"And I'll bet they don't have the money to pay the duty." Gertrude's anger sought an appropriate target as she glared at the noisy scene before her.

"Nope. They spent every penny we gave them on the contraband they hoped to smuggle into Yencheng and make their fortunes." Gertrude thought Dr. Nethery was finding this interruption entirely too amusing.

"Well, I'm not going to stand here and gawk at this foolishness," she growled. "I'm going on." She turned and stomped off in the direction from which she had come.

"We have three more rivers to cross today," he called out after her. "Make sure your coolie knows the road. And don't get too far ahead."

Three hours later Gertrude sat waiting in her rickshaw which was resting on its long, brown handles on the ground, drumming her impatient fingers on the armrest. Her coolie sat idly by in the grass, wrapped in his long coat, leaning against a rock asleep, apparently content to be doing nothing. He had gotten her to the top of the rise above the river and she had paused there, hoping to see from this high vantage point the serpentine approach of the carts winding around the hills and along the road on the other side.

She and her coolie had crossed the third river more than an hour ago. She thought they'd not been traveling all that fast although she hadn't had to bargain for all the carts with the boatman at the last river or wait for them all to cross. She stood up on the small platform used for a footrest as she traveled, shading her eyes against the bright overhead sun. There was no sign of anyone on the road leading down to the river's edge where the boatmen now sat smoking and conversing in their small craft on the far side of the river. She had already used her best Mandarin to question the coolie about the road, throwing in a few words she'd learned of the local dialect. He had bowed and nodded, assuring her that this was the road to Yencheng.

She shook her head and sat down heavily. *Where is everyone?*

"Miss Green! Hello! Miss Green!"

Her eyes climbed the barren hill on the far side of the river, searching for the source of the strident greetings.

"Miss Green, you'll never get to Yencheng by going that way." She could see the small figure of Dr. Nethery, standing on the road waving his arms, motioning her back across the river. His voice sounded irritated, angry. *What have I done?* she demanded of herself. She felt irritated. *I didn't get too far ahead.*

The coolie had also heard the incensed voice. He rose quickly and grabbed the handles of the rickshaw, throwing Gertrude roughly back into the seat, as he raced back down the hill toward the river crossing.

A somber group of travelers stood at the head of the 16 carts which had paused at the fork in the road, and watched the rapid approach of Gertrude's rickshaw. Gertrude was hunched forward speaking forcefully while the coolie trotted as fast as he could, watching the ground, trying to outrun the raging storm that sat on the seat just behind him. The rickshaw paused only a moment while Gertrude stepped to the ground. The group could not hear distinctly the words she used but they observed their effect as the coolie and his rickshaw scampered for safety near the rear of the procession of carts.

Gertrude tromped across the intervening ground, her face livid. She ignored the glowering eyes and dark face of Dr. Nethery, consumed with her own fury.

"What happened?" Dr. Nethery measured his words precisely, biting off each syllable.

"He did it deliberately," Gertrude fumed, turning and firing a parting glance at the retreating coolie. She flung her right arm toward the river in a wide arc. "He intended to make a wide circle back to meet you at the correct river crossing." Her words were a staccato of machine-gun fire. "He wanted it to look like he was coming from the opposite direction so the customs officer wouldn't search him for contraband."

Dr. Nethery's hard, dark eyes locked onto Gertrude's green ones.

"I've been sitting there for more than an hour," she snapped, blinking hard, the fire in her eyes being quenched by small pools of moisture which appeared in their outer corners.

Dr. Nethery's mouth twitched and his face cracked, struggling to suppress a grin. His face softened and contorted by turn, barely maintaining control. Now he looked to Thelma for help.

"We're so glad you're safe." Thelma stepped forward, holding Gertrude's bicycle out to her. "We were all so worried about you."

"Well, you weren't half as worried as I was." Gertrude touched the corners of her eyes with the back of her dirty gloves. "And not half so glad that I'm found," she said as a small smile creased the black streaks on her cheeks. She squeezed Thelma's arm and accepted the metal-framed steed from her, stepping through the low-slung girdle and placing a heavily shod foot on the uppermost pedal. "It will feel good to pedal awhile after sitting in that rickshaw all morning," she said, pushing off.

Dr. Nethery and Herbert followed behind Thelma so as not to reveal their mirth.

After crossing the River Has—which they nicknamed the River Jordan because it was the last river to cross before coming to Yencheng—the traveling five found relatively quiet lodging in a tiny mud hut with few onlookers. It was a small village, and only 39 *li* from where they'd begun early that morning.

"I've been thinking about that remark about being a Russian," Winston said, rising from his low perch. "It worries me, and I don't like it."

From where she was bent over the washing pot cleaning her bowl Gertrude looked up and watched him beginning to fitfully prowl about the small room. She glanced at Thelma. *What's his problem?* their eyes silently asked each other.

"The Russians aren't liked or trusted in this part of the country," he continued, stroking his beard with both hands. "If they think we're Russian . . ." Suddenly he turned on them. "I'm going to shave off this beard." He strode to his own suitcase, opening it on the floor. "Save a little of that hot water for me," he called out. Standing erect, he thrust a flashlight at Herbert. "Here, Herbert, you hold the flashlight." He paused momentarily. "Mrs. Smith, where is that little mirror I saw you looking at the other day?" His intensity was infectious, causing Thelma to scramble for her personal effects.

When she tried to hand the mirror to him, he said, "No, you hold it. Like this." He adjusted her hand. "I can at least see part of my face at a time. You there, Miss Green," he called.

Gertrude stood watching, much amused at the spontaneous construction of an operating room directly over the oil lamp balanced on its small upright box. "Yes, Doctor," she answered mockingly, holding up her rice bowl now full of hot water.

"Staunch the blood if I cut myself," he said seriously as he dipped the sharp razor in the water and cautiously began to scrape his tender, sunburned left cheek.

Miss Ma's Chinese curiosity was entertained as the group danced about the oil lamp, waving the mirror and flashlight, issuing adjustment orders, emitting cries of pain. She applauded gleefully as a child when the doctor stepped away from the group, gently rubbing his smooth and tender chin.

"I wish we could do something that easy, Thelma, to transform ourselves into respectable looking Americans." Running her fingers through her own dirty hair, Gertrude laughed and pointed at Thelma's grimy, windburned face and the straggling wisps of hair peeking from under her ever-present turban.

Thelma peeked in the small mirror she still held and grimaced, then grinned as Gertrude made a ridiculous face to emphasize that she knew she looked the same.

"Easy!" Dr. Nethery turned, hands on hips, to face them. "Do you think that was a pleasure with my wind-sore face and all these nicks on my neck?"

It was Herbert's turn to chortle at the hilarious scene before him, the doctor dabbing at his face with a bloody cloth and the women making grotesque faces by turn in the mirror.

"Poor doctor," each woman said in turn. They turned to each other, pulling down the corners of their mouths in exaggerated clown-sad sympathy before falling into each others arms with gales of exhausted laughter.

The next four days continued to bring numbingly cold mornings, burning afternoon sun, and the incessant wind. The countryside became flatter, the villages more monotonously similar, the soil more sandy, the roads more impassable. The traffic on the roads increased, the carts continued breaking down at an alarming rate, and the bicycle accidents became more frequent.

The only joyous part of the day was breakfast. The hot water, with Postum added to take away the vile taste, warmed them to face the cold day, and the Post Toasties with hot water filled them until lunch time. Dr. Nethery always added two tablespoons of Merry Brand condensed milk, a Japanese product much like Eagle Brand in the United States, to his cereal.

"When you need energy, when you need pep, drink Merry Brand," was his comical commercial each morning as he ceremoniously added it to his meager meal.

But the humor was wearing thin. Gertrude no longer smiled and no longer attached her high praises for Postum to the end of his commercial plug. In fact, she hardly spoke at all. With a forced laugh for Herbert's benefit Thelma occasionally tried to repeat Gertrude's Postum commercial. But she failed miserably, for her heart wasn't in it. Even Miss Ma was growing weary of the wind and the sun and the constant travel.

On the fourth day, Wednesday, Dr. Nethery and Miss Ma separated themselves from the main party to search several side roads and villages, seeking information or someone who might be looking for their caravan. Gertrude, Thelma, and Herbert were left to travel the main road with the carts and the coolies, separated from the other two for more than 24 hours. The result was to separate the group of two from their cots and the larger group from their strong right arm to set up the cots. That evening Gertrude and Thelma fearfully barricaded their door with boxes and bicycles against imagined intruders. The congenial relaxation of suppertime was sorely absent.

On their reappearance on Thursday the smaller group of explorers reported that none of the small villages produced an advance welcoming party, however, they had plenty of company at night. Dr. Nethery and Miss Ma managed to find "a million others" who shared their straw sleeping arrangements and left their red marks to be scratched and examined in the morning.

By Thursday evening, Gertrude and Thelma were exhausted. They'd spent much of the day taking turns riding in the spare rickshaw with no congenial sarcasm from either of them about who was not able to keep up. Even questions by some of the locals about whether Gertrude was a man or a woman had failed to raise more than the perfunctory remark that they were all becoming less and less recognizable, even to each other.

When they did not reach Yencheng that evening as planned, the weary group ate a silent supper in the small village of Deng Tsai still 18 *li* from their destination. Tempers flared when the rowdy children outside started shouting about "the devils from the American hospital" and began throwing stones at the door and front windows of their small abode. Dr. Nethery ran out the back door and around the side of the small house, grabbing one of the children by surprise. Her terrified screams sent the other children scrambling and soon brought the local Chinese soldiers who told them all they would have to see the magistrate in the morning to examine their baggage for "customs."

The following morning they quietly left Deng Tsai earlier than usual without eating breakfast.

Chapter 42

BEGINNING AGAIN

Yencheng, Honan Province
Sabbath, March 23, 1940

Dearest Mother:

Well here I am in my new place. The trip is over and am I ever glad it is. We arrived yesterday morning in Yencheng after riding our bicycles for 12 days from morning 'til night.

When we arrived on the edge of Yencheng, we could see the smoke stack of the railroad roundhouse and railroad bridge and knew we were almost there.

As we rounded the corner and climbed the hill to the front gates of the mission compound, we could see the people lining the path into the compound to welcome us. And there were the Chinese characters "Seventh-day Adventist Mission and Hospital" over the gate. Even from the front gate I could see that it was a large and beautiful compound with hospital buildings, school buildings, and a church.

In the foreign section of the compound Elder Effenberg was waiting on the steps to welcome us into Dr. Nethery's house. And I tell you, it was the most beautiful house I had ever seen, with a real table for dinner and all the hot water we wanted for baths.

So the great adventure bicycle trip is over and I intend to write a long travel letter to all of my friends so you can get the whole story.

Mrs. Thelma Smith and her son, Herbert, will be living in the apartment right under mine but both apartments will have to be fixed up before we can move in. The whole front is screened porch. There is a living room, dining room, kitchen, two bedrooms and a bathroom. I have a swell piano that Elder

Effenburg tuned recently and I also have my accordion which the people here will love, but they haven't seen it yet. And my battery radio works great. It made the trip just fine and I can get all over on it. So I am all set.

This is a really lovely place with trees and plants and flowers everywhere which help to divide the compound into four sections. The hospital section has three buildings for the men's hospital, the women's hospital, and an out-patient building. The education section is for the ten-grade school which has about 400 students and the church. The other two sections are areas for the Chinese housing and the Western foreigners' housing plus the gardens and orchards and a swimming pool!

The hospital is very busy. We have more men than women patients partly because of the war and partly because the men's hospital is bigger. The hospital was built to hold 60 patients but our average daily list is 115-125. Even then we have to turn many away who have come from a long way off. Even the patients' dining room and the classrooms have been turned into wards. Dr. Nethery and Dr. Tsao, the Chinese doctor, are kept very busy seeing everyone, sometimes 150 a day in the outpatient department. Our most commonly seen diseases include bladder stones, relapsing fever, cholera, kala-azar, venereal disease, and abscesses caused by the needling of the Chinese doctors. There are eye diseases and TB and malaria. And there are the gunshot wounds.

We also have a Refugee Kitchen which has been running now for about 2 years. It provides a place to eat for those who have been chased from their homes and their work by the war. We have rented a small piece of land next to ours and built a wall around it. Each morning from 5:00 a.m. to 8:30 a.m. 10,000 refugees are fed in two shifts of 5,000. They sit on the ground back to back in rows with their bowls held out. Our coolies pass down the rows and dish out the cereal which is really like cornmeal mush. It gives a fair picture of what the Scriptures says about the feeding of the 5,000 except there they had women and children besides.

I went to Sabbath School this morning and guess how many members they have? 1,093! This doesn't count the 150 to 200 visitors and the eleven branch Sabbath Schools they conduct in the afternoon all around. I went to one this afternoon in the larger nearby town of Loho and there were 93 people there. This is surely a live working church. It is so nice to be in a place where the gospel is going out and where there is a real mission work with so many good results.

Well, I am sending this letter to mail with Elder Effenburg when he goes back to Shanghai. I will write you all the time but from now on I can't tell you when you will receive my letters. Dr. Nethery just got some letters yesterday that were written in September of 1938—one and a half years ago! At that rate you may see me before you see the letters. Actually he says it takes about three months for the mail to go through so here's hoping for the best.

I am wondering how you are as I have not heard from you in quite a while. I hope you received all the boxes and pictures I sent from Shanghai. Take care of yourself and remember me to everyone. Tell them I am fine and feeling wonderful. This is a swell place and I like it heaps.

Well, it's time for supper and I am eating at Dr. Nethery's house until we get settled in. Bye-bye for this time and hope this finds you well.

From your loving daughter who loves her mother,

Gertrude

"Mrs. Yu, I need the self-retaining retractor . . . now." Dr. Nethery held the lower abdominal wound open with his right hand, his index finger pointing to the fascial plane that Dr. Tsao needed to separate to find the bladder, his other fingers spread uncomfortably to expose the surgical field. His left hand blindly waved about behind him, impatiently awaiting the missing instrument. "Why is it not in the room?"

"It's coming, doctor," the strong, long-faced Chinese nurse said smoothly, standing with one foot holding open the swinging door of the operating room that led into the hallway, unruffled in the face of his anxiety. "We have only two of these retractors so we keep them in a special place." She turned and barked into the darkness of the hallway in the local dialect that she thought the Caucasians would not understand, producing an anxious, scurrying Anne Feng bearing the offending instrument.

Gertrude noted that Mrs. Yu had a silky, patronizing voice for the foreigners and a sharp, demanding voice for the Chinese who worked under her. Gertrude pictured the conniving witch in her childhood book about Hansel and Gretel, and smiled to herself.

"But we're doing only one surgery today." Dr. Nethery ignored the condescending tones of his operating room supervisor, dismissing her mixture of nursing passivity and Oriental frugality. "Please, have everything that we need in the room," he said. His eyes darted to the head of the table, imploring Gertrude to do something about this woman, to fix this recurring conundrum.

Gertrude held the gauze-encased ether mask steadily in her left hand, supporting the patient's chin with two fingers and feeling the pulse under the chin with a third finger. The ether can rested in her right hand, its pungent wick limply poised for the next application of anesthetic.

Sorry, Doctor. I'm a bit preoccupied, Gertrude mused mentally. Yet standing before her was the personification of the perplexing dilemma which had confronted her for two months now. *What did these people expect of her? What was the proper way to work with them?*

This wasn't the Shanghai Sanitarium, a Western hospital in the International Settlement where everything was run by the Western foreigners, lots of them on every floor and in every classroom. This was Yencheng, in the heart of China. And she was the only Western nurse here.

Gertrude searched for possible strategies, recalling her clinic work in Mr. Chen's courtyard and the passionate appeal of Dr. Hwang. How had she related to these Chinese men? But they were the older teachers and she was the younger student. Now she was the teacher but not always the elder. And she was a woman, although this was not nearly as much of a problem for the Chinese as it was for the brethren of the church. This last thought simultaneously raised her ire and brought her thoughts back to her struggling surgeon, the operating room, and the bladder stone they were removing.

Better pay attention and worry later, she thought as she skillfully tipped the ether can.

Gertrude and Dr. Nethery stepped out of the door of the Men's Hospital into the bright May sunshine, quickly making their way down the concrete steps and along the brick walkways that led to their offices in the Outpatient Building. Gertrude, quite agile and strong at age 31, and long of limb, had no trouble matching the rapid strides of her much taller companion. She noted the new, green fruit filling the branches of the plum and peach trees which shaded their path. *It is a wonderful time of year on this beautiful compound,* she thought.

"Miss Green, I need your help," Dr. Nethery said, breaking into her reverie.

"Yes, doctor," she replied, expecting a change of clinic schedules or a special order for one of the hospital patients.

"I need you to take charge," he said emphatically.

"Of what, doctor?" She responded more to his tone of voice than to his statement.

"Of that business back there, of Mrs. Yu, and the nursing staff, and . . . everything."

When he halted and turned to her, Gertrude saw confusion and frustration on his face—or was it irritation?

"Look, you've been here two months now . . . ," he began.

"And you've been here how long?" Gertrude stood her ground, looking him in the eye. *I'll not back down from you, Winston Nethery,* she thought. *It only encourages you to be more pushy. Besides, something else is bothering you. What is it?* She searched his face and felt herself mellow at the years of questions and frustrations she saw etched there.

"I've been here a little over two years . . . and, no, I haven't found a solution for Mrs. Yu either." He offered with a weak smile. "But I think you are having a hard time taking control . . . being sick and all," he added.

Gertrude remembered her recent days in bed with a cold and those stomach cramps . . . the frequent Japanese airplanes overhead going south to bomb near Wuhan . . . and the news on her radio of the ever-advancing war. "I think that's all over now," she said with more conviction than she felt.

"Good. I hope so." He turned and began walking, but not so quickly now. "Mr. Fan in the pharmacy is very upset. He says he is still losing medicines and doesn't know where they're going."

Gertrude looked up and met his gaze searching for her reaction. She nodded in response, knowing that they were thinking the same thing. Being cut off from supplies by the war, stealing from the pharmacy was about the worst crime anyone could commit.

"I am planning another trip out to Shanghai to get more supplies and medicines . . . and to bring back Marie and Skippy. But not until after she delivers the baby," he said. "The medicines have to last until at least July or later."

"Can Mr. Fan be trusted?" Gertrude asked the obvious first question.

"With my life," he affirmed with a vigorous nod of his head.

At 24 years of age Wang Shueh Wen was the youngest of the nursing supervisors. His muscular physique, full head of unruly black hair, and large, square smiling face made him stand out among the Chinese wherever he went. And his industriousness and quick mind made him an instant favorite with Gertrude. One morning, during her Director of Nurses morning rounds through the Men's Hospital, she spotted Mr. Wang working at his desk during an unusually quiet moment and approached him.

"Brother Wang, may I speak with you?" She addressed him by his Christian title, using the local dialectic version of Mandarin that she was beginning to understand and adopt as her own.

"Yes, Miss Green." He quickly stood and bowed in respect.

She gave a quick small bow as she knew was expected of her by her rank. "Mr. Wang," she began again, "I have been here more than two months now and I have not attended a single meeting of the nursing school teaching staff."

He stood still, blinking but not speaking.

Did I say something incorrectly? Gertrude wondered at his non-response. She tried again. "What day does the teaching staff have their meetings?" She spoke slowly, choosing Chinese words and sentence construction that she was sure of.

"Monday evenings, Miss Green," he answered promptly.

"Will there be a meeting this Monday evening?" she asked carefully.

"Yes, Miss Green." He replied and bowed as if in response to a command.

"Thank you, Mr. Wang." Gertrude tried a disarming smile but Mr. Wang seemed reluctant to return it. After an awkward moment, she nodded, turned and left.

Monday evening when Gertrude arrived in the small treatment room they used as a conference room, she found Mr. Wang, Miss Ma, and Mr. Yu in quiet conversation around a small square table. When she entered the room, they all stood and bowed with their hands folded in front of them. Gertrude returned their bow with a gentle nod of her head and took the remaining seat, after which they also resumed their seats.

For several moments no one spoke.

"Oh, I can't stand this," Gertrude suddenly burst out in English, making everyone visibly jump.

"I'm sorry," she quickly said in Mandarin, "I just don't know what is going on. Who is in charge here?"

"You are," Miss Ma said.

"But who was in charge before I came?" Gertrude asked in confusion.

"It does not matter now," Miss Ma said simply. "Now that you are here, we need your experience to tell us what to do."

"But why do you trust me? What can you possibly know about me?" Gertrude struggled to make her thoughts and her emotions translate into understandable Chinese.

"Oh, we know a lot about you." This time Mr. Wang spoke, more enthusiastically, Gertrude thought, than he had last week during their awkward, formal meeting in his office.

"We have known about you for some time now—the move of the Shanghai Sanitarium, the opening of the Range Road Clinic, and the facing down of the Japanese guards on the Soochow Creek bridge." This last comment was spoken with pride as if describing a win by a favorite sports team.

"We had word of your work from the Chinese workers in Shanghai and Wuhan." Mr. Yu's voice was surprisingly quiet.

Gertrude turned her attention quickly in his direction. His severe black eyes were full of traditional formality but Gertrude heard kindness in his tone.

"And from Doctor Miller," he added.

Ah, Harry Miller. I might have known, Gertrude mused inwardly.

"This was his first hospital," Miss Ma said, reading Gertrude's thoughts. "He still keeps in touch with us."

Gertrude adjusted herself in her seat, processing what had just transpired. Clearly these people had been waiting for her to call this meeting, which she had done inadvertently in Mr. Wang's office last week. They expected her to be the Director of the Nursing School as well as the Director of Nurses, and all because of what? Her nursing degree? All of them were RNs. Because she was Caucasian? She wasn't sure. But she knew she needed to talk with someone and soon.

Over the next hour Gertrude learned that these three were the main teachers in the school of nursing. Mr. Ren did some nursing duties, but his primary responsibility was finance and collections, something they all thought he did with great skill and exceptional honesty. Thinking about Dr. Nethery's problem in the pharmacy, Gertrude carefully couched her questions about Mr. Fan in terms of the nursing school and discovered that he also could teach and do some occasional nursing supervisory work. But they assured her that he worriedly stood guard over his pharmacy so much that he had little time for teaching.

And what about Mr. Cecil Tang? she asked. It seemed that he worked in various capacities, some teaching, some supervising. But he had no specific assignment as many of the others did. And why not, Gertrude wondered at the time. Did he not have a relative in power or was he new, or had he not been given an opportunity because of some other social reason? As his broad smiling face and crinkling eyes came before her mind, she made a mental note to find out what he could do and to put him to work.

Also before the meeting was over, Gertrude discovered that no one had the experience to teach hydrotherapy. And because the Chinese were afraid the patients would catch cold, and because the Chinese do not traditionally bathe during the cold season, no one was teaching hygiene, especially the bathing techniques. As a result, Gertrude found herself with two more jobs, including teaching one of her favorite topics—hydrotherapy. Gertrude remembered Miss Ragsdale's parting advice that she should insist on teaching only. Maybe this is what she meant.

As the expected hot weather of June made Gertrude's upstairs apartment more unbearable, she spent many nights relaxing in the downstairs apartment with Thelma and Herbert playing "Shanghai Millionaire." Herbert was glad for the table game and the company as there were no other children on the missionary side of the compound. And as missionaries working constantly in the Chinese language, Thelma and Gertrude had no other women with whom to share their thoughts in English where they were able to express more clearly what they were feeling.

"Do you think he's asleep?" Gertrude asked abruptly after Herbert had been in bed for about 15 minutes.

"Of course," Thelma replied. "He's never had a problem sleeping, even when he was a baby. Comes from all the traveling we do." Thelma cocked her head thoughtfully. "Why? What's up?"

"I need some advice." Gertrude sat up, leaning forward. "I'm just not sure how to take charge. I mean, I'm feeling like a duck out of water, working in Chinese and all." She found the words coming easier as she realized she was speaking in English. "I can speak Chinese all right but

I'm just not sure how forceful I should be. I'm the only English-speaking nurse here, excepting Miss Ma, of course. Actually the only Western nurse here. Do you know what I mean?"

"Yes." Thelma gave a little laugh. "I'm walking in the same shoes as the Chinese would say." She laughed again. "We can't seem to get away from the Chinese, even here." She waved her hand to the four, very Western, wainscoted walls of her apartment. "The bookkeeping is the same but the people and the culture and the . . . well, what can I say? It's China. I've been here for years and it's still different. It's not home. It's China."

"In Shanghai, I had people I could talk to," Gertrude said. "There I knew what was expected of me." She became more earnest as she came closer to understanding her own frustration. "If I needed correction, I had people I could count on to correct me." The faces of Geneva Beatty and Grace Dale briefly floated through her mind as her voice became husky and her eyes misted over. "Here I don't have anyone." She touched a finger to the corner of her eye to catch the tear before it could run down her cheek.

"You have me," Thelma offered gently.

"Yes, I know, dear" Gertrude smiled. "But you're not there in the hospital when I'm about to open my big mouth and say something I shouldn't."

"Do you do that?"

"You know I do," Gertrude said with an emphatic shake of her head and a burst of laughter. Then gathering her seriousness together she asked, "Who can I talk to who will know?"

After a few quiet moments Thelma said, "Talk with Pastor Chang. I've spoken with him about my frustrations at not having the time to do the Bible studies I was trained to do. He seemed to understand and was very sympathetic." She paused. "And he's Chinese and will understand your predicament . . . I think."

Gertrude recalled the tall, dark pastor with the rugged face of a farmer, the square jaw and large forehead that made him look almost European, and the soft eyes that lit up when he preached.

"Perhaps so," she said more to herself. "That's who helped me before. The Chinese."

"And don't forget to pray," Thelma added softly.

"Oh, I've been praying," Gertrude retorted sharply as if in answer to a criticism.

"I don't mean just praying, Gertrude," Thelma said firmly. "I mean, being in a state of prayer all the time." Her round, brown eyes were lit with a fire that Gertrude didn't usually see there. "And I'm praying for you, too," she added, her eyes softening.

"I know," Gertrude mumbled in instant contrition. "Thank you."

Chapter 43

FINDING HER VOICE

July was exceptionally hot. The frequent opportunities for afternoon swims in Dr. Nethery's concrete block swimming pool were only distant memories the next day as the noontime sun and afternoon heat beat down on the hospital buildings and clinic. Of course, there was no air conditioning. No one in Yencheng went to the mountains during the heat of summer as they'd done in Nanking. There was too much work to be done in the hospital. There was also the fear that, without the Westerners around, everyone would lapse into laziness and squalor. And there was the ever-present threat of thievery.

Gertrude had spent the early morning teaching hygiene to the new freshmen students—in Chinese, of course. This was followed by administering the anesthetic for an operation, a session with Miss Ma and Mr. Yu reworking the floor schedules for the junior and senior nursing students and the staff nurses, and morning rounds in the Women's Hospital and now the Men's Hospital. It was approaching lunch time, the hottest part of the day.

As she reached the final few steps of the large open staircase to the second floor of the Men's Hospital, Gertrude heard the clamor of many voices and saw several of her new male student nurses coming from one of the few private rooms at the far end of the hall. At the same time, three female floor nurses pushed their way in. *Did a patient fall out of bed? Was one of the typhoid patients dying? And what were the female nurses doing here in the Men's Hospital?* With a deep breath Gertrude brushed several stray curls back under the edge of her beloved nursing cap and quickened her steps toward the commotion.

Entering the room, Gertrude saw several people gathered around the single iron bedstead which all but filled the small room. Rather than administering emergency care to the patient, the nurses simply stood about the bed, occasionally bowing like her mother's weighted metal bird that tipped forward to pick up toothpicks from a bowl. Gertrude's green eyes narrowed as the corners of her mouth sank and her face grew long and serious. She took a deep breath through her nose and exhaled noisily.

The three nurses melted away from the bed toward the walls, leaving two young female servants—Gertrude judged by their common cotton, ankle length pants and ordinary jackets—plumping pillows and arranging some expensive embroidered bed coverings around Mrs. Cho. Mrs. Cho had accompanied her husband, General Cho, to the hospital just five days ago.

Immediately on his arrival by barge, Dr. Nethery had removed a bullet from the general's chest. Now he was convalescing nicely in the private room next door. In the meantime, Mrs. Cho was scheduled for a hysterectomy at the end of the week. But she had been housed in a nice private room in the Women's Hospital. What was she doing here—on the second floor of the Men's Hospital?

"Mrs. Liu." Gertrude addressed the charge nurse who was cowering against the wall, caught between her unexpected guest and her Director of Nurses. "What is the meaning of this? What's going on here?" Gertrude's crisp formal Mandarin pronunciation, bereft of any local dialect, electrified the room, causing the servants and Mrs. Cho to hesitate in their nest building and look at her.

"Honorable Miss Green." Mrs. Liu spoke formally as she bowed to Gertrude, something Gertrude had discouraged the nurses from doing but which she did not stop now. "Mrs. Cho was lonely. She missed her husband and wanted to be next to him." Mrs. Liu's tone of voice was servile . . . and fearful. "She requested to be moved here next to her husband."

"Mrs. Liu, this is the Men's Hospital. Female nurses do not like to work with the male patients and therefore we separate the patients. It is not a system that I particularly like but it is the system we have."

Gertrude spoke firmly with purposeful, measured cadence while trying to decide if Mrs. Liu was one of the major players in this game or only a pawn. Using her conversation with Mrs. Liu as a shield, Gertrude's heightened instincts swept the room. As the social and cultural realities of the situation fell into place, she fought to control her anger, reining it in and focusing its energy, awaiting the first move of the one person who would dare assume this much authority.

"I do not have extra female nurses that I can put here on this floor for just one patient. Mrs. Cho cannot stay here."

"Miss Green, is it?" Mrs. Cho spoke as to an underling, without using a title or any formal greeting, emphasizing her status as a married woman and belittling Gertrude's unmarried situation. "I wish to be left here next to my husband." She spoke with a condescending nod of her head is if she were dismissing one of the servants who stood next to her bed.

"Mrs. Cho." Gertrude moved quickly and decisively into the position of power that Mrs. Cho had too quickly assumed was her own. "This is a hospital, not a hotel. The patients are not in charge." She paused for effect. "I am in charge. And you will return to the Women's Hospital immediately." Gertrude's green eyes challenged her adversary to speak.

Mrs. Cho met Gertrude's gaze for a moment. Then her eyes closed slowly and fell away as she sullenly turned over into her large pillows.

"Mrs. Liu, please ask the student nurses to take Mrs. Cho back to her room in the Women's Hospital," Gertrude said with final authority.

A resounding and resolute "Yes, Miss Green" was the reply Gertrude heard as she turned and left the room.

> SDA Mission
> Yencheng, Honan, China
> July 25, 1940

Dearest Mother,

It's about time I was getting a letter off to you. If I remember right the last one was about how awful hot it was then. For the past week the weather has been fine with a breeze most every day. I am wondering how you are because I haven't had an American letter in ages. Don't know where they are all gone to, but nothing I can do about it.

This last week the Juniors gave the graduating class a picnic. They had never done this before and didn't know what to do. So I explained what it was and that they did it everywhere else. So they made all the plans and arranged for the eats. They hired two boats on the river and tied them together, putting mats down to sit on.

We started out at 4:30 p.m. with a lot of firecrackers. What a noise! We had music and jokes and way up the river there was a nice stopping off place where we ran races and played games until dark. Then we came back to the mission compound by moonlight. They all so enjoyed it and didn't want to come back so soon. It gave them a change from their work and they were all so happy.

Dr. Nethery and Thelma Smith went along on the picnic as well. This was just the ticket for Dr. Nethery who has been working too hard and worrying about how quickly the supplies are running out and wishing he could see his wife who gave birth to a little girl, their second child, almost three months ago. He is talking about going out to Shanghai again to get more supplies and bring back his wife and family. But he is not going until the new mission leader, Elder Wilkinson and his wife get here. Mr. Dixon, the Union Auditor and Treasurer, has been here for the last few months helping out but he has to get back to his other duties. And Dr. Nethery doesn't want to leave two "helpless" women here by themselves. But I think we can take care of ourselves pretty well.

Thelma Smith and I got to talk on the boat coming back from the picnic. She is the local treasurer and bookkeeper for the hospital, and the school, and the mission which keeps her hopping, I'll tell you. That and raising her son, Herbert, without a husband. He was killed by bandits very soon after they arrived in China. Thelma could have gone home to the States then but felt the Lord calling her to stay and do Bible studies, which is what she was trained to do and why she came to China.

But the bookkeeping has kept her so busy that she has almost no time for anything else except schooling Herbert. That's another story, with so few books available. But all of us are pitching in and helping out each other where we can.

My garden is producing as much as ever. Plenty of tomatoes, corn, okra, carrots, and onions. The gardener has done a fine job and is planting a second crop of string beans. We even have a watermelon growing in our own yard! We've had lots of plums and peaches and loads of strawberries just like we had from the college in Chiao Tou Tseng. Mercy, wasn't that a long time ago!

Well, here it is already the end of July, the time goes so quickly. Dr. Nethery mentioned that his furlough would be coming up soon and I said that in one year and five months I would be going home also. We all are so tired that we are not sure if we want to come back or not. The war is dragging on. I still don't like it when the Japanese fly over our town toward Wuhan or out toward Chungking. But they have not bombed anywhere around here now for over two years, certainly before my time, at least. And we are beginning to learn to live with it. My battery radio works wonderfully well. We listen to the news every morning at 4:30 and every evening at 8:30 so we don't feel so isolated.

Well, I will close this letter for today, hoping it finds you well and happy. I guess you should address my letters to Shanghai at Box 1281 and they can send them on to me. That way I might get them. Because now I am getting nothing. Write soon.

Loads of love to my Darling Mother from her daughter who loves her,
Gertrude

The letter from Mukden, China, that Gertrude held in her hand was obviously written in Marie Nethery's hand but the words were straight from the heart of 7-year-old Skippy, Winston James, Jr.

"When you come to see us again, I want you to stay a long time," his mother had faithfully written from his dictation.

Gertrude laid the letter back on the desk in front of Dr. Nethery, who had sat with his head in his hands while she read it. With a slight shrug of her shoulders, she sat resignedly in the chair opposite him, making no comment, knowing what was coming.

"It's only one more reason I have to go out," he said finally, looking up.

"I know," she replied with a worried sigh. "We've had no more supplies since the last carts came in with Elder White. We are almost out of sulfanilamide, salygan, Syrup of White Pine, and any number of other medicines. And there are only six tins of ether left."

Winston Nethery slapped the desk top with his immense hands and heaved his generous frame to a standing position. Even though she'd been watching him, Gertrude flinched at this unusually intense display of irritation.

"If Wilkinson had come overland like we did, instead of coming up river, he would have been here by now," he snapped as he began to pace back and forth in front of her within the confines of the small office.

"There's a war on, doctor," Gertrude remarked to his back. "I'd rather he got here safely with those supplies in six weeks than lose them trying to get them here in 10 days."

He turned on her with a dark scowl. "I'd a lot rather be in our little war here than in Europe about now," he barked. Returning abruptly to his pacing, he opened his mouth to speak again, then paused, staring at the wall of bookcases that had so quickly confronted him. "There's not enough room to pace in here," he remarked, his mouth twitching with the foolishness of his outburst. "Probably not enough room to be upset either."

"Probably not." Gertrude kept a straight face and waited. She knew this boss needed a little time to let off steam before he could contemplate the serious problems they faced. She watched his hands pull down the corners of his ever-present vest over his belt buckle then slip behind his back and clasp together. *Now we're getting somewhere,* she thought.

"I'll take Mr. Fan with me." He was thinking out loud, trying on ideas for size and comfort. "We'll send out an order for supplies before we go and he can intercept them and bring them right back in, in case Elder Wilkinson takes longer to get here than he planned." His upper body pivoted halfway around, seeking Gertrude's approval.

"And I'll place Cecil Tang in the pharmacy until Mr. Fan gets back," she joined in the planning process. "He's the only one who doesn't seem to have an area of responsibility."

"But Dixon is gone." Dr. Nethery stopped, stymied by this new complication. He faced Gertrude, arms extended in serious supplication. "How can you manage the painting of the Men's Hospital and the building of the hydrotherapy room?"

"And who do you think you would have asked to look after those little items if you were going to be here?" Gertrude retorted with a twinge of irritation. "We'll manage just fine."

"Well, Wilkinsons will be here soon." He shrugged with reluctant acceptance.

"We'll be fine," Gertrude repeated. "You just get that family of yours— and those supplies—and get back here as quick as you can."

On Wednesday, August 14, at 4:30 a.m.—with Gertrude's medicine order and Thelma's request for sixth grade books for Herbert—Dr. Nethery and Mr. Fan set out on their journey to Mukden and then Shanghai.

Chapter 44

WORKING WITHIN THE CULTURE

S. D. A. Mission
Yencheng, Honan, China
August 19, 1940

Dearest Mother—

Well, at last I have received a letter from you! It was written May 31 and is 3 months old but a late letter is better than none. I do hope you are feeling much better now that the summer weather can pep you up.

Dr. Nethery left here last week to go to Mukden to get his wife and son—and new baby daughter he has not seen yet. They will go to Shanghai for medicines and supplies and then make the same trip we did to get back here. At present Mrs. Smith and her son Herbert—and me—are the only foreigners here. We are expecting Pastor Wilkinson and his wife, Nellie, to arrive most any day now. They have had a difficult time getting out of Pengpu with the supplies they are bringing. When he arrives, we can have graduation because he is bringing the senior student nurses their new uniforms.

I am busy in the Hospital getting new methods started and new things built. I have to boss the carpenters and the painters and everyone around. Many times I don't know much about it myself, but I pretend like I do. I am having the Men's Hospital all repainted and it looks wonderful. The ceiling and the walls halfway down are cream and the lower walls are light green with a dark green border.

There are two children in the hospital about twelve years old who have no home. Their fathers and mothers were killed by bombs. They are not sick anymore but they have no place to go. They have never gone to school. So Thelma and I have arranged for them to go to our school starting the next Monday. We are having a lot of fun getting them clothes made and shoes and socks, two pair each. It costs Shanghai $6.50 to send them to school for half a year, which is about 4 cents of your money for each child. I will have their pictures taken when they are all rigged up and send you one. They are too cute for words.

I am anxious for another letter from you but I suppose they will drift in gradually. I hope that you are sending them to Shanghai again and not mailing them air mail here which doesn't get them here at all. Hope Aunt Belle is better and also Walter. The summer weather should have helped him some, too.

Well, I don't have any more special news today so I had better close, hoping this finds you well with Loads of Love from your daughter who loves you.

Gertrude

Within one week of Dr. Nethery's being gone, the problems began.

In the middle of August Mr. Yu contracted typhoid fever and became one of the patients. This increased the teaching load on Miss Ma, Mr. Wang, and Gertrude just as the new freshman class started its work on the wards and the makeup hydrotherapy and hygiene classes for the juniors and seniors were getting underway. Gertrude had to press Mr. Ren and several others into service as temporary teachers and ward supervisors.

On Friday of that same week Dr. Tsao got into trouble during a surgery for removal of an immense bladder stone. Although Dr. Nethery had instructed Dr. Tsao in how to perform this procedure many times, he became confused when the stone refused to budge and angry when Gertrude suggested he lengthen the incision to give more working room. After several tense minutes, Gertrude gave Anne Feng some rudimentary instructions in managing the anesthetic mask, then quickly went to the other end of the table where she thought to assist Dr. Tsao. In fact, he was so upset that Gertrude had to take over the surgery, making a joke about being only a nurse and having to "deliver" the stone like a baby. To help Dr. Tsao save face she pretended to be the assistant while guiding him in the closure of the now gaping wound.

On the following Monday evening, the night watchman and Mr. Ren found the cooks from the second-class kitchen drinking in their room, being more loud and disruptive than even the Chinese would tolerate on their side of the compound. When Gertrude asked who would have to take the necessary disciplinary action, Mr. Ren told her it would be the Medical Superintendent.

And since Dr. Nethery is gone . . . ., Gertrude said in her mind and left the sentence unfinished.

In the middle of clinics on Tuesday morning, an excited coolie burst into the OPD building, calling for Miss Green to come to the Men's Hospital. Thinking it might be a complication from last Friday's bladder surgery, Gertrude quickly made her way to the second floor of the larger of the two hospital buildings. At the top of the stairs, Wang Shueh Wen was waiting for her.

"Is it the bladder surgery from Friday?" she asked as she mounted the last step.

"No, he is doing quite well." Mr. Wang spoke barely above a whisper. "It is another problem entirely, Miss Green."

What problem didn't I know about when I made rounds this morning? Gertrude considered as she trailed behind his quick, shuffling steps to the large five-bed ward.

She remembered the four patients in the ward; all were reasonably well this morning. Now one of the small, steel framed cots had two folding screens around it, providing privacy as well as "protection" for the other patients who greatly feared the dead body and the disembodied spirit. She peered around the edge of the screen, confirming the presence of the body covered completely by a white sheet. A graduate nurse and two students hovered over the man in the next bed. One of the students was holding up the patient's chin.

"Mr. Wang, what happened?"

Just that morning Gertrude had seen the patient folding his quilt at the end of his bed. Now he was comatose and breathing only four or five times a minute. She bent over and smelled his breath. "No alcohol and no sweetness," she said aloud.

Mr. Wang nodded in agreement. "The students found this man and that one over there when they came to take them down for hydrotherapy."

Gertrude glanced over her shoulder at the shrouded body behind her. "Did they come in together? Did they know each other?"

"They were brothers," Mr. Wang said quietly.

Gertrude stepped forward and lifted the patient's eyelids. His pupils were pinpricks in motionless eyes. "This man looks very like the ones we sometimes receive from the opium dens," she said, straightening up.

Again Mr. Wang nodded. He reached across the bed and retracted the quilt from the patient's left arm. His finger traced down the large vein to a small trail of dried blood coming from a puncture site. "That man over there has one also," he said, looking up at Gertrude.

Gertrude met his gaze. "Have they had any visitors? Any family?"

"I have asked carefully," he said, replacing the quilt. "No one but our people has been here today."

She held his gaze for a moment longer, then turned quickly and left the ward, heading for the outpatient building and the pharmacy.

The door was unlocked; there was no sign of Mr. Cecil Tang. Gertrude marched directly to the drawer where the morphine was kept. She had counted these vials on Sunday and none had been dispensed since that time. Now two were missing. Only she and the pharmacist had access to this room and this drawer.

"May I help you, Miss Green?" Cecil Tang stood directly behind Gertrude, bowing slightly at the waist.

More in anger than in fright, Gertrude's head turned quickly. A disarming smile covered his round face. With hands folded in front of him, he exuded helpful virtue and placid innocence. Yet his eyes darted from the drawer to her face to the floor, and remained there. *Was he frightened? Had he already heard about the patients in the Men's Hospital? What would he say?* Deliberately Gertrude turned her mind from spontaneous anger to calculated confrontation.

"Yes, Mr. Tang," she replied coolly, peering again into the drawer. "Please tell me where the two missing vials of morphine are."

"I did not know any vials were missing," he said earnestly.

"Did you take them?" She spoke calmly, letting the complete turn of her body to face him carry the increased weight of her words.

"I did not take them, Miss Green," he answered, looking directly at her, his eyes crinkled with that irritatingly constant smile.

What was it Dr. Hwang had said about the smiling Chinese face?

"Then where did they go?" Gertrude fretted aloud, losing her concentration for the moment. "Who has access to this room?" She focused again on the simpering minion before her, wondering why he was such a poor source of information. "Mr. Tang, who comes in here besides you and me? Do you keep that door locked?" She walked toward the door, looking for signs of a forced entry, wondering if the lock even worked.

"It is not useful to lock the door, Miss Green," he said, swiftly moving with her. "The latch on the window next to it is broken." His quick hands darted forward, demonstrating the broken lock before she could discover it for herself. "Anyone at all can reach through the window and open the door."

"Then why not fix it?" she asked, perturbed at the obvious laziness. Her green eyes pierced him and held him in place like a bug is held with a pin. "I want that window fixed today and the door constantly locked. And the lock on the morphine drawer always locked. It is that understood, Mr. Tang?"

"Yes, Miss Green." The smile was unchanged, but the eyes did not look up.

"Who might have come in here?" she asked suddenly.

"As the person in charge, I think that is for you to find out." His voice was a hiss but the smile remained fixed in place like a mask.

The rest of that Tuesday anyone who crossed Gertrude's path was told that absolutely no one was allowed in the pharmacy except her and Mr. Tang—under penalty of immediate dismissal.

On Friday Mr. Yu died. He had been regaining his strength nicely on a simple diet of rice soup and pudding. But Mrs. Yu, the unteachable OR supervisor, decided on her own that she would feed him noodles, pomegranates, and peaches. He obstructed, perforated, and hemorrhaged. In 24 hours he was dead.

Gertrude had thought that Pastor Chang would receive her in his office. But as she came up the walk she saw his tall form standing in the arched doorway of the church. He held open the door to the sanctuary, inviting her in. She was struck again by the contradictions of his face. There was farmer's ruggedness with the dark lower face and the light colored forehead, the full eyebrows of the Northern Chinese and the soft eyes beneath them where a fire was always glowing. And the glasses. She'd forgotten about the scholarly glasses.

He let the door close behind her then glided across the short entryway, preceding her into the sanctuary. As she followed his long, swishing Chinese gown into the high arched vault of worship her burden of responsibility slid off like a heavy coat. She sat in the front pew as a student and a supplicant.

"How can I help you, Sister Green?" he asked, standing a respectful distance from her. He seemed haloed in the rose and aquamarine light that streamed in through the stained glass Gothic windows on the northeast side of the church.

Beginning slowly at first with the cascade of events of the past two weeks, Gertrude gradually unfolded her quilt of anxiety: the patchwork of her additional responsibilities, her cultural loneliness, and her burden for the student nurses.

"I can do the work, honorable pastor, and I can speak the language," she said, her Chinese words flowing freely, "but I am not sure if I'm doing what needs to be done. Everyone seems to be waiting for me to tell them what to do. And when I ask for advice in a committee, it's like I have stunned them into silence." She found herself on her feet. "What do they expect of me, Pastor Chang? I can't do this by myself. I need their cooperation"—her rising voice halted temporarily as she stumbled over this Chinese word. "I need their help. Yes. And I don't know how to get it." Her mind was drained and empty but her heart felt lighter.

Pastor Chang, arms tucked into the sleeves of his dark, silk gown, turned toward the window behind him. Extracting one hand, he tilted open the bottom transom, then beckoned her to join him.

"What do you see, Sister Green?"

"I see the plum tree that is planted between the church and the compound wall."

"The plum tree did not ask to be planted there. God arranged for the plum tree to be there. The plum tree does not ask what it should do there. It just grows where it is planted."

Gertrude looked up into the intensity of his gaze.

"God has planted you here, Sister Green. Grow where you are planted." His arms were again hidden in his sleeves as he turned his back and walked away. Then he turned and added solemnly, "Do not ask man what you should do. Ask God. Are you asking God?"

"Every day, honorable pastor, every day." Gertrude's voice was barely a whisper.

His eyes now smiled though his face retained its serious demeanor. "Because you are the Westerner, the Chinese expect you to know what to do. When you expose your ignorance in public, they think you do not know—and it frightens them. Ask them individually in private and they will help you." Again he paused, the fire in his eyes burning brightly. "Anyone who can move a general's wife, can do what you need to do."

So you know about Mrs. Cho, Gertrude reflected to herself as her ears burned a bright red.

"Now that Dr. Nethery is gone, everyone knows you are the leader and they are watching to see what you will do. They will follow a strong, determined, and confident leader." Pastor Chang slowly nodded his head in self-confirmation.

"Strong and determined is not the problem," Gertrude quipped. "It's the confidence part that's difficult."

Pastor Chang picked up the large pulpit Bible behind him and thumbed through a few pages. "A scripture for leadership, Sister Green." Then he read: "Romans 12:11 and 12. 'Not slothful in business; fervent in spirit; serving the Lord; rejoicing in hope; patient in tribulation; continuing instant in prayer.'" He lay the Bible back in its cradle. "Shall we pray, Sister Green?"

Yes, Lord, a constant state of prayer, Gertrude prayed silently as she folded her hands and closed her eyes.

The following morning Gertrude summoned Cecil Tang to meet her in Dr. Nethery's office. From behind the big desk she told him that if she did not hear in 24 hours who it was that took the medicines, he, Mr. Tang, would be dismissed. She sent him back to the pharmacy without allowing him to say a word.

Then she sent for Mr. Ren and asked him if the cooks knew what the rules were concerning drinking on the compound.

"Yes, Miss Green, the rules are explained carefully whenever anyone is hired."

"Dismiss them, then. And make sure they leave the compound today."

The next day Mr. Su in OPD registry did not come to work. When a coolie was sent to fetch him from the Chinese section of the compound, his room was empty. From some unknown source the rumor quickly spread that he was the one who had taken the morphine from the pharmacy. Every day as part of her morning and evening rounds, Gertrude checked the window and the door of the pharmacy to be sure they were locked.

THE LIFE AND TIMES OF GERTRUDE GREEN

ABOVE: Gertrude, age 14, in one of her favorite costumes.
When she gave her life to God she "knew" she must stop dancing. Though she
didn't know why at the time, God's plan for her was so much bigger than that.

LEFT: Gertrude at Nanking language school, on the porch of her apartment.

BELOW: Mr. Chen, the Christian language teacher.

LEFT: Students at Nanking language school where Gertrude studied when she first came to China.
Front row, L – R: Dr. Mary Wilkinson, Ruth Atwell, and Gertrude Green.

BELOW: Ashey, the Chinese boy Gertrude befriended.

ABOVE: At left, Dr. Charles and Grace Dale.

RIGHT: Nursing Station in the Shanghai Sanitarium.

ABOVE: Traveling by sedan chair, several missionaries made the eight-mile trip up the mountain to Kuling, 1937.

LEFT: Gertrude, Thelma, and Herbert Smith, Jr. with their bicycles on the way to Yencheng.

BELOW: Gertrude (right) and Thelma Smith.

LEFT: Pastor Chang, of the Yencheng Hospital Church.

BELOW: Clinic Building, Yencheng Hospital.

LEFT: Elder Merritt and Wilma Warren in 1953. Elder Warren was a spiritual support to Gertrude during the bombings and the long winter trip to freedom.

BELOW: A few of the 10,000 war-displaced refugees that the Yencheng Hospital fed every day. After a grueling eight-day trip by bicycle, Gertrude and others reached Yencheng, 1940.

LEFT:
Bringing the injured to Yencheng Hospital.

ABOVE: Workers at Yencheng Sanitarium Front row, second man from left, Dr. McMullen; next, Elder Warren; near center, Gertrude Green; Otis Erich; Elder Christensen; Dr. Paul Hwang; Pastor Peng; second from right, Thelma Hwang, 1947.

RIGHT AND
FAR RIGHT:
This picture of
Gertrude Green
appeared in the
newspaper with this
article in January, 1948.

BELOW:
Shanghai Sanitarium
and Hospital on
Rubicon Road.

Former Portland Nurse Reported Captive of Reds

NANKING, Jan. 8.-(AP)-The government's Central News agency reported without confirmation today that three American missionaries and a child were believed to have been captured by Communists withdrawing from Yencheng, on the Peiping-Hankow railroad.

The Americans, Mr. and Mrs. Eric Mullen and their child, and Miss Gertrude Green, Seventh-Day Adventist missionaries, are overdue on a trip from the mission in Honan province to Hankow.

(In San Francisco, church officials identified the missing missionaries as Dr. Raymond Wesley McMullen, his wife, Zora, and son, Ronald, in addition to Miss Green.

ABOVE: The Graduation of Nurses—at the Range Road Clinic. Front row, fourth from left, Mildred and Allen Boynton; Gertrude Green; Dr. Harry Miller; Dr. Herbert Liu; Dr. Andrew Chen.

FAR LEFT:
Gertrude's mother,
Lena Schwader Green.

LEFT: Range Road
Clinic in Shanghai.

施洪奉
Grenella Shih
馬秀英
Lucy Itoh

馬高山
Nathan Ma
劉錦棠
Franklin Liu

馬威華
Irene Ma
范麗華
Marian Tan

學生

DIH MIE STUDIO
海寧路二四〇號下浦東路

同顧校長留影於上海

一九四九

ABOVE: Gertrude with her nursing students whose education was interrupted by war. They followed her from Yencheng in 1941, to Hankow in 1948, to the Range Road Clinic in Shanghai where they finally graduated in 1949.

ABOVE: Gertrude's diary, her letters, her special closing and signature (inset).

Chapter 45

ADMINISTERING THE HOSPITAL

September marked a new beginning for Gertrude and the Yencheng Sanitarium and Hospital. On the first of September Elder and Mrs. Wilkinson arrived with the carts of much needed supplies and 28 boxes of medicine. For the next three days Gertrude stocked the shelves with the pharmaceuticals while Mr. Wang made a detailed inventory of the new supplies and the old. The exercise turned up several medicines that had been reported as having been used up including the tetanus toxoid. Gertrude's suspicions were again aroused and her resolve to monitor the drug supplies was doubled. Fortunately Cecil Tang was gone for the week, requiring no confrontation or explanation of Gertrude's increased personal vigil over the pharmacy.

The graduate nurses' uniforms also arrived in the carts, just in time for graduation on September 15. Thelma assisted Gertrude in producing a graduation ceremony complete with candle lighting and "Florence Nightingale" with her lamp. Gertrude arranged for the electricity to be turned on for one night in the church, allowing her to set up colored footlights. And Nellie Wilkinson, an artist of some accomplishment as well as a nurse, contributed her expertise by assisting with the decorating of the sanctuary.

To complete the festivities, the next evening Gertrude hosted one of her famous parties for all the students and new graduates, celebrating both graduation and the Moon Festival. The students planned the program, insuring participation by everyone. And Gertrude stretched the Sanitarium's food budget to buy the Chinese favorites: peanuts, watermelon seeds, and pears. The graduate students soon educated the freshman class that Miss Green was a severe taskmaster to those who shirked their studies and an endearing friend to those who worked hard.

Because of her instinctively insightful decisiveness and her tough, no-nonsense administration, by the end of the month Gertrude had become the *de facto* head of the hospital board. When Mr. Ren asked about the prices to be charged for the new medicines, it was Gertrude who established an across the board increase in medicine charges to meet the rising costs caused by the war's short supplies. When Elder Wilkinson sent Mr. Hwang and then Mr. Lao Da to deliver medicine to the outlying clinic in Lanchow, it was Gertrude who countermanded the orders saying that each of these men were vital to the functioning of the hospital and could not be stranded by the war in another city and be unable to return to Yencheng. When various board members wanted their relatives to join the freshman nursing class that was now two months into their training, it was Gertrude who insisted that their entrance fees be doubled and that they get no ward work for some time as they had missed much practical instruction and would require much extra work by the instructors to catch them up to their classmates.

By the middle of October in the minds of those living on the compound, foreign and Chinese, Gertrude had replaced Dr. Nethery as the "superintendent" of the Yencheng Sanitarium and Hospital.

"What items should we put on the list or . . . uh . . . how do we go about this?" Thelma sat at the kitchen table, pencil poised in the air, wavering in uncertainty.

"Well, they're not going to allow us to have just anything we want." Gertrude's eyes narrowed in frustration. "Why did the Red Cross stop giving us the money to buy the supplies anyway? Why are they making us order the supplies and then telling us to come pick them up for free?"

"Because they don't have the money," Thelma guessed. "But they do have the supplies. Some of the world is still recovering from the Depression. And some of the world is fighting a war." Her practical mind ran through the logic. "The organizations who help the Red Cross probably have the supplies but don't have the money to ship them. So that's what the Red Cross is doing—they're shipping us the supplies."

"But we still have to get them across the battle lines at Kweitah." Gertrude was thinking of the difficult logistics of moving supplies by bicycle and cart where the trains were not running. "I already have Mr. Fan stranded there trying to get out the last batch of medicines."

"And I don't know what to write down," Thelma said, pencil still poised above the paper.

For the next 30 minutes Gertrude sat up straight, elbows on the table, fingers pressed to sides of her temples, and from memory ran through the rapidly diminishing pharmacy list and hospital supplies list. Thelma dutifully took the rapid-fire dictation like the good scribe she was. And during the following hour the two of them prioritized the list, starting with the most pressing needs.

Then it was Thelma's turn. The amount of supplies for which they were eligible depended on the daily patient census, both hospital patients and clinic patients. These numbers had to be multiplied by the preset dollar amount per patient in Hong Kong dollars and converted to the National Chinese currency. Gertrude watched mesmerized as Thelma rapidly and deftly performed the necessary calculations. With this dollar-weighted, finalized list Thelma began filling out the Red Cross order form in her neat accountant's writing.

"But I'll bet they don't have any wheat flour," Gertrude said as she sat back in her chair exhausted.

Thelma's pen stopped scratching on the paper as she looked up, perplexed.

"For the refugee feeding program," Gertrude said with a sigh. "When they used to send us the money to buy supplies, we could set some of it aside to buy the wheat flour and the onions for the gruel we feed them. Now there will be no money. And I doubt they are sending us any wheat."

"Will you have to discontinue the feeding program?" Thelma asked.

"Probably. I'll have to talk with the board about it."

Through the hand-stitched curtains she had made herself, Gertrude stared out into the early dark of evening and over the low stone wall that separated the foreigners' part of the compound from the hospital grounds. Thelma followed her gaze to the collection of two-story buildings that had become Gertrude's life-consuming occupation.

"When do you think Dr. Nethery will come back?" Thelma guessed at Gertrude's thoughts.

"The question is how," Gertrude answered with a halfhearted laugh. "I've encouraged him to come by the rail lines we used, only to find out all traffic has stopped by that route. I've sent my letters to him in Chungking, thinking he would be coming up through Burma and drive in by truck from the west, only to hear he is still in Shanghai."

"If there's any way he can come, he'll come," Thelma said, trying to drive away the discouragement she could see in Gertrude's eyes.

"I hope so," Gertrude smiled, "I'm tired of being the doctor and the nurse."

"What about Dr. Tsao? Or is there a problem?"

"He knows how to do only certain things." Gertrude shook her head, trying to clear away another spider web of difficulty. "He doesn't know how to do bowel obstructions and he doesn't know when to do appendectomies." She was on her feet and beginning to pace in the tiny kitchen. "He lets the nursing students tend the wounds without looking at them himself. And he's still making old Chinese medicine diagnoses—like dropped stomach." She turned abruptly. "Your stomach can't 'drop.' It's not physically possible," she said angrily.

"Sss-o-o-o . . . what do you do?" Thelma asked cautiously in response to Gertrude's rising tone of voice.

"I try to help him," Gertrude said with sudden compassion. "He does the best he can. I can't shame him; cause him to lose face." Her speech was halting; her shoulders sagged as if under a great weight. "But his fragile ego bristles if my suggestions are too obvious."

Gertrude searched Thelma's face for comprehension of her difficulties but saw only sympathy and consternation. *She doesn't really understand*, Gertrude surmised. *She doesn't really know what it's like to carry all the responsibility.* And Gertrude began to feel like Alice in Wonderland, as if somehow the room were getting larger and she, Gertrude, were getting smaller. It seemed as if she were very small, stretching up high but unable to reach the top of the very tall table next to her where the bottle that contained all the answers sat waiting.

"He's all you have," the voice of Thelma said quietly, intruding into her imaginary world.

"Yes. Yes, that's it exactly," Gertrude said slowly, surprised to find herself at her normal height. She quickly picked up the bottle on the table and read the label. It was cough syrup.

There are no magic answers, she reminded herself, smiling sheepishly. *Only godly friends sent by the Lord to help in time of need.*

"Well, at least we have your radio," Thelma said, bouncing away from the table.

Seeing Gertrude's confused expression, Thelma pointed to the clock and added, "to stay in touch. Look at the time!"

"The Shanghai news broadcast!" Gertrude squealed as she raced Thelma to the living room.

S. D. A. Mission
Yencheng, Honan
October 15, 1940

Dearest Mother:

Well, at last a letter arrived today and I was so happy that I hardly knew what to do. I have received only two letters written in June and no others. But today I received the letter you wrote Sept. 2 and the letter you wrote at camp meeting in July.

This is as far as I got last night as all the folks came in to hear the radio broadcast so I couldn't write anymore.

I was glad to hear you could go to camp meeting and that you met the Bransons there. Yes, they are very nice people and they sure do love each other. I suppose you told Elder Branson that I was your daughter and that I am fine and all. I am wondering what he said bad about me.

I am keeping very busy every day carrying Dr. Nethery's work and mine, too. I go on duty in the morning at 7:00 and come home at 12:00 for dinner. After dinner I teach classes at 1:15 and get home at night about 6:30.

Today I have an exam to give and another one tomorrow. I am writing up procedures for the hospital so that we have more definite ways and everybody will know how to do everything. I am assisting in all the operations now and giving the anesthetics and making rounds twice a day to make a general inspection of the entire hospital. And I have to tend to the bills and decide what things need to be fixed. Then in the evening I have to see about the students' study period. I light a lamp and see that they all get started on their work. So my day is long and busy.

We use kerosene for the lamps which used to be expensive at $18 a tin. It was $6 a tin in Shanghai. Now it is $50 a tin. Prices are simply awful. The coal for my kitchen stove is over $60 for half a ton which lasts only about one and a half months. But I have to burn it anyway.

It is Harvest Ingathering time here and we do it just like you do in the States. We divided up the small village of Loho into sections and each section is canvassed door-to-door by a solicitation band from the church membership. I am the leader of my band. There are only four in our band and our goal is $40, but we already have $85. We went out today and raised $10 in one hour. The Chinese love to go out and solicit funds, especially when we tell them that the Americans are helping and that the Chinese ought to be willing to help their own people. We rarely get less than $5.

Next month we are going to have a Tent Meeting up in the town of Loho. It will run for one month and meet every night. I have charge of the music. The nurses will give health demonstrations for 15 minutes each night and Mr. Wang will do the health lectures. I am very interested for the students to be involved with helping people who are not in the hospital. We are very busy now so my senior students are seeing patients in the out-patient clinics. I will try to get them to also be involved in doing Bible studies with the interests that come out of the Branch Sabbath Schools and now from these meetings.

This town is packed full of people and every spare lot is being built up into houses and stores. If we can't find a place for the tent for the meeting, I don't know what we will do.

We hear on the radio that all Americans are to be evacuated from the Orient and that America is sending over three special boats to get us. I am wondering if our mission will consent to let us go; I suppose they will not. But we have to receive word from the American Consulate first, and letters take so long to get anywhere I think we would not know when the boats come. We could hear it on the radio since the battery for my radio is still working. But it takes so much electricity to charge it and the electricity is on only one night a week so that we can take our X-rays. We may have to find another way to work the radio.

Our compound is really a very peaceful place and it is very lovely. Wish you were here to share in my bounty. My boy does all the cooking and his wife does the cleaning. I am having wonderful pumpkin pies. And I am safe and eating well. Goodnight and hope to hear from you soon.

Loads of love to my darling mother from her true and loving daughter, Gertrude

Chapter 46

GETTING THROUGH CHRISTMAS

Gertrude stood gazing into the little gold-edged mirror she'd hung over the bureau in her bedroom. "Gertrude, you need your haircut," she said under her breath. Her hair was longer than it had been in years. But where to get it done? There were no professional hairdressers in Yencheng to cut it or style it as there had been in Shanghai.

Maybe I can roll it around the edges like the new styles in the magazines, she thought as she grappled with two handfuls of unusually long, brown locks, twisting her head sideways to see if it would lay neatly down the back of her neck. The hairdo in the mirror did not come close to duplicating the image she had in her mind.

Maybe I can get Mrs. Wilkinson to help me.

Gertrude thought of the beautiful decorative border Nellie Wilkinson had hand painted all around the top of the nurses' study room then tried to picture the blond, petite, artistic Nellie Wilkinson cutting and setting her hair . . . with what? The unmanageable tresses tumbled from her hands which were poised halfempty above and behind her head.

Are these new hair styles done with regular hair pins? She would have to find out.

The gray-green eyes of a 32-year-old looked out at her from the mirror. With her forefinger she absently traced the edges of her face from the corners of her eyes to her chin. Front on, her face appeared to be more full than when she was younger, especially her jawline. Turning her head from side to side, she closely examined the hairline at her temples but found no hint of gray. The skin over her forehead was still smooth and the prominent cheeks were firm, especially when she smiled broadly. She grinned at herself and liked the effect. "Need to do more of that," she said out loud, smiling spontaneously at her own silliness and vanity.

What am I becoming? A matron? She was pensive again. Her eyes wandered to the envelope lying on top of the bureau, the old Range Road address in Shanghai written in Dick Richard's strong, shipboard-efficient handwriting. She brushed the letter lightly with the back of her hand, remembering that it had found its way through the battle lines to Yencheng when Mother's letters were struggling to find China. Although she had answered two previous letters from him, she knew there was no lasting relationship here and that she would not see him again. She dismissed the letter along with her truant thoughts concerning its writer from her mind.

Who am I? she thought. She could hear the voices of Herbert and his mother in the apartment below hers. *Not a wife. Not a mother.*

Walking through her kitchen, Gertrude gravitated toward the chatter of voices that she knew to be the Chinese students who invaded and inhabited Nellie Wilkinson's newly painted apartment just across the lawn. Hidden in the dark shadows of her screened-in porch, Gertrude observed the milling about of the blue-clad nursing students, remembering her own early days as a probie and the generous nurturing of the nursing students by the staff at the New England Sanitarium and Hospital.

She looked beyond the happy chirping at the Wilkinson cottage, beyond the vegetable gardens where Yang, her cook and gardener, and his wife were picking the last of the corn, over the walls that separated the foreign and Chinese sections of the compound to the very edges of their world—the dikes that surrounded and protected them from the river. She could see patients unloading from the little flatboats, making their way up the hill to the hospital gates.

"I am not a wife, O Lord," she prayed softly. "But I am a mother—a mother to all of this."

She opened the screen door and descended resolutely into the missionary work of mothering that had become hers.

On entering the church sanctuary Gertrude paused. The soft light through the stained glass warmed her and encouraged her, reminiscent of her home church in Rochester, removing her temporarily from China, drawing her closer to her mother. Then Gertrude moved on swiftly between the wooden bench pews through the sanctuary of the church toward the pastor's study. As the colored light from the windows followed her, she sensed a strengthening and an inner peace. She needed it.

Pastor Chang arose from behind his desk and bowed respectfully as Gertrude entered his office. Sensing motion to her right, Gertrude turned slightly in time to see the diminutive Dr. Tsao in the corner following his pastor's lead, although the bow was only a slight lowering of the shoulders and a nod of the head.

All the better, she reasoned to herself. *Another opinion will be helpful.*

"Miss Green," Pastor Chang offered. "Would you like to sit?"

"No, no, I can't stay." Gertrude's Chinese flowed effortlessly. "But I wanted to ask your advice, actually present an idea." She turned to Dr. Tsao. "And Dr. Tsao's advice is always valuable."

Dr. Tsao bowed again, more deeply and with his eyes lowered.

"I know we have not found a place to set up the tent for the evangelistic meeting in Loho," Gertrude hurried on.

"That is so," Pastor Chang murmured.

"Mr. Wang has come to me with an idea for a dispensary in the town, a place to see patients so that they don't have to come all the way out to the hospital. And I am wondering if we might hold the evangelistic meetings in a storefront, remake it into a clinic after the meetings and use it as a Bible study center in the evenings?"

"Mr. Wang has found such a storefront?" Dr. Tsao asked quietly.

"He has," Gertrude said, turning to face him. "As you know we have no extra money just now. But, if we can turn the storefront into a profitable clinic, we will regain whatever we spend in renovations."

"And we will have our evangelistic center in the center of Loho." Pastor Chang's eyes sparkled as he completed Gertrude's thought with uncharacteristic emotion. "Is this a good idea, honorable doctor?" he asked, regaining his composure and politely seeking to include Dr. Tsao in the discussion.

"As usual, Miss Green, has come up with an excellent plan." Dr. Tsao said, nodding slowly. His large eyes set close together made direct contact with Gertrude for the first time but his full mouth and dark face did not change.

I wonder when I will get used to the Chinese face that looks solemn as a judge while hiding genuine pleasure, Gertrude mused.

"Now, if I could just find a place to buy coal for less than $120 a ton," she said, thinking out loud, mentally moving on to her next problem. When both Chinese faces registered questions, she added, "I am building stoves in hydrotherapy so that the students will continue to give the patients their therapeutic baths even when it is winter and the weather is colder." Her shoulders rose and fell in resignation. "But the coal is too expensive."

"I know where we can get a better price for coal," Dr. Tsao offered. "I will arrange for delivery."

Now it was Gertrude's turn to bow in thanks.

"And I have sent a man to help Mr. Fan get our medicines out of Kweitah," Dr. Tsao continued.

Gertrude's eyes and mouth opened wide in astonishment. "I know that for the right price paid to the right people Mr. Swen was able to bring things in from Tsingtao. But we don't have the money to get the supplies released . . ." She stopped as Dr. Tsao fixed her with his gaze. "It is your money, your own personal money, isn't it?" she said aloud, not recognizing the social blunder she had committed by revealing his generosity.

"China is my country, too, Miss Green," Dr. Tsao said with quiet firmness. "The gospel and our mission here as a Christian hospital is in crisis. The war approaches and we are stretched beyond our means. It is no time to be personally greedy."

Gertrude observed this short, thickly set Chinese doctor as if for the first time, the thinning hair brushed severely back over a slanting forehead, the dark, desert-like Mongolian features. She was used to imagining this face scrunched down in anger when challenged or vacuous when facing a difficult medical problem. *You are a Christian, too, aren't you?* The thought startled her.

"It is truly a Chinese miracle, honorable doctor," Gertrude said with a genuine gratefulness she had not felt previously for this man.

"We will give the credit for miracles to God," Dr. Tsao said quietly.

If they were to have any peace and quiet, Thanksgiving would have to be held at Thelma Smith's house. Carrying food to Gertrude's upstairs apartment was a lot of work and Nellie Wilkinson had failed so far to teach the

Chinese students not to barge into her house unannounced. Elder Wilkinson was on a pastoral trip through the northern reaches of Honan Province with Pastor Chang which left the three women and Herbert to celebrate their North American Pilgrim holiday without him. The weather was bitingly cold. Winter had come.

"Thelma, I'm just about frozen," Gertrude grumbled as she pushed through the door into Thelma's downstairs apartment, a duplicate of the one Gertrude occupied directly overhead. "I don't think my feet have ever thawed out since that bicycle ride last March." She set the large saucepan of sweet potatoes on Thelma's undersized kitchen table that had been pulled to the middle of the room and set for four.

"Wherever did you find the flowers?" Gertrude momentarily brightened, touching the autumn colored mums being held erect in a squat vase which occupied the center of the table.

"They were hiding in a corner near the church," Thelma explained, standing guard at the stove where she labored over a bubbling pot, threatening it occasionally with a large spoon. "You should take a lesson from the Chinese women," she said over her shoulder. "Dress in those double layered pants they have and long jackets."

"Not very fashionable," Gertrude retorted.

"And who's to notice? Not me." Thelma turned with laughter creasing her round, dark cherubic face.

"I suppose not." Gertrude's face darkened again and would not be cheered.

"Still upset about the radio?" Thelma asked softly.

"If I had known . . ." Gertrude bit off each word vehemently. "He told me that he could wire up those flashlight batteries to work just as well as the regular battery." Gertrude eyes flashed the fire of an avenging angel. "When I heard that little sizzle in the back of the radio, I knew we were done for. For two cents I could have sizzled him right there."

Thelma took a deep breath and cast her eyes heavenward as she prepared to endure the same story she had heard five times in the last 24 hours.

"We don't have the radio news broadcast, Thelma. We don't know anything about what's going on out there." Gertrude flung both arms out in large circles, encompassing the wide world that was cut off to them. "Despite your letters and your subscription money, we haven't seen a news-paper since . . . when?"

"About six weeks ago. And that one was a month old," Thelma sighed.

"And no magazines and no letters." Gertrude began pacing around the table. "You'd think Dr. Nethery would send us something. He's all so comfortable there in Shanghai; he could think of us here once in a while." Gertrude stopped and began counting on her fingers, her voice rising. "We have no morphine. We have almost no iodine or Mercurochrome. We are almost out of Balsam Peru and Plain One catgut suture for ties. And I have only two tins of ether." Gertrude stopped, worn out by the rant and the aching realization that the situation was not imagined; it was real. "We're cut off from the world, Thelma," she said in more subdued tones.

"I know," Thelma said with a quick nod, her dark head cocked to one side like a small, brown wren. "I've been there before."

The enormity of Thelma's personal burden careened into sharp focus as Gertrude stopped short. For a moment she remembered the death of Thelma's husband, the raising of Herbert, the traveling about as a widow in a war-ravaged China.

"Tell me—how do you do it?" Gertrude demanded as she confronted Thelma across the table, her voice and her mood rising to its previous hot intensity.

"I pray a lot. And I cry a lot." Thelma said, a small, brave smile slowly spreading across her face. She gazed at the troubled surface of the soup before her, the bursting bubbles releasing memories of persons and places, joys and sorrows. Faithfully, she dipped in her spoon and stirred, the steam of her years of struggling alone in China rising around her. "And I try to remember why I am here."

"Well, I can tell you, I'm not going to be here any longer than I have to be," Gertrude spewed in a second wave of volcanic indignation. She turned away sharply, pacing again. "I'm going to be out of here before next September or know the reason why!"

"What will they do without you?" Thelma spoke her thoughts aloud, her spoon hovering over the watched pot, her voice echoing the darker future that her mind now imagined.

"You mean the ones who stole Dr. Nethery's bicycle from Elmer Wang?" Gertrude spat out the caustic, accusing words like hot chili peppers.

"The nursing students, Dr. Tsao, . . . and Dr. Nethery, if he ever returns." Thelma's voice was plaintive and forlorn. She turned to face Gertrude. "And the patients. What about the patients? Like the general?"

Gertrude's face clouded over and her eyes closed, shutting the door on her anger and her fear, now mostly spent. The Chinese general who had been shot through the upper arm, shattering his shoulder, came into focus behind her closed eyelids.

"Dr. Tsao doesn't know what to do with that one," Gertrude agreed as she quieted. Her mind quickly reviewed the facts of the case, diverting into that activity which gave her the greatest sense of purpose and fulfilled her own greatest personal need—the mental gymnastics of figuring out what to do to help a patient. "I've looked in Dr. Nethery's books for a better way to cast him—with his arm in the air—like an airplane." Gertrude demonstrated the position. "The new position also helps us to irrigate his wounds and clean out the infection," she added, animated in her pursuit of a concrete, solvable problem.

"But they can't do it without you," Thelma stated firmly, advancing on Gertrude, her soup spoon at the ready, slowly dripping on the floor.

"I know," Gertrude murmured with reluctant recognition. Her arms slowly descended from the airplane position as she shifted her gaze out the window in the direction of the hospital buildings. "I know," she repeated, acknowledging the reality that Thelma saw clearly.

"OK," she sighed, her eyes downcast, her head bent submissively. "Until Dr. Nethery returns."

Retreating up the stairs to her own apartment for the green beans, Gertrude began to pray as hot tears of exhaustion flowed down her cheeks. "God, You'd better do something. I'm so tired. I don't know how much longer I can last."

The small office they used as a boardroom on Sunday afternoons erupted in Chinese chatter as Mr. Fan entered. Gertrude paused in her presentation, knowing what many of the rest did not, that Mr. Fan had returned late last evening. She had met him at the hospital front gate to see what medicines and supplies he'd managed to bring with him. Together they had secreted away his meager gleanings, hiding them in the pharmacy. They hardly seemed worth Dr. Tsao's financial sacrifice and the 10 weeks Mr. Fan had been stuck on the Japanese side of the front lines, not to mention her continual confrontations with Cecil Tang.

"We are all excited to have Mr. Fan back with us," Gertrude said as the greetings began to abate. In the far corner of the room she noted Mr. Ren's reserved demeanor and near her right elbow Dr. Tsao's keen interest in Mr. Fan's sudden appearance. Mr. Ren and Dr. Tsao were old friends from school days and Dr. Tsao had been promoting Mr. Ren among the hospital staff to take over the pharmacy in Mr. Fan's absence.

How do I keep my pharmacist and my best collections manager in place while not making my only doctor angry with me? Gertrude's mind raced ahead to the disaster that awaited her if these next few moments did not go well.

"You will all be pleased to hear that Mr. Fan will return to his position as head of the pharmacy. Mr. Tang will return to his floor supervising duties and relieve the pressure on those of us who have been filling in for him." Out of the corner of her eye, Gertrude watched Dr. Tsao's jaw tighten. "This change will allow Mr. Ren to return to his excellent work in the collections and billing office. With the financial situation as it is, we need his expert touch there now more than ever to collect the money as only he is able to do." When several people nodded in the affirmative, Mr. Ren bowed his head to acknowledge their confidence. Gertrude watched a flicker of eye contact between the two old school chums signal a resignation to their fate.

One more hurdle cleared. Gertrude exhaled a quiet prayer of thanks, her pulse slowing perceptibly.

Next the very young, very enthusiastic Wang Shueh Wen described the new dispensary being constructed in the larger town of Loho. The large central waiting room would soon be ready to accept the transfer of the evangelistic series from the well-attended tent meetings in the field next to the new clinic. The two examining rooms that were completed were being used for Bible studies. The rest of the internal construction would be finished and ready for the opening of the dispensary on January 1.

Mr. Wang announced that he would be living in the back room on the premises by next weekend in preparation for the opening date. Gertrude had agreed to this move only if he continued teaching anatomy and physiology to the nursing students three afternoons a week at the hospital *and* if he promised to begin a new outpatient clinic practicum for the senior students at the dispensary.

With the added income and the convenience for the local merchants, the dispensary was turning out to be an excellent investment that would pay for itself within the first year. In addition, Gertrude noted Pastor Chang's eyes glowing with joy throughout the presentation. For once Gertrude felt she had gotten something right.

"On this next item . . . ," she paused to get their attention, "I need some suggestions. The local town leaders want us to begin the refugee feeding program again as the war is causing a great strain on their local budget."

Last Tuesday, Gertrude had met with a local delegation of leaders. By tactful questioning she had learned how the local and provincial governors retained their appointed positions of power from the central Chinese government by funding local needs out of their own personal finances. She also knew that, by virtue of the war effort, several of that town's delegation were on the verge of bankruptcy. Much political clout could be gained by being able to assist them on this issue.

"Although the Red Cross has stopped sending us money which we were able to use for this purpose, Mr. Loewen, who is now in Chungking . . ." Several heads nodded in recognition of the beloved Loewens who had lived in the apartment Gertrude now inhabited. ". . . has collected 1,000 Chinese dollars from the Harvest Ingathering in Szechuan which was specified for Yencheng. Dr. Nethery has written to say that he has obtained 5,000 Chinese dollars from Shanghai and that there are 3,000 Chinese dollars left over from last year's Harvest Ingathering here in Yencheng and Loho." Gertrude remembered with pride the $40 her own small Ingathering band had collected in two days from the merchants immediately surrounding the hospital.

"As you know the ground next to the hospital where we used to have the refugee kitchen doesn't belong to us. And now the man who owns it wants to sell it—for $6,000 dollars. The question is: should we spend the money and buy it?"

No one spoke as she contemplated the options again. To spend the Ingathering money on the land would mean they would have no money left to buy food for the refugees. To not buy the land meant moving the refugee kitchen somewhere else probably too far away for the hospital people to service it—

or not to feed the refugees at all. For a fraction of a moment she considered the hospital's reserves of $5,000 in gold, the only commodity that was retaining its value in China's rampant inflation. The gold reserves were the last, final hope they had in a crisis of securing the drugs and supplies they needed to keep the hospital open. *No,* she decided in her own mind, *the refugees come second to the hospital. Now if I haven't made Dr. Tsao mad at me . . .*

"Miss Green." The voice came from near her right elbow. It was Dr. Tsao.

"Miss Green," he said, "two friends of the hospital have offered to buy the land and donate it to the hospital."

No one is acting surprised by his announcement, she mused, surveying the faces before her for some flicker of reaction. *So much for my secret discussions with Dr. Tsao and his friends—or the Chinese know how to control their startled reactions.* Gertrude did not know which it was.

"Good. The money from Dr. Nethery should arrive from Shanghai just after Christmas and we can schedule the refugee feeding program to reopen on January 15. We will run it every other day to make the money last longer," she announced, fulfilling her part in the plan she and Dr. Tsao and Pastor Chang had discussed previously.

But I don't know for how long, she worried to herself. *Dr. Nethery, when are you coming home?*

Gertrude scooted the kerosene lamp across the large desk and closer to her work space, partly to see the typewriter keys better and partly to keep her hands warm. She had moved into Dr. Nethery's office just after Christmas because it was on the other side of the wall from the hydrotherapy room where the wood burning stoves kept the patients, the water baths, and Dr. Nethery's office on this side of the wall warm 16 hours a day. But tonight even the Primus stove near her feet wasn't sufficient to warm her.

The thin, white paper perched in the typewriter with only the date and "Dear Dr. Nethery" printed on its surface. Gertrude stared at it, imagining all that she wanted say, trying to logically arrange the worries and pressures, the decisions and the stories that haphazardly bubbled up and overflowed from her heart.

The Women's Hospital currently housed only eight women patients but more Chinese soldiers and injured civilians were being admitted every day.

Every day she was in surgery with Dr. Tsao, helping him with bladder stones and amputations. "There is no end of work to do," she typed.

The first-year nursing students were showing up on time and actually doing better than the third-year students because she'd taught them to be careful in their work. She was bonding with them as a friend and a respected mentor and they were trying to please her.

"And you thought these new students wouldn't amount to much," she wrote, admonishing the Dr. Nethery who existed only in her mind and on her paper. "Guess we fooled you."

I should tell him about the increases in the price of the rooms and the clinic appointments. It's the only way we can keep up with the inflation of money. She remembered the long, agonizing discussion with Thelma and Mr. Fan. They had to charge enough to pay the bills but they didn't want to keep out people who needed medical care. "Well, you are not here to make these decisions so we did the best we could on our own. Hope you approve." Her cold fingers rattled over the typewriter keys in stiff, short strokes.

She hammered out her anxieties over the diminishing supply of vital medicines and about the drugs and supplies she and Thelma had ordered from the Red Cross which remained tied up in Kweitah and Kaifeng without passes from the Japanese to allow them across the battle lines.

"We think the Japanese have found them and used them up and just won't tell us." The rhythm of her vented anger on the keys brought temporary warmth to her fingertips.

"We caught Cecil Tang red-handed," she wrote as the topic of medicine shortages took another form. "He denied knowing anything about the missing sulfa tablets and narcotics until Mr. Wang and Mr. Fan and I confronted him and threatened to bring in the police and search his room. Then he broke down and admitted everything.

"When we went to his room, he brought out the drugs we knew about and several other items we didn't know were missing. He's been running quite a lucrative business on the side. But he has been dismissed and will have to make his ill-gotten living off of someone else. Good riddance to bad rubbish, I say."

She stared at the last sentence. *Why am I so angry?* And her immediate response was as vehement as it was audible. "Because he's messing up all the hard work we're doing. Everyone is trying so hard to make a go of it and he's—"

What had she said?

"All the hard work we're doing . . ."

But she didn't want to stay here another minute! She began typing furiously onto paper what came roiling to the surface.

She wanted an early furlough in the spring. Just as soon as Dr. Nethery got back, she wanted out from under all the responsibilities that had been piling up since last August. And when her furlough was up, she wasn't coming back!

There! It was on paper in black and white.

"*. . . all the hard work we're doing . . .*"

The images passed before her eyes: the tall, sad-eyed Mr. Fan who shared her passion for accuracy in the pharmacy and honesty in the hospital staff; the young, energetic Mr. Wang who managed the clinic and the Bible studies in town with equal skill; the tall, dark Mr. Ren who had the tact and skill to collect payments from patients with Christian courtesy in the worst of financial times; and Pastor Chang whose very eyes glowed with the gospel as he nurtured and encouraged them all.

Gertrude arose from the desk and walked to the window, gazing into the darkness at the shadows of buildings and trees that defined the meaning of her life here in China. With one finger she traced the outline of the Men's Hospital rooftop in the moisture her warm breath deposited on the cold windowpane.

She was a part of them and a part of the Yencheng Sanitarium and Hospital. She was part of "*. . . all of the hard work we're doing . . .*"

Returning to the desk, she typed more slowly. "The general with the bad arm is doing much better with the new cast and traction that Dr. Tsao and I have set up," she wrote. "The arm is draining nicely and the general is getting his feeling and hand motion back again.

"We will still be here caring for the patients when you return." She paused and then typed on. "I will remain here for as long as you need me to, certainly until next fall when my furlough is due. But who knows if I will be able to get out even then."

She paused and reconsidered what she had written, but only for a moment. *There it is. So let's move on,* she lectured herself severely.

"It is three days until the Chinese New Year holiday begins," she typed with the smooth rhythm she'd learned at Simmons College. "The nursing students want to have a party for Chinese New Year and I will not oppose them. I put all my efforts into Christmas and will leave them to do what they will."

And the stories about the struggles and the heartaches, the victories and the successes of the Yencheng Adventist Sanitarium and Hospital, isolated in central China by an ever intensifying war, continued to flow onto the page as she typed on.

Chapter 47

SURVIVING CHINESE NEW YEAR

On Friday, January 24, 1941, Gertrude made out the special nursing schedule for the Chinese New Year holiday season that would last the next three weeks. Her isolation from her own family made Gertrude especially sensitive to the need for everyone to have time at home with their families. The nurses loved her for her thoughtfulness and Gertrude had very few unexplained absences on the wards.

It was winter. The patient census was down because of the holiday. All nursing classes were suspended for three weeks. In fact, all activities on the compound were curtailed. In the education section, the grade school and high school classes were on holiday, and the church attendance was at an all time low as people were visiting their families elsewhere in the province. Even the Japanese planes which flew over several times each day, pursuing the war to the west toward Chungking, were ignored. Gertrude had even cancelled the early morning worship exercises normally held for the nursing students, and she could sleep in on the days she was not on duty.

Tuesday was not going to follow its regular schedule. Because of the Chinese New Year celebration dinner Monday noon and the special program at the Women's Hospital that evening, and no morning worship with the student nurses, Gertrude decided to treat herself by sleeping an extra two hours. So sitting at her kitchen table in her house dress at 7:25, Gertrude did not hear the first squad of Japanese bombers until after their initial approach and the first bomb began to fall.

In disbelief she stared upward, as if to penetrate the ceiling with her gaze. Unconsciously, she followed the ever-increasing scream of the plummeting projectile. A massive explosion in front of her apartment building showered her and her entire kitchen with glass from the front windows that now no longer existed. As she struggled to comprehend what had happened, she distinctly heard her cook shout from below, "What was that?" With crystal clarity her mind registered the scratching sounds of running feet on gravel and then quiet, followed within seconds by a second screaming whistle.

Like a punch in the chest, fear and self-preservation struck Gertrude with the peril of her situation. She dived under the table crying out, "O God, save me!" as the second bomb landed in the front yard, collapsing the entire front wall of her apartment into Thelma's apartment below. A large part of her roof was blown away, and bricks, pieces of wood, and hot metal fragments rained down on the tabletop over her head. The apartment building shuddered beneath her knees and Gertrude was convinced that the entire structure would soon collapse and she would die, trapped in flaming rubble.

Peering between the table legs, her eyes strained to see through dust and debris, Gertrude saw that the stairway was still standing. It was strangely back-lit by dusty sunlight streaming in where the front of the building used to be. With the drone of airplane engines dying away in the distance, she half ran, half crawled to the head of the stairway and scrambled to the ground. As she frantically cast about for a safe haven, the ominous hum of approaching aircraft drew her attention to the south. Shading her eyes from the gray-orange sun, she could make out three low shadows looming larger as the noise of their approach became deafening. Gertrude turned and bolted blindly for the laundry room she instinctively knew was directly behind her, huddled in the half basement under what was left of Thelma's apartment.

Flying through the door, she flung it shut and dashed for the back wall. She threw herself behind the wash tubs and against the dirt wall just as it jumped toward her, two dull thuds echoing through the room from the direction of the hospital and drumming dirt clods on the hollow washtubs over her head. Almost simultaneously, a horrendous explosion visibly moved inward the front wall of the tiny refuge. The door of the washroom burst open and slammed against the wall with a resounding crash, its hinges ripping loose from the door frame. The invisible concussion filled the air with clouds of dirt and tattered tree branches. Directly overhead Gertrude heard the hot metal shrapnel as it rained and sizzled on the linoleum floor in Thelma's kitchen.

Survival speculations and the images of her friends collided in Gertrude's confused thought processes. Except for the cook, she had heard no human sound. *Where was everyone? Where could they have gone? What was lower in the ground than the wash room? Oh! The root cellar near the Wilkinson house!*

Gertrude scrambled quickly over the debris, aiming for the dusty shaft of light that was the doorway. Not daring to touch the door frame for fear of bringing down the structure above her, she dashed free of her shaky prison and began running across the lawn, skirting two large craters which occupied the greater part of the lawn in front of her apartment building. Focusing into the distance on the top half of a door that peeked out over the three steep steps into the root cellar, she ran the fastest race of her life. The sound of another wave of death approached from the south.

Gertrude threw herself against the door. It crashed open on the fear-strained faces and opened mouths of Thelma, Herbert, Nellie, and Gertrude's cook and his wife all huddled in the far corner. Even as she slammed the door and threw herself on the floor, Gertrude felt the ground shudder with two concussions close together, but further away.

After 15 minutes of silence, Thelma whispered, "Have they gone?"

"I don't know," Gertrude responded in a shaky voice that she didn't recognize as her own. Only then did she realize that she had crawled across the dirt floor and now lay huddled between Thelma and Nellie.

During the next hour they heard the recurring overhead passage of airplanes and distant explosions in the direction of the village of Loho but nothing more fell on or around the hospital compound. Then for another half hour there was silence. Still no one moved.

Emerging from the root cellar at last, Gertrude and Thelma were still shaking so violently, they had to physically support each other so they could walk about the compound and survey the damage. Besides the missing front wall and most of their apartment building roof, both Wilkinson's and Nethery's houses had lost walls and all the doors and windows on the sides that faced the common open courtyard. None of the houses had any plaster remaining on the walls or ceilings.

Only one bomb fell in the Chinese section of the compound. It landed on the wall in front of Dr. Tsao's home, destroying that end of his house. Two large bombs in the hospital section had made the Men's Hospital uninhabitable. The Women's Hospital was less damaged, although it had no window glass remaining. Except for window damage, the church building was untouched as were the school buildings.

But for Gertrude the most fearful effect of the bombing was the complete absence of human sound. She could see that the male hospital was completely empty. In fact, all patients who could flee, including the wounded general, and all the male nurses were gone. Gazing through the glass-less windows of the female hospital building, Gertrude saw two or three of the nursing staff moving around, but no sounds of either patients or nurses. As Gertrude and Thelma slowly shuffled past the Chinese section where the noise of celebration had filled the air just yesterday, there was neither sound nor movement.

In two hours Gertrude's world had completely changed—physically, emotionally, professionally.

Shakily, the two women emerged hand in hand through the front gates of the compound, drawn by the rising smoke of several fires in the village of Loho a few *li* to the north. Suddenly Thelma gasped and snatched her hand from Gertrude's grasp. Gertrude turned fearfully to see Thelma covering her wide-opened mouth with her hand, then followed her gaze to the huddled, bloody masses of ragged clothes and grotesquely entangled bodies stacked closely against the mission's compound walls on both sides of the gate. Thousands of refugees who normally lived in the surrounding fields, waiting, living for their next free meal, had huddled against the American compound walls, thinking the Japanese would honor American neutrality and not harm them. There they had been murderously strafed in their precariously exposed position. Not one remained alive.

Large tears welling up in her dark brown eyes, Thelma began, "A thousand shall fall at thy side and ten thousand at thy right hand . . ."

"But it shall not come nigh thee," Gertrude finished, her gray eyes also overflowing, her heart filled simultaneously with gratitude and shame. So far as she could tell, not one person in the compound—the obvious target of the bombing attack—had been injured or killed. But those who had come from the outside for nurture, sustenance and—at the last—for protection had died.

For the next three days, Gertrude, Thelma, Herbert, and Nellie Wilkinson with 20 female nurses in tow, traveled on foot to sleep in the small, one-room, Adventist chapels of various nearby villages. Fearfully, they traveled under cover of darkness, leaving the hospital compound before dawn and returning after dark. Each day they became more thoroughly convinced that their houses were unlivable, in imminent danger of collapsing, and that the Japanese would return any day to finish the destruction they had started. With every sighting or sound of Japanese airplanes, the women leaped for the nearest hiding place, huddling there, shaking uncontrollably long after the true danger was past.

Several more bombing runs assaulted Loho and the surrounding villages, but none returned to the Yencheng San. Only later was it learned that the presence of the two generals who had been patients at the San had been magnified in the intelligence-gathering community into a war council of generals at the hospital. This was the reason for bombing the hospital.

> Yencheng San
> Yencheng, Honan, China
> February 9, 1941

Dearest Mother,

It is quite some time since I have written to you, but there has been much happening since I last wrote. We are living in a world of hate and war, and therefore we never know what will happen from day to day.

Chinese New Year was on January 27 and we all had a very gay time, a big dinner, and everybody happy. But on January 28 the planes came to our place very early, about 7:25 a.m. Little did we think they would bomb us, but that is what they did. I was still in the house when the first bombs fell, and I was showered with glass from the broken windows. I managed to get out of the house before another blast. But the bombs just continued to fall.

When it was over, we looked around. The two largest bombs fell in my front yard, twenty feet from the front door. They were intended to hit our home, but the mercy of the Lord pushed them away. Besides the two big ones, there were three smaller bombs in our yard. And the hospital compound received three bombs.

Of course, you can imagine that we have no house to live in now—doors and windows are all blown out—and everything is ruined. Even the quilts on my bed have ten large shrapnel holes in them and the foot of my iron bed was broken in two pieces. I have no ceiling, all the plaster is gone, the front porch is gone, and Mrs. Smith's front wall downstairs is all caved in. In the yard there isn't a tree left anywhere.

At the hospital, the front windows are all out, but we are so thankful to God, not even one person was hurt. Even though now our hearts beat faster than usual, we are so thankful to God for the wonderful promises of His Word—His protection over us.

Three faithful nurses stayed at the hospital to help me discharge the last of the patients. Now the hospital is empty. And we are not living there either. Mrs. Wilkinson was made very nervous by all the noise and destruction and our legs were exhausted from walking every night to one of our nearby chapels to sleep. So Thelma Smith, the treasurer, collected all the records of the multiple enterprises on the compound along with all the available money—which was in heavy silver dollars. And I collected all the valuable medicines and assets I could carry. And on Jan 31 we moved in two hand-drawn carts to Yao Chiao, the village of one of our nurses, where we are living Chinese style. Elder Wilkinson remained behind to protect the compound.

Now do not worry about me, Mother. If the Lord spared my life once, He can do it again, and all I ask you to do is to pray for me here.

War is a terrible thing. I would like to get out, but there is fighting on all sides. A little later the Lord may open the way and I can come home.

Remember me to everyone.

With lots of love, your daughter,

Gertrude

February 16, 1941

A. W. Cormack
6840 Eastern Ave. N. W.
Tacoma Park, Washington, D.C.

Dear Sir:

Again I have read in the papers that the Dep't of State has requested U.S. citizens to leave the Orient and has included unoccupied China in this request. A short time ago I wrote you regarding my sister, Miss Gertrude Green, who is in unoccupied China and asked what your plans were in regard to her. You merely stated you were keeping in touch with the Secretary of State which as far as I can see was a matter of "passing the buck" as to the responsibility for her welfare.

I am aware of the fact that even though my sister is in unoccupied China that it will be necessary for her to travel for approximately two weeks thru occupied territory to get to Shanghai. I have also been informed that this trip is none too pleasant and treatment is none too courteous. As time goes on there are increasing reports of insults thru this territory. Miss Green's family and in particular her mother is concerned over this situation. Miss Green would be glad to come home if given a chance in spite of the fact that she is enjoying her work there.

I sincerely hope that you will give my sister's welfare serious consideration immediately and act promptly for her best interests.

Yours truly

Ruth L. Green, MD

Chapter 48

LIVING IN THE COUNTRY

Mary Wang, one of the faithful student nurses, had taken the all-female group—and Herbert—to live at her village. However, Mary had neglected to tell them that they would be living in a dirt-floored, one-room hut, flimsily attached to the tattered skirts of the village. They would be sleeping on a half dozen small, shabby cots that had been borrowed from generous neighbors. And there was no spare food to be found in the village anywhere.

Gertrude learned another precious lesson about Chinese peasants and winter in China. The Chinese farmers harvest barely enough food to see them through the harsh winter with just enough left over to plant their new crops the following spring. Especially following the Chinese New Year celebration, no vegetables and no greens were to be had. The best Mary and her fellow students could serve the sojourners was *shi fan*, a gruel made of wheat, and then only twice a day.

Once the bombing raids in the Loho-Yencheng area had ceased and Gertrude and Thelma had stopped quaking at every small noise, they attempted to assert some order over the utter chaos of their lives.

Thelma spent her days conscientiously bargaining with the Yencheng San workers who sought her out, some asking, some demanding a financial settlement from an unsure employer with a dubious future. Cautiously and carefully she disbursed what each worker needed immediately and promised a final settlement at a later date. In the back of her mind she prayed she would find a brave local banker who would honor a bank draft against the division's accounts at a Shanghai bank .

Gertrude and her nursing students spent their daylight hours among the villagers in the market, scrounging for food and interviewing every prospective itinerant about potential escape routes and the possible location of the sure-to-be-advancing Japanese army.

"Thelma, I've got onions," Gertrude sang out as she trudged heavily between the frozen wagon ruts leading to their isolated humble abode. Dressed in the long quilted pants, heavy Chinese jacket, and thick boots that Thelma had sensibly advised at Thanksgiving, Gertrude could easily have been mistaken for a tall Chinese farm wife excitedly announcing her precious purchases upon returning from the morning market.

Even with her short stature, Thelma's head nearly touched the lintel of the low door frame where she stood gazing after the distant, receding form of the last hospital worker to visit her. At the sharp sound of Gertrude's voice ringing in the cold air, she turned to focus a grim countenance on Gertrude as she approached.

"Well, I knew our situation was desperate," Gertrude chided, laughingly, as she approached, "but what kind of pickle did you swallow?"

"I'm sorry. Do I look that bad?" Thelma apologized, retreating into the dark interior.

"It's just that I depend on your cheerfulness to sustain me," Gertrude said as she ducked into the doorway. She pulled the short, flimsy door shut behind her and bolted it. "Although I agree, there is little to be cheerful about."

"Where's Nellie and Herbert?" Gertrude peered into the dark corners of the small hut but found them empty.

"Herbert took Nellie out for some fresh air," Thelma said quietly. "She was beginning to shake again. I thought she could use some sunshine and open space."

"Probably so," Gertrude nodded in agreement. "She still hasn't recovered from the bombing raid, has she?" As her shoulders unconsciously shuddered, to herself she added, *Frankly, neither have I.*

"Well, here's the last of the vegetables in Yao Chiao," Gertrude announced, plunking down the three smallish, yellow orbs onto the squat, slatted crate used as a sideboard and cupboard, "unless there's a root cellar hidden somewhere that I don't know about. But no need to complain while we have plenty." Gertrude turned to Thelma for a response and saw her sitting on her cot, staring at the dirt floor.

Looking up into the ensuing silence, Thelma managed a small smile, "No, I suppose not."

Gertrude quickly crossed the small room, seating herself on the cot opposite Thelma. "OK, tell Aunt Gertrude all about it." When Thelma's smile broadened, Gertrude sat up straighter and added, "It's going to be hard to get me down after finding those onions. So what's the problem now?"

"Well, for starters, I'm about out of money," Thelma sighed, extending her hands to demonstrate her dearth of cash. "I can't go on promising our workers any further payments until I can find someone who will take a draft on our Shanghai bank."

"Well, we're not likely to find anyone here in Yao Chiao with that kind of money, that's for sure." Gertrude shook her head as she mentally reviewed the few poor people she had met in this small village while searching for food and information.

"And one of the workers brought this letter from Dr. Nethery this morning," Thelma added as she placed the already-opened envelope into Gertrude's eagerly outstretched hand.

Gertrude quickly scanned its first few sentences. "Kweitah. So that's where you've been, Doctor," she said aloud. Looking up at Thelma she added, "Well, I guess we know now why the Japanese asked him to wait a few days. They thought he was trying to get back to warn us about the bombing raids they were planning."

Thelma nodded. "We should be thankful that he and Marie and the children weren't traveling on the Kweitah Road during the bombing," she said softly as if the Japanese might hear her even now.

Gertrude shuddered at the gruesome thought of such an obvious target for the Japanese airmen. "But I surely wish you were here, Doctor, with all of your supplies," Gertrude said, returning her attention to the letter. "Our hospital will need them now more than ever."

"That's the next problem," Thelma said quietly. When Gertrude looked up inquisitively, Thelma continued, "That last worker—who just left— brought word from Fan and Lao Da that there's widespread looting on the compound."

"What!" Gertrude stood swiftly, spilling Dr. Nethery's letter onto the floor. "Who would do such a thing?" she asked, looking incredulously about as if she might find the culprits hiding in the darkness of their small house.

"Some of the graduate nurses," Thelma said with a shake of her head. "Lao Da and Fan caught them trying to break through the iron bars on the main storage room next to Dr. Nethery's office. They'd already stripped the hospitals of everything they could carry."

"Everything?" Gertrude asked. Her mind grasped at the 'impossible' possibility as she sagged limply down on the cot.

"Lao Da convinced them that they'd get no severance pay if they continued looting. So they left."

"I should think that they have their settlement already," Gertrude said as she straightened up, firelight flickering into full flame in her eyes. "Thelma, we need to return as soon as we can," she said, her voice hardening, "if we're going to have any hospital or school left at all."

"I agree," Thelma answered, confident that Gertrude would take things in hand as soon as they returned to the compound. "Oh, I almost forgot," Thelma added, handing over a small envelope with the familiar 'avion' symbol on it. "This came also. It's for you."

Gertrude took the airmail letter, not glancing at the return address, knowing it was from her mother who insisted on sending airmail letters, and absently opened it as she reviewed in her mind what steps she would take to salvage the Yencheng Sanitarium and Hospital. As her eyes carelessly scanned the first few sentences, her left hand suddenly flew to her mouth, the empty envelope fluttering to the floor.

"What is it, Gertrude?" Thelma asked, her arms anxiously braced on edge of the cot.

Gertrude looked up as large tears overflowed onto her cheeks. "My father died," she said softly.

For the next five days a blizzard, such as Gertrude had not experienced since living in New England, raged over central China, burying everything and everyone in a blanket of deep snow and frigid air. Sequestered in their living quarters, even in the daytime the sojourners stayed in their beds fully dressed, in order to stay warm. During meal preparations they huddled together in the small, separate but warm kitchen hut. On the coldest days they built a fire in the middle of the dirt floor of their sleeping room. Even though it filled the room with smothering smoke, they achieved a modicum of warmth and the hint that they could survive even this.

Gertrude developed a bad cold and deep, debilitating cough that kept her in her bed even as the weather warmed and the snow began to melt. Because she'd sold her personal supply of Phecol cough syrup to the hospital to restock the pharmacy, she had nothing with her now to calm the cough. She was so wearied from coughing she could not eat even the two small meals of *shi fan* the nursing students prepared for them each day. By the end of the third week Gertrude had lost 14 pounds and looked skeletal. And the meager food supply in the small village of Yao Chiao was depleted.

On February 19, three weeks after the bombing raid, Gertrude and Thelma repacked their two hand carts with their few remaining supplies and possessions. Traveling only with Herbert and Nellie Wilkinson over the muddy, rutted roads and melting snow, they struggled back to Loho in search of a more promising food supply and the remains of the Yencheng San.

Chapter 49

RETURNING HOME

After observing that her apartment building had not collapsed, Gertrude boarded up what was exposed, closed doors on what was not needed, and set up temporary living space in its back half—the kitchen, dining room, and back bedroom. There was no plaster on the walls and the paper that now covered the windows rattled frighteningly in the night wind. Although she had moved her stove into the center of the three rooms, the cold wind entered easily through the numerous gaps in the ceiling and windows, making attempts at warmth useless.

Very quickly it became obvious that there had been widespread looting of the compound, including Gertrude's apartment. Her cook had taken all of her sugar, kerosene, salt, and canned goods. In addition, all of her dresses, three coats, two umbrellas, all of her white nursing duty stockings, her Chinese dresses, the silk shirts she'd purchased for the boys back home, white duty slips, a vanity suitcase, two manicure sets, all her bed sheets and pillow slips, and 11 bath towels were nowhere to be found.

Fortunately Thelma's cook proved to be more trustworthy than the others. He had bundled up all of her things and buried them in his back yard. And he had prevailed upon Dr. Nethery's cook to do the same and secure the Netherys' things at their house in Yencheng.

With the return of some of Thelma's "unearthed" canned goods and a few hearty meals, Gertrude began to regain her strength and her ability to contend with the devastation that confronted her.

The looting of her apartment made Gertrude angry. The looting of the hospital by her fellow workers brought heartbreak and despair. An inventory of the men's and women's buildings revealed that little remained of the hospital's already depleted supplies. Although most of the iron bedsteads remained in the wards, all linens, towels, blankets, and mattresses were gone. Even the storage cabinets and the new stoves in the hydrotherapy rooms had been taken.

As Gertrude slowly walked through the operating room she could only gaze in shock and amazement at the broken glass in the locked metal cabinets and the resulting empty shelves. No scissors or scalpel handles remained. All the carefully wrapped sterile packs were gone. All of her anesthesia equipment had been taken. Only the large light hanging from the ceiling and the heavy operating table remained undamaged and intact.

Running her hand along the shelf above the scrub sink, Gertrude found, hiding under a crumpled towel, four of the dozen new "mosquito" clamps she had brought in with Dr. Nethery on their bicycle trip. She cradled them carefully, even tenderly, in her hand, as one might hold a very tiny, premature infant tenuously holding to life. Of all the new equipment that had come in with them, these were the only things that remained.

". . . all the hard work we're doing . . ." The words she had written, the thoughts that had shaped her resolve to remain in Yencheng returned in intense irony. Too despondent to weep, she stared about at the decimation caused by those she had trusted. *Dear God,* she agonized silently, gripping the small, metal instruments in her hand, *what was it all for? Did it mean nothing to them?* Her eyes gazed upward, her gaze penetrating the ceiling, driven by the agony in her heart for her students and her friends. *God, didn't we teach them anything?*

When Wang Shueh Wen had discovered his fellow workers breaking down doors to steal all they could, he had rescued the meager stores of the pharmacy and much of the equipment from the clinics and had taken them to the dispensary in Loho. With barely enough supplies to support the dispensary and certainly not nearly enough to run a hospital, Gertrude decided to leave them safely in his keeping. If Doctor Nethery was going to return, he would need to bring enough supplies to start over. There remained nothing with which to run a hospital in Yencheng.

On Sabbath, March 1, three solemn women and Herbert were gathered in the rear, undamaged section of the Wilkinson house. Elder Wilkinson had gone with Pastor Chang visiting and encouraging church members who also had suffered from the recent bombings. The four friends, isolated from their world, shared their Sabbath hours huddled close to the kitchen stove. Nellie led them in singing a few hymns with Gertrude accompanying them on the accordion. Thelma guided them in a short study of Scripture. Herbert offered a prayer. Then without the aid of household cooks or nursing students, the three women prepared and served the Sabbath meal.

"What did you do this morning when the airplanes went over?" Nellie Wilkinson asked quietly, her eyes furtively averted from the others seated at the table. Her small, elfin face, pinched in fear and shame, was bowed beneath her curly blond tresses.

Gertrude glanced up from her plate. "I hid under my bed," she admitted, "and put my fingers in my ears." Her ears flamed bright red as if in response to the mention of their involvement.

"Me, too," Thelma added. She lay down her fork resolutely. "I don't think any of us have anything to be ashamed of." She regarded the other three faces now turned toward her. "My heart still pounds and I shake uncontrollably at just the thought of that day."

As if on cue, Gertrude's hand began to tremble. Surreptitiously she rested her spoon next to her plate, pressing her arm against the edge of the table until the shaking subsided.

"What do we do now?" Herbert asked in the ensuing silence.

Three pairs of female eyes turned to the one person who had expressed what all had been thinking for the past week but which no one had voiced until now. Everyone's hands were motionless, the food on their plates ignored. Everyone was internally consumed with the topic that all had been avoiding since their return to the devastated compound. Despite their best efforts to recover the work in Yencheng, the proximity of the Japanese army assured that there would be no patients in the hospital and no students at the school. Their presence at the Yencheng Sanitarium and Hospital no longer served any useful purpose.

It was as if Herbert had pulled the plug in a bathtub full of water. Words ran out in a torrent as everyone began to talk at once.

"What *can* we do?" Nellie asked quickly.

"Dr. Nethery said in his last letter that he is returning to the States,"

Gertrude said with a deep sigh of resignation. "I can't blame him. I have no patients and no nurses to care for them. There's nothing for him to do here."

"Well, Division headquarters was plain enough in their last communication," Thelma began.

"After they dallied for the last three months," Gertrude interjected darkly.

"Yes . . . they did dally." Thelma nodded and laughed in reluctant agreement. "But they did say—finally—that we should leave here."

"But we'll never go anywhere so long as my husband thinks there's one more soul who needs to be saved or one more stick of furniture here that he's responsible for." Nellie's voice quavered noticeably.

But Gertrude heard the firm bite of conviction as well. *A little anger might do you good, Nellie Wilkinson. Give you a bit of backbone,* she ruminated silently.

"Your husband will send you out even though he has to stay," Thelma said quickly, trying to encourage her timorous friend.

"Out to where?" Nellie asked, the pitch of her voice rising higher. "I couldn't travel alone. I just couldn't."

"Yes, Mother, out to where?" Herbert asked, caught up in the flurry of increasingly anxious conversation.

"Chungking, probably," Thelma said, rapidly considering the alternatives. "That's where the Chinese National Government has gone. And that's where the missionaries in western China will go as well, I think." Then focusing on the distraught mission president's wife, she added confidently, "And you won't have to go alone, Nellie. You can travel with us." She nodded in Herbert's direction as he nodded vigorously in turn, his mouth full of the breakfast he had rediscovered.

Having retreated into her own thoughts, Gertrude felt more than heard the silence as the weight of everyone's gaze rested on her, awaiting her response. Looking up, she met Thelma's questioning eyes with anxious uncertainties of her own.

"I can't go to Chungking. If I go there, I will be trapped and unable to get out of China." Gertrude was speaking rapidly, thinking outloud as she attempted to sort out her frustrations and her fears. "I gave up my furlough to stay here when Dr. Nethery left. It was due last September, you know. And I haven't seen my mother in more than four years," she continued, looking away from the group, stifling the anger that rose inside her. "The Japanese Army is coming soon—so none of the Chinese will stay and help run our hospital here. Besides Dr. Nethery isn't coming back and no one will come in to replace him." She pushed back from the table and stood as one does when resigning their position. "I know I promised I would stay until he returned. But now . . . there's no reason for me to stay." She turned and walked away from the table, distancing herself from the other three who would be going somewhere else without her.

Like a kite in a shifting wind she turned quickly and confronted the three of them. "Why did God send us here? What did we think we were doing? What was it all for?" As she spoke her voice lost it's strident tone, quieting to a husky whisper.

Thelma spoke first. "Those who looked after us while we were here— Mary Wang, Dr. Tsao, Mr. Fan, Pastor Chang. They all knew that we gave them the best that we had. We loved them and they knew it." Her eyes warmed as she spoke, became sparkles of light as she finished.

"And those precious souls who committed their hearts to Jesus during the evangelistic campaign," Nellie added, ever the pastor's wife. "The ones you played the accordion for."

"And the patients . . . and the workers . . . and the students," Gertrude spoke aloud, nodding in self-confirmation, searching for meaning in each word as she spoke it. "For me, it was always the students."

In one quick motion Thelma pushed back her chair and stood, then hesitated. Gertrude watched as Thelma took a few cautious steps in her direction, extending one hand, palm upward and open. When Gertrude extended her own hand, Thelma walked forward with increasing confidence until the two old comrades were hugging tightly while standing in the middle of the chilly, meager remains of their once substantial compound in central China.

"I just needed to hear it," Gertrude said over Thelma's head in the direction of Nellie. "We were just beginning to get a program started here." She shook her head in disbelief.

In rapid succession visions of five years in China swam through her mind: the Chinese language school, Ashey and Gert Loewen, the Shanghai San and the Wuhan San, and a cold bicycle trip across China to Yencheng. It had all passed so rapidly.

"And now I'm taking almost nothing home with me. It seems like I've accomplished so little." Her gray eyes misted over as she hugged Thelma ever tighter. "I just needed to hear it again."

Two days later Gertrude left Yencheng, riding in the most comfortable and readily-available conveyance in Loho, a Chinese wheelbarrow. She was followed by two carts drawn by coolies. The carts held two trunks and several suitcases containing what worldly goods she still possessed, plus the remains of the Nethery household extracted by threat from their cook and hastily packed in available containers in a 24-four hour whirlwind of activity.

In Hsuchang she was joined by a couple from the Lutheran Mission who accompanied her along back roads and over river fords to Wangtien. After a fruitless interrogation of a stoic Gertrude by the Japanese in this battlefront, war zone city, she was allowed to travel on to Shanghai by rail.

With her back salary now firmly in hand from the Division headquarters, Gertrude spent two weeks carefully shopping to replace her winter coat, her dresses, and other necessary wearing apparel. She splurged only once, buying a lovely silver fox scarf. She also purchased another trunk, sorting, updating, and carefully repacking the Nethery household possessions along with her own. At 7:00 o'clock on a rainy Tuesday evening, April 8, 1941, Gertrude settled into a comfortable cabin on the SS Cleveland for an uneventful cruise to Honolulu, Los Angeles, and San Francisco.

GENERAL CONFERENCE OF SEVENTH-DAY ADVENTISTS
Takoma Park, Washington, D.C.
April 11, 1941

Mrs. Lena Green
88 Bryan St.
Rochester, N.Y.

Dear Mrs. Green:
Further to my letter of April 10. I was very happy this morning to be able to send you by telegram information that had just come in by cable from

Shanghai informing us that Nurse Green will arrive in the States by the S.S. "Cleveland." The telegram to us did not give the date of the steamer's expected arrival, but upon checking with the agent here in Washington this morning, we are informed that the vessel is expected in San Francisco on the twenty-fourth, and so we included this in the message to you.

We are glad indeed for this definite word that your daughter is safely on her way to the homeland, and feel confident that you will have already shared this information with Dr. Ruth and other members of the family.

Yours sincerely,
A.W. Cormack

SS *Cleveland*
At Sea, April 21, 1941

Dear Mother:

Just a short note while sitting quietly waiting for them to call me to dinner. I know you will be shocked to hear from me like this but things moved very fast. I was able to write to you when I finally got to Shanghai but I was not sure if you received that letter. Everything is so confused by the war.

I will just tell you that I escaped by the skin of my teeth before the Japanese army captured everything the Japanese air corps had not destroyed at our hospital in Yencheng. As I wrote before, the trip to Shanghai was uneventful except for the short stop in Wangtien where the Japanese interrogate everyone who is coming from the free Chinese territories. They really thought we were going to tell them something. Well, they got nothing out of me, I can tell you. I just played dumb and I hope they thought so or I would be very disappointed in my acting.

I am feeling much better since I got out of that place and especially since I got on this quiet boat. But now I am homesick for Yencheng and wish I were going the other way. But it was not an easy experience with all the bombing. I still shake and tremble when I think of it all and to even hear the sound of a plane nearly kills me. I just start trembling.

I had a radiogram from Ruth telling me she will be waiting for me to arrive. I will be stopping in Los Angeles first to leave off the trunks and things

I brought home for the Netherys who had to leave Yencheng without any of their things. I packed them up—what was left of them —and brought them out with me. And I will see them in Los Angeles before traveling up to San Francisco. I hope Ruth does not mind waiting for a little while until I have visited in So. California.

While visiting Ruth, I will go to the General Conference meetings in San Francisco and then I will be coming east to see you. I can hardly wait to see you.

From your daughter who loves you,
Gertrude

Chapter 50

A MISSION ASSIGNMENT IN THE STATES

Sitting in front of her third-story window in the Glenhurst Building, Gertrude cradled in her lap the latest letter from Thelma Smith in Chungking, China, and gazed out across the familiar grounds of the New England Sanitarium and Hospital. The early morning sun, promising a warm June Sabbath, played among the full-leafed trees along Doctor's Row and sent showers of sparkles rippling across Spot Pond beyond the main road. It was one of her favorite places in all the world, and the beginning of summer was her favorite time of the year.

In front of her and to her left, the hospital building stretched out along the ridge of the hill like a large battleship, imposing itself upon the ground, occupying the heights, and commanding the surrounding countryside. Newsreels of the war, battleships belching forth fire and destruction, sprang into her mind.

Funny how everything reminds me of the war, she thought.

The war. Gertrude's thoughts slipped back to her return to the States in April, 1941, on an open-ended furlough—"until the fighting stops and it is safe to return," she was told. She had attended the Seventh-day Adventist world church's General Conference session in San Francisco that May. She'd had a joyous summer with her mother and an extended family reunion in Rochester, New York. But there had been no call to return to China. It was still too dangerous, she had been told—because of the war.

Officially Gertrude had been, and still was, under missionary appointment to the Seventh-day Adventist Church to return to China. Officially she was now in the States on furlough only. At the same time Hong Kong and the

Philippines were full of displaced workers from China. Many missionaries from the Far East and from Europe were still in the States awaiting the call to return to their postings. There were more missionaries in the States now with no place to go than there were places to send them. Even with her Chinese language skills there was no place to use Gertrude at the moment.

When I left Thelma Smith and the others in Yencheng, I knew I would not be able to get back into Chungking in Nationalist China. Remembering the tearful parting at the front gates of the Yencheng San compound, Gertrude clutched more tightly the letter from Thelma in her lap. *Dr. Nethery had tried to get back in from Burma into Chungking and was unsuccessful then. It's even more unlikely now.*

Her mind did a full turnabout and asked the question she had been trying to avoid. *Would I have gone back if they had asked me?* In response her whole body shuddered at the exquisitely vivid memories of her last three weeks there . . . no supplies . . . diving airplanes . . . screaming bombs . . . extreme cold . . . student thievery and vandalism. *Don't know. They never asked.*

Because waiting around with nothing to do seemed such a waste of time. In September 1941, she had decided to attend classes at Washington Missionary College in Washington, D.C., to complete her bachelor's degree in nursing. Even now she could see the cut flower arrangement on the tiny kitchen table and the red chair where she had been sitting, writing letters, that Sunday afternoon in December. Her friend from the apartment next door had come bursting in, shouting for her to turn on the radio. Japan's surprise attack on Pearl Harbor had brought the United States and Great Britain into the war against Japan. And all her friends and coworkers who had remained in Shanghai, Hong Kong, and the Philippines had been made prisoners of war.

And the letters had stopped coming.

Thelma Smith and Nellie Wilkinson got to Chungking. Gertrude placed the letter in her lap on the desk where several neat, individualized stacks of letters reminded her of those who had escaped to the western parts of China. *But the ones who had gone to the Philippines . . .* Gertrude had not heard from them since January 1942. Again she shuddered to think what she would have been doing now if she had been waiting in the Philippines to return to China. Gertrude glanced at the *Farmer's Almanac* abover her small kitchen range.

It was June 1943. Gertrude now had her Bachelor of Science degree in nursing but the war still continued in China and throughout Southeast Asia. Last year she had been offered the position of assistant director of nurses here at the New England Sanitarium and Hospital. And she'd taken it because no one was going to return to the Far East, at least, not in the foreseeable future. So far as she could tell, the war had engulfed that entire region of the world in hatred and betrayal, darkness and destruction.

Why would I want to go back? What did I accomplish there anyway?

Finding herself staring into the empty hands that lay folded in her lap, Gertrude looked out again at the view before her. The familiar red, peaked roof of Langwood Hall, the nursing dorm, rose above the treetops on her right. This was where she had begun her nursing career 14 years ago.

As did many of those who are now over there . . . somewhere . . .

She was scheduled to give her "missionary talk" this morning to the student nurses' Sabbath school, in the Langwood Hall chapel. The pages of outline she'd written last night on the backs of squares of paper torn from old nursing forms lay folded neatly in her lap, under her hands. She turned her hands over and touched them, then slowly spread them out for review.

She would tell them about nursing in a foreign country—about teaching in the Chinese language, and traveling on bicycles. She'd tell them about having limited supplies and learning to substitute what you have for what you need, about mattresses made of straw, and bed linens that are washed repeatedly until they are gray and falling apart. And she would tell them of the spiritual needs of the patients. She'd tell about holding Sabbath schools for patients on the ward, finding Chinese-language Bibles and hymnals for them. She'd tell how she played the accordion and how she taught the nursing students to do Bible studies at evangelistic meetings.

Gertrude collected the tattered-edged notes from her lap and stood, retrieving her thick Chinese Bible from the corner of the bed nearest the door. As she reached for the doorknob, she glanced back at the window and the view it afforded her of her beloved Spot Pond.

Her life had come full circle. She was once again at the New England San. To be sure, she was a returned missionary with stories to tell. But China was far away. This was home.

She opened the door and stepped into the hallway.

And I will not talk about the war, she resolved, quietly closing the door behind her.

As Assistant Director of Nurses, Gertrude's primary responsibilities were to give guidance to the nursing supervisors, manage the ward nursing through the ward charge nurses, and oversee the nursing work schedule throughout the hospital. Compared to Yencheng it was a light load, and she was happy for that. She had managed to arrange one day off a week for every nurse in the hospital, had fought for the idea in nursing council, and had struggled with the schedules until it was a reality. But it was her only crusade of the year. Mostly she had "kept her head down" and avoided unnecessary trips to the administrative offices, the better to sustain her sense of quiet relaxation. It had made for a pleasant year.

That's why the early morning summons to the office of Dr. Wells Allen Ruble was so unusual.

Why would he want to see me at this time of day? she questioned as she took the back stairs to the second floor of the main hospital building.

From her previous years of experience as his office nurse Gertrude knew that early Monday morning was Dr. Ruble's planning time. *While the sun is coming up, he sits in his office and plans out his week.* In her mind's eye she could see his slender silhouette rise from behind his massive desk and walk to the window where he'd stare out at the front road and Spot Pond, thinking out some particularly difficult problem. She knew his routine and his habits.

Standing in front of the familiar office door, she knocked gently on the familiar opaque glass where his name was printed in black letters.

"Come in." Gertrude heard his quiet baritone call out to her. *Did it have a touch of quaver in it?* She wasn't sure.

As she'd pictured, he stood before the window with the opened drapes held loosely in his right hand. He held himself remarkably erect for a man of his age, but his square, spectacled face topped with thin gray hair, remained ageless. The office, like the man, had not changed in 14 years. The same two green chairs sat facing each other in front of the same immense desk.

Nothing new here, she observed, *except you're getting older.* Then she remembered that she herself would be 34 in three months, and winced.

"Good morning, Miss Green," Dr. Ruble said pleasantly, turning to face her. He moved with quick, even strides to his desk and began searching for a piece of paper. "Do come in and have a seat." He waved absently at one of the straight-backed, green chairs. "I have a message for you here . . . somewhere." He continued his search, opening several drawers, until the truant was found hiding under his daily schedule. Extracting the elusive, yellow Western Union form, he spread it on the nearly empty desktop and looked up to see Gertrude still standing beside her chair observing him.

Unconsciously, Gertrude smiled and stood waiting for her elder to be seated. When he hesitated, she gave a small bow and continued waiting. She saw a small smile twitch the corners of his mouth as he sat. Suddenly aware of her Chinese mannerisms, her smile diminished as she lowered herself into the old familiar chair. *It's my Chinese habits,* she groused at herself. *A lot of good they'll do me here in the States.*

He glanced down at the crumpled telegram in front of him and up at Gertrude. "The people at the Portland Sanitarium and Hospital are searching for a director for their nursing school," he began.

The Portland San is in Portland, Oregon, were her first thoughts. Observing a shadow of sadness pass over the fatherly face before her, she leaned forward, her mind grasping for understanding as her hands clutched the green cloth covering the arms of the chair.

"Are they asking for me?" She spoke loudly, incredulously.

"They've practically asked for you by name." He leaned forward, placing both elbows on his desk. Pressing down the folded edges of the telegram with his long, thin fingers, he began reading. "'Experienced in nursing, teaching, and administration. Stop. Difficult situation. Stop. Need immediately.'" He gazed up at her. "There aren't many available with your qualifications, Miss Green."

" . . . who don't have a family and a permanent position," she snapped, her green eyes flashing with anger and irritation.

He folded his hands in front of him and studied them. "Seems like we're always sending you away just when we've gotten used to having you here . . . in the family," he offered quietly.

"The Lord giveth and the Lord taketh away."

My bicycle . . . my radio . . . my clothes . . . my furniture . . . my friends . . . my nursing students . . . my apartment . . . my hospital. O Lord, what else is there left to take away? As she listed each item in her mind, her shoulders sank a bit and her frame relaxed until she was sitting back in the chair, her mind submissive and her body tired.

The words of the telegram floated up from her subconscious mind. "Why do they need someone immediately?" she asked, her analytical faculties beginning to pick at the words like an old sweater, seeking the thread of understanding that would unravel their mystery. "What's so difficult about the situation?"

"They're grappling with the same situation we're facing here," he said, removing his glasses and pinching the bridge of his nose. Gertrude recognized the signal of perplexity in his movements. "According to our teachers, the new regulations for nursing schools in the United States call for a stronger curriculum, more classroom teaching, and a connection to a recognized educational institution." He paused, his face resting in his left hand, his brow furrowed in contemplation. "We've started our own discussions with Atlantic Union College but, as you know, the college is 50 miles away. That's a long way to go to use the library." He smiled weakly at his own joke. "It's a problem not easily solved."

"The boys at the college seem to manage the distance . . . whenever they're looking for a date," she quipped. "Especially on the weekends."

"Yes, I suppose they do." He nodded and laughed, putting his glasses back on his face.

"But why the urgency?" Gertrude asked, still not satisfied.

He drew in a deep breath. "I don't know exactly." He ran his finger along the edge of the telegram, studying it as if the elusive truth might be hiding there. "But I understand they're about to come up for review."

"And they think they'll lose their accreditation." Gertrude finished the thought. She sat back considering her conclusion and the questions it left unanswered, questions that could only be answered in Portland, Oregon.

"What do you think, Miss Green? Will you go?" His eyes followed her as she stood.

"I think I need to pack . . . and visit my mother in Rochester . . . on my way to Portland, Oregon," she answered with a small twist of her head and a firm nod.

406

Chapter 51

THE PORTLAND PUZZLE

In July of 1943, the Portland Sanitarium and Hospital was one of the premier private health institutions in the Pacific Northwest. Perched on the northwestern slope of Mt. Tabor (a smallish hill by comparison to the majestic Mt. Hood just to the east) the west facing, cream colored brick hospital was well removed from the congested, grimy downtown area of Portland, Oregon. All the windows on the second floor provided a view of the surrounding lush, verdant mountain foliage in the daytime and the lights of the city of Portland to the northwest at night.

From 1928 to 1938, the hospital had added a modern operating suite, a new laboratory facility, 15 semiprivate rooms in the East Annex, and two new, large ward rooms on the first floor. Immediately to the south of the hospital across Yamhill Street and slightly down the hill stood the Nurses Home, the dormitory for nursing students, a three-story brick structure—four stories on the downhill side—of matching color to the hospital. In addition to modern two-bed dormitory rooms with hot and cold running water, the Nurses Home provided nursing classrooms, laboratories for bacteriology and diet therapy, a nursing procedures room with beds and cupboards, and a chapel.

Most recently the hospital had committed to providing the community with a separate maternity department, the most modern on the Pacific Coast, including a 30-bed nursery, two state-of-the-art birthing rooms, and four labor rooms along with the accompanying maternity ward. With more than 15 operations preformed daily and more than 2,000 births a year in maternity, in 1943 the Portland Sanitarium and Hospital provided its nursing students with a wealth of clinical learning opportunities in all the areas of modern medicine as well as delightful living accommodations.

Yet the modernization of nursing education and the establishment of national standards for nursing schools was catching up with the Portland San. In 1917 the National League of Nursing Education wrote the first guidelines for an ideal nursing school curriculum. In the 1930s and early 1940s further studies struck the death knell for many hospital-affiliated nursing schools. The studies suggested that hospital-sponsored nursing schools were producing inferiorly trained nurses because the hospitals did not have sufficient numbers of qualified teaching staff, were not affiliated with institutions of higher learning with qualified pre-nursing faculty and adequate library facilities, and were unable to provide a sufficient variety of patients for clinical teaching material.

With her well-traveled, small brown suitcase in hand, Gertrude alighted from the Belmont Street trolley across the street from the hospital at about 1:00 p.m. on a beautiful Portland summer day. At the edge of the road she paused to take in the magnificent view of this large, attractive hospital building in its natural surroundings of tall Douglas Fir trees, azaleas, ferns, and mountain flowers. The gentle breezes coming up the slope of Mt. Tabor tugged at her broad-brimmed hat, causing her to catch at it absentmindedly. Mentally she reviewed the list of specific problems she suspected were plaguing their nursing school program. As she stepped briskly across the street behind the departing trolley, she felt sure the problems would quickly be obvious, even if the solutions took some time to implement.

As Gertrude entered the spacious lobby, she noted that it was filled with patients waiting their turn in the clinics. *A good indication of a busy hospital,* she thought as she approached a mother who was struggling with a crying infant. *But we'll see.*

"How long have you been waiting to be seen?" Gertrude asked quietly.

"Since before lunch," the mother answered, shaking her head as she searched in her bag for something to placate the distraught infant. "And I don't think I can hold out much longer."

Gertrude patted her on the arm, nodding sympathetically. Crossing to the other side of the lobby, she approached a frail, elderly man seated and leaning forward heavily on a cane.

Gertrude leaned down and spoke in his ear. "How long have you been waiting here?"

"About an hour," he croaked in response. His red, watery eyes blinked rapidly several times as he stared up at her.

Who's in charge of the registration desk? Gertrude wondered as she stood erect. Her careful gaze followed the line of waiting patients as it bent around the far end of the room and disappeared through a doorway on the opposite wall of the lobby.

Walking through the doorway Gertrude entered a corridor and saw the familiar blue dress with white-trimmed, short sleeves and white covering pinafore of a student nurse, standing in the doorway of an office on the left. She was motioning for another patient to come in. Gertrude quickly approached her.

"Good afternoon," Gertrude began pleasantly, "I'm Miss Green, the new director of the nursing school."

"Yes, ma'am." The student nurse stared blankly at her interrupter.

Glancing past the student nurse into the small office, taking in the desk piled with charts, Gertrude continued, "Where is your supervisor?"

"I don't have one, ma'am. I'm working all alone," the student nurse answered with a sigh as she absently brushed several stray wisps of red hair back over her ear.

Gertrude pursed her lips, considering, as the situation became clear to her. *It's good to train student nurses in triage of patients, but this is not an educational exercise, is it?*

"Well, there's a young mother out there who needs to get in quickly." Gertrude nodded toward the outer office.

"Yes'm. I saw her." The student nurse nodded in response. "I'm working as fast as I can."

"I'm sure you are, my dear," Gertrude said quietly with a smile. "I'm sure you are."

Gertrude, you'd better get settled in before you get too involved, Gertrude lectured herself as she turned and went in search of the administrative offices and the arrangements for her apartment.

"I'm sorry, Miss Green. None of the graduate nurses live in the nursing dorm. Even the Dean of Women does not have an apartment at the Nurses Home," said the business manager and administrator of the Portland San.

Seated in a comfortable chair in the small, unpretentious office of the hospital business manager, Gertrude listened and took the measure of the man. *Hair cut short and neatly combed. Wireless glasses over dark, handsome eyes. He always looks at me as he talks. A strong, square, boyish face with the trace of a smile playing in the background. A modern single-breasted suit and colorful, striped tie. He is sure of his work and sure of his words. An able administrator, if ever I've seen one,* she summarized to herself. Gertrude smiled as she heard the words, "No apartment." *I like you, Ralph Nelson. But I've worked with your kind before.*

Gertrude scooted forward to the edge of her chair. "I notice that many of your nurses are the wives of the doctors or the interns."

"Why, yes, they are. We try to help the interns all we can," Mr. Nelson assured her.

"And many of the single nurses live together, I assume, two or three to a home or an apartment," Gertrude said, smilingly weaving her clever web.

Mr. Nelson nodded in assent.

"I am not married, Mr. Nelson. I do not have any friends here that I can room with." Gertrude did not harden her tone, yet her pronunciation became decidedly more crisp and distinct. Her faced tightened into a Chinese smile as she fixed the hospital manager with her intense green eyes. "Now that I have given up my job at the New England San and come all the way across the United States to help you with the nursing school, what can you do to help me?"

He sat transfixed, unable to break eye contact and unable to speak.

"I can assure you, Mr. Nelson, that I have lived in some very humble situations." Gertrude thought back to the two weeks following the bombing raid on Yencheng and inwardly shuddered. "In Hong Kong I set up housekeeping on the stairway landing between first and second floor. My bed was outside on the roof balcony, but, fortunately, it was not the rainy season." Smiling naturally again, Gertrude softened her gaze, sat back and waited.

She thought she could see visions running through his mind—of the new Director of Nurses living on the roof of the Nurses Home dorm, exposed to the weather and to the view of all the patients on that side of the hospital.

"I don't think that will be necessary, Miss Green," he said finally. "I'm sure we can find something suitable for you."

When Gertrude's trunks arrived from the Johnson Street Railway Terminal later that afternoon, they were taken up to a small, hastily thrown together, two-room apartment on the back side of the top floor of the Nurses Home. In one room was a bed, a desk, and a stand-up closet. In the other room was a hot plate and what passed for a refrigerator—a chest cooler full of ice such as held soft drinks for sale at a local gas station. A table and chair completed Gertrude's kitchen setting. The whole was sparse, compact, and private, suiting Gertrude just fine.

On Thursday morning Gertrude met all of her teaching staff for the first time. Anne Stratton, the Director of Education and Gertrude's second in command, had juggled schedules and exerted firm pressure to make sure the directors of the major nursing services, who were also members of the nursing school staff, attended. Gertrude had insisted that they all be present. She needed to evaluate every aspect of the nursing program, including the nursing instructors, if she was to understand the problems she faced.

As Gertrude questioned her teaching staff about the problems and possible solutions for the nursing school, she discovered that there was hardly a fresh idea among the lot of them. Anne Stratton was the only instructor with a bachelor's degree. One of the instructors did not even have an RN degree. None of them had a teaching certificate or a higher degree. Almost all of the teachers were older, former graduates of the Portland San nursing program and as such were unable to imagine methods and procedures beyond what they'd been taught.

The younger few were reluctant to challenge the opinions of the older instructors. And all of them deferred to the Board of Trustees whenever Gertrude challenged a currently held policy or suggested a new nursing concept or a new approach to a situation. In frustration, Gertrude asked if anyone ever made any decision without first consulting the board. No one responded.

After finishing lunch in the spacious patient dining hall, Gertrude followed the ample frame of Anne Stratton, RN, BA, on a tour through the wide corridors, the well-appointed wards, and semiprivate rooms of the Portland San. They visited the well-equipped operating rooms, the excellent laboratory and

X-ray departments, the new nursery, and the modern maternity department, reviewing the numbers and types of patients visiting each area every month.

"There's certainly nothing wrong with the facilities or the variety of patients you care for," Gertrude said, striding alongside Miss Stratton as they crossed Yamhill Street. They were headed for the small, pillared front porch tucked in the inside corner of the L-shaped Nurses Home building.

"Oh, no," Anne returned quickly. Gripping the handrail and pausing on the third step of the porch, she turned and looked down at Gertrude, her salt-and-pepper, short, wavy hair blowing around her nursing cap. "According to our internal study, the kinds of patients we have are not the problem at all." She turned and marched up the stairs, holding open the door for Gertrude.

So what do you *think the problem is?* Gertrude thought as she passed through the door.

After taking Gertrude on a tour of the teaching facilities built into the Nurses Home, Anne led her to a small office next to the nursing procedures lab. Offering Gertrude a chair, Anne sat in the chair opposite her. Her broad face with round cheeks was missing its usual smile. In just a few days Gertrude—like all the employees of the Portland San—had learned to expect an ever-present, broad smile on Anne's face, exposing a gap in the middle of her upper front teeth. Now the smile, and the gap, was missing. But Gertrude noted that her dark-circled eyes behind wire-rimmed, owlish glasses sparkled with intelligence and intensity.

You know something, but you want me to figure it out for myself, Gertrude mused. *Why? What have you got to lose by telling me?*

On the small, waist-high table between them lay several piles of educational material. In one stack Gertrude recognized articles from the National League of Nursing Education concerning nursing schools. Next to these were study guides for evaluating nursing schools and a large report entitled "Results of the First Grading Study of Nursing Schools." Gertrude picked it up and read, "Confidential Copy for School Number . . ." with the number penciled in on the front cover. In neat handwriting next to the number was the notation: Portland Sanitarium and Hospital.

"I see you've done your homework," Gertrude said, picking up the report and thumbing through the first section on the student body.

"Yes, we did our own internal study as well as participating in the national study," Anne said, motioning toward the papers Gertrude held in her hands. "We know that we have sufficient clinical teaching material. And we have excellent facilities in which to work." Anne readjusted herself in her seat as she warmed to the subject on which she'd spent the greater part of her professional efforts for the last two years. "And I have worked very hard on upgrading our curriculum. I've been working on my Bachelor of Science degree in Teaching here in Portland and using the school as my project."

"Good for you." Gertrude nodded approvingly, remembering the social life she'd sacrificed while taking evening classes even as she continued working at the New England San. She looked admiringly at the young woman across from her, only two years her junior, who was doing the same thing.

"We have established a working relationship with Walla Walla College on the eastern side of Washington State," Anne continued. "They are willing to support our first two prenursing years of a four-year degree program." Gertrude noted that here her voice lost its enthusiasm. "But the negotiations on this are still not settled."

"Where's the holdup?" Gertrude asked sharply, looking up.

"The Board of Trustees of the hospital," Anne said quietly.

Before Gertrude could respond, Anne continued. "The nursing students are of excellent quality. But for the last few years they have not done well on the state board exams." Gertrude watched her pause for a moment and look away as if remembering a previous time. "When this school began, Portland San nurses always scored the highest on the exams." She looked back at Gertrude, almost pleadingly. "But now, every year, we have nurses who fail one or two subjects. And many of our graduates don't even bother to take the board exams at all, thinking they'll be nursing only a few years before they get married and put their nursing behind them."

"Education is everything to a nurse, Miss Stratton," Gertrude said, pronouncing each word carefully for emphasis even as Anne nodded vigorously in assent. "Since my early days as a student at the New England San, I have tried to learn everything I can as often as I can from everyone that I can." Gertrude's voice grew louder with each syllable. Then she paused as the obvious question blossomed into full flower in her mind. "Why aren't the girls learning, Miss Stratton?" Gertrude's eyes lit up, knowing she had hit upon the missing piece of the puzzle.

"They're not attending their classes, Miss Green."

Anne's face mirrored Gertrude's intensity as the two of them mentally moved toward Gertrude's decisive discovery. "They're kept from their classes by extra ward duties, by cleaning and scrubbing, by—"

"By working alone at the patient reception desk . . . and elsewhere," Gertrude interjected, now able to guess that the scene she'd witnessed in the hospital lobby was being repeated throughout the hospital. Then a second question proposed itself. "Who is insisting that the nursing students do all this menial housework instead of attending their classes?"

"Dr. Holden," Anne said.

Gertrude sat back and considered the name. "Dr. William Holden," she said aloud. "The medical director of the nursing school and the senior surgeon on the hospital staff—according to the nursing school handbook I read." She tapped the little tan handbook on the table as she spoke.

"And the major voice on the Board of Trustees—besides Mr. Nelson," Anne added. "He says that the only thing nurses really need to know is how to empty bedpans."

"Oh, he does, does he?" Gertrude snapped, making the air crackle.

"He's been here since forever, since before the new hospital was built," Anne said, speaking quietly as one does in the presence of greatness. "He's very powerful."

"Are you afraid of him?" Gertrude asked with a slight tilt of her head.

"Most of the nurses are," Anne demurred. "They won't oppose him." She paused thoughtfully. "And many think he's right. They had to do it when they were students here and they think the new nursing students should have to do it as well."

"Which is why no one's making any headway on the nursing school," Gertrude said, nodding in understanding. She sat up straight and leaned forward, placing her forearms, sphinx-like, on the table. "Now that I know where the problem is, Miss Stratton," she began, "are you willing to be a co-conspirator with me in fixing this nursing school?" The glowing green of her eyes and the lack of a smile revealed Gertrude's earnestness.

"I will follow you, Miss Green," Anne responded, equally serious. "I love this school with all my heart."

"Good." Gertrude straightened up with a deep breath of commitment, knowing now where the battle lay. "You take care of getting the discussions going again with Walla Walla College and I will take care of Dr. Holden. It's my specialty, Miss Stratton—dealing with physicians." With this remark Gertrude watched Anne's famous smile spread across her face.

Gertrude reached for the small nursing school handbook on the table. "Now according to this description of the nursing school, you don't have any classes in office nursing. Is that a subject you would like me to teach? It's also one of my specialties."

Over the next week Gertrude joined the anesthesia call rotation and gave anesthetics for five of Dr. Holden's cases, three during the daytime and two at night. Unobtrusively, she studied the man carefully. He was extremely kind and courteous with his patients, praying with each one of them before every surgery. He was demanding of the operating room staff, using his age and senior staff position to command competence and respect. He allowed no silly remarks or behavior in the OR and tolerated ignorance poorly. He was exceptionally competent as a diagnostician and displayed wonderfully skillful hands at the operating table. He was forthright, intelligent, hardworking. In short, he was a typical Seventh-day Adventist Christian surgeon.

Gertrude was impressed, as were most people, with the power and presence of Dr. Holden. From all of her experience with other physicians she compared him most favorably with Dr. Harry Miller. But she had yet to encounter him outside the operating room or in a social setting.

Chapter 52

THE REAL CONTROVERSY

During the next two weeks, after meeting with the various nursing floors and department supervisors to learn their unique problems and perspectives, Gertrude took firm hold of the reins of the Department of Nursing at the Portland San. Also, at Anne Stratton's urging, she began her teaching responsibilities by redesigning the two senior classes called "Professional Problems I and II" which Gertrude renamed "Professional Adjustments." In these seminars she planned to expose the senior students to nursing administration, office nursing, higher education, and teaching. Her thirty-fifth birthday was just two months away and Gertrude, an old hand at nursing administration, had returned to the love of her professional life—teaching.

Wednesday afternoon at 4:20 found Gertrude stalking the halls of the hospital, looking for her students. At the first meeting of her new Senior Seminar she'd waited in the classroom a full 15 minutes. When only two of the 15 students appeared, she had asked the two where the others were. Their response had been a vague reference to the nursing floors in the hospital and something about "ward work." Now Gertrude was on the prowl.

She found three of the senior students cleaning in the kitchen and two of them on their hands and knees scrubbing the clinic hallways. After informing their supervisors of their absence and instructing the students to leave their mops and pails "right where they are," she sent them all to the classroom to await her arrival. On the medical floor Gertrude found three of her seniors cleaning the nursing station.

"Alice, Helen, Ruth!" Gertrude called out as she approached the desk, addressing each of them by their first names. "It's time for class, girls. Leave everything right where it is." In answer to their wordless, startled expressions she responded sharply, "I'll speak to your supervisor. Now go."

As the confused students began filing out of the work station, they were confronted by the evening nurse supervisor who had been getting reports from around the hospital of work stoppage and disappearing students.

"Girls, where are you going?" she demanded.

"They're going to my classroom," Gertrude said, stepping out of the workstation. She made shooing motions with her hands, herding the girls around the startled supervisor and down the hall. The supervisor, recognizing the new Director of Nurses, stared in awe, mouth agape, as Gertrude purposefully passed within inches of her. Gertrude paused, staring directly at her, green eyes aglow like a mother bear protecting her young, then growled, "These girls are students. They are not slaves."

Gertrude did not follow the students to the classroom. She headed for the surgery floor. Five of her cubs were still missing.

She found them in the East Wing Annex doing what nurses had been doing since Florence Nightingale was in the Crimea: cleaning patient rooms, washing windows, scrubbing sinks, and mopping floors. Gertrude knew that all of these activities were required in a hospital environment to prevent the spread of infection and to protect patients from one another. All of these activities were the proper concern of nurses who cared about the safety of their patients. But Gertrude also understood that in a modern hospital like the Portland San, the nursing staff was fully occupied in assisting with complex medical procedures, distributing powerful medicines, administering physical treatments, and meeting the spiritual and emotional needs of the patients. Housekeeping duties were to be performed by the janitorial staff under the watchful eye of the nursing personnel, but even in China this was considered the work of coolies—day laborers hired to do menial tasks—and not the proper work of professional nurses. Her students were not coolies.

From the medicine prep room to the back hall storage and through every patient room, like a naval destroyer on patrol, Gertrude thoroughly searched the surgical floor for her students. She did not raise her voice, made no boisterous scenes, disturbed no patient care situations. Yet where she found her students, she extracted them, leaving their cleaning supplies bobbing in the wake of her ever-expanding convoy.

"Miss Green, what are you doing?"

The power and command of the vaguely familiar male voice slowed Gertrude's forward progress. Her eyes darted side to side in search of its owner.

Ten feet to her right stood the diminutive Dr. Holden, bespectacled and round faced with a high-domed, bald head ringed with a gray fringe of hair. His sparse eyebrows and deep cheek wrinkles made him appear old, craggy, weathered. His dark eyes and heavily hooded eyelids gave his face and demeanor quiet intensity. His lab coat added professional authority, the authority with which he brought Gertrude to a halt.

In his left hand he held a patient's chart in which he'd been writing just moments before. Surrounding him was his own entourage of interns and ward nurses, including the surgery floor supervisor, one of Gertrude's teaching staff. His pen, with which he'd been writing, was poised in midair, held like a scepter. But it was the regal tone in his voice and the commanding authority in his glance that held her attention and brought everyone in the immediate area under his power.

"Dr. Holden." Gertrude addressed him politely, but impassively. Her voice carried its own power; her tone was collegial and not subservient. "I'm collecting my class."

"But they're doing their work here," he said, indicating the wide expanse of the surgery floor with a casual wave of his pen.

Gertrude's green eyes locked on his, startling him in their intensity. "Cleaning is not their work, Dr. Holden. Nursing is their work. And if they are to be good nurses, they must attend their classes." The severity of Gertrude's countenance broke into playful smiles as the perfect words sprang into her mind and then from her lips. "Besides, if they don't come to my class, they will be good for nothing but emptying bed pans."

Gertrude glanced about her for her charges. "Girls," she commanded, her voice hardening with authority as she moved forward, "Come with me. Now."

The following week Gertrude was scheduled to meet with Elder Vernon G. Anderson, president of the Oregon Conference of Seventh-day Adventists and chair of the Board of Trustees of Portland Sanitarium and Hospital. Typically, presidents of local conferences are extremely busy in the summer: running the annual camp meeting schedule, preparing for Fall Council meetings, and every other year organizing the year-end constituency session. This summer Elder Anderson had the unfortunate additional burden of trying to salvage a nursing school which was in danger of losing its accreditation—and of welcoming a new nursing school director who in three weeks had already earned a reputation for challenging the system and confronting his senior surgeon.

Seated across from him in his office at this first meeting, Gertrude observed Elder Anderson to be tall even while sitting down, affable, handsome, and about her age. What she wasn't prepared for was his frankness.

"Miss Green, we need to change the way we do things in our nursing school," were almost the first words out of his mouth. "We are in grave danger of losing our school."

Realizing that social pleasantries were not on the agenda, Gertrude sat up straighter, preparing for a serious discussion. "I've spent the last three weeks studying your situation, Elder Anderson. I agree. You are in danger, but it's not as grave as I first thought."

"Then you have discovered what the problem is." It was a statement and not a question.

"It's not the teaching or the facility or the clinical material." Gertrude sounded objective and detached, summarizing the conclusions she had often repeated to Anne Stratton. "It's not one of the usual things that plague a hospital-based nursing school," she added, playing for time. To herself, she thought, *Don't tip your hand, Gertrude, until you know which team this man is playing for.* Aloud, she hedged. "The nursing students aren't going to classes."

"But do you know the real problem?" Elder Anderson asked, leaning forward, one hand extended, imploring her for the honest answer.

She read sincerity in his earnest eyes and answered bluntly, "Dr. William Holden."

His shoulders sagged. He slumped backward into his chair. Retracting his imploring hand into his lap, he sighed deeply as one who has just heard confirmation of a death in the family. "Yes, I know."

"I've trained physicians before," Gertrude asserted, sensing approval of her confrontation with the surgeon.

"You misunderstand me, Miss Green." Elder Anderson looked up, catching Gertrude off guard. He spoke quietly but his hands became animated, emphasizing each word. "Dr. Holden loves the Portland Sanitarium and Hospital. He and Mr. Nelson literally built it from the ground up."

"That doesn't give him the right to destroy it by insisting on the old ways," Gertrude retorted, unwilling to surrender her righteous position.

"He doesn't . . . insist on the old ways, Miss Green," Elder Anderson remonstrated with an upraised index finger which he withdrew as he retreated. ". . . except in the area of nursing."

"Men!" Gertrude exclaimed, boiling over in exasperation at her old bugaboo—male authority figures in the church hierarchy, especially those who cover for each other.

"Not all men," Elder Anderson quietly insisted. But he ignored her pointed barb. He wasn't biting on Gertrude's baited hook. He was thinking.

Gertrude watched, her ire cooled by curiosity, as he agilely turned his large youthful torso halfway around in his chair and reached back for the leather-covered Bible lying on the corner of his desk. For the second time in less than five minutes she was caught unprepared by his next comment, delivered offhandedly while his head was turned away from her.

"Have you had much experience handling men, Miss Green?"

Gertrude's face colored as the memory of Dick Richards and a few other young men in blue worsted uniforms with two rows of gold buttons surfaced in her mind. When she saw shock and then a twinkle in the bespectacled eyes of her questioner, Gertrude realized she had misunderstood his meaning and her blush deepened even more.

"I'm sorry," Elder Anderson apologized, suppressing his mirth. "I was thinking along the professional line."

"Yes, of course you were," Gertrude mumbled, struggling to reassemble her composure. Quickly other more mature images replaced the blond-haired, blue-suited sailors. She saw Mr. Chen, her Chinese teacher and mentor in Chinese civility; Dr. Miller with a brilliant mind and an unrealistic view of the real world; Mr. Ren, the excellent accounts collector who wanted to be a pharmacist; and Dr. Tsao, the struggling clinician but faithful Chinese Christian doctor.

"Yes, I've had to manage many male egos." Gertrude spoke with her chin in the air, her embarrassment forgotten, her confidence restored by years of successful encounters.

"Along these lines?" Elder Anderson asked, expeditiously opening his Bible and turning over a few pages as one does who is intimately familiar with the book. "This is Romans, chapter 12 and verse 18," he announced without looking up. Then he read, "If it be possible, as much as lieth in you, live peaceably with all men."

Gertrude was listening intently, absorbing his words and his implied but obvious meaning. She watched his gaze rise from the page and engage her, a gaze of intense hopefulness such as he had exhibited when asking if she had discovered the real problem with the nursing school. She held his gaze, realizing the enormously delicate task he was asking her to undertake.

"You know who the problem is," she said after several moments of silence.

"I do," he responded evenly. "Don't fight him, and don't embarrass him. Work with him . . . and change him."

What have you learned in 14 years, Gertrude? she mused, retreating into her thoughts. *What would Dr. Ruble do? What would the Chinese do?* A flicker of hope, an idea began to emerge.

But will you support me in this? Her eyes narrowed as she focused again on Elder Anderson. Without him she would be out on a limb all by herself.

"I will help you, Miss Green," he said, reading her eyes and her thoughts. He leaned back in his chair, his hands folded near his face, his index fingers extended together like a church steeple, touching his lips pensively. "I would like for you to come to dinner this Sabbath as my guest," he said finally. "We will be going to the home of Dr. Holden, which is just down the street from the hospital."

Gertrude recognized the ploy. *A social encounter away from the hospital. On ground that is comfortable to Dr. Holden. On a day when everyone is expected to be pleasant.*

"I would be happy to come," she announced with a smile. "I never miss a meal."

"Good," he said with a nod but without smiling. "I will be praying for you."

Chapter 53

WINNERS AND LOSERS

The dinner had gone well. Dr. Holden and Mr. Nelson had been strategically seated among the out-of-town guests who had plied the first two for every particular concerning the history of the institution. As the meal progressed to apple pie a la mode, Gertrude sat quietly eating while absorbing the glorious details as told by the two mutually admiring old friends, both of whom had given their entire professional lives to the same mistress, the Portland San.

Gertrude also observed the third member of the vocal triumvirate, Elder Vernon Anderson. Deftly he monitored the questions asked and the answers given, inserting his own questions to elicit some important detail that went unmentioned, stimulating one or the other of the narrators to add his particular slant on an item.

She caught his eye once and held it long enough to communicate silently, *You're doing this to make sure I understand him, aren't you?*

Elder Anderson's only reply was to nod his head ever so slightly, closing and opening his eyes slowly. An ocular bow.

With a slight arching of her eyebrows she telegraphed back, *OK, I'll take it from here.*

Her opportunity came after the meal when Dr. Holden, worn down by the marathon of table conversation, sought out his favorite leather chair in the far corner of a smallish room that in earlier times would have been called the parlor. The other female guests were helping Mrs. Holden clear the dishes and Mr. Nelson had been detained at the table, caught in a knotty conversation by two men.

Gertrude followed Dr. Holden into this small private world decorated with doily-covered jardinière, beadwork string-shade lamps, and other family heirlooms from the previous century. Under other circumstances Gertrude would have gloried in exploring this room with Mrs. Holden, learning the family history of each treasure displayed here. But today she had other work to do. As the only other person in the room she had her choice of seats so settled herself into a smaller, feminine rocker immediately to Dr. Holden's left.

Seeing the Bibles and devotional books lying on the round, linen-covered lamp table between them, Gertrude guessed that this was the private corner where Dr. and Mrs. Holden had their worship time and their intimate conversations. For a moment she reconsidered, *Gertrude, you were too hasty. This is their sacred space.* About to rise, she was startled when Dr. Holden addressed her.

"So tell me, Miss Green, where did you work before you came to Portland?"

Gertrude turned to the right and found herself the subject of his steady, assessing physician's gaze, a friendly smile playing about his lips. Under such close scrutiny, she squirmed in the chair, seeking a more comfortable position before speaking. "I've been at the New England Sanitarium and Hospital for the past year and a half. Before that I was in China for six years." She spoke confidently, holding eye contact but without challenging him.

Aware of her own discomfort, she asked herself, *Why?* and got a curious answer. *Because a steady eye and a smiling face mean something different in China than they do in the West. Be careful, Gertrude"* she admonished herself. *"We're playing mind games here, but not by Oriental rules. Relax. Enjoy him. Pretend he's a Norwegian fifth mate in a blue coat with gold buttons."* This mental image brought her within a hair's breadth of laughing out loud but accomplished the outward warm smile and the internal comfortableness she needed.

She observed that her mention of China brought an alertness to his eye as he turned his whole body toward her. "Did you work with Harry Miller by any chance?" he asked. "He was my intern at the Chicago Clinic." His eyes wandered to the far wall as he began reminiscing. "He would have taken my place there as chief surgeon when I came out here to Portland . . . if he had not gone to China."

"You would be proud of him, Dr. Holden." As she spoke, Gertrude nodded with genuine affirmation. "He does excellent surgery."

"Thyroid surgery is his specialty, I hear," he said as he returned his gaze to her.

"There's a lot of thyroid disease, especially in the interior of China far from the sea." She was lecturing now as if speaking to the nursing students and caught herself. "But he does more than thyroids. We started the Wuhan Hospital together and he oversees 12 other hospitals in China."

"And what was your role, Miss Green?" he asked casually.

"Director of nurses and superintendent of the nursing school," she said proudly.

"Same as here?" His eyes were half closed, hooded and unfocused, his torso slowly turning away from her.

"Same as a lot of places, Dr. Holden. Shanghai San, Yencheng San, and New England San," she replied, counting on her fingers for emphasis, stretching her credentials just a bit.

"And did you run all of your programs with the same disrespect for the nursing role?"

She paused, confused and unguarded, not knowing if he was baiting her or if he was serious in his accusation. She searched his face, looking for clues and found none. *Proceed cautiously*, she advised herself, remembering Elder Anderson's counsel and parting plea.

"The nursing role is changing, Dr. Holden." Now it was her turn to search the flocked wallpaper on the far wall for wisdom. She spoke quietly, her words aided by the memories of the last 14 years—shopping in Wuhan for curtains, learning to speak Chinese in order to teach in the language in Shanghai, running clinics in Mr. Chen's courtyard in Nanking, assisting Dr. Tsao in surgery in Yencheng.

"When I was a probie at the New England San in 1927, the nursing role was primarily personal care for the patient. But in the last ... uh ... 17 years," she said, doing the math quickly in her head, "the nursing role has changed so much I hardly recognize it anymore myself. We have to think more and do more than we were ever taught to do."

She sat up straighter, turning toward him, appealing for his understanding. "We have become the assistants to the physician, the pharmacists at the bedside, the hydrotherapists in clinic as well as the directors of personal patient care. We no longer just give bed baths and empty bedpans."

At this last remark she saw his mouth twitch into what wanted to be a smile, but the effort faded quickly. His dark eyes blinked rapidly in consideration of her polemic, then became serious. "And what about the patient, Miss Green? In all of this newfound knowledge and responsibility, what about the patient?" His gaze was steady. He was looking for a serious answer.

"The patient always comes first, Dr. Holden. The whole patient." Gertrude was preaching now, as if she were addressing her nursing students. "Especially the spiritual condition of the patient. In all of my years of teaching, that has never changed." She had made her appeal and she wanted him to respond, to come forward as a penitent down the aisle and be converted at the altar of modern nursing.

"But the nursing students must learn what nurses have always learned," he said after a moment of silence, averting his eyes. "And you pulled them away from their duties."

"If they had been doing nursing duties, if they had been directly caring for patients, I would have left them to their duties," Gertrude said quietly and firmly, drawing his gaze back to hers and holding it there.

"I like you, Miss Green. I like you very much," Dr. Holden said with a nod of his head. "I just don't like what you stand for."

And so it went for the next three months. On one or two Sabbaths every month, Gertrude would be in the home of Dr. Holden, discussing China, Dr. Miller, church administration, and medicine in general. They cooperated admirably in surgery and worked together on the administrative committee for the upgrading of hospital services. But neither was able to convert the other when it came to the basic principles of nursing duties.

Behind the scenes was Elder Anderson, president of the Oregon Conference of Seventh-day Adventists and, by virtue of his office, chair of the hospital Board of Trustees. He manipulated seating assignments at meetings, arranged social gatherings where both would be present, and kept the lines of communication open between the two antagonists. And he continued to support and approve the changes Gertrude was making at the nursing school.

In the late fall of 1943, everything changed. The North Pacific Union of Seventh-day Adventists, the oversight organization for the several church conferences in the Pacific Northwest, held its constituency meeting—and elected Elder Vernon G. Anderson as their new president. By the spring of

1944, in a special session, the Oregon Conference Committee elected Elder C.A. Scriven, a longtime friend of Dr. Holden, as their new president and, by virtue of his office, chair of the Board of Trustees of the Portland San. Gertrude's secret sponsor was no longer in charge.

For the next six months Gertrude struggled to get programs approved and changes made. While she became the lightning rod that attracted the brilliantly flashing bolts of attention from the board, Anne Stratton functioned surreptitiously under the cover of the ensuing thunder, completing the affiliation of the nursing school with Walla Walla College. The nursing school had been transferred from the hands of an institution whose main interest was to get the work done into the hands of an institution whose main interest was to educate nurses. The nursing school was safe from extinction but the six months of constant conflict with the board left Gertrude battle-scarred and weary, like a worn out warrior ready to retire from the field and be replaced by fresh troops.

It was late September and a warm Thursday, shortly after noon. The Portland San Nursing School had successfully weathered the opening months of another school year. The probies of the new nursing class had passed their first two months of orientation classes without anyone dropping out. Several of the older "Holden" nurses on the nursing school staff had been eased out of leadership positions and teaching roles and had been replaced by bright, new faces. These were the recent graduates who had blossomed under Gertrude's exacting tutelage and had excelled on their state board exams. They understood and would teach the new role of nursing to the incoming freshmen students.

The two leaders of the nursing school were taking a breather, Gertrude sitting opposite Anna Stratton in the hospital cafeteria which had been closed for about half an hour and was now empty of other patrons. They were dawdling over their favorite dessert, strawberry shortcake, enjoying the last of the berries being harvested in the Willamette Valley just south of Portland. Gertrude remembered another place and time when she had seen fields of ripe strawberries while riding in a rickshaw along a dusty road going into another school, the school at Chiao Tou Tseng, the school that no longer existed. Absently she twirled her spoon in a circle beside her plate.

"A penny for your thoughts," Anne said, her head twisted sideways and bent low, trying to peer up into Gertrude's downcast eyes.

"Sorry," Gertrude said with a laugh and an upward tilt of her chin. "I was somewhere else."

"On the other side of the world, I bet." Anne straightend and nodded her head knowingly. "A large country where the people wear pajamas and eat lots of rice," she said as she pressed the tines of her fork into the ripe berries and soft pastry, releasing cascading rivulets of red juice and whipped cream across the small round plate in front of her.

"And lots of strawberries," Gertrude responded wistfully. The memory of strawberries in China resurrected thoughts of Sun Ya's restaurant. Another memory came flooding back and Gertrude's face broke into a broad smile.

"What?" Anna asked clumsily around the mouthful of berries. She dabbed hurriedly at the corners of her mouth with a paper napkin.

"I had a lunch like this with a nursing instructor that I was replacing . . . in Shanghai. Letha Coulson." Gertrude stared intently into Anne's attentive eyes, her hands pressed firmly on both sides of her plate, her smile disappearing. "But I never got to finish what I started over there. Every school I taught in was disrupted before we could complete our task, before we could get the girls —and boys—through all their classes." Gertrude could see the startled, questioning gaze in Anne's eyes, her search for the missing information that would lead to understanding Gertrude's sudden change of demeanor. Gertrude decided she was not up to a long explanation. "And now I'm turning this school over to you," she said, abandoning her intensity and returning to her original thought and to the strawberries before her.

"And you'll be going to Porter Sanitarium and Hospital in Denver when?" Anne asked quietly, sensing that Gertrude had retreated from some memory she would not share today.

"At the end of next month," Gertrude responded mechanically.

"And it's not a permanent position." Anne parroted what Gertrude had told her previously, wondering why Gertrude would go to a place with no future for her.

"No. I have an appointment to China . . . when the war is over. And they know that."

"So you'll be returning to China?" In their past conversations Anne had never gotten a clear answer on this point, or what any of Gertrude's future plans were.

Gertrude looked up, her full fork poised halfway to her mouth. "I don't know," she said in a voice that was genuinely puzzled.

"Don't you want to go back?" Anne asked, surprised.

"No," Gertrude said spontaneously as the memory of approaching airplanes and whistling bombs echoed in her head. Quickly she retracted her response. "I don't know."

"Don't know what?" Anne asked, not understanding.

Gertrude cocked her head thoughtfully as if considering this question for the first time. "I don't know what God wants me to do."

"Has He released you from your commitment?" Anne asked cautiously.

"No."

"Then what is it you don't know?"

Gertrude turned the question over and examined its under side. "What *I* want to do," she said finally.

"And it's not Denver."

"No, it's not Denver." Gertrude sat back in her chair, retrieving her napkin from her lap. "I like working in the operating room. But my real love is in obstetrics," she said, pushing away her half empty plate.

"I know," Anne said, remembering. "You told me about the research studies you were a part of at Boston Lying-In."

"It was a hard time," Gertrude said, quickly brushing aside the painful memories of those dark days, "but I've always liked helping with childbirth."

"So?" Anne chased one last, elusive strawberry to the edge of her plate.

Gertrude leaned forward, folding her hands on the table in front of her. "While I'm marking time, I'm looking into attending some midwifery classes. They're being held in New York City." As she described her new educational endeavor, the cadence of her speech increased rapidly, her voice rising with enthusiasm, her hands rising from the table, animated. "I can't get into the class that starts this March but I'm on their list for next year. And I would be closer to my mother in Rochester."

"And then you'll return to China?" Anne asked absently, finally catching the errant berry.

There was that question again. It caught Gertrude in the middle of her exuberance, both hands lifted in midair. For a moment it froze her into a statue of supplication, arms raised, head tilted upward. Then she twisted her head, lifted her eyebrows, and shrugged, backing away from the decision she must make sooner or later. "I don't know. We'll see," was all she could manage as she slowly lowered her arms.

Chapter 54

THE ABYSS

Seven months at the Porter Sanitarium and Hospital in Denver, Colorado, did not change Gertrude's mind. While she had talents for running an operating room, in fact, for running almost anything, in her heart she wanted to deliver babies.

The obvious path to prepare for such a venture was to become a physician. Despite her proven ability to learn and teach in Chinese, administer hospitals, and organize the moving of entire hospitals, Gertrude had always been convinced that her sister, Ruth, had all the brains. Gertrude was sure she wouldn't have the brains for medical school. The pathway for nurses to assist in child birthing was midwifery. It was a practice as old as giving birth, but given professional respectability by the establishment of training programs and the awarding of professional credentials, first in Great Britain in the late 1800s and later in the United States in 1931 at the Maternity Center Association in New York City.

The midwifery program in New York City began its six-month training programs in October and March. The number of applicants was so great that Gertrude could not find a placement in the class until March 1946. The position at the Porter San was a temporary one, lasting only until June 1945. Gertrude had nine months to wait until her classes would start, with no imminent call to return to China in the foreseeable future.

To be sure, the war in Europe was at an end. The German government had surrendered to the Allies. Hitler was dead; an apparent suicide. The east coast of the United States was celebrating but the west coast was preparing for possible invasion and the naval bases in San Diego, Los Angeles, and San Francisco still hummed with activity. Civilian and Coast Guard airplanes patrolled the western coastline, daily flying over American coastal cities, watching for enemy submarines. The war in the Pacific theater continued.

Although in May the Allies had captured the island of Okinawa, the actual invasion of the main Japanese islands was not planned until after the smoke and fire had settled in Berlin, until the Army personnel in Europe and their equipment could be moved to the staging areas in the Philippines. Besides no one knew how long it would take to root out the Japanese from China, Burma, and Mongolia, and to overcome them in their homeland. If it had taken two months and almost 50,000 casualties to conquer Iwo Jima, how long would it take to capture and control the rest of the Japanese home islands? No one knew.

How long could Gertrude wait before she would be forced to answer the question, "Are you returning to China?" No one knew. But she knew one thing for sure. She wasn't going back as long as they were still fighting. She wanted nothing to do with war, ever again.

May 30, 1945
Long Beach, Calif.

Dearest Gertrude,

Happy Memorial Day! I am sitting with my feet up and relaxing for a change. Nice to have a holiday in the middle of the week. There have been no calls for delivering babies and I am having a good time of it.

I have the spare bedroom all prepared for you when you come at the end of June. You will have your own little private world for a while. I know that you like your private space. Not like the tight quarters we had in Shanghai in the apartment, huh? How did we survive all cooped up like a bunch of skunks in a den? Well, your space is awaiting you here and should do you very nicely for the next six months.

Your job working for the Doctors Coston is all arranged. Their internal medicine office is easily reached on the streetcar and I know you know how to ride one of those things, although the Long Beach streetcars aren't nearly as posh as the Shanghai trolleys. Ha!

I don't know what you will do on your time off. Their practice is in internal medicine and I think that will seem tame compared to supervising an operating room and being on call. But maybe you will appreciate the quiet time for a change of pace. I don't think you will get much rest when you go to the midwifery school next March. Still can't imagine why you would want to subject yourself to such torture. Ha!

We are only three blocks from the ocean here on Wisconsin Place and Broadway. On your time off you can walk down to the beach and watch the sun go down. My mother-in-law, Mother Jones, who lives under us here in the duplex, makes that walk most days. Sometimes, if I get home in time from making rounds at the hospital, I go with her, especially on Friday nights when we have sundown worship together on the beach to welcome in the Sabbath.

Be sure to bring some warm things. The sun goes down rather late in the summer and the wind off the ocean can kick up cold and blustery sometimes, even if we are in California.

I'm looking forward to the famous Gertrude Green hot chocolate this winter. We will have a chance to gas a bit about the old days in Shanghai and listen to some Victrola records I have. I know you and I share the same taste in music, classical and opera. I have pictures to show you of how I completed the rest of my trip around the world. And you can tell me how you escaped China without becoming a prisoner of war. See you at the train station.

Love,

Geneva Beatty Jones, MD

Since returning to the States, Gertrude had always been in cities that were located somewhat inland: Melrose, Massachusetts, Portland, Oregon, and definitely Denver, Colorado. Tonight she had dangled her legs over the low sea wall and watched the sun go down over the Pacific Ocean. Not since Shanghai and Wuhan had she lived so close to such a large body of water. It lived up to its name: Pacific Ocean. On this, her first week in California, her walks on the beach every evening and the cooling, onshore breezes which accompanied the sunset "pacified" her soul.

Walking up Lisnero Avenue from the beach, Gertrude looked happily at the palm trees lining her way. Then crossing Ocean Boulevard in the semi-darkness, she noted the dimly lit street lights. Their globes had been painted black as part of the imposed blackouts. Dark green window blinds in Geneva's home served the same purpose. The blinds certainly weren't attractive, she mused, and didn't match anything Geneva had in her home.

But the shades kept the room in semidarkness most of the time which helped cool the upstairs of the duplex where Geneva and her husband lived. Anything which ameliorated the California summertime heat was welcome. However, they were not allowed to open the blinds at night and let in the wonderful breeze. The neighborhood air raid wardens made sure no stray light source would offer a tempting target to any Japanese bombers who were rumored to be preparing for an invasion of the west coast of the United States. Someone said that a bombing had happened up on the Oregon coast. Still on Lisnero Avenue, Gertrude hurriedly crossed First Street.

I'll probably be by myself again tonight, she guessed as she passed under several spreading deciduous trees. They blocked out the available starlight, making the night even darker. *Geneva's not much company anyway. Never was a game player like the rest of us. But I'll have time to write Mother and catch up on several other letters I should have written when I was in Denver.* Remembering a letter she owed her sister, Ruth, Gertrude began considering ways she might travel to San Francisco where Ruth had been transferred to be on the psychiatric staff of its mental hospital.

Then thinking of her physician sister reminded Gertrude of the new physicians she now worked for as office nurse and receptionist. The Costons were very pleasant and ran a well organized office. This job would be easy and the trolley—they called them streetcars here in California—ran right out to their office. Gertrude was approaching the darkened corner of Lisnero and Second Street.

Somehow the Lord knew I needed a job and a quiet place to live. She paused a moment before crossing the street to ponder the infinite knowledge of the Lord of Heaven and how He would know what she needed. *I'll get plenty of practice riding the streetcars here. The line runs out to the SDA Church on Third Street. And I'll have to learn how to go by myself if Geneva is busy delivering babies. We can't waste gas-rationing coupons on trips to church.* Gertrude continued up Lisnero Avenue toward Broadway, thinking about the next nine months. They would be long enough and quiet enough to consider the decision she yet had to make.

Without thinking Gertrude turned her head to the right and peered upward into the night sky through the bougainvillea that wrapped the darkened side of the house next to her.

What's that sound? That droning sound?

Gertrude knew about the blackouts and about the coastline air patrols by civilian, light aircraft. But these sounded like heavy engines, military aircraft engines. More than one, she was sure of it.

She began walking faster, trying to get out from behind the tall house in order to see more clearly. But the night was too dark. All she could discern was the ever-increasing drone of the aircraft engines.

Gertrude panicked and broke into a run, crossing Broadway at a diagonal. Because of the blackout the street was practically deserted and traffic was nonexistent. As she ran up Wisconsin Place, Gertrude put her fingers in her ears. She didn't want to hear the next sound she knew would be coming—the whistling scream of falling projectiles.

Hearing the pounding of feet on the stairway, Geneva laid aside her book, arose from her living room chair, and hurried to open the stairway door. Below her was an apparition that resembled Gertrude, her cream-colored blouse disheveled and pulling out of the waistband at the front of her skirt, her brown hair tousled, her purse dangling wildly by its strap from her left elbow. Gertrude was attempting to bound up the stairs while keeping her fingers in her ears. Without her hands to steady her, she bumped from side to side into the thin, hanging handrail on the one side and into the striped, papered wall on the other.

As the light from the open doorway at the top of the stairs fell on her face, Gertrude looked up and began screaming at the top of her voice, "They're coming! They're right here!"

"Who?" Geneva shouted back.

"The Japanese! Don't you hear them?" Gertrude made a desperate lunge at the door from the top riser, almost falling. "They're coming!" she gasped as Geneva caught her, dragged her into the living room, inadvertently dislodging one of Gertrude's fingers from her ear.

"Those are our planes," Geneva said, still shouting as she slammed the door behind her with one hand. "We've got good watchmen out there." Still holding onto one of Gertrude's arms, Geneva turned her around and spoke in a quieter voice. "Those are our planes. They're just patrolling the coastline." Geneva grasped both of Gertrude's arms, drawing her close and staring intensely into her panic-filled eyes.

"Are you sure?" Gertrude was trembling from head to foot, ready to run at the slightest provocation.

"Yes, I'm sure."

Gertrude stood quite still and listened as the drone of aircraft engines faded away in the distance. "Oh, Geneva, I was so afraid." Great tears of relief welled up as she melted, crumpling into a small pile in the middle of the floor.

Geneva knelt beside her, cradling Gertrude's head on her shoulder as she would a small child, rubbing her back with her free hand. Gently she lifted her up. "Come. Sit down. Catch your breath." She guided Gertrude to the couch. "What's wrong? Tell me about it."

Gertrude had told no one. Not her mother, not her sister, not anyone at the New England San or the Portland San. For the first time since it happened, for the first time since returning to the States, Gertrude told the story of the New Year's Day attack, told of the bombing of the hospital and the twisted piles of dead refugees against the outside of the compound walls and the hiding afterward, of the living in a small shack in the cold, of the pneumonia, and the devastation and the ransacking of the hospital by the Chinese nurses, *her* Chinese nurses, told of friends unaccounted for and a work unfinished. The story came pouring out like milk from a great pitcher turned upside down, gushing and splashing, with all of the loud screams and accusations, all of the wild arm gesticulations that usually accompany spilt milk. When the story ended, Gertrude leaned back into the cushions on the sofa, exhausted, her hands in her lap, her eyes red and puffy.

"Dear God, girl, you've been through hell," Geneva said, feeling as exhausted as Gertrude looked.

" 'Dear God' is right," Gertrude responded, looking up accusingly.

"Well, I didn't mean it the way it sounded," Geneva apologized.

"I do." Gertrude's mouth was set in a tight, thin line that quivered on the ends. "Dear God! Dear God! Dear God!" Her shoulders heaved and shook as she looked heavenward with eyes that could not cry anymore.

"Whatever do you mean?"

"Dear God, why did You let those terrible things happen?" Gertrude's conversation was not with Geneva anymore. "What about the work we were doing?" she shouted, straightening up and raising her fist to the ceiling.

"What work?" Geneva was confused, wondering if she were being addressed. "We were just running hospitals like all the rest of the missionaries, doing what we were supposed to be doing."

Gertrude turned her gaze on Geneva, speaking rapidly. "Didn't you see the nursing students doing Bible studies with patients, giving health talks for the evangelistic meetings?" She slowed, thinking. "No, that was in Yencheng, not in Shanghai. You weren't there."

"We baptized more than 40 people, Geneva. God blessed us. I know He did." Gertrude was making her final appeal, her voice rising, her arms animated. "You didn't see the way God provided for our medicines when we didn't have any. How He provided food for the refugees that we fed when we didn't have the money to feed them. The sacrifices we made. Oh, Geneva, we worked so hard. And it was all gone in an instant!"

She stopped and the room became completely silent. "And I thought I was going to die," she whispered. Her ashen face reflected the undiluted fear that abruptly replaced her vehemence of the moment before.

Silently Gertrude tried to retrieve her emotions, gathering them as one would gather clothes blown from a clothesline in a wind storm, stooping and picking them up without close examination, just getting them off the ground, getting them inside and out of sight of the neighbors. Geneva's open mouth and awed silence told Gertrude that an uncrossable abyss lay between them. *She wasn't there. She doesn't know. She doesn't understand. She's still sitting at the other end of the couch.* Gertrude lowered her eyes and her voice, wrapping her arms around herself.

"You're right, Geneva. I've been through hell. And I don't ever want to go there again," Gertrude said, trying to close the door on further discussion.

"You don't want to go *where*, Gertrude?" Geneva's professional antennae tingled. As so often happened with her patients, her clinical sixth sense told her a piercing insight was about to be breached.

"China. I don't want to go back there," Gertrude said evenly, quietly. "I don't want to experience the horrid sights and sounds of that war. I don't want to work where I can never finish anything I start." Gertrude looked up again. "I don't want to go back there."

"Do you have to go? Can't you just resign or something?" Geneva said, clumsily trying to force a positive conclusion from the obvious truth of the moment.

"I can't resign. I'm a missionary. I promised." Gertrude spoke with spontaneous firmness. The phrases were truths that she acknowledged and affirmed in her own mind as she said them, even though she had not consciously considered them previously.

"Whom did you promise?" Geneva proposed this more as a statement, ready to argue the point.

"God."

The room went silent again.

"And He has not released me from my promise." The sadness in Gertrude's voice was palpable.

"How do you know He hasn't?" Geneva asked, not at all certain how one can get out of a promise to God.

"I've prayed every day since I arrived in the States. I wanted to know if I had to go back." Suddenly Gertrude sprang from the couch, activated like a jack-in-the-box by the energy of her pent-up frustrations. She paced the length of the living room, speaking rapidly. "I was so frightened, Geneva." She stopped to face Geneva, pointing her finger accusingly. "I have never been frightened in my life of anyone or anything. You know I haven't." Her hands were fists of frustration thrust defiantly out from her sides as she continued to pace. The anger crackled in her voice, anger at God . . . and at the weakness Gertrude saw in herself. "But that day I was scared beyond belief." She turned and faced Geneva, her eyes blazing.

"I didn't want to go back, not if I had to face that again." Her voice calmed; her hands relaxed. "And I have been praying to be released. And I have been waiting."

"Waiting? Waiting for what?" Geneva asked, attempting to follow the conversation, attempting to ride out the roller coaster of Gertrude's emotions that Geneva knew only too well.

"An answer. Dr. Haysmer said I would know."

"Who's Dr. Haysmer?"

"A surgeon I knew at the New England San." Gertrude smiled at the memory. "We did a Bible study on prayer one day. And he told me I would know what God wanted me to do."

"So . . . what do you know so far?"

Gertrude closed her eyes and recited with certainty the thoughts and words that had flooded her mind whenever she had prayed during the past three weeks. "That my heart is still in China. I have nursing students back there who haven't finished their courses. I have a hospital that was bombed out and Chinese workers who died defending the Gospel work that we were trying to do." Gertrude's face radiated with the intensity she felt inside. She opened her eyes and fixed Geneva with an intense stare. "Every time I have asked to be released, all I can see are the Chinese faces I came to love."

"So you can't stay here . . . and you can't go back." Geneva spoke the obvious conclusion, then shook her head as people do when they think they are seeing double. "Gertrude, you'll have to make up your mind somehow. You can't stay suspended in midair forever. You'll tear yourself apart."

Gertrude slowly nodded her head in affirmation of the diagnosis of her doctor friend.

Chapter 55

THE DECISION—REPRISED

GENERAL CONFERENCE OF SEVENTH-DAY ADVENTISTS
Takoma Park, Washington, D.C.
February 13, 1946

Miss Gertrude Green
88 Bryan St.
Rochester, N.Y.

Dear Sister Green:

It is my distinct pleasure to inform you that the first boat carrying missionaries who are returning to their assignments in the Orient will be leaving April 11, 1946, from San Francisco. I know you have been looking forward to this good news as have we all. The end of hostilities with the Japanese this last August will allow us to return to spreading the gospel throughout this territory and the world.

We have been in contact with our national workers in Shanghai, Tokyo, Singapore, Bangkok, and Manila. They have done a marvelous job in keeping open and running many of our institutions there. They are anxious and willing to have us return and take up our work.

Please contact this office at your earliest convenience so that we might make arrangements for your arrival and housing accommodations in San Francisco.

Yours sincerely,
A.W. Cormack

New York City, New York
July 6, 1946

Dear Geneva,

A hearty New York hello to you! We have just finished a 4th of July holiday on the calendar but it was no holiday from having babies, I'll tell you. So now I have Sabbath off and am able to catch up on some of my mail. It is so reassuring to write to people here in the States and know they will receive the letter before the end of the month. Not like when I was in China.

My time here in New York is almost at an end and I have sure learned a lot. Some of it was review from my time in Boston but a lot of it was learning what I should have known while delivering babies in China. But no crying over spilt milk I always say.

All in all it has been an interesting experience. For many of the people here, delivering babies is a lot like what I did in China. The babies are delivered at home and the families are supposed to get together all the stuff they will need for the delivery. But many times they don't have the money to get everything. When we go to the homes for the deliveries, we take everything just in case.

In China we had a large group of curious onlookers at every delivery. It's the same here in New York, especially among the Greeks and the Italians. Everyone has a grandmother or two. And everyone is an expert, shouting orders and telling the new mother what to do. It can be a real circus. Sometimes we need the police just to get in the door.

Everyone who is taking our midwifery class is on an overseas assignment. Some are going to government embassies and some are missionaries going back to their assignments in Africa or in the Orient. It's like the end of the war has opened the flood gates and all the overseas people have come pouring out. I feel right at home with everyone else.

When I finish in August, I will have my certificate in midwifery. In some states here at home this certificate would allow me to assist in delivering babies in the hospital and to deliver babies on my own in the home. In China, having the certificate will not matter. However, the training will be invaluable. I will be able to teach a whole unit on midwifery to my nursing students.

You remember that I received the letter at your house from the General Conference calling me to come join them on the first boat trip back to the

Orient in April. Well, it seems that a series of dock strikes has kept everyone here in the States. No one has gone anywhere. The seventh floor at the Palomar Hotel in San Francisco is so full of Adventists that you can't get any water on that top floor on Friday evening. So many are taking their Sabbath baths that the water pressure drops too low for the water to flow!

I am staying in touch with the folk there in San Francisco. If the strikes continue, they will still be waiting for me after I finish here in August, probably even after I go home to see my mother and pack up my things.

Yes, I am probably committed to going to China—I think. I'll bet you're surprised at that decision. I know I am. But I don't see any other way around it. The war is over and the people there are waiting anxiously for us to return. Maybe this time I will be able to actually get through a school year and see all of my nurses through all three years of their training.

I will be sure to write to you before I leave for San Francisco. Who knows? Maybe I can come see you again before the boat leaves.

Much love,

Gertrude

When the midwifery classes were finished at the end of August, Gertrude returned to work at the New England San. Letters from the General Conference Secretariat, which was responsible for staying in contact with the missionaries, continued to follow Gertrude—from Long Beach, California, to New York City to Melrose, Massachusetts. And Gertrude continued to avoid making the final commitment to returning to China.

> Sunday afternoon
> August 11, 1946
> Stoneham, Mass.

Dearest Mother:

Oh, what a hot day. I am sitting here with practically no clothes on trying to keep cool. It feels like the hottest day yet. I was supposed to go to a wedding at 2:30 and got all dressed when a call on the phone said they were terribly busy and could I please come back to work, so no wedding for me. It really has been terrifically busy with patients coming in by the droves. I just keep hopping every minute.

Our graduating class from 1929 is having a reunion tonight and we are going out for supper. Not everyone can come but there will be a lot of them there.

Well, on the China business, I guess it is nearly settled that I shall go. They wanted me to sail Sept. 12, but that is far too soon and I am going to write them and tell them that will be impossible.

Really I have prayed much over this matter and said that if the Lord wanted me to go that I wanted definite evidence from Him as to whether I should go or not. And in one letter I told them "No." And even through all this, Dr. Miller and Professor Griggs were still very determined it should be me. Even though some of the other girls on the list to go have college degrees and much advanced education, they still want me in preference to all of them. Just the way it all came out I really feel it is my duty. So the only thing now before the final decision is my physical examination which I am having tomorrow.

If the Lord can use me better in the foreign land, I have consecrated myself to His service and want to do His will. I really feel he has used me here at the New England San to help others and I have built up a department for them that is worth something. In fact, Dr. Ruble can't find anyone to take my place. He says whoever steps into my place will have a very hard time filling my shoes. That makes me feel good—and makes up for the lack in pay.

I have a very nice plan in mind for you and me. And I want it to work if only you will do it. When I leave here, I will come home for a while. I will pack my trunks and then start for California. But I want you to go along. You see, my fare gets paid, and with the money I had saved for myself to go to California, I am going to take you. We can have a fine trip together and you can spend a while with Ruth. You know so many other people there that, if you liked it out there, you could maybe find a swell job. I really want this thing to work out. This is *your* opportunity and you must plan on it.

I have written quite a lot and I hope somehow or other you will under-stand. I know you have always said that I have a mind of my own and must decide my own way. The Lord is leading me this way, I know, and by faith I must walk therein.

Well, mother, I love you and I will say good night and God bless you.

Oodles of love from Your Loving Daughter,

Gertrude

At the end of October, 1946, Gertrude went home to Rochester, New York.

When she had first returned to the States in 1941, Gertrude had left what few things she had brought with her from China at her mother's house. Her books, her trunks, and her teaching materials acquired at Washington Missionary College where she had earned her Bachelor of Science in nursing had been stored there. To these she now added her books and tools of the newly acquired skill of midwifery and what little she had brought from the New England San.

The upstairs room that Gertrude had shared with her sister, Ruth, was stacked with the collected paraphernalia of her last five years. Nothing had been organized and nothing had been thrown away. The room reflected what her life had been like for the last five years—education and life experiences heaped upon one another, stacked in a corner, and added to over time. But no choices of consequence, no lasting decisions of direction or commitment had been made. Gertrude was only marking time, marching in place, moving neither forward nor backward.

Life with her mother was quiet and without stress. The limitations of rationing were easing. They could now buy canned fruits, other than plums—which had been plentiful even throughout the war. Butter from local country farms could also be purchased in limited amounts. Gas rationing was easing, although the troops were still overseas as occupiers of various conquered countries and some things were still hard to get. Besides, it was easier and cheaper to go to church on the streetcar than in her brother Fred's car.

And the letters from the General Conference urging Gertrude to join the missionaries, preparing to leave from San Francisco, continued to arrive. Gertrude wrote to various friends who were members of the missionary throng holed up in the Palomar Hotel. She kept track of their acquisitions for overseas, of their continuing delays because of the shipping strikes, and of their various adventures in the City by the Bay. But her answers to the General Conference offices about her plans for joining the group were vague.

In the waning light of sundown coming through the window Lena Green stood at the kitchen sink and listened, her hands in the dishwater, motionless, silent. Having prepared her own luggage weeks before, she had sent Gertrude upstairs after supper to continue packing her things. Lena had said that she'd do the dishes. At first Lena had heard the noise of scraping boxes and trunks being scooted about on the floor overhead. But now there was silence, and had been for more than half an hour.

Lena slowly turned from the sink, unconsciously wiping her hands on her apron. She crossed the kitchen, walking toward the dining room, staring at the ceiling as if trying to visually penetrate the wood, trying to discern what was *not* happening upstairs. As she lowered her eyes, her gaze fell on a legal-sized envelope propped against the glass bowl centerpiece on the dining room table. She pushed the black-buttoned wall light switch to "on," then approached the table, reaching out and picking up the letter. "General Conference of Seventh-day Adventists" was on the return address. She turned it over in her hand. It had not been opened.

She remembered that several of these official-looking letters had come in recent weeks. Gertrude had not shown much interest in them and had not shared their contents with her. But Gertrude shared almost all of her correspondence with her mother, usually at the table over dinner, where they would laugh over someone's wild antic or discuss some serious problem.

Lena walked to the foot of the stairs and peered up into the gathering shadows. She slowly mounted the stairs, the unopened letter in her hand.

In the darkened hallway upstairs Lena could see no light coming from any of the rooms.

"Gertrude?" Mrs. Green called out.

"What?" Gertrude cried out, leaping in her skin and jerking her head toward the doorway. She had been sitting on her bedroom floor with her back to the door, staring at her half-filled trunk. Now she was turned halfway around searching, wide-eyed, the darkened hallway for Japanese soldiers.

"Gertrude, *liebchen*, I'm sorry," Lena Green said, rushing into the room. She knelt beside her oldest daughter, her arms encircling the trembling shoulders. "What's wrong?"

"Nothing's wrong," Gertrude said, pulling herself together. "I was just thinking. I didn't hear you come up the stairs." Gertrude clumsily patted her mother's arm and pulled away from her embrace. Stumbling to her feet, Gertrude reached out and randomly selected several items from the piles of linens and undergarments stacked on her bed, her back to her mother.

With some difficulty Lena Green arose from her crouched position. "Gertrude, you were shaking just now. And you sounded so . . . so frightened."

"You just startled me, that's all," Gertrude mumbled.

Wanting to reach out but not knowing if she should, Lena brought her hands together in front of her in a rubbing, washing motion. Her left hand settled into her right hand, cradled as one cradles a tender, ripe fruit to protect it from bruising.

"Gertrude, you've been up here in the darkness for more than half an hour and you haven't made a sound," Lena said. "What's wrong?"

Slowly Gertrude turned around, her eyes downcast, the linens in her hands held tightly against her chest. "I don't know what to do." She looked fully into her mother's face. "I don't think I can go back to China."

"Whatever do you mean?" Lena asked, totally bewildered. "I thought you . . . I thought we were going to California."

"Every time I think about going to China, I can hear those airplane engines and the scream of falling bombs in my head." Gertrude was shaking her head from side to side. "I don't think I can do it."

"But the war is over, Gertrude. What could possibly happen now?"

"I don't know." Gertrude's voice became sharper, harder. "God seems to have a surprise waiting for me around every corner."

"God didn't start the war," Lena Green said quietly.

"But He didn't prevent it either," Gertrude said, trying not to snap at her mother. "I lost two babies for Gert Loewen. I lost my nursing students twice . . . actually three times. I lost all my personal belongings at least four times. And I lost my hospital and all my supplies." Gertrude's voice was getting softer. "And I almost lost my life."

"But you didn't," Mrs. Green said. "As you wrote me many times, 'Don't worry, Mother. The Lord is taking carry of me.' And I didn't worry." Lena slipped her hand behind her apron and into her skirt pocket. She withdrew a small Bible. "Ever since you left, I have carried this with me constantly," Lena said, holding the small book carefully in her left hand and patting its cover with her right.

"I didn't worry, Gertrude, not because you told me not to, but because the Lord had given me a promise." Lena opened her small volume at the bluebird bookmark which peeked out from the top of the gilded pages in a place where it seemed to have always resided, and began to read.

"'The eternal God is thy refuge, and underneath are the everlasting arms: and he shall thrust out the enemy from before thee; and shall say, Destroy them. Israel then shall dwell in safety alone: the fountain of Jacob shall be upon a land of corn and wine; also his heavens shall drop down dew. Happy art thou, O Israel: who is like unto thee, O people saved by the Lord, the shield of thy help, and who is the sword of thy excellency!' (Deut. 33:27-29)."

Lena looked up from the precious book. "It goes on. But I think you get the idea, *nicht vahr?*"

Gertrude nodded and sat down on the edge of her bed.

"I didn't worry because the Lord gave me this promise and I've clung to it with all my might," Lena Green said. "It sustained me through those years, Gertrude, when I lost you to China, when I lost Ruth to her illness in California . . . and when I lost your father." Her voice quavered as two big tears formed at the outer corners of her gray eyes.

Gertrude looked up in time to see one tear slip over the edge and stumble across the care lines etched on her mother's cheek. She reached up with one hand and drew her mother down on the bed beside her.

"You loved him, didn't you?" Even as the eldest daughter, Gertrude had known only partially of the struggles and heartaches which had passed for a relationship between her mother and her father. Unconsciously, Gertrude slipped smoothly into her "compassionate nurse" role.

"Of course, I did," Lena said with a fleeting smile as she wiped the tears from her face. "But God didn't cause the losses, Gertrude. And God didn't prevent the losses. He used the losses." She took hold of Gertrude's two hands and pressed them together between her own, trying by every means possible to transmit her faith to her daughter. "He used them to teach me to trust, and He used them to make you grow. And He used them to accomplish His purposes in China and elsewhere in spite of all that the devil could throw at Him."

Gertrude searched deeply her mother's gray eyes. She knew that they looked exactly like her own when she was calm, and pondered, *Oh, Mother, if I could just take you with me, just have you by my side, everything would be all right.* Aloud she said, "You really believe that, don't you?"

"With all my heart, *liebchen*. 'And underneath are the everlasting arms,'" Lena repeated. "Never forget it, Gertrude. As long as you live, never forget it."

Lena released her daughter's hands and turned to the half-empty steamer trunk. "Now what can I do to help you pack?"

In September, 1946, Gertrude gathered her trunks, suitcases, and boxes—and her mother—and boarded the train in Rochester, New York, heading west. On arriving in San Francisco, she moved her luggage into storage and herself in with one of her missionary friends on the top floor of the Palomar Hotel. Her mother moved in with Ruth.

For the next six weeks Gertrude and her mother visited friends, traveled to Los Angeles, and shopped, adding a few carefully selected, on-sale items to her already well-packed trunks. All the while she waited with the other missionaries until the multiple dock workers' strikes were sufficiently ameliorated to allow the stranded ships to leave the docks.

On December 2, the SS *General Meigs*, recently decommissioned as a troop transport, steamed out of San Francisco Bay. Tucked safely away on one of the lower decks was Gertrude's dormitory class room, shared closely by 11 other women. On deck, wrapped in her long, fur-collared coat and head scarf, Gertrude watched the Golden Gate Bridge pass overhead. The chill, biting wind reminded her that she needed to find a shop in Shanghai where she could purchase—at a good price—the quilted, heavy Chinese coat and pants that Thelma had recommended. Just like the first time, it would be winter when she arrived in China.

Chapter 56

RETURNING TO CHINA

There was no time or inclination to reconsider her decision to return to China. Gertrude was having too much fun on the ship. The holiday spirit that had pervaded the missionary group living in the Palomar Hotel carried over to the *SS General Meigs*. For many of them China had become their entire life's work. After having been gone for more than five years, everyone was delighted to be returning.

Unfortunately, the women's dormitory cabin was in the forward end of the ship near the officers' quarters. There the up and down motion of the boat was more noticeable and initially all the women suffered from motion sickness. Gertrude was the first to recover—in slightly more than two days—and she never had a recurrence, not even in the midst of a typhoon.

Except for these temporary inconveniences Gertrude luxuriated on the deck of the ocean liner in her lounge chair, rented for the entire time aboard, and feasted in the dining room where excellent food was served. Well, excellent except for the vegetables which seemed always overcooked and "filmy."

Meal after meal she eagerly listened to the conversations. Many of the returning missionaries had stayed in China some months after Gertrude had left in April, 1941, leaving just prior to the United States' entering the war in December of the same year. Some of the others had kept up religiously with the news of unfolding events in postwar China. Gertrude anxiously listened for any fragment of information she might hear about the hospital in Yencheng and those who had served there with her.

Gertrude gripped the edge of the dining table with her left hand as the ocean liner climbed to the crest of a steep wave. Her right hand was occupied with the important job of transporting food to her mouth. For Gertrude, eating was a top priority.

Because a typhoon had passed 12 hours previously, the ocean waves were still rough and unpredictable. To keep the dishes from sliding around, the porters continually wet down the linen tablecloths. Since the tables were bolted to the floor, Gertrude's only concern was to make sure her chair didn't slide away from the table. Yesterday during the typhoon she had unintentionally entertained the entire dining room by sliding across the floor on her chair and hitting the opposite wall. Today she wanted to concentrate on the conversation—not be its topic.

I've got a grip on the table, my eyes on the food, and a fork in my hand while the deck of the ship keeps rolling under me. How am I supposed to concentrate on what people are saying? Gertrude's frustrated consternation turned humorous as she imagined watching herself from across the room. *I must look like a performer in a Chinese acrobat show, trying to keep five plates spinning on tall, wobbly sticks.* She managed a small snort of a chuckle and a shake of her head just as the thread of the conversation recaptured her attention.

"I know Dr. Miller was asked to intervene between the Young General, General Chang, and Generalissimo Chiang Kai-shek. Something to do with the Communists in the west and the Japanese in the north, as I remember." Gertrude didn't need to take her eyes off her plate, recognizing the voice of Elder Branson, the returning president of the China Division.

"Yes, there was a disagreement among the Nationalist Chinese Army as to who posed the bigger threat at the time, the Communists or the Japanese." Gertrude looked up to confirm that this was Elder Abernathy, the newly appointed secretary for the China Mission.

"I just remember how brutally the Nationalists eliminated the Communist insurgency in Chungking. I don't suppose that's been forgotten." Gertrude couldn't see who was speaking from the other end of the table and didn't recognize the voice. It obviously belonged to someone who had been there at the time.

"Mao's people were just speaking up for the common folks, same as we were doing." This came from someone across the table. Gertrude tried to observe them more closely but was jolted into grabbing for the table as the bow of the boat rose sharply, threatening to tip her over. *Isn't anyone else having a problem staying upright?* she groused as the descent of the boat tossed her forward against the table.

"We're told by the State Department," Elder Branson observed, casually picking up his fork after letting go of the table edge, "that the Communists will stay in the Northwest near the source of their strength, the common border people. The Nationals will stay in control of the rest of China."

Gertrude tried to conjure up the few rag-tag Communists she had seen around Loho and the hospital at Yencheng. She had a hard time imagining such a poorly equipped group as being any challenge to Generalissimo Chiang Kai-shek and his newly reinforced army. *With all the financial assistance from the United States, I don't see how . . .*

"The northwest has always been the breeding ground for revolutions in China." It was Elder Abernathy. Gertrude thought he sounded like a lecturing history teacher. "Look at India, Africa, the Dutch East Indies. The world's ripe for revolution." He picked up his dinner roll and waved it in the air for emphasis. "I wouldn't be surprised to see some kind of autonomy happen— in the Philippines, for instance."

"But it will be peaceful, won't it, dear?" his wife asked anxiously.

"Oh, yes. The Filipinos were our allies." He nodded his head reassuringly and considered the roll he still held. "The war's still fresh in everyone's mind, and we'll treat 'em right." He bit into the roll.

The war wasn't still fresh in Gertrude's mind, but she remembered it well enough. *The Chinese were our allies, too. All of them. They all must be tired of war by now. I know I am.* Even as Gertrude's thoughts drifted back to the scenes of Yencheng as she'd last seen it, the ship's bow sliced through the crest of another wave and settled precipitously. Her left hand shot out to keep her from hitting the table edge as the fork in her right hand pinned escaping green peas to the wetted tablecloth. "You would think—on an ocean liner—they'd have sense enough to serve them in a cream sauce," she muttered.

Patrolling the railing on the Bridge Deck, Gertrude had been the first of the passengers to see a yellow color swirling in the ocean waves. Ever since the ship had passed Okinawa and the Ryukyu Islands south of Japan, Gertrude had been watching for this sure sign that the Yangtze River was still dumping its silt load into the East China Sea. Now watching the yellow color deepen as each sea mile brought her closer to the continent, Gertrude felt her heart being drawn back to the country and the Chinese people she had come to love, erasing from her consciousness all qualms of returning to China.

Upon being instructed to do so, Gertrude was one of the first to arrange her luggage on the Promenade Deck for the customs inspection. Excitedly she'd clambered down to the Main Deck to inform the other missionaries that they were entering the mouth of the Yangtze. Then she had joined the crowd on the Bridge Deck who were watching the harbor pilot and the customs officials being brought aboard as the ship headed south into the Wangpoo River toward the docks of Shanghai.

With building anticipation, for the next two and one-half hours Gertrude waited in the passport lines, dashed down to her cabin to retrieve her declarations documents, then cornered and coerced the customs officer into examining her luggage first. As the *SS General Meigs* drew alongside the Hongkew Wharf and others waited beside their luggage for the customs officer, Gertrude, wrapped in her long fur coat and head scarf against the biting cold, stood on the Bridge Deck, searching the crowd on shore for the familiar faces who waited there to welcome home the returning missionaries.

"Gertrude! Oh, Gertrude!" Mrs. Branson called out as she saw the fur coat-clad figure hurrying along the Promenade Deck passageway. "Did you see Mrs. Sevrens and the Lees down there on the dock? It looks like half the China Division is here to greet us."

"Yes, I saw them," Gertrude answered brusquely. She quickly surveyed the luggage piled around Elder Branson and his wife. "But right now you'd better grab some of these coolies"— she gestured to the two young Chinese men dressed in rough, simple garb who followed her— "and get this luggage off the boat."

"She's right, my dear." Elder Branson sheepishly nodded to Gertrude's wisdom.

"But how do we do that?" his wife asked, gazing dumbfounded from Gertrude to her husband.

"The coolies are swarming aboard on the gangplank right there," Gertrude said with a thrust of her forefinger at the midpoint of the ship nearest the wharf. "But you'd better hurry. The amount of money they will demand is going up by the minute." With a chatter of rediscovered Mandarin flung over her shoulder at the two young men, promising them great rewards for following her, Gertrude pushed through the swarms of passengers toward her luggage near the bow of the ship.

Very soon it became apparent that there was more work than there were coolies. Predictably the price for coolie work shot through the ceiling. To keep her coolies from abandoning her halfway to the loading and unloading area, Gertrude, in her most convincing Chinese, had to promise them more money and to threaten them with severe loss of face and loss of the money they had earned thus far. No sooner had she hugged Mrs. Sevrens and Mrs. Boynton on the wharf than her attention was drawn to the Bransons and the Hills who were waving frantically from the railing of the Promenade Deck. They pointed dramatically to their luggage still stacked around them and exaggeratedly shrugged their shoulders and shook their heads. Gertrude got the picture immediately.

Dr. Miller, you were here to help me when I arrived in China the first time, she mused. *Now it's my turn.*

Enlisting three of the husky young men from the crowd of mission compound greeters, Gertrude rushed back through the disembarkation gate to the wharf side. Leaving two of the young men stationed on the dock directly below the missionaries still stuck on the ship, she convinced two local stevedores to loan her a long length of rope which she and her remaining assistant carried aboard the ship to her stranded companions. Over the next 30 minutes the two teams lowered each piece of luggage over the side of the ship and carried it to the waiting mission vehicles. After assuring herself that all of her deck luggage had made it onto the two old Dodge trucks, Gertrude hastily squeezed into the backseat of the compound sedan next to Elder and Mrs. Branson.

She rode in silence, taking in all the little Chinese shops that had sprung up along Ping Liang Road. The street, she noted, was as crowded as usual, but the rubble and debris from the war were nowhere to be seen.

"It's all been cleared away," she said softly to no one in particular.

"Yes, it has," Elder Branson agreed. "They've done a lovely job in rebuilding their country. At least what we've seen so far."

Gertrude turned her head slightly to the left to note Elder Branson's spectacled boyish face peering over her shoulder, then turned back to the unfolding street scene just beyond the car window. To her, Elder Branson seemed as genuinely curious and pleased with what he saw as she was.

"I wonder what they call those things," Gertrude said, pointing with her finger, tapping on the window. "They look like a rickshaw attached to a bicycle."

"They're called pedicabs, I've heard," Elder Branson murmured. "Something the Japanese brought in. Looks like they were popular enough to stay after the Japanese left."

Gertrude nodded her understanding and continued to gaze out the window, smiling in recognition at familiar sights, noting with curiosity those things that were new and different.

"How does it look to you?" Elder Branson asked, quietly breaking into her reverie.

"It looks like home," she whispered softly, never turning her head.

"I wonder how things are in Yencheng," he said a bit more loudly.

"I wouldn't know," Gertrude answered honestly. She turned her gaze fully on him. "But I'd give a good, gold U.S. dollar to find out."

He continued peering out the window. "After we get settled in . . . the first of next week some time, come talk to me. We'll see what we can find out."

One week stretched into three weeks as Gertrude, along with the offices of the China Division of Seventh-day Adventists, was consumed with the many activities of settling so many people into a foreign country.

Like an amphibious invasion, several waves of boats deposited returning missionaries on Shanghai's shores to be housed on the burgeoning Ningkuo Road compound. The compound already held the China Division Printing Press, the Far Eastern Academy teaching staff and boarding students (grades nine to 12), children of missionaries in the Far East, the reconstituted China College, and the headquarters of the China Division. To these were added all the returned missionaries who would be moving to their assignments throughout China once they got their household goods through the tedious process of customs clearance.

Housing was at a premium. Two and three families were in temporary quarters together. The division president, Elder Branson, and his wife moved in with the Milton Lee family. The Hills and the Abernathys, the new missionaries, took up temporary quarters with the Clarence Miller family. And Gertrude moved in with Miss Landrum, the division cashier, known to her friends on the compound as Landy.

With so many mouths to feed in such cramped quarters, a community dining room was established at Far Eastern Academy. Crossing a construction area on their way to the dining hall one evening, Gertrude fell, hitting her head hard against the concrete walkway. Seconds later she hit her head again when Miss Landrum fell on top of her. Gertrude remembered very little of what happened the rest of the evening and had a splitting headache for the next several days. Despite the pain she spent the next seven business days standing in lines eight hours a day with everyone else to get her four large trunks, her two radios, and her record player through customs.

And then came Christmas. With just two days left to prepare, Gertrude and her friends invaded the Bund of Shanghai on an all-day shopping spree. They visited many of their old familiar stores along Nanking Road, Szechuan Road, and even Bubbling Wells Road beyond the previous hospital site in the old U.S. Marine barracks. At noon they all met at Sun Ya's where the new missionaries were initiated into the Shanghai life with a wonderful Chinese meal, including the delicious fried noodles that Gertrude had not tasted for five years.

Christmas Day was excruciatingly cold, another educational experience for the new missionaries. For their Christmas party the Chinese contractor for the compound sent a large cake on top of which sat a church and steeple, made of sugar. Lighted by a small electric light bulb, the church provided decoration in the dining hall for the next several days.

On Sabbath Gertrude attended the Range Road Clinic Church. The following Tuesday she and a large contingency from the compound met another boat at the wharf bringing another 18 missionaries to Shanghai. The following Thursday, the Chinese national mission employees on the compound hosted a welcome party in the community dining hall for all of the returning missionaries.

It wasn't Gertrude's party, but as usual she was making the rounds. Being so busy with customs officials and Christmas, she had not been to the hospital to see her old friends. Tonight she made up for lost time.

"Gertrude! Gertrude, over here!" Mary Woo shouted in English. Gertrude moved quickly to where a diminutive, round-faced young Chinese woman stood next to a table, waving her arms over her head.

"Where have you been?" Mary asked, greeting Gertrude with a Western-style hug. "I've been looking all over the dining hall for you."

"I'm trying to see all my former students," Gertrude said with a laugh. "But there are so many of them." She reached out her hand to the older and taller Chinese woman at the table. "Are you having a good time, Edith?"

Edith Chang, who was more reserved and Chinese in her demeanor, despite her name, nodded deeply. "I am, Miss Green. Thank you."

"Thank you again, the both of you," Gertrude said in Mandarin for Edith's sake, "for inviting me to your lovely apartment for dinner last Sabbath."

The conversation continued in Mandarin and English as Gertrude related what she had heard at the other tables while listening and comparing what these two friends could add or confirm. The Chinese grapevine was accurate, but only in the conglomerate.

Gertrude's ears perked up when Mary said, "Have you heard the rumor about Dr. Hwang in Yencheng?"

"Dr. Hwang?" Gertrude's mind raced back to a memory of a short, bald Chinese doctor in owlish glasses whom she had met at Professor Quimby's office at the Chiao Tou Tseng school. *But he was murdered,* she remembered. "Who?" she asked as if she hadn't heard correctly.

"Dr. Hwang. Dr. Paul Hwang," Mary repeated. "He and his wife, Thelma, are currently leading the work at the Yencheng Hospital. It is said that he is stealing the hospital's money and using it to buy property for himself and his family."

"That's not true," Gertrude snapped, her green eyes flashing. "He would never do such a thing. It's not even possible." Gertrude watched as Mary Woo physically drew back.

"Do you know Dr. Paul Hwang, honored teacher?" Edith Chang's voice was calm, steady and respectful, but her eyes were alert, searching Gertrude's face carefully.

Gertrude saw the serious Chinese face and reconsidered her words of a few moments before. *Careful, girl. You're about to step on a landmine. This is China. Think. What did you just say?* Gertrude snapped her eyes two times and took a deep breath. She spoke in slow, deliberately calm Chinese. "Yes, I knew Dr. Paul Hwang and his wife before they were married, when they both lived here in Shanghai. Paul Hwang was a medical student under Dr. Dale at St. John's. Thelma was one of my nursing students—for a while." She remembered the short, sturdy Australian Chinese girl who had publicly corrected her boyfriend, and the earnest young man who'd sung in the choir for which Gertrude had played the piano. "Neither of them is capable of such an act." The pitch of her voice rose despite her attempt to control it.

"Who isn't capable of what act?" a male voice said behind Gertrude.

Gertrude whirled to face a handsome Chinese man, approximately her height and only slightly older. "Dr. Paul Hwang." she blurted. "Oh . . . Dr. Chen." For the second time in less than five minutes, Gertrude fought for control of her emotions as she bowed slightly to one of the attending staff at the Shanghai Sanitarium, currently operating in the Range Road Clinic.

"Miss Green," Dr. Chen returned with a short bow. "I have heard of these rumors also. I can assure you, they are false." He nodded again to Gertrude, his face a mask of Chinese seriousness, his eyes engaging her completely.

You've forgotten how to play this game, haven't you? Gertrude derided herself. *Only those who defend the guilty need to show such emotion. The innocent can afford to be calm; they have nothing to hide.* It was a lesson in Chinese culture—one she'd obviously forgotten—from her former teacher, Mr. Chen.

"Why do we hear such rumors, honored doctor?" It was Miss Chang, seeking information in the appropriate and respectful Chinese way.

"I suspect someone is trying to discredit him. They want to replace him with one of their own choosing," he said, looking from one to the other to make sure he was understood.

That means a family member, Gertrude thought. *Chinese politics, even in the church.* As the information sank in, her mind rushed on, *This is someone more powerful than Paul. I need to get to Yencheng.*

Gertrude sensed the stiffening of her female companions and saw Dr. Chen bow slightly and back away. As she turned, a familiar voice rang out.

"Miss Green, may I speak with you for a moment?" It was Elder Branson.

"Yes, of course." Gertrude turned to her companions. "Excuse me," she said with a small bow. "Duty calls."

As she approached Elder Branson, Gertrude grasped at a small hope. *A*

Western mind! Maybe he can do something about getting me to Yencheng to help Paul and Thelma. Aloud she said, "Elder Branson, I need to go to Yencheng right away."

"Yes, I know," he replied.

"You do?" She was incredulous.

"Yes." He handed her a letter that was not in an envelope. "I received a letter . . . actually, you received a letter from the people at Yencheng . . ."

"You read it?"

"Yes." He shook his head, his eyes sparkling with mirth. "Miss Green, you must stop interrupting."

She paused, thinking. "How did they know I was here?"

"When I heard the rumors, I checked with certain people to see if they were true. Then I found out where the rumors were coming from to see how much time we have. Then I wrote to Dr. Paul and Thelma, telling them you were here."

"You let them know you were aware of the rumors without saying so." Gertrude's mouth twitched with a smile of her own.

"I did." He nodded, his face reflecting the seriousness of the situation. "And they wrote to you, asking you to come quickly. They gave it to Elder Hartwell to carry back here, knowing he would give it to me." He reflected a moment before he continued. "The power play is not a particularly serious one, but we do need to get you there soon."

"You play the political game very well." She nodded in appreciation, intending a compliment.

"It's not a game, Miss Green," he said. "We are here to do the Lord's work. But we must do it within the Chinese culture, their customs, their ways of communicating. Wise as serpents, but harmless as doves, you know. I'm sure you learned how to do it when you were here before."

"I did." Gertrude recalled a medical clinic in Mr. Chen's courtyard and a hospital business meeting with Dr. Tsao. "But I've forgotten a lot."

"Welcome to China, Miss Green." Elder Branson said seriously.

Gertrude looked at the folded letter in her hand and realized she already knew what was in it without reading it. Then she considered the workers and the hospital it represented and realized she did not know anything about what was happening in Yencheng.

"I suppose this means I have to go through customs all over again to get out of Shanghai."

He laughed. "Welcome to China, Miss Green."

Chapter 57

RETURNING TO YENCHENG

On Board the *SS Lung On*
February 14, 1947

Dearest Mother:

Here I am on my way to Hankow. I can't say that I am enjoying it so much but at least I am on my way, if that means anything. Wish it didn't take so long to get to Hankow. This is a small boat and we should get there sooner than some other boats. We didn't even stop in Nanking. We will make our first stop tonight in Anking and then the next stop is Kiukiang and then after that we will be in Hankow. About three more days yet.

This is our second day on this tub. No heat and it is plenty cold weather, I can tell you. I have on my padded Chinese jacket to keep warm and my stadium boots. Really those stadium boots I bought last winter are surely grand and what I would have done without them I do not know. My feet would freeze if I didn't have them. Everyone else out here wishes they had a pair. By next winter I will need another pair because I will have these worn out by that time. They look awfully big and bulky, but that doesn't bother me any because they keep my feet warm. You know how I have suffered with cold feet all my life.

I wanted to write you again before I left Shanghai, but I didn't have the time for that because I was so busy packing and getting my things ready to go. I do believe it is more difficult to get out of Shanghai coming up here than it is to get into Shanghai. I had to go through just as much customs business to get my things out of Shanghai and much worse, if you ask me. At least I am on my way now and that is a help.

I received your last letter and was glad to get the clipping from the newspaper about Fred. Well, he is all engaged and everything is fine. Now you will lose another son pretty soon or, I should say, gain another daughter. I wonder if I will ever help you out with another son. I guess not at the present rate of my goings on. Well, anyway, it was a nice write-up and I'll keep that clipping.

I am glad that Walter and his new bride, Amelia, are getting on well. I know that they should be happy and that it is nice for you as they will come over often to see you.

This morning I met two single ladies on the boat; one is Canadian and one is American. They are Mennonites and work at their mission in Chumatien which is on the rail line between Hankow and Yencheng. They are going to their mission just like I am and will be taking the same train north out of Hankow. I am hoping to be able to share a compartment on the train with them. Getting a compartment on the train is always risky business; you get to share with whoever gets there first.

Did you have fun unpacking the chest I sent? I am wondering if the vases came through OK? I bought a small one just like it to take with me to Yencheng. It is made of teakwood, which is the best kind of wood out here. I also bought a set of tables which are made of mahogany, which is not considered such a nice wood. But they will do for some tables for my living room.

I bought them last week just before the exchange rate went down to $17,000 Shanghai to $1.00 U.S. Can you imagine what it is like to carry a million dollars around in your baggage? I just throw my money in a shopping bag and go to town. It is impossible to carry it in a pocketbook. Some carry their money in a box; some just carry great bundles of it in their arms and not even cover it up.

Well, I can't think of anything more to write about today. Tell everyone hello and that I am traveling around China now just like I did when I was in the States. I guess when I get to Yencheng I won't be traveling so very much. But I may get down to Hankow as the train connections there are not too bad.

Toodle loo for today and I may add some more to this letter before I mail it in Hankow.

Loads of love from your loving daughter and
Heaps of good wishes,
Gertrude

In Hankow, Gertrude found herself in the interior of China once again.

As casually and as comfortably as diving into a swimming pool, she plunged into the Chinese culture with all of its scents, colors, and sounds—and loved every minute of it. The language was Chinese; not an English speaker could be found. The street traffic of every imaginable conveyance was Chinese—although Gertrude noted that the market vendors and the pedicab drivers were much better dressed than before the war. Inflation didn't seem to be hindering the local economy. The markets, where she purchased dozens of crates of pears, apples, pumpkin seeds, and other Chinese delicacies for her friends and soon-to-be students in Yencheng, were definitely Chinese. As she had said to Elder Branson, she was home.

At 5:30 p.m. Gertrude arrived at the train station with her usual entourage: three pedicabs piled high with trunks, her old beat-up brown suitcase along with several newer suitcases, and the crates of fruits and nuts. After making sure that all this was safely loaded on the freight car, she took her brown suitcase and went in search of the two young Mennonite missionaries and a compartment to share with them.

"Now where do you suppose they've gotten off to?" Gertrude grumbled after walking the length of the railway station platform twice and peering into all the passenger coach car windows as best she could. She turned and gazed the length of the platform, her long fur-collared coat flapping in the stiff, cold breeze. It stirred the husks and wrappers scattered by the food vendors, swirling the trash around her feet. *Gertrude, you should have kept your padded Chinese jacket on. You're going to freeze out here,* she mentally lectured. *You'd better find a compartment or you'll be sleeping sitting up all the way to Yencheng and Loho.* At that, she marched smartly to the first-class cars and stepped on board. *I'll watch for you girls out of the window, but it will be from my compartment.*

On the second car, third door down, Gertrude found an unoccupied compartment, entered it and claimed it for her own. Setting her small suitcase on the seat beside her, she settled herself near the window, occasionally gazing out in both directions for the truant young missionaries.

"Oh! A thousand pardons!" emanated from the now opened compartment doorway in Mandarin Chinese.

Gertrude looked up in time to see a startled, round-faced Chinese man in an ill-fitting double-breasted Western suit being jostled from behind by two more, similarly dressed Chinese men. The first two men each carried two suitcases and the third carried a suitcase and a large brown paper bag. From the spicy smells, she guessed that it contained supper for himself and the other two.

Giving a slight nod of recognition, Gertrude—in her most polite Chinese—welcomed the three men inside. "Please, my older brothers, come in and share this humble compartment with me. I am very small and will take up almost no space at all." *Sorry, girls,* Gertrude thought with a glance out of the window. *There's no polite way to refuse hospitality in China, especially on a crowded train.*

Over supper and for the next four hours Gertrude and her three guests shared their family lineage, their home towns, and their work assignments. Gertrude discovered that the three men were bank accountants and clerks who were going to Chengchow to help set up another branch of the Bank of China. They, in turn, were quite familiar with the Yencheng Sanitarium and Hospital, one of them having cared for a relative there in the recent past.

When the porter came in to make up the four bunks, Gertrude observed him looking out of the corner of his eye from her to the three men as he listened to their conversation in Chinese and tried to figure out her relationship to them, and which bed she would occupy. The older of the men, also observing the porter's shifting gaze, immediately suggested that Gertrude take one of the lower, more comfortable beds. Gertrude politely—and gratefully—accepted his suggestion. She hated sleeping up in the air, "perched on the edge of the world," for fear of falling. And in the present company, she couldn't imagine how she would have maintained her modesty while climbing into the sky.

The small toilet at the end of the car allowed Gertrude to wash her face in private but was not spacious enough to allow her to change into sleeping attire. *Too bad you didn't wear your Chinese coat and pants,* Gertrude chided herself while looking in the small mirror she kept in her handbag. *They would have made excellent pajamas.* She looked down at her Western apparel and shook her head. *Tonight you get to sleep in your clothes. Won't be the first time.* A smile creased her face as she wondered what her German mother would have done in this situation. *She's very adaptable, very practical, just like me.* Gertrude opened the door and sidled down the narrow corridor. *Half a world away, and she's still that close. Mama, I miss you,* she thought as she turned the small brass knob to the compartment and entered her Chinese world once again.

Twenty-four hours after leaving Hankow, and after making numerous stops at small towns and villages on the way, the train pulled into the railway station only a mile from the Yencheng Sanitarium and Hospital. Clutching her travel-worn brown suitcase firmly in her left hand, Gertrude emerged from the compartment car onto the steps leading down to the platform. From her compartment window she had seen no one she recognized waiting for her in the crowds. Now from her new vantage point she again surveyed the three or four dozen station workers and passengers scurrying to and from the train, searching for a familiar face.

"Miss Green! Oh, Miss Green!" The male Chinese voice speaking English stood out distinctly above the cacophony of melded voices, animal and human, that flowed upward and beat about her feet like irregularly advancing waves.

Gertrude spotted him, his arm raised in greeting, threading his way through the baggage and boxes being unloaded four cars down. His angular face, large chin, and high cheek bones, appeared older now, showing the drawn lines of worry and care. His thinning, black hair was cut short, riding high above his ears and wire-framed glasses. He was short, even by Chinese standards, but his carriage was straight and his steps were measured and even, as one who carries the weight of authority and responsibility. He was no longer the young medical student she had known in Shanghai but he was the same Paul Hwang whom Gertrude had accompanied on the piano at the English church services. Gertrude waved in response.

"Honorable Miss Green," he said respectfully, in English, as he approached. "I am so glad you have come. May I carry your bag?"

Gertrude tried to read his intense eyes and serious face as her mind filled with endless questions. *You are a doctor now, Paul. Why are you addressing me as 'honorable'? What do you think I know about your situation here? What do you expect of me?* Gertrude composed herself. "Honorable doctor, I am humbled to be called to work here in Yencheng under your direction."

"No, Miss Green," he said simply, "I will be working under your direction."

He had her full attention as he laid his hand on hers on the handle of the old brown suitcase. "There is much controversy here in Yencheng as to who is in charge. The old patriarch, Wang Jing Bo, has his favorites. The school headmaster, Liu Shun-ming, has his favorites. But I am nobody's favorite—except for Pastor Pung."

"But you have been appointed by the China Division as the Medical Director of the Yencheng Sanitarium and Hospital," she said sharply, still clinging to her suitcase with both hands, as if unwilling to let go of a truth that now seemed in jeopardy.

"May I carry your bag, Miss Green?" Paul Hwang repeated, looking intently into her eyes.

For a moment Gertrude felt herself being held by the steady gaze of another Dr. Hwang. *How like your father you have become, Paul,* she thought as she relinquished the suitcase into his hands. She accepted his extended hand of assistance and descended the steps from the train car to the platform.

As he turned and began working his way off the platform and away from the train station, she fell in step beside him.

"When the missionaries went home after Pearl Harbor," he said without looking at her, "the Chinese accepted the challenge of attempting to keep open all of the church's institutions. But it was done according to Chinese tradition." He gave her a sharp look. "And Chinese politics." He glanced forward in time to move sideways and avoid a stack of crates. Gertrude scooted around them on the other side and hurried to catch up with him.

"Chinese politics always involves family and favorites—and a regrettable struggle for power." He nodded as if to confirm to himself the truth of this statement. "With the return of the foreign missionaries, much of this struggle will end."

"How will we . . . how will I end it here?" Gertrude knew she was the "foreign missionary" he referred to. She also knew she was the student and Paul was the teacher as she attempted to understand ever more deeply the Chinese cultural mindset and the situation into which she was about to be immersed.

He abruptly stopped walking. She continued on for two or three steps, until, realizing she was alone, she turned and came back to stand facing him.

"The Chinese will assume that the foreign missionary will take charge. And I know you will." His face was serious; his black eyes intense. "And that will end the struggle."

"And will it also end these groundless accusations against you and Thelma?"

"I think it will . . . Yes." He rubbed his nose. His voice was more quiet, less certain.

"I hope so, Dr. Paul, if it is, as you say, all about politics."

Gertrude noticed him look past her to her left and twisted her head around to see a small Chinese woman with a round face, dark complexion, and very Western hair style rapidly approaching. "Is that Thelma?" she asked.

"It is," he said. "She is beautiful, is she not?"

"She is, Doctor Paul." Gertrude looked back to see Paul's eyes sparkle, then rotated about to wave at Thelma. "Her face looks tired."

"She is the financial manager for the hospital," Paul said from behind her. "The accusations have been hard on her."

"We'll work through this together, Dr. Paul," Gertrude said confidently. "One problem at a time."

"Thank you, Miss Green," he said softly.

Chapter 58

REBUILDING YENCHENG HOSPITAL

The Great Plain of China lies between Peking (Beijing) with the Great Wall in the north and Wuhan on the Yangtze River in the south, between the mountains of Xian and Chungking in the west and the East China Sea. It is bisected from south to north by the railroad from Hankow through Chengchow to Peking, from west to east by the Yellow River. This flat, broad plain is the bread basket of China wherein lie the wheat fields, the grain staple of northern China. This plain also contains the vast tributaries—most generally running west to east—of the Yellow River, the Yangtze River, and the Huai River that regularly overflow their banks every spring, guaranteeing soil fertility and crop productivity for the sustenance of China's millions.

In the very heart of central China's interior, in this great plain, is Honan Province. It was here around 200 BC, that the first Chinese emperor to unite all of the kingdoms of China established the Qin Dynasty. It was the first of many to rule the Middle Kingdom. Into this province, in 1903, came the Drs. Harry and Maude Miller and Drs. Arthur and Bertha Selmon. They followed the railroad lines to establish their medical missionary presence, first in Sinyang, 150 miles north of Hankow, and later in Shangtsai, 210 miles north of Hankow. In 1915 Dr. and Mrs. D.E. Davenport extended this incursion into Honan province another 60 miles by following the rail lines farther northward and opening a 30-bed hospital in Yencheng near Loho.

On a flat plain, such as Honan Province, prudent Chinese villagers build dikes as tall as a two-story building and as broad as a baseball field. They are as long and serpentine as a coal train, and run along the banks of the rivers and canals that traverse their towns and meander among their permanent structures. Near the small city of Loho, at Yencheng, the Seventh-day Adventist missionaries bought a section of the top of the dike where the She River and the Loho canal converge. Over the ensuing years the mission created, on this broad flat space, four large open spaces or "yards," divided from each other by low walls. Each division or yard contained one of the organizations that serviced the numerous churches and the people on the vast plain of Honan Province.

One large area contained the mission offices, the printing offices, the church, and the primary and secondary school which eventually accommodated 400 students. One large yard held the homes of the foreign missionaries—apartment buildings and individual homes. A third large yard was reserved for the Chinese workers in all of the institutions. The last large enclosure contained the hospital buildings: a 60-bed, two-story hospital for men, a separate 24-bed, two-story hospital for women, plus surgical suites and a third clinical building which included laboratory, X-ray, and offices. With the accompanying gardens and orchards, various outbuildings, water purification system, and a concrete block swimming pool built by Dr. Nethery, the entire compound covered several acres.

Surrounding the compound was a high wall with several gates. One of the gates opened onto the river to admit patients who might arrive by boat. Another gate conveyed tradesmen and compound workers to and from the villages of Yencheng and Loho. When Gertrude had last seen it, a third gate, the main gate, had heavy wooden doors which swung from the pillars of a large arch on which was displayed the sign, "Yencheng Seventh-day Adventist Mission and Hospital."

Then the war came.

"There are lots of fruit trees missing," was Gertrude's first audible observation as she and Dr. Hwang began an inspection tour of the hospital compound, entering this section by the path between the Women's and the Men's Buildings. *And the grass and the bushes and the flowers are also missing,* she added to herself. *Interesting, how we don't notice the beauty in this world until it is missing.*

Dr. Paul walked resolutely toward the square two-story, stone-fronted clinic building with the arched portico on the far right, its oval driving path in front of the entryway empty of the greenery that once adorned it. "The Japanese stripped away every source of firewood they could find," he said, "including the floors and walls of the buildings. They didn't leave any trees standing, even in the surrounding villages."

Gertrude paused, facing the three buildings. "All of the floors?"

"And many of the walls, especially in the Men's Building." Paul turned toward her, purposefully not looking at the dilapidated hulk of the Men's Building that sat like a corpse on the far side of the compound.

Gertrude could see the ragged holes in the outer walls caused by the bombing on that terrible day many years ago. Other gaping cavities, whole sections of external wall missing, allowed her to see completely through the interior framework to the low yard wall immediately behind it. Throughout the skeletal building no window frames and no doors remained. Gertrude assumed that the other two buildings would have been in a similar state.

"We started our repairs here in the Women's Building," Dr. Paul said, drawing her attention to the central, now more substantial structure. "We keep all the patients here because that's where the operating rooms are."

"And in the clinic building because that's where you have to see the new patients," Gertrude said, turning her attention to the two viable buildings where Paul and Thelma had concentrated their first efforts.

Then the obvious question struck her. "If there are no trees, where did you get the wood for the floors?"

"In Chengchow," he replied. "There is an organization operating there— the United Nations Relief and Rehabilitation Association—which is making numerous materials available free to any organization that is trying to rebuild after the war. The only stipulation is that we have to go get the materials and transport them here."

"And you've been doing that?"

"Yes, I have personally gone several times," he said evenly. "The China Division has sent us some money and we have raised some ourselves. But it is not easy to find people you can trust. So I had to go myself, which makes it hard to tend to my medical work."

"And that's the money they've accused you of stealing?"

Dr. Paul hung his head with the shame of the accusation.

"The rumor is that you have built yourself a nice house here on the compound."

Dr. Paul raised his head slowly. Gertrude could see the pain behind the resolute gaze.

"You are welcome to visit our three rooms, Miss Green, at any time. They are over there in one of the apartment buildings in the Chinese section," he said, motioning with his head. "But you must be careful as the floor in one of the rooms is still partially missing." His eyes were intense, almost points of fire. "Thelma had to line up the play pen and our traveling trunk so that Jeannie would not walk off the edge."

"If I thought you had taken the money, Dr. Paul, I would not have come to help you." Gertrude was careful to show no inappropriate outward emotion to add to his embarrassment. "But I would like to visit your home, honorable doctor, and meet your little child."

"Thank you, Miss Green." He bowed his head ever so slightly. "We were hoping you would come for supper tonight."

It was Gertrude's turn to respond with a courteous nod of the head.

"But first. Come see what we have done with the hospital." Dr. Paul turned and marched toward the Woman's Building with Gertrude close behind him.

Over the next several weeks it happened as Dr. Paul Hwang had predicted. Local politics and directives from the division offices converged to appoint Gertrude to chair the hospital board in addition to her duties as the Superintendent of Nurses. Dr. Hwang retained his position as Medical Director.

Recalling her previous experiences in Yencheng—the excellent leadership advice of Pastor Chang and the on-the-job training as the board chair after the departure of Dr. Nethery, Gertrude met individually with the various department leaders and the local political power brokers, seeking their concerns, ideas, and advice. After discussing these ideas and formulating a plan with Dr. Hwang, Gertrude called a hospital board meeting and presented the plans, which, not surprisingly, met with the complete and unanimous approval of the board.

In accordance with Chinese custom, the male patients would continue to be housed separately on the top floor of what used to be the Women's Building. The women would continue to be treated on the ground floor. Three ground-floor rooms of the old Men's Building would be rehabilitated to provide office space which would free up more treatment areas in the clinic and hospital. One of the new rooms would contain the new X-ray machine that had been promised to Dr. Paul by the United Nations Relief and Rehabilitation Association (UNRRA). On its arrival it would be the only X-ray machine in the entire province of Honan.

Dr. Paul would stay in Yencheng, seeing patients, doing surgery, directing the hospital. Thelma would continue managing the financial well-being of the hospital under the long-distance oversight and patronage of Elder Merritt Warren, the Central China Union president, from his office in Hankow. Gertrude's role was to take the transportation money—plus a young lab technician as a traveling companion—and make the train trip to Chengchow to retrieve the necessary supplies for the next phase of the rehabilitation of the Yencheng Sanitarium and Hospital.

Gertrude sat in the corner of the freight car, resting atop the boards for which she had feistily bargained in Kaifeng, her padded Chinese coat and trousers and her stadium boots further cushioned by a wrapping of blankets. The motion of the moving train gently bumped her shoulder rhythmically against the slatted wall. The flash of torches or small kerosene lanterns from the occasional railway station flashed across her eyes from between the slats of the car, piercing the thick darkness and keeping her in a perpetual state of semiconsciousness. Rain water, sporadically splashing through the cracks, wet her face with a fine mist.

The spring rains of April had begun halfway through the two week trip, making the loading of her precious cargo of windows, slippery with rain, all the more tedious. Looking to her right, she could see them stacked against the side of the car, carefully layered in between with surplus army blankets and bolts of muslin, which she would turn into bed sheets. Across the floor, stacked three feet high on her precious boards, were boxes of nails, doors, sacks of cement, hospital beds, metal pipe—everything she and Dr. Paul had placed on their "want" list. In the far corner stood 55-gallon drums full of all the medicines she could talk away from the warehouse managers of the UNRRA. The medicines would restock their meager pharmacy supplies. The 55-gallon metal drums would become stoves in the various wards and on the various floors. No floor space on this freight car was wasted.

The trip had taken longer than she had anticipated. Most of the supplies had been available in Chengchow. However, she had to go to Kaifeng to get the boards. A different supplier, a different warehouse. But she was not going home empty-handed. Those three rooms on the ground floor of the Men's Building were desperately needed so they could move the offices and expand the treatment areas in the other two buildings—and the rooms could not be repaired without the wood. And in the back of her mind were plans for nursing school classrooms and labs like she had had in Portland, which would mean even more rooms to rebuild.

So she'd left her supplies to be guarded by the young lab tech, who was now sound asleep at the other end of the freight car, and had gone on alone to Kaifeng to bargain and cajole her way to half a freight car load of wooden boards. She had ridden in the freight car back to Chengchow, had her supplies—and her helper—loaded on top of the wood, and was now riding shotgun on the freight car back south to Yencheng.

Two weeks is a long time to be without regular meals and an indoor bathroom, she mused. Her meals had been purchased from rail-side vendors. Bathroom breaks came whenever the train stopped, but she and the lab tech had to alternate taking turns. The freight car could not be left unguarded for a minute, for the materials the hospital had received for free from the UNRRA were worth a small fortune on the black market.

I can understand how someone might think the temptation to sell these things for personal profit would be overwhelming. Gertrude imagined her boxcar full of the inflated Chinese dollars and smiled. *They obviously didn't know Paul and Thelma like I do.*

She reached under her leg and straightened a small wrinkle in the blankets, then leaned more heavily on the side of the car, closing her eyes. *Tomorrow we'll be in Yencheng. Then maybe I can get some more sleep.*

> June 14, 1947
> Yencheng Hospital
> Yencheng, Honan, China

Dearest Mother:

It was good to get your recent letter; in fact, two came at once. So I had a delightful Sabbath today catching up on all the news about Fred and Walter and their wives or soon to be. I think you must be having the grandest time at camp meeting with your friends. We have camp meetings in China as well. But this year we are so busy rebuilding our hospital that we have no time to attend anywhere.

Well, we have finally finished the ground floor rooms in the old building that I told you about. Dr. Paul made a trip to Kaifeng and returned with the X-ray machine that was promised to us by UNRRA and CNRRA and we now have X-rays, but only for two hours on Wednesday nights when there is electricity. Our offices have been moved to the old building so we have treatment rooms for hydrotherapy and massage and a classroom for the nursing students all in the regular hospital building. That will be nice this winter when we won't have to take anyone outside to get them to therapy.

Thelma Hwang and I were able to contact many of our former nursing students who had not completed their classes because the hospital was closed during the war. I had a fine time getting everyone back into their correct classes and we had to work like sixty to find a place for everyone to live. Having them here has been a real help in staffing the hospital which is getting busier now that Dr. Hwang can give his full attention to the medical work.

I was supposed to get some help here from Miss Edith Johnson. But the China Division Committee decided they need her worse than I do. Trying to get the nursing school programs started again in all of the China hospitals is a big task and they have asked her to do it. So I will have to carry on as best I can by myself.

I thought I was going to lose Dr. Paul Hwang as he had requested to take more training at the Shanghai San. There are many American physicians there now with recent training in surgery. He thinks he needs to learn something from them but I think he does very well just as he is. But doctors are hard to find for all of our hospitals, so Dr. Paul will stay here for now.

We have a wonderful gardener here who is raising flowers to replace the ones that used to decorate this whole compound. By next year he hopes to find some replacements for the fruit trees that disappeared during the war. But for now the walkways around the hospital and the church are looking beautiful again.

I should be able to move back into my old apartment in another month. I have been living in Thelma Smith's old apartment that was directly under mine. I'll be glad to be "home" because I like living up where I can see out.

We waited until we had the hospital fixed up the way we needed it. Then we used the scrap lumber and what was left over to begin fixing up the houses. There will be more people coming here, we are told, so we are getting all the housing ready for them. The school and the publishing house should be up to running full tilt this fall and a new mission director is coming some-time near the end of the year. So we're working hard to have everything ready when they arrive.

My, it just seems like there is never an end to the work around here. But it feels so good to be getting everything back in shape. I am speaking Mandarin all the time except when I am with Thelma Hwang. She was raised in Aus-tralia so I get to practice my English with her. And I just love their dear little daughter, Jeannie. I spend a lot of my spare time with them.

Well, that is all from this gabby old lady here in central China—I will be 39 in September, you know. I am always glad for letters so tell everyone there to write as often as they can and I will answer every letter.

From your daughter who loves you very much,

Gertrude

Chapter 59

EXPECTING COMPANY

During the hot, humid days of August in northern China every person, regardless of age or physical condition, toiled long hours every day until the wheat harvest was gathered in. To be released from work to go to the hospital, someone had to be desperately ill. With few inpatients and a very light load of outpatient clinic visits, Gertrude was in her office preparing for the afternoon nursing class when she heard her name anxiously called through the open window.

"Miss Green! Come! Come quickly and see!"

Looking up from her book, Gertrude recognized one of the teachers from the grade school, the older sister of one of her senior nursing students. As she struggled to shift her focus from the topic in the book to the voice outside, a series of increasingly unsettling questions raced through her mind in rapid succession. *Why is she calling to me? What is she doing out of her classroom? What could be so serious that she would come all the way over here to the hospital section . . .* Her mind had barely formulated the last question when Gertrude dropped the book on the desk. "I'm coming," she called as she dashed for the front door.

Following the teacher across the compound at a rapid pace, Gertrude was out of breath when they reached the large, wooden double gates which normally stood open during the day but were now shut and bolted with a large crossbar firmly in place.

"Why are the gates shut?" Gertrude gasped, trying to catch her breath.

"Come. Come and see." The teacher was whispering but pointing animatedly at the peephole in the gate.

Gertrude applied her eye to the dime-sized opening drilled through the heavy plank. At first she could discern only a crowd of men moving past the gate, going north.

Workers, probably, all going to the fields. Dismissing the scene as one she thought she witnessed daily, she was about to turn away when something unusual caught her eye. *They're all dressed alike. And what are they carrying? Something over their shoulders.* She had assumed that many were carrying what looked like large clubs or harvesting flails. All were carrying satchels or back-packs. *Those aren't clubs. Those are guns!*

With renewed concentration Gertrude scanned to the left and right as far as the tiny aperture would allow. The procession of soldiers continued un-interrupted; the successive ranks were unending. "Who are these men?" she said softly.

"It is part of the Communist Army," the teacher whispered close to Gertrude's ear.

Gertrude turned and stared at her. "I thought they were up north."

"They are . . . but more are traveling from here to join them every day." The teacher's eyes were as large as silver dollars. The Chinese gape of fear hung on her face like a heavy weight, her mouth hung open and her lower eyelids sagged.

"Where are they going?" Gertrude forced herself to think objectively, to stave off the heaviness she felt rising up in the pit of her own stomach.

"To cross the river on the railroad bridge."

"Are we in danger here?" Gertrude had returned to staring at the passing horde through the heavy gate, her hands resting on its reassuring thickness. She was thinking of her pharmacy full of medicines, the cash Thelma kept hidden in the safe, her nursing students—all free for the taking.

"Generalissimo Chiang Kai-shek's army patrols the railroad from Kaifeng to Hankow . . . and all of the villages in between. While he is still strong, I think they will not bother us." The teacher's voice was quieter, steadied by the reassurance of her own testimony.

Emboldened by the teacher's favorable report, Gertrude felt her confidence returning. She turned from the gate. "Why can't people just learn to get along?" she asked, her fear turning to irritation and disgust. Shaking her head, she marched off toward the hospital, the teacher following a safe distance behind.

Four weeks later, on a Wednesday evening in September, Gertrude was supervising the taking of X-rays on several patients with leg and arm fractures. Electricity was available only two hours each week—on Wednesday evenings—so Gertrude's Wednesdays were permanently booked far into the future.

As she walked down the row of waiting patients, reassuring herself of their names and conditions, Gertrude's mind was only partially on the business at hand. The day's mail had brought a telegram from the Division headquarters that a new physician, Dr. Raymond McMullen, would soon join them at the Yencheng Hospital.

She knew the new doctor had arrived in China only a few months before and had not had sufficient time to learn the language, certainly not the nine months that she had enjoyed. *I know they're short of physicians. But sending him out here where almost no one speaks English before he's ready will make it doubly hard for him to adjust.*

She checked the chart of the last patient waiting at the end of the line, an elbow fracture. Two days ago she and Dr. Hwang had worked for more than an hour getting it into an acceptable position. Although the bones had felt right when they finished, she was especially curious to see if they'd been successful in their attempt.

It probably means I'll have to find a translator to help Dr. McMullen in clinic. That means tying up one of my nurses or students. I wonder who made that decision. She grimaced and shook her head.

"Miss Green, the machine is getting hot."

"What?"

"The tube in the machine, it's getting hot." It was the senior student nurse assisting her tonight, a quick, observant learner. She was standing in the doorway of the room where the precious X-ray machine did its work.

Gertrude strode into the room, placing her hand on the housing surrounding the rotating armature. It was almost too hot to touch. "Turn it off. The oil coolant isn't working again." She looked at her watch and anxiously thought about the limited time they had to take X-rays. Dismissing any thought of attempting to fix it herself, she said, "Call Dr. Hwang. He was an X-ray technologist before he became a doctor. He fixed it last time. He'll know what to do."

Ten minutes later Dr. Paul hastened into the X-ray room. "I was on the second floor making rounds," he apologized. "I came as fast as I could. I know we have only a limited time to take the X-rays before the electricity is shut off." He headed for the tool cabinet and selected a screwdriver, then turned to the gargantuan machine that was their mechanical prima donna in every sense of the word—high notoriety and high maintenance.

"I'm just glad you know something about this dragon, Dr. Paul. I wouldn't want to be working on it myself," Gertrude said, appreciatively standing close by to offer any assistance he might need.

He paused momentarily to give a short, formal bow in recognition of the compliment then quickly turned his attention to the hoses and housing that concealed the secret inner workings of the machine.

Gertrude watched him remove a curved plate. He reached inside and made some unseen and undisclosed adjustment. She watched his eyes close momentarily in studied concentration. He opened them slowly, then took a deep breath and removed his hand.

"You may start the machine again," he said to the student nurse as he screwed the housing plate into position. When he left the room, Gertrude followed him.

"Dr. Hwang," she called out to him in English.

"Yes, Miss Green." He turned and faced her.

"I received a telegram from Division headquarters today." She paused, wanting to penetrate the stoic facial facade he wore as a mask, yet not embarrass him. "Do you know about the new physician who is coming here to Yencheng to help us?"

"I've heard a rumor."

"So you knew already?" Gertrude tried unsuccessfully to take the sharpness out of her voice.

"You know how Chinese rumors are, Miss Green," he responded quietly, politely. "Some parts are true and some parts are not true."

"What part is not true?"

"That he's coming here to help me."

"Then why, pray tell, is he coming at all?" She was growing tired of the big Oriental mystery game.

"He's coming to replace me," he said simply, without emotion.

"What do you mean, replace you?" Tiredness was becoming irritation.

Dr. Hwang pursed his lips in thought, then retracted them into a thin, serious line before speaking. "He is the foreign missionary. He will be placed in charge here in Yencheng, a large hospital connected to a significant mission compound which serves the needs of the large population of the Central China Union and the consultation requests of several outlying medical clinics. I will be moved to a smaller hospital in an—u'mm—how do you say? An out-of-the-way place."

"Why?" Gertrude was stunned almost speechless.

"Because that's the way it is done, Miss Green."

"But that's not fair!" she blurted out—in Chinese—out of force of habit.

"What would be fair, Miss Green? That they send *him* to the small hospital where he has no translators and no English-speaking nurse to help him run his hospital?" He advanced toward her, intently holding her gaze with his own. "I am happy to serve the Lord and the Chinese people as a physician, Miss Green. It does not matter if I serve them here or in another place."

"But I need you and Thelma here," she said quietly, her eyes misting over. "And Jeannie. I would miss her terribly, Paul. I'm teaching her to sing 'Jesus Loves Me' in Chinese."

"I know." He lowered his eyes to avoid embarrassing her further. "But it's only a rumor after all, Miss Green. Perhaps it is not true."

But Gertrude knew about Chinese rumors.

Just a week later Gertrude received a telegram from the Central Union Office requesting that she come to Hankow to accompany Dr. and Mrs. Mc-Mullen and their 5-year-old son on their train trip to Yencheng. Not recognizing her own independent spirit as anything other than normal, she wondered why someone would want to appear helpless by asking for assistance in riding a train. She soon discovered that their helplessness extended beyond their inadequate language skills.

Without seeking guidance from the office and thinking to save money, Dr. McMullen had purchased third-class tickets for the train ride north. As third-class tickets did not allow travel in a compartment, Gertrude and the Mc-Mullens had to sit upright on hard wooden benches for the entire 24-hour trip. The live animals, communal eating and sleeping arrangements, card games, and constant conversation common to third-class travelers made sleep for the Westerners a fleeting dream at best.

Because the railroad system on this line had been built by the Belgians, the coach cars were of the French design with long wooden benches the full width of the car and a narrow aisle along one side. The smallest McMullen soon proved himself to be an excellent escape artist, crawling under the benches, over the baggage, and through the lives of the Chinese passengers. Because of the car design, Dr. McMullen found it exceedingly difficult and increasingly embarrassing to retrieve the child. Mrs. McMullen proved equally inept at controlling or correcting him. Gertrude, normally a lover and defender of all children, found herself growing to dislike this small boy.

At every station stop Gertrude vainly attempted to find vendors who were selling food that might entice the McMullens to eat. Except for pears, apples, and white rice, they were not inclined to eat anything that was unfamiliar to them. Even after setting up housekeeping on the compound in what had been the Nethery home, they continued to eat their meals in Gertrude's apartment until a cook could be found who was able to fix Western-style food.

Gertrude stood at the head of the operating table. Her hand rested lightly on the hand of the senior student who held the anesthesia mask on the patient's face.

"It is not necessary to press down hard with the mask," she instructed quietly near the student's ear. "It is more important that your hand be relaxed so that you can feel the patient's pulse—here—under your fourth finger." She guided the student's finger as she spoke. "That and the breathing let you know when to add more ether." Even as she taught, Gertrude listened with a sinking heart to the conversation between the two physicians.

"I cannot see what I'm doing," Dr. McMullen repeated as he struggled to tie a ligature deep in the abdominal cavity. "I don't know if I'm tying off the artery or the vein." He withdrew his hand, which held the catgut string, tied in a knot around thin air.

Dr. Hwang deftly thrust a surgical sponge on a ring forceps into the wound followed by a clamp which controlled the bleeding that had begun again. "I am sorry that we do not have electricity," he apologized. "We operate near the window, like this, to get all the available light. I will try to expose the area more clearly," he said, lifting on the retractor again.

Taking a deep breath, Dr. McMullen rested his hand on the patient's chest.

"It's not your fault, Dr. Hwang," he said. "I just can't see what to do."

"May I try?" Dr. Hwang asked carefully.

"Please. Do try" Dr. McMullen took the retractor from Dr. Hwang and lifted.

Dr. Hwang accepted the proffered tie from the operating assistant, reached inside and quickly tied off the bleeder.

Later, Dr. Hwang emerged alone from the side entrance of the main hospital building, heading down the pathway toward the clinic and his office. Gertrude, seeing him through the window, darted out through the main door, hurrying to catch up with him.

"You're very patient with him, Dr. Paul," she said as she fell in step with him.

"He is very good in the clinic," Dr. Hwang replied, looking straight ahead.

"But not in surgery," she said firmly.

Dr. Hwang slowed his pace and lowered his head, speaking almost in a whisper, as if he might be overheard. "It seems to me that he was not very well trained in surgery."

Gertrude lowered her head as well, but not her voice. "Then how am I going to get these surgeries done when you are gone to the new hospital in Taishen?"

"The Lord will provide, Miss Green," he replied uncertainly. Wanting to brush her off, yet remain polite, he quickened his pace while walking in an awkward, bent-over position, attempting a bow as he moved away hastily.

"The Lord will not come down here and do these surgeries." She kept pace with him, walking bent over as he was, in order to be at his eye level—and almost shouting.

Dr. Hwang stopped walking and stood up. Gertrude stood erect as well. He looked about at the new flowers along the pathway as if searching for an appropriate response.

"No, I suppose not," he said quietly. In his uncertainty he turned to face her. "What am I supposed to do?"

"I don't know." It was Gertrude's turn to be uncertain, to flounder for the words. "I feel like I'm back doing what I did with my Chinese surgeon, Dr. Tsao. I will be forced to step in, to help Dr. McMullen while trying not to bruise his fragile ego." With a deep breath of frustration she turned away, her arms folded across her chest. "I thought that having an American-trained physician would not make that necessary."

"It is not a matter of what country the doctor is trained in, Miss Green."

"No, I suppose not," she said offhandedly. Belatedly detecting the hardness of his voice, she thought, *What did you just say to him?* She turned quickly to meet his penetrating gaze. "I'm sorry. I didn't mean it like that." Her hand moved out in reconciliation but she quickly withdrew it. *Don't invade his private space,* warned the voice of Mr. Chen in her head.

After a few seconds he brought his hands together in front of him and bent at the waist in a soft bow. "It is . . ." A puzzled expression crossed his face. "It is . . . O.K." His eyes softened. "I understand."

"Paul, I need you here," she said plaintively.

"I am not gone yet, Miss Green." Gertrude heard his voice change, take on the qualities of a teacher, the qualities of his father's voice.

"The China Division is trying to repair all of the old hospitals and get them open. Mr. Wood, the Division builder, is still struggling to repair the old Shanghai Sanitarium on Rubicon Road. There is not enough material or enough people to get all of this done and build a new hospital at the same time." He paused. "I am not gone yet," he repeated.

Gertrude was processing what he had just said, trying to understand how he could know such things and how this would coincide with the directive she knew had come from the Division office. "But you're supposed to go there . . . to Taishen . . . at the end of the year. When they get the new hospital built."

"That is still three months away, Miss Green," he reasoned. "I think it will take them longer than three months to build a new hospital in Taishen."

Gertrude stared at him and blinked three times as what he had said sank in.

His eyes lit up. "We have an old saying in Chinese." He wrinkled his brow as if trying to recall some ancient proverb. " 'Take no thought for the morrow, for the morrow shall take thought for the things of itself. Sufficient unto the day is the evil thereof.' "

"That's not Chinese," she said with a laugh.

"No?" he said, his eyes dancing. "Well, it could be."

Throughout the month of November Gertrude waited apprehensively for word that construction on the new hospital in Taishen had begun—although she had little time to worry about such things.

During the second week she hosted two field secretaries from the General Conference—Professor Cossentine and Elder Bradley, both of whom she had known while working in Denver—and Professor Quimby, her former academy teacher and old friend from Chiao Tou Tseng, now the head of the Church's education work in China. They were visiting the various educational institutions in China and wanted to see the secondary school at Yencheng and learn how Gertrude's nursing school was implementing the new nursing school guidelines adopted in September.

The following week, just prior to Thanksgiving, she hosted three physicians from the Chinese National Relief and Rehabilitation Association (CNRRA) who had supplied the hospital with the X-ray machine as well as much of their new equipment.

When extremely cold weather suddenly descended on central China, Gertrude was delighted that she had ordered two fuel oil stoves from Shanghai for the offices on the first floor of the old, drafty Men's Building. Even with kerosene selling at one dollar (U.S.) per gallon, she felt the hospital could afford to be prepared for winter. She felt even better since there had been no word about moving Dr. Hwang to southern China.

What she was not prepared for was the news that the Communist Army was marching south. In an unexpected move in midwinter, intended to catch the Nationalist Army off guard, they were threatening to take Chengchow and Kaifang and cut the railroad lines linking Peking with Hankow—and Yencheng—halfway between them.

Yencheng, Honan
December 6, 1947

Dearest Mother:

This is Saturday night and I thought I would get a letter off to you tonight before I get started on such a busy week next week. I received your most recent letter this last week in just seven days. Can you imagine such good time? I surely was surprised because letters coming from Shanghai now take about six or eight days. And for your letter to come all the way from New York in seven days surely is wonderful.

Our weather has not been so nice lately. The cold weather that descended on us like a lion two weeks ago has not let up at all. If it wasn't for my stadium boots, I don't know how I would keep my feet warm. The wind is terrible and it is hard to get our hospital laundry dry in weather like this. We hadn't had a frost before and suddenly it just froze everything. I covered my strawberry plants with straw to keep them from freezing. You know how I love strawberries. I was so looking forward to strawberries next year.

With all the new lovely things that we have managed to put together here, our situation is not so very good and it looks more serious all the time. The Communists will probably take over this entire area about the first of the year. Now I have started repacking all of our things and shipping them to Hankow so we won't lose them. I got twenty-one cases of drugs sent off yesterday on the train. It sort of breaks my heart to have to work so hard for a place then have to see it pass off the scene of action again. Now I will be extra busy all this week getting things packed again in boxes and getting them off for Hankow. Dear me, it is disheartening.

I need to pack my own things and send them down to Hankow because what I do not send I will probably lose. It is sad to think of all this moving just after getting settled, but that shows that we are not to plan on anything as secure in this world. I should be packing my own things right now, but I just don't have the heart for it. I know I must, but I thought I would get this letter off to you first and then when I start packing I won't have to worry about stopping to write to you.

Although an air mail letter costs 43,000 Chinese dollars—just over 50 cents U.S., I guess I will be able to send you only air mail letters from now on. I think everyone will have to wait awhile for regular mail.

You will be receiving a check from the General Conference for $200. It is for that stove that you wanted that you said you would have to wait for until spring. Well, you can buy it now, or if not, you can buy a fur coat if you want to. The price for fur coats here is simply awful at $1,000 U.S. or more. I couldn't pay that price so I just couldn't buy any. Maybe you can look and see if you can find one for $200. Or you can take the money and take some out of my bank account there and get the stove. I told Miss Landrum in Shanghai to wire the money to the States and the General Conference would send it on to you.

Well, I had better close this letter and get started with my packing. I hate to do this, but maybe I had better. I hope this finds you well and I am wondering if you will go to Ruth's for Christmas. Remember me to Aunt Emma and Aunt Mary. Give my love to Amelia and Walter when you see them.

Loads of love from your loving daughter,

Gertrude

Chapter 60

MAKING THE DECISION

Morning and evening, as was her daily custom, Gertrude had her own private prayers. She had worship with the nursing students every morning at 6:00 o'clock and every evening at 7:00 o'clock. But Gertrude's personal prayer time was taken in the privacy of her bedroom, sitting up at the head of her bed with her legs tucked under herself, her pillows tucked in at her back against the headboard. Unlike her public prayers, her private prayers were conversational in tone and demeanor. She guilelessly displayed her thoughts and concerns to God as an innocent child would show her colored drawings to a trusted parent, without apparent priority, in no particular order.

This Saturday evening was no exception. In a haphazard manner, similar to the letter she had just typed to her mother, Gertrude's thoughts tumbled out, one upon the other, to God.

Lord, you know the Communists are coming. As surely as winter is coming, they are coming. And I don't know what to do with everyone. Dr. Hwang is Chinese. They will force him to go with them and care for their army. You know what they are doing to families. Don't let them do that to our Chinese workers. And my nursing students. Some don't have homes nearby where they can go to escape whatever it is that conquering armies do to young, unmarried ladies.

Lord, we're having a board meeting tomorrow. Everyone of any authority on the compound will be there. And I have to chair it. And I have to act like I know what I am doing. And I don't. There are so many chiefs on this compound. I know it will be a big mess. I need your help. Show us the way.

Still praying, still thinking, Gertrude slipped down between her sheets and pulled the quilts up under her chin. Still beseeching God for the wisdom she needed, she fell asleep.

The next morning, for more than two hours, Gertrude sat at the head of the long table in the conference room at the school. Arrayed in front of her, sitting down both sides of the table were the leaders of the various compound organizations: the Chinese school principal, the Chinese publishing house director, the Chinese first elder of the church, the Chinese mission director, and several others. Behind each group leader perched a cadre of Chinese underlings, individually murmuring criticisms about every presentation and noisily sharing their opinions among themselves. The low level, constant buzz of Mandarin caused Gertrude to imagine, *Is this what it sounds like in a beehive?*

So far, Gertrude and Dr. McMullen were the only "foreign missionaries" to arrive in Yencheng. And thus far in the meeting, Dr. McMullen had said nothing. Two hours passed, and still only the Chinese were talking.

Gertrude herself had said little. She mostly listened and thought carefully about what was being said. But in her heart a fire of indignation was building in intensity, swelling to forest fire proportions.

I can understand why the Division brethren insist on having expatriates at the head of the various church organizations. All I've heard so far is fear and indecision: "The Communists are too frightening to face." "The hospital will be burned down." "We can only work with the Communists if they give us certain concessions." "Can I have so-and-so's house?" "We can't work with the Communists at all." "We should run away." "I just want to go home."

No one seems to have any backbone. And everyone is thinking only of themselves.

Gertrude scribbled a short note on her pad and slid it in front of Dr. Hwang who sat to her immediate left: *No one has any idea about how to work together. What's wrong with everyone?*

Hardly looking down, he quickly answered her incredulous inquiry with a note of his own: *They are afraid. Remember what Thelma said.*

Gertrude flashed back to three nights previously when she'd eaten supper with Paul and Thelma at their small apartment. Gertrude had been telling them what she was doing to prepare for the coming crisis, then asked what the Chinese were doing to get ready.

Thelma had looked up with her dark, penetrating gaze, her chopsticks poised above her plate like a predatory bird, and had quoted an old Chinese proverb: "In a crisis, the Chinese know 36 ways to escape the danger. The first is to run away."

Gertrude tried to hide the tightening of her jaw as she thought, *So far this morning—except for Pastor Pung—that's all I've heard from this group: how to run away and how to make it profitable for me or my organization.*

As if reading her mind, Paul pulled the notepad back and quickly scrawled: *Forgive them. They don't know what they are doing.*

As she read it, Gertrude recognized the Scriptural reference to Jesus' dying words on the cross. Her heart softened, allowing her own self-revelation to follow, *Neither do I.* Her face a stoic bastion of non-emotion, her eyes ranging over the sea of emotion-filled Chinese faces before her, Gertrude prayed quietly, *Lord, we don't know what we're doing. We need wisdom. We need a prophet.*

Then, at the far end of the table, Pastor Pung stood. His aged, skeletal features and long gray beard asked for a respectful silence—which he received, somewhat reluctantly, from the others. Although he raised his arms in an inclusive gesture to all the participants, his rheumy eyes, peering through perfectly round glasses, focused only on Gertrude as he spoke.

"Please. Let us thank our charitable chairwoman for patiently allowing all of us a chance to speak. Unfortunately, we have not come upon a plan that will help us prepare for what is about to happen."

Hearing a sudden, sharp intake of air from Paul Hwang, Gertrude realized Pastor Pung had just done what no one else was "elder" enough to do—politely criticize the entire group for their failure to find a workable solution to their problem. Her ears also told her that all conversation had ceased. It was absolutely quiet.

Taking advantage of the silence, Pastor Pung continued. "I move that Miss Green telegraph the mission officers in Hankow and ask them to come immediately and help us. Let us all pray to God that He will give them the wisdom to know what to do."

Following a hasty "second" by Dr. McMullen, the Mandarin buzz began again in earnest, eventually culminating in a yes vote on the motion and a welcome adjournment.

With a sigh of relief, Gertrude nodded her thanks to Pastor Pung, who bowed slightly in return, arose quietly, and left the room without speaking to anyone.

CHINA TELEGRAM SERVICE

SUNDAY, DECEMBER 7, 14:23 PM   HONAN MISSION UNION HANKOW
REQUEST MISSION OFICERS COME IMMEDIATELY STOP IMMEDEIATE THREAT NORTH STOP INDECISION

MONDAY, DECEMBER 8, 12:30 PM   YENCHENG HOSPITAL YENCHENG
BRIDGE OUT MINKIANG STOP ONLY TROOP TRAINS NORTH STOP COME NEXT AVAILABLE

THURSDAY, DECEMBER 10, 8:35 AM   YENCHENG HOSPI-TAL YENCHENG   TROOP TRAIN TODAY STOP THREE AR-RIVE FRIDAY AM

Thursday evening Gertrude had hospital cots set up in her bedroom to accommodate Merritt Warren, the Honan Union Mission president, Otis G. Erich, the secretary-treasurer of the mission, and Jerald E. Christensen, the newly-appointed "foreign" director of the Yencheng Mission.

In the crisp, cold air of a December Friday noon, Gertrude led the officers on an extended tour of the Yencheng Mission Compound, the four of them walking soldier-like, two by two in tandem. Elder Christensen, thin in body and face with chiseled cheek bones and pointed chin, stayed close to Gertrude's side. Through wireless glasses his thoughtful eyes seemed to caress every building as he questioned her closely about its occupants, seeming to memorize the information she gave him with an intensity she had not seen since her encounters with Dr. Miller. His boyish, tooth-filled grin and deep dimples, which she had seen at their initial introduction, were not in evidence now.

All of this is now his responsibility, she thought as she watched his serious contemplation. *What a time to be trying to grasp the basics.*

Following closely behind the other two, Elder Warren, older and shorter than the other two men, and Mr. Erich, taller by several inches and wider around the middle by several inches than the rest, were already familiar with Yencheng and its environs.

To the casual observer, this group appeared to be getting the same tour of the grounds that Gertrude had given the General Conference men and the Chinese CNRRA men just a few weeks before. In fact, this group was walking outside so as not to be overheard and not to give rise to wild rumors. The three men were earnestly absorbing Gertrude's report on the high anxiety level of the workers and the inability of the Chinese to decide what to do.

"Dr. Hwang and Dr. McMullen are attending to clinics this morning and making rounds on hospital patients twice a day to make it appear that we are still busy," Gertrude said quietly as they walked down several steps, crossing over a low wall into the hospital part of the compound. "In fact, most of the patients have gone. Just checked themselves out or disappeared in the night."

"I noticed that few students are in attendance at the school." Mr. Erich nodded over his shoulder to the school building they had just passed. "And not many teachers there either."

"No, they've all gone home, those that could get home," Gertrude said. "We had 300 students in the school, but not now."

"These are all hospital buildings?" Elder Christensen asked as his eyes swept over the three large buildings standing in a semicircle. He was still trying to grasp the enormity of the largest mission compound in central China.

"Yes, the far building is what used to be the Men's Building." Gertrude swept her arm forward, pointing for emphasis. "We've managed to repair the ground floor for office space and were just beginning to get the second floor ready for nursing school expansion." She blinked twice, her eyes growing gray with the contemplation of her dream project that would never be completed. "I have—that is, I *had* 30 nursing students. All but 16 have gone home or to the homes of relatives that live south of here. Those remaining are the boarding students in the school—they don't have anywhere to go—because all the roads north are blocked by the Communist army." Gertrude stopped walking and turned to address the men directly. She kept her voice low but the intensity was unmistakable. "The families of many of the students and hospital workers have moved to the compound here. Some are living in the

Chinese section and some are living in the empty rooms of the school itself. That's the reason you fellows are staying at my house. We have very little activity here, but lots of people.

"Without local families to take them in—and if we don't keep the institutions here open, most of these people will starve when winter comes."

"The Chinese seem fairly certain that the Communists will be here shortly." Elder Warren spoke aloud the conclusion he had already drawn from what he had seen and heard. "We would do well to heed the wisdom of the locals and leave while there is still time to do so in an orderly manner."

"Judging by the agitation I saw in the board meeting last Sunday, I'd say the time is just about gone." Gertrude gazed about her at the reason she had returned to China, her "home" here in Yencheng. *Don't listen to your heart. You've been here before. When the enemy comes, you have to leave*, she admonished herself.

Elder Christensen had turned away from the group, looking back over the other areas of the compound they had already visited: the church, the print shop, and the school. "Are you sure we have to abandon all this?" he asked, trying to speak hope into the others. "Are you sure we can't continue our work here in spite of the Communist presence?" He turned to face them. "I've worked with robbers and dissidents before—here in China," he reasoned.

"I have too, Jerald . . ." Elder Warren began.

"The Communists are *not* robbers," Gertrude cut in, her eyes flashing green fire. "They're different. They tear apart families. They kill intellectuals. They destroy society—as we know it. They want everyone to be as backward and ignorant as they are."

Now it was Elder Warren's turn to interrupt. "What Miss Green means to say is . . ." He nodded his head deferentially to Gertrude. "The Communists do not work well with doctors, teachers, administrators . . . or with those who promote Western Christianity."

"I think our teachers and doctors will be in great danger if they try to continue working here," Mr. Erich said thoughtfully.

"It makes me angry . . . and it makes me sad," Gertrude spoke more calmly. "We have worked so hard and now we have to walk away from it all . . . again." For a few moments no one spoke.

"Gertrude, make the rounds of your leadership people in the hospital this afternoon. Find out what they are willing to do and if they have a safe place where they would go if they could. And tell them that we're having a special meeting Sunday morning." Elder Warren turned and spoke to Mr. Erich. "Otis and I will talk with the school officials—those who are left—and the pastors." He turned to Elder Christensen. "Jerald, you talk to the printing house people. I think you know some of them from your days in Chungking during the war."

Elder Christensen nodded absently, absorbed in his own thoughts. "Correct. Several were workers of mine there."

"Supper is at my house at 4:30, boys," Gertrude said with a matronly grin. "Don't be late. Elder Warren, you're speaking at sundown worship at 6:00 o'clock."

"I'm never late for meals," Otis Erich said with a laugh, hitching up his belt over his ample tummy. "I'll get him there on time."

The two of them retreated in the direction of the school as Gertrude headed for the Women's Building, leaving Jerald Christensen still staring at the complex of hospital buildings and slowly shaking his head.

Yencheng Sanitarium and Hospital
Yencheng, Honan
December 13, 1947

Dearest mother:

Here it is another Saturday night and I thought I would follow last week's example and write to you late in the week, rather than at the first of the week, and be ahead of what I usually do. I have had a very busy week. We decided to pack all the hospital supplies and send them to Hankow so as not to lose them to the Communists. It has been a big job. I have the inventory to make for the 100 cases of drugs and supplies. They are in boxes now ready to go.

The weather has been real cold, but somehow I am getting used to it. I don't seem to mind as much as before.

Brother Erich and Elder Warren and Elder Christensen arrived yesterday morning and are staying here at my house. I had to round up some beds for them. They are having supper at the doctor's house tonight so I have time to write to you. They have come to hold committee meetings to see whether we should move our hospital or stay where we are in the present situation with the Communists. Elder Warren has had two wonderful services at the church—last night and again this morning. We had over six hundred in church this morning as everyone is here for the major workers' meeting tomorrow. Elder Christensen is the new Honan Mission Director so he will be staying longer than the others.

I tell you those Communists are really terrible. Not far from here is a town they have taken over. Those who fled came and told us all about what they did. Mr. and Mrs. Smith can like it and talk for it, but I tell you, we know what Communism is all about in all its bad forms. They pin numbers on everybody and mate them up by the numbers so that families are broken up. They make people put their babies on the ground and make the mothers march around in a circle and then pick up the baby that is right in front of them which of course is not theirs. They dig holes in the ground and stand a child in the hole for a day and a night with a number on their back. Then they give the child to whoever has that number. They do not honor the family system. It is simply terrible. The Chinese people fear these Communists worse than they ever feared the Japanese. I tell you the Smiths can have it!

I am keeping nice and warm in my house, not the whole house, but the kitchen and dining room. I moved my things from the living room and it is quite cozy now with fewer cracks for the heat to get out. My little kerosene heater and my kerosene cook stove are the best things I purchased in San Francisco. When Mrs. Longway heard I was out of wicks, she sent three along with the men who came up from Hankow. McMullens have the wickless type of kerosene stove and it is too difficult to work with. I am so thankful I have the wick type.

I used my last lemon filling for pie yesterday and I have one butterscotch pudding left. The union men who are staying with me surely liked my lemon pie. I am looking forward to the arrival of the next boxes in the mail. I just love to cook and regret that I don't have more time to do more of it.

Christmas is coming soon, but I have no idea that it is Christmas or anything else. I suppose the stores are all busy at home and things are humming around there aplenty. I guess I told you that $200 was coming to you from the General Conference for your birthday and Christmas present combined. Hope you receive it before too long. I hope that you have a very happy Christmas. Maybe Fred and Gloria will come up.

I must close for tonight and find myself a bite to eat. Give my love to Aunt

Mary and Aunt Emma and all the rest.

With loads of love from your loving daughter,

Gertrude

At 2:30 a.m. Gertrude was awakened by a loud rapping on her door. Already that night she'd been awakened three times by the occasional explosions that reverberated from north of the village of Loho. As she scrambled from her cot near the stove in the dining room, she remembered her guests in the bedroom and grabbed her robe, quickly pulling it on.

"Miss Green! Miss Green!" came a strident voice on the landing outside her door.

Gertrude jerked open the door in time to hear the not-so-distant sporadic rattle of machine gun fire.

"Miss Green, the Communists are coming!" It was the tall male nursing student from the second-year class, pointing toward the north, his eyes round as saucers. "They've blown up the railroad bridge north of Loho. They attack in the night and come take what they have conquered in the daytime. They will be here tomorrow to blow up the railroad station! They always do."

"Mr. Wen, I can hear them very clearly," she snapped. "They have kept me awake nearly all night. I have no doubt what they are doing."

"We should go now. Are you coming?" His voice was high pitched and quavering.

"No, I am not coming, Mr. Wen. I must stay here and do my work." Gertrude said, even as she flinched with the next explosion. "I must be free to do my work as usual." She inhaled slowly and exhaled, her hand clutching the doorknob. "I cannot make the patients nervous, nor the students nervous, Mr. Wen. And neither should you," she said more quietly. "Please, return to your quarters. I will see you at morning worship at 6:00 o'clock." Gertrude shut the door silently and returned to her bed, knowing she would not sleep.

Mr. Wen was not at the morning worship. Neither were the other three male nursing students. Neither was the Communist Army which seemed satisfied with its conquests of the evening before to the north of Loho.

Before she went back to her apartment to make breakfast for her house guests Gertrude decided to check on the wards to see which patients were still here and which had disappeared in the night.

At the far end of the second floor she spotted Dr. Hwang in one of the ward rooms. He was standing near a window in the pale early morning light, writing on a chart.

"Good morning, Miss Green," he said quietly in English. "Did you sleep well last night?"

"You know I did not, Dr. Paul," she said with mock exasperation, catching the merriment in his eyes that danced behind his glasses. "Did you?"

"No," he said, the merriment fading quickly. He continued writing for a moment. When he finished, he looked up. "We have only five patients left, counting the gunshot victim I have downstairs where I can watch him more closely."

Gertrude nodded as she looked around at the empty beds along the side wall. "I heard a large explosion this morning, bigger than the rest. Any rumor as to what it was?"

"It was the railroad bridge north of Loho."

"The train from Peking will not be coming, will it?" Gertrude absently gazed out the window as if searching for the truant train.

"No."

"Have you told Elder Warren?"

"Thelma and Jeannie are over at your apartment now, telling him."

Knowing that the Chinese almost never came into the "foreign missionary" part of the compound, Gertrude turned to him, studying his face. "She's very close to Elder Warren, isn't she?"

"She calls him Father Warren," Dr. Hwang said. Through the window his eyes sought out Gertrude's apartment crouching behind the trees just beyond the three hospital buildings. His face did not betray the anguish of his soul. "He was her major support . . . before you came." He paused, his eyes blinking twice. "He never lost faith in us."

"He's a prize, all right."

Paul turned his head and his eyes toward her. He tilted his head slightly to one side like a small puppy, his brow wrinkled in puzzlement.

"He has value," she explained. "He's worth keeping. A true friend."

Paul nodded in understanding.

"I'll see you at the 10:00 o'clock meeting," she said as she turned and made her way downstairs, heading to breakfast with her house guests.

The meeting was well attended by all the leadership of the entire mission compound. Gertrude watched from an aisle seat as Merritt Warren, flanked by Mr. Erich and Elder Christensen on the dais, addressed the quiet, somber group. He outlined briefly what had been learned overnight, that the Communists had control of the entire area just north of Loho and along both sides of the railroad track for 50 miles south. Only the area around Loho and Yencheng and the railroad corridor were still under the control of the Nationalist Army of China. He added that the prevalent opinion among the local political leaders was that the Communists would be in control of these areas by the first of January.

Today is the fourteenth. Gertrude did some mental arithmetic. *That's a little over two weeks. And it includes Christmas. What will that be like around here?*

Each of the leaders of the major organizations reported on what had been done to prepare for the inevitable Communist takeover. When it came to Gertrude's turn, she related that during the past two weeks she had sent much of the hospital supplies south by rail to Hankow. She had completed the inventory of the OR, pharmacy, and clinic supplies that still remained. Very few patients were in the hospital. Very little would be required to care for them.

The decision to close the school, the publishing house, and the hospital was obvious. The decision of what to do with the people who were stranded on the compound was more complex. The group decided to meet again the next day to discuss how to shut down the various organizations and what to do with the people who had nowhere to go.

Chapter 61

FACING WAR AGAIN

The small company of foreign missionaries plus the Hwangs had agreed to gather in back of the church sanctuary after lunch for a prayer meeting. Dr. Raymond and Zora McMullen were especially anxious to be reassured of what would happen to them. They had arrived only three months previously with hardly enough Mandarin-speaking ability to survive in peace time, let alone in a war zone. Paul and Thelma Hwang were torn between their Chinese cultural roots and their obvious identity with a Western religion and a Western medical education, neither of which would endear them to the Communists. Elder Jerald Christensen had left his family in Hankow when the emergency trip to Yencheng became necessary. He needed to decide whether to return to his family or to take up his responsibilities at his newly assigned post, dangerous as it might be.

Having sent the union officers on ahead to the church, Gertrude tidied up her kitchen and dining table while turning over in her mind all these possibilities along with her own options. Descending her outside staircase, Gertrude remembered the last time she had left Yencheng. There had been bomb craters in the yard that now lay before her, smooth and flowered. The hospital had been ransacked by the nurses. The houses were in ruins. The compound walls were layered with the bodies of dead refugees. None of that was true now.

Why am I running away? The hospital is in perfectly good working order, she argued as she passed the three buildings that she had thought would be her world for the foreseeable future. *Who knows but that the Communists might pass right on by and ignore us completely. After all, America is not at war with the Communists.*

There were two problems, she reminded herself. There were almost no patients in the hospital nor would there be until the Communists had gone. And there were 13 nursing students plus other Chinese workers and their families who had nowhere to go and no one to care for them in the coming winter. *I need to go to Hankow for their sakes,* she decided. *Once I get them settled there and the war situation settles down here, perhaps I can return with Dr. Hwang and my supplies and take up where we left off.*

Gertrude entered the rear of the church just as Elder Warren rose to speak. She slipped into a pew next to Thelma, who reached out a hand to her. Gertrude enfolded Thelma's hand in hers and squeezed. Jeannie, sitting quietly on her mother's lap, felt the bodily movement and looked around to see what had happened. On seeing her "Aunt" Gertrude, Jeanne quietly slid onto Gertrude's lap and settled there with her dolly cradled dutifully in her folded arms.

"I have two announcements to make that will affect us all," Elder Warren began as he stood between two pews in front of the assembled group. "Elder Christensen has informed me that he will be staying here in Yencheng even though I have reminded him that it might be too dangerous." As Jerald Christensen rose from his seat, Elder Warren turned and invited him to speak. "Elder Christensen. Please."

"I realize that to stay behind is dangerous and I am glad that my family is not here. But I have just been called to this field to serve, and I can't leave the work like this," he said.

Gertrude took a deep breath, mentally reviewing her own decision, as she watched him sit down.

Elder Warren spoke again. "Dr. Paul Hwang has informed me that he too will be staying in Yencheng to keep the hospital open and care for the patients who remain there."

Gertrude drew in a sharp breath as she snapped her head around in the direction of the Hwang family. Thelma's face never changed. Perhaps she already knew. Paul did not move.

Instead Dr. McMullan stood, shuffling off 5-year-old Ronnie to his mother. "But I'm the one who should be staying," he blurted out even as he was rising. Zora McMullen stiffened as her hand flew to her mouth, almost dropping their child.

Slowly Paul stood. He looked directly at Raymond McMullen and spoke slowly and distinctly. "I want to tell you. At this time you do not know the language or the people and what they will do in a crisis. This is unfair to ask you to take care of this, whether we stay open or we close. I have been here enough time to keep the hospital open and whatever the Lord will direct, I am willing to accept that. But it is better for you to retreat with the party and with Elder Warren. I think your wife will need you."

"But what about your wife?" Dr. McMullen protested.

From the pew beside Gertrude came a sharp reply. "I have to get the money of the hospital and the school out of the city," Thelma said in her crisp Australian English. "If I do not, the Communists will take it to finance their war. Mr. Erich has been working with me to get all of the accounts closed. We will carry the money with us—on our persons—to Shanghai."

Dr. McMullen opened his mouth to respond and felt a hand slip into his and pull downward. He gazed down into the pleading eyes of his wife and sat down.

"The Lord is glorified. The Lord has people He can use," Elder Warren said solemnly. "May the Lord bless you in your wisdom," he said to the two men. "I know that the Lord will be with you."

"Elder Warren," Gertrude said, moving Jeannie to her other knee so she could see him better. "I think I need to stay here and help Dr. Hwang." Paul had said that Dr. McMullen would need someone to help him run a hospital. Now Gertrude would need to help Dr. Paul Hwang run this hospital. She was certain of it.

"But I will need you to care for all the women and children who must go out with us, Gertrude," Elder Warren said. "I think I will need both you and Thelma to manage all of them."

"There are 36 Chinese," Thelma said, never thinking of herself as one of them. "Plus all of us. Without Paul and Elder Christensen, that makes 44." Her accounting mind did the sums easily.

Suddenly the front door of the church rattled loudly as it was flung open.

"Miss Green! Miss Green!" It was one of the hospital workers, speaking in excited Mandarin.

"I'm here," Gertrude responded, standing up and handing Jeannie back to Thelma.

"Miss Green, the stationmaster says that only one more train is coming from the south," he said, advancing into the darkness of the church sanctuary.

"It cannot go on to Peking because the bridge is out. It will return to Han-kow at 4:00 p.m. Because the Communists will probably blow up our train station, there will be no more trains. He says to come at 4:00 p.m. today if you want to go to Hankow."

Gertrude had made her way to the messenger during his frantic speech. Patting him on the arm to thank him and to calm him, she turned to the group. "What do we do?" she asked no one in particular.

"We have a 4:00 o'clock train to catch," Elder Warren said without humor. "Gertrude and Thelma, you two pack for yourselves what you need. One suitcase for each that you can carry and one trunk each. Then organize the women and children who have to go with us with the same instructions." He turned and pointed at Elder Christensen. "Jerald, go to the train station and buy the tickets we need." Jerald nodded. "Mr. Erich and I will talk with the publishing house people about hiding the printing presses. Then we will organize the wheelbarrows needed to carry all the luggage to the station." He looked at the McMullens. "With Ronnie there, you will have all you can do to pack for the three of you.

He paused a moment until he had made eye contact with each one. "Leave what must be left to continue the hospital work. Take only one suitcase and one trunk per person, that's all. Leave everything else." He paused again. "But let's seek the Lord in prayer before we go."

Eight adult heads bowed while two small children looked on.

It took almost no time at all for the news to spread across the compound that the foreign leaders were "abandoning" the mission and its work. Absolute panic ensued. Almost everyone deserted their work stations and stampeded to the railway station.

Gertrude did not run from the church, but her pace rivaled that of most professional walkers. Bounding up the staircase to her apartment, two steps at a time, Gertrude attempted to think and to pray even as she tried to organize her priorities, her possessions, and her responsibilities.

Think, Gertrude, think. Dear Lord, what do I need to take for the nursing students? What do they not have that they must absolutely . . .

She stood still in the middle of her kitchen floor.

Get hold of yourself, dearie. You've done this before. This is only a 24-hour trip, not a month's leave of absence. A wide smile spread over her face with the thought of Dr. Miller's dismay at her large collection of luggage when she first arrived in China.

She took a deep breath and considered. Slowly a plan unfolded of packing Christmas gifts purchased, extra underwear, uniforms purchased for her graduating senior nurses, and enough clothes for her to stay in Hankow until she could return to Yencheng or until . . . whatever happened next. At any rate, she would be near a store somewhere, for sure, in 36 hours. In 20 minutes Gertrude had packed her trusty brown suitcase, a slightly larger, plaid companion bag, and the metal-banded stateroom trunk that stood at the end of her bed. She placed them by her front door. Then Gertrude took her large medical bag from her closet and headed for the hospital.

From the pharmacy and the supply room, she selected medicines, suture kits, gauze rolls, and bandage kits. Whatever came to her mind that she might need, she confiscated and tucked inside her medical bag. *Lord, what do I need to take?* was her continual prayer. The only answer: *You never know what you'll need.*

Gertrude returned to her apartment to retrieve the packed luggage. She was about to call her cook to bring around the wheelbarrow when an unbidden thought—almost audible—pressed into her mind. *Dress warmly. It's the middle of the winter.* Unconsciously, quizzically, she peered at the living room furniture and the far corners of the kitchen. Finding no one there, she paused for a moment, then headed for the bedroom. She emerged dressed in her padded Chinese pants, her long, padded Chinese coat, and her stadium boots—all covered by her long fur-lined overcoat and topped off with her fur traveling cap.

As she reached for the glass doorknob on the front door, she paused and looked back at her desk area. Turning, she crossed the small space, closed the black lid of the case over her portable typewriter, and picked it up. Hefting it for appreciation of weight, she carried it to where her luggage awaited, setting it on the floor on its little, brass button feet. Then she opened the front door and called for the cook.

Carrying her portable typewriter, Gertrude emerged from between the high and heavy wooden wings of the compound front gate followed closely by her cook *cum* gardener. He was pushing the flat wheelbarrow he used for transporting pots to the garden, only now it was loaded with Gertrude's trunk and two suitcases. She was preparing to defend her extra suitcase until she saw Merritt Warren laboring with Raymond McMullen about the gigantic suitcase he was attempting to transfer from a wheelbarrow to a small cart parked in from of him. Sitting on the ground next to Zora McMullen and her small child were five more large suitcases awaiting their turn to be loaded.

"Dr. McMullen, this is too heavy to carry and too cumbersome to be lifted easily, like a trunk," Elder Warren explained in a calm voice that did not match the pained expression on his face.

"But I can't leave my dresses behind," Zora interjected, as she struggled to control their 5-year-old Ronnie. "Heaven knows what the Chinese will do with them.

Do all Texas females sound that childish? Gertrude thought. Gertrude had never thought Zora McMullen was other than a foolish and impractical Southern belle.

"Besides we need things for the boy," Dr. McMullen panted, heaving the monstrous valise onto the small horse cart.

"Raymond," Elder Warren said, purposefully using the doctor's first name and avoiding any professional appellation, "at least repack the other suitcases. You cannot carry those five and the boy, too. One of you will have to carry Ronnie. One of you will have to carry two suitcases." He paused for emphasis. "You do have smaller suitcases, don't you?"

"We do," Dr. McMullan responded, his short, thick body still breathing heavily with the exertion of transporting all of their suitcases to the front gate on the wheelbarrow.

They argued about this before they came here. Gertrude watched the furtive eye contact between husband and wife and knew the truth.

"I strongly suggest that you repack those other bags into two smaller suitcases that you can carry," Elder Warren advised. "Otherwise you might be forced to leave behind essential items—at a moment's notice—when you least expect it. And have everything at the station by 4:00 o'clock."

Gertrude eyes narrowed as she thought back to a particular day when the Japanese airplanes were firing and the rickshaw pullers were running through the market and she lost two rickshaws full of luggage. *He's right. You never know when something will be left behind.*

Zora McMullen hung on her husband's arm, attempting to protest while he wheeled the five large, varicolored bags back through the gates to their home. Elder Warren had turned his attention to other travelers who were adding more than their share to the growing pile of luggage. Gertrude spotted Paul and Thelma Hwang standing near the wall on the far side of the gate, engaged in a family embrace with Jeannie. As she approached them, she saw Thelma brushing away tears and heard Paul's quiet words.

"If anything happens to me that I don't see you again, be sure to bring up Jeannie for Jesus," he was saying.

Thelma's lower lip trembled, though her black eyes and upturned face were clearly focused on Paul. Jeannie, resting in the crook of Paul's arm, looked from one parent to the other trying to comprehend in her 2-year-old mind what was happening.

As she got closer, Gertrude saw Paul look her way, then beyond her, and smile shyly. As she was about to turn, Elder Warren stepped up beside her.

"Paul, will everything be ready by 4:00 o'clock?"

"Yes, Father Warren," Paul replied. He shifted Jeannie into his two hands and placed her in the arms of Elder Warren. He placed his hands together in front of his chest and bowed at the waist. "Please take care of my family in Hankow. You know my brothers and where my family are in Shanghai."

"Brother Paul, they will be to me as my own," Merritt Warren said.

Gertrude observed this exchange of vows, knowing she would never feel the heartache of separation from a spouse or the anxiety of care for a child. She missed the intimacy but did not miss the responsibility. It was going to be hard enough caring for the 36 Chinese women in their entourage.

Paul reached behind him and came up with a long, rounded package, a case of sorts, that had been sitting against the wall. "Take this with you," he said, handing it to Thelma.

"It's your French-made violin," she said, recognizing it. "Why take it?"

"It may be worth something, maybe $80, if you need the money," he said.

Gertrude watched Thelma's face cloud with worry. Then Thelma thrust the violin case into Gertrude's arms and reached down for her ever-present business briefcase. The violin or the money had triggered some concern, Gertrude surmised.

"Paul, I have my control pass and my Australian passport. But I can't find your papers." Thelma attempted to hold her briefcase open, balancing it on her small, outstretched arm while rummaging through it for the missing papers.

Elder Warren touched Gertrude on the arm. Handing Jeannie to her, he said, "Help them be ready to go by 4:00 o'clock. I have to see what I can do about getting this mountain of luggage to the train station." And he turned away.

The Yencheng railroad station was a scene of panic and chaos. Men, women, and children were running about, shouting and gesturing, trying to purchase nonexistent tickets or barter for space on a train that had not yet arrived. Every contraption of Chinese transportation was being driven or ridden to the station, each loaded with bedrolls, boxes, and crates of live animals.

Walking on each side of the hospital group of people, Gertrude and Thelma herded them through the teeming masses like a barge through turbulent water. Spotting Jerald Christensen standing near the main track, Gertrude pointed toward him and Thelma nodded in acknowledgment. Together they turned their charges in his direction until they had them "corralled" near where they hoped the train would stop.

Elder Warren, Mr. Erich, and Dr. McMullen were riding herd on a dozen coolies as they ran a shuttle service of wheelbarrows back and forth to the station. Soon a large pile of footlockers, small trunks, great bags, and bedrolls had accumulated next to the women. They, in turn, had used the luggage to create a small housekeeping area in which they were caring for small children and attending to family chores.

"We have more than 100 pieces of luggage stacked here," Elder Warren whispered, sidling up near Gertrude's left elbow and causing her to jump.

Mercy, this man can move quietly, she thought, collecting herself. *He's spent too much time in China.* She whispered in turn, "Seems like about the right number, considering we have 44 in our group."

"The difficulty will be trying to load it all on the train in a short time," he responded. "This pandemonium will be nothing compared to what will happen when that train arrives."

Out of the corner of her eye Gertrude could see him surveying the surging masses that surrounded the train station and covered all the various tracks along its loading platform. She imagined the stampede for the train, and nodded.

"I'm going to have the coolies remain here to take back what we can't load on the train. I hope people have packed their essentials in small carry-along bags," he worried.

"I wouldn't count on that," she said with a dry laugh.

"Probably not."

"And I wouldn't count on anything being here when we get back."

This time it was Elder Warren's turn to nod in agreement.

At 4:00 o'clock all 44 of the emigrating group from the Yencheng Mission Compound were present. All 100 pieces of luggage were stacked about them in a makeshift fort. But the train did not appear.

At 4:30 the masses milling about the station became restless. Ripples of rumors spread over the crowd, crashing into one another in splashes of excitement and anger: "The train is not coming." "There is no train." "The train has turned back." "The Communists are coming from the north on their own train." Several groups besieged the stationmaster's office, thrusting hands angrily through the ticket window bars, demanding answers, demanding money. The stationmaster closed the ticket window shutters and locked the station.

"What are they saying?" Dr. McMullen implored, shouting to be heard above the din.

Gertrude hurried to where he was huddled on the ground with his small family, his wife's face buried in his shoulder. She knelt beside them.

"Best I can tell," Gertrude said, "they all seemed to think there was a train coming from Peking, going south. We know that's not true. The bridge north of us was blown up last night."

"Then what are we waiting for?" Dr. McMullen pressed.

"The train that is coming from the south, from Hankow." Gertrude tried to remain calm, tried to speak objectively. "We know it can't go north and will have to return south. And we will be on board when it does." She touched him lightly on the shoulder and stood up to view the near riot that was unfolding around her.

Thelma moved next to her, holding Jeannie on her hip. Gertrude watched

Thelma's hard face and black eyes scan the crowd, disgust oozing from every pore. *She thinks she is Chinese until the Chinese do something she despises, then she disowns them and thinks she is Australian. If I live here 100 years, I think I will not understand the Chinese.*

Gertrude followed Thelma's gaze between the stacked boxes and into the crowd that was beginning to disperse. The people's anger was being replaced by fear as they realized that *no* train was coming which birthed an accompanying conclusion that the Communists *were* coming. Within half an hour, no one remained at the station except the small mission band inside their fortification of luggage.

By 7:30 that evening everyone had eaten the meager meal they had intended to eat on the train. Darkness was settling in. Elder Warren and Mr. Erich had circulated among the group all through supper, reassuring them with the tickets that Elder Christensen had purchased, reassuring them that a train was coming up from Hankow. Suddenly from out of the darkness came a voice and then the figure of a man running toward the train station. He was shouting to the stationmaster, still locked in his station.

"The Communists are coming. They are only five *li* to the north."

Everyone inside the little fortress heard him plainly. The stationmaster heard him and responded by rushing out of the station, closing and locking the door, the two of them running away into the darkness. Inside the little fortress, the whispering started.

Gertrude scooted over next to Elder Warren. "I think you'd better talk to Thelma," she said softly in English. "Those coolies aren't going to stay out here if any shooting starts."

"I already have," he whispered back. "She's talking with Otis about how much money they can spare. We're going to need those coolies if we have to move everything back to the compound."

Gertrude peered through the darkness to her right and saw Otis Erich and Thelma Hwang huddled in the far corner with the coolies. Thelma's voice rose and fell in rapid, forceful Mandarin. The coolies would stay for a little while. *But how long should we stay here?*

At 9:00 o'clock machine gunfire began up north. The evening's offensive was beginning; the Communists were on the move. And the whispering began again inside the small enclosure, but no one moved.

The young children who were still awake heard it first. When she saw them standing and pointing, Gertrude stood up to listen, peering down the tracks to the southeast. She couldn't see it. *They probably have their headlight turned off*, she guessed. But she could hear it. The train was coming!

By the time the train ground to a halt, Gertrude and Thelma had the women and children, including Mrs. McMullen and her son, organized and prepared to board. The space between the first passenger car and the preceding boxcar was lined up perfectly with the luggage.

"Thelma, Gertrude, get the women on board," Elder Warren called out in Mandarin. In English, he added, "Men, let's get these bags loaded before that engineer figures out what's happening and decides to back out of here in a hurry."

Merritt Warren, the smallest of the three men, leaped up into the gap between the cars, calling the two coolies to follow him. From there he could direct the flow of luggage, watch the coolies, and help Gertrude and Thelma with the female escapees. While she hustled the women and children up the steps and into the car, Gertrude saw Mr. Erich and Dr. McMullen toss boxes and bags up to the three men in the gap. They were stacking some bags in the passageway normally used to pass from car to car, stashing many of the trunks and larger bags in the boxcar immediately forward of the gap. Thelma led and Gertrude pushed their charges into the aisle of the already crowded, third-class car until they were standing body to body so closely it was impossible to fall down.

Just as she was wondering where to put the men, Gertrude saw Elder Warren squeeze through the doorway and began piling the smaller hand bags and carry-on cases on top of the passageway suitcases. When they had stacked the doorway full of bags, Elder Warren took the money for the coolies from Thelma and handed it over the luggage to someone who presumably paid the coolies and dismissed them. Then Raymond McMullen appeared up near the ceiling, crawling over the bags and into the car. In a moment, and with a little more difficulty, Mr. Erich followed him. With a lurch the train began backing along the track by which it had arrived.

We're on a third-class car with no heat, no beds, and little food, Gertrude sighed, *but in 36 hours we'll be in Hankow.*

A powerful explosion shook the train and its passengers. Gertrude shot a glance at Elder Warren as the same thought passed between them, *The railroad bridge in Yencheng.*

Chapter 62

RIDING THE TRAIN THAT WOULD NOT GO

The train stopped, jolting Gertrude awake. She had slumped against Mr. Erich in the packed conditions and had slept while standing. Gertrude looked around for the others. She knew that Thelma was at the other end of their group although she couldn't see her in the dark. The McMullens were pushed together to her right against the wall, in the corner, held upright by the press of the crowd. She could see Dr. McMullen's head moving and assumed he was awake also.

In her bulky clothes Gertrude tried to bend over and look out the window to see where they were. No lanterns were lit anywhere; shadows of buildings were barely visible.

"I think we're in Suiping," said a tenor voice far above her.

Gertrude tried to draw back and was unable to. She looked up a good 12 inches into the shadowed face of Otis Erich. "I'm sorry to be using you for a pillow," she apologized.

"It's OK," he mumbled quietly. "We're all doing it. I don't think Elder Warren has moved since we left Yencheng."

Gertrude could just make out Merritt Warren's silhouette against the baggage in the doorway. The train started up again; the rocking motion was hypnotic. Gertrude's eyes gradually closed as she drifted into sleep.

When the train stopped again, lantern light was coming in the window and people were walking about outside. Gertrude squinted at her nursing watch, trying to twist her arm around into the light to see the dial.

Two a.m. She calculated the time since leaving Yencheng. *Two and a half hours. About 60 or 70 miles. One quarter of the way to Hankow. Where are we now?"*

She bent sideways and peered under the upper edge of the window. The sign above the station said, "Chumatien."

By the time most of the passengers were awake, Gertrude, Otis Erich, Elder Warren, and two of Gertrude's nursing students had managed to stack enough luggage into the corner opposite the McMullens to create a small path where even Mr. Erich could squeeze out of the train car. Not that anyone would want to. It was snowing outside and a cold wind was blowing.

Answering the call of nature and in search of food for the others, Gertrude had already been outside and was coming in the door as Thelma and Jeannie prepared to squeeze their way out.

"Hope you're ready for *kongee*," Gertrude said as they passed. "That's all I can find."

"What's *kongee*?" Zora McMullen asked from the far corner.

"It's flour and water soup, Zora, the flour sometimes becoming little lumps, like small dumplings," Gertrude tried to explain. "In good times there are vegetables cut up and stuffed in the dumplings. But these aren't the good times."

"What do you mean?" Dr. McMullen asked.

"It's the beginning of winter. The Chinese have just a few vegetables to see their family through until spring. They won't sell them to us. It's a bad time to be traveling and trying to eat from the vendors out there." Gertrude pointed to the window. Turning to the students, she said, "Sarah, take Annabelle with you and this money. I think you can find enough *kongee* for all of us. But make them sell you the pot to carry it in and don't pay a fortune for it." Gertrude had already found bowls enough to go around.

Before the girls returned, Elder Warren entered the car.

"Good news and bad news," he said, brushing the snow from his hair. "The Communists have blown up the bridge just south of here. But, the stationmaster assures me that the bridge will be repaired quickly and we can be on our way."

Gertrude glanced around at the third-class passenger car that now held four times the number of people it was designed for—people in various stages of dressing and feeding families—and slowly shook her head. It was going to be a long trip to Hankow.

"Oh, by the way," Elder Warren added, "the Bank of China got several people and three or four money boxes on the train in Suiping. They're in the car on the other side of our boxcar."

"Makes us all the more attractive to the Communists," Gertrude noted with a wry smile. "It's nice to know we have such rich neighbors."

By mid morning the wind had picked up. A blizzard was blowing outside. The Nationalist Chinese Army guards, who had been posted around the station and the train, went inside—somewhere. The passengers on the train who had been milling about on the station platform had crowded back into the cars. The body heat being generated in such cramped quarters inside was preferable to the raging cold outside. As the darkness of the blizzard brought on an early evening, there was no food available except for what little nourishment a few had with them and the *kongee* they'd eaten at breakfast. The adults were able to do without. The children were crying.

Over the heads of the nursing students Gertrude could see Thelma halfway down the aisle. She was shifting from foot to foot, holding Jeannie first on one hip and then on the other. Thelma had no place to lay her and no place to sit down.

Gertrude pushed and squeezed her way between the people standing in the aisle. "Thelma, I'm coming," she called out in English.

"Oh, I didn't know what to do," Thelma said as Gertrude lifted Jeannie's sleeping form over her shoulder. "I prayed and prayed for strength but I just couldn't hold her up anymore."

"I know," Gertrude said as she hoisted Jeannie with her other arm. *I didn't know a 2-year-old could weigh so much,* she thought. "I'll just stand here and hold her for a little while. Give you a chance to rest a bit."

Most of the small children had cried themselves to sleep and the larger children had stopped asking for food. But Ronnie was still crying. Gertrude could see Dr. McMullen in the far corner trying to hold the sobbing boy and at the same time to comfort his wife who was crying almost as hard as the child.

In the graying interior shadows of dusk, Gertrude caught the form of Merritt Warren heading for the McMullen corner.

"The boy is too old to be crying like that," Thelma was saying in English, not quite under her breath. "He's 5 years old already. You'd think he would run out of tears after a while."

I would be embarrassed to be making such a scene. Gertrude, only half listening, shook her head slowly in righteous disapproval. *Zora McMullen is of no more use now than she was on the compound. Dr. McMullen pampers them both.* Gertrude repeated in her mind all the phrases she and Thelma had shared.

"He's pampering them both," Thelma echoed aloud.

Gertrude heard a commotion in the McMullen corner. Was it Zora striking out? Was it Raymond McMullen clutching at a falling child? Whatever it was, Gertrude had seen enough. It was time to put a stop to this childish temper tantrum, both mother and son. Gertrude handed Jeannie back to Thelma and made her righteous way to the front of the car.

As she determinedly approached the small bellicose conference in progress, Gertrude heard the strident voice of Zora McMullen speaking between sobs.

"He's all I have." Zora choked out the words. "I never see my husband. I didn't, even when we were in the States. He's always working!" Tears flowed from her eyes. Her chest heaved with sobs. "My family is 7,000 miles away and I don't speak very good Chinese." She stopped with a gasp, and blew her nose. "Actually, I hardly speak it at all. And Ronald is all I have. He's all I have! And now this!" Zora spread her arms as best she could in the crowded car. "I know I could lose him," she cried. "I could lose him."

Her arms went limp, dropping to her sides; her head sagged onto her chest as if drawn down by a great weight. She looked like she had stopped breathing.

Gertrude stopped just short of the group, a vision, a memory forming in her mind. *Gert Loewen looked just that way when I accompanied her to Hawaii.* Gertrude could see her sitting in the deck chair, so forlorn and alone, even in the presence of others. *Why is it different now? Why do I not have the same feelings for Zora that I had for Gert?*

For all the times I've had to leave things behind, lost things I liked—what is it now— five or six times? I have never come close to losing a child. I will never be a mother.

Gertrude stepped forward and held out her arms to Dr. McMullen who, though startled, handed over the quietly crying child. Gertrude hoisted him on her left arm, slid the other arm around the shoulders of Zora McMullen and held them both close.

By 7:00 p.m. the blizzard had let up; the snow had stopped falling and the wind had abated. Elder Warren called a leadership council on the loading platform outside the train, away from ears unaccustomed to hearing all sides of an argument and to discussing all options, even those that might be unpleasant.

Elder Erich's large frame made an excellent windbreak, especially as he was flanked by Dr. McMullen's chubby girth on one side and Gertrude in her long fur coat over her padded Chinese winter clothes on the other. Elder Warren and Thelma, the smallest members of the group, stood facing them.

"It's obvious to everyone that this trip is not going as planned," Elder Warren began. All heads nodded. "So, there is a decision to be made and I don't want to make it alone."

"If it has to do with getting off this train, I'm for it," Gertrude interjected. "I don't think we can stay here another night without heat."

"And without food," Thelma added.

When all heads nodded again, Elder Warren continued. "I thought you would all agree. But the questions is, Where do we go if we don't stay on the train? The stationmaster tells me that the Communists are coming from the south as well as the north. We can't stay here."

"I don't want to be out in the open where someone can drop a bomb on us," Gertrude said, eyes flashing angrily. "These Communists . . ."

"Don't have airplanes." Otis Erich completed her sentence.

"But they have guns and they have dynamite," she shot back.

"What Mr. Erich means to say," Elder Warren interposed, "is that the Communists may not be our worst enemy."

"The weather is," Dr. McMullen observed.

"Quite correct," Elder Warren said. "It's the middle of the winter." He paused. "The other enemy is that we are missionaries."

"Why is that a problem?" Dr. McMullen asked, his voice rising incredulously. "I thought they liked us."

"In a time of war, everyone is suspected," Elder Warren explained, "especially foreigners —and especially foreigners who espouse a Western religion. In a world of corrupt governments and high taxes, revolutionaries and destruction . . ."

"And bandits and looting," Thelma added.

"Yes, the criminal element as well," he acknowledged. "We are seen as one more destabilizing force, suspected by everyone."

"Which is why we can't go to a hotel tonight," Otis Erich observed. "We would put the hotel manager in great danger. The Communists would burn the place down if they found us there." He thought a moment and added, "And we can't go to the Catholic mission. I know the people there, and they would take us in. But the Communists . . ."

"And the Chinese people . . . they don't like Catholics." Even in the shadows under the platform overhang, Gertrude could see the strong firm line of Thelma's mouth as she spoke. Gertrude knew it was true. She had heard these same sentiments from patients. The Catholic Church had treated people harshly and had taken sides in local government political squabbles, usually on the side of repressive government policies. It was true. The Catholics were not liked.

"So where does that leave us?" Raymond McMullen asked.

"Now, where are we again? What town?" Gertrude was thinking aloud. "Chumatien," she said with conclusive satisfaction as she recalled her train trip from Hankow. "I traveled with two young women, Mennonites, I think, who were coming here to Chumatien. Yes, one was American and one was Canadian," she concluded. "And their mission is somewhere here in this city." She looked about as if she might spot their building in the immediate vicinity.

"OK. It's a long shot," Elder Warren said, glancing at Otis Erich for a confirmatory nod. "Otis, you and Raymond find us some coolies to transport the luggage. Thelma, go prepare Mrs. McMullen and the other women for the move." He turned to Gertrude with a nod and a smile of thanks. "Let's go find your Mennonites, Gertrude. See if they'll take in some Seventh-day Adventists."

The Mennonites were easy to find and exceedingly gracious in welcoming the entire party to share their small, but warm quarters. With the judicious application of money Mr. Erich and Dr. McMullen organized a wheelbarrow convoy to transport—over the railroad tracks and through the snow—the 100 pieces of luggage from the train. Likewise Gertrude and Thelma Hwang guided and accompanied the women and children past the ditches and over the stone slabs that crossed open sewers, to the Mennonite mission compound.

By Monday midnight Merritt Warren had extracted a promise from the stationmaster that he would send for them when the train was ready to move, the cook was standing guard at the gate, listening for any word of approaching Communists, and 44 Seventh-day Adventist refugees were lying under warm blankets for the first time in 36 hours. They slept in their clothes in case they had to run quickly, but the children's stomachs were full and the adults felt well hidden—and exhausted. No one cried that night.

Chapter 63

RETURNING HOME

On Tuesday morning the blizzard returned with a vengeance. Every two or three hours the faithful cook reported what news he had heard. Villages all around had been looted and burned by bandits. The militia, the police, and all the city officials had fled Chumatien. Stores and the hotels were being looted by the poor and the opportunists. There was no word of the Communists.

With nothing else to do, the missionaries waited. They held prayer meetings twice a day. They read their Bibles and chapters from *Christ's Object Lessons*, a Seventh-day Adventist book based on Christ's teachings in His parables, that happened to be in the Mennonite library. They played with and fed their children. When the rumors of looting came, they hid their valuables in an unused potbellied stove in the back of the kitchen and stayed out of sight. They waited for news from the train.

Wednesday morning the snowstorm finally let up. Elder Warren, guided and protected by the watchful, trustworthy cook, went in search of information about their train. Two hours later he returned. He slowly removed his coat, looking directly at no one, his face as inexpressive as a Chinese stone statue, while everyone pressed around him clamoring for news. Still without speaking, he motioned them all into sitting positions around him and sat on a chair in their midst.

"I have good news and bad news," he said solemnly in Chinese. Gertrude translated this into English for the benefit of the McMullens.

"During the lull in the snowstorm, the stationmaster found that the train had been booby-trapped. If the train had moved, it would have been blown up." Darting her startled eyes back and forth between Elder Warren and the McMullens, Gertrude strained to contain her anxiety while she translated. "The good news is that the train officials removed the booby traps and immediately sent the train back to Yencheng—yesterday."

"That's the good news?" Gertrude snapped, forgetting about her translation duties.

"You haven't heard the bad news yet," he said in English, fixing her with a level gaze. "Better translate what I said for Zora and Raymond." Fuming, Gertrude turned toward the McMullens and translated his last words. When she'd finished, Elder Warren continued in Mandarin, "The bad news is that on the way to Yencheng, the train was captured and burned by the Communists. Some of the people were taken captive."

Gertrude's eyes darted to Elder Warren's face, looking for more hopeful information. *Did any escape? Are you going to tell us more?* Watching his face, she slowly translated what he'd said, being careful to leave out the word "some." He listened while she spoke, never changing his expression.

"I assume that the money from the Bank of China survived—in the hands of the Communists," she said evenly, in English, when she had finished translating. *But the bank officials probably did not,* she thought, watching his face for any sign.

"I would assume so," he said, his head slowly nodding, his lips pressed in a tight, straight line.

"But I have other good news." His manner brightened. "I found a telephone." He turned to look at Thelma with a smile. "And I talked with Dr. Hwang in Yencheng."

"You did? Is he all right? What's happening?" Suddenly Thelma was up on her knees, and Jeannie, with her mother's arms around her waist, was dancing up and down, caught up in Thelma's excitement.

"He's fine," Elder Warren reassured her. "In fact, everything is quiet in Yencheng," he said, scanning the whole group. "The fighting is all around them, and they have many new patients. Wounded soldiers, and some villagers. But the hospital has not been molested. In fact, Dr. Hwang and Elder Christensen have invited us back—if we can get there."

"Is that a good idea?" Dr. McMullen's tone of voice suggested that it wasn't.

"I don't know," Elder Warren reflected. "Let's talk about it."

The Chinese women began discussing among themselves what all of this might mean for their families still caught in the crosshairs of the Communist onslaught around Yencheng. The five—very informal—committee members convened in the kitchen, tightly packed around a small table meant for four and more easily accommodating two.

In 20 minutes they'd outlined and explored three options: one—return home to Yencheng; two—find a truck or horse cart to take them over the motor road to Junan to the east and catch a train south from there; or three—stay where they were. Option two put them on the open road to Junan in the middle of the winter. Option three? Chumatien was becoming more unsafe by the hour. Reluctantly, they decided to return to Yencheng. After the noon meal, Elder Warren and Mr. Erich would return to the train station and try to find out if any train was scheduled to go north.

As the other committee members bumped against each other in their struggle to exit the kitchen, Elder Warren reached across the table and touched Gertrude on the shoulder. She paused, half standing, looking up at him.

"I'm sorry that you aren't still in Yencheng," he said sincerely. "I know I'm the one who insisted you come on this trek."

"I know. I've thought of that." Gertrude eyed him critically, then looked away to avoid a confrontation.

"But I don't think Thelma could have looked after everyone by herself," he added, leaning over the table to speak more quietly. "And Thelma couldn't have consoled Zora."

"I've thought of that, too," she said, her voice softening as she sidled out from the behind the table and followed the others out the room.

As evening descended, the cook reported that 100 Nationalist Chinese Army soldiers had returned and had set up guard positions around the station. Just before dark all of them had pulled out. What were they planning? What were they getting ready for? With the ever faithful cook as a guard, Elder Warren went out into the gently falling snow to the railroad station to find out.

Half an hour later he returned. "Get packed," he shouted as he came through the door. "Otis, Raymond! Find some coolies. Get everything moved to the train station. Gertrude, Thelma! Get everyone packed up. There's a train coming through here in one hour. We need to be on it."

"Why do we always have to travel in the dark?" Gertrude muttered as she began searching about for her truant belongings.

"I don't know, Miss Green," Elder Warren said in his quiet, steady voice. "You'll have to check with the military."

Gertrude hadn't intended to be overheard. She twisted around and found his eyes fixed on her. The voice had been gentle but the stare was intense. *I know, I know,* she telegraphed as she dropped her embarrassed gaze. *Gertrude, behave yourself. Others are watching.* She busied herself packing her eating utensils then arose to go find the Mennonite girls.

Otis Erich pulled on his heavy coat that made him look like a giant beehive. "It's a troop train then, is it?" he asked.

"It is," Elder Warren responded. "The stationmaster kindly gave us permission to ride along."

"I hope that's within his authority," Mr. Erich said, lumbering into the narrow hallway behind the short, groundhog-like silhouette of Dr. McMullen.

"Me, too," Elder Warren answered, mostly to himself, as he placed his shaving kit in his small suitcase and tidied up his own little corner of the room.

Through the continuously falling snow and with the help of the Mennonite missionaries, Gertrude and Thelma led the female members of the group through the back streets along the southern wall of the city to the railroad station. There Gertrude found Elder Warren cajoling the Army captain in charge of the troops into allowing the coolies to load the luggage into a steel gondola car that was half full of coal. The train was made up of nine gondola cars of coal filled with loudly protesting soldiers, declaring that they were already overcrowded.

Gertrude stood staring at the train of coal cars half filled with coal and half filled with complaining soldiers. *Something isn't right. Soldiers don't travel in coal cars.* The coolies were pushing the luggage over the edge of one of the cars; Mr. Erich and Dr. McMullen were inside catching it. Behind his back Elder Warren waved her forward, obviously telling her to get everyone loaded, even as his discussion with the Army captain continued.

Elder Warren was still climbing up the short ladder into the car as the train pulled out of the station. At the last minute the stationmaster came running along the side of the moving train, shouting to the Army captain in charge of the troops. "The Communists are along both sides of the track nine *li* north of here at the next station," he yelled. "Tell the engineer to keep the train moving slowly and not stop."

Military orders passed quickly among the soldiers who began to chamber rounds into their rifles and unsheathe their bayonets.

"I knew this didn't look right," Gertrude shouted above the chugging of the accelerating steam engine and the clickety-clack of the train wheels on the iron rails. "The Communists will be shooting right in here at all of us!" She pointed vigorously at Thelma and Jeannie while trying awkwardly to stand up on the lumpy coal.

"Miss Green, I would suggest that you sit down." Elder Warren steadied himself with one hand on the side of the gondola as he followed his own advice and sat down near the outside edge of the car. "I would further suggest that you move everyone to the outside edge of the cars—and that you begin as many silent prayer meetings as you can among those around you." He turned away and began organizing those within his immediate vicinity.

Gertrude plopped down on the rough lumps of coal, staring at the man who had insisted that she come on this outing and who was now going to get her killed. As the fire of her indignation receded from full flame to simmer, she looked about her at the women and children interspersed among the soldiers in the coal car. *I think they will be in less danger if they . . .* While her mind envisioned the inevitable gun battle, she imagined the places in the coal car that would be safest. She started moving among the group, starting with Zora McMullen and Ronnie.

Within a few minutes the train began to slow down as if it were approaching a station stop. The whispered message passed through the ranks of the Nationalist Chinese soldiers, from coal car to coal car. "There they are!" The men huddled against the sides of the car, rifles at the ready.

Gertrude did not need to look over the top of the coal car to confirm that the Communists were walking just beyond the dusty steel side against which she leaned. The rhythmic thud-thud of marching feet filled her ears. She gazed upward, trying to see through the heavily falling snow into the black night, and heard the rattle of mess kits and knives inside haversacks. The Communists were a mere three feet away. She pulled Jeannie close to her and continued to fervently pray that Ronnie McMullen would remain quiet.

The train slowed but did not stop. The flicker of two kerosene lanterns at the railroad station illuminated the snowflakes falling upon them. Shadow patterns danced over the cars for a moment and were gone. The train began to pick up speed.

An hour later the train crawled into the railroad station three miles from Suiping and ground to a halt. At the Army captain's shouted command the Nationalist Chinese soldiers tossed supplies and ammunition over the sides of the gondola cars and awkwardly climbed down after them. Gertrude and the others peered over the sooty edge of the car as the soldiers formed ranks along the track and marched away.

"I'm going to find out what's happening," Elder Warren told the group. He scrambled up the face of the piled coal to the top of the ladder at the end of the car and disappeared over the side.

In 15 minutes Gertrude and Otis Erich saw him striding back from the station, stepping over parallel railroad tracks, avoiding the slippery, steel rails.

"The Army is not going any farther," he called up to them. "Neither is this train. It's returning to Chumatien." Coughing from trying to shout into the cold wind, he waved them off with his hand and headed for the end of the car. Once inside he gathered the committee of five around him, huddling with them in the center of the car, and continued. "The stationmaster says he will try to find an engine and car to take us the rest of the way."

"How did we get so lucky?" Otis Erich asked.

Elder Warren nodded in the direction of Raymond McMullen. "He remembers when Doctor here took care of his family in Yencheng." Dr. McMullen raised his eyebrows and shrugged his shoulders incredulously.

"The Chinese never forget a favor done to the family," Thelma said sagaciously.

"So. We unload here beside the tracks and wait for our chariot to take us to Yencheng," Elder Warren said, standing erect.

"And be waiting out in the open for a mystery train that won't come, like we did in Yencheng." Gertrude glared up at him from her crouched position. "I don't think so. Not in this snowstorm."

"H'mmm. Maybe you're right," Elder Warren said, gazing over his shoulder at the expanse of railroad tracks beyond the edge of the gondola car. After a moment's thought he said, "OK. Gertrude, you and Thelma take the women up to the station and wait in their baggage area. It's sheltered on three sides and away from the wind. Otis, you and Raymond help me unload this luggage by the track over there."

"And when you're unloaded, send Dr. McMullen to stand guard with us," Gertrude said, also rising. "He's a friend of the stationmaster. Can't ever have too many friends."

By 8:30 that night the women and their sleeping children were bedded down in the baggage shed while Dr. McMullen and Gertrude crouched in the shadow of the doorway, watching Elder Warren and Mr. Erich alternately build a windbreak of the luggage and beat their arms along the sides of their bodies like penguins to stay warm.

Noting movement in the shadows to the east across the switch yard, Raymond McMullen nudged Gertrude and pointed surreptitiously. She stared hard into the darkness and the dwindling snowfall until the shadows took the form of men, marching in three columns, moving northwest across the switch yard, and disappearing beyond the edge of the station into the night.

"Who are they?" Dr. McMullen whispered.

"Probably Communists," Gertrude murmured anxiously, "judging by their clothes. No uniforms. Besides the Nationalist soldiers marched away to the west, toward Suiping." *And what's to keep them from finding us, once they find the luggage?* she agonized. With her eyes she estimated the distance from the Communist Army to where the 100 pieces of baggage was stacked—out in the open along the tracks, the lanterns of the station highlighting them from behind. "Don't they see the suitcases—and the guys?" she wondered aloud.

"I don't know," Dr. McMullen answered. "Maybe they're too busy trying not to be noticed. Maybe they can't see through the falling snow." He paused. "Maybe . . . Someone is hiding the luggage from their sight." He looked to Gertrude for confirmation of his epiphany.

Her body shuddered at the thought. "Maybe," she whispered. *Dear Lord, let it be so.*

The last of the poorly dressed Communist fighters quickened their pace, hurrying into the darkness just before a new sound came from the south.

Gertrude and Raymond McMullen turned their gaze in time to see a switch engine pulling a small coal tender into the outer edges of the lantern light.

"Our ride is here." Raymond smiled and stretched out his hand like a maitre d' indicating a choice table.

"And we just got the kids settled," Gertrude said, indicating with a nod of her head the shadowy figures behind them for which she felt a sudden rush of compassion and responsibility.

Gertrude peered through the darkness at her watch. *11:00 p.m. How could it not be 4:00 a.m.? This night is so long and my feet are so cold.* She sat huddled in a corner, her legs drawn up under her long coat. She and Thelma had brought folding camp cots to sleep on, but so far they hadn't used them. They'd slept standing up or had been in such cramped quarters that there was no room to set them up. Now they were trying to sleep on the coal in the small tender.

Gertrude looked up into the clear night sky. The snow had stopped falling, but December's frigid north wind continued to blow. *We're going to freeze to death,* she concluded. Though wearing her padded Chinese clothes and fur coat, a head scarf tying her fur cap tightly to her head, she shivered almost continuously.

They had all climbed inside the coal tender and the switch engine had pulled ahead and over two tracks. There it had stopped, and the engineer and fireman had disappeared into the railroad station.

"Gertrude, help me." The low command came across the small tender as Elder Warren motioned for Gertrude to join him. He was squatting beside Thelma who was lying face up, asleep. Jeannie lay on top of her, face down.

"The child's legs are cold," Elder Warren said, rubbing the small limbs vigorously. "They're freezing. We've got to get them warm."

"Get them up. Make them move around," Gertrude commanded irritably, trying to lift the child who was limp in her hands. Thelma lay motionless, undisturbed by the commotion above her.

Roughly Gertrude handed the child to Elder Warren. She turned and grasped Thelma by the shoulders, shaking her awake.

"Thelma, you've got to wake up," Gertrude said insistently into the ear of the fluttery-eyed Thelma. "Wake up. Get up and move around. You're freezing."

"Gertrude, I'm so cold," Thelma mumbled. She stumbled over the coal but managed to stand up and stagger to the end of the tender and back.

"Keep your coat tucked in around you," Gertrude ordered as she placed Jeannie inside of Thelma's Chinese coat. On her knees, twisting to her left, she moved them into a small gap next to the outside wall of the tender, out of the wind. Still holding her little girl, Thelma sank down to the floor.

Over her shoulder she heard Elder Warren mumbling.

"What are you doing?" she asked gruffly, straightening herself to face him.

"I'm praying," he answered simply. "I've been praying all night."

"For warmth, I hope."

"For warmth, yes. But more than that." He glanced sideways at her. "I've been praying about Wilma and the kids in Hankow. I've been praying for the people of this Conference I was elected to lead. I've been praying for people I've worked for, tried to reach all my life, people I've wanted to see saved for Jesus' kingdom."

He pointed upward. "Do you see that constellation up there?" She glanced up. "That's Orion. It's actually a hallway of stars, a tunnel. Some say that it leads all the way to heaven itself."

Gertrude looked up again, more sharply, half expecting to see a glorious radiance emanating from somewhere in the heavens. What she saw was a cold night sky with faintly twinkling stars. *Not a very helpful prayer right now,* she thought.

"I've been praying for the faith and the strength to meet Jesus when He comes down through that hallway of stars," Elder Warren said, "which means I need the strength for me and for all of these"—his glance indicated those who slept around him—"to survive this freezing cold night." He smiled. "So you see, it is a more practical prayer than you might think."

Perhaps, Gertrude thought, as she stood and stripped off her fur coat.

"Gertrude, you can't. You're just as cold as they are," Elder Warren argued.

"I may be cold, but I'm not dying," she muttered. Draping the long fur coat over Thelma and Jeannie, Gertrude tucked it in around Thelma's feet and shoulders. Stiffly she stood and made her way to her corner.

How does one develop that kind of faith? she wondered as she squatted against the side of the car. *By sleeping out in the freezing cold? By praying for others?* Her thoughts turned to Thelma and Jeannie . . . and to her own mother, and . . .

"My feet are freezing," Gertrude shouted. "I can't stand this any longer."

"Gertrude! Wake up!" She blinked and tried to focus on Elder Warren who stood over her, shaking her.

"My feet are so cold," Gertrude cried. Her body shook violently. "I just can't do this." Slowly she pushed herself up. She stood for a moment to get her balance, then clumsily tried to walk.

"Go down and put your feet against the fire box wall in the engine," Elder Warren said, suddenly remembering the oven in the woodstove of his boyhood kitchen and an old trick from his childhood about how to get your feet warm. He steadied her as she carefully stepped down into the cab of the engine.

Twenty minutes later and much warmer, Gertrude climbed back into the tender and hastened across the coals.

"Let's get the others down there—in the engine," she said to Elder Warren.

"Good idea," he said, rising quickly. He stopped. "I'm sorry you weren't in your warm bed in Yencheng. This has been an awful night for you."

She nodded. "One of the worst of my life."

That night, far to their north, in Yencheng, and unknown, of course, to Gertrude and the rest, the Communists destroyed the railroad station and all 12 train engines at the roundhouse. They also burned down the Women's Building and several other structures at the Yencheng Sanitarium and Hospital.

Chapter 64

HIDING IN THE MIDST OF THE ENEMY

For the rest of that early Friday morning Gertrude did not sleep. Comforting crying and hungry children and warming mothers near the firebox in the engine occupied her fully. It had been five days since the hopeful band of missionary refugees had left Yencheng. Two of those days had been spent in situations where food was not easily obtained. Now, after everyone had been warmed and "pottied," the first order of business was food. Gertrude and Thelma went looking.

Returning from a futile search of the few shop houses huddled near the railroad station, they rounded the corner of a lean-to shack to see smoke rising from a small bonfire in the middle of the main track. Elder Warren and Mr. Erich were trudging through the snow across the rail yard, returning to their switch engine. The mothers and children milled about near the tender car, waving their arms and trying to keep warm. Gertrude and Thelma pushed through the cold, gusting wind toward the destitute little flock.

"Did you find anything?" Elder Warren called as they approached.

"No," Gertrude replied, shaking her head. "What's going on over there?" She canted her head toward the fire.

"The stationmaster won't talk to us, but we think he is burning all his papers," he conjectured as the four of them assembled near the front of the motionless engine. He gazed across the open switchyard tracks to the uniformed Chinese official who had returned to his fire with another armload of documents.

"And his equipment, including his telephone," Mr. Erich added as Dr. McMullen wandered over to join the conversation.

"He knows someone is coming and he doesn't intend to be here when they arrive." Dr. McMullen motioned to the frantic activity at the fire, then glanced over his shoulder at his wife and child doing their warming exercises with the rest of the women and children.

"You're right, Doctor," Elder Warren said, following his gaze. "Neither should we. Otis and I will go look for some kind of transportation. The rest of you better get all the luggage out on the ground."

"Where are we going?" Thelma Hwang asked.

"Yencheng . . . or Suiping, if we have to. It's only three miles that way," he said pointing west. "Otis and I will search for some kind of transportation. Doctor Raymond, you organize the folk here to get all of the luggage out of the tender."

"Let's pray you have more luck than we did, trying to find something to eat," Gertrude called after the two retreating figures. She turned up her coat collar and followed Raymond and Thelma back to the coal car.

Before they could get all the suitcases and trunks out of the coal car, Merritt Warren and Otis Erich were back.

"There's no one here. Absolutely no one," Elder Warren said when the small committee had assembled around him. "Every scrap of transportation has fled to the west, and the Communists are coming from the north and the south." His face was set firmly, his mouth in a thin, straight line. "We have to leave now."

"But how will we carry our luggage?" Thelma asked.

"We won't. Except for what we can carry, we leave everything right here." Elder Warren looked over Gertrude's head to the women and children behind her, his grim features softening with compassion. "Tell everyone to go through their luggage. Put only what they can carry in one small bag. We leave in 15 minutes."

As the news spread, crying and wailing erupted among the people forced to abandon their warm bedding and extra clothes. Children, already hungry, and now sensing the emotions of loss and crisis, added their howls to their mothers' tears.

In 15 minutes the small band was tramping out a new road in the snow—walking westward toward the walled city of Suiping. Mr. Erich and one of the larger women, dressed in heavy clothes to look like a man, stayed behind to guard the pile of forsaken luggage.

"We'll look for some kind of transport to send to you. If you don't hear from us within two hours, leave it all, and come," Elder Warren told them.

Elder Warren led the group to the Lutheran Mission compound on the north side of Suiping. Pastor Li, the Chinese minister in charge, welcomed them warmly, explaining that the American missionaries who'd served there had already been pulled out because of the intense fighting. After learning the size of the party, he suggested that the nursing students and Chinese mothers with children should stay in the servants' quarters. There they'd be with other Chinese Christians from the city and not so likely to draw attention to themselves. Then he personally led Elder Warren and the other foreigners to the foreign missionary's house. It was empty as all the furniture had been put in storage under lock and key. As the two groups parted to go their separate ways, Thelma and Jeannie joined the group of foreigners going to the house.

Immediately after they'd set down their bags in a large echoingly empty room, Elder Warren asked Pastor Li to help him find someone with wagons to retrieve the luggage that had been left behind. Meanwhile, Gertrude sought out the compound workers to arrange for food for her group. Fortunately there was plenty of food, and a Christian farmer was found who had two ox carts. On hearing the need, he hitched up his oxen and immediately headed east, accompanied by Elder Warren, Dr. McMullen, and several of the Lutheran workers.

By noon Gertrude had made sure that everyone in her temporary family was fed and Elder Warren, oxcarts packed with luggage, came through the large bi-winged compound gate.

"Did you get my typewriter?" Gertrude shouted, crunching through the snow toward the small caravan.

"We got everything," Elder Warren said as he reached up to receive the first of the suitcases being handed down. "But we were none too soon."

"We weren't sure what to do." Mr. Erich, one of the two left behind to guard the luggage, stepped from behind the second cart. "Almost as soon as you were out of sight, we saw looters near the shanties by the tracks. We kept circling the pile, marching as if we were soldiers on guard duty." His tenor voice rang out with laughter. "I don't know how long the ruse would have worked, since we obviously had no guns."

"Well, we saw the looters closing in as we were approaching," Elder Warren said, reaching up for a small black box with brass-studded feet. "We made lots of noise and they all scattered." He handed the typewriter case to Gertrude.

"I would have done more than make noise if I'd been there," Gertrude said, her eyes snapping with anger. "If anybody had stolen my typewriter ..." She lovingly examined the case, then brushed a hole in the snow with her foot and set it on the ground. Having secured the most important item, she was ready to receive the rest of her luggage.

Silhouetted by dim, rectangular patches of twilight struggling through war-weary, dirty windows, Gertrude sat on a hard wooden bench next to Thelma and Jeannie in the Lutheran chapel. It was Friday evening. Sabbath was about to begin. Pastor Li had gathered all the Christians from the compound for a prayer meeting and had asked Elder Warren to take the service. Now he stood before them all, introducing his text.

"Please turn with me to Psalm 25," he said.

I am so glad to be out of that cold wind. Gertrude pulled her fur coat more tightly around her and wiggled her toes inside her wool socks and stadium boots.

"'Unto thee, O Lord, do I lift up my soul. O my God, I trust in thee,'" he read slowly in Chinese.

Two rows back, Gertrude heard one of the nursing students translating for the McMullens. *That big room should be sufficient for all of us, at least for now.* Gertrude mentally ran through the list of those staying in the big house, then switched to the names of the mothers, children, and nursing students in the servants' quarters. *I need to go look at those servants quarters, find out if they're warm enough.*

"'Let not mine enemies triumph over me.'" For the benefit of the Suiping Christians, Elder Warren began a short explanation of what his group had been through in the last five days.

Lord, how much more do we have to put up with before we can find a train going to Hankow? This was supposed to take us 36 hours at the most. Gertrude's thoughts remained in the last 36 hours. *I've never been so cold in my life. I thought my feet were frozen.* She rubbed her boots together as she remembered the aching pain in her feet. *What was it that Elder Warren was praying about last night?*

"'The troubles of my heart are enlarged: O bring me out of my distresses,'" he intoned.

That wasn't it. He wasn't praying about our troubles—exactly. Gertrude closed her eyes and tried to remember. *He was praying about going to heaven. No, that's not right. He was praying . . . something about strength and faith for others.* She shook her head. *How do you think about those kinds of things when you're so cold and hungry? Lord, increase my faith—like that. So many are depending on me right now. I have to be strong.*

"'Consider mine enemies; for they are many'," he read.

Lord, I can deal with the Communists. But I can't deal with the cold. She was crying silently, large tears welling up and spilling down her cheeks. *I was so cold. Please. I don't want to be cold like that again.*

"'O keep my soul, and deliver me.'"

Lord, I need to get home and take care of my mother. In a few years, I think, she'll need me. She glanced around at her charges, huddled together on the wooden benches, then up at the vaulted ceiling above her. *We're in a Lutheran chapel . . . in the middle of a Communist attack . . . in the middle of China. And there's no way to escape.*" Her whole body shuddered as if she were back in the coal car. She squeezed her eyes tightly shut, swiping at her tears with her coat sleeve. *Please. If something should happen to me . . . please take care of my mother.*

"'For I put my trust in thee.'" Elder Warren closed his Bible and sat down.

At the close of the meeting while the others filed out, Elder Warren motioned for Gertrude to join him near the front of the chapel. Working her way down the side aisle, Gertrude saw Pastor Li introducing Elder Warren to a tall Chinese gentleman. He was bigger than most Chinese, broad in the shoulders, erect posture, black hair swept straight back, and dark, attentive eyes that swept the room occasionally even while he carried his part of the conversation.

Military man of some kind, Gertrude guessed. *But there's no uniform.*

"Miss Green," Pastor Li announced, bowing as she approached. "Major General Li Deh Shem."

"Miss Gertrude Green, I believe," the general said in perfect English, bowing politely as befitted his social status.

Gertrude took a deep breath and bowed somewhat lower, attempting to hide her bewilderment. "General Li," she said. *How does he know my name? Where did he learn to speak English like that? Where is his uniform? Is he a spy?*

"General Li graduated from George Washington University in Washington, D.C.," Elder Warren said, attempting to answer the question he saw in Gertrude's face. "He retired from the Nationalist Chinese Army at the end of the war with Japan."

"Like General Chiang Kai-shek, I am also a Christian," the general added. "Because I have several Western connections, I am also avoiding contact with the Communists." He bowed again.

"Not an easy thing to do in this part of China right now," Gertrude commented as she bowed again.

"He and his family also plan to stay with us." The pastor extended his arms grandly as if to enfold them all in his flock. "And I will wait for the Communists at the city gate."

"Please, do not let my elder brother endanger himself unnecessarily," Elder Warren implored him. "But please, if they come at night, do not open the compound gates until morning. Our group needs to have a good night's sleep."

"But what should I tell them about you, if they ask?" Pastor Li asked, his voice quavering and his eyes widening.

He will not protect us, Gertrude realized. *He will lead them right here to the compound.* "Elder Warren—" she began.

"Tell them the truth," Elder Warren answered, glancing at Gertrude and holding up his hand for silence. "Tell them that we are American missionaries."

"Don't you know what will happen to Americans if the Communists come? Aren't you going to hide?" General Li objected, losing his Chinese composure.

"Where would we hide?" Elder Warren said simply. "We are strangers—foreigners—and a large group. We have done our best to keep out of trouble. Now we must trust in the Lord to take care of us."

"I thank you for your generosity." General Li was addressing the pastor. "But I must take my family to a safer place." He turned to Elder Warren. "The Communists certainly will not spare you. And if they find me here with you, they will not spare my family. Goodnight to you all." He bowed stiffly, turned on his heels and left.

Pastor Li awkwardly excused himself and slipped away.

I am surrounded by people who want to save their own skins or are bound to get us killed. "You are going to let him give us away?" Gertrude's statement was not intended as a question.

"Two things frighten the Chinese, deception and surprise. Frightened Chinese act unpredictably," Elder Warren instructed gently. "I do not want the Communists to be deceived or surprised by our presence. 'Wise as serpents; gentle as doves,' Miss Green."

As she lay, fully clothed, under a warm blanket, Gertrude glanced about at the restless forms lying on pallets in the large empty room they shared just off the main living room. On her immediate left, Thelma sang softly, trying to get Jeannie to sleep. Mercifully, Ronnie had collapsed into sleep after his noisy and rather public bath behind makeshift curtains in the far corner. Gertrude could hear Zora and Raymond whispering across his sleeping form which lay between them. Across from her, on the opposite wall, slept Mr. Erich. Gertrude listened with a nurse's attentive ear to his gradually increasing snore. Elder Warren was outside, she remembered, at the compound gate, standing the first of three watches the men had divided among themselves.

Outside the city, all the small villages were being burned and destroyed. They'd seen the glow of the fires in the sky as they left the chapel after the evening worship. The city of Suiping was the same as Chumatien had been: abandoned by the magistrates and the militia. Now looters and bandits were sweeping away whatever was not protected or locked up.

Lord, what is going to happen to us? Gertrude thought desperately. She clutched her Bible to her chest, praying quietly, fervently, almost angrily. *How do we get out of here, and where do we go? The Communists are all around us.*

"Are you cold?" The question came unbidden to her mind.

No, she answered without thinking. She paused—and realized that no one in the room had spoken. *"It is what you prayed for."* Suddenly she knew! *It is what I prayed for! O Lord, forgive me!* she cried out in her mind. *Increase my faith, my little mustard seed faith.* She rolled over on her right side, facing the closed door that led into the next room, and fell into a fitful sleep.

"Miss Green. Miss Green, wake up."

Gertrude looked up into the face of Sarah, her senior nursing student. She knelt next to Gertrude, gently shaking her awake.

"Yes, Sarah, what is it?" she asked quietly, remembering the sleeping children. Her mind grasped for comprehension. *What's Sarah doing here? She was sleeping in the servant's quarters.*

Looking across the room she saw Dr. McMullen, who had the third watch of the night, kneeling between the pallets of the two church officers—Elder Warren and Mr. Erich. She saw him speak but could not hear his words. Quickly the two men threw off their blankets and stood. They spoke briefly with Dr. McMullen, then crossed the short distance to the door and slipped into the large living room, closing the door behind them.

"They're coming, Miss Green." Sarah spoke again, urgently.

"Who?" Gertrude asked, trying to focus. *What time is it?* Her watch read 8:00 o'clock. The sunlight streaming through the window indicated morning.

"The Communists. We heard them. We saw them marching on the other side of the wall from the servants' quarters and heard them talking loudly to Pastor Li."

Gertrude sat up quickly, shaking off her blankets. Behind her Thelma raised up on one elbow. "What is it?" she asked.

"Three generals and two armed soldiers are coming with Pastor Li," the student gasped, running her words together.

"Shhh, Sarah," Gertrude hushed her. To Thelma she whispered, "I knew he was going to give us away."

Together Gertrude and Thelma arose and stood next to Dr. McMullen who'd cracked open the tall bedroom door. A moment later the heavy thumping of boots sounded on the front steps of the house. Through the crack in the doorway they peered across the empty space of living area and watched Elder Warren reach for the large brass door handle.

"Please, let our brothers come into our house," Elder Warren said, stepping aside as he opened the great front door of the missionary home, graciously establishing who was in control of the house and who was the invited guest.

"Those are the Three Red Devils, the Communist generals," the student whispered. "I have seen that one on the right, General Yi, at our hospital in Yencheng."

"You have?" Gertrude whispered.

"Yes. They used to be in the Nationalist Chinese Army. See the medals?

Those are Nationalist Army medals."

"They're not in the mood for pleasantries, are they?" Dr. McMullen observed.

The three generals stood in the middle of the large living room, glowering about them at the empty space and the doors that exited it.

"Are those American planes that are coming over and dropping bombs on us? Are they?" General Yi turned and stared fiercely at Elder Warren.

"Yes, my brother, I suppose they are," Elder Warren said politely. Gertrude saw that he was searching for further words of explanation.

"I know you are not military men, but are ordinary citizens." The general offered his own assessment.

"Yes, just so." Gertrude saw Elder Warren's face relax. "More than that, we are Seventh-day Adventists. We do not believe in war. Our men are willing to take care of the wounded and the sick, but we do not bear arms," Elder Warren continued, warming to his opportunity. "We worship the One God of Heaven as understood by your first emperor many years ago. We attempt to live as our Lord lived while He was on earth—by helping the poor, the sick, and the weak. We operate many hospitals in China—"

"Yes, I know of your hospital in Yencheng and I know about the good work of Dr. Hwang," General Yi cut in. "We have been watching him for some time now. He is doing just as you say."

"How does he know Paul?" Thelma whispered loudly. "What has he done?"

"Thelma, be quiet," Gertrude said in a sharp, hushed voice. "You'll give us all away."

"What is upstairs?" It was General Yi again, speaking sharply.

"Nothing. The foreign missionary is away and all his furniture has been removed to storage."

"Show us."

"Certainly."

Gertrude watched them all march up the stairs, the soldiers with rifles bringing up the rear.

"Are they going to explore the whole house?" Dr. McMullen asked.

Gertrude frowned. "If they do, they'll certainly find us."

Suddenly realizing their danger, as one body they all turned and fled to their pallets, leaving the door slightly ajar.

From under her blanket Gertrude heard boots thudding on the ceiling above her. When the boots descended the stairs, she held onto Sarah who was huddled with her, physically trembling. In an instant the door to their bedroom sanctuary would creak open and rifle shots ring out.

"What is this thing?" It was a question in Chinese from one of the generals.

They've stopped in the main room, Gertrude thought, *but what are they looking at?*

"It is called an organ." Elder Warren clumsily attempted to explain in Chinese. "It makes music."

The generals began to talk excitedly among themselves, apparently unconvinced.

"Gertrude, come and play the organ," Elder Warren called out in English.

The generals were silenced by the foreign tongue. Gertrude heard restless feet scraping on the floor.

"Nurse Green." This time Elder Warren spoke slowly in Chinese. "Come and play the organ."

Gertrude was trembling violently. "I can't," she managed to gasp after a few moments.

"Gertrude, you must come," Elder Warren said, his voice even and calm. "The generals must hear the music that comes from the organ."

O Dear God, I cannot do this. I am so frightened. I know they will kill me.

Slowly Gertrude got to her feet and tugged her long Chinese coat down over her padded pants. From under her Chinese Bible she retrieved her Chinese song book. She shoved her pointed fur hat more firmly on her head to hide her disheveled hair. *I must look a sight,* she thought. Without a mirror she could only imagine what her face looked like after spending the last 24 hours on two different coal cars. She pushed open the heavy, solid wooden door and stepped into the room.

From somewhere someone had found three chairs. In the middle of the room the three generals sat in a row, facing the organ. The armed soldiers stood behind them, their rifles held across their chests. Mr. Erich and Elder Warren, lined up like two waiters in a fine restaurant, stood in front of the generals, but facing her. Elder Warren silently extended his arm while bowing, inviting her to sit at the organ.

With trembling arms, Gertrude place the songbook on the music rack.

Dear God, don't let me drop the book, she prayed. Opening it somewhere near its center, Gertrude smoothed the pages while searching with her feet for the organ's pedals. As she began pumping air into the bellows, she heard the restless movement of feet again. *They don't know what I'm doing. Play, Gertrude, play.* Tentatively Gertrude began to press the keys, concentrating all her energies on reading the musical notes. She proceeded onward through the stanza and into the chorus of the hymn. Incapable of appreciating how the music sounded, she focused all her fearful anxiety into the notes on the page, into reading them precisely, into not making any mistakes.

From the corner of her eye, she saw Mr. Erich approach the organ. He touched her lightly on the shoulder and pointed to the words of the first stanza. Then standing erect beside the organ with hands folded in front of him—*like an angel,* Gertrude imagined—Mr. Erich began singing.

"Under His wings I am safely abiding . . ." He continued on through all the stanzas, repeating the chorus each time. Gertrude concentrated on the music, never rushing him, and never knowing how their music was being received by their "guests."

As the notes of the last chorus died away, the generals said to each other, "Very good, very good." They stood and without any further word marched out of the house.

Elder Warren followed them to the door, watching them march past Pastor Li at the compound gate without a nod or a bow. "That was what we feared the most," he said with a nod, "and we are still alive." Gently he shut the tall double doors, latched them top and bottom, and threw the deadbolt.

Chapter 65

PLAYING WITH FIRE

The presence of the Communists brought peace and stability to the city of Suiping. Although the magistrates and the city's militia did not return, the looters and bandits withdrew to the countryside allowing the citizenry and the missionaries freedom to move about the city. The Communists assumed the same freedom to enter the missionary house unannounced throughout the rest of the day, precluding any opportunity to hold organized Sabbath services. With Thelma looking after the women and children, and food readily available, Gertrude—with her medical bag—took her junior and senior nursing students on a tour of the town, observing the Lord's admonition to "do good on the Sabbath" by seeking whoever might need medical assistance. They did not return until late afternoon.

Gertrude walked through the front door of the large house followed at a distance by four chattering nursing students excitedly discussing the young Communist soldiers milling about in the courtyard of the Lutheran compound. In the middle of the main room over hot drinks and fruit, Elder Warren and several of the others were having a lively discussion with General Yi and several of his staff officers.

Gertrude's gaze quickly found Thelma who stood near the door to their sleeping quarters. Thelma was clutching Jeannie close to her, her right hand hovering near her mouth, her eyes wide in terror. *What's wrong? What did he just say?* Confused, Gertrude shifted her gaze and her attention to General Yi, who was balancing his teacup on his knee, speaking loudly and gesturing grandly with both hands.

"After we had captured the city of Loho we burned down the hospital in Yencheng," he said proudly.

"You didn't! You burned my hospital?" Gertrude shouted angrily, advancing on the men, her medical bag swinging wildly in her left hand.

All heads turned toward her and conversation stopped. Gertrude heard the sharp intake of air coming from the vicinity of Elder Warren's chair. Her eyes caught the face of General Yi which contorted from a startled frown to a broad grin.

The general laughed out loud, but his eyes were not laughing. "You speak Chinese very well, Nurse Green," he said, his broad grin woodenly affixed to his face.

That irritating, smiling face, she fumed. *Cecil Tang had such a face when I caught him stealing drugs.* The man confronting her now was not Cecil Tang. An icy chill touched her spine. *A smiling Chinese face is dangerous. Watch yourself!* Gertrude recoiled from her anger and stepped back, fighting to betray no emotion.

"Of course I speak Chinese, honorable general," she said, bowing slightly. "I would not be able to carry on my work as a nurse if I did not."

The general eyed her medical bag. "Do you care for everyone?"

"It does not matter to me who they are. They are all the children of the Lord," she said firmly, regaining a small portion of her courage. "I care for all of them. I cared for some of your soldiers today."

"Yes. I know you did," he said, and turned back to Elder Warren.

Gertrude shifted her gaze from the back of the general's head to Elder Warren's face. From behind his wire-rimmed glasses his eyes reflected a mixture of compassion and warning. Trembling inside, Gertrude headed for their sleeping quarters.

As she passed Thelma near the door, Thelma hissed, "You're going to get us all killed."

I came very close, didn't I? Gertrude kept her gaze fixed on the floor. *And I was going to be so brave with the Communists.* Gertrude passed through the door and shut it quietly.

Just before the evening meal, a snowstorm of leaflets fell from the sky, dropped by Chinese Nationalist Army airplanes, warning the populace to depart as the city would be bombed the next day. Over supper a huge discussion ensued over whether they should risk the ire of the Communists in running away or whether they should pray that the bombs would not find them. Everyone but Gertrude agreed that the more immediate danger seemed to lie in running away.

"I am petrified of falling bombs," was all Gertrude had said during the discussion. She had told no one in the group of her previous ordeal during the bombing of the Yencheng Hospital compound.

Just before sundown and the close of the Sabbath, a second small crisis erupted. Elder Warren discovered that Paul Hwang's violin was missing.

"One of those soldiers parading around in here today took it," he said, shaking his head in disgust at his own carelessness.

"Paul liked to play it for special music whenever he preached at a church," Thelma said sadly.

"I will go with you next time you make your health rounds, Miss Green. Please let me know when you're going," he commanded. "I will figure out something."

The next morning, at the request of Pastor Li, Elder Warren presided over the Sunday church service. Partly because they had missed their own services the day before and partly to show solidarity with the other Suiping Christians, at 11:00 o'clock the Seventh-day Adventists sat lined up on the chapel's wooden benches with the Sunday-keeping Lutherans.

Ten minutes into the service, during the second stanza of the opening song, the air raid sirens in Suiping began to wail. Gertrude, who was at the piano, missed playing for the rest of that stanza and the one following, frozen in place while the sirens ascended and descended their own scale twice in slow succession. When nothing further happened, Gertrude managed to play through the offertory and to accompany the singing of the Doxology which followed the morning prayer. Then as Elder Warren read his scriptural passage for the sermon, Gertrude, now on her wooden bench in the congregation, heard the unmistakable sound that haunted her dreams and paralyzed her with fear—the whistle of a falling bomb.

Gertrude clutched the seat board beneath her with both hands. *I cannot run. I cannot scream,* she whimpered silently again and again while the crescendo of sound filled her brain. She jerked reflexively with the percussive explosion. Rationally, she knew that the bomb had landed well to the south of the chapel and the compound, somewhere in the center of the city. But emotionally she recoiled as if the bomb had exploded in the seat beside her. Her fingers were just beginning to unlock from her seat when the next whistle began.

How can I survive this? She gasped while her frenzied mind fought off hysteria. She scanned the room, searching for visual clues as to how to survive. Everyone else's eyes were riveted on Elder Warren. Gertrude frantically shifted her gaze in the same direction, desperate to discern in his instructions where to find a safe haven.

Elder Warren gazed over the heads of the people as if seeing a distant vision unavailable to the rest of the congregants. With serene confidence he continued his sermon until the pitch of the falling missile reached a certain decibel level. He paused while the bomb finished its flight and the explosion ended its existence. With the bomb's having no further consequence, he continued with his sermon as if there had been no interruption.

Visually clutching onto her spiritual mentor, Gertrude grew evermore amazed as the bombs fell ever closer and Elder Warren's sermon skipped forward like a game of hopscotch—pause, consideration, jump; pause, consideration, jump. During the pauses, Gertrude held her breath. After each explosion Elder Warren continued preaching and Gertrude rejoiced in her ability to continue breathing. After the last bomb had fallen, Elder Warren paused one last time, gazed at the ceiling and waited. When no further sound followed, he spoke the last remaining sentences of his sermon and sat down.

No one spoke or moved. Everyone sat in awe and amazement that the Lutheran chapel was still standing. Each one without exception concluded that God had surely intervened to preserve them. In her heart Gertrude knew without a doubt that they had all been preserved by the courageous, persevering faith of one man. She also considered the possibility that in the future she would be able to survive the falling of a bomb without an anxiety meltdown. But she wasn't sure.

After two minutes when no one had moved to lead the closing hymn or to offer any closing remarks, Elder Warren stood and approached the small rostrum. "I think we should have the benediction and go to dinner," he said, "in case we have a repeat performance."

All the heads in the room bowed low.

That night the sky to the north was lit up by a fire somewhere just over the compound wall. Elder Warren and Gertrude decided to investigate to see if there was any danger of it spreading to their buildings.

In the main street in front of the compound and to the north they saw several groups of soldiers on guard duty, standing around barrels in which the soldiers had built fires to keep warm. Apparently someone had tossed firebrands from the barrel into the empty house of the city magistrate which was almost total consumed, the flames dying down and not spreading beyond the compound wall surrounding it.

"Nobody's celebrating their little childish deed," Gertrude commented, inclining her head toward Elder Warren. "They're all standing around, saying nothing."

"There's the reason," Elder Warren said. He was already hurrying toward a tall Chinese soldier at attention who was being severely reprimanded by one of the generals.

"Your men are not to be destructive. They are not to loot. They are not to steal," he shouted into the face of the tall sergeant. The general was livid. "If it happens again, I will know and I will personally punish the guilty one *and* the person in charge. Is that clear?"

What kind of words are these—coming from a Communist general? I thought all Communists were destructive. Gertrude paused in her thinking. *But they haven't destroyed us . . . and I don't understand why.*

"Good evening, Brother Warren." The general had spotted them. "You are out for a walk so late in the evening."

"Good evening, my brother," Elder Warren answered, bowing politely, his arms folded over one another. "We were checking on the fire, hoping it would not spread to our compound. It would be too bad to destroy such a pleasant village unnecessarily."

"Those were American planes today," the general said flatly, his face expressionless.

"Those were Chinese Nationalist Army planes, that the Americans gave them. Yes, my brother. I am sorry." Elder Warren bowed as he spoke to show his genuine concern.

The general's face remained passive, unmoved. He nodded and turned away.

"Look over there," Elder Warren whispered to Gertrude, pointing to a fire barrel just up the street from where they stood.

"It's Paul's violin case." Gertrude recognized it immediately but wondered how they would get it back.

"It is indeed," Elder Warren said, moving quickly in that direction. He walked past the general and up to the pile of stones where the violin case stood leaning. Ignoring the soldiers standing nearby, he picked up the violin and tucked it under his arm. "Goodnight, my brother," he said as he passed the general, who turned and watched him stride toward the Lutheran compound.

Gertrude hurried to catch up. Coming along side, she whispered, "Won't they be angry? Won't they burn down our compound?"

"I don't think so," Elder Warren said, more firmly than was his custom. "They were told not to destroy and they were told not to steal. They would be in trouble if they did anything now."

Gertrude looked over her shoulder at the general who was eyeing the soldiers at the barrel, then turned and hurried after Elder Warren who had already reached the compound gate.

Suiping, Honan, China
Monday, December 22, 1947

Dearest Mother:

Well, it is some time since I wrote you last and I presume that you have not received even that letter because the next day we started on our long journey of evacuation from Yencheng because of the Communists. At the present we are not so far from Yencheng, but we were caught by the Communists here in this place. The Lord was very good to us in letting us not be bothered by them too much.

At this present minute while I sit here typing this letter to you, we can hear guns and cannons going off everywhere because the National government troops have just a few minutes ago taken this city back again. We are all feeling much better that the Communists are gone and now I am writing this letter hoping that I can get to Hankow and get it mailed to you. We have certainly been through a terrible week of trouble. It is now more than one week since we left Yencheng and have traveled on open boxcars, coal cars and even slept one night on a coal car on top of the coal out in the open. But I will try to write up an entire story of just what we have been through and send it later. What a life we have been living.

We surely are glad that the government troops have come in now. The villagers are beginning to return and we are hoping to find some food as things are getting a little short where we are staying. But the Lord has watched over us and blessed us so very much. Here it is almost Christmas Day and it certainly doesn't seem much like Christmas to us sleeping on the floor with barely anything to eat, but then we still have our lives—so I will not complain.

I presume that everything I have in Yencheng will be lost. I could not bring anything with me and so I have very little hope that much will be left there if I ever get a chance to go back and see about it. We are going to try to get some carts and leave for Hankow tomorrow if we can. It means that we will have to walk about four days to get to the place where the trains are still running south. Here's hoping that the Communists do not get there before we do and break up the railroad and bridges. I hate to leave my little home in Yencheng and all my things, but then I am thankful that I still have my life.

Christmas Day we will probably be traveling on the road. I guess everyone at home is busy as can be buying last minute presents, but we don't have to worry about all of that. Our big Christmas present this year is our lives being spared. We are all very grateful for this.

I hope you are enjoying a nice Christmas Day and I hope your Christmas present got to you—the $200 I arranged for the Gen'l Conference to send to you to buy your stove or whatever you need. Take good care of yourself. I will probably add a letter on to this when I arrive in Hankow. Say hello to everyone one for me—to Walter and Amelia and Fred and Gloria and Aunt Mary and Aunt Emma.

Loads of love from your most loving daughter,
Gertrude

Chapter 66

LEAVING ON SHORT NOTICE

As soon as the fighting stopped, Thelma and the younger nurses went scrounging for food while Gertrude, with her medical bag, took her older nursing students on another foray for medical cases to treat. And now that the Communists were gone, Elder Warren and Mr. Erich went in search of any kind of transportation that could get them out of town, Dr. McMullen stood guard over the rest of the group. All agreed to meet back on the compound for a meal by 1:00 o'clock.

At the dinner table, everyone congratulated Thelma and her girls on their find of rice, turnips, and flour for *kongee*—everyone except Mr. Erich.

"I am very happy for your efforts, ladies, but I almost never eat *kongee*," Mr. Erich said as he munched on his small bowl of rice with stewed turnip pieces. "I tried to eat it when I first came to China, but it made me ill."

"Well, it's the best we could do," Thelma said, trying not to sound peeved.

"And it's all we're likely to have for some time in the future," Gertrude added.

"It was certainly better than *we* were able to do," Elder Warren said smoothly, changing the subject. "We couldn't find a truck or a cart anywhere. Maybe things will have settled down a bit more by tomorrow. We'll try again then."

On Tuesday morning, the Nationalist Army marched out of the city to the north in pursuit of the Communists, leaving only a small contingent of troops in the city to hold it. The major topic of conversation on the street—that the bandits or the Communists would return—made its way to the dinner table in the large missionary house by early afternoon.

"I know," Mr. Erich said between mouthfuls of rice. "We heard about it all morning long while we searched for something to carry us out of here."

Pastor Li came hurrying in the front door of the house. "Brother Warren, we have visitors," he announced.

"I hope they brought their own food," Thelma remarked from her end of the table.

Elder Warren arose from his chair in time to meet a tall Chinese man with military bearing coming through the door.

"Welcome, my brother," Elder Warren said warmly, extending his hand.

"General Li, how good to see you." Mr. Erich stood and offered his chair. "Come, sit and eat with us."

"No, thank you. I know that food is scarce," the general said, eyeing Thelma, "and I've already eaten." The general bowed to the ladies at the table.

"But what about your family?" Gertrude asked.

"They are well hidden and well cared for, thank you, Miss Green."

"When the Communists came, we didn't know what had happened to you," Elder Warren said, voicing the concern of all.

"I could say the same for you," the general replied. "When I saw the Communists go into your building, I knew you would be done for. I thought I would hear shrieks, cries, and gunshots. Instead I heard soft, sweet music and then singing."

"Well, as you can see, thanks to Miss Green's organ playing and Mr. Erich's singing, we are still here," Elder Warren said and proceeded to describe the encounter more fully.

General Li shook his head in disbelief. "Since your God is obviously taking care of you, perhaps I should have come to you sooner," he said, standing straighter. "As you already know, it is impossible to find any transportation out of Suiping and the situation here is unstable at best. Pastor Warren, my brother, please come with me to Chumatien. We can hire carts there, bring them back to Suiping and take everyone south. I will join my family with your group and I will lead you."

"We appreciate your offer to . . . guide us, honorable general," Elder Warren replied carefully. "As you say, the situation here is unstable, but it may not be advisable for the rest to wait here for carts to come from Chumatien." He paused. "But the decision is not up to me."

"Please, discuss it among yourselves then," the general said urgently. "But we haven't much time."

Is he just in a hurry . . . or is he nervous? Gertrude wondered. She let her eyes cut toward him for just an instant. *Why did you come seeking us now, and what are you really looking for?*

Elder Warren spoke. "It isn't up to any of us," he said quietly. "We need to pray about this. The Lord has taken care of us this far and we would not want to be out of His will now."

"Yes . . . of course," the general said. Confused, he bowed and backed out of the room, closing the door.

"I don't think he understands," Mr. Erich commented, glancing at the closed front door.

"Neither do some of the rest of us, quite frankly," Gertrude said.

"Nor do I," Elder Warren said. "But God understands and it is His understanding that counts the most."

The remains of dinner was set aside as the members of the small advisory group knelt together in prayer. After praying for guidance, the group discussed the situation thoroughly and prayed again for guidance. At the end of the prayer meeting, everyone agreed that having the group wait in Suiping for carts to come from Chumatien did not seem to be the Lord's plan for them.

When Elder Warren went to tell the general of their decision, he was disappointed. "I was hoping that we could work together," he said.

"Perhaps we will, my brother," Elder Warren told him kindly, "but we believe this plan is not the Lord's will for us."

"After what I witnessed last Saturday, I will not argue with your God," General Li said with resignation.

In the warm light of early evening Gertrude, in her long Chinese coat and stadium boots, stood at the compound gate watching Suiping come alive in the melting snow. Others of their group stood nearby, also watching. The coolies and the farmers had arrived from the countryside, churning up the slushy roads with their carts and wheelbarrows. The magistrate directed workers in the cleanup of what was left of his house next door. The militia, with the help of the nationalist troops, had made its presence known on the street. Small shops were open for business and the noodle vendors plied their trade on the street corners.

"Our chance to hire transportation has markedly improved," Mr. Erich said smiling, his round cheeks bunched up hopefully under slitted eyes that crinkled at the edges.

"Don't we need some money to do that?" Dr. McMullen asked.

"Never a problem in China," Gertrude assured him. "There's always money out there. The difficulty is knowing who has it, and you can't tell by looking at the clothes. The plainest of clothes can hide the richest of men."

"I'll ask around," Elder Warren told them. "I will find someone, a businessman probably, who will take a note on our bank in Hankow. Then we'll hire a truck and be on our way." He turned to Dr. McMullen with a knowing smile. "Care to come along and see how this miracle of financing is done in the middle of a war?"

As the others returned to the house, Elder Warren and Dr. McMullen set off in search of a loan and a truck. In two hours they returned with coolies and carts.

"A very pleasant businessman gave us our loan," Elder Warren announced to the group as he removed his heavy coat and hung it on a hook next to the door. "We couldn't find a truck."

"But we found carts and coolies," Dr. McMullen announced proudly, hanging up his coat. "The coolies have promised to return in the morning. They will help us load our luggage and take us the 15 miles to Chumatien."

Gertrude watched Merritt Warren's eyes, noted the way he held his hands folded together in front of him, as if he were holding something back. "What else did he say?" she asked.

"Who?"

"The man who gave you the loan."

Elder Warren regarded her, his smile coming easily. "You don't miss much, do you?"

"I try not to."

He sat down heavily. "The town seems to be quite stable now. Everything seems to be back to normal." He looked up at Gertrude. "The man said, 'You have helped us, especially Nurse Green, but now you should go.'" He shook his head. "I'm unable to discern the danger, but he was quite insistent. I put a lot of faith in their intuition."

"It is their country and not ours," Gertrude responded.

"Well, let's get some sleep," he said, rising. Hands outstretched, he herded the others, like goats, ahead of him to their sleeping quarters. "Maybe it will be made more clear to us tomorrow."

After a leisurely breakfast on Wednesday morning, Gertrude and Thelma started organizing the women and children, gathering their carried baggage and sleeping bundles from the servants' quarters and piling it near the compound gate. The men brought out the larger trunks and suitcases. With the arrival of the coolies and their carts came other willing hands from the village as well as the usual crowd of curious onlookers. The atmosphere was more like the entertainment of loading a circus rather than the preparation of refugees fleeing a war.

Gertrude drew Elder Warren aside.

"I've been approached by two other villagers," she confided, "bearing the same message you received yesterday. They spoke to me quietly and said, 'You should go now.'"

"Perhaps we should pay attention," he said. Looking about at the lively carnival around them, he added, "Let's see if we can get this process finished quickly and get moving."

By noon the caravan was proceeding through the muddy streets of Suiping headed for the South Gate of the city and the road to Chumatien. But they hadn't gone far when the carts ground to a halt.

Gertrude hurried forward from the carts in the rear that carried the smaller children. She was looking for Elder Warren.

"What's the holdup?" she asked, hustling up to Otis and Raymond who stood at the head of the line of carts, their hands on their hips.

Otis Erich pointed ahead to where they saw the wavy, salt-and-pepper hair of Elder Warren walking toward a barricade of overturned carts, military equipment, and stones and timbers from surrounding houses. The barricade was manned by Chinese Nationalist troops and faced the South Gate.

"How do we get through there?" Gertrude asked. The barricade covered the entire street. When her companions answered with shrugs of shoulders, she folded her arms in frustration and joined them in their vigil.

An hour later—with the intervention of several city officials—the troops opened a small gap in the barricade and allowed the missionary band to exit the South Gate.

"What was that all about?" Gertrude asked Elder Warren when they had guided all the carts through the great stone arch of the gate and were trudging along on the road.

"I don't know. They wouldn't say much," he said, looking back at the city gate that had swung shut on its huge hinges. "My guess is that it has something to do with the warnings we were given."

"But I thought the Communists were north of us," Gertrude reasoned.

"Maybe they were guarding the back door. I don't know," he said. "But I do know this," he added firmly. "When the Lord sends a message to leave the city, we should do it as quickly as we can."

"Look up ahead. Right there," Raymond McMullen shouted, pointing from where he was walking beside the second cart.

In the far distance Gertrude saw a large, black truck coming toward them. The carts prepared to move to the side of the road to allow the truck to pass, but it slowed as it approached, then stopped. A tall Chinese man alighted from the passenger side and strode toward them.

"It's General Li—with a truck," Elder Warren said in disbelief as he waited for the man to reach them.

"Pastor Warren," General Li said, offering his hand. "I was afraid I would be too late."

"Too late for what?" Elder Warren asked, confused.

"There is a Communist push coming from the north to the south. It's rumored that they will take Suiping today."

"There's been no fighting there today," Gertrude reassured him.

"That is good," he said, his steady black eyes searching the distance beyond the city. "In the middle of a pitched battle, they would not be as generous to you as they were the last time. But come." He motioned to the coolies to move their carts forward. "The truck is for you. Load all of your luggage aboard as quickly as you can."

Despite their protests, he was already moving the luggage into the truck and helping the women to climb in. "Quickly! Quickly!" he urged.

"What was that?" Gertrude turned her head as she heard, in the far distance, the distinctive popping sound of gunfire. The others had heard it also.

"It has begun on the north side of the city," General Li lectured. "Go quickly now. The militia will not be able to hold them off for long."

"Aren't you coming?" Dr. McMullen asked anxiously.

"My family are still in hiding in the city," he said, looking in that direction.

"General Li," Elder Warren said. "If we had known, we could have brought them with us."

"I know," he replied. "You warned me. But we will be all right. We are Chinese and we can hide among the Chinese." He waved them away. "Go now. Hurry."

He turned, setting off on foot for the city gates. "I will meet you in Chumatien," he called back.

Gertrude turned to Thelma. "We can't leave him behind," she protested.

"It is his choice. We must leave," Thelma said flatly as she hoisted Jeannie up into Dr. McMullen's waiting arms.

The sounds of battle grew louder, seemed wider, spreading through the city, coming closer.

"Come, Gertrude," Elder Warren beckoned.

He clambered up the fender and stepped gently on the hood of the old truck, then offered a hand down to the bewildered Gertrude. "Come ride up on top with me," he said. "I like to see where I'm going and not where I've been."

As they neared their destination, from her vantage point, sitting atop the truck cab, Gertrude could see the devastation inflicted on Chumatien. The Communists had blown up the roundhouse and its locomotives as well as the railway station. The Nationalists had wreaked their own destruction, bombing the city with the same government planes that had visited Suiping on Sunday. Terrified and exhilarated, Gertrude clung to the edge of the cab roof while the driver followed a circuitous route around the gaping craters in the road and the bricks and mortar that had spewed forth from shops and houses. The truck was heading for the one place they all knew well in Chumatien.

The Mennonite mission compound was one of the few places left relatively untouched, and the two young women at the mission were delighted to see them.

"We've been running an inn ever since we last saw you," the girls told them over hot drinks in their living quarters.

"We were hosting the Communists until two days ago," one said.

"And we've lived through our bombing here and the taking of Junan to our northeast," the other added.

"Good thing we didn't go there," Thelma interjected quietly from the rocking chair where she held her sleeping child.

"We had a very active church there," Mr. Erich remembered.

"We hear that the Communists are about six miles away, and are set to come back and retake this city," the Canadian girl said with a sigh. "And the bandits will probably come if the Communists don't. There's been no militia or police protection for days now."

These tidbits of news, given in soft Chinese sing-song whispers, made the rounds through all 36 of the women and children now encamped in the living space they'd occupied just one week before in this same room.

After a few minutes Elder Warren said, "I don't think this is a good place for us to remain for too long. We need to keep moving south." All heads nodded in agreement. "I'll go and try to engage the driver of our truck to take us farther on. And I'll see what I can find out about the roads south of here." He stood to put on his coat.

"I'll go with you," Dr. McMullen said, rising from the couch near his wife and sleeping son.

"Otis will accompany me on this one, Raymond," Elder Warren said, winking at Gertrude. "You might want to stay here with your family and plan something special."

"Oh? Why's that?" Dr. McMullen asked.

"It's Christmas Eve, Doctor," Gertrude said gaily. "You and Zora can help me fix up this 'inn' for when our travelers return. We don't want them to have to sleep in the stable." Addressing her hostesses, she said, "Girls, what can we put together for a small Christmas celebration for all of our folks?"

Chapter 67

DECIDING ON A COURSE OF ACTION

Christmas Day dawned crisp, clear—and cold. Despite the holiday marked on the calendar, the missionaries and their companions did not spend the day celebrating. They were preparing to travel. During the morning worship, Elder Warren explained what he'd learned the night before. The road south of Chumatien ran through low lying mountains where bandits were reported to be hiding. The road to the southeast went to Minkiang where they'd been told a railway repair train was fixing a bridge and preparing for a trip back to Hankow. The distance to Minkiang was 50 miles, easily done in a day's drive, even over roads normally used by horse carts. After a season of prayer, everyone agreed that Minkiang was their destination.

Following a Spartan breakfast of *kongee* and some canned fruit donated by the Mennonite girls to celebrate the day, the group of refugees began the now familiar process of packing up. The men concentrated on loading the large items while Gertrude and Thelma organized the female cadre.

Having her own bundles ready and having made the rounds to make sure the others were getting ready, Gertrude paused and considered a nagging thought that had been bothering her all night. Putting action to her thoughts, she disappeared through a rear doorway of the overcrowded sleeping room. In a few minutes she reappeared. Peering over the field of waving bedroll fasteners and cooking utensils that undulated like windblown wheat in the center of the room, she spotted Thelma changing Jeannie's diaper against the far wall.

"Thelma, the two Mennonite girls are coming with us," she shouted across the expanse.

"That makes 46," Thelma retorted loudly, not looking up.

"It's not safe to leave them behind," Gertrude shouted back, irritated at Thelma's apparent stinginess.

"That's two more mouths to feed," Thelma replied tersely.

"Right," Gertrude called out with more restraint. "I'll see what food they've got that we can carry." She disappeared in the direction of the kitchen and the pantry.

When the Mennonite missionaries revealed that they'd be taking a small cache of canned goods and their own truck, Gertrude stepped outside to report their good fortune to Elder Warren.

"That *is* good fortune for us," Elder Warren said, his frosty breath hanging in the air around his head. "Our driver was worried that the truck would be overloaded and get stuck in the muddy parts of the cart tracks they use for roads."

"But it's only two more people," Gertrude reasoned. "How could that be a problem?"

"Actually we have six more people," Elder Warren said, pointing to the canvas-covered rear of the hulking truck, idling in the snow.

Gertrude saw a tall Chinese man in a heavy military overcoat handing up bundles to two people in the back of the truck. "General Li," she said with a laugh, "like a bad penny."

"And his wife, two children, and two servants," Elder Warren finished up the list.

"I hope they brought food for themselves," Gertrude carped. "Thelma's already counting biscuits and bowls. She's sure we're going to starve before we get to Hankow."

"First, we have to get to Minkiang," Elder Warren said, his hands thrust into his pockets and his lips pursed in deep thought.

You're worried, aren't you? This is taking longer than even you thought it would. Gertrude watched him trace a pattern in the snow with his toe.

"Yes, the general brought their food supply—and maybe enough for some others," he said, looking up with a smile. "Well. An extra truck." His smile broadened and his eyes brightened. "That means we can divide up our people and not overload either vehicle." He shook his head as if he were trying to clear his vision. "The Lord continues to bless, Miss Green. Never doubt. The Lord continues to bless."

At 11:00 o'clock the caravan pulled out of the South Gate of Chumatien and turned into the two muddy tracks that led to Minkiang. Gertrude had so enjoyed the view from her catbird seat of the day before that she again accepted Elder Warren's hospitality and joined him on top of the truck cab. Grasping the edge of the small luggage frame bolted there, her padded pants legs dangling over the passenger side windshield like bolts of cloth, she looked all about. In front of them the mountains were covered with sparse pines. Behind them lay the city and its gate. Strung out along the road back to the city, traveling in their own bunches like sausage links, were several more truck caravans. Obviously, many more were following their example and escaping from Chumatien.

From her vantage point Gertrude saw ahead and to their left several crouched men running down a long slope, heading for a rocky outcropping under which the truck would pass shortly.

"Do you see them?" she asked in a hoarse whisper.

"Yes," Elder Warren said. "Looks like we'll have company in just a bit."

"*Wan-dao! Wan-dao!*" The shout rang out in the crystal clear air and echoed from the nearby rocky walls.

"I haven't heard that word since I was traveling on the river in western China," Elder Warren said as he banged on the top of the truck to get the driver's attention. "Pull over!" Elder Warren shouted to the driver the same word that the bandits had used. "Stop the truck!" he added, beating on the cab roof again for emphasis.

Gertrude held tightly to her baggage rack, but in her mind her hands were folded tightly in supplication. *Dear Lord, protect us . . .* was as far as she got. In front of them a man ran out of the bushes, holding a hand grenade high over his head. *He's going to pull the pin and throw that grenade under our truck!*

Elder Warren stood up on top of the truck, his right hand in the air. "Wait, my brother. Have a heart for your elder brother," he pleaded loudly but calmly in Mandarin. "Your elder brother is a missionary. Have a heart for the women and children in our truck who are escaping from the battlefields all around us." Slowly, very slowly, he began to climb down from the truck. The man held his hand—with the grenade—over his head, but did not move.

Elder Warren was on the ground. Gertrude watched him walk slowly to the front of the truck and bow with his hands folded in front of him. "Please, your elder brother begs permission to pass through your territory."

"Who are you?" barked the bandit.

"I am Pastor Warren and these"—he gestured toward the truck—"are poor missionaries from the Seventh-day Adventist Hospital in Yencheng. Mostly women and children."

"What do you have in the truck?"

"We have only what clothes we could carry and our bedrolls. We have only enough food to get us to Minkiang where we hope to get on a train for Hankow and out of the war zone."

The man with the grenade remained motionless.

Dear Lord in heaven, move on his heart. Let him believe Elder Warren.

"Please, my brother," Elder Warren continued, "the truck following us has more of our women and children. There are so many of us that we required two trucks. We did not want to be stuck in the mud on this poor road."

The man with the grenade lowered his arm. "It is true, my brother. You do not want to be stuck on this road, especially at night. There are bandits all along this way," he said, his face never changing. "You should move along quickly." At that, the man stepped off the road and out of the way.

"Let's move along," Elder Warren said to the driver through the window. As the truck eased forward, he climbed up on the cab roof and motioned for the Mennonite truck to follow.

Gertrude scooted around in her seat, watching behind her as the trucks cleared the narrow spot in the trail. In the distance she saw other trucks coming out of the trees, approaching the same outcropping of rocks. Up on the slope, the men, now in miniature, crouched along its edge, their guns trained on the approaching trucks.

"*Wan-dao!*" echoed up from the hills around them.

"Will they be robbed?" she asked, still turned around.

"I don't know," Elder Warren said. "I can't prevent it. I can only take care of those who are in my keeping."

Gertrude straightened around in her seat. "Don't you care what happens to them?" she asked rather sharply.

"It is not a question of caring, Miss Green," he insisted, turning to face her fully. "It is out of my control, out of my sphere of influence, to use a

Chinese political phrase. The Lord provided for us because . . ." His voice dropped and he spread his hands wide, as if he were about to catch something in his lap. "Because, Miss Green, we are His. Because we have chosen to be His. That is our choice." He cupped his hands in front of himself and looked at her again. "We place ourselves in His hands and He decides what will happen. He sends the sunshine or the rain. That is His choice."

Gertrude looked over her shoulder at the distant truck that had stopped in the narrow gap behind them. "Sort of like the five wise virgins who could not share their oil?" she asked, straightening around.

"Something like that, yes, I think so," he replied. "We cannot share what is not ours to give."

For the rest of the afternoon their mountain trek was interrupted only once, for half an hour, getting one of the trucks out of a muddy hole. As they had been warned, it was a frightening experience being stuck in the mud in bandit country.

Arriving in Kioshan as the sun nestled behind the hills, the missionary band sought out the militia barracks. Elder Warren needed information about the road that went farther south. What kind of road was it? Would it be safe to travel after dark? How far was it to Minkiang?

Gertrude stood leaning on the passenger door of the big truck and listening to the conversation between Elder Warren, General Li, and the militia commander. *We need to decide something pretty soon, fellas,* she worried as she stood erect, stamping her feet to get them warm. *We either need to get going or stop and feed the people.*

"The road is passable for a truck of your size," the militia commander said, "but there are a few bandits, in small groups. You could get through with 12 armed men as guards."

"I am not certain we want armed men on our trucks, my brother," Elder Warren argued to both men, struggling to maintain his Chinese politeness. "We do not want to antagonize the bandits, if they should appear."

"Armed men will not antagonize them. Armed men will make them stay far away," General Li insisted.

"It will take an hour to organize such a group of men," the militia commander offered.

"Please organize such a group," General Li commanded.

"But where will we put them?" Elder Warren asked. "On the fenders? On the hood? Our trucks are already loaded."

Gertrude turned away and wandered back to where Thelma stood at the rear of the truck.

"Well, what did they decide?" she asked sharply, pointing with her chin at the wrangling controversy in front of the barracks.

"Nothing, really. Typical of men," Gertrude replied shaking her head, "except that we have an hour, at least, before anything happens. Let's feed the people."

"Good idea," Thelma answered.

An hour later it was dark and the threat of being stuck in bandit country at night frightened everyone—except General Li. They had traveled only 15 miles so far. Minkiang was another 35 miles through the dark along mountain trails that were poorly marked and not well known, even to the militia. Despite the general's opposition, the decision was to stay in Kioshan for the night.

The militia commander suggested that, as they were missionaries, they should inquire at the Lutheran mission. He pointed to the mountain slope in the southwest corner of town where the city walls, like a great serpent, climbed up and around a large compound and a mission hospital. Once there, they discovered that the mission director, an American doctor, had gone to Hankow to get a medical exam for his wife. The Chinese doctor invited them to stay in the foreign director's house if they would sleep on the floor. The nursing students and the Chinese women and their children were housed in the hospital basement with the hospital workers. General Li and his family, the Mennonite girls, and the missionary group from Yencheng—including Thelma and Jeannie—found sleeping space in several small bedrooms that surrounded and opened into a large living room on the first floor of the big house.

After Jeannie had been put to bed, Gertrude and Thelma baked bread, biscuits, and crackers on a wood stove in the kitchen. Otis Erich, whom Gertrude had been treating for diarrhea for the last two days, was glad to see some solid food. Gertrude assigned him sleeping quarters in the room next to hers so that she could look in on him if need be. The contents of her medical bag were proving to be a godsend.

During the evening prayer time, with General Li in attendance, they discussed what they would do in the morning. If it rained in the night—and it looked as if it might—the road would be impassable. If it didn't rain, they would try to get everyone into one truck to attract less attention from bandits. During their prayer time they asked the Lord to send whatever weather He saw fit to send.

At 4:00 a. m. it began raining—hard. At 5:00 a.m. Raymond McMullen stepped into the large empty living room and found Gertrude and Thelma silently staring out the massive windows at the city and valley before them.

"Looks like the Lord has decided for us," Dr. McMullen offered.

"Indeed He has," said a voice from the opposite side of the room. Elder Warren and Mr. Erich stepped into the shadowed room from their quarters.

"It's a beautiful view from up here," Mr. Erich said, "even in the rain."

"That's all we'll do for today. Just look at it," Thelma said, rather less impressed.

"And see what we can find to restock our food supply," Gertrude added. "I used the last of the flour last night baking the bread."

"Sounds like we have some things to be thankful for and some time to find things we should ask for," Elder Warren observed. "Maybe we should have a little prayer meeting right here."

As the group knelt down and began to thank God for the rain, General Li stood quietly in the doorway to his family's sleeping quarters, observing with astonishment that these strange Christians were thanking God for the rain which would keep them in the very danger from which they wished to escape.

All day Friday it rained and grew steadily colder. Gertrude and Thelma went to the hospital and enlisted the help of the local hospital workers to pinpoint every shop and local merchant where they might find food for 52 people. Borrowing umbrellas for everyone, they sent the nursing students and the women without children into the city to the targeted areas, Gertrude and Thelma covered the farmers' market themselves. By evening, although the pickings were slim, they had garnered enough flour and rice to feed the entire group for another two days.

In the evening Gertrude sat with her feet up on the cooler side of the kitchen stove, steam slowly rising from her wet woolen socks.

"My stadium boots are leaking," she said. "They're wonderful for being out in the cold, but I never intended to live in them. They're falling apart."

"It's starting to snow," Thelma said, standing by the lace-curtained window.

"Been getting colder all day," Gertrude said, not looking up. She rubbed her feet where they ached in the arches.

Although it stopped snowing during the night, the cold wind continued to blow. The mud and water on the streets and trails froze solid.

A brilliant sun rose over the mission house the next morning, with no obstructing clouds and no chilling wind. It was a perfect day for traveling, except for one small detail. It was the Sabbath day.

"Where are you going?" Gertrude called, peering out of the kitchen door, her stirring spoon held at attention in her right hand. Their arms loaded with sleeping bundles, the two Mennonite girls had exited by the front door, the last one trying to shut it with her foot.

"We're loading up our truck," they called back from the front porch.

"But it's Sabbath," Thelma said, plainly puzzled. She stood in the doorway of her sleeping room dandling Jeannie on her hip.

Her spoon still at the ready, Gertrude followed the girls to the front porch where both trucks were parked in front of the house, the engines running. Beyond, she saw several more trucks waiting in a line at the compound gate, their drivers pacing back and forth on the road to keep warm.

"What is this?" Gertrude asked out loud to no one in particular.

"This is a caravan of trucks that are ready to travel over the frozen roads on a perfectly lovely day," Elder Warren said, stepping through the door behind her. "The general has spread the word of our ability to escape the Communists and the bandits. Now everyone wants to travel with us." He pointed down the hill to the right where three smaller trucks and a tiny car marked the tail end of the line. "Those last three trucks belong to the local bank."

"But we won't be going anywhere today. It's Sabbath," Gertrude said, her eyebrows arching in confusion.

"So I've been telling General Li," Elder Warren said. "But he insists that we should go." He pointed to the gate. "You can see that some of the others out there have hired guards to accompany them."

On closer inspection Gertrude saw several men in uniform walking about and the muzzles of rifles pointing out of the canvas flaps on the back of one of the trucks.

"Well, does he remember that we're the ones who hired our truck?" Gertrude said, shaking her spoon, her voice rising with her ire.

"That's the next step," Elder Warren said, carefully detouring around the spoon. He stepped off the porch into the crunchy remains of the snow, walked to the truck, and spoke to the driver who then turned off the engine.

Behind her Gertrude heard the rush of footfalls and stepped aside just in time to avoid being run over by the general's two servants loaded with bags and bedrolls. They were followed immediately by General Li. As they approached, Elder Warren intercepted them and told them to put their load on the ground.

As General Li approached him, Elder Warren spoke, bowing only slightly. "My brother, this is the Sabbath day. We will not be traveling on the Sabbath day. We will pay our driver for today—for the truck which we hired. But we will not be traveling today. You are welcome to travel with us tomorrow. On Sunday."

Gertrude watched as the general's face registered irritation, then anger, and finally, curiosity. "I am a Catholic, Pastor Warren, a good Catholic. And I would travel on a Sunday if my safety required it. Do you put your religion before your personal safety and the safety of the others you serve?"

"My religion *is* my safety," Elder Warren said calmly and firmly. His gaze never left the general's face.

"I will not argue with the Seventh-day Adventists," General Li said, bowing deeply. He stepped around to the rear of the truck and spoke to his servants. They picked up their loads and started for the house.

"What are they doing?" It was the American Mennonite girl standing in the doorway behind Gertrude.

"They're taking the general's things back in the house," Gertrude explained.

"But look at the beautiful day. Aren't you going today?" she asked, her arms spread wide.

"No, this is our Sabbath," Elder Warren said as he trudged toward the house. "We never travel on the Sabbath."

"But look at the wonderful day the Lord has given us that we may go," the Canadian girl argued, standing behind her friend in the doorway.

"You have your own truck. You can go," Elder Warren said kindly. "We will not stop you. But as far as we are concerned, we will not travel today. Tomorrow, on Sunday, we will go. Are you willing to travel tomorrow?"

"Yes. We are." The girls looked at each other, their brows drawn down into tight knots, their mouths in a pout. They turned and reentered the house. For the next 15 minutes Gertrude heard them talking loudly in their room. Then they tromped past her to their truck and talked to their driver. The two trucks started their engines and drove around back of the house. The two girls marched to the house, their faces set in firm lines. They would not make eye contact with Gertrude.

A few minutes later the truck drivers that were waiting at the gate started their engines and drove down to the road going south. From the porch Gertrude watched them drive through the gate and turn left into the trail indentations in the snow. She followed them with her eyes until the last little car disappeared behind short, scrubby trees at a bend in the road. The hacking coughs of their engines echoed briefly from the narrow valley beyond, quickly receding into the distance.

The Sabbath noon meal had been meager but filling. Gertrude had arranged to serve it in one of the larger rooms in the hospital to accommodate all those who had attended the worship services in the chapel. Gertrude had hoped the fellowship over food would repair some of the hard feelings of the morning. General Li and his family had attended the Sabbath worship service and the dinner, but the young Mennonite women had come only for the meal. Now everyone was back in the big house, most having retired to their sleeping rooms. Because she felt it was too cold outside for a Sabbath afternoon walk and because she was glad for a day of rest, Gertrude sat by the big windows facing west into the city, reading her Bible.

Below her on the city streets she heard, then saw, a commotion. Someone was coming in the South Gate, someone walking. They were soldiers in uniform but they were not marching, just stumbling along, at intervals, in groups of two or three. Watching them pass, the villagers came out of their houses, streaming along behind the soldiers like a kite's tail, twisting and winding through the streets. The cacophony of curious chatter filtered up to the mission house on the hill.

"Who are they?" asked the deep voice of General Li.

"I don't know," Gertrude answered, only half turning to acknowledge him, never taking her eyes from the scene.

"They look like the guards who went with the caravans this morning," he said, his voice growing quieter. "I will find out."

Gertrude heard his footfalls on the hardwood floor. The front door opened and closed.

When General Li returned, everyone had gathered in the living area near the big windows, discussing the spectacle in the streets below. As he entered the tall double doors, all eyes turned to him and all talking ceased.

"It is as I thought," he announced, hanging his heavy military coat on a peg in the hall. "They are the guards who went with the trucks this morning, at least what's left of them."

"What do you mean?" Zora said. Her voice sounded small and far away.

"All the cars and trucks that traveled toward Minkiang from here were looted, blown up, and burned—by the Communists," he said. His voice grew more solemn with each phrase. "All the people were shot, except for those who could escape." He nodded with his head toward the window. "The ones you see down there."

"That could have been us . . . if we'd traveled today," Thelma said, looking around the room, making sure everyone understood what she meant.

A few furtive glances passed around the room, but no sounds. The McMullens were the first to retire to their room. The Mennonite girls said nothing and looked at no one as they went to their room. Gertrude sought out Elder Warren's face. His eyes were moist, his face serious but calm.

We cannot share what is not ours to give, Gertrude remembered, then added from what she had learned in the last 24 hours, *and what others will not receive from us.*

Chapter 68

PREPARING THE GROUND

After Jeannie awoke from her nap, Thelma was ready to go out for a walk. "Father Warren, come walk with me," Thelma cajoled. "The sun is so beautiful. And I'm so tired of hiding inside dark buildings."

In turn, Elder Warren held out his hand to Gertrude, who was seated on the floor near the window. "Want to come with us?" He gave her his best smile. "The sunshine will make it seem warm."

"Sure," Gertrude said, rising to his good humor, laying aside her Bible. "I haven't had that long, fuzzy coat on for at least 24 hours." She stood and made for the hallway. "Let's see what happens."

Together they crunched through the crusty mud and snow, breaking a new trail down the hill to the hospital. The distance was less than 400 yards but the effort of walking on the rough, uneven, breakable surface and of breathing the cold, dry air made it seem three times as far.

Their path led them down to the middle of the drive that circled behind the house under the large living room windows. To their left were the doors that led to the basement rooms dug into the knoll under the house. To their right, beyond the broken-glass top of the compound wall that went down the hill from them and below their view, the grand vista of Kioshan and its cradling valley spread out before them.

Gertrude brought up the rear of the column on their return trip. Looking back, she noticed a line of soldiers marching around the bend in the road. It was where the caravan had left from earlier that day. Even as she pointed them out to the others, more soldiers appeared, followed by green, canvas-covered military vehicles pulling large gun carriages. Everyone paused to watch.

"Look over there," Thelma exclaimed, pointing to a split in the hills on the southwest side of the city. "There's more of them!"

"Those are Nationalist Chinese troops," Elder Warren said, thinking out loud. "But where did they come from and why so many?"

"Will General Li know?" Gertrude asked, watching entranced as thousands of troops and their equipment poured into the city.

"Let's go ask him," Elder Warren said, pointing to the living room window above them where a tall silhouette stood outlined in the sunlight.

"They are Szechuanese," General Li called out voluntarily as Gertrude and the rest entered the house, hanging their coats in the front hall and hurrying to the window.

"The 20th Division of the National Army, General Yang Sen's division," he explained in a quieter tone as they gathered around him.

"Are they moving north? Are they chasing the Communists like they did in Suiping?" Gertrude reasoned.

"If they've just come from the south, that means the road to the south of here is open and safe!" Thelma exulted.

"Maybe," he answered to both women's comments. His gaze scanned the troops that now spread through the city like ants swarming over a discarded apple core. "Wait here. I'll find out." He turned and headed for the door.

"There goes one very cautious man," Gertrude commented as the door shut behind the General.

"I'm sure he thinks it has kept him alive thus far," Elder Warren commented.

Within one hour Nationalist Chinese Army soldiers were digging trenches and building barricades in Kioshan. They shored up breaches in the city walls and repaired the canal moat that surrounded the western two-thirds of the city, even as more troops continued to pour in. By sundown and the close of Sabbath vespers, the soldiers were inside and outside the Lutheran compound, placing machine gun nests and building perimeter defense lines.

When Gertrude and Thelma went outside to talk with the few soldiers who spoke Mandarin, they found that the army was not here to chase the Communists. The Nationalist Army in the north, which had ridden the coal cars with Gertrude and supposedly had been chasing the Communists out of Suiping, had been routed in Junan. They were fleeing south while the

Communist armies of the Three Red Devils, Gertrude's music-appreciating generals, were close on their heels. The 20th Division had been sent to stop the Communist armies that were flooding down from the north and the east. The place chosen to stop them was Kioshan.

"General Yang's 20th Division is digging in for a siege," General Li confirmed, when he joined them all for prayers just before bedtime.

"And we'll be caught right in the middle of it," the Canadian girl complained bitterly. Gertrude watched her flounce her skirt over her knees with obvious irritation. "We should have left this morning like we wanted to."

"I do not think you really wanted to end up like the trucks that were burned by the Communists," General Li said carefully.

Not to mention what happened to the passengers, Gertrude thought with a wince.

"Well, we won't be any better off here," she retorted, tossing her skirts once again.

"I agree that we need to leave as soon as we can," the general lectured, looking about to be sure everyone was listening. "We can't be on the roads at night. It's too dangerous. But if the weather remains cold and the roads are frozen, we can leave early in the morning, if my brother agrees." He looked with deference to Elder Warren and nodded.

"I agree with my experienced brother," Elder Warren responded politely. "I've asked the truck drivers to come before daylight and to help us pack out."

"Besides praying for cold weather, we need to pray that the road to Minkiang stays open," Gertrude observed, thinking aloud as she considered their options for the morrow.

"Let's keep that in our prayers as well," Elder Warren said as he bowed his head and folded his hands.

Everyone else did likewise.

Gertrude awoke with a start. *What was that sound?* she wondered. Her watch said 1:00 a.m. In the distance she could hear rapid gunfire. *Machine guns?* Another explosion that sounded like distant thunder, then silence.

Gertrude got up from her portable cot, put on her long Chinese coat and quietly—so as not to awaken Thelma or Jeannie—opened the door into the living room. General Li was silhouetted against the night sky, gazing out of the large windows at the flashes of light that periodically illuminated various parts of the darkened city below.

"You are up early, Miss Green," the general remarked quietly.

"What are they doing?" she asked, ignoring his humor.

"They're exploring. To see where the weaknesses are in the line," he replied.

"Who are?"

"The Communists. They are here, Miss Green, all around the city," he said, his voice soft and deep, now completely serious. "They are trying to see how close they can get to the city wall."

"How close are they?" Gertrude squinted into the night, seeking to detect movement in the wavering shadows in the far distance, trying to attach objective meaning to the indiscernible.

"We will see when the sun rises."

Sunday morning breakfast consisted of *kongee* and General Li's explanation of how the Communists had surrounded the city in the night, cutting off their planned escape. Mr. Erich, much weakened by diarrhea, lay on Gertrude's cot, sipping hot rice broth made with the water drained from yesterday's vegetables. He wanted to be near the others and not miss out on their discussion. Gertrude worried about him because he was visibly losing weight.

"The 20th Division has excellent equipment," General Li explained as the others sipped their thin *kongee* broth. "They control the city and the roads"—he paused to swallow—"and they are able to pick off the Communists in the daytime with ease."

"Which means the Communists will attack after dark," Dr. McMullen concluded.

"Just like they did in Suiping," Thelma said, shaking her head. "No sleep."

"I'm afraid so." The general scanned the serious, attentive faces of those seated around the table. "But we are relatively safe in the daytime. We are fortunate that no one is positioned on the hill above us. It's not possible to shoot a cannon, or a gun for that matter, straight up or straight down hill. It's too hard to determine the trajectory."

"We are fortunate?" Gertrude snapped, setting her cup down with a thump. "We are relatively safe? We are surrounded and cut off from our escape road." Her eyes glowed green as her hands traced out their situation on the table top. "We are searching for food in the daytime"— she glanced over her shoulder at Otis Erich on the cot—"and getting no sleep at night. And we are fortunate?" The words rose with a flourish. Her hands spread wide in disbelief.

"But our death is not a certainty. Be thankful, Miss Green. It is not over yet." The general leveled his eyes, holding Gertrude's gaze with his own.

"Yes . . . ," she said, not lowering her eyes. *You have great faith, General. But in what,* she pondered, allowing consideration of his logic to abate her anger. "Yes. I suppose you're right, honorable general," she conceded, resting her hands on the table. Lowering her eyes, she nodded to his wisdom.

"Our compound, up here on the hill, means we are in an excellent defensive position, yes?" Dr. McMullen, wiping his mouth on the back of his hand, spoke aloud the conclusions he was mentally drawing from the general's explanations.

"Yes," he answered, appreciative of Dr. McMullen's military insight. "An excellent position. If I were General Yang, I would place all my big guns right here in this compound. I am sure he is more willing to lose the city than he is to lose this position on the hill."

"Which means we will be the center of the attack," Elder Warren concluded solemnly. Gertrude saw Elder Warren's face crease with concern when General Li confirmed his deduction.

"Yes, the bullets will come right into the house at night," General Li said. "There will probably be no glass left in any of the windows of this building."

Mr. Erich raised up on one elbow on the cot. "We should move to the basement at night, when the fighting is the worst," he said.

"The Nationalist Army is already filling the basement with its command centers," the general informed them. "One room has telephone communications wired in from over the entire city. Another room has wireless communications for all of central China."

"Let's go talk to the general, or whatever officer is in charge," Elder Warren interrupted. "Mr. Erich is right. We need to be in the basement at night."

After half an hour of explanations and polite pleadings, Elder Warren and General Li convinced the commanding officer to allow the missionary band to occupy the last room in the basement—the room on the outside western wall, the room just below the large windows, the room facing the direction from which the attacks would come.

As Gertrude already knew, food was a problem. All roads leading into the city, including the roads south, were controlled by the Communists. No food or ammunition could come in—neither for the army nor for civilians.

The daily foray into the city for food produced nothing, even with Thelma's reluctant offer of more money. Nothing remained in the regular shops or the farmers' market. Even the family gardens had been stripped— what had not already been hidden by the civilians—by the soldiers. In whispers, one or two farmers informed Gertrude that, under penalty of death, the army general had banned everyone from selling food to anyone who was not a soldier. They assured her that not even the most ardent entrepreneurial Chinese was willing to take such a risk for profit. By 11:00 o'clock Gertrude had returned to the compound and was discussing a food rationing plan with Elder Warren. He would present it to the entire group, including those at the hospital, at the noon meal.

Intense fighting around the perimeter of the city filled the night hours. The hard ground in the basement on which Gertrude's and Thelma's cots rested jumped and thumped with every huge explosion. Gertrude slept fitfully, getting up frequently to peer through the single, small, dirty glass window in the concrete wall that faced the city.

Frequently she shared the view with General Li. They did not speak nor point, but stood guard over the incendiary display below them for a few minutes before exhaustedly returning to their respective beds.

Lying quietly on her cot after an especially extended sentinel posting, Gertrude listened uneasily to the uproar beyond the front wall. *Why is no one else awake except me and General Li? What do we share in common? Fear? I don't think he's afraid. Anticipation of the outcome? I have no anticipations. I have no idea what's going to happen. Responsibility for others? Perhaps. The need to know so we can plan what we will do?* She stiffened through a series of rolling concussions. *A lack of faith?* She momentarily considered the thought as her hands reflexively folded on top of her chest. *Dear God, protect us and get us out of here . . . and please increase my faith.*

Despite the intense fighting of the night before, Monday morning revealed no serious incursions into the city. The decrease in hostilities in the "relative safety" of daylight permitted increased activities of maintenance and preparation—for the next night.

As General Li had predicted, the Nationalist Army moved heavy guns into the compound. The general watched and talked with the soldiers, gathering intelligence for his own private analysis. Elder Warren circulated with the general among the troops, speaking to the officers in the Szechuanese dialect, asking about their families and their home towns.

Gertrude and Dr. McMullen worked with the Chinese doctor in the hospital, organizing emergency ward rooms and treatment areas for the Chinese soldiers and civilians injured in the fighting. She and her graduate nurses and nursing students were a welcome replacement for the many hospital workers who had abandoned the hospital when the soldiers appeared. While the Chinese physician treated the patients, Gertrude organized nursing teams to oversee the hospital wards. And along with her senior nursing students, she accompanied teams of stretcher bearers in scouring the city for wounded who could be treated in the field. The more seriously wounded were transported to the hospital.

Thelma organized the women in their group who did not have children to search the city for food. Thelma was infinitely less successful in her endeavors than the others.

Entering through the back door of the big house into the kitchen, Gertrude smelled the pungent aroma of wheat *kongee* on the stove and heard the rise and fall of several voices speaking Chinese in the living room.

But I don't understand the dialect, she thought. *And there's another voice I don't recognize.* Puzzled, she strode across the room in a dozen quick steps and pushed open the door.

General Yang Sen stood in the middle of the room with several of the officers whom Gertrude had met previously. They faced Elder Warren and Dr. McMullen who had their backs to the kitchen door. Because they were speaking in the Szechuanese dialect, she understood only enough words to know that the general and Elder Warren were observing the age old oriental ritual of asking after each other's family. Elder Warren, who had served in southeastern China for many of his early years, was asking about the general's home town and mentioning villages and people he knew who might be friends of the general.

Screwing her eyebrows down tightly, Gertrude concentrated on the flow of words, listening for familiar phrases. *Something about . . . Elder Warren's family . . . no . . . his friends. Elder Warren says that . . . something about food . . . not enough for everyone . . . oh, that's us! The general is asking . . . how much food we have.*

"None," Gertrude said loudly, advancing on the group.

"Ah, Miss Green." Elder Warren turned abruptly, aware of her presence for the first time. "I'm not the only one who walks softly," he said in English with a twitch at the corners of his mouth. In Mandarin, he made his introductions, "General Yang Sen. Miss Gertrude Green."

The general clicked his heels together and stiffly nodded. "Miss . . . Green . . . the nurse, I believe," he struggled to speak in halting English. "I know . . . of you . . . work."

"I have observed your work also, honorable general," Gertrude said in smooth Mandarin. She indicated the view afforded by large windows. "The enemy has not entered the city."

"Not yet," he said. He paused, glancing out the window as if for confirmation. "And the food, Miss Green?" His attention shifted, first to Elder Warren then to Gertrude. "There is none?"

"I have heard . . . that there is an order for no one to sell any food—except to a soldier," Gertrude observed, her voice calm, her gaze steady.

The general turned and spoke to one of his officers.

He wants a bag . . . a sack. Gertrude struggled to understand the general's Szechuanese dialect. *He wants it filled . . . with rice . . . cabbage and . . . vegetables!*

"General," she blurted out in English.

He turned abruptly, looking at her sharply.

"Honorable general," she said in Mandarin, taking care to control her tone. "I know that vegetables are hard to find this time of year. The villagers need them to survive the winter and the wounded soldiers need them worse than we do."

"I appreciate your concern," General Sang Yen said, his face softening, "for the soldiers. I know of your kindnesses in the city already. I can assure you that the soldiers will be cared for as well as the missionaries." He gestured his largess with a generous sweep of his arm.

"Just so, honorable general." Gertrude folded her arms and bowed deeply. *You will be a powerful general indeed if you can make more vegetables grow in the winter,* she mused.

Within the hour Gertrude, Thelma, and Zora were in the kitchen with ample flour for baking bread and with vegetables for adding to a rice stew, newly bubbling on the stove.

"I'm glad for the rice and the vegetables, especially for Mr. Erich," Gertrude said. With an apron, found in one of the drawers, tied over her heavy Chinese clothes, she hovered over her work space, her floured hands molding small mounds of wheat dough. "He needs something of substance. He is getting weaker every day."

"How do you walk so straight?" Thelma asked.

Gertrude's hands stopped shaping the little buns. Her head came up as she turned to face Thelma. "What?"

"How do you walk so straight?" Thelma paused in her stirring of the stew. "You know, how do you walk upright? You walk straight up." She lifted her face from the steam rising from the pot and looked over her shoulder. "You talk to important people as if you have no fear. You face hard tasks and know what to do."

Zora stopped peeling the turnips and was listening as well.

"Everyone knows you because of the way you walk. Are you not afraid?"

Now turned completely, Thelma's small, round face was a study in genuine puzzlement—and adoration.

Gertrude faced them both, thoughts and memories racing through her mind. *Oh, girls, if you only knew.* Considerations of self-pity and self-revelation flitted by and vanished. Self-assurance seemed out of place. *Not with my lack of faith.*

"I don't know," she began. "I pray for the Lord to increase my faith." The words came out unbidden. Lamely, self-consciously, she attempted an explanation, "I'm trying to learn to wait on the Lord and to rely on Him."

"I think you're more Chinese than you know." Zora voiced her observation, cocking her head to one side as if considering a bug pinned under a glass.

"Not any Chinese *I* know." Thelma laughed disdainfully, struggling with her own assessment. "Maybe more American?"

"I don't think so," Gertrude tried again. *It's not the country you're from. That's not it.* She shrugged. *Then how do I explain it?* "I don't know," she mumbled.

Immediately after the mid afternoon meal, when the men had gone outside to watch the soldiers at work and the women were clearing the table, they heard a low rumbling which gradually increased in volume.

Gertrude stared up at the ceiling. Her two hands clasped the front of her apron, crumpling it into a ball. "What's that noise?" she shouted as she rushed for the front door and flung it open. Racing out on the porch, she held the apron to her mouth, shouting, "What is that noise?"

"They're airplanes," Elder Warren called out from down on the road. He hurried toward her. "Our airplanes!"

"Will they bomb us?" she cried, running into the yard, in the snow. She stared in the direction of the increasingly thunderous drone.

"The Communists don't have airplanes, Miss Green," General Li said, approaching the porch from the other side of the house. "They're what I've been expecting because of the clear weather. They are supply planes. Come. Stand up here on the porch where it is safer."

The general assisted her as the three of them climbed up on the porch and strained to look past the corner of the house toward the southwest. Dark shapes materialized as if emerging directly from the sun, flying low, on a collision course with the hills behind them. At the last moment dark boxes blotted the sky, large white canopies blooming above each one. Simultaneously all the aircraft pulled up sharply and to the left. The little group watched anxiously as the large pallets of supplies swung from their parachutes, drifting down, falling in a continuous line into the city and up the hill, some falling inside the compound, some landing dangerously close to the house.

As the Nationalist soldiers ran to retrieve the pallets, sniper fire erupted from all along the perimeter. From inside the city machine guns instantly replied which brought, in turn, gunfire from outside the city.

"I expected that," General Li said, pointing to pursuit fighter planes directly behind the bulkier supply planes. The fighter planes made strafing runs where the flashes of fire revealed the enemy's position.

Soon the air was filled with light bombers and fighter planes. They pummeled the enemy from the air as another wave of supply planes flew another aid mission to the city.

Gertrude couldn't take it. "I just can't stand the noise of airplanes," she sobbed into Elder Warren's chest. When the bombing and shooting had started, she'd wrapped her arms around his waist. She could not bear the sound alone.

"The army needs those supplies, Miss Green," General Li spoke emphatically, "and so do we. There is food in those boxes."

Gertrude looked up as a large container landed directly in front of the house and rolled once, its parachute falling over it like a large handkerchief. "It's not the food I mind, General," she shouted over the din. "It's the airplanes I'm deathly afraid of." She lifted her head, her fear turning to anger. "How am I going to visit the hospital? How can I go out in this hail of lead and minister to anyone?"

"See them like the hand of God," he retorted, pointing upward. "They cover us. They protect us. They supply our needs." He extended his hand. "Come, I will take you to the hospital. I will accompany you on your rounds. We will be safe—under the hand of God."

Timorously she released her grip on Elder Warren's coat. Placing her hand in his, Gertrude allowed General Li to lead her off the porch and around the house in the new path they had made in the snow on Sabbath afternoon. They hugged the edge of the house, walking past the wall of their sleeping quarters, toward the hospital. All around them airplanes bobbed and weaved, containers fell from the sky, and the sporadic rattle of gunfire punctuated the deadly conversation of war.

Chapter 69

PREPARING THE HEART

Wearily Gertrude emerged from the hospital at dusk. She paused to observe the gold and scarlet hues painting the sky above the setting sun and the shadows of evening advancing up and over the western hills just beyond city walls. The sharp trill of a bird drew her attention to the fruit trees clustered at the far end of the building.

Fruit trees and birds—odd things to find on a battlefield. Her medically trained mind made observations and cast about for explanations. *The hospital is down the hill from the house. No bullets have been flying in this direction. That's why the trees are still in place.* She scrutinized the western sky. *No more planes. No noise of any kind. Just the wind.* She gazed up at the house on the hill, the large gun emplacements bristling all around it, like unruly hair sticking out from under a hat brim. *It's peaceful now, but that will change as soon as the sun goes down.* Gertrude wrapped her long fur coat more tightly around her body, lowered her capped head, and trudged up the hill toward the house—alone.

Approaching the western wall of the house, Gertrude saw several soldiers stacking large objects that looked like fat, black sausages in tiered piles along the ridge in front of the door to their basement sleeping quarters. Another soldier was transferring small white boxes from a wheelbarrow to a growing mound directly under the small basement window.

"What's all this?" Gertrude barked, striding up the hill.

The young soldier backed away from the oncoming apparition in the long flapping coat. He held two white boxes—one in each hand—at arms length as if to ward off evil. "Oh, this is nothing," he stammered.

"No," she insisted, stopping next to the pile. She picked up one of the unmarked boxes and turned it over. "What are in all these little white boxes here in front of the window?"

"Nothing," he said again. He lowered his gaze to the boxes he held in his hands and would not look at her.

"It has to be something." She squinted at the box in her hand, trying to penetrate its covering. She waved it at him. "You have to tell me what it is," she commanded in a tone she used to speak to lazy or obstinate students.

"It is nothing," he mumbled, shaking his head. "It's only TNT."

"It's what?" Now it was Gertrude's turn to hold the little white box out at arms length, as far from her body as possible.

"It is only TNT," he repeated.

Not stopping to take off her coat or hat, Gertrude marched straight into the house and into the living room. Elder Warren stood in the center of the room, a suitcase in each hand, conferring with Dr. McMullen and General Li, whose backs were toward the front door. She advanced on the group, which had bundles, boxes, and suitcases piled around them, waving the little white box in her outstretched hand.

"Do you know what they're stacking out there against our wall?" she fumed as she barged across the room. Using the offensive box like the prow of a ship, she rammed under full sail through the luggage and the conversational group on her way to the window.

"It looks like TNT," General Li said, glancing at the box as it passed him, then returning to his conversation.

"And it's stacked out there against our wall!" she snapped, yanking back the edge of the loosely hanging window drape and gesturing wildly with the little box at the soldiers laboring in the muddy snow.

"Along with all the other munitions that came in the air drop," General Li explained, his voice developing a sharp edge. "Their ammunition needs to be where they can reach it easily."

"They have to move it!" Her voice—strident, shrill—filled the room like a train whistle.

"Gertrude!" Elder Warren's voice cracked in the air like a whip. "We can't move the boxes."

She looked at him, her eyes wide, blinking rapidly.

He gentled his voice when he knew he had her attention. "We can't impose on their hospitality any more than we already have."

"But if it blows up, it will kill us all in our sleep." Her voice was plaintive, begging them to see the reasonableness of her demand.

"No matter where it is located, Miss Green, if it blows up, it will destroy the entire house." General Li spoke insistently. "There is no escaping the destruction."

"It's in the Lord's hands, Miss Green," Dr. McMullen said, releasing a deep sigh of resignation.

"Can't we just try to help the Lord a little?" She looked from one male face to another, tears spilling down her cheeks. "Can they move it out a few feet?"

For a few moments no one moved. Then General Li nodded stiffly and said, "I will ask." He stepped around the suitcases standing beside him and walked out the front door without putting on his coat.

"Gertrude, can you come help us?" Elder Warren asked quietly, breaking the ensuing silence. "General Li was instructing us on how to build a barrier in our basement room. We've been taking all the luggage down there and putting up a wall in front of the small window and the door—to protect us."

"Of course," she sniffed, setting the small offending box on the window sill and wiping her eyes on her coat sleeves.

With small bundles under her arms and suitcases in each hand, she struggled behind Elder Warren and Dr. McMullen out the door. Single file they went down the path to the basement, stepped over the black sausages—mortar shells, she was told—that were lined up in the muddy depression they used as a pathway. In the gathering darkness, Gertrude saw soldiers moving little white boxes to a new pile—a whole two feet in front of the wall. General Li's statement, *If they blow up, they will destroy the house,* rang in her ears.

Up ahead, backlit by the flickering light of an oil lamp, the weak and emaciated Otis Erich stood outlined in the open basement door, waiting to receive them.

"We are stacking the luggage away from the window and the door," he said as he relieved Gertrude of her suitcases. He added them to the barricade he'd begun to build out from both walls and across the room, the ends of which overlapped in the middle, allowing a small passageway between them.

"If the enemy tosses hand grenades in the window, they'll go off in front of the barricade." He indicated the narrow open space between the window and the growing pile of luggage.

"And if the enemy bangs on this door in the night," Elder Warren added, opening the outside door, testing it to be sure it cleared the barrier, "we don't want to waste time getting the door open. It is impolite not to welcome your guests. Any hesitation shows fear or opposition."

"Wise as serpents, gentle as doves," Gertrude recited from memory. She shook her head, trying to understand how this simple Scriptural wisdom, which was so obviously out of place on a battlefield, just might save their lives.

"Just so, Miss Green," Elder Warren encouraged her. "But let's not tell the others and worry them unnecessarily."

Gertrude nodded numbly and followed the men out the door to get another load of luggage. *OK, we won't tell the others,* she mentally agreed. *But what do I tell myself? How do I stop shaking every time I think about hand grenades and mortar shells—and boxes of TNT outside my window?* Her trembling hand grasped the edge of what felt like a very thin and insufficient door and closed it behind her.

When the missionary band, with General Li and his family, gathered in the dimly lit basement room for evening prayers, they were joined by General Yang Sen. General Li had told him how the God of the Seventh-day Adventists had saved them from the Communists in Suiping and from the bandits on the road from Chumatien. With Thelma next to her and Jeannie cuddled on her lap, Gertrude sat on the floor leaning against the front of her cot, as General Yang beseeched them for their prayers.

"I want your prayers for my soldiers," he entreated them, standing in the center of the small room, bent at the waist in supplication.

An unusual position for a Chinese general, Gertrude considered as she watched him turning slowly, searching the deeply shadowed faces of each person. *What is he seeking?* she wondered. *Reassurance? A miracle? Does he think our prayers work like magic? That we have some special power or unique ability to reach God when others can't? What does the Chinese mind know about God?"*

"The Communists will bring everything they have against us tonight," he said soberly. "They have moved in their large mortars. These are so powerful they can reach all the way up the side of this mountain and drop shells on the roof of this house, shells which can penetrate all the way down to the basement."

Gertrude closed her eyes, shuddering at the thought. Instinctively, she hugged Jeannie tighter.

"They know this is where the ammunition is stored," General Yang continued earnestly. "They saw it come in on the parachutes."

Elder Warren slipped up beside him and touched his arm, interrupting his graphic description of their situation. Gertrude saw the general flinch and stiffen, now standing up straight, his eyes scanning the room—in fear?

"You have our solemn promise, honorable general," Elder Warren said reassuringly, stepping back a pace. "You will have our prayers. In fact, we would be pleased and honored if you would join us for prayers now." He motioned toward a place of prominence for the general next to Mr. Erich in the circle of worshippers.

The prayer meeting had begun some minutes earlier—as it had every night since they arrived in Kioshan—with a reading of Psalm 91: "He that dwelleth in the secret place of the most High shall abide under the shadow of the Almighty. I will say of the Lord, He is my refuge and my fortress: my God; in him will I trust."

As in previous nights, there had been a discussion of their situation listing specific items for prayer including their food shortage and the necessity of rationing the next day, the condition of the medical cases being tended in the hospital, and the continuing poor health of Mr. Erich. And then General Yang had made his vivid, desperate plea for their prayers.

Now, just before going to bed, their community worship was drawing to a close. It was time for prayer. The children would sleep the sleep of the innocent and the exhausted. But Gertrude knew that most of them would sleep fitfully, if at all. Filled with anxiety and apprehension, the adults would awaken with every explosion. Already she heard through the walls the increase of noise and activity in the nearby rooms where the Army had its headquarters. Telephones rang. Messengers called to one another. Outside in the distance, sporadic rifle fire had already begun; machine guns speaking to each other in short sentences. Tonight promised to be worse than last night.

"Let us pray," Elder Warren said, kneeling on the dirt floor.

Gertrude looked around at the others as they knelt beside their beds on the floor. Now with the barrier of suitcases in place, the room had become a small, intimate cell. It was rather like what she imagined rooms in a monastery would be, certainly smaller than anything she'd lived in at Union Springs Academy, in nursing school, or even in Shanghai.

"Our Father, which art in heaven . . ."

The Mennonite girls occupied the back corner against the outside stone wall. Next to them, in the center of the back wall, the McMullens huddled together, kneeling on their pallets, 5-year-old Ronnie tucked unresisting between his mother and father whose arms enfolded each other.

They are a family, a close family. Gertrude longed for the intimacy of their closeness and envied them. Images of Ruth in San Francisco and her brothers and mother in Rochester swam before her eyes as tears began to flow. *My family . . . is not here. My mother is on the other side of the world. She cannot pray for me like they are doing for each other. It's not even night where she is. And I have no husband . . .*

". . . our lives are in Your hands . . ."

General Li, his family, and two servants crowded into the other back corner and spilled into the center of the room. Through slitted eyes Gertrude watched him. He was erect, even on his knees. Somehow he hovered over his wife and two children like a great eagle, his gray-green military overcoat spread wide to shelter them.

". . . Your angels watch over us and protect us . . ."

In the front inside corner of the room, immediately behind the barricade, Gertrude remained seated with the sleeping Jeannie on her lap, Thelma, on her knees, nestled in tightly on her left. Thelma's hair gave off the pleasant odor of wood smoke, from the cook stove, Gertrude assumed.

O my Father, this is all that is left of my family. Gertrude thought back over the years of mothering nursing students, of being a sister to fellow missionaries, of huddling with "family" in small rooms and in dank basements in times of crisis.

The big guns surrounding the house thundered to life, shaking the ground. As if given permission to speak, every cannon in the valley answered them. The battle had begun in earnest. With the first heavy explosion, Thelma grabbed Gertrude's shoulder, her left hand squeezing Gertrude's forearm like a vice.

". . . commit our lives to Your keeping . . ."

O Lord, I am going to die . . . right here. Tears flowed freely down Gertrude's face. *There's no way to escape, nowhere to go.* Her chest heaved and she began to sob aloud, her breath coming in gasps. Thelma rose up on her knees and cradled Gertrude's head on her shoulder, as the two of them cried together.

" . . . the soldiers whose lives are in danger . . ."

Across the room General Yang arose from his knees and slipped out through the short runway in the barricade.

O God, why did I ever return to China? This is what I left behind. This is what I feared the most—always on the run . . . never completing anything . . . never being of any use to anyone. Gertrude's mind rambled, past frustrations mingling with present fears. Lifting her head from Thelma's shoulder, she tilted it back in emotional exhaustion, silently imploring heaven. Her mouth open and her eyes closed, she rasped out each breath. To her left, across the room, General Li's wife had collapsed in a heap and the McMullens cried quietly on each other's shoulder. Gertrude couldn't see the Mennonite girls. She raised her head and opened her eyes.

What will happen to all of us? And to the others?" Her mothering instincts engaged, pushing aside her personal anxieties. *What do I do to help them?* She looked at Elder Warren for assistance.

"It's going to be a long night, my friends," he said as he rose to his feet. His voice was husky but calm. "We should try to get some sleep if we can."

He lifted Jeannie from Gertrude's lap, then nodding to Thelma to lie down on her cot, he placed the little girl beside her mother. With a nod to General Li, he crossed the room to the McMullens, patting them both on the shoulder. Red-eyed, Raymond McMullen looked up at him, then began to help his family lie down on their pallets. After pausing in the far corner to whisper with the Mennonite missionaries, Elder Warren sat down on his own pallet, elbows resting on his knees, his head in his hands. Numbly Gertrude arose and, fully dressed, lay down on her cot.

For the next several hours, brilliant flashes of the battle filled the small window and reflected over the barricade, illuminating the cobwebs in the beams overhead. The ground shook almost continuously with the roar of the cannonade, kicking up fine dust from the floor into a misty fog.

Gertrude's gaze shot upward when the windows in the living room above them shattered, shards of glass skittering like gravel across the floor above them. At intervals she heard the other windows in the house, higher up and farther away, meet the same fate with the gentle bursting sound of dropped watermelons.

Gertrude sat up and looked down at Thelma's cot. Despite the shouting and the clatter of running soldiers coming from the adjacent rooms, despite the continuous, deep-throated thunder of the big guns, Jeannie slept peacefully in her mother's arms. Thelma's eyes were shut but her mouth moved as her hand caressed the little head cradled on her shoulder. Gertrude suspected that the other parents in the room were praying too.

"I'm not sleeping either." Elder Warren's whisper was so soft, Gertrude almost didn't hear it. She peered through the darkness, searching for his face in the recurrent flashes that lit the room. He still sat with his knees drawn up, his arms wrapped around them, his coat cascading like a tent around him. He obviously hadn't moved all night.

"What are you doing?" she asked.

"I'm watching and I'm praying, and I'm listening," he whispered.

"What are you watching . . . in the dark?"

"God in action," he murmured. "I can see the parents here in this room protecting their children. And I can imagine God doing the same." For an instant a shard of light reflected off his glasses. He was nodding in affirmation of his own conclusion. "After General Yang's graphic description of the mortars, I would have expected one or two to hit the house by now, wouldn't you?"

He's right. I heard the windows break, but the house has not been hit. At least not so far as I can tell. She was astonished at the reality of his conclusion.

"Right now I am feeling like a child in His arms, as if a dome of angels has been placed over this house and we are safely inside," he said softly.

Gertrude lay back on her cot. *Outside the world is coming to an end. In here we are safely in the arms of Jesus.* She closed her eyes. *Can I believe that?* Quietly the words of Psalm 91 washed over her: *He that dwelleth in the secret place of the most High shall abide under the shadow of the Almighty. I will say of the Lord, He is my refuge and my fortress: my God; in Him will I trust.* Tears of peaceful relief flowed gently down past her nose and along the creases in her cheeks, stinging her lips with their saltiness. "He cares for me. He cares for *me*," she repeated, as she brushed away the wetness with the back of her hand.

Gertrude heard the door open as sunlight shot across the ceiling, momentarily brightening the room. Looking around, she saw the Mennonite girls straightening themselves as best they could, preparing for the day. Everyone had slept in their clothes, prepared to flee at a moment's notice. No one had time—or the privacy—for morning ablutions. Elder Warren was gone, as were Dr. McMullen and General Li. Otis lay crumpled on his pallet, sleeping the exhausted sleep of the ill.

Gertrude stepped through the basement door and walked out into the cold brightness of a pale-blue winter sky. Squinting up at the house rising above her, she thankfully noted that it was still intact. She looked behind her. The ground along the ridge toward the city and the ground down the hill toward the gate was pockmarked with holes, craters ringed by grass clumps and tree limbs that had been torn out by the blast of shells. Around her feet the ground had been beaten down by a multitude of soldiers' feet. The little white TNT boxes were gone, as were all the mortar shells. From the front of the house, she heard Elder Warren's the rich tenor voice speaking in the Szechuan dialect with someone—*an officer, perhaps?*

She rounded the corner of the building and heard Elder Warren explaining to Dr. McMullen what the officers—there were three of them—had said.

"They say that they were outnumbered five to one, but they had the superior firepower. The Communists threw everything at them last night and will do it again tonight, they say, but they'll never surrender."

"It can't be any worse than it was last night," Gertrude said in Mandarin as she approached the group, intending that the officers would know she understood them.

"No, probably not," Elder Warren answered in Mandarin, turning toward her. "Good morning, Miss Green."

"Good morning, honorable pastor," Gertrude returned, bowing properly, remembering to play her part in showing respect in front of the officers.

"There were several breaches in the walls last night and three times the Communists broke through down there near the South Gate," he continued in English for Dr. McMullen, pointing down the hill. "But they were beaten back with a terrible loss of life for the Communists, if I understand these officers correctly."

"How long can they hold out against such odds?" Dr. McMullen wondered aloud.

"That's a question best left until General Li returns at breakfast, I think," Elder Warren said slowly.

The rest had begun to eat their breakfast rations when General Li entered the house. They sat at the table with their coats on, the room darkened by the paper they'd placed over the broken windows. One small oil lamp cast a flickering glow over the weary, stricken faces of those who waited for his report.

The general hung up his greatcoat in the hall in silence, and Gertrude knew the news was not good. General Li never greeted anyone when the news was bad. Instead of taking his usual place next to his wife at the end of the table, he strode to the head of the table. Leaning over, he conferred quietly with Elder Warren, the acknowledged spiritual leader of the band of 16 who had survived two horrid nights in the missionary house high on the hill.

Gertrude watched Elder Warren's face. She saw that his head leaned forward with intense listening. She saw his brows knit together as he asked two or three terse questions. When Elder Warren closed his eyes and slowly nodded, General Li stood erect and looked out over the heads of his audience, focusing on the back wall, avoiding eye contact.

"General Yang Sen requests that we evacuate today to the hospital basement," he said in a tight, sharp voice.

"Why?" Gertrude spoke without thinking. "It was perfectly safe here last night."

"That's not what you said last night," Thelma said in a hollow voice. She stared into her bowl of *kongee* and stirred it slowly.

"Why must we leave the house?" Zora's shrill voice rang out, cutting off Gertrude's rejoinder, drawing her attention to the other side of the table.

General Li looked down at Elder Warren who nodded again slowly, his eyes downcast, his face grim.

"General Yang says they have no more ammunition," he began slowly. "He says that there are no more supplies. They will fight on as long as they can, but when their ammunition runs out tonight, they will have to surrender. He thinks that, if we stay in the house, we will be killed when the Communists overrun this position. Those in the hospital will probably be spared as the Communists will think that they're hospital workers."

"These generals? These are the Three Red Devils we met in Suiping, right?" Thelma's biting words gave voice to her fear, converting it to anger. "Don't you think these generals will recognize us?"

"Probably so." It was Elder Warren who answered her sarcasm with simple truth.

"So we will be dead no matter . . . where we stay." Thelma's voice trailed off as she recognized the real meaning of her angry conclusion. Gertrude watched her play with her bowl and glance at Jeannie who sat beside her, intently laboring over her *kongee* with an adult spoon.

"I think we would have more of a chance if we viewed the battle from a distance—at the hospital," General Li observed. "Then we would have more of a chance to escape—if that became necessary." No one spoke. No one ate. "The Communists will probably blow up this house rather than try to take it room by room. It's what I would do, if it were me."

Elder Warren rose and stood beside the general. "My brother is wise in the ways of war. And I think my brother knows what is the best course of action." He turned to face General Li and bowed low. "I will ask you to lead us in these matters and I will follow your instructions."

Gertrude scraped back her chair and stood. She wanted to be angry but could only muster enough strength to be resentful. "We might as well go and die with the rest of them as to die here alone," she said, her voice as hollow and tired as she felt. She walked behind her chair and pushed it forward. "I will be closer to my patients there," she reasoned, grasping for some semblance of a rational act she could perform in the midst of events that were beyond anyone's control. She looked down at the half-eaten muffin on her plate. "We don't have much. I think we can be packed in 20 minutes, yes?" Several heads nodded around the table. "OK, then."

By midmorning they had all moved their sleeping accommodations into the unoccupied spaces in the hospital basement. During the rest of the day Gertrude concentrated intensely on her nursing duties, organizing care for last night's wounded, and settling Otis Erich onto a hospital cot for hourly rehydration with the last of the rice and vegetable water.

By twilight, when Elder Warren convened the evening prayer service in the hospital lobby, every person had heard about the grim report given by

General Li that morning. Seated on the floor in families and in intimate groups, a continuous circle of solemn faces looked up as Elder Warren—in Mandarin—began reading Psalm 18:1-7. No one had to explain the meaning of, "Then the earth shook and trembled." And everyone—even General Yang who sat with General Li and his family—appreciated verses two and three: "The Lord is my rock, and my fortress, and my deliverer; my God, my strength, in whom I will trust; my buckler, and the horn of my salvation, and my high tower. I will call upon the Lord, who is worthy to be praised: so shall I be saved from mine enemies."

Gertrude sat on a chair near the reception desk surveying such a scene of solemn worship as she'd never before witnessed. *Everyone here, even General Li, I think, knows that only the hand of Providence can save us.* Occasionally, she reached out and patted Mr. Erich's hand, lying on a recliner to her immediate left. Her touch reassured him while she checked his pulse and his warmth at the same time. When General Yang silently arose and slipped away, Gertrude silently prayed, "Dear God, protect us. It's about to begin."

Chapter 70

RINGING IN THE NEW YEAR

The room in the hospital basement was much larger than the small, cell-like enclosure the group had occupied the night before. Near the ceiling's supporting pillars, small lamps or candles flickered. They illuminated the makeshift nursing stations around which Gertrude had arranged little pods of patients, moved downstairs from the vulnerable spaces upstairs.

In between the temporary "patient wards" were the clustered sleeping pallets of hospital workers from Kioshan and the Chinese women and children immigrants from Yencheng. Tucked in around these who had previously established residential living spaces in the basement were the refugees from the big missionary house on the hill. Just above their heads, drifting like fog on the night air, floating in the tattered ends of the shadows, was the quiet rustle of human voices. The children were sleeping; the parents were awake—some praying, some encouraging one another, their soft voices like a wind whispering through foliage. Hovering over them all was the funereal pall of darkness.

Silent as a wraith, Gertrude glided from patient area to patient area, checking on her nursing students and her patients. From time to time she glanced toward the far end of the large room where Thelma's cot stood close to Elder Warren's pallet. He sat in the same position as the night before, arms draped around his knees. Gertrude knew he was praying. Otis Erich slept on Gertrude's cot next to Thelma. She knelt on the floor, praying over Jeannie who slept snuggled under a blanket.

Gertrude would not sleep, not tonight. Having her student nurses and her patients gave her focus, gave her something to do. She was glad beyond words to have something to think about other than the disaster that crouched like a wild animal in the dark corners of the room—a room that was their prison and their sanctuary.

Bent over a nursing station table, Gertrude glanced up at the ceiling when the first faint whistle of a flying mortar shell crescendoed into a *whump* somewhere on the Lutheran compound, followed by an explosion. The hospital was far enough away and the basement walls thick enough to mute the rifle and machine-gun fire. But the high-pitched screams of the mortars penetrated into their inner sanctum and the earth-shaking concussions reverberated through the floor. Gertrude hurried through the narrow aisles to the far wall. Two more mortars landed before she could crouch down next to Thelma.

"Are you all right?" Gertrude whispered as she draped an arm over Thelma's shoulders.

"I can't hear what's happening!" Thelma growled under her breath. "In the house basement we had all the radio messages and the telephones and the soldiers running in and out of the other rooms. We knew what was happening. Here there's nothing."

And we complained about all the noise, Gertrude reflected as two more explosions made the floor jump. "They're getting closer together," she whispered.

Thelma nodded as, without conscious thought, she lay her body across her sleeping child.

The barrage continued for the next five hours. The mortars came frequently but always off to the north toward the house on the hill, the explosions seeming to increase in intensity as well as in frequency. The small familial clusters, Christian and pagan alike, huddled in the darkness of the basement and prayed for each other, each to his own god. No one moved.

Then at 2:00 a.m., it suddenly became deathly quiet.

"Do you hear anything?" Thelma Hwang panted after a few agonizing minutes of silence. "Father Warren, do you hear anything?"

Gertrude strained her ears for the expected sounds of murderously victorious troops overrunning the compound. But there was no sound of gunfire, no grenades exploding, no running or shouting soldiers. She heard no sound of any kind. Slowly she stood up, as if being nearer the ceiling would give her an advantage.

"Surely the final assault will come soon," Elder Warren whispered. He also stood, listening intently.

For more than an hour the group remained silent, waiting, as if by a noisy commotion they would invite the invading enemy in to kill them, as if by remaining silent they could remain hidden forever.

Gradually various ones in the hushed room began to stand, to move about, to speak in audible tones, to ask questions. The anxiety of waiting for the inevitable mounted.

"If they're going to do it, I wish they'd hurry up." Gertrude looked around to find the source of such a ridiculous request. Clutching his wife's sobbing form, Dr. McMullen knelt on one knee, his fisted right hand balled in defiance, his face a mask of dark anger.

"I would go out and find out what's happening," Elder Warren said softly. "But I'm unfamiliar with the compound around the hospital. I don't want to stumble about in the shadows and become a target for some nervous soldier."

"Let me see if I can find a guide for you, someone who knows the grounds," Gertrude said. Her eyes cast about in the shadows as she went in search of a local hospital employee who could act as guide. She returned a few moments later with an ill-clad but willing gray-bearded elderly man, a grounds worker who possessed his own flashlight. After a few hurried words of instruction, a borrowed coat for the old worker, and a prayer for safety, Gertrude stood by the open doorway and watched the old man and his flashlight, followed by Elder Warren, disappear up the stairs into the darkness.

While they were gone, Gertrude made her rounds of the nursing stations and the missionary groups, encouraging her nursing students, praying with frightened Chinese mothers, reassuring nervous hospital workers, conferring with the Chinese doctor. Inside her head, as a constant prayer, Psalm 91 went around and around: *He that dwelleth in the secret place of the most High shall abide under the shadow of the Almighty. I will say of the Lord, He is my refuge and my fortress: my God; in him will I trust.*

Forty-five minutes later, Thelma called out, "Gertrude, look!"

Rising up quickly from her crouched position beside a patient bed, Gertrude saw a shaft of light flash down the stairwell followed by two shadowy figures. She hurried toward them.

"There's no one out there, Gertrude," Elder Warren said, shaking his head in disbelief. "We walked all around the hospital and up the hill toward the house. Everyone is gone."

"Everyone? No soldiers? Nobody?" Gertrude struggled to understand the incomprehensible.

"Nobody. You want to come see?"

"Yes. Yes, I do." Snatching up her coat, Gertrude said to Thelma, "Come on, let's go see this."

Hastily pulling on coats and mittens, Gertrude, Thelma, Raymond McMullen, and General Li followed Elder Warren and the old Chinese gentleman up the stairs and out into the chilly, star-filled night.

Down in the hollow where the hospital sat, there was not a sound. The compound wall was high and the city could not be seen. Above them the big house on the hill rose up like a hollow specter in the starlight. From its open basement doors squares of light spread out on the ground like empty garden plots, undisturbed by movement of any kind.

"You know what this is like?" Thelma whispered, pausing, her frosted breath visible in the cold air.

"What?" Gertrude asked, gazing up at the silent, star-studded wonder before her.

"'Silent night, holy night,'" Thelma quoted. "And there's the stable just like in the Christmas card pictures." She pointed to the light coming from the open basement door up on the hill.

"You're a week late," Gertrude chided. "Christmas was a week ago. Today is January the first. In some places in the world this is New Year's Day."

"I still prefer Christmas." Thelma's upturned face shone serenely in the starlight. She reached out and clasped Gertrude's mittened hand in her own.

Gertrude gave a tug and started forward. "Come on, you old silly, we'd better keep up."

The troupe cautiously trudged up the hill behind the wavering flashlight. The house grew larger and blocked out the sky to the north. The basement doors were wide open, the lanterns within casting elongated rectangles of light on the snow. The large cannons on the west side of the house stood silent and unattended. Gaining the crest of the hill, standing in front of the door to their old sleeping quarters, Gertrude looked across the valley to the west. Fires burned in various parts of the city, but there was no gunfire of any caliber.

Excited Chinese voices drifted up from the front gate of the compound below them on the road. Taking the flashlight from the wary old man, Elder

Warren led the group down the drive. Calling out a greeting from a distance, he cautiously approached two figures near the gate, pointing the flashlight at the ground as he walked. Judiciously applied beams revealed them to be celebrating soldiers who were supposed to be standing guard at the gate.

"What's happening?" he asked in Szechuanese as he approached.

"The Communists have withdrawn," they responded, their faces split by wide grins. "They ran away."

"Why?" he asked, hoping for some more clearly rational explanation.

"We don't know, but they are gone."

After a whispered conference, everyone agreed that venturing out among the celebrating soldiers might be dangerous. Retreating back up to the top of the hill near the house, they stared down at the valley for several minutes, trying to discern what mysterious event had transpired that would stop the fighting so suddenly and so completely. With parting sidelong glances at the city of Kioshan below them, the missionaries quietly returned to the hospital basement and explained to everyone that there would be no more fighting that night. Everyone could go to sleep.

Without exception, all were stunned into silence. Amazingly, without the usual chatter of Chinese gossip, all settled down on their makeshift beds and fell into a deep slumber. Even Mr. Erich seemed to feel better knowing that something like a miracle had delivered them all. As for the little scouting group, they were suddenly very tired.

In the morning the kitchen help served a late breakfast of *kongee* from a large communal kettle. The various family groupings carried their bowls to the pot and back to their sleeping areas and the hospital workers likewise fed the patients. When General Li's wife, accompanied by her servants, returned to the Li sleeping area with her family's breakfast bowls, Gertrude noticed that General Li was not with them.

"He's gone out to find out what happened," Thelma commented as she helped Jeannie with her bowl. "He always has to know everything."

"He thinks by knowing everything he can survive," Gertrude said.

"Does he know the Lord?" Thelma asked, looking up at Gertrude. "Does he know it was the Lord who stopped the fighting last night?" A cry from Jeannie drew Thelma's attention. She grabbed the child's bowl, preventing a spill.

"How do you know the Lord stopped the fighting?" Gertrude asked abruptly. She had stopped eating and was holding her bowl in both hands, gazing into the distance, beyond the walls of their fortress basement. She tried to imagine how God could have stopped a war. "How did He do that?"

"I don't know." Thelma shrugged dismissively. "I just know He did."

Elder Warren stood and stretched. "Who would like to go for a walk?" he asked, looking around. "Find out for themselves what the Lord did last night?"

Dr. McMullen stood, then looked at his wife for confirmation. She nodded, her eyes softer and more peaceful than Gertrude had seen for a long time.

"We're coming, too." It was the two Mennonite girls who were already snuggled into their coats.

"I need to stay here with Jeannie. She needs a bath," Thelma said. "I need one, too, but I think that may have to wait. No privacy." She raised her eyebrows with a chuckle, then shrugged off her attempt at a small joke and turned away.

Wrapped warmly against the cold, Elder Warren, Gertrude, and the rest ascended the basement steps into the bright sunshine of midday. For the next 90 minutes they wandered the streets and climbed the small hills that bordered the high wall south and west of the city. Thousands of dead Communist soldiers lay everywhere in piles inside the wall or stacked in crevices and gaps as part of the wall, some appearing to have been there for as long as three days. The stench was nauseatingly overpowering. With their noses covered, they abandoned their plans for a long walk and quickly crossed through the center of the city, back up the hill to the Lutheran compound.

As they entered the front gate, they were greeted by screams and cries for help—in Mandarin.

"Where's that coming from?" Gertrude called out, stepping up quickly beside Elder Warren who was striding up the drive toward the big house. "It's not Szechuanese, is it?"

"It sounds like it's coming from over there," he said, pointing beyond the house to the garage area where the compound cars and trucks were stored.

Moans and cries of pain from behind them caused Gertrude and the Mennonite girls to turn and look as three groups of stretcher bearers came plodding through the mud, entering the compound gateway. On each litter was a wounded Communist soldier, his arms dangling helplessly over the edge of the stretcher or flailing weakly in the air. The stretcher bearers turned up the drive, heading for the garage area.

Her long fur coat flapping about her legs, Gertrude splashed through the mud back down the drive past the astonished Mennonite girls and followed the soldiers. "Come on," she called out, waving to her companions.

The muddy parking area in front of the truck barn was covered with stretchers, set haphazardly about in the sun, bearing the bodies—some alive and some dead—of Communist soldiers. Their faces were covered with mud, their bodies bleeding, their lips parched and split open.

Gertrude ran to a Nationalist soldier who carried a pistol on his belt and looked like he might be in charge.

"Who is taking care of these wounded men?" she demanded.

"No one," he answered without emotion. "They are from the army of the enemy."

"Then we will take care of them," Gertrude said, her feet spread apart, her arms folded across her chest.

The soldier paused a moment, studying the American missionary before him, dressed in Chinese clothes and a Western fur coat—with a knitted, peaked cap on her head. "That is good," he said. "We know you are missionaries. We know you take care of everyone." He turned away to direct the newest arrivals to an empty spot on the ground.

Gertrude watched him walk away. *Dr. Miller, you were right,* she thought. *This is not our war. Our war is with sickness and disease. We have no enemies, only very sick patients who need our care.*

As Elder Warren and Dr. McMullen approached the garage area, Gertrude confronted them. "Dr. McMullen, what can we do for these men? We've got to help them."

"Not much, I'm afraid. There are too many, Gertrude," Dr. McMullen said, shaking his head. "Besides, what can we do for them? The hospital has no surgical supplies or intravenous fluids."

"Well, I can't just let them lie there," she said in frustration, turning about to view again the broken human remains of war. "I'm a Christian nurse. I have to do something."

"Let's go back to the hospital," Elder Warren suggested. "Let's see what we can find."

At the hospital Thelma gathered a basket of wheat crackers that Gertrude had baked the day before. Gertrude collected spare bottles from various places in the hospital and filled them with water.

"Come on, girls," she said to her nursing students, "this is nursing at its most basic. You won't see it any worse than here."

With everyone carrying scraps of food or bottles of water in various makeshift backpacks and baskets, Gertrude led the Mennonite girls, her nursing students, Thelma, and Dr. McMullen back to the parking area where they ministered with what they had to the suffering Communist soldiers. When every wounded man had received water and food and had been prayed with, the group returned to the hospital. Gertrude vowed to return that evening with her own workers to carry the ones she could help to the hospital.

"I found out what happened last night," Gertrude told Thelma as they trudged down the now well-worn path to the hospital.

"You did?"

"Yes. I was talking to one of the soldiers back there and he told me everything."

Gertrude gazed out at the city on their right and up to the mountains that rose above them on their left. "I'll tell everyone when we get back to the hospital."

At 1:30 that afternoon, the missionary group from the big house, including General Li who'd returned, and his family, gathered in a large, informal circle in the hospital basement. Crouched on the floor near their sleeping mats, they shared the remaining warmed-up *kongee* from the morning's pot. Mr. Erich, propped up on one elbow on Gertrude's cot, sipped his warm vegetable broth, ate her wheat crackers, and tried not to look hungry.

"Gertrude, I can't wait any longer," Thelma said, after settling Jeannie with her small bowl and spoon. "You said you were going to tell us what you learned from the soldier this morning."

"Well, yes. Yes, I need to tell you all," Gertrude said, slurping down a spoonful of *kongee* broth and wiping her mouth on her coat sleeve. "This is what he told me—and I can hardly believe it." She set her bowl on the floor beside her and enthusiastically rose up on her knees. "He told me that they—the Communist army—were ready to make their final push into the city when they saw a huge army—a tremendous number of troops with all kinds of ammunition—coming right at them from all around the wall. He said the commanders sent up a red flare, that's their signal for retreat, and all the Communist soldiers retreated way back into the hills and mountains.

"I think the Nationalist Army must have had some kind of reserves, or the Lord kept them hidden away until the last minute. I don't know. At any rate they made some kind of desperate push and scared the Communists away. Anyway, that's what he told me," she said with a finishing flourish, sinking back down. Reaching for her bowl, she confided more quietly to Thelma, "However it was that the Lord made it happen, I'm glad He did."

Thelma wasn't looking at her. She was studying General Li. Thelma glanced quickly at Gertrude, caught her eye, and jerked her head ever so slightly toward the general's rugged face. Gertrude followed her gaze, and could hardly believe what she saw.

Gone was General Li's sober control. His eyes were wide open. His jaw had dropped and his lips were parted in a plastic grin. The spoon in his right hand slowly and mechanically lowered itself to the bowl cradled in his motionless left hand.

A frightened Chinese face, if ever I saw one, Gertrude concluded, staring at him, *but why?*

"General Li, what's the problem?" Elder Warren had also seen the look of severe fright.

Slowly the general swiveled his head toward Elder Warren, his gaze at once frightened and quizzical. He let out a deep, audible sigh and snapped his eyes shut twice in rapid succession before closing his mouth. "I hardly know what to say or what to ask, my brother," he said, his deep baritone so soft that Gertrude could hardly hear him.

"What do you mean?" Elder Warren asked gently.

"You know, you all know," he said, his gaze sweeping around the circle of faces, his voice growing in volume. "I told you at breakfast yesterday what General Yang told me. The Nationalist Army was completely out of ammunition. Completely. Last night—this morning—they were laying down their arms. They were preparing to surrender when they saw the red flare go up. They didn't know that it was a signal for retreat. All they knew was that the Communists suddenly withdrew, broke off what General Yang thought was the final attack." His voice became almost a whisper. "The Nationalist Army had no army, my brother." He looked earnestly into Elder Warren's face. "The Nationalist Army was ready to quit. They still do not understand what happened."

"They did not make a final push?" Gertrude asked, completely astonished. For the second time in less than 12 hours she tried to understand the incomprehensible.

General Li turned to face her. "No," he answered plainly.

"Then what was it the Communists saw?" Gertrude's mind staggered before the gradually emerging truth that Thelma's miracle of salvation had suddenly grown to unimaginable proportions.

"'The angel of the Lord encampeth round about them that fear him, and delivereth them.'" Elder Warren quoted Psalm 34:7 in hushed, but firm tones.

But in Gertrude's ears the words roared like crashing waves on a beach, the turbulent, churning surf of Truth washing over her, upending her mind, and tumbling her thoughts in the sand, scrubbing them clean of fear and doubt. "You mean like the story of Elisha and the Army of the Lord?" she whispered.

"Exactly like that," Elder Warren said, speaking more loudly, more confidently. "'Fear not; for they that be with us are more than they that be with them'," he quoted again.

"The Nationalist Army has lost more than 1,000 men," General Li said, sounding like an echo, like a man in a dark cave talking to himself, searching for a way out. "But there is no accounting of the Communist dead. Some are estimating more than 10,000."

Gertrude sat transfixed, the magnitude of the miracle of their deliverance slowly becoming reality. Other instances in her life came to mind, times of deliverance, of protection. When it happened, she'd hailed them as interventions of the Lord. But had she really meant it? "We said the same thing when they bombed us in Yencheng in 1941," she remembered aloud, speaking from a vivid memory, her green eyes aglow with intensity. "'A thousand shall fall at thy side and ten thousand at thy right hand; but it shall not come nigh thee.'"

"You act like you are not surprised," General Li interposed, desperately needing an explanation. "You act like you always knew that the Lord would take care of you. Does He always do this—for you?" He was leaning forward, examining earnestly Gertrude's face, then Elder Warren's, Mr. Erich's, and the others.

Elder Warren spoke first. "Of course, we are very happy and blessed. But, no, we did not know if the Lord would preserve our lives. After all, the history of the Christian church is full of martyrs."

"Yes, I know," General Li said huskily. "I helped to create some of them."

"God does not always prevent disaster," Elder Warren continued. "In faith, we just leave it up to Him to decide what to do, what is the best course for us."

"That's the hard part," Gertrude confessed, staring at General Li. She wanted to share with him all that she thought she understood, all that had occurred to her in these last few moments of reflection, all that was becoming more clear. She wanted him to know, but she wanted to capture the moment of truth for herself. "The hard part is waiting on the Lord and letting Him be in charge. I'm still not good at it. But after last night I think I will do better."

For the next three days, Friday, the Sabbath, and Sunday, Gertrude and her friends remained in Kioshan. No one was allowed to leave or enter the city for no one knew who was a Communist. For the next three nights, in her dreams, Gertrude saw piles of dead bodies, smelled the stench of three-day-old death, and heard the silence of a star-filled night.

China Daily News – Tuesday, Jan. 6, 1948

GOVT CLAIMS THREE RED DEVILS ROUTED

Nanking, Jan. 5—AP—The forces of the "three Red devils," communist generals one-eyed Liu Po-cheng, Chen Yi and Chen Keng were smashed at the Peiping-Hankow rail town of Kioshan, according to a report received today from the Hankow correspondent of the government Central News Agency.

Powerful units of the still fledgling Chinese Air Force were said to have hammered at and "finally routed" the communist forces. It was the second massed Red approach on the southern section of the rail line and the anti-government forces were already reported at the outer perimeter of the important railway station before the Nationalists wielded their air weapon to succeed in "clearing all communists" from the rail line, as reported.

Chapter 71

TRYING TO MAKE SENSE OF IT ALL

On Monday, January 5, when no further attacks came from the Communists, General Yang Sen gave permission for the gates of the city to be opened. While Thelma organized the Chinese women and children and Gertrude, with her students, scrounged the city one last time for food, Elder Warren and Dr. McMullen procured a truck and driver. During the fighting the truck had lost a tire on each back wheel, leaving it unable to carry all the luggage and the people. To carry the extra weight, General Li hired two large horse carts and drivers to accompany them. By the time everyone was loaded and orders were issued and passed down the line of command to open the barricades at the South Gate, it was 1:00 p.m.

Marching on either side of the first horse cart, Gertrude and Elder Warren hurried to keep pace as the driver urged the horse to follow the truck just in front of them. Already it had passed the last barricade and was accelerating through the gate. Looking up as they passed under it, Gertrude examined the thick, battle-scarred masonry arch above the gate. Turning her head to the left to gaze at the heavy walls which had so recently held out the enemy, she saw in the distance the Lutheran Mission house standing on the knoll above the city.

Such an obvious and easy target, yet there it stands, she reflected. "There's our stone, our Ebenezer," she shouted, pointing, speaking loudly so she'd be heard above the rattle and bang of the horse cart. "Who was it said that—in the Bible?" she asked, trying to remember the scriptural reference.

"Samuel. When the Philistines were defeated . . . by the hand of the Lord," Elder Warren shouted back. " 'Hitherto hath the Lord helped us.' "

Hitherto . . . h'mmm, she considered, striding quickly to keep up with the cart. She focused her gaze forward into the narrow defile which dropped down between and cut through the white and brown speckled wintry hills before them. *And what's going to happen to us now? Before we get to Wuhan? Oh, Lord, you have preserved us this far—hitherto. Please get us home.*

Because the truck had to wait every two miles for the horse carts to catch up, after three hours the group had traveled only 15 miles. Minkiang, their original destination when they had stopped in Kioshan a week and a half ago, was another 15 miles farther.

At the top of a rise Elder Warren and Gertrude hurried ahead of the horse carts to where the truck was waiting for them and approached its passenger side. General Li and Dr. McMullen scrambled down from the roof of the truck where they had been riding, plopping into the slushy, muddy snow that covered the ground. Propped up with pillows and blankets, Mr. Erich leaned out the passenger window, resting on his forearm.

I've got to get you to a hospital, Gertrude vowed, wincing at the sight of his face, thinned almost beyond recognition.

"It's January. The sun will set in another hour, especially in these mountains," Elder Warren said, his breath forming great clouds in the cold bright sunshine.

Mr. Erich searched the western sky with tired eyes. "And we can't be out here in the dark. We're moving so slowly we'd be sitting ducks for every bandit around."

"There's a small village just below us," General Li suggested, momentarily looking back over his shoulder to indicate the direction. "We could stay there until morning."

After a thoughtful moment, five tired heads all nodded in agreement and five weary travelers took their respective positions in the caravan and traveled on.

Fifteen minutes later, emerging from a small stand of pines, Gertrude and Elder Warren saw the truck stopped ahead of them in the middle of the road. They were 100 yards from a ramshackle gate and some roughly thrown-up fortifications. Halfway between the truck and the gate two men in heavy, shabby coats, rifles slung over their shoulders, were in deep conversation with General Li.

"Looks like they were expecting company," Gertrude remarked.

"Of the unwelcome kind," Elder Warren agreed.

Simultaneously Gertrude and Elder Warren quickened their steps, leaving the struggling horses and carts to follow along behind, and hustled forward. As she passed the truck, Gertrude critically eyed Mr. Erich who was leaning out of the passenger-side window, trying to overhear the conversation ahead of him. She looked up and caught the eye of Dr. McMullen who was still perched on the roof. A silent agreement of apprehension passed between the two medical minds concerning the rapidly weakening secretary of the Honan Conference. Up ahead General Li slogged his way through the muddy track back toward the truck.

"The guards say that the villagers don't want us to stay. Our luggage and our truck are an open invitation for bandits to loot their village," he said as he reached them. He glanced back at the guards. "They've had a tough week, hiding from the Communists and keeping out the bandits."

"Well, we can't stay out here in the dark," Gertrude said, "with all these helpless people." She looked back at the horse carts that were approaching but her gaze rested on Otis Erich.

"We can go on," Otis shouted.

"What?" Elder Warren returned as loudly.

"We can go on," Otis repeated, waving his arm, beckoning them to his side of the truck. "General Li and I can go with the truck and the luggage— on to Minkiang," he said as they approached his window. "Without the carts to slow us down, we can make it in another hour or hour and a half. The rest of you stay here in the village with the carts and come on tomorrow."

Gertrude looked up at Raymond McMullen on the roof. *Who will take care of him?* she asked silently. Dr. McMullen shrugged a silent answer in return.

"I will look after Mr. Erich and find a safe place for the truck," General Li offered. "If that is acceptable with my elder brother."

"And I will look out for your family as if they were my own," Elder Warren responded with a slight bow.

After some shifting of luggage and passengers between the carts and the truck and a short prayer for safety from bandits and for health for Mr. Erich, the migrants parted company. While Elder Warren and Dr. McMullen fanned out through the village searching for shelter, Gertrude stood beside the lead horse and watched the quickly receding truck. Its canvas cover rippled in the wind as it quickly traversed the short main street of the village and disappeared through the far gate.

"I'm not sure what it was used for," Thelma said. She held her kerosene lantern high, peering around in the shadows of descending twilight at the large, three-sided building. It had a steep low-hanging roof and a three-foot-high wall across its open face, all surrounded by a high, thick wall and a massive front gate. The enclosure and its courtyard were big enough to hold horses, carts, and people. "Those big haystacks make me think it was a stable for horses." She pointed to the two large bread loaf-shaped straw stacks pushed against the wall, that faced the street.

"They can be a warm place to sleep," Gertrude responded as she pulled her cot from the horse cart. "Heaven knows I've slept in worse."

As night descended, the company of 44, plus the drivers, stacked what little luggage they had in a half-moon wall formation before the front gate and ate a quick, sparse supper.

"If someone comes in the middle of the night, how do we get out of here?" Gertrude asked over her *kongee* bowl. "I didn't see a back door."

"I know," Elder Warren answered, not making eye contact, intent on balancing his bowl, his spoon, and his small crust of bread. "I asked the same thing, but the landlord said there was no rear opening in the back wall." He looked up, waving his bread toward the back wall. "I checked. He's right. The rear wall is actually the outside wall of the village on this side. There are only slits to fire guns through."

"Let's pray no one has to fire any guns," Zora McMullen said softly.

"Let's pray there are no bandits," Gertrude worried aloud, peering into the shadows along the back wall, as if an exit might have materialized there since she last checked. "The villagers are obviously expecting an invasion at any time and there's no way out of this place."

"Except through the front door," Dr. McMullen said, his puzzled face reflecting consternation that Gertrude did not seem to know this.

"A lot of good that will do us if the bandits come in that way," she snapped. "It's the only way in and the only way out!" She stood suddenly, dumping her bowl and its meager contents on the ground. "We're trapped in here," she announced, wheeling about and stalking off to her cot near the back wall.

At 8:30, after evening vespers, everyone had settled into whatever sleeping accommodations they thought would provide the most warmth—some burrowed into the haystacks, some huddled along the rear wall. An hour later Gertrude sat straight up. "Mercy, what was that?" she asked no one in particular. Her blanket, wrapped askew around her shoulders, cascaded to her feet. "Is it bandits?"

"What?" Thelma answered sleepily. "I don't know!" She raised up on one elbow, not yet totally awake.

In the street, just outside the front wall, people were running and yelling. Someone was pounding on a door, though not on their gate.

"Is it bandits? Is it?" Gertrude was on her feet, shouting.

"Gertrude! Gertrude, calm down," Elder Warren called out. He came scurrying from behind the luggage wall where he'd been sleeping on the ground. "It's all right. It's not bandits," he assured her more quietly as he ducked under the edge of the roof and approached the back wall.

Thelma was on her feet, standing next to Gertrude, tugging at her arm. "Gertrude, what's the matter?" she whispered sharply, both irritated and puzzled. "Sit down. Be quiet,"

"It's bandits. I know it is. And we can't escape," Gertrude sobbed as she sank down on her cot next to Thelma.

"It's not bandits, Gertrude," Elder Warren assured her again. "I think it's soldiers being rousted out to go to Kioshan, probably to take supplies and reinforcements because of another attack. That's what I'm hearing out there on the street." He raised up on his toes to peer over the makeshift barricade where the top of the gate could just be seen. "No one has come to our gate."

"I don't understand, Miss Green," Thelma said, her brows drawn down in a matronly scowl even as she held Gertrude's hand while she sobbed. "You always walk so tall. Remember what you said to General Li about trusting the Lord?"

Gertrude slowly nodded as her crying subsided to sniffles and blowing her nose. "I was so worried about not having a back door. And about the bandits." She looked up into Thelma's disappointed eyes. "I'm sorry. I still can't do it . . . let the Lord be in charge." She blew her nose again. "I'll be all right. I'm just tired. I'm sorry." Gertrude looked up at Elder Warren. "I'll be all right—after I get some sleep." She slipped her hand from Thelma's grasp and lay down on her side, swinging her tattered stadium boots up on the cot. "I'll be all right," she repeated as she closed her eyes.

But the following morning Gertrude wasn't all right. Always before she'd recovered from her emotional roller coaster tirades in a remarkably short time—overnight, or even more quickly. Always before she'd presumed that someone else's misunderstanding had caused the difficulty, exhibiting little insight into her own culpability. Always before she had the chameleon-like ability to switch from anger to good humor, from sobbing to laughter— sometimes within seconds. But not this time. This time it was different.

For two weeks she'd lived with the unappeasable pressures of food shortages and concern about Mr. Erich's deteriorating health. She'd gone through unrelenting military attacks and aerial assaults. She'd endured painful cold and physical exhaustion, and most fearful of all, the inexorable prospect that death—her own death—could come at any moment. Her faith in herself had become hard and brittle as Christmas ribbon candy, and now it had broken. In her own mind, her faith in God had proven to be insufficient.

She awoke angry—mostly at herself—for being such a fool as to believe that it would be different in China this time around and for being such a weakling in the face of danger. Especially after making such a public statement of faith. What a worthless missionary she'd turned out to be!

From the break of day until noon, Gertrude and Elder Warren walked on either side of the lead horse cart as they slowly made their way to Minkiang. For the first hour, other than for exchanging essential information, Gertrude spoke to no one except herself.

A fine example of a missionary you turned out to be, Gertrude Green, she upbraided herself. *You give a wonderful testimony of faith and at the first sound of a little ruckus in the street, you fall apart. No more backbone than a piece of rope.*

Actually I have plenty of backbone and lots of sass! she vehemently repudiated her own argument. *I'm not afraid of people—usually. And I'm not afraid of situations that I can figure out. It's when I can't control a situation. It's when something is out of control . . . out of my control.*

And you don't think God can handle those situations?

I guess not. I don't know. Yes, I think He can handle them . . . I believe He can.

Then why do you carry on like the roof is about to fall in?

"You're unusually quiet this morning," Elder Warren remarked. Gertrude shot a glance up over the horse's withers to see Elder Warren trudging through the muddy snow, looking down, watching his steps, and glancing up occasionally to smile at her.

"Not in my head, I'm not," she said, averting her eyes.

"You want to talk about it?" he asked in his best pastoral voice.

"What do I say?" she began. "I'm a failure as a missionary." She kept her head down and her gazed fixed on the ground. Shrugging her shoulders, she continued to plod forward.

"Oh, you mean that business last night?" he said lightly.

"Of course, that business last night!" she said, her voice rising, suspecting him of poking fun at her. She shook her head in disgust. "Didn't you see how Thelma looked at me?"

"Sounded like pretty common stuff for a Christian," he said off-handedly. "You and the apostle Paul. Pretty much in the same boat."

"What do you mean?" She risked a glance at him again, her curiosity, for a moment, overriding her anger.

"Romans, chapter seven, of course," he said, his voice casual and conversational. "The lament of Paul. You know: that which I want to do, I don't do. And that which I hate and don't want to do, that's what I find myself doing." He chuckled. "Please excuse the rather free Warren translation. The King James Bible and the American Standard Bible both make this passage unbelievably difficult to understand."

"And you think that's me?" Gertrude spoke sharply, defensively, knowing in her heart that it was true.

"It's me, and every other Christian I know," Elder Warren said. "It's me. That's why I know the passage so well. I get to review its teaching and its implications in my own life, oh, about once a week or so. We all know what is right and none of us can do it." Gertrude saw that he was not laughing at her. He was gazing at the ground, his eyes reflecting on some unknown thought or incident he probably would not share. "And so we wait upon the Lord to do it for us. But that's not the way He works."

She inhaled the crisp, cold air and blew out a vapor cloud of anger and resentment. "Dr. Haysmer said that I'd learn to wait on the Lord. But I have not learned it. I don't even know what I'm waiting for."

"We are waiting to be changed—from our old nasty selves to our new wonderful selves. We're waiting to be changed on the outside. What we say and what we do. We want to *do* right." Elder Warren shook his head. "But the Holy Spirit works on the inside. He wants us to *be* right. The book of Romans, chapter 12, uses the word 'transformation.' It's talking of a gradual process of change on the inside—on the heart." He peeked under the bobbing neck of the horse that walked between them. "Are you familiar with Ezekiel 36:26, Miss Green?"

"'A new heart also will I give you, and a new spirit will I put within you: and I will take away the stony heart out of your flesh and I will give you an heart of flesh,'" she quoted from memory. "It's one of the first texts I can remember learning as a youth at the Missionary Volunteer meetings on Sabbath afternoon."

"Good for you," he approved, looking down again to be sure of his footing. "Yes, He starts on the heart. The Holy Spirit works on the heart, Miss Green." He glanced up and Gertrude caught the glint of joy in his eye, like when he was preaching. "Do you happen to remember the next verse there, verse 27?" he asked.

"No, not off the top of my head," she apologized. "I'm not very good at recalling long passages of Scripture."

"OK," he said. "Let's see if I can remember it." He cocked his head, thinking for a moment. "'And I will put my spirit within you, and cause you to walk in my statutes, and ye shall keep my judgments, and do them.'" He gave her a sidewise glance.

"It's a promise, Miss Green. By the indwelling of the Holy Spirit and His transforming power He makes it possible for us to actually do what we knew to be right but could not do on our own." Gertrude did not reply as Elder Warren paced off a dozen steps of silent contemplation.

"Do you remember your baptism, Miss Green?"

What a strange question, she thought. "Yes, of course," she said aloud.

"Did you give your heart to Jesus?"

Gertrude recalled vividly the decision she had made. *What was it now, 23 or 24 years ago?* She thought of the extreme changes it had brought to her life.

"I gave Him my heart . . . and my life." Her steps quickened as she remembered the confrontation with her dance teacher. "I was a dancer, Elder Warren.

I was a professional dancer with dance students of my own. And I was only in the eighth grade." Memories came flooding back—of the costumes she'd worn. Of Mother and of home and the dining room rug that they'd rolled up together. "When I met Jesus, that all changed. I gave my life to Him—completely."

"Do the same thing—again. Now." he said. "Give your life completely to the Holy Spirit."

Gertrude heard the intensity in his voice, felt the urgency of his earnestness as his hands split the air in emphatic gesture. He stared hard at her. "Stop fighting the Holy Spirit, Miss Green."

"What?" she gasped, more shocked at the idea than at the cold air she had rapidly inhaled.

"Stop fighting the Holy Spirit," he repeated, never shifting his gaze from her face. "Let Him do His work in you." He sensed her discomfort and shifted his gaze to the ground in front of him. "We Adventists, we think that the time of Jacob's trouble is about the end times and about the great tribulation we will pass through with all of its persecutions. You know, a lot like the last two weeks that we've been through. And we miss the fact that at the time of Jacob's greatest trouble, at the River Jabok, Jacob was not fighting with his brother. He was fighting with the Lord." Elder Warren glanced over at her again. "Jacob was struggling to retain control over his own life, Miss Green. He was facing a situation with his brother Esau that he couldn't control, but he didn't know how to let God be in control. He didn't know how to surrender. He didn't know how to wait on the Lord."

Her eyes blinked rapidly, her thoughts whirling at the possibilities. "Do you think the Holy Spirit is waiting for me to give Him permission?" she asked.

"He can't work in you, and He can't work through you, until you do."

For the rest of the morning, Gertrude crunched through the frozen mud and snow beside her equine companion, arguing with herself and berating herself like a stern teacher with a willful pupil.

To give Him permission, do I need more faith? How do I get more faith?

Dr. Haysmer said to wait for it. She tried to remember exactly what he had said to wait for, but could not.

Wait for what? For faith? Haven't I been through enough already that I should have developed some faith somewhere along the line?

How can I wait on the Lord to work and continue doing my work at the same time?

Do I stop working? Do I stop trying? Who will take care of Mr. Erich, and the others, if I do that?

How do I wait on the Lord? What am I waiting for Him to do? What is He waiting for me to do? Give Him permission to do what? How do I do that?

Occasionally gazing heavenward, she could see, just above her head, the lingering fog nesting in the tops of the trees, rendering the surrounding mountains veiled and indistinct. In her mind, just beyond the grasp of her reasoning, a confusion of doubts and faith swam and swirled about each other It seemed to hide, as in a hazy, obscuring fog, the understanding she so desperately wanted but could not reach or see.

Chapter 72

CROSSING THE LAST BRIDGE

As they approached the outskirts of Minkiang, Elder Warren picked up his walking pace, getting several yards ahead of Gertrude and the horse cart. Glancing back at her, he pointed ahead. "Let's work our way to the rail yards," he called out. "Hopefully they've found us a train home."

Gertrude nodded absently and responded, "Yes, hopefully."

Minkiang was the apparent end of the line for every refugee fleeing from Honan Province and points northwest, refugees who now had nowhere else to go. The thoroughfares of the city were choked with families camping in makeshift "home" spaces on the street. Horse carts, stretchers, and wheelbarrows simultaneously crisscrossed the narrow streets in every direction. Stacks of abandoned household items obstructed forward motion on every hand.

The only benefit of such uncontrolled chaos for Elder Warren, Gertrude, and company was that the wet streets were totally devoid of the snow or slush that had delayed their travel through the mountains. Thousands of walking, running, stomping feet had erased any trace of solid precipitation. The singular disadvantage of such uncontrolled chaos was that after an hour, the Adventist missionaries and their companions had traversed only halfway to where they knew the rail yards to be.

"Elder Warren! Elder Warren!" A deep authoritative voice rang out above the tumult of the churning masses. Stepping toward them out of the crowd they saw a tall Chinese figure in a heavy military overcoat.

"General Li." Elder Warren, all five-foot-five of him, stretched up on tiptoe and raised his hand over his head in a spontaneous and genuinely warm

American greeting as he strode toward the general. "Well, there's no sign of an impending attack here, is there?" he said, shaking the general's hand.

"It's true. No one is running or hiding here," General Li responded with a smile, looking about him. "Miss Green," he said with a nod as she approached the two men. "But there is no train leaving here either." Gertrude watched his face lose all expression, his eyes rapidly, suspiciously interrogating the faces of those standing or passing near him. "Two bridges are out just south of here. Taken down by the Communists last week," he muttered, inclining his head toward them, as if the information he had imparted was a closely held secret.

"Where is Mr. Erich?" Gertrude asked, doing an area search of her own, scanning the buildings and the street immediately behind the general for the truck.

"He's fine, Miss Green. Very weak, but able to sit up." He smiled in appreciation of her concern. "He's with the truck in a safe spot around this corner and down an alleyway." She watched his eyes scan the crowd again after revealing another of his small secrets, the whereabouts of the truck.

"If there is no train here, where do we go to find one?" Elder Warren asked.

"Forty-five *li*—15 of your miles," General Li said, nodding politely, not knowing if they understood the Chinese distance measurements. "It's farther south, beyond the last bridge over the river."

Gertrude met Elder Warren's gaze and held it. *What now?* her eyes asked, half hoping, half expecting he would know.

His eyes lit up and a smile momentarily lifted the corners of his mouth. "We're still waiting, Miss Green," he said with a slight twist of his head and a shrug of his shoulders.

"For what?" General Li was lost in the conversation.

"For the Lord—to do whatever it is He is going to do," Gertrude answered, shaking her head in resignation.

A startling crash resounded behind her, followed immediately by shouts and cries of resistance, "Stop that! What are you doing? Help!"

"Gertrude! What's happening?" Gertrude subconsciously picked out Thelma Hwang's voice, calling out from the back of the second horse cart.

Gertrude's head snapped around in time to witness the tailgate of the second cart crash to the ground, as had happened to the first cart. The drivers of both carts were roughly forcing the women and children out of the carts and into the street. Most had grabbed up their belongings before being pushed out but some of the women had fallen, dropping their bedrolls and their belongings. The drivers were throwing out whatever was not being hand carried by someone. Children were slipping, falling, and crying as they clutched at their mothers. Thelma had managed to protect her belongings and had Jeannie firmly in tow. Gertrude rushed toward her own battered, brown suitcase and her cot that lay upside down in the street.

"Men! My brothers," Elder Warren called out, rushing past Gertrude toward the drivers.

"Those drivers overheard what I said." General Li spat out the words through tight lips. He hurried to assist his two servants who had surrounded his family, threatening with a raised fist one of the drivers who had come too near.

Despite Elder Warren's pleadings and Thelma's offer of staggering sums of money, the drivers refused to go farther. Having heard General Li's pronouncement, they rightly assumed that they would be asked to travel even farther and face even greater danger. They would hear none of it and continued to empty the human cargo from their carts. Within 15 minutes the carts and their drivers had melted into the swirling mass of humanity, leaving the missionary band and their luggage as another of the impediments to traffic in the street.

We're only 15 miles from the train. Lord, you've left us out in the street. What could You possibly have in mind? Gertrude shouted silently to the only One who could hear her.

"Let's find Mr. Erich and the truck and have a prayer meeting," Elder Warren instructed, taking charge of the confused group that surrounded him. "We could use some divine direction about now."

When no divine response came to Gertrude's cry for understanding, she did what she always did when her grasp of the situation was unclear. She set aside the unanswered questions and found something practical to do.

Checking to see that Thelma had Jeannie and all their belongings, she picked up her typewriter, cot, and suitcase and fell in line at the rear of the entourage. Then she scanned her group of charges—nursing students and hospital workers—to make sure they were all accounted for. Last, she took up the rear guard, sending senior students to herd in stragglers behind Elder Warren and General Li as the group pushed through the congested street toward the alleyway and Otis Erich.

"Lord, we are stranded," Elder Warren prayed, his hands folded over the hood of the old Dodge truck. "We have a large party, lots of luggage, and inadequate transportation. We are in a city full of refugees just like us. That means we have no place to sleep tonight except on the street."

Gertrude gazed about at the mothers and children huddled in the shadows around the front of the truck, squeezed into the tight, dark alley. Dr. Mc-Mullen, head bowed and eyes closed, held Ronnie, seated in his arms as Zora clung to him, silently weeping. With his back against the far wall so as to watch both of the alley entrances, General Li stood behind his family, arms outstretched, encompassing them.

Gertrude watched until his vigilant, sweeping gaze met her own. The two defensive warriors locked eyes in appreciation and respect for what each had contributed to the journey, the sacrifices each had made to protect their charges.

So like you . . . and yet so different, Gertrude thought, examining the strong, chiseled features etched into his face. *How do I share my faith with you when I am so uncertain of it myself?*

"Lord, we came here looking for a train. In fact, we've been looking for a train for almost—" The unmistakable blast of a steam whistle interrupted Elder Warren's prayer.

"Where did that come from?" Gertrude spoke aloud the question registered in the eyes around her that had popped open.

"The railroad yards," General Li said in a half whisper, almost in disbelief. He craned his face upward and to his left, as if trying to see over the oppressively overhanging shop houses and second-story balconies, their laundry poles hanging crisscrossed just above their heads.

"But there are no trains," Thelma pronounced loudly, incredulously.

"Let's go see," Elder Warren suggested as he edged his way past Gertrude, slipping between the shop house wall and the truck.

"What did Elder Warren say?" Thelma asked. She reached beneath herself, adjusted the folded sleeping blanket on top of the lumpy coal and settled herself back once more against the inside wall of a coal car.

"He quoted the Scriptures where it says, 'Before you call, I will answer,'" Gertrude said. "Then he went off with the general and found the army commander here in Minkiang." Gertrude shook her head as she seated herself next to Thelma, wrapping her heavy coat around her knees and pulling it closed at the throat. "Turns out the commander had this military train headed out of town. It also turns out that he comes from the same city in Szechuan where Elder Warren worked back before the war. Before you know it, they're talking about old times and the commander is saying, 'Sure, you can ride on my military train.'" Gertrude folded her mittened hands prayerfully in her lap and gazed up at the stars overhead. "One minute we're praying for a shelter or a truck and the next minute we're on a train, headed for Hankow."

Out of habit, Gertrude raised up to do a "bed check," counting all the students and women with children scattered over the small, fist-sized lumps of coal that half filled the gondola car. In the far corner she saw Zora McMullen and Ronnie propped against the wall, sitting with General Li and his family. Just in front of her, Dr. McMullen knelt next to Gertrude's cot which had been set up in the center of the car. He was spooning hot broth into the mouth of Otis Erich who lay listlessly on the cot, covered by a blanket, his head on a makeshift pillow. Toward the front of the car the Mennonite girls were arranging their luggage to make a bed of sorts on top of the coal. Everyone was covering themselves as best they could, preparing to weather another night train ride in an open gondola, in the cold.

"The train hasn't gone anywhere yet," Thelma remarked stolidly, stroking Jeannie's hair as the blanketed child slept with her head in her mother's lap.

Rising from her padded perch to one knee, Gertrude peeked over the edge of the car. The stationmaster was on a ladder, lighting a smudgy lamp that hung from the corner of the station house roof. The soldiers who had helped them load their luggage were gone, all loaded in the train cars, she supposed. Only a few stood shivering at attention, standing guard on the platform. Elder Warren and the area commander were nowhere to be seen.

"Nope, no movement. And it's getting dark, too," Gertrude agreed. "I'd better go find our benefactor and Elder Warren. They're probably still comparing notes on the towns of Szechuan."

The train lurched, banging the railroad cars in their coupling links and throwing Gertrude sideways. As she grabbed for a handhold on the wall, she saw Elder Warren at the far end of the car doing the same while clambering down inside, followed by the commander himself, clutching at the ladder to keep from falling.

Regaining her balance as the train picked up speed, Gertrude pointed to the man in uniform and said, "Unless he gets off at the next stop, we just got another mouth to feed."

For the next hour the military train backed—for it was traveling backward—southward down the tracks with no lights on. Gertrude sat quietly, wrapped in her blanket and her long, wool coat with the fur collar, staring at the cold stars above her, thinking about the last 24 hours, and praying.

When the train slowed and stopped, a murmur rolled through the Chinese women. Dr. McMullen rose to his feet near Mr. Erich's cot, peering over the car's edge into the darkness.

"There's nothing out there. No village. Nothing. Where are we?" he asked.

"The commander went to check on the bridge that was supposedly repaired," Elder Warren said softly. "He wants to make sure the Communists haven't undone the repairs before the train crosses it."

For 20 minutes the train sat, engines idling. Solicitously Gertrude ran her eyes over the various groups huddled in the car, but she made no remarks.

"Will bandits attack us?" It was a question whispered in Mandarin Chinese by one of the mothers. Like a brief breeze in rustling leaves, the question arose, passed over the other mothers and died out with no answer. Gertrude remained quiet. With a lurch and the resonant clatter of car couplings being mashed together, the train engine pushed its cars backward over the bridge.

When the echo of empty space below the bridge trestle became the muffled thud of solid ground again and the flicker of lanterns and shadows signaled the approach of another station, the train cars stopped rolling once more. Gertrude watched Elder Warren stand and dust off the back of his coat.

"Please. Your attention, everyone." His voice was crisp and his Chinese words carried clearly in the cold night air. "We must get off the train here. This military train stops here to do more repair work. It goes no farther. Our brother, the army commander, will find us another train to take us on to Singyang."

Gertrude held her wristwatch over her head, above the edge of the car and peered at the small dial in the flickering light. *Almost 10:00 o'clock. Lord, I hardly dare ask. Where do we sleep tonight?*

Hearing that their wait for another train or engine might be a long one, Gertrude organized a party of soldiers to lift Mr. Erich, still on her cot, up and out of the coal car and to carry him into the station house where he could be warm. Many of the Chinese families had already bedded down in the car and wanted to stay on the train. Zora and Ronnie and the Mennonites followed Dr. McMullen into the station as he accompanied his patient on the cot. After assuring herself that her students had enough blankets, Gertrude helped Thelma lift the sleeping Jeannie onto her shoulder and make the trip up and over the side of the coal car and safely down the ladder.

As she entered the station house behind Thelma carrying Thelma's cot and her own suitcase, Gertrude could hear the excited stationmaster, shouting into his phone that he had 20 or 30 Americans and that he had been ordered to get a train to take them out. *We aren't exactly all Americans,* she mused, remembering the Chinese and the Canadian Mennonite among them. As she followed Thelma to an unoccupied corner, she thought about General Li. With his Chinese roots and American education, she wasn't sure which category he belonged in, but probably Chinese. Finding an open spot against the wall and farther away from the potbellied stove, Gertrude slipped down into a sitting position. Her long coat dropped open revealing her heavy Chinese coat and padded pants. *Actually, ol' girl, I'm not so sure which category you belong in either,* she thought with a smile. Then she remembered that Thelma Hwang carried an Australian passport. *But the good ol' Red, White, and Blue— whatever it takes to get a train . . .*

Until past midnight, the stationmaster continued his phone calls, encouraged by occasional threats from the army commander who officiously strode in and out unannounced. By turns shouting and begging over the wire, the harried stationmaster sought for any conveyance that would rid him of his unwanted foreign passengers.

Elder Warren crossed the room and squatted beside Gertrude. "Not sleepy?"

"Not with that caterwauling going on," Gertrude said, pointing with her chin at the barred window behind which the stationmaster was shouting into his phone.

"Me either." Elder Warren sat down with his back against the wall, his feet stretched out in front of him. "You've been uncharacteristically quiet today," he noted, folding his hands in his lap. "Been praying?"

"Yes," Gertrude said with a shy smile. "For courage . . . and for understanding . . . and for the patience to wait."

"A lot of things happened today . . . upsetting things."

"Yes." Gertrude nodded vigorously. "Lots of chances to practice waiting."

"Yes, lots of waiting today," he agreed, ducking his head in reflection on the day's events. He pulled his knees up and wrapped his hands around them, his fingers interlaced. "What are you waiting for?" he queried.

Twisting her head to the right, Gertrude looked at him sideways. "This may sound silly," she said, her eyes bright green with seriousness. "I'm waiting for Him to talk to me. I want Him to tell me what He's going to do."

"Doesn't sound silly at all," he responded. "Actually, it's quite biblical. Kings and prophets have been asking God to do the same thing for millennia."

"Do they ever get any answers?" She knew what she wanted the answer to be.

"Oh, yes. Daniel and Ezekiel had dreams and visions, the usual way God spoke to prophets. Moses and Elijah actually heard a voice, the not-so-usual way." He paused, his eyes searching the opposite wall for a better example. "But David. David is like a lot of us. David got his information from his life experiences . . . and from his prayers . . . and from his wise friends."

"I used to think I was a lot like David," Gertrude remembered.

"I think you are," Elder Warren said a resolute nod. "Intense, loyal, decisive, and courageous—most of the time." He shot a small smile her way. "And David was emotional. Quick to speak and act. Sometimes without considering the consequences." His left hand touched the floor as he turned to face her. "Why do you think David wrote, 'Wait patiently on the Lord'? He was telling us that he was learning that lesson himself the hard way. By experience."

Gertrude missed his reference to experience as a more pressing, more personal question sprang to her mind.

"Does God talk to you?" she asked, looking directly at him. Challenging him to tell the truth.

"Oh, yes. He has His own special way to communicate with me."

Gertrude saw in his eyes the honesty of understanding and experience—and pain.

"Unfortunately, I haven't always listened, or been willing to listen. But I always know it's His voice." His eyes, which had temporarily misted over, became bright and clear. "But the question is, 'Does God talk to *you*,' isn't it? And the answer is yes . . . He does."

"But I don't hear Him," she protested. "I'm trying. I'm waiting and I'm listening, but I don't hear Him."

"That is the problem, isn't it? To distinguish His voice from all the other voices . . . including our own."

He fumbled in his coat pocket, the folds of which momentarily entangled his right hand. For a moment he struggled, twisting about, his left hand trying to free him from the coat, until he extracted his small traveling Bible, the one Gertrude had seen him use many times in the last three weeks. Getting comfortable again, settling back against the wall, he held the Bible in front of him in both hands, reverently as an offering, and gazed at it.

"That's one reason we study the Scriptures, to hear what His voice sounds like, to listen to the kinds of things He says to other people. It's one of the reasons we talk with our Christian friends, to hear what He sounds like when He talks through them to us." Gertrude followed his gaze to the far window where the outside lanterns revealed a light snow blowing in swirls about the corner of the building. "Some hear Him best in the wind or in the mountains. Some hear Him in the voices of small children." In the corner, Ronnie slept soundly in his mother's arms; Jeannie breathed quietly in her favorite position, with her head resting in Thelma's lap.

"For every person God has a special way of speaking." He looked at her again. "How does He speak to you, Miss Green?"

"I don't know." She met his gaze, her eyes now gray with uncertainty. "I'm not sure."

"Keep waiting; keep listening. You will know." He clutched his Bible to his chest. "And when you know, you will never mistake His voice again. You won't always want to listen, but you'll know."

Chapter 73

SINGING THE CLOSING HYMN

On the far side of the room, the door to the office opened and a small Chinese man in heavy winter clothes and an official looking hat padded toward them in his worn, black silk slippers.

"Oh, honorable Americans," he said, bowing low, "a train will be here at 1:00 a.m. to take you south to Singyang."

In the next 45 minutes Gertrude and the nursing students awoke all of those who had chosen to remain on the train and transferred them to another, emptier coal car. Dr. McMullen and Elder Warren found three soldiers to help them move Otis Erich, on his cot, and the heavy luggage to the waiting car. General Li assisted his family, Thelma, Zora, and the children.

At the appointed hour, through swirling snow, a hulking steam locomotive, black and green and larger than most other engines, backed into the rail yard and coupled itself to the now almost full open coal car, forming a train of one engine and its tender and one coal car full of refugees. At 2:30 a.m. they arrived at the rail station in Singyang, 160 miles south of Yencheng and 80 miles north of Hankow.

Immediately Elder Warren and General Li stomped off into the dark in search of a train to take them on to Hankow. Thelma and the nursing students took charge of the other women and children, getting them out of the coal car and off the train. Dr. McMullen, his Mandarin improved somewhat, found men loitering about—even at that time of the early morning. With Thelma's promises of money, they were persuaded to help him unload Otis Erich and the luggage.

Gertrude watched anxiously as the cot carrying the limp form of Mr. Erich was set gingerly on the gravel amid the railroad ties, now sporting a light blanket of snow. Gertrude looked up into the darkness at Dr. McMullen, perched on the edge of the coal car. A coating of snow lightly dusted his coat and cap, giving him an apparitional appearance.

"If we don't find some water or warm broth from somewhere, we're going to lose him," he said before he disappeared, ghost like, back into the car.

"Sarah," Gertrude called out, turning to the huddled mass of women who had built themselves a lean-to of their luggage in the lee of an idle boxcar only a dozen feet away. "Bring the other senior girls and come over here." When she was surrounded by her best and brightest students, she said, "Sarah, you are in charge. You and the others carry Mr. Erich over there. Start a fire and keep him warm. Anna, come with me. We have to find warm broth—if we are to save him."

"At 3:00 o'clock in the morning, Miss Green?" Anna questioned.

"Don't worry, dear. The Lord will help us find it."

Within the hour, Gertrude and Anna returned, carrying between them a medium-sized kettle full of hot soupy liquid, the steam rising from it mixing with the fog that had settled down over the rail yard.

"Where did you find that?" Dr. McMullen called out, advancing toward them. He leaned down and sniffed, then wrinkled up his nose. "What's in there?"

"You don't want to know," Gertrude answered, shaking her head at Anna to silence her. "It's been boiled and it's edible."

When Elder Warren returned with news that they all had tickets on a train leaving at 8:00 a.m., Otis Erich was awake and taking small mouthfuls of the mysterious soup.

The boxcar rocked gently from side to side as it clickety-clacked through the morning hours on its way to Hankow. Until well past noon many of those who had been awakened off and on throughout the night sat on the floor in clumps, leaning against each other, sleeping with their backs against the benches that had been placed crosswise in rows. Across the aisle from Gertrude, Thelma and the McMullens sat on benches, nodding off. Immediately in front of Gertrude, lying on the floor, were the sleeping children of General Li and the cot carrying the gently snoring Otis Erich. The half-empty pot of soup, sitting on the floor near his head, sloshed back and forth with small plopping sounds. The heavy luggage and the small hand luggage all had been loaded in another baggage car. This car was full of travelers— no, refugees—Gertrude's group and many others who were escaping the coming Red Tide washing down from the north.

Sitting up on the bench and peering out through the slatted sides at the passing wheat fields and walled farm compounds, Gertrude felt like she was riding in a Chinese third-class rail car. Behind her and receding from her current reality with every mile they traveled, was a world of war such as she had never before experienced. Ahead of her and getting closer was a world in which she imagined hot showers, sufficient food, medical care, military protection—all the essentials she'd not had just six hours before. *Funny, how the basic needs of life become so important, so critical when you don't have them.* Gertrude regarded a farm compound as it slid past her view. She noted the boxy house, the five-foot-high mud walls, the rake-back hay wagons sitting in the enclosure, and the bread-loaf haystacks—like those some of her charges had slept in two nights ago. *How are these people managing this winter?* she wondered. *Do they have the basics for survival?* From what she'd witnessed in Kioshan and the other little villages, she knew that in the midwinter, even in the good times, no one in China had anything to spare. Surely it was worse in the midst of a war.

In front of her, General Li was making his fourth or fifth trip across the front of the car, pacing like a man in pain. *In pain?* Gertrude heard him let out a soft grunt of discomfort as he sat down on the floor next to his wife. Within five minutes he was on his feet again with a moan, and pacing. Gertrude stood and walked down the narrow aisle, intercepting the general as he turned around in the far front corner of the car to begin pacing back again.

"What's wrong with you?" she asked in an—appropriately Chinese— abrupt fashion, standing in his way, blocking his forward progress.

"I have hemorrhoids," the general answered honestly, taking no offense.

"Wait here," she ordered.

Gertrude returned to her seat and retrieved her medical bag from under the bench. For the past three weeks, this bag—the one she'd filled with every conceivable medication and item on the day they left Yencheng—had accompanied her every day as she ministered to villagers. Now she returned to where the general was standing very stiffly, very uncomfortably.

"I think I have something in here for you," she said, holding the bag up high to see in the dim light of the boxcar interior, rifling around in the bottom of the bag with her free hand.

"You seem to have something in there for everyone, Miss Green," he said.

"The Lord helped me pack before we left Yencheng," she remarked offhandedly. Her hand touched a wrinkled paper-wrapped object and closed over it. "Aha! Here it is," she triumphed holding aloft the Anusol rectal suppository in its wrapping. *Now, how to put this where it will do the most good—in this crowded boxcar?* she thought as the reality of the situation struck her.

Placing the suppository in the general's hand, Gertrude delicately explained what it was for and how to insert it. It was wrapped in paper, like a firecracker, with twists at both ends.

General Li turned over the bullet-sized lump and considered the possibilities.

"Honorable Miss Green, my expertise is in military matters, not medical treatments," he said quietly. "I do not think I know how to do this. Can you do this for me, my little sister?"

Recognizing the formal, and very honorable, Chinese relationship she had just been invited into, Gertrude bowed politely and said, "Of course, my older brother. I would be honored."

Backing General Li into the front corner of the car where his family and his servants were encamped, Gertrude had him take down his pants and assume the knee-chest position, his head pointed toward the center of the car and his buttocks toward the dark corner. Much as she had done years before in nursing school, with the first difficult patient she had had to catheterize by herself, Gertrude mentally reviewed what she would need to do—mostly in the dark, mostly by feel.

Then in one swift, well-practiced motion, she inserted the suppository.

Upon returning to her seat, Gertrude kept her eyes modestly averted, finding things to look for in her medical bag, until she was reasonably sure that General Li was clothed again. Looking up she saw him seated comfortably on the floor next to his wife, on his face a calm Chinese stoicism, in his eyes the most grateful look of thanks that she had ever seen on a Chinese face.

A small thought blossomed in her mind. *What was it I said to the general? "The Lord helped me pack my medical bag?" Is that true? Did You help me pack?* She paused. *Did You help us find the soup for Mr. Erich? Did You get us on this train? Is that how You talk to me, Lord?* She received no audible response.

Two hours out of Hankow the train slowed and stopped. Having just dozed off while sitting upright on the bench, Gertrude raised her head. *Are we in Hankow?* she asked silently. Peering through the slatted boxcar wall, she saw only blackness. There were no lights of a city anywhere. A glance at her watch by the light of a small lamp swinging slightly in the top of the car told her it was 10:00 p.m. *Where are we?* she wondered, remembering that she had guessed they would reach their destination about midnight.

"Where are we?" It was the voice of Zora McMullen.

Those who had been awake already were peering through the sides of the car. Others were stretching, sitting up, and looking about. Gertrude saw Thelma sit up and draw a deep breath, gazing about in the semidarkness to get her bearings, to remember that she was in a boxcar that had been moving but now sat motionless.

"Where are we? Is it bandits?" It was Zora again, more loudly, more shrilly.

Dr. McMullen sharply told her to hush. "You're going to wake Ronnie."

"It will be all right, Zora," Gertrude heard herself say. "We've just stopped for a bit. The Lord is in charge. He will take care of us. Go back to sleep, dear." Gertrude smiled at Thelma who was staring at her so impolitely. *You really are Chinese, aren't you, Thelma?*

Softly Gertrude began singing. "O safe to the Rock that is higher than I, my soul in its conflicts and sorrows would fly; . . ." When she reached the third line, "So sinful, so weary, Thine, Thine would I be," Elder Warren added his rich baritone. By the time they reached the chorus of "Hiding in Thee," several others, even some who were not in the Yencheng group, joined in the familiar hymn, singing quietly. For more than an hour they sang softly, like a lullaby, working their way through several songs of faith and confidence—"The Lord Is My Light," "'Tis So Sweet to Trust in Jesus," "Anywhere With Jesus," and many more. Some of the refugees hummed when they didn't know the words. All joined in on the familiar choruses. When they began "Under His Wings," Otis Erich's quavering tenor voice joined in, unable to be silent any longer.

At 11:30 p.m. the boxcar lurched as the train rolled forward and slowly gained speed. Gradually the singing died down as various members of the spontaneous choir grew tired and fell asleep. When the train stopped again, they were in Hankow. It was 1:30 a.m. Thursday, January 8, 1948.

The *Democrat and Chronicle*, Rochester, New York
WASHINGTON, Jan. 8 (INS)

Chinese Communist forces were believed today to have kidnapped an American missionary couple, their four year old son, and a nursing director serving as Seventh-day Adventist missionaries at Yencheng.

In addition, two other veteran Adventist missionaries were reported as "whereabouts unknown."

The missionaries were reported kidnapped and missing in a cable from Jerald E. Christensen, director of the Honan Mission in Yencheng. He also reported that the main sanitarium at Yencheng had been destroyed in a Communist raid, and that he apparently was the only one to reach Shanghai safely.

Reported missing and "feared taken by Communists for medical service," were: Dr. and Mrs. Raymond McMullen, their son, Ronald, and Miss Gertrude Green, the nursing director.

Reported missing and "whereabouts unknown" were: Merritt C. Warren, superintendent of the Central China Union Mission, Hankow, and Otis G. Erich, its secretary-treasurer.

GENERAL CONFERENCE OF SEVENTH-DAY ADVENTISTS
TACOMA PARK, WASHINGTON 12, D.C.
January 8, 1948

Mr. Walter Green
88 Bryan Street
Rochester, NY

Dear Mr. Green:

We have today received a cablegram from Elder Branson, president of the China Division, indicating that several of our missionary families located in the Yencheng province have made an effort to withdraw from that area in order to avoid the difficulties which might arise because of pressure from the Communist forces. The cablegram states that they are deeply concerned lest your sister may not have succeeded in securing transportation out of that province. They express fear lest the Communist forces may have held her for medical service. The mission sanitarium at Yencheng was destroyed.

We deeply regret the necessity of passing this rather uncertain information on to you, but feel that you would rather know the situation and you may be sure that we shall notify you immediately if further information reaches us from the China Division.

We pray that God's protecting care may be manifested on behalf of all our missionaries in China.

Very sincerely yours,
Norman W. Dunn

NWD:ema

(When Walter showed this letter to his mother, Lena, she immediately scribbled the following in her own handwriting across the bottom of the letter.)

Walter received this after we heard it over the radio and read it in the newspaper.

Chapter 74

ENJOYING A RESPITE

On arriving in Hankow, one of Gertrude's first tasks was to let her mother know that she was safe. She quickly added a short, hurried, somewhat jumbled note to her December 22 letter. She'd written it while hiding in Suiping but, not surprisingly, the letter had yet to be mailed. At her first opportunity, she sent the entire letter in the next airmail packet.

Jan 8, 1948

Well, here I am in Hankow, arrived last night by train and I tell you I am glad to be here because we surely have been through quite a lot, but the Lord has wonderfully protected us all the way. I had this letter written to you on the way so will just get it off to you right now before I write too much more so that I will not hold it up. I will write again in a day when I get some rest and have a chance to think about what I am doing. For now, I will close. I am fine and I am safe. Don't worry about me.

I have lost everything in Yencheng. The Communists burned our whole hospital and looted everything out of our houses and everywhere. Well, I have my life and that is what is most important. The Lord has been good to us. There were several of us together which made it good.

Now I will mail this to you and hope that you receive it in good time. I will write more in a day or two and remember me to everyone around there. Will close now and take this to the Post Office to mail.

The address here is 17 Li Hwang Pei Road

Hankow, Hupeh, China

Loads of love to my mother from her loving daughter,

Gertrude

One week later, when she had had "a chance to think" about what she was doing, Gertrude wrote the longest letter she had written to her mother since excitedly telling about her bicycle trip to Yencheng in 1940.

> 17 Li Hwang Pei Road
> Hankow, Hupeh, China
> January 16, 1948

Dearest Mother:

I know that I should have written you before, but I just haven't felt like writing any letters since I arrived here in Hankow. I was able to help Mr. Otis Erich call his wife when we arrived here at 1:30 a.m. to let her know that we had all arrived safely. But I had him admitted to the Wuhan Sanitarium immediately and have been nursing him back to health over the last week. Most of the women and children traveling in our group had places to stay with relatives in the Hankow area. My nursing students I took to be enrolled in the nursing school here at the Wuhan Sanitarium.

Today I came over here to beautiful East Lake at the San to stay with a friend of mine, Mrs. Boynton, that I used to know in Denver. This sanitarium is the place where I was located when I was here in China before with Dr. Miller and helped him open it.

I hope that you received my other letter that I started to write on my trip out from Yencheng and mailed it when I arrived here in Hankow. I presume you have sort of been worrying about me when you didn't receive any letters from me for such a long time. I had no way to write to you because I was on the road all the time. I wrote you a letter the night before we had to evacuate Yencheng (letter of Dec. 13, 1947) but I am sure that you didn't receive it because the train I went out on the next day—it was burned by the Communists and I am sure that my letters to you were also very likely on that train.

[For the next three pages, Gertrude recounted in detail the trip from Yencheng to Hankow.]

I got out with just a few things. I guess everything I own I have lost in Yencheng. The Communists burned our hospital in Yencheng. They threw two incendiary bombs on it. They have only one thing in mind to fight for and that is to destroy everything. They have destroyed the railroad. They say that the railroad is only for the rich and they don't want any. Well, if you could see just about only poor people are riding on the railroad here in China and no one could say it was just for the rich. They told us when we saw them that they wanted to destroy everything and then they would all be poor together. Can you imagine how any country could continue to exist on such a plan as the Communists have?

I guess those packages you sent will never get to me now. It makes me sick to think my house and everything is gone. I am supposed to go to Shanghai any day. Just waiting for a boat to take me down the river. They are having meetings down there and want me to attend. I still need a good rest after such a long siege of being on such a tension for so long and not being able to sleep at night. I lost twenty pounds weight, but I have gained some of that after getting good food to eat here in Hankow . . .

Ten days later, still full of her long tale about escaping from the Communists, Gertrude wrote another long letter. This time she wrote from Shanghai.

> 526 Ningkuo Road
> Shanghai, China
> Monday, January 26, 1948

Dearest Mother:

Well, I have just arrived in Shanghai yesterday morning and I was so busy seeing everybody that I didn't get around to write you yesterday. Everybody was so interested to hear about our escape out of Yencheng that I have talked until my throat is sore.

It took us five days to come down on the boat from Hankow which is much longer than usual. We had such bad weather, storms and rain, snow and cold and fog that we had to drop anchor every little bit. The boat did not go at night either because they were afraid of Communists all along the river. We had to stay in bed nearly all the time on the boat to stay warm.

Now the weather is very cold again. In Hankow the weather got real warm and nice and then suddenly winter descended down with a vengeance. It snowed all day yesterday.

I have been waiting for a letter from you, but up to the present I haven't received any word and so I shall be worried until I hear from you and know that you are all right. When I got here yesterday I had a lot of letters waiting for me from all kinds of friends telling me that they were so glad that I was safe. My, I certainly didn't know that I was so popular and my name was all over the radio and in the papers and in the TIME magazine. I was surely surprised to hear all of this. Well, I guess no one knew anything about us for so long that they thought we had been captured by the Communists.

[At this point Gertrude wrote two more typed, single-spaced pages, needing to talk out once again their escape from Central China.]

I will try and write a regular big story of the whole trip getting in all the interesting items after I have had time to collect my brains together and feel like sitting down and getting started at it.

I am feeling just fine. I have gained back all my weight on the good meals I have been eating. Everything tasted so good to me that I ate like a pig. I hope that I hear from you very soon and that you are well and not had any cold since I last heard from you.

I think I am going to stay in Shanghai now, so maybe it will be better. There are plenty of Communists here, too, but there are plenty in the U.S. too. What can we do about that now? The Lord said that things would be worse and worse toward the end of time, so I guess we cannot look for anything better . . .

By February, Gertrude had "collected her brains together" and was able to write a letter to her mother that wasn't about the four-week trip out of Yencheng. While her focus on the medical work was returning, she was still concerned for her own safety, and for the reasons behind what she had lost in Yencheng and why they continued to elude her.

> 526 Ningkuo Road
> Shanghai, China
> Feb. 2, 1948

Dearest Mother:

I surely was glad to receive your first letter last Friday. You can imagine how shocked I was to receive it from California, but I was pleased about hearing from you there. Little did I dream of what was going on all during the long time that I was not in contact with civilization. Your letter was most welcome and I am so glad you went to California for Christmas. It must have been a lovely Christmas indeed with Ruth and Louise.

The Big Division meetings are over now, except for some committee work that has to be done. Personally I do not care to stay in Shanghai if I can go somewhere else that is fairly safe. I would like to go to South China to a place outside of Canton (the place where Dr. Paul Hwang had thought he might be sent). It is a very lovely place and they are just going to start a new place for a hospital there. Sounds good to me, but I don't know whether they would let me go there or not. I am going to ask to go there. It is not so very far from Hong Kong,

It is wonderful that you are having such a wonderful time in California. My, to think you do not need to cook or do anything, just play with Louise. It is so nice that she is a nice little girl. I'll bet she loves her grandma. I suppose that Ruth has a nice home and everything.

I have decided that on this earth I am not ever supposed to have such a thing as a nice home and family, or even a house. Every time I get one, I don't have it for very long. Maybe the Lord knows that I might be satisfied there and then not do my work right. Not even when I was in the States— I lived the last two years before I came back to China in a suitcase. Now my home is gone again. I guess I never will eat fresh strawberries again. After putting in 500 plants up there, now I am gone. Everything in my house is gone, including my rugs, and I know you wanted a rug so badly . . .

In January, Gertrude had enrolled 14 students from Yencheng in the Wuhan Sanitarium Nursing School, six in the second or junior year and eight in the senior year. By March, the Wuhan Nursing School was clamoring for Gertrude to come help them teach, especially the obstetrical courses, as these extra 14 students had overwhelmed the teaching staff.

Wuhan Sanitarium and Hospital
P.O. Box 40, Wuchang, Hupeh, China
March 28, 1948

Dearest Mother:

I wanted to get a letter off to you all last week, but I was so busy trying to get classes ready for my students here, that I just let it go and go. I arrived here in Hankow by boat last Sunday evening, just one week ago. I had a good trip up the river and it took only four days.

I received your last letter telling me about your trip home by plane. I am so glad you had such an enjoyable time and that you like plane travel. It surely gets one places fast. I'll bet everyone was anxious to hear about your good time in California. I'll bet most of all you miss you little granddaughter, Louise. She must be very cute, at least her pictures are—quite a serious look-ing child. I suppose it will be lonesome for her as well as yourself.

I got a letter from Ruth yesterday. She told me that Elder Bradley got in early and brought her coat from China. She went down to San Francisco and got it from him on the 15th. She likes it very much and says it is just what she wanted. I'm glad she is satisfied. She only had to pay $25.00 duty on it. I paid $180.00 and with the $25 duty she sure could not get anything decent like it in the States for $205.

What about Fred? All the time you have been out there you have never once mentioned him. Does he come to see Ruth and what does Ruth have to say about him? It is too bad that they have broken up, or maybe it is only temporary. Ruth has never written me about it.

I got a darling white fur coat and bonnet for Louise. I looked all around and didn't find anything that I wanted, and then finally I saw a cute set all lined in white satin and the bonnet is adorable. It may be too big for Louise right now, but children grow so fast that by next winter she probably can wear it and the hem can be turned up or let out as needed.

I will have a cute little house to live in here, like a little dollhouse, made of red brick with small rooms. But it is big enough for one person and easy to clean. The kitchen is small also and it has a bathroom. I don't know when I will get my things from Shanghai. In the meantime I am living with Mr. and Mrs. Boynton who used to be in China and then when I was in Denver, they were there.

I hope to get in a garden soon, the ground is all plowed. When I think of all those seeds you sent me and were left in Yencheng. I wonder about where they are, probably somebody stole them. Makes me sick. Think of all those strawber-ries I put in and now I won't have any, also makes me sick when I think of it.

I have bought several pieces of material for Dr. Beatty and have sent them to her. She pays me well for them. Now I should have some money coming from

Ruth for her fur coat. I have your fur coat packed in a chest that I am sending home to you. I wanted to send some things home, so decided to buy another chest and pack it full of some things that I do not want to lose, because this evacuation business scares me to death because I lose so much. I am having it shipped directly to New York and Rochester, so when it gets there you will have to take it through Customs and sometime in the near future I will send you a list of everything that is in it. Most everything is used. I took your coat and powdered it with a powder puff on the neck so that it looks like it is used. You can sponge it off, I guess. Therefore you can prove that it has been used.

How is Aunt Mary and Aunt Emma? Hope everything is going nicely at home and that you get your room rented soon. Tell Walter and Amelia hello and also Fred and Gloria when you go down to see them. I must close for today. I must get busy and do some studying. Take good care of yourself and don't work too hard.

Loads of love from you loving daughter,
Gertrude

By June, Gertrude's life had taken on a semblance of normality. Her garden was in full bloom and producing both vegetables and flowers in abundance. Her shopping days were full of pricing and buying things for other people, with the occasional purchase for herself. Packages from her friends arrived daily from the States. She had time for canoe trips with the Boyntons on East Lake in front of the hospital.

Wuhan Sanitarium and Hospital
Wuchang 3, Hupeh
June 7, 1948

Dearest Mother:

Well here it is—another week passed by, but so much has transpired and now the graduation is over and I feel like dropping down in a heap after so much planning and busy getting everything ready. Last night was the last, it was graduation and very beautiful. Everyone liked it very much and everything went off just beautiful. I was so happy because when I am responsible for something like that it just kills me to have anything go wrong, so I try to think of everything when planning so that it won't be left to the last minute.

We had five students graduate. These poor students surely have had a hard time because when they started training over five years ago, they had to stop because the Japs came in and took Yencheng. Because they were only first-year students, they did not take them to another hospital to finish, so they had to wait to come back into training after the Japs were defeated. They came back into training at a hard period just when everything had to be built up and then, when the Communists came into Yencheng last December, they had to flee again and were out of their course for over three months. Then I came back up here to help them finish up their class work and so here they are now—graduated at last. You can imagine how extremely happy they all are. Now that it is all over I am completely let down and tired out today. I suppose it will take a couple of days to recover from the hard work. It was fun and I was glad to do it for the students who were so very appreciative.

I will try to enclose a list of the things that are in that chest. I thought I already put on the list how old most of the things were. I presume that there will be some duty on that stuff. It is all my own personal stuff. Inasmuch as I lost everything up in Yencheng, the things that I was able to save by having stored them in other places besides Yencheng, I didn't want to lose, so sent them home. If the Customs man wants to open the chest and see for himself, just give him the list. And if he charges duty, just pay what he says and say nothing.

I still have to continue to teach classes to the second-year students. I am teaching every day and have another bunch of exam papers piling up that I need to look over. That is a job I do not like and worse to do in Chinese. By rights classes should be over, but because we evacuated and did not have classes for three months, we have to make up this summer. My program is not nearly as heavy as it was before graduation, but I am plenty busy enough although I have time to breathe and take things a little bit easier.

I am hoping that this year I can get a vacation. I want to go to Tsingtao, a place up on the coast where I can go swimming. They say it is nice and a wonderful place in the summer. I hope so. I will try to make arrangements to go there if possible . . .

In her letters of July and August, Gertrude described her new refrigerator and new stove with small oven, her surprise at receiving an extra Feather-Lite Singer sewing machine which she could always use, all of the shopping and baking and gardening that she accomplished throughout the summer. She also described the rampant inflation in the country.

"Mother, I want you to notice the postage on the outside of this letter. It is costing me now to send an airmail letter one million one hundred thousand dollars. $1,100,000! You can tell your friends that you got a letter with over a million dollars in postage on it.

This money is crazy as can be. I understand that the government is coming out with some new kind of money tomorrow. It is going off of all these millions and we are going back to what we used to have when I was here before. It is going to be dollars, but not millions of dollars. The new money will take only four of them to equal one U.S. dollar. The present currency takes fifteen million dollars to equal one U.S. dollar. The new money will certainly make a lot more sense than these millions that we carry around now but at least I can say that I was a millionaire."

At the end of August Gertrude had one more surprise for her mother.

Wuhan Sanitarium and Hospital
Wuchang 3, Hupeh
August 22, 1948

Dearest Mother:

Well, here I am starting to pack again. I started today and have one trunk finished with most of my books in. It is such a job, I am just glad I have it cool to do it. There is no other way but that I just have to go back to Shanghai and take charge of the Clinic. To think of leaving this lovely place is hard, because it is a gorgeous location, but I guess I have to go where they need me most. Elder Branson wrote quite a strong letter telling them that I should be released and go to Shanghai.

I have my vacation coming. Mr. and Mrs. Boynton and their daughter Carolyn are going to Hong Kong for their vacation and want me to go along, so I have decided to take two weeks and go there first and then come back here and get my things and then take a boat to Shanghai. When I deposit my things I shall start for Peking and Tsingtao right away for the rest of my vacation which is four weeks altogether. I think it will be fun to take a trip down to Hong Kong where there is ocean swimming and they can go every day because they live close to the beach. And I am looking forward to swimming in the ocean at Tsingtao . . .

What Gertrude did not tell her mother was that Elder Branson had insisted that Gertrude be released to come to Shanghai. He wanted more than for her to run the Range Road Clinic. He wanted her to bring the second-year Yencheng students from Hankow to attend the Shanghai San Nursing School as seniors because the Communists were closing in on Wuhan and would probably be in control of that city by year's end.

She also didn't tell her mother, probably because she didn't know, that the Communist army had broken out of the northern corridor between Kaifeng, Yencheng, and Hankow and was fighting its way through Northeast China toward Peking, Tsingtao, and the seacoast. In September Gertrude vacationed and swam in the ocean at Tsingtao, visiting Dr. McMullen and his family who had been assigned to the clinic in that city. From there she rode the train down to Shanghai. In November, 1948, the Communists began their siege of Peking engulfing Northeast China, including Peking, Tianjin—and Tsingtao—and advancing all the way to the sea coast by January, 1949.

Chapter 75

SHARING ANOTHER THANKSGIVING

GENERAL CONFERENCE OF SEVENTH-DAY ADVENTISTS
TAKOMA PARK, WASHINGTON 12, D.C.

November 11, 1948

PARENTS OF MISSIONARIES IN CHINA:

Dear Friends:

Today the General Conference Committee has been giving study to the troubled situation in China. We have been in touch with the Department of State in Washington and have also been watching all news which seems to cast light on the developments. We understand that the viewpoint of the American observers in China is that the military situation is deteriorating rapidly, and there is the likelihood that Communistic forces will approach much nearer to the Yangtze Valley and the cities of Nanking and Shanghai, even to the point where these cities may be occupied by Communistic forces. At the same time, winter is coming on and it is possible that means of communication now open may be closed a little later because of unfavorable flying conditions and also because of freezing of the waterways in North China.

All these considerations led the American consular authorities in China to advise Americans that those who plan to evacuate should do so now. We are informed that naval vessels are standing by and will be ready to evacuate all who are wanting to go. We have been told, however, that not all the Americans are planning to leave at this time; in fact, it seems that the ma-

630

jority of Americans are staying on, including American consular officials in Mukden, Peiping, Tientsien, Shanghai, Nanking and Hankow.

We are told that the food situation is the worst in Shanghai, and that the American Community is being supplied from stores which are available to Americans on a ration basis. However, since the stringent currency regulations have been cancelled, supplies are again moving from the country into the cities and are appearing in the shops, though at higher prices.

The General Conference cabled to Shanghai asking about the general situation. The answer of the brethren included instructions for continuing to send new missionaries, some by air, some by boat and some to language school in safe places, concluding with these words, "conditions still uncertain." I refer to this cable and the other bits of information to indicate that there seems to be no immediate danger to those who are in the various cities, and all seem to be getting on quite well.

We are hopeful that it will be possible for most of our missionaries to remain at their posts of duty, for we know that they all would like to do this. We do not wish any of them to remain, however, to the point where their lives will be in danger. We know that certain missionaries of other boards remained in Tsinan when the Communists took control of Shangtung Province and messages have come through from them which seem to indicate that they are all right. We are endeavoring to keep in close touch with developments day by day and wish to assure you that we will continue to take every possible precaution for the safety of our missionaries in China.

Surely the Lord will watch over His work and those who have gone out to take the gospel abroad. Let us pray that this new convulsion in war-torn China may result in the awakening of the minds of the people and the saving of many souls in the kingdom of heaven.

Sincerely you brother,
W. P. Bradley, Assoc. Secretary

WPB:hs

526 Ningkuo Road
Shanghai 19, China
November 22, 1948

Dearest Mother:

I was pleased to receive your letter yesterday when I got home from the hospital. I wanted to write last night, but my typewriter was here at the hospital and I hate to write by hand any more, because I can do it so much faster with the machine. Guess people can read it better, too. We had a house full of company last night so I didn't get to do anything, but play a game.

Well, I'm still not in my apartment. The painting is finished and my things have been moved to the Clinic from out at the Shanghai San on Rubicon Road, but the plumbers haven't finished the bathroom yet, so I can't move in. I have a nice oil heating stove in the living room and just this morning I got my gas stove fixed in the kitchen. The gas isn't as strong over here as at home and so the holes that gas comes through have to be bored larger. So that was done this morning. The kitchen is now ready, all white, trimmed in red. It is cute. I only hope I don't have to go off and leave it right away.

I shall be glad to move in because I just hate to ride these awful crowded buses with such dirty people all around me. If you think your buses are crowded at home, you haven't seen anything yet. I smash about two ribs every time I get off and on. They are almost more than I can stand. When I move to the Clinic, I won't have to ride out from Ningkuo Road any more. And I will be near enough to town that I can walk or take a rickshaw.

So you received a letter from Elder Bradley from the General Conference. It was nice of him to write you. He was one of the three men from the General Conference who visited me in Yencheng just before the evacuation. He is very nice.

It is hard to know the true situation of things here in Shanghai, but things have not looked too well throughout all of China with the upset of this money and with the Communists gaining so much ground. All of north China has been evacuated of our missionaries. My, I am so glad that I was fortunate enough to get to see that place before things got worse up there. The folks in Hankow all have to evacuate, too, so it is good that I am already out of there. They have to close our hospital there and most everyone is leaving for Canton down south.

At present we do not have to evacuate Shanghai as things have been much improved. Food is now available again; all of the stores are open and have their shelves well stocked with goods. Of course there is the threat of the

Reds coming into Shanghai. Everyone thinks that during the time they would be coming into the city, it would be better to be somewhere else, Hong Kong or the Philippines, or some other safe place. Then after the new government took over, they could all come back. I don't think that any new government in China will be entirely Communist. But the people of China do not want the government that is existing now and so I feel sure that there will be a new government soon.

This present government cannot go on. This country is run the worst of any I know and most of it is just plain stupid, if you ask me. The people have no confidence in it. They have been swindled out of so much money by the government with the change of money and the price fixing.

As I say, the conditions in Shanghai are so much better than they were. Before, no one could get any rice or flour or anything. Prices are high now, but it can be gotten.

The poor Chinese are the ones that I feel sorry for. How can they afford to buy things on their little pay, when it is almost impossible for us to pay the price that is asked? What will happen over here is a great question. There is no doubt that the Communists are gaining control of most of China. There are a lot of Chinese who have turned to the Communists simply as a means of doing something to get rid of the present government.

It is a sad situation. But we are carrying on many, many evangelistic meetings all over China. I guess the people now believe what we preach. The meetings are well attended. Here in Shanghai Elder Detamore is holding meetings. They have to have two meetings on Sunday nights, at 5:30 and at 7:00 because the crowds are so big. This will be the last chance to hear the gospel. My, these are just like the times that the Bible predicts. How anyone who knows this truth can spurn the words of prophecy, I do not know as it is so plain. I am so happy that I believe and have accepted this wonderful Truth. While everyone in the world is gripped with fear for what will happen to them, we have a hope and know that these things must come to pass, but our joy is fuller looking for the coming of Jesus to take us to a better home to live.

I surely do thank you for sending me the recipe for the nice creamy rice pudding. I lost my recipe book in Yencheng last year so that I have not had any book to cook by. Oh, yes, I did remember your recipe for potato salad. I am glad for the bumper crop of celery I had this year in my garden. As much celery as potatoes is the secret to Lena Green's potato salad—and mine, too.

I think maybe the boat strike will be over before long. When it is, I was hoping that you might send me a new pair of Stadium boots like my old ones with the fleece lining. The ones I got when I was home, I have worn for three years and they are pretty messy. And I also need some index cards, the three by five size without any alphabet letters on them. But I tell you what. You should hold up sending any more packages for a while until we know what is going to happen over here. I don't want to lose any more stuff than I have to. Some days it looks like we will be coming home right away and then again we don't know. So just to be safe, hold everything else until you have word from me to send them on.

I had a letter from Ruth this last week, didn't have much to say. She writes big on the page, I guess, so it gives the appearance of a long letter, but there isn't much news. Is she getting a divorce? She says nothing to me—I guess she wouldn't have the "face" to tell me anything about it. When she first got married, she kept writing me to hurry and get married and not to be so particular. I wrote back and told her that it was me who had to live with him and if I wanted to be particular that was my business. Guess she wasn't so particular and that's what she got. I feel sorry for her, it is not a nice thing to happen, but people can't always be so cock-sure.

I was absolutely flabbergasted when Truman got elected again. I thought for sure that Dewey would get it without any trouble. I guess we have to take it and like it. Good men never get political jobs these days. Truman is so weak that the politicians can run him the way they want and that is the way they like it.

I feel terrible about this Christmas. I planned to send some gifts, but I am living in such a muddle that I cannot get around to do anything. I bought Christmas cards, but they haven't been written yet. Maybe I will get them off yet.

I am busy in the hospital, too. My, the way they have been doing things is surely a mess. Every day I find out something different and have to straighten it out. I am teaching also, so you see I have a full day. Now with this moving down here and packing my stuff, it is a job indeed.

I hope that you all have a very pleasant Thanksgiving. I expect to have a nice time. I will go to Branson's and Hill's for my Thanksgiving dinner. We always have such good food there. I am sort of privileged to be invited there. I am sure it will be nice there at home with Fred and Gloria and Walter and Amelia all together. Remember me to Aunt Mary and Aunt Emma and to everyone you know. Really the letters that need answering are stacking up and I cannot write a decent letter while we sit in such suspense at the present time. So tell everyone I think of them anyway even if I don't write.

I hope this finds you well. I am fine. My cold is all better and I am taking some Vitamin tablets and I think they help. Take good care of yourself and I am thinking of you all the time.

Loads of love to my dear mother from your daughter,
Gertrude

Even though she was 20 years Gertrude's senior, Rachel Landrum was a fast walker, which was a good thing because Gertrude set a blistering pace. They'd started out from Rachel's house, walking together down the main road of the China Division Headquarters compound on Ningkuo Road toward Elder Hill's house where Thanksgiving dinner was being held. He lived at the back of the Division compound near the new Signs Publishing House where he was manager and superintendent of all SDA church publishing for China. He'd been given an especially large house to serve as his office and as an unofficial location for meetings and training sessions for the colporteurs and administrative staff. The publishing house and its dedicated workers kept the presses running efficiently through 16-hour days to meet the increased demand for Adventist Christian literature.

"Gertrude, wait up," Rachel called out when she had fallen behind several yards.

Gertrude had been thinking about how different the winter was here in Shanghai from what it had been in Yencheng. Here was darker and dreary, with a penetratingly wet coldness like they'd known in Rochester, New York. Remembering the Thanksgivings they'd celebrated there on Bryan Street and the wonderful cooking of her mother and her aunts, the warm memory of delicious, home-cooked food made her realize how hungry she was. So she walked even faster.

Looking around, Gertrude was surprised to hear her name being called.

"What? What's wrong?" she called back. Seeing how far Rachel had dropped behind her, she paused and waited for her to catch up.

"I think your potato salad must be lighter than my stuffing," Rachel puffed. She tried to hold up her blue and white serving dish as evidence of its increased weight while running with a skittering, awkward bounce.

Puzzled, Gertrude looked down at her own offering for the Thanksgiving dinner, then glanced up smiling when she realized Rachel was joking. "Did I get too far ahead of you, dearie? I'm sorry. It's just that when I'm headed for a meal, nothing gets in my way." She laughed aloud. "I guess I'm hungry."

"Me, too," Rachel admitted, "but mostly for someone to talk to." Breathing hard, Rachel slowed to a walk to catch her breath. "This month I've spent nearly every waking moment working on the Division accounts or else trying to find time to search for the material for my wedding dress. Mrs. Butka is helping me, but she's about the only other person I get to talk with."

Yes, I'm going for the talk, but I'm going to listen too, Gertrude mused. *It's at these big dinners where you hear the latest news about what's happening—things they never tell you in committee meetings or in written reports.*

Responding to Rachel's comment about her upcoming wedding to a pastor in the south of China, Gertrude offered, "Well, you can use my new sewing machine if you need to. It's got a new kind of serging foot on it. Would save you time from doing it by hand."

"That'd be a help," Rachel said as she fell in step with Gertrude again. After a few moments she added, "You won't be needing it for your own wedding dress, will you?

Gertrude glanced at her out of the corner of her eye and frowned. "Of course not, silly." Seeing the wry grin, Gertrude softened and said in mock offense, "You knew that." She looked down at the potato salad she'd carefully made that morning from her mother's recipe, and drew a deep breath. "No, I don't think I'll ever need my sewing machine for that particular task."

"Not ever?" Rachel asked, lapsing into her own reverie. "I've waited a long time—and sometimes thought I'd waited too long—but always in the back of my mind ..." Looking over at Gertrude's pensive face, Rachel abandoned her own history and asked, "Wasn't there ever that someone special . . ., you know?"

In an instant Gertrude's mind flashed images across her internal screen—

a young intern at the Boston City Hospital, a blond Norwegian fifth mate in a heavy peacoat, and several other handsome men who had attempted to attach themselves to her. "To tell you the truth, no, there never was. Not really."

Gertrude laughed a short laugh aloud, two short bursts of mirth. "Several Chinese men, some younger and one older man, used to travel up to Yencheng from Wuhan to see me. The staff at the hospital thought it was amusing at first. But when I let everyone know, in no uncertain terms, that I really wasn't interested, the staff began to protect me, run interference for me. Like in those American football games. And those men, they finally gave up."

"You still have a long life ahead of you," Rachel encouraged. "Look at me. I've been cast as the old maid for years now . . . but look at me!" She extended her favorite serving dish before her like an offering. Spreading her elbows wide in joyous celebration, she did a slow pirouette in the middle of the street, her heavy coat fluffing out at the bottom, filling like a hot air balloon with the motion.

You would have made a good dancer, Rachel Landrum, Gertrude adjudged appreciatively. *You've waited a long time—through internment in the prisoner of war camp in the Philippines, through all your service here in China. And finally it happened for you. You have every right to celebrate.* Gertrude stood watching Rachel turn in a full circle, like a small child in a playground game. *And you are genuinely happy, aren't you?*

As Rachel turned, Gertrude's mind revolved through her various assignments throughout her career. In every instance she always had nursing students to teach, physicians to coddle, hospitals to run, people to care for—even in the hard times, even in the dangerous times. In every instance there were always people who required her attention and her devoted service.

And there was the uncertainty. There was the pain she'd seen in the faces of Gert and Marvin Loewen with the loss of two infants, the memory of her mother's unhappy marriage, and now, apparently, Ruth's recent divorce.

Marriage! Would there be happiness in it for me? Devotion and service confined to one person? No, I don't think so. Not for me, Gertrude concluded, *not for me.*

"I'm too busy with my work, Rachel," she said, trying to put in words what she was thinking without revealing more than she intended. "You know how busy I am. And the times—they're too uncertain to be making a decision like that. You never know what will happen." Gertrude tried to make a joke, tried to lighten what had become an entirely too serious topic of discussion. "I have a hard enough time trying to keep up with the Lord, let alone trying to keep up with a man."

Rachel had stopped turning and was examining Gertrude closely, scrutinizing her inner being, or that part of it that she'd come to know since Gertrude had moved in with her while the apartment at the Clinic was being made ready. Gertrude squirmed internally like a bug under a magnifying glass.

"You're married already, aren't you . . . to your work." It was a statement and not a question.

It was a thought that had never before crossed Gertrude's mind. She considered it. "I guess I am," she said, turning and marching off in the direction of the festive dinner that awaited them.

The Thanksgiving dinner did not disappoint. Because of boxed cake mixes, Jell-O, shredded coconut, Kool-Aid, and other nonperishable items sent from the States to various people in attendance, the repast was marvelous and every bit as American as any Thanksgiving dinner stateside. But more than the food, the information that circulated around the tables was invaluable and exactly to Gertrude's liking.

From the various names dropped by several parties, Gertrude learned that Dr. Gregory and Dr. Lonser were moving to Shanghai and that Dr. Lee would be taking their place in Wuhan, setting up a city hospital in the Hankow city clinic and offices and closing the Wuhan San.

So we will replace American doctors with Chinese doctors in areas where the Communists have already taken over, she concluded. *Let's hope we have enough to go around.*

From the intense conversations and stressed expressions on the faces of Elder Frost and Dr. Butka, Gertrude was able to surmise that the efforts to rehabilitate the Shanghai Sanitarium on Rubicon Road were coming to an end.

I would not be surprised to learn that you, Dr. Butka, will be going back to America soon, Gertrude remarked to herself as she studied the weary face of a man she'd come to admire. *After all you have tried to do here in China, you deserve a rest. Let some of the younger ones, like Dr. Slough and Dr. Gregory carry this fight now.*

Then a more perplexing, more practical thought crossed her mind. *If the San is closed, the Range Road Clinic, my clinic, will become the major hospital in Shanghai—the only Seventh-day Adventist hospital in Shanghai.* A dozen situations—from the six nursing students from Yencheng now in the senior class to the increased patient load on the nursing staff—presented themselves. *When you get back to the clinic, you've got some planning to do,* she told herself. *Wonder when the powers that be were going to let me know this?* Gertrude was more than a little irritated at this obvious omission.

From the quiet remarks and innuendos that passed between division president Elder William Branson and Elder Nathan Brewer, the division secretary, Gertrude understood that the decision had already been made to move the China Division headquarters to Hong Kong. And not only that, but a list of people would soon be made public—those who were slated to be evacuated in December from Shanghai to Canton and from there, on to other assignments in the Far East.

Whose names are on that list and who is staying behind in Shanghai? The word "behind" bothered her just a bit. *No one has spoken to me about going or staying. Am I on that list to evacuate? Do I want to be?* She thought of her Yencheng nursing students and winced. *And if people are being sent home, where will we get the staff to carry the workload and teach the students?*

The clouds of uncertainty were closing in on Shanghai. The winds of war were blowing ever closer and, unconsciously, Gertrude began to shiver in the ensuing cold.

Chapter 76

REVIEWING THE REASONS WHY

At 5:00 a.m. Gertrude, wrapped in her Chinese silk dressing gown, common black silk slippers on her feet, sat at a small dining table in her darkened sixth-floor apartment. As the director of the School of Nursing she enjoyed having a kitchen/living room (previously a large ward room) and bedroom (formerly a private patient room) in the southeast corner of the top floor of the Range Road Clinic building. It was the tallest building in the small business district of Chapei, 10 blocks north of the Soochow Creek, the northern edge of downtown Shanghai.

On the table her Bible and the Sabbath school lesson quarterly lay open before her in a soft circle of light cast by a small kerosene lamp. With her favorite fountain pen she scratched out responses to the questions posed in the study guide. The new kerosene-wicked cooking stove she'd recently purchased stood against the far wall. It was turned down low, bravely warming the bone-chilling January air that seeped slowly into her apartment through 40-year-old walls. This was the place of her morning and evening worship, her place for devotional prayer and Bible study. This was her personal sanctuary in Shanghai.

If she had crossed this corner room which served as her kitchen/living/dining area, she could have gazed out the south-facing window down Szechuan Road, across Soochow Creek and along the Bund—the International Business District. At this early hour she would have seen, in the far distance on the right, tall, dark buildings of international businesses standing at attention in the early morning shadows. They seemed to be watching over the houseboats there on the left, nestled, low-slung, along the waterfront. The baguette-shaped houseboats were small dwellings, bumping and jostling quietly just across the broad avenue from their lofty guardians, small, pale lights swinging from the points of their moorings. She could have watched small scurrying figures escaping the shadows on the waterfront, hurrying to occupations as street sweepers, rickshaw drivers, street market entrepreneurs—all harbingers of the thrumming commerce that would erupt on the streets of Shanghai at first light.

Directly under her south-facing window she could have looked across the street and down into the playground of a school that now had been expropriated to be a Nationalist Army hospital. This hospital regularly sent patients across the street to her clinic for X-rays. At this early hour, of course, the hospital grounds would be dark and deserted.

However, for her place of prayer—her Bethel—she preferred the east-facing window where she'd purposefully placed her table and chairs. From this window she could look east to where the Wangpoo River bent acutely in that compass direction reflecting sparkles of moonlight from its ruffled surface. She could see past the Ningkuo Road compound which contained the Seventh-day Adventist China Division offices, now crouching unseen in the darkness that engulfed the eastern industrial warehouse waterfront of Shanghai. Beyond that were the far distant pastoral lands where the Wangpoo River joined the broad Yangtze River near the sea.

Gertrude preferred this eastern vista for her worship because the water and the distant, more rural setting reminded her of East Lake in Wuhan and of her beloved Spot Pond at the New England San.

Now she stopped writing and stared at the fountain pen, her nursing pen, which she held in her right hand.

Lord, you know I can't leave this place. Not now, not with my nursing students depending on me. They've been enrolled in three different schools and have been through two different wars trying to get their nursing education—and I just can't abandon them. Not now, not after all that.

A sound, a droning, a continuous motor sound rose up from the street below. Gertrude raised her head. *What's that noise?* The noise grew louder with overtones like thunder, or was it explosions? *What is that?* Gertrude placed her palms on the table and half raised herself from the seat, trying to see out the south-facing window.

The noise grew in intensity and variation, now mixed with the sounds of . . . *screaming*? Gertrude closed her eyes and shook her head, lowering herself into her seat, rejecting the fear that attempted to invade her sanctuary. She turned to the east and opened her eyes, gazing out the window. Concentrating on the faint pink, gray, and orange along the rim of the earth, she prayed.

"He that dwelleth in the secret place of the most High shall abide under the shadow of the Almighty."

The rumbling diminished. The voices quieted and receded into the shadows of early morning.

"I will say of the Lord, He is my refuge and my fortress: my God; in him I will trust!"

The thunderous explosions became the coughing and wheezing of a delivery truck filtering up from the street below, crossing the creek, and fading into the city.

Lord, I don't want to run away this time. I don't want my fears to chase me out. I want to stay and finish something for once.

A camp meeting tune emerged from her memory, a tune she had taught her nursing students. Voices and a piano, or was it an accordion? The voices were those of nursing students leading patients in singing in an evangelistic meeting tent somewhere in the interior of China. The music became clearer and more distinct: "I shall not be, I shall not be moved. I shall not be, I shall not be moved . . ."

Gertrude smiled at the reminiscence and allowed the voices to direct her eyes to the river below as it reached out for the sea in the far distance.

"Just like a tree planted by the waters, I shall not be moved."

She picked up her pen, pulled her lesson quarterly a bit closer and began to write.

On the second Sunday of January, 1949, Gertrude stepped into the hallway outside her apartment as the faces of Allan and Mildred Boynton bobbed into view in the stairwell.

"Hi," Gertrude cried. "I heard the echoes of your footsteps on the stairs."

"That's quite a trek up those stairs," Allan Boynton huffed. Tall, rail thin, and gray haired, the new superintendent of the Range Road Clinic reached out a helping hand to his wife, equally thin and graying, whose struggle up the stairs was a bit more labored. "I'm used to climbing up only to the second floor offices," he said.

"Well, welcome to the domain of the higher-ups," Gertrude laughed. "Come on in." She held open her front door.

"You have a lovely place here, Gertrude," Mildred Boynton complimented as she entered the large corner room. "And such a grand view."

"Not like we had in Denver," Gertrude responded, closing the door and rushing to her stove where a pot was about to boil over, "but it'll do in a pinch."

"No, not like we had in Denver," Mildred agreed. "Porter Memorial Hospital had just a little more space to spread out in, huh? But then, we were not in the middle of a war there, were we?"

"Just pull out those chairs there at the table and sit," Gertrude called over her shoulder. "I've been looking for a couch—in my spare time—but I just haven't found one that's small enough to fit in this room."

She turned from the stove as Allan lowered himself into the easy chair by the bedroom door. Mildred had pulled out a white, curved back chair and was sitting at the table by the window where Gertrude had her worship time.

"I'm so glad that you came to dinner today," Gertrude announced, bowing slightly. "You were so gracious to me during my stay in Denver and again in Wuhan, I wanted to return the favor on your arrival in Shanghai." She shook her head with irritation. "But I just couldn't get you invited until today. So many things to do with the nursing school and the clinic and all. Sunday is a slightly less busy day since we don't have classes today."

"No need to apologize, Miss Green," Allan Boynton rejoined with a wave of his hand. "I, for one, am very appreciative of all the work you're getting done here at the clinic."

"Well, I'm not sure how we would get the work done if you hadn't come from Wuhan to take over its management, what with Elder Landis leaving last month," Gertrude said, turning back to the stove on hearing a lid rattle.

"We did lose a lot of people, didn't we?" Mildred said aloud, but mostly to herself as she gazed thoughtfully out the east window.

"Just the entire China Division, the college, the academy, and the language school *and* most of my Caucasian nurses!" Gertrude's voice was sharp, rising in volume and emphasis as each word was delivered. "Those three evacuation planes wiped out just about everything."

"I'm sure the brethren felt the need to protect the work here in China," Allan offered in a subdued voice. "I think they remember that they waited too long to get everyone out when the Japanese were invading."

"I'm sure you're right," Gertrude said, calmer this time. "I know Rachel Landrum felt that way. She didn't get out the last time and ended up in a concentration camp in the Philippines." Gertrude kept her back turned and found something to keep her hands busy. "I know Rachel was glad to evacuate this time," she added quietly, remembering the wedding gown she had helped Rachel pack in the top of her steamer trunk.

"But some of us seem to be gluttons for punishment, eh, Gertrude?" he offered, trying to lighten the mood.

"Well, I'm not sure I'm a glutton except when it comes to strawberries," she laughed, "but I chose to stay." She turned and faced them both, a dinner plate in her hand. "I wanted to stay this time for the sake of my nursing students." She spoke emphatically, warming to her topic as they both nodded their heads in understanding. "You know. You were there when we arrived in Wuhan from Yencheng. Those students had been trying for six years to get their degree, and I just can't abandon them now. Besides, we can use their help after they graduate."

"We understand." Allan sat up straighter, his gray eyes blinking rapidly. "We feel the same way about the Range Road Clinic. We were here before, before the war with the Japanese. So much hard work has gone into this institution since we got it from the Red Cross in 1927." He shook his head, pausing to correct himself. "I should say, when the Lord procured this clinic for us in 1927. It was a beacon of hope in this community then and it can still be—whether the Communists eventually take over Shanghai or not."

"Well, I'm no lover of Communists," Gertrude said, filling the plate from the pots on the stove, "but they can't do any worse than is being done right now."

"Oh, look." Mildred rose and walked over to the small washing machine sitting in the corner behind the bedroom door. "What a cute little washing machine!" she said, bending over to look inside the tub. "And just the right size for this apartment."

"It's called a 'Monitor,'" Gertrude told her. She carried her first plate to the table and returned to the cupboard for a second one. "It saves me just oodles of work—and the wringer is so easy to use."

Mildred straightened up as if she'd been pinched. "Oh, Gertrude, forgive me." She rushed to the center of the room. "I should have offered to help. What can I do?"

"You can sit down in that chair and eat. My refrigerator isn't big enough to hold the leftovers," Gertrude laughed, handing the filled plate to Mildred.

On Monday, January 17, Dr. Harry Miller flew into Shanghai. At age 70, with thin white hair and a heavy face that had sagged into jowls, he was making another whirlwind visit to the Far East. As on his other trips, he came to do goiter surgery, his specialty, to assess the current crisis and how it was affecting the hospitals he'd so lovingly helped establish, and to further pursue his dream of making soy milk available to the masses of Asia by establishing a soy milk plant in Hong Kong. On Tuesday and Wednesday he would do goiter surgery in Shanghai. On Thursday and Friday he would do surgery in the Philippines. After a Sabbath rest he would fly to Hong Kong for a business meeting. Then he would return to his farm and soy milk laboratory in Mount Vernon, Ohio—and to his wife, Marie, who had recently become ill again.

But this Monday evening he was in Shanghai, examining and preparing patients for their goiter surgery, touring and becoming familiar again with the operating rooms that he'd use the next morning. And perhaps most important, he was seeing first hand how the Range Road Clinic had taken over the functions of a hospital—functions that used to take place on Rubicon Road at the premier Seventh-day Adventist hospital in China—the Shanghai Sanitarium and Hospital.

"Well, it's not the Shanghai San, now is it, Gertrude?" Dr. Miller commented as he ascended the staircase. Coming down the first floor central hall, he had noted the various cracks in the walls, the holes left where plaster had fallen, and the scarred and warped doors on the clinic offices that needed to be replaced. Now he pointed to the corners high up in the stairwell as he spoke.

"Well, we don't have a chandelier in the foyer, if that's what you mean," she joked. "Actually, the San looks worse in some spots." She was standing behind him, waiting for him to start up the stairs. "Dr. Butka and Mrs. Sevrens have been trying for more than two years to get the San back on its feet and working again. But the damage done by the Japanese during the invasion, and the decay that set in during the Japanese occupation—water pipes freezing and bursting and all—would require more money than they have to spend. There are just too many other hospitals here in China that need to be repaired. At least, that's what Elder Frost tells me."

You might stand as straight and as tall as ever, but you don't climb stairs as fast as you used to, Gertrude observed as she slowed her usually quick ascent to match his. *But then, you're 70 years old.* "We still have the surgery suites on the second floor," she said, indicating the door just above him. "Even in the same old rooms. It would be too hard to move the lights and the scrub sinks."

Reaching the landing, Dr. Miller reached out a strong, steady right hand and turned the brass knob. Passing through the doorway, he stepped into the wide hallway lined with tall wooden doors. The upper half of each door framed a large, clear glass window. Behind the windows were operating tables and glass wall cabinets full of wrapped instruments. Gertrude slipped through the doorway and stood beside him.

"We've had to press together just a bit," she explained. "We moved Mr. Boynton and the administrative offices up here to the second floor. Over there"—she pointed to the southwest corner of the building. "And the children's ward is over there behind those doors. We moved the women's ward, including OB, to the third floor, and moved the men's ward to the fourth floor."

"Because people are living on the top two floors," he said, looking up at the ceiling as if he could see the upper two floors of the building.

"All the unmarried nursing personnel are living on those top two floors, as well as all the nursing students," she answered. "Some are living 10 to a room. I have no classrooms and no nursing laboratory." Her voice was rising. She felt herself rising up on her toes.

"Yes," Dr. Miller said matter-of-factly, nodding his head as if he knew already. "Some of your classes and the religious services are being held in that little chapel next to the hospital."

He turned and looked at Gertrude, a wry smile playing in his lips, his soft blue eyes lit with mirth.

You knew all of this already, didn't you? she thought, staring hard at him. *Why am I taking you on a tour of this place if you already know everything?*

"Are you ready to run the Shanghai San from this little six-story building?" he asked, his eyes losing their mirth, becoming colder, more serious.

"We're already doing that, at least for those who can't get out to the San," she retorted. "But I could do it a lot better if I had more staff and more equipment."

"I think I heard that there are too many other hospitals in China that need the money for their own repairs," he said, repeating what Gertrude had told him not five minutes previously. He turned his head, gazing down the corridor past the OR doors, seeing beyond the outside wall—as if he were seeing all the way west to the Shanghai San miles away on Rubicon Road.

"They will close the Shanghai San in about six weeks," he said flatly. "They don't have the money to keep it open or to repair it." He swiveled his large white-topped head around and stared down at her. "They will send Dr. Butka home to the States and what's left of the expatriate staff to other hospitals outside of China. Only Chinese doctors and nurses will be serving in the other Chinese hospitals—under the Communists. After your experience traveling from Yencheng, I think you know why."

It was Gertrude's turn to look beyond the walls of the building, to remember escaping through the south gates of Suiping as the Communists were returning through the north gates to kill all the Americans. Her gaze fell to the floor and her face broke into a broad grin as her shoulders shook with an audible chuckle. "I'm remembering," she explained quickly, "what Mrs. Smith said. She's a friend of my mother, back in the States. She talked about how kind and generous the Communists are." Gertrude snorted through her nose in disgust, her smile gone. "Little does she know."

Dr. Miller continued to stare at her. "This Range Road Clinic and Hospital will be the only Seventh-day Adventist medical facility in Shanghai. There will be no other staff coming. Are you ready for that?"

Gertrude gazed into his blue eyes, deep with wisdom. *This is why we're on this little tour, isn't it? You wanted to prepare me for this.* "I'm not afraid of them, not any more," she said, her voice firm and steady.

"It's not about the fear of them," he responded. "He who is with us is greater than he who is with them."

"I know that. I learned that." Gertrude felt uncomfortable and wriggled inside her skin. *Why is he prodding me, goading me?* It was as if he were testing her. "I've already been tested on that point. 'A thousand shall fall at thy side

647

and ten thousand at thy right hand; but it shall not come nigh thee,'" she quoted emphatically. "I lived that . . . and I learned."

"It's not about the fear of them," he pressed on. "It's about the fear of the unknown, the unknowable, the undoable. It's about the thing which the Lord asks us to do that we cannot do—no matter how hard we try."

"What are you saying?" she blurted, irritated that he did not give her credit for her new understanding. "You're the 'China Doctor'. You can do anything you set your mind to do."

Dr. Miller broke off his steely gaze and took a deep breath. "How I wish that were true," he murmured, raising one eyebrow. "I'm just a man, made of clay, like every other man. An earthen vessel, unworthy to hold precious spiritual things, like human lives. Every move I make, every plan, every scalpel I hold, I hold it with all the skill I can muster."

Gertrude watched him become animated, watched him transform into the younger, stronger man she had known in Wuhan. His long arms came up; his large hands unfolded, now slicing the air, now formed into rounded cups, offering his lifetime of learning.

"But it's all worthless unless I'm working with the Holy Spirit." He quickly corrected himself. "Or I should say, the Holy Spirit is working with me. I wait on Him to direct, to confirm that I'm on the right track. This work that I'm doing with the soy, trying to make a milk that is nutritious as well as tasty to the palate, trying to make nutrition available to the Chinese and others who are unaware of what their own culture has known for thousands of years." He paused, gazing into his own hands. "I'm on the right track, but I'm always watching and waiting, trying to work simultaneously with Him."

He held it out to her, the wisdom distilled from a lifetime of work in China, the understanding gleaned from gains and losses, the secret of success when working with the Lord. In his extended right hand he held his precious elixir out to her.

"I'm glad I chose to stay in Shanghai," she said with defiance. "It's what the Lord wanted me to do. I can't quit this time. My students need me." She wasn't sure she was getting through to him. *Why don't you understand me? I have faith in the Lord that I am doing the right thing this time.* Yet her words didn't feel right and she tried again. "I'd rather be in Shanghai doing something than in Canton or Hong Kong doing nothing, just sitting around doing nothing."

"I'm glad you stayed, too," he said with a tired smile, lowering his arm.

On April 20, the Communist Army crossed the Yangtze River in the north, separated into two armies and began a two-pronged advance toward Shanghai.

At the Range Road Clinic and Hospital, Gertrude carried the responsibilities of both Director of Nurses and Director of the Nursing School. Edith Johnson, who was the last American nurse with Gertrude, had already departed for Hong Kong. In addition, Gertrude was the Director of Clinical Services at the doctors' offices and the clinic which had been moved many city blocks away to a rented residence on Tsingkiang Road. As Dr. Miller had predicted, the six-story building on Range Road was now the Range Road Hospital and Gertrude was the last American nurse working there.

Draped by an OR cover gown which protected her operating room attire, Gertrude stood impatiently at the door of the administrator's office and knocked. Mentally Gertrude ran through her morning schedule. She'd teach another lesson in anesthesia for her senior nursing students, check on her junior students at the clinic offices, and prepare another nursing schedule for the month of May—all to be done before noon. In a far recess of her thoughts lurked the faint notion of graduation in September for her senior students. Absentmindedly, she banged on the door with her fist a second time.

When the door flew open Gertrude leaped back. She'd expected a voice to summon from inside the room, not someone to open the door.

"Gertrude," Allan Boynton said with a laugh, even before the door was completely opened. "Come on in." He stood in the open doorway, a tall angular man, stooped at the shoulders, a generous nose in a long face, and sparkling eyes to match his mirthful demeanor. "I guess you didn't hear me call out to you."

"How did you know it was me?" she asked, still taken aback, not moving toward the door.

"No one else bangs on my door like that," he said, "except you." Leaving the door ajar, he retreated into the room. "Come on in."

He crossed the room to lean his tall frame against the large wooden desk that occupied most of the small room, his long, thin fingers resting on the desk's edge on each side of him. "What can I do for you?" he asked.

"Well," she began, catching her breath and following him into the room, "you could begin by finding me some more staff. You could make me extremely happy by telling me that some of the Chinese nurses we have asked to come from the States are coming to help me—us."

"Boy, I wish I could." He shook his head, folding his arms across his chest. "We could use help in the clinic, in the laboratory, and on the floors. Believe me, Gertrude, I've tried. It's just, somehow, no one wants to volunteer to come work in a war zone."

Gertrude sank into the straight-backed padded chair near the door. It was the only chair in the room besides the short green leather rolling secretarial chair that sat behind the desk.

"In fact, it's almost impossible to convince the State Department to issue visas and traveling permits to China," he added. "But I do have some news."

She looked up, her mouth a straight noncommittal line, weariness and hope struggling to coexist on her face.

"You knew that Dr. Lonser and his family are returning to the States on May 18," he said.

"Leaving us with Dr. Herbert Liu and Dr. Andrew Chen—good men, good doctors. We can manage," she stated flatly. *Dr. Miller predicted we'd have only Chinese doctors in Communist China hospitals,* she reminded herself.

"And the residents," he added.

"Yes, the residents." She nodded without interest. "We could hardly function without them."

"What I just learned this morning . . . " Allan Boynton paused, reaching back on his desk for a telegram. ". . . is that Dr. Harry Miller will be flying in on May 9 to help staff the clinic and hospital during this . . . this difficult transition time."

"Harry Miller?" She was astounded. "But why? Marie has been sick recently. Is he going to leave her at home?" Gertrude sat straight up, her eyes bright green with amazement and unbelief.

"Dr. Miller is known to both Communists and Nationals alike," Allan Boynton said, still studying the communication he held in his hand. "The Division leaders, in counsel with the brethren at the General Conference, think he'll be able to negotiate with whomever takes possession of this country in the next few months—and help preserve our hospitals and our church work."

"Oh, they do, do they?" Gertrude shook her head vigorously as she spoke. "Do the brethren also realize that he is a 70-year-old man with a sick wife— who is likely to get stuck here with the rest of us for some time if the Communists take this city?"

"Since Dr. Miller was a former president of this division, I'm sure the brethren are quite aware of his age," Allan Boynton said firmly. "Besides," he added more gently, "it was his idea. He wanted to come."

On a cool May 9, strikingly attired in a flashy red jacket, Gertrude watched from the terminal door as Dr. Harry and Mrs. Marie Miller and one other passenger alighted from the Pan Am Clipper that had taxied to the airport terminal. Before the ground crew could even reach the plane, the pilot hauled up the stairs and closed the door, revved his still-running engines, and fled to the runway. Minutes later the plane was airborne.

Now there's a pilot who didn't want to stay in a war zone any longer than necessary," Gertrude noted wryly as she watched the ground crew scramble out, huffing mightily, to give the abandoned passengers a proper welcome.

Each carrying a single suitcase, the Millers approached the terminal entrance as Gertrude stepped through the door and onto the tarmac. When they were within earshot, Gertrude raised her arm in greeting and called out, "Welcome back to China, Dr. Miller."

Chapter 77

PREPARING TO BE BRAVE

The large dining room of the Kung Teh Lin restaurant was filled with a celebrating throng of Chinese church members and hospital workers. As she gazed out over the milling throng, Gertrude only half listened to the conversation of the women clustered around her. *By the looks of this celebration, you would never know that Shanghai is under siege,* she ruminated. Mentally she compared the sumptuously laid serving tables with the latest rumors of Communist troop movements north, south, and west toward the heart of Shanghai. *You would never know that we are about to be in the middle of an attack coming from three directions at once!*

It was the evening of May 10, a Thursday by the calendar, a holiday—if judged by the jubilant mood of the Chinese welcoming Dr. Harry and Mrs. Marie Miller's return to China. Gertrude glanced up at the dais at the far end of the room where the Millers were surrounded by admirers and devotees. *They really do love you, Dr. Miller. Almost worship you. And why not? You came to join them in their darkest hour.* She wrinkled her brow with a studious stare. *Can you really save them?* she wondered.

"He says he wants to take all the equipment back out to the San." Hazel Sevrens was speaking to the group of women, her voice raised just enough to be heard above the din. "He says he wants to reopen the San under the Communists."

"He wants to do what?" In her shock, Gertrude spoke loudly, forcefully, her attention snatched away from the scene of admiration at the far end of the dining hall.

"He wants to reopen the San out on Rubicon Road," Hazel repeated.

"He says he needs the large flow of patients to support the nursing school."

"Does he know how hard you all worked to bring that equipment safely across the front lines?" In her mind Gertrude could still see Elder Frost's red Chevrolet leading the caravan of cars and trucks driven by Dr. Lonser, Dr. Liu, and the others. What a parade they had made, arriving in front of the clinic multiple times that day, blocking traffic as she and her workers had helped unload the equipment.

Gertrude turned to Mildred Boynton, seeking someone who would understand what folly Dr. Miller had proposed. "It was just—what—10 days ago you moved everything over here? And through the Army's roadblocks no less." Gertrude could not believe that Dr. Miller wanted to risk the loss of all that they had saved. "Does he know that the Communists will soon be in control of that part of the city? Does he even know there's a war on?"

"Gertrude, it's not that bad out there at the San," Hazel insisted. "Really it isn't." She nodded her head and rolled her eyes, waving her hand dismissively. "I know, I know. When I got back last week, I had everything moved into town. But Dr. Miller wants to try. He thinks he can work with the Communists. That's why he came back, you know. He's treated many of their generals, and they know him."

"We live at the Medical Clinic on Tsingkiang Road, you know, the same place Dr. Miller is staying," Mildred added earnestly, convincingly. "All our Chinese workers out there are saying that the Communists are being very civilized to the towns they've captured to the west of Shanghai."

"I heard Elder Longway give a report at the Division headquarters last week," Olga Oss chimed in. "He said that Brother Coberly called from the East China Training Institute in Chiao Tuo Tseng to say that the Communists had already 'liberated' their school. He reported that there was no looting or destruction of buildings and no killing of civilians at all. In fact, he said that all their Chinese families and teachers and students were safe and well. It sounds like the Communist army is one of the most well-behaved armies on record." The other women in the group nodded vigorously in agreement.

"Well, they're not the Communists I know," Gertrude shot back, her green eyes glaring at the raised dais in the front of the room and its respected occupant. "You just wait until they change their mind and decide to destroy or sell off everything you have in order to finance their war—or to kill you all in your beds." She had turned her gaze on the group, her lecturing finger pointing at each of them in turn.

"He's not getting any of my equipment," she ranted, "and I'm not sending any of my nursing students out there to the San." She lowered her shaking finger, wondering in disbelief at the gullibility that had seized everyone. "I've worked too hard to get those kids graduated from nursing school and we will have our graduation at the end of September—war or no war."

The National Garrison Commander had amassed 250,000 Nationalist Army troops in Shanghai, vowing to defend it to the last. Extensive defensive breastworks, artillery positions, and garrisons of soldiers were established throughout the city and around its perimeter, even on the grounds of the Shanghai Sanitarium and Hospital on Rubicon Road. Everyone expected widespread destruction and loss of civilian life in the ensuing struggle.

On Sunday, May 22, the Communist army threw their attacking force against the city of Shanghai from the west and the south. At the Shanghai San, as well as in other parts of the city, the Nationalist Army ran away. The only destruction at the San was caused by the Nationalist Army shooting back at the buildings of the San after the Communists had occupied them.

On Monday, almost unnoticed, the Communists 'liberated' large sections of Shanghai to the west and to the south. By Tuesday, they were concentrating their efforts on the northeast section of Shanghai to which the Nationalists had retreated. This section contained the Range Road Clinic and further to the east, the Division Headquarters on Ningkuo Road.

The bell system at the Range Road Clinic "dinged" the code that signaled a telephone call for the director of nurses. Standing in front of the desk on the large men's ward on the fourth floor, Gertrude was supervising a major change of beds and personnel. She picked up the telephone and informed the operator where she was. Then holding the receiver against the side of her head, she pressed down on the handset cradle with the fingers of her left hand. Within seconds the phone rang.

"Hello. Gertrude Green," she said absently, her mind on her nurses and patients.

"Hello, this is Olga Oss," said the voice on the other end of the line. "Is that you, Gertrude?"

"Yes, Olga, it's me," Gertrude said. She closed her eyes momentarily in the solace of a friendly voice. The image of Olga's strong Germanic face, bright blue eyes, and golden hair was angelic in its comfort. "How's the Ningkuo Road crowd doing?"

"We're fine," Olga said. "We're far away from the fighting, but we're preparing just in case."

"Well, we're right here on the edge of it," Gertrude said, her eyes open again. Directly in front of her the nurses were pushing extra beds together. They were creating an isolation typhoid ward at one end of the hall to handle the sudden upsurge of typhoid fever in people who'd been drinking contaminated water. The other end of the men's floor held a ward full of injured refugees just recently admitted. They were mostly civilians, but included some soldiers who were too severely injured to be admitted across the street at the army hospital. "We're kind of busy here, Olga. What can I do for you?"

"Well, John and I—actually several people out here at headquarters—we were wondering if you shouldn't come stay out here with us—tonight, you know, well, until the worst of the fighting is over."

"Why would I do that?" Gertrude asked, mostly to herself. "My work is here, Olga."

"Yes, I know, Gertrude." Olga's German accent rolled the r's in Gertrude's name, making it sound like an engine starting up. "I know how intensely you feel the responsibility for your nurses there at Range Road. But you are the only foreigner there. The only one actually living there."

"And you think my presence here might make it more dangerous for the workers . . . when the Communists come in," Gertrude said.

"I'm just remembering what you told . . . ." The phone line crackled for a moment, covering up Olga's voice. ". . . the Communists that you knew about."

"I'm not afraid of them, you know," Gertrude intoned quickly.

"I know, Gertrude. 'A thousand shall fall at thy side,'" Olga repeated the scripture they had all heard Gertrude quote whenever she told the story of her escape from Yencheng. "I'm not suggesting that you're afraid. Just that it might be safer for the others."

Gertrude pushed back a stray wisp of hair, newly escaped from under her nursing cap. "So what are you thinking?" she asked after a moment's reflection.

"Elder Longway said he could send his car for you this evening—when the fighting usually begins in earnest," Olga suggested. "You could stay here a few nights with John and me—where it's safer—and go back to the clinic each morning. Just until the fighting stops."

"You mean tonight?"

"We already have your room prepared."

The thunder and volley of the artillery rumbled continuously. Gertrude sat on the floor of the dining area in Olga's house, her legs wrapped in a blanket and drawn up to her chest, her back huddled in the corner made by Olga's sideboard and the inside wall. With every explosion she flinched, a shudder that made her toes cold with the remembrance.

Lord, we've been here before, she prayed silently. *Increase my faith and make me strong.* She sat in silence, waiting for the next round. *I didn't run away this time, You know.*

"Gertrude, are you still awake?" Olga called from the other end of the heavy chest where she and her husband, similarly wrapped, sat in the dark.

"It's 2:00 o'clock in the morning, Olga," Gertrude grumbled, glancing at her nursing watch. "Of course I'm awake. What else would I be doing at this time of day?"

"I'm sorry, Gertrude," said a huskier German voice. "I truly thought it would be safer here."

"It's OK, John." Gertrude tried to sound repentant. "I know you meant well. It's probably just this noisy at the Clinic, if not worse."

"True. Most of the noise seems to be out to the north and west of here."

A loud concussion shook the ground, rattling the dishes in the dining room hutch. Gertrude wrapped her arms tighter around her bent knees and drew them closer to her body.

"Sorry. It was to the north just a few minutes ago," he apologized.

"Are you frightened, Olga?" Gertrude asked, her voice adopting a more professional, compassionate tone.

After a few seconds the quavering answer came back. "Yes. Are you?"

"Not so much," Gertrude responded honestly. "I've been through worse." In her mind's eye she saw a tall house on a hill with all the window panes missing, the light from the open basement doors spread across the snow in uneven squares.

"I won't be coming back tonight for a repeat performance," she said with a laugh. "I would just as soon be in my own bed as huddled here on the floor. It won't be any noisier, and it will certainly be more comfortable."

Now it was Wednesday evening. Standing beside her stove, looking out the south-facing window of her apartment on the top floor of the Range Road Clinic building, Gertrude slowly stirred the vegetable soup in the large mug she held in her hand. As the soup cooled she gazed south along Szechuan Road, across the creek to where the long shadows of the ponderously massive buildings on the Bund engulfed the houseboats on the waterfront, the pinks and yellows of the setting sun fading into twilight.

The Communist Army always attacks at night, Gertrude remembered, recalling the midnight vigils she had shared with General Li. She brushed the surface of the soup with the bowl of the spoon, crowding the chunks of vegetables to one side, and filled the spoon with the red, speckled broth.

Throughout the daylight hours of Wednesday, while directing the emergency preparations of the clinic, Gertrude had heard the occasional isolated rattle of machine guns and the echoes of small arms skirmishes emanating from the west.

Out near the Marine hospital we used to occupy on Bubbling Wells Road, she now guessed, peering past downtown Shanghai to the west and into the maze of roads and buildings that was fast disappearing into the shadows of night. She lifted the steaming spoon to her lips, carefully testing her meager supper.

From the broad boulevard of the Bund large army trucks had moved northward all day, crossing several of the Soochow Creek bridges into the Chapei District. They had flowed northward along North Honan Road toward the North Railroad Station and streamed eastward along the Wangpoo River toward the warehouse district along the river—and the Division Headquarters on Ningkuo Road.

Hazel Sevrens was really confused when she called today. Gertrude smiled at the thought, lifting the mug to her lips for a second test, drinking a small portion of the soup. *The Communist takeover on Tsingkiang Road was so quiet, she wasn't sure if they had been "liberated" or not.* She placed the serving spoon in the cast iron spoon trivet on the edge of the stove.

She considered the reports from Hazel as well as similar rumors that had filtered in from the Russian church to the south on Joffe Road and the people out on Yu Yuen Road, comparing them to her own experiences with the Communist Army. *Lord, it would be nice if it went the same here with us,* she prayed quietly. *But somehow I don't think it will.* She tipped up the mug, drinking carefully, peering over its edge into the settling darkness beyond the bridge—into the heart of Shanghai.

The Bund was quiet, the boulevard deserted, the houseboats empty.

It will be starting soon, she surmised, savoring the American canned soup and its seasonings with which she rewarded herself each night at supper time. She swallowed a large, warm gulp. Supper time was her private time and, frequently, her prayer time, a short respite from the pressures of the day. Tonight she needed it more than ever. She took another drink.

Lord, strengthen me, prepare me. You know I'm the foreigner they all look up to—even Dr. Liu. As Thelma said, I need to walk straight, or upright, if that's the right translation. She drank again from the mug, a last swallow.

Time to check on my own troops, she decided. Setting the empty mug in the sink, she paused for a quick look in the mirror beside the door. Adjusting her nursing cap, she headed for the stairs.

Chapter 78

FACING THE FIRE

Girls! Girls! Come out of there!" Gertrude shouted in Chinese as she yanked open the door to the X-ray developing room. In the darkened room, reeking of sharp chemical smells, she could make out a dozen nurses huddled around the developer tank in the far corner near the sink. "If a bomb shell lands in here, I will lose half of my nursing staff." Her spoken fears did not inspire anyone to budge.

Through the clinic windows down the hall just behind her, the sky lit up like daylight as a shell burst across the street near the Army Hospital. It shook the floor and puffed small clouds of dust from the joints between the ceiling tiles.

"But there are no windows in here," Lucy Hoh, a senior nursing student, whimpered in a hoarse whisper. She was half kneeling, clinging to the edge of the sink.

"Come on, get out of there," Gertrude shouted again. Entering the dark room, she pushed her way into the midst of the crowd and began shoving girls toward the door. *Stay in control, Gertrude,* she reminded herself, struggling to contain her anger. *You were frightened by bombs once yourself.*

"You're on the wrong side of the building," Gertrude lectured with an even tone, fluttering her hands and clapping them together as her frightened chicks rushed before her into the hallway. "The attacks are coming from the south. You need to get yourselves and the remaining patients into the rooms on the north side of the building."

For the moment the only noise coming from the outside was the sound of feet running and men shouting. To the west, the glow of fires against the night sky reflected orange off the walls of the clinic waiting room. It lit the large open space where the waiting room chairs had been removed earlier that day, space that Gertrude planned to use as an emergency triage area.

Using her flashlight, she examined the tired, frightened faces huddled before her in the narrow hallway. These were some of her junior and senior nursing students and members of the senior class from last year who were now graduate nurses, more valuable than her students for taking care of patients—but just as frightened now.

Two more explosions rattled the clinic windows to her right. Without looking at the source of the brightness which filled the room, she said, "Don't panic," and held out both arms as if to press them all against the opposite wall. "We'll be OK if we don't panic." *Or take a direct hit,* she thought.

"Where are the boys?" she asked, realizing that two senior male students were missing. Her eyes darted among the group as if somehow her tall senior boys were hiding, crouched down among the girls. "Where are Franklin and Nathan?"

"They're upstairs," Geneva Shih offered.

"Looking after patients?"

Geneva shifted her feet, wilting under Gertrude's steady gaze. "They said that Dr. Liu was up on the roof, watching the attack," she half whispered.

"Men!" Gertrude snorted. "They'll get themselves shot is what they'll do. All that the Communists can tell is that they're Chinese men. They won't know if they're nurses or soldiers." Her eyes widened with the sudden realization that the clinic was the tallest building in the area. "And the Communists will think the Nationalist Army is hiding in here and really start shelling the place."

"All right," Gertrude commanded, her eyes narrowing with concentration. "Girls, I want you to get back in your teams of two, just like I assigned you this morning." She pointed to the team members and directed them together with quick strokes of her hands. "Go to your assigned wards and make sure everyone has been moved to the north side of the building. Where you can, move them into private rooms and shut the doors."

"Girls," she said, pointing to the graduate nurses. "Go check on the student groups that were assigned to you. Make sure they're at their stations. Then barricade them and yourselves in the rooms as best you can. Then stay put so I can find you if I need to."

She turned from the group and made for the stairs. *And I will go get my men off the roof before they get us all killed.* Multiple disparaging remarks with which she might pummel them passed through her thoughts and were lost as her mind raced on to more immediate practical concerns—her patients.

Someone needs to check on the tuberculosis patient who was bleeding, she planned silently as she reached the second floor landing. *I wonder if anyone moved that patient with the broken back who is on the circle bed?* Mentally, she ran down the list of patients with special needs. She was so engrossed in her calculations that she did not hear the clattering footsteps on the stairs until the men were almost on top of her.

Tall Dr. Liu was in the lead. Senior nursing students Nathan and Franklin, tall as they were, were dwarfed by his height and large frame. The three men stumbled to a halt on the stairs above where she stood on the fourth floor landing. She gazed up at them with blazing green eyes, darting from one prey to another.

"They were shooting at us," Dr. Liu offered lamely, raising his arm to point above his head.

And saved me the trouble, she fulminated silently. "They thought you were soldiers," she lectured. "They thought you were attempting to shoot at them."

She watched the light of awareness flick to life in Dr. Liu's eyes.

"Oh, Miss Green," he said, lowering his head in shame.

"It is nothing, my brother," she quickly replied, attempting to save face for him. "You are safe and that is the important thing." *Men are fascinated with war. Will they ever learn?* she wondered, forcing herself to display no outward sign of her inward anger and horror.

"Dr. Liu, I am concerned about the tuberculosis patient on the men's ward." Gertrude feigned ineptitude. "I think he started bleeding again."

"I will check on him, Miss Green," Dr. Liu said, his eyes registering thanks for her offering of respect.

"Franklin, please accompany your uncle Dr. Liu and assist him in any way you can. Nathan, please come with me," she ordered.

Gertrude led Nathan Ma back down the stairway, leaving Dr. Liu and Franklin on the men's floor. "Nathan, I think I will need your help to move our circle bed patient to a stretcher. In our preparation for others, I think we forgot to move her."

As Gertrude emerged from the stairwell onto the women's floor, the south side windows lit up and a series of concussions resounded along the hallway. Gertrude flinched inwardly. *Lord, give me courage. I have faith that we can do this together.* Without turning, never slowing, she said, "I think they're getting closer, don't you?" She didn't look behind her to see what effect her words had on her younger companion. She continued praying and kept walking.

As they reached the door of the private room, cries and small arms fire echoed up the side of the building followed by two more large concussions at close range. The door quivered on its hinges, shaking itself loose from Gertrude's grasp as she attempted to open it.

"I thought so," Gertrude shouted as she shoved the door inward against the sounds of war that reverberated through the broken window. The empty stretcher sat next to a large chrome double circle mounted on wheels. Attached to the circle was a stretcher-like aluminum frame which allowed the circle to be rotated, thus turning the patient over without having to be moved from her bed. Lying on the stretcher, ashen-faced, the immobile patient peered over the white sheet that covered her to her chin.

"Let's get her moved," Gertrude called, directing Nathan Ma to the head of the bed. "Undo the screw at that end," she instructed, "and hold the frame steady." As she spoke she reached for the screw that held the stretcher frame to the circle at the foot end of the bed.

Through the gaping, jagged window pane to her right came the scream of an approaching projectile.

"Miss Green!" Nathan yelled.

Instantly, Gertrude squatted—a reflex, done without thought. A few inches above her head a mortar shell whistled in the window, flashed through the open door, and burst the window in the room on the opposite side of the building. It exploded in the street beyond them with a deafening roar and a shower of concrete pieces which rattled on the side of the building.

"We don't have time to be messing with the screws!" she shouted, standing up. "Let's just grab the sheet and pull her over onto the stretcher."

Quickly, each undid the corner tucks in the bottom sheet and swiftly pulled patient and sheet onto the stretcher.

"Let's take her to the other end of the building. They're not shooting at us down there," Gertrude exclaimed, leading the way through the door and tugging the foot of the stretcher behind her.

171 Wutsin Road
Shanghai, China
May 28, 1949

Dearest Mother:

Well, here is my first letter since the last one that I had mailed in Hong Kong. During the ten days since then the Battle of Shanghai has come and gone. I think I told you in that last letter that the battle was all around us, but on the outside of the city so that we did not fear too much. In fact, we used to stand by the hour on the top of the Clinic to watch the battle going on. We could see the big shells fly across from one direction to another and then big fires were started in different places. For days we would watch the battle from our front row seats.

On Tuesday afternoon, May 24, I decided to go out shopping to look for a kerosene stove in case the gas should be cut off due to the battle. I went at noon and walked from the Clinic a great distance up Nanking Road looking everywhere, but never did find a stove. The streets were so crowded with people it seemed like everyone in Shanghai was out. Soldiers were racing every which way in trucks. I finally decided to get back to the Clinic because I have had to take all the X-rays for the last six weeks and I needed to get back and catch up. I waited and waited for a bus to come along and I began to be a bit frightened. The crowds were disappearing and the other people waiting on the bus were getting upset. I finally got back to the Clinic about 2:45.

When I got back I was told that the war was creeping up to where I had been shopping. My, was I thankful to get back.

Each night the shells have been louder and getting closer all the time. We could hear fighting all night long so loud that it was almost impossible to sleep. The people at Mission Headquarters on Ningkuo Road thought that as I was the only foreigner at the Clinic, it might be better if I went out and stayed with them. But I wished I hadn't. It seemed like the firing was worse out there than at the Clinic, although it was bad at the Clinic, too. The next morning I went back to my own place.

I was terribly busy those days because so many people were wounded and came to the hospital for treatments and X-rays, both for our patients and the army hospital across the road. So I worked like everything.

The next night, Wednesday, we had terrible fighting right on the streets all around us here at the Clinic, because we are not far from the Soochow Creek where the Nationalists decided to make their last ditch stand. We could not sleep because we were afraid that shells would come at us any minute and machine gunning and everything.

The next day, Thursday, there was sporadic gunfire most all day long and hardly anyone was on the street. Then in the afternoon there was suddenly fighting right on the street in front of the Clinic. The Communists took the Army hospital across the street from us and for the rest of the afternoon fired sporadically at any passing trucks carrying Nationalist troops.

We were terribly busy the whole time because the shooting was so close. We had to move the patients from the rooms on the front of the building to safer places. I couldn't stop to be frightened, just worked and worked to get patients to a safe place. The Communists liberated our section of the city at 1:20 a.m. that night. After that everything quieted down quite a bit.

I have felt exhausted ever since. Now everything is quiet and people are out on the streets and everything is going on as if nothing ever happened. Stores are not opened yet but the streets are crowded. I have stayed in as I have nothing to go out for and it has been raining steady since then. Today is Sabbath and I had a good sleep this afternoon.

No one in all of our mission here in Shanghai received any injuries of any kind. The Sanitarium was banged up quite a bit. Several large shells hit it and it will have to be repaired. We got only one shell here at the Clinic and the Division had several.

This letter, I hope, gets through to you, but I don't know how it will. The Post Office always has some method though. I wanted you to know that we are all right and things are over and quiet now. You know that we are on the Lord's side and He always cares for His children. I thank God for His protection and for giving me courage to face the struggles we have had here. Keep writing.

Loads of love to my mother—lovingly,
Gertrude

Chapter 79

CONFRONTING THE IRRATIONAL

Through June and July the members of the international community of Shanghai continued to operate their businesses inside China as though nothing out of the ordinary had happened. However, because of the continuing conflict, no foreign boats docked in Shanghai, no air service came to the airport, and no mail service connected China with the outside world.

At the beginning of August, in response to warnings from the U.S. Consulate of dangerous and consequential instability in China, the General Conference of Seventh-day Adventists instructed all foreign personnel to begin evacuating from mainland China. Of course, without transportation and without a governmental procedure to process evacuees, it was impossible to comply with those instructions. In fact, only eight foreigners were left who represented the SDA Church in eastern China; specifically, in Shanghai: Elder Samuel Frost and Elder Ezra Longway overseeing the old Division Headquarters, Elder John and Olga Oss and Elder Clarence Miller representing the publishing and evangelistic work, Dr. Harry and Marie Miller, working as his secretary, representing the health work . . . and Gertrude.

Despite the dire warnings, at least in the beginning, the fledgling Communist government did not harass or hinder anyone's activities in Shanghai, including those of the city's hospitals. In fact, for Gertrude the work only increased.

Dr. Miller found a Chinese workman to repair the elevator at the Shanghai San. This lifted his spirits and he decided to pursue the restoration of the San as well as doing most of the surgeries and teaching of some of the nurses' classes. Therefore, Gertrude had to oversee the students at the Rubicon Road San, supervise students at the Medical Clinic on Tsingkiang Road, and teach

classes at the Range Road Clinic. In every case, the bus ride from one location to the next consumed more than an hour.

Because of staff shortages, Gertrude was taking all the X-rays and giving
anesthetics for surgery at the San and the Clinic. In her spare time she attended to the administrative duties of being Director of Nurses for all three
institutions as well as Director of the Nursing School. Consequently, as the
work hours grew longer Gertrude's patience grew shorter.

Gertrude did not knock. Hardly slowing in her stride, she pushed open
the door to the small second floor office shared by Drs. Liu and Chen, and
barged in.

"Where are the resident physicians?" she demanded. "I have patients who
need care and I can't find any of our ward physicians. Where are they?"

Dr. Herbert Liu, large and imposing, sitting behind his desk, looked up
with a start. His narrow eyes from under hooded eyelids registered surprise
and defensiveness. Dr. Andrew Chen, small, wiry, and spider like, half arose
from his seat as if he were about to dart behind it.

"Miss Green," Dr. Liu began, a Chinese smile slowly spreading across his
face, "it is considered impolite—in my culture and in yours—to barge in on
conversations without knocking."

Gertrude glared at him, ignoring the faintly hidden warning. "I have no
time for niceties, Dr. Liu," she barked. "I am trying to care for patients in
three facilities and to manage nurses in three different places. I have no time
to be polite."

"You do know what has been happening recently, I'm sure," Dr. Liu responded icily, the stiff smile never leaving his lips. "The Communist government
has begun to arrest any physician or nurse who cares for a patient who happens
not to get well. These medical people are being imprisoned for a situation that
is beyond their control. They are frightened, and they have fled."

"I know the Communists, Dr. Liu," Gertrude returned. Her gaze was unrelenting as she advanced by small steps into a room darkened and made
smaller by the absence of windows, a room already filled with men and desks,
and now completely overcrowded by her unwelcome presence. "I know their
unreasonableness and I expected something like this would happen."

"But Miss Green, we've been doing fairly well under the Communists,"

Dr. Chen interjected. "The famine we all feared has been averted. Inflation has been stabilized. People are allowed to go about their business unmolested. I'm sure we can work something out with these people."

"Give them time, Dr. Chen, and you will get to know them as I do." The fire in her flashing eyes drove him behind his chair as he'd considered earlier. "Every morning I hear them torturing the Nationalist soldiers across the street at the Army hospital. Their screams for mercy are so loud I am sickened and cannot eat my breakfast. Believe me, you have only begun to see what these Communists will do."

She stood her ground, her left hand tightly gripping the faceted glass doorknob. Alternatively, she scanned Dr. Liu's Chinese face of anger and Dr. Chen's Chinese face of fear. *This is always the Chinese reaction,* she adjudged contemptuously. *Always anger or fear. When are you people ever going to understand?*

"Your residents need to show the face of courage to the Communists. They should do their duty in caring for the patients—at any cost. Their fight is with disease and not with the Communists." Her voice was strident, her emotions rising precipitously like an ocean tidal wave. "This is their country. If they are going to be the doctors we now depend on to run our church hospitals, they had better start walking tall and showing some backbone."

The doctors were quiet, their facial expressions softening into—respect. Gertrude realized that they weren't looking at her, but at someone directly behind her.

She instantly recognized the quiet, firm voice that spoke behind her. "Sometimes people do not have enough courage to do their duty. Sometimes they feel that they must evacuate to a safer place."

Gertrude turned and saw emerging from the hallway's shadowy light the thinning, but still wavy gray hair and kind blue-gray eyes of Dr. Harry Miller. Although slightly taken aback, she was determined not to be dissuaded from her assault. Dismissing his remarks as a poor attempt to make excuses, and condescendingly impudent, she plunged ahead.

"Dr. Miller, I am a missionary nurse. I have tried my very best to share with others the power of the gospel. I have tried to tell them that the gospel can strengthen them and give them the courage to face whatever might come at them." She momentarily closed her eyes to more clearly marshal her thoughts and the face of General Li appeared. "I tried to share this with General Li, a Chinese general I met on my journey from Yencheng."

"I know General Li, Miss Green," Dr. Miller interrupted. "I have spoken with him about the 24-day ordeal you all experienced together. He was very impressed with the courage of all who traveled with him and told me the whole story of what happened."

"You cannot imagine how hard I prayed for General Li," she effused, rushing on, not looking into his eyes, barely hearing his last remarks. "I wanted to share with him what he did not understand, that the gospel is supposed to supply the courage to do what needs to be done." She drew a deep breath; her green eyes narrowed as she returned to the focus of her ire. "These residents. They are supposed to be Seventh-day Adventists. They are supposed to know this."

"You have prayed so fervently for others," he replied quietly. "Have you prayed for yourself?"

For the first time since he'd spoken, Gertrude looked fully into the face of Dr. Miller and saw sympathetic fatherly strength, understanding kindness . . . and something else. Gertrude shifted uneasily from foot to foot. *What is it? What did I miss?* she pondered, suddenly uncertain.

He spoke quietly and with tenderness, but with a sharpness in his voice that warned her to pay attention. "There are times when people simply do not have the knowledge or the courage to do what is required of them," he said. "Sometimes—whether in Wuhan facing the Japanese or in Suiping facing the Communists, or in a little village north of Minkiang facing bandits— sometimes the fear of injury or death, or even failure, is just too great. Then the Holy Spirit has to do for people what they cannot do themselves."

With every mention of a place name or description Gertrude shuddered with the realization that he was talking about her fears, her lack of courage, her lack of understanding. *Dr. Liu and Dr. Chen do not know. But he knows all about me. He's not telling them, but he's telling me that he knows.* Gertrude was struck dumb with the reality of her own inadequacies.

As the recognition of her weaknesses pressed down and smothered her, making it difficult to breath, shame and anger welled up from the pit of her stomach and overflowed. Snapping her eyelids rapidly to hold back tears, she turned on her heels, quickly brushed past the elderly Dr. Miller and fled, her nursing shoes stomping out a rhythm on the terrazzo floor.

Beginning the first of August, the Provisional Committee of North China, made up of mostly Chinese workers under the leadership of Elder Hsu Hwa, began directing the Seventh-day Adventist church work in mainland China. They communicated with and sought instructions from the Division offices and Elder Branson, the president of the Division in Hong Kong. But they were responsible for directing the work according to their best judgment.

FIRST COMMITTEE MEETING OF THE NORTH CHINA PROVISIONAL DIVISION OF THE GENERAL CONFERENCE OF SEVENTH-DAY ADVENTISTS

August 8, 1949

49/1 <u>RETAINING FOREIGN MISSIONARY WORKERS</u>

WHEREAS, the General Conference has wired the foreign missionaries in China to plan to evacuate at the earliest possible date and whereas we feel that the work in this field still needs their help at this time, it was

VOTED, That the following telegram be sent to Elder McElhany of the General Conference asking permission for those who wish to volunteer be allowed to remain at their posts.

COPY OF TELEGRAM:

"FOREIGN MISSIONARIES PREPARING EVACUATION AC-CORDING GENERAL CONFERENCE DIVISION INSTRUCTIONS STOP DUE IMPROVED CONDITIONS NO OTHER DENOMINA-TION PLANNING COMPLETE WITHDRAWAL STOP WE BELIEVE IF FEW MISSIONARIES REMAIN WILL BE GREAT STABILIZING INFLUENCE ON WORKERS CONSTITUENCY AND HELP SAFE-GUARD PROPERTY AND FUTURE DEVELOPMENT DENOMINA-TIONAL WORK STOP PROVISIONAL COMMITTEE EARNESTLY REQUESTS RECONSIDER AND PERMIT VOLUNTEERS REMAIN REPLY URGENT STOP COPY SENT HONG KONG WASHINGTON HSU HWA"

49/2 <u>CALL FOR HO PAO CHUNG AND YEN SHU PING</u>

VOTED, That we send a telegram to the China Division asking that Ho

Pao Chung and Yen Shu Ping return to China by the *SS General Gordon* to connect with our work in this field.

Meeting adjourned with prayer by Li Su Liang

Hsu Hwa, Chairman
H. H. Tan, Secretary

Chapter 80

FAILING AS A NURSE

It was 4:30 on a hot afternoon during the second week of August. The stench of human bodies on the sweaty bus ride from the Shanghai San had been insufferable. The walk from the bus stop to the Range Road Clinic had been almost entirely in full sun. As she opened the front door of the tall brick clinic building Gertrude desperately wanted to get in out of the heat.

"Miss Green! Oh, Miss Green!" It was Marrion Fan and Irene Ma, coming directly for her across the lobby. "Come quickly. Please, come quickly!"

"Whatever is the matter, girls?" Forgetting the sweltering atmosphere, Gertrude hurried toward her two best senior nursing students. In their panic to communicate, they were speaking English, something they almost never did.

"It's a patient on the women's floor," Irene said rapidly, switching to Mandarin in midsentence.

"She received a transfusion of blood this morning and has been convulsing ever since," Marrion cut in.

"Where's the head nurse?" Gertrude questioned as they headed for the stairs.

"She's with the patient, but she's afraid to touch her," Irene said. She was puffing hard, trying to keep up with Gertrude who was taking the ascending steps two at a time. Marrion bounced up the stairs behind them.

Gertrude burst through the stairwell doorway onto the women's floor, startling the head nurse and the junior student nurse who were working at the central nursing desk. "Where is she?" Gertrude called out. Her arms streamed out on each side, flailing the air, as she charged the desk like an irate mother duck, her two young duckling protégés following close behind.

The head nurse momentarily eyed the oncoming attack and stepped behind the desk. The junior nursing student was frozen in space and time, unable to dodge the onslaught, unable to remember social courtesies such as like rising from her chair to offer it to the Director of Nurses.

"Miss Cho, where is she?" Gertrude repeated. She leaning forward, the knuckles of both hands placed firmly on the front edge of the desk, hovering above the desk like an owl about to strike.

"At the end of the side hall—down there." Miss Cho, the head nurse, pointed down the hall. She had backed away from the desk until her backside seemed to be firmly attached to the wall under the clock.

Gertrude abruptly abandoned the desk and started for the hallway. She looked to her right, then over her shoulder for the reluctant head nurse. She halted in mid-stride. Her two faithful students narrowly avoided colliding with her. "Come, Miss Cho," she urged, beckoning to the head nurse with a downturned hand in the polite Oriental fashion. "Come, I need you to help me think."

The head nurse sprang away from the wall, rapidly shuffling forward to catch up.

"How long has she been convulsing?" Gertrude asked, moving forward again, not looking at her colleague.

"Since about 10:30 this morning," Miss Cho replied, shuffling her feet mightily to keep up with Gertrude's long strides.

For the second time Gertrude stopped abruptly, the nursing students ready for her this time. "Has no one done anything for her?" she snapped in exasperation. "Where's Dr. Chen?" Her eyes, locked on to the frightened face before her, were pinpoints of light.

"There's a man in the patient's room," the nurse answered in a half whisper. "We think he's her brother."

"But Dr. Chen?"

"He was here several times before noon, but he has not returned since her brother came." Miss Cho's hands came up in supplication, her interlocking fingers raised to her chin. "The doctors are afraid. They have all run away. Oh, please, Miss Green, please do something!"

Gertrude looked away, staring out the window at the end of the hall. *Dear God. Give me strength. Patients are dying and my help is running away in fear. Do I have to do everything myself?* Shaking her head, Gertrude started forward again, resolutely turning the corner into the side hallway.

"Miss Green. What about her brother?" Miss Cho implored.

"He will have to look after himself, Miss Cho," Gertrude replied in all seriousness. "I don't have time to care for the patient and the family at the same time. Come on."

The roller blind at the window was pulled down and the room was deeply shadowed as they entered. Gertrude sensed more than saw the bed shaking with the patient's persistent convulsions. The room reeked of body odor, sweaty sheets, and urine. She hurried forward, placing her hand on the trembling forehead. The woman's skin was burning up.

"What's her temperature?" Miss Green asked, her mind dominated by numerous clinical considerations.

"We don't know."

"Marrion, get me the thermometer over there," Gertrude commanded, nodding with her head toward the bedside stand.

Marrion Fan hurried to the opposite side of the bed. Retrieving the bedside thermometer from its small, upright alcohol bottle, she shook it down and handed it to Gertrude.

"We can't put it in her mouth," Gertrude voiced her thoughts aloud. "She might bite it in two. Let's put it under her arm."

With effort Gertrude raised the patient's quivering arm, stiff with convulsions, and placed the thermometer in her armpit. Gertrude held it there for the requisite two minutes, then removed it. She walked to the doorway to read it in the hall light.

"Oh, boy," she whispered with a whistle, "It's off the scale! Must be 109 degrees." Striding back to the bed, she asked, "Are we sure it was the blood transfusion that did this?"

"We don't know," Miss Cho responded. "She was admitted because of anemia and she didn't have a fever when she came in."

"Well, she does now—and a whopper." Gertrude stood gazing down at the quivering sheets in the bed, her eyes blinking rapidly. *What's to be done now? Where do we start? How do we find out what's happening?* She paused. *First things first.*

She looked up. "OK, girls. First things first. A patient with convulsions for seven hours and a fever of 109 degrees. What do we do first?"

"We need to cool her down," Irene answered confidently.

"You bet. And right now." Gertrude flashed a grin of approval. "But what about the convulsions?"

Irene and Marrion stared at the tremulous patient and said nothing.

"Phenobarb, girls. Phenobarbital for convulsions." Gertrude turned to the head nurse who was standing behind her. "Miss Cho, listen carefully. If we are to save this patient, we must act quickly." Gertrude began ticking off items on her fingers. "I need all the ice the kitchen can get me, and bring me basins, too, small ones and large ones. And I need two capsules of phenobarb." She gazed at the ceiling, thinking. "We can't get them into her mouth . . . so bring me a rectal tube and a syringe . . . and a needle. We'll punch holes in the capsules and place them rectally with a small amount of ice water." She looked again at the head nurse. "Send me two more helpers in here . . . and hurry, Miss Cho. There isn't much time."

By the time the ice arrived from the kitchen, Gertrude, with the help of the students, had cleaned up the patient and remade the bed with the patient in it. They had placed the phenobarbital rectally and irrigated the patient's colon with water to help dissolve the medicine and begin its absorption. Now placing the pans and basins under the woman's arms, in her groin, between her legs, and down the sides of her body Gertrude instructed the girls to fill them with ice.

"Now we watch and wait," she said quietly. "And pray."

Within half an hour the ice had turned to slush in the pans, wetting the bedding as the convulsions slopped the water over the sides. Gertrude sent the two helpers to the kitchen for more ice. Under her directions, the nursing students soaked towels in the ice water and placed them on the patient's chest, abdomen, and limbs. "But don't wrap the head," she instructed. "We want to cool the brain, not freeze it." . . . *if she still has a brain,* she finished the thought to herself.

At 6:00 p.m. the patient's temperature had not budged and the convulsions had not relented. In another hour the new ice had melted and more was retrieved from the kitchen.

Dear God, Gertrude prayed, *You know that if we don't get this fever down and the convulsions stopped, this patient's brain is going to turn to soup, cooked right inside her skull.*

"Girls, let's send some blood to the laboratory for a CBC slide and wet mount for parasites. See if they can tell us anything about what is the cause of all this." Gertrude was thinking hard, trying to cover all the bases.

"And let's get a rubber sheet and put it under her," she continued, still thinking aloud. "We're going to have another soaking mess in this bed, if this keeps up."

It took the four helpers and Gertrude 15 minutes to remove all the pans, roll the convulsing patient off her wet sheets and onto the rubber sheet, and replace all the pans and basins. "Let's dump out the water and fill them up again," Gertrude instructed.

By 7:30 the patient's temperature was down to 104 degrees but she was still convulsing. Every half hour they resoaked the towels and placed them again on the woman's trunk. Every hour they got more ice from the kitchen, dumped the water, and filled the basins again. In between those times and duties, Gertrude wiped the sweat from the woman's face—and prayed.

Gertrude sent the girls off to eat supper, but she never left the bedside. *God, help me figure this out,* she implored silently. *Help me understand. Why is she still convulsing? What more can I do?*

When Marrion and Irene, returning from supper, entered the room Gertrude was bent over the patient, mopping her brow, her back to the door. "Leave the light off, girls. It's cooler in here in the dark," she instructed without looking up, anticipating what they were about to do. Irene lowered her hand which had been half raised toward the button switch on the wall. The girls glanced at each other, wondering at Gertrude's ability to read their minds.

"Where is Dr. Miller?" she asked, glancing up at them.

"He's in emergency surgery out at the San," Irene answered, hurrying around the bed to feel the towels to see if they were drying out. "He won't be coming here tonight."

"Dr. Liu is out there with him," Marrion added from the foot of the bed, avoiding direct eye contact with her mentor.

She's afraid that I'll be upset, Gertrude surmised. She drew a deep breath. "Well, we'll just have to do the best we can by ourselves." She glanced at Marrion to offer a smile of encouragement and saw her furtively peeking at the far corner of the room.

For the first time since entering the patient's room, Gertrude peered into the shadowed corner. Sitting in a metal-tubed chair was a man—at least it looked like a man—although it was hard to tell in the darkness. His arms were folded across his chest, his legs were tucked up under him tailor-fashion in the seat of the chair.

I don't know if you're her brother, she thought, gazing at the apparition. *Whoever you are . . . I hope you are praying as hard as I am.*

"Girls, you have other duties and I've kept you from them long enough," Gertrude said. "You go along and I'll ring for you if I need you."

By 9:00 o'clock the patient's axillary temperature was down to 102 degrees but the convulsions still continued. The laboratory provided no help. Her red cell count was low, but the white cell count was only a little elevated. No parasites had been found. Gertrude rang the bell. "It's time for more ice," she said when two heads appeared in the doorway.

When the hourly chores of ice changes and towel placements were completed and the nursing students had gone, Gertrude stood at the foot of the bed staring at the quavering mummy lying there. Her face was blotched red and white; her lips were blue-gray.

Dear Jesus, what do I do now? Do I add more phenobarb? I don't want to stop her breathing. I'm not sure I'm making any headway. I thought for sure she would stop convulsing when the fever came down. She rubbed her tired eyes. *Lord, I've done all I know how to do—and I'm afraid it's not enough. She's not ever going to wake up and I can't do anything about it.*

For two more hours Gertrude mopped the floor, exchanged the ice, wiped the patient's face, and checked the patient's temperature. Only once did she glance into the corner at the silent enigma crouched in the chair, and then only to be irritated at his presence. She never stopped praying.

The nursing students had gone to bed. The night shift had come on at 11:00 p.m.

"Miss Green, can I get you anything?"

Startled, Gertrude snapped her head around and saw a small Chinese silhouette backlit by the light in the hallway.

"No," she answered quickly, returning to the patient. She paused, her hands, towel-encumbered, hovering near the woman's face. Slowly she turned to face the nurse at the door. "No, thank you," she said with a slight bow. "Her temperature is down to 100 degrees. I'll stop the ice now." She turned back and looked at the patient. "But she's still convulsing," she mumbled, even more softly.

As midnight approached, Gertrude, having less physical work to do, prayed without ceasing. *Jesus, I need You,* she begged desperately, her hands clutching the cold iron bedstead, her eyes closed as much in weariness as in prayer. Two trails of tears slowly coursed over her cheeks and down to her chin. *I need for You to take care of my patient. I can't do anything more. You'll have to do this. I can't. I want to, but I don't know how.*

The bed stopped shaking.

Gertrude's eyes flew open and an audible gasp escaped her lips. For just a few seconds, the patient didn't move at all. The noise of the iron bedstead shaking had made a continuous unnoticed rattle of metal on metal. Now everything was still.

Then the bed began to shake again.

Gertrude slipped to her knees on the wet floor, clutching the foot of the bed, and for a full five minutes prayed her prayer over and over like a mantra, like a magical incantation, trying to get the bed to stop shaking once more. But the patient continued to convulse.

Slowly Gertrude got to her feet. Slowly she walked to the head of the bed and picked up the towel lying on the pillow near the patient's face. As she wiped her face once more, she prayed. *God, I don't know what to do. How do I get You to work for me? What do I say? How do I get You to answer me?* She let out a slow breath of resignation and wiped away her own tears. *I will do what I can . . . until I can't do it anymore. Don't give up on me.*

The bed stopped shaking again. The patient lay quietly while Gertrude wiped her mouth and eyes. For five minutes, all was quiet. Then the convulsions started again.

For the next hour and a half, Gertrude alternately knelt by the bed in prayer and tended the woman's bodily needs as the minutes between convulsions gradually lengthened. At 2:30 a.m. the convulsions stopped completely.

Employing 20 years of nursing skill, Gertrude cared for her patient in the blessed silence. Once again she changed the bed linen. She medicated the woman's parched lips and rubbed body lotion on her hands, elbows, and feet that had chafed against the bedding during the convulsions.

All during her ministrations, she prayed.

O Jesus, take care of my patient. After all that fever and all those convulsions, I don't know what's left of her brain. She hasn't responded at all, not one flutter of purposeful movement. Please, has it all been for nothing? Give me just one sign.

Gertrude stood at the foot of the bed, gazing down on the peaceful face lying on a clean pillowcase. The chest rose and fell in deep sleep, the cheeks were mostly clear of the blotchiness, the lips faintly red. *Jesus, please talk to me. I need You.* A faint breeze stirred, rattling the roller blind in the window casing.

Gertrude shook her head, turned, and walked from the room.

The sound of her nursing shoes echoing on the terrazzo floor alerted the personnel at the nursing desk of her approach.

"She's quiet now," Gertrude murmured softly, as all nurses do at night. She had reached the desk and now fixed both nurses with a steady gaze. "Call me if anything changes, if anything happens." She made sure she had their full attention. "Immediately. Anything at all." She lowered her eyes. "I'm going up to my apartment and get some sleep." She turned and headed for the stairwell.

Chapter 81

LISTENING FOR THE VOICE

A t 8:00 a.m. when Gertrude opened the stairwell door to the women's floor she had quickly pulled it partly shut again to avoid colliding with two freshmen nursing students as they whisked by, breakfast trays in their hands.

"Good morning, Miss Green," they called out in unison.

"Good morning, girls," she answered absently as she scanned the corridor for Miss Cho, the head nurse.

"Miss Cho," she called on seeing her emerge from a private patient room. Gertrude hurried toward her. "Miss Cho, I left orders to call me if anything happened to the patient at the end of the hall."

"Yes, Miss Green," Miss Cho responded, bowing respectfully—deeper than Gertrude thought necessary. "The night nurses told us in report this morning."

"But I didn't get called."

"No, Miss Green."

Anxiously Gertrude waited for a further explanation. Miss Cho stood respectfully, looking at her, but saying nothing. Gertrude opened her mouth to remonstrate with the head nurse when she remembered, *The Chinese do not answer questions that they have not been asked. It is highly impolite to presume to speak to superiors about topics before they bring them up.* Gertrude closed her mouth and took a deep breath. *Calm down, ol' girl.*

"Miss Cho, what has happened to the patient since last night?" she asked politely.

"She is being discharged, Miss Green," Miss Cho said with another bow.

"What!" Gertrude was unable to control herself.

"Dr. Chen has made rounds already this morning, and has discharged her." Miss Cho was not smiling. "She awoke this morning and wanted something to eat," she added, her face a study in seriousness and respect, "so we fed her."

"Good morning, Miss Green." It was Irene who had come running down the hall when she saw her instructor. "Did you hear about our patient?" Irene was dancing up and down in her excitement, treating Gertrude like a Chinese girlfriend and not like a respected instructor. "Come see," Irene said, extending her hand.

Hand in hand, the instructor and the student turned into the side corridor and hurried down to the end of the hall. Barely containing herself, Irene stepped back respectfully and allowed Gertrude to enter the patient room first.

With roller blind up, the morning sun streamed in through the window, brightly lighting the room. In the center of the room Gertrude found an empty, well-made bed. In the far corner, perched on the metal-tubed chair from the night before was her patient, bright eyed, rested, her hair brushed—and ready to go home.

"Good morning, Miss Gho," Gertrude said in her best professional voice.

"Good morning," the patient replied. "You are Miss Green, yes?"

"I am, my sister" Gertrude responded with a polite bow.

"I understand that I owe you my life," Miss Gho said, not rising, not addressing Gertrude with any terms of familiarity or politeness.

"It was the Lord God of heaven who saved your life," Gertrude responded. "Your sister was only a tool in His hands." When the patient stared back at her with vacuous eyes and no response, Gertrude went on. "Do you remember anything about the events of yesterday?"

"No, not at all," Miss Gho answered, coming to life again. "I awoke this morning and felt rested and hungry. That's all I know."

"I am glad we were able to care for you." Gertrude studied the inscrutable Chinese face before her and weighed her options. "May I pray with you before you go?"

"Do you always do that?" Miss Gho's eyes were narrow and suspicious.

"Yes. Always," Gertrude answered honestly.

"Very well."

Walking up the corridor beside Irene, Gertrude was lost in her own thoughts. *Lord, what happened in that room? Nothing I did seemed to work; nothing I did made her better. But here she is—well, and ready to go home. I don't understand. You worked the miracle but You didn't speak to me. So many pieces out of place.* She turned to Irene. "Those were unusual clothes she was wearing. Not expensive, but not the sort you see on the street every day. More like a uniform."

"Those are the clothes, the uniform, of the Communist Party members," Irene explained, laughing. "They are supposed to look ordinary— but they all look alike."

"Communists? And her brother?" Gertrude stopped and half-turned toward the room that they had just left. "Where is her brother? How is she going to get home?" She looked at Irene, puzzled.

"Her brother left early this morning. Just after Dr. Chen discharged her," Irene said simply. "He said he would send a car to pick her up later today."

"A car? Her brother has a car?"

"He is one of the high officials of the new Communist government in Shanghai."

Allan Boynton, manager of the Range Road Clinic, sat squeezed in behind his desk in his small office on the second floor. He exchanged occasional anxious glances with Dr. Miller who sat across the desk from him, slouched in a straight-backed common chair crowded against the wall. Dr. Miller's shoulders drooped under the weight of his 70 years, his long, crossed legs uncharacteristically sticking straight out into the area occupied by Gertrude at the opposite corner of the desk, her back against the door.

Sitting on a metal stool borrowed from a nearby operating room, Gertrude held two cheap, yellow papers in her hand. Adjusting her glasses, she read the large letters of the top telegram message.

BRANSON ADVENTIST HONGKONG

PERSONAL CONVICTION LORD LED COMMITTEE CALL US SHANGHAI STOP DEVOTED TO CHINA PATIENTS UNUSU-

ALLY INTERESTED MESSAGE APPRECIATIVE MEDICAL SERV-
ICE STOP HOWEVER CAN SEE HANDWRITING WIDESPREAD
EVACUATION PLANNED STOP LIMITATIONS INCREASING
CHINESE LEADERSHIP IMPERATIVE STOP CONFIDENCE IN
COMMITTEE ADVICE STOP PLANNING GORDON STOP DUE
CRITICAL SITUATION SUGGEST SMALL MEDICAL BEGIN-
NING HONGKONG MILLER.

Without looking up, she shuffled the bottom yellow page to the top and continued reading.

DR. MILLER 30 TSINGKIANG ROAD SHANGHAI

COMMITTEE APPROVES YOUR EVACUATION HONGKONG
HOPE SMALL MEDICAL UNIT HERE COMMITTEE HAS SENT
FOLLOWING MESSAGE LONGWAY OSS QUOTE STILL CON-
VINCED FULL EVACUATION WISE SINCE PRESENCE FOREIGN-
ERS MAY SERIOUSLY COMPLICATE WORK NATIONAL LEADERS
STOP WE HAVE HOWEVER REQUESTED GENERAL CONFER-
ENCE DECIDE MATTER AND CONCUR ANY DECISION THEY
MAY MAKE STOP SHOULD THEY AUTHORIZE VOLUNTEERS RE-
MAIN EVERYONE SHOULD HAVE UTMOST FREEDOM FOLLOW
PERSONAL CONVICTIONS REGARDING GENERAL CONFER-
ENCE EVACUATION INSTRUCTIONS PLEASE HAND COPIES ALL
MISSIONARIES UNQUOTE BRANSON

Gertrude squirmed on the hard, cold metal seat, seeking a more comfortable spot as the contents of the telegraph messages slowly sank in.

"There was a previous telegram?" Staring at the papers in her hand, she
spoke it as a question but understood the answer already.

"There was," Mr. Boynton said. "Elder Longway and Elder Oss want
to stay. They are concerned about the publishing house and the literature
evangelists."

"You know Ezra Longway—the beacon of eternal hope, the eternal op-
timist," Dr. Miller chimed in with a grin.

"I would have thought that was your title," Gertrude responded. Slowly
she removed her glasses, peering up at Dr. Miller from under disquieted
eyebrows before returning her gaze to the telegrams now lying in her lap.

"Yes . . . well . . ." It was Dr. Miller's turn to squirm. He hoisted himself up in his chair, withdrawing his feet from in front of the desk and out of Gertrude's space.

Allan Boynton drew his long, thin fingers down the side of his lean, narrow face. "I think we need to lay out a plan for our evacuation," he said, thinking out loud. "The *SS General Gordon* is due in here at the end of September. Considering the long processing lines . . ."

"I have six senior students who graduate at the end of September," Gertrude interrupted. "I'm not going anywhere until I see them graduate."

"Miss Green, considering the situation, I think it unwise to do anything other than prepare to . . . ," Dr. Miller counseled, leaning forward, his elbows on his knees.

"I don't know how you know these things. Really, I don't." Gertrude stood up, cutting him off. "In February you were sure that we were all going to be replaced by Chinese. Yet when you arrived in May you were ready to repair the San and move our whole operation back out there. Now you're sure we should pack up and go home."

"Believe me, Miss Green, that is not my choice." Harry Miller looked up at her earnestly, pleading for understanding.

"Oh, it isn't?" Gertrude retorted, waving the yellow telegrams in the air as evidence to the contrary.

"No, Gertrude, it isn't," Allan Boynton interjected forcefully.

Gertrude turned on him, fists clenched, ready to confront two foes if need be, ready to defend her courage and her faith in God that she would be allowed—for once—to finish what she had started.

"We have been asked to leave," Allan Boynton continued, "by the Communists."

"Asked to leave?" Gertrude repeated the words, twisting her head to the side, trying to see the words he had said from a new perspective.

"Dr. Miller had an important patient visit him in the clinic three days ago, a man from the Communist high committee. He requested that Dr. Miller and all our remaining foreigners leave China immediately."

"The Communists don't request anything from anyone." Gertrude shook her head in rapid staccato, rejecting the idea altogether.

"They do if they know you personally. They are still Chinese, after all," Dr. Miller explained quietly. "He is one of my patients. Actually, he has been a patient since he was in the Nationalist government years ago. Now he is one of the head people in the Communist high committee." Dr. Miller looked into his hands helplessly. "The committee sent him with the request and I have to honor it." He looked up at Gertrude again. "They are being polite, at least, for now."

Slowly Gertrude sat down, remembering the sudden shift of attitude by the Communists of her experience. "Yes. I suppose they are."

"I'm sorry for your disappointment," Dr. Miller consoled. "It's not my choice to leave either . . . but I think it is the Lord's choice. He seems to have made that plain enough."

"I wish He would send me a message that plainly," Gertrude returned, her vexation appearing again.

"Hasn't He already?" Dr. Miller asked.

"Not yet," Gertrude snapped, "not with my name on it, anyway." She looked away in embarrassment, unable to control her frustration.

"Maybe this is it," Dr. Miller suggested.

Purposefully, Gertrude stood up, firmly placing the telegrams on the corner of the desk. "Well, I have students whom I will see graduate before I leave."

"Considering the long lines in the emigration offices, I suspect you will get your wish," Mr. Boynton said, leaning back in his chair.

As usual Gertrude led the pack, marching up Nanking Road toward the Chocolate Shoppe. Olga Oss's yellow braids, not curled up in their usual bun, bounced rhythmically on her shoulders as she matched Gertrude stride for stride. Marie Miller straggled along behind, occasionally having to trot a few steps in order to catch up with them.

"Gertrude. Please," she finally called out. "I can't keep up."

Gertrude looked over her shoulder and saw Marie Miller had slowed to a walk, her head down, breathing heavily.

"Oh, Marie," she cried, running back to her. "I'm sorry. I'm such a glutton," she apologized, linking arms with the older woman, gently propelling her forward. "Whenever there's a meal, I'm always the first one to the table or know the reason why."

Olga paused where she was while the other two caught up to her.

"How are you doing?" Olga asked, swinging in on Marie's other side, peering closely at her face for signs of illness.

"Oh, I'm OK." Marie smiled weakly. "I'm just so tired of standing in that line."

"It didn't take them long to get their bureaucracy in order, did it?" Gertrude sniped, screwing up her mouth in disgust. "Paperwork and long lines." She began walking faster in order to let Olga see her face and get her reaction, gradually pulling ahead of the other two.

"Actually, they're not very good at it," Olga responded with a grimace of her own and a sarcastic laugh. "They have farmers who can barely write their names telling us what to do."

"Yes, they should come take lessons from our church. We're much better at bureaucracy than they are," Marie said with a smirk. The spontaneous, uproarious laughter broke the group apart and halted it momentarily. When they recovered, they formed up again with Marie in the middle, allowing her to set a more reasonable pace.

"But they have their own special brand," Gertrude noted. "They make everyone stand in line. Makes no difference who you are. You stand in line like everyone else."

"Yes. Did you see the German attaché standing in line just ahead of us?" Olga asked.

"That's the idea of Communism—I think," Marie said, wrinkling her brow, unsure of her own analysis.

"You bet. Everyone suffering together at the lowest possible level." Gertrude shook her head in amazement at the ludicrous idea before pointing ahead, the first to spot the sign. "And there's the Chocolate Shoppe," she called out happily.

When everyone was seated and had ordered, Gertrude leaned back in her chair, inhaled deeply the wonderful scents wafting in from the kitchen, and spread her arms wide. "I always say—if you have to stand in line all morning and can't get into the office you need by noon, go to the Chocolate Shoppe!"

"So long as you can get back by 1:30," Olga sang out in a like comical manner.

Marie Miller sat playing with her napkin, seeming not to notice them.

"Marie, how are you feeling?" Gertrude's professional antennae picked up on Marie's quietness.

"I'm doing fine . . . now," she reassured them with a small smile of embarrassment, patting each of them on the hand.

"But you weren't feeling fine . . . before you came over here . . . to China, I mean." Gertrude sensed more than a tiredness of standing in lines.

"No, I wasn't," Marie admitted, looking down at her hands which she folded together on the table in front of her. "But I got well . . . quite suddenly, actually. One could say . . . miraculously." This time when she looked up, her smile was warm and enthusiastic.

Gertrude examined the face before her, pale and pinched, the hair frizzy and losing its natural wave, the neck old and wrinkled with the weight loss of illness. It was there . . . in the eyes, she decided.

"Does God talk to you?" Gertrude asked simply.

"You mean like in nature or in the Bible?" Olga piped up.

"I mean, does He talk to you?" Gertrude's gaze never left Marie's face. "How do you know it is for you? Does He say your name?"

Marie steadily returned her gaze. "For each one of us, I think He has a special way of communicating, a way that we will not mistake for someone else. For me, it was getting well." Looking away for a moment, Marie drew a deep breath and continued, "Harry knew that the Lord wanted him to return to China . . . but Harry didn't want to leave me behind." She looked back at Gertrude who continued to stare at her. "I was the one who was convinced when I got well." She lifted her hands from the table as if offering a gift, shifting her gaze from Olga to Gertrude and back again. "The circumstances—my illness and my sudden recovery—they just said to me, 'Trust in the Lord. He is watching over you.'"

She looked directly into Gertrude's eyes. "Haven't you ever been in circumstances that told you that the Lord was watching over you, that He was in control?"

"I'm afraid to let . . ." Gertrude shook her head and looked away. After a few seconds, she cocked her head sideways and tried again. "I don't trust myself to know what the circumstances mean, Marie. Circumstances always involve others." Gertrude placed both hands on the table, palms up. "Nothing has my name on it, so to speak. You know what I mean?"

Marie Miller gathered Gertrude's left hand in both of hers. "I will pray that the Lord will call your name, Gertrude," she said softly as Olga grasped Gertrude's other hand.

Gertrude nodded. *Dear God, hear the prayers of this good woman . . . if You don't hear mine.* "I just pray that I can see my students graduate," she whispered.

"We'll pray for that, too," Marie said, patting Gertrude's hand.

Gertrude had spent the morning waiting in lines and visiting offices on the main floor of what had been the Nationalist Government Building. At the last office they had directed her to the second floor to validate her passport. At least, that's what they said should happen.

Half of these people haven't a clue what they're doing, she groused to herself as she grasped the hand-carved banister, her footsteps ringing out on the marble stairs. *I had to help the last person find the papers he wanted to check. It's a good thing I can read Mandarin Chinese.* She moved to the right side of the broad staircase as five people came clattering down past her, gesticulating with their hands and vehemently discussing some apparently unjust cause in Spanish or in Italian, she wasn't sure which. She paused on the staircase and watched them as they descended. *I'm not the only one who's less than satisfied with how things are going,* she concluded. Having justified her irritation, she marched on up the stairs to her next appointment.

On the other side of the counter, the man examining passports was more than efficient. He wasted no motions, flipped quickly through her documents, had his die cut stamps all in a row, and used them with precision. Gertrude was impressed.

The man's face was devoid of expression. Gertrude doubted if he actually saw her at all. He looked up at her as if she were a post and spoke officiously. "Now for your next step you will have to go up to the third floor. Up there you will have to write Chinese. If you can't, you will have to bring someone who can write for you."

Gertrude stared at him incredulously, the man she was so sure knew his business. "Oh, no. That's not the truth. My next step is to be fingerprinted," she announced.

"No, you don't have to be fingerprinted," he said, looking down at the short wooden stems of his stamps which he was rearranging for some reason known only to himself.

"But I want to be," Gertrude insisted. "I am not afraid of fingerprinting. I want to be."

"No. You will not be." The man was dismissive, waving her away with his hand.

"But I don't want to miss any step that I am supposed to take." Gertrude could see herself having to stand in all those lines again when it was discovered that she had not completed all the steps. "I know the steps that others before me have taken and the next step is fingerprinting," she explained.

"Please, you do not have to be fingerprinted." The man was actually looking at her, making eye contact, and rubbing his hands together.

He said 'please.' Does he know me? Gertrude struggled to concentrate on winning her argument and accomplishing her task even as this new conundrum niggled at her. "But just let me," she insisted. She searched his face for weakness. "I'm going up there," she announced, gathering up her papers and pulling away from the counter.

"No. Don't." The man knocked over two of his stamps.

Gertrude turned back and dropped her papers on the counter. "Please, I don't want to do this all again," she implored, her arms spread in a half circle of ardent petition.

The man placed his hands on the counter, his eyes darting to the corners of the room—a frightened mouse looking for cover or escape. "I will tell you," he hissed, leaning across the counter. "There are only two people in all of these"—he pointed with his uplifted chin at the people waiting behind Gertrude at the door—"only two people who don't need to be fingerprinted. You and Dr. Miller."

How do you know who I am?

Gertrude stared at the man, her mouth open but no sound coming out. *With all the people in Shanghai, how could you know me personally—by name?* She snatched up her papers in both hands, held her arms tightly across her chest, and walked out of the office.

Gertrude maundered along the wide hallway, mindlessly avoiding collisions with those who passed her, not seeing any of the people standing in the lines that trailed out of the various offices. When a wooden bench materialized before her, she sat down.

What was going on back there? Who in the Communist high command knows me by name? I'm just one of several thousand who is try— She shuddered and closed her eyes, leaning heavily against the back rest. *The patient with the fever. Her brother. They know my name.* She took a deep breath and tried to understand if that was a good thing or a bad thing.

"Only two . . . you and Dr. Miller," he had said. *He practically called me by name.*

Another conversation elbowed its way to the front of her thoughts, demanding a rehearing. *"Haven't you ever been in circumstances that told you that the Lord was watching over you, that He was in control? I will pray that the Lord will call your name, Gertrude."*

Startled, Gertrude opened her eyes and looked up. *Lord? Is that You?*

Chapter 82

GOING HOME

Walking the second floor corridor toward the staircase, Gertrude looked at her watch. It was 11:15 a.m. *If I hurry, I will have just enough time to get up to the third floor and write whatever it is that they need me to write in Chinese.*

Reaching for the banister, she looked up. Elder Frost was turning the corner on his way down. Anyone who saw his frosty bouffant hairstyle and round cherubic face would know immediately that he was a minister in some Protestant denomination.

"Gertrude," he called out cheerily, "where are you going?"

"I'm going up to that place on the third floor," she answered, watching him descend the staircase toward her.

"Where you have to write in Chinese?" he questioned.

"I can write Chinese," she quickly answered. "I've been reading and writing Chinese for years. All my students answer on their exams in Chinese. I have to read it."

"But now you'll have to write it, and it's not medical stuff," he warned, throwing up his hands in mock horror. "I finished the five-year course in Chinese, but I'm afraid to try." He walked down two more steps to where she stood at the foot of the stairs. Crooking his left arm, he made a small, stiff bow, extending his right arm as a gentleman cavalier might doff his hat. "I'm going to lunch and will return this afternoon with someone to write for me. Care to join me?"

"Thank you very much, kind sir." Gertrude made her best curtsey, laughing. "But I think I will go up right now and get this over with. I think I can write for myself."

"Very well," he said, giving a small nod of his head to their mock formality. "But don't be surprised." He turned to go with a parting wave of his hand. "I know I won't be. I want to get it right."

With a chuckle, Gertrude shook her head and waved in return, then turned and started up the staircase.

The sign over the entrance to the room struggled—in English—to say, "If your not writing Chinese, you have to bringing somebody for writing for you."

Well, I am going to try, she thought, studying the sign. *I don't know how much I have to write. Let's give it a shot and see if I can write Chinese. If not, I can come back this afternoon with someone to help me.*

The room had multiple stalls like bank teller windows, each with iron grating and a place underneath to slide papers through. Gertrude approached an empty stall and stood there waiting. Through the narrow wrought iron bars she could see the clerk crouched down, his head under the counter. Gazing about at the cracks in the plastered walls and the single bulb light fixtures hanging from the 15-foot ceiling, she wondered, *What do they do in this room? Collect taxes? Bookkeeping?*

The clerk—*youngish,* she thought, *for such an assignment*—emerged from under the counter and stood up, placing a paper in front of her. "Can you write in Chinese?" he asked without looking at her.

"Yes, of course I can," she responded confidently. The clerk turned away and began separating papers into two piles.

Papers of previous people who are evacuating? she wondered. *Separated into those who could write Chinese and those who could not?* With a shrug, she dismissed the thought as idle and of no importance.

Setting her passport and papers neatly to one side, she retrieved her nursing pen from her purse. Unscrewing the cap of the pen, she looked at the questions on the paper before her.

"Your name . . ."

Gertrude had a name in Chinese. She wrote it down.

"Your address . . ."

She kept writing.

"How old are you? . . ."

She continued to write—in quick, delicate strokes—the box-like Chinese characters of the Chinese language. Finally she had everything written except her profession.

"What is your work?"

The word for "nurse" was comprised of two Chinese characters. One was "kahoo" and the other one was "hoosut." She knew how to write one of them, but the other character had so many strokes that she could not remember them all.

She wrote down the one character she knew.

I know that the character has this stroke and this stroke. She made the strokes in her mind, hoping to stimulate the memory of the rest of the strokes in the Chinese character. She stared at the blank spot on the paper. Nothing came to her mind. It was as blank as the paper.

Come on, Gertrude. You can do this. You've written everything else. Don't block up now. She imagined the time she had wasted. She glanced at her watch. Lunch time was over. *The lines will have formed outside already. By the time I go back to the clinic and find someone to return with me, it will be late in the day, probably too late to get back up here. Come on, Gertrude, ol' girl.*

Nothing.

Gertrude leaned her elbow on the counter, her head on her hand, staring at the little iron bars before her. *How far back in the lines will I have to go?* she worried. She thought about all the places that she'd visited that morning and about what had happened to her.

She paused. *Lord, is this one of those circumstances?* She wasn't sure what to do, what to ask. *Lord, if You can help me, I surely need to remember that second character.* She waited. Nothing came to her mind. She waited 30 seconds longer and began to worry. *Lord, am I being presumptuous? I don't know what to do.*

Gertrude looked from side to side at the other stalls in the room. Most of them contained people who had Chinese helpers. Only one other stall contained a single person like herself, a Caucasian working alone. *I should never have come without someone to help me,.* she fumed. *I should never have been so cocksure of myself.* She remembered Elder Frost's warning that she had taken so lightly.

"Sometimes the Holy Spirit has to do for us what we cannot do for ourselves." Dr. *Miller told me that,* she remembered. *Well, right now I would certainly be glad to*

have someone write this character for me. She looked about her again at those who were busily scribbling on their own forms and shook her head. *No one's going to help me,* she agonized, her anger melting into frustration to the point of tears.

"Please, my younger brother," she said suddenly, pushing her paper under the cage bars and across the counter. "Please, what should I do? I am a nurse." She pointed to the line that asked her occupation. "Only this one character. I can't remember all of the strokes."

The clerk, a full 15 years younger than Gertrude's 41 years, glanced over at the paper, up at Gertrude's anxious face, and down at the paper again. She watched his eyes move from her to the paper and back again.

What do you think? she implored silently of this young man. *So young, you could be one of my nursing students. I know you're not supposed to help me, but . . .*

The clerk snatched the paper down under the counter and scribbled something on it. Glancing sideways in both directions, he quickly slid the paper back up on the counter in front of her.

Gertrude scanned the paper, moving down the page with her finger. He had written the missing character in the blank space. She looked up. He was busy stacking his papers.

"I think I am done," she announced, pushing the paper under the iron bars once more.

The clerk turned indifferently and pulled the paper across the counter. Gertrude watched closely as he scanned down the page. Inking an official-looking stamp, he pressed the die surface to the paper in the upper right corner.

"Is it all right?" she asked.

He looked up at her and blinked his eyes as if clearing them. Giving a quick, short nod, he whisked away the paper and placed it on one of the stacks before him. She could not tell which stack—the good stack or the bad stack—and continued working, his back to her.

Taking a deep breath, she picked up her papers, turned from the counter and the little caged window and left the room.

As she descended the wide marble staircase, Gertrude spotted Elder Frost coming up from the first floor accompanied by one of the Chinese secretaries from the Division Office.

"Well, how did it go, Gertrude?" he called out when he recognized her.

"I wrote everything up there but the one character. And the man wrote that one for me."

"He's not supposed to do that, is he?" he asked thoughtfully as he reached her. "Why would he do such a thing?"

"I don't really know," she said. *I think I know why . . . but I'm not really sure . . . at least, not sure enough to tell you.* She grinned. "Maybe he thought I did a really good job."

"Well, good for you," he sang out, his voice echoing in the stone-lined building as he started up the stairs. "As you can see, I brought my help with me. Can't take a chance. Want to get it right."

Gertrude nodded and paused, watching him as he turned on the landing above her and disappeared up the stairs, his helper in tow. Turning, she continued her descent to the bottom of the staircase and headed for the front door, wondering where she might find some lunch at this time in the afternoon.

On the second weekend of September Gertrude sat with Dr. Harry Miller on the flat roof of the Range Road Clinic, the time-honored place for taking pictures. Dr. Herbert Liu and Dr. Andrew Chen sat to the left of Dr. Miller. Allan and Mildred Boynton sat to Gertrude's right. Surrounding them on three tiers of steps, one of the largest classes of senior nurses to graduate from the Shanghai Sanitarium Nursing School posed for their graduation picture. The photographer had just finished a separate picture of Gertrude surrounded by the six senior nursing students who had followed her from Yencheng as freshmen in 1941, to Wuhan as juniors in 1948, and to Shanghai as seniors in 1949.

As the photographer arranged all 37 students for this final picture, Mr. Boynton tilted his head toward Gertrude and whispered, "I got the notice of our departure put in the newspaper for the next three days."

"Are you worried," she quipped, "that Mildred might have run up some debts? Maybe a tab at the Chocolate Shoppe that she hasn't paid?"

"I'm not worried," Allan Boynton said with a grin, "but the Communist Chinese government is. We all got included. We're all famous in Shanghai— one more time." He leaned over to listen to Mildred then whispered in Gertrude's ear, "Mildred says that sounds more like a stunt you'd pull."

Gertrude leaned out and eyed Mildred Boynton with an impish grin. "Not me, my dear. I never run up a tab. I always pay my bills." She sat up straight as the photographer moved behind his camera. "Pay as you go is my motto."

Suddenly she turned to Mr. Boynton. "But who's going to put up the money for our guarantee? They won't let us leave unless someone guarantees they will pay any of our debts that show up after we're gone."

"... or go to jail for us if need be," Allan Boynton added, without moving.

The photographer stepped out from behind his camera, trying to decide who had moved and made the blurring motion he had seen through his lens.

"A businessman over on Peking Road is guaranteeing for all of us," Dr. Miller said, turning his eyes out of the sun now that the photographer wasn't ready.

"He would do that for us?" Gertrude asked, turning to her left.

"For a price, a good price, I might add." Mr. Boynton spoke as if *he* might have had to pay the sum asked.

"He's a friend of mine," Dr. Miller whispered, facing the sun once more. The photographer was standing behind his camera, waving his hands to get their attention. "A former patient."

As the photographer snapped the picture, Gertrude prayed silently, *Thank You, God. After all that I've been through—finally—I got to complete something here in China.*

On September 20, 1949, Gertrude stood behind her trunk on the wharf in a line with the rest of her party, Dr. and Mrs. Miller to her left, the Boyntons to her right. In front of her the government inspector was digging through her trunk, throwing her linens, her nylons, her nursing uniforms out helter-skelter onto the rough boards. He had already created havoc with Mrs. Miller's clothes. Now he was doing the same with Gertrude's things.

As she took deep breaths and clenched her fists, she heard a "tsk, tsk" sound from her left. Glancing over she saw Harry Miller slowly, imperceptibly, shaking his head, his eyes closed.

I know, Dr. Miller, she fumed. *He's just showing off, just demonstrating how much power he thinks he has. He wants everyone to see how the capitalist dogs waste their money on finery. Well, I'd like to see him tramp the floors of that hospital every day like I do—without those good, tight nylons in place.* The inspector had found another pair and flung them in the air. *He's going to snag those nylons,* she raged, *and then I'll really be upset.* She closed her eyes, blocking out the inspector's exaggerated motions and the falling nylons.

The gentle undulations of the wharf under her feet made Gertrude think of previous trips to the docks. *I'm glad that I sent that last shipment to Mother,* she thought. *The two trunks, the two wooden boxes, and the burlap roll with the rug in it.*

Gertrude had no medical equipment or books in her trunk. She knew the Shanghai nursing program would need every scrap that she could leave behind. She only regretted that she had lost so much in Yencheng, things that would have been useful to the students in Shanghai.

When the inspector finally moved on to the next group, Gertrude and her companions stepped around to the front of their luggage.

Well, there's nothing for it but to get on with life, she thought, carefully picking her nylons off the rough timbers of the wharf.

On September 27, Gertrude and her party arrived in Hong Kong, and from there they scattered to their new missions stations. The Frosts, Marie Miller, and several others sailed for the United States. The Boyntons moved to Korea where Allan Boynton had been appointed as the manager of the Seoul Sanitarium and Hospital. Dr. Harry Miller flew to the Philippines to review the medical work there and—with hands still steady at age 70—do surgery.

On October 19, Gertrude sailed to Singapore to join the staff at the Singapore Sanitarium and Hospital.

88 Bryan Street
Rochester, New York
November 14, 1949

Dear Sis,

I am hoping that this letter finds you OK. Amelia assures me that if I write to the last address Mother had for you in Hong Kong, it would catch up to you eventually.

I don't have much to say. It's not a long letter, just a note really.

Mother is very sick. Actually the doctor says she has advanced cancer of the uterus. We all knew that she was getting weaker but just thought it had to do with the hard winter we had last year and the fact that she is getting older. Now we have found out that it is cancer.

Gloria and Amelia have been wonderful at taking care of her, taking turns with her in the hospital and at home. But Mother keeps asking for you. She knows that you are safely out of China, although she thinks that Hong Kong is still in China. Actually, I guess it is—but it belongs to the British.

Anyway, I know that you recently moved to Singapore but I don't know where. Is it possible for you come home, even for a little while?

I hope this message finds you well.

From your brother,
Walter Green

On New Year's Eve, Gertrude Green, former missionary nurse to China, landed in Honolulu on a Pan Am flight from Singapore by way of the Philippines. On New Year's Day, January 1, 1950, her Pan Am flight touched down in San Francisco.

EPILOGUE

Gertrude stood up, leaning heavily on her walker, all 91 of her years pressing down, trying to force her back into the chair. Her knee, still recovering from surgery, began to throb. She shook it from side to side to relieve the ache.

Dr. Schwarz was used to waiting for the older residents to gain their balance before speaking. He watched Gertrude's eyes. When she looked up at him, he said again, "Yes, Gertrude? You wanted to say something?"

There were so many things Gertrude wanted to say, so many stories to tell. She stood for a few seconds longer, trying to put into words what it all meant.

What is the sum total of it all? What did I learn—about myself? About life? Do I have something to say?

"Yes. Yes, I do." Gertrude drew in a deep breath and gathered her thoughts. *You've never been at a loss for words before, ol' girl. Don't block up now.*

"I know of those who dread the time of trouble, but I do not. I have been through what I think is a time of trouble."

Several in the front rows turned about in their chairs to see more clearly who was speaking.

"If you have faith in the Lord, He will take care of you. I know I should not be here. I should have been dead over and over again. But I'm not. You see me."

Everyone was absolutely quiet, straining toward her. Everyone was listening to Gertrude tell her story ... and their story. Gray heads nodded in understanding, confirming that the truth she spoke was their truth.

"I have outlived any other member of my family." *Well, almost,* she thought as she remembered that Fred was still alive. She wrinkled her brow with a short twitch and went on. "And why the Lord has allowed me to live this long, I do not know."

She shuffled her feet to get the numbness out of them, then planted them firmly again. "Never fear the time of trouble," she said in clear tones. "If you have your faith in the Lord and what He has done for you, He will carry you through. I thank the Lord every day for that care He had for me and everyone who went through that terrible, terrible experience."

Her left hand began to shake, making the walker squeak rhythmically, as the memories of that "terrible, terrible experience"—in bits and pieces—flashed through her mind. She gripped the walker firmly with both hands.

"It strengthens your faith and makes you stronger in the Lord," she said finally. "Yes, we were afraid. We had our prayer meetings. But the Lord answered so many prayers in the early part that we knew that He was taking care of us."

I did know it. Gertrude squeezed her eyes closed, her lips tightening in a thin, straight line as she prayed, "Thank You," one more time. *I did know it.*

"It was a time of trouble," she said aloud, opening her eyes, staring at her feet—her dancing feet, imagining them cold and numb in worn stadium boots—"especially those six weeks walking from the Communists."

She stood there silently, all the words drained out, staring at her feet.

The applause began on the far side of room, just a few hands quietly coming together, old hands, the loose skin padding the sound. A few more joined in and Dr. Schwarz did likewise. Someone stood up and continued clapping. Then everyone was standing and everyone was clapping, applauding, celebrating— quietly, as older people do—for themselves and for Gertrude, celebrating the truth that she had put into words for all of them.

Dr. Schwarz knew the Bible study was at an end for the day. His lips twitched beneath his generous moustache as he forced a smile to keep back the tears. He gathered his papers from the small podium and zipped his Bible into its black leather carrying case. Shaking a few hands, he quietly made his way to the back door and slipped out.

Several older women near Gertrude reached out and touched her hands or patted her on the arms. One or two pressed closer, giving her a hug and a generous whiff of lilac water as they passed by. Two old friends, standing near, watched the tender touch of warm human flesh on their dear friend, watched Gertrude's facial expression change from worried memories—to surprise of the moment—to joy at being the center of so much unexpected attention. They watched her gray eyes brighten until they sparkled emerald green.

POSTSCRIPT

Gertrude stayed in Rochester, New York, caring for her mother until her death in April, 1950. In March, 1951, she returned as a missionary nurse to what was then the Far Eastern Division of the Seventh-day Adventist Church—that division extending from Korea in the north to Indonesia in the south. She flew to Bangkok, Thailand, where she served at Bangkok Adventist Hospital from 1951 to 1993—42 years.

Gertrude initially performed in all those capacities in which she'd served previously— anesthetist, radiology technician, OR supervisor, nurse midwife, director of nurses, and nursing school director. As the staff of the hospital grew, Gertrude gradually turned over many of her duties to others, finally concentrating on midwifery. In 1955, she founded the School of Midwifery, which she directed and taught in until her retirement.

Gertrude returned to China on several occasions, but always as a tourist, never again as a worker. Her mission post was in Bangkok. She learned to drive a car and became a terror and a known hazard on the streets of Bangkok, driving until her retirement at age 86. It was said that on the city streets around Bangkok Adventist Hospital, Gertrude was known by every fourth person because she had attended their mothers at their birth or had delivered their own babies, sometimes up to three and four generations.

For the rest of her professional life Gertrude continued to study nursing, participating in several international studies of maternity. She read nursing journals and kept up with the latest information available and passed it on to her midwifery students, many of whom came from other countries in Asia to study under her. In Thailand, the Philippines, Indonesia, and other countries of Southeast Asia every student who graduated from Gertrude's Midwifery School was immediately snatched up by the medical system. Everyone knew that Miss Green's midwifery students were the best—knowledgeable, hardworking, outstanding midwives.

In 1961 she received her Master of Science degree in Maternal Child Health from Boston University. In 1970 Gertrude was honored by the Association of Seventh-day Adventist Nurses by having her name recorded, along with nine others, as a charter inductee into the association's Hall of Fame. In 1971 she earned her designation as a Certified Nurse-Midwife from the American College of Nurse-Midwives. In 1997 Gertrude was honored as the Woman of the Year by the Association of Adventist Women. She was also named an Honored Alumna of Atlantic Union College and of Columbia Union College.

In 1997 Bangkok Adventist Hospital invited Gertrude back to Thailand for a special celebration during which the midwifery building in which she had served for so many years was named the Gertrude Green Building.

On her retirement, Gertrude moved to Hendersonville, North Carolina, to live at the Fletcher Park Inn and be near several of her missionary friends. In 2002, Gertrude developed difficulty with the healing of wounds on her feet, and was diagnosed with Raynaud's Disease, a condition of poor arterial circulation of the extremities. Following surgery to amputate both feet, Gertrude developed respiratory problems and died on March 12. She was 94.

BOOKS TO ENRICH YOUR RELATIONSHIP WITH JESUS

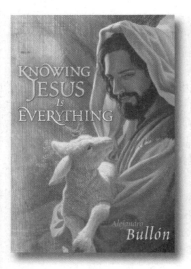

Knowing Jesus Is Everything

The Christian life is too difficult—if you don't know Jesus personally. No matter what you do (or don't do), you don't stand a chance without Him. Alejandro Bullón offers guidance for pursuing a genuine friendship with Jesus. 978-0-8280-2381-8

Savior

You've read the greatest story ever told—but never quite like this. Written in modern language without the disjointed interruption of chapter or verse, Jack Blanco merges the four Gospel accounts into one fresh, unified narrative. This is the timeless, captivating story of Jesus, our Savior. 978-0-8127-0469-3

Revelation's Great Love Story

Larry Lichtenwalter explores the final book of the Bible and unveils a side of Revelation that is seldom portrayed: Christ's passionate love for humanity. Open your eyes to the extraordinary love of our Savior for His rebellious, undeserving children—and the incredible reasons we can love Him in return. 978-0-8127-0460-0

3 Ways to Shop

- Visit your local Adventist Book Center®
- Call 1-800-765-6955
- Order online at www.AdventistBookCenter.com